The Art of Digital Video

For Chrissie

The Art of Digital Video

Second Edition

John Watkinson

Focal Press
An imprint of Butterworth-Heinemann Ltd
Linacre House, Jordan Hill, Oxford OX2 8DP

 A member of the Reed-Elsevier group

OXFORD   LONDON   BOSTON
MUNICH   NEW DELHI   SINGAPORE   SYDNEY
TOKYO   TORONTO   WELLINGTON

First published 1990
Second edition 1994

British Library Cataloguing in Publication Data
Watkinson, John
    Art of Digital Video. – 2 Rev. ed
    I. Title
    621.38833

ISBN 0 240 51369 X

Library of Congress Cataloging in Publication Data
Watkinson, John.
    The art of digital video/John Watkinson. – 2nd ed.
    p.   cm.
    Includes bibliographical references and index.
    ISBN 0 240 51369 X
    1. Digital television. I. Title.
    TK6678.W38   93–39376
    621.388–dc20   CIP

Composition by Genesis Typesetting, Laser Quay, Rochester, Kent
Printed and bound in Great Britain by Clays Ltd, St Ives plc

Contents

Chapter 7 Digital interfaces and broadcast 384

Chapter 8 Rotary-head tape transports 412

Preface

In 1990 the first edition of this book appeared. At that time, digital video equipment was beginning to show its promise, but it remained an expensive way of producing television. Analog equipment was still the most cost-effective choice, particularly in recording.

The rate of progress has been so great that the overall cost of ownership of digital video equipment is now less than that of analog.

Techniques which were still in the laboratory, such as data reduction and motion estimation, are now commercially available. Devices such as workstations based on hard disks are now in everyday use. The serial digital interface has established itself as a standard and testing methods have evolved to measure its performance.

The rate of change of the technology has been so great that a new book is required. As a result this is not a revision, but a complete rewrite. It was a goal of this rewrite that someone who already has the first edition would still consider this edition good value. There are a number of changes here compared with the first edition. Firstly, there have been requests to lower the assumed level of the book to make it accessible to a wider audience. This is consistent with the increasing market penetration turning digital equipment from a specialist to an everyday subject. This book now contains an introductory chapter which is a small book in its own right. All of the basic principles are introduced there at a tutorial level. Secondly, as a result of presenting a great many training courses around the world, newer and better explanations of certain subjects have occurred to me and these have all been incorporated in the text. Finally, all relevant new technology is included. New material includes transform coding for data reduction and motion estimation, advanced PAL decoding, 16:9, signature analysis, noise-shaping audio converters, workstations and an introduction to the new DVTR formats.

When this book was first written, there were two DVTR formats, and it seemed a good idea to treat them both in depth. Now there are six DVTR formats (not including high definition); detailing them all would distort the content and so only the principles of DVTRs with carefully chosen examples are included here. DVTRs are now a subject in themselves and are given comprehensive treatment in a companion volume entitled *The digital video tape recorder*.

Whilst a great deal has changed, there are some things which have not changed. The original approach to the subject has been well received and is not changed here. Every subject is explained in plain English with the minimum of equations. Even transform coding has been explained in this way. Theory is illustrated with practical examples and there are plenty of new illustrations.

The first edition undoubtedly dealt with a specialist subject, but the rate of progress has been so great that now this is a mainstream book dealing with devices and techniques which are becoming commonplace in the facility and broadcast industry. Perhaps in the next edition the qualifier *digital* in the title will be starting to look superfluous.

Acknowledgements

I must first thank David Kirk, who invited me to write a series on digital video for 'Broadcast Systems Engineering', which he then edited, and Ron Godwyn, who succeeded him. The response to that series provided the impetus to turn it into a book. BSE is no longer published – a victim of recession – but it deserves a place in our memories.

The publications of the Society of Motion Picture and Television Engineers, the European Broadcasting Union and the Audio Engineering Society have been extremely useful.

I am indebted to the many people who have found time to discuss complex subjects and to suggest reference works. Particular thanks go to David Lyon, Roderick Snell and Tim Borer of Snell and Wilcox, Takeo Eguchi, Jim Wilkinson, David Huckfield and John Ive of Sony, Steve Owen of Panasonic and Yoshinobu Oba of NHK, Luigi Gallo of Accom, Graham Roe, David Stone and Robin Caine of ProBel, Dave Trytko, Joe Attard, John Watney and Fraser Morrison of Ampex, Roger Wood of IBM, Tom Cavanagh and Steve Lyman of CBC, Kees Schouhamer Immink and Peter de With of Philips, Ab Weber, John Mallinson and Peter Kraniauskas.

Thanks are also due to Margaret Riley of Focal Press for her endless support.

John Watkinson
Burghfield Common, England

Chapter 1
Introducing digital video

1.1 Analog video

The first methods used in television transmission and recording were understandably analog, and the signal formats were essentially determined by the requirements of the cathode ray tube as a display, so that the receiver might be as simple as possible, and be constructed with a minimum number of vacuum tubes. Following the development of magnetic audio recording during the Second World War, a need for television recording was perceived. This was due to the various time zones across the United States. Without recording, popular television programmes had to be performed live several times so they could be seen at peak viewing time in each time zone. Ampex eventually succeeded in recording monochrome video in the 1950s, and the fundamentals of the Quadruplex machine were so soundly based that modern analog video recorders only refine the process.[1] Study of every shortcoming in the analog production process has led to the development of some measure to reduce it, and current equipment is capable of excellent performance. The point to appreciate, however, is that analog production equipment has become a mature technology, and has almost reached limits determined by the laws of physics. The process of refinement produces increasingly small returns.

As there is now another video technology, known as digital, the previous technology has to be referred to as analog. It is appropriate to begin by contrasting the two technologies. Comparison is only possible in areas where the two technologies overlap. The real strength of digital video lies in areas where no comparison is possible because such processes are simply impossible in the analog domain.

In an analog system, information is conveyed by some infinite variation of a continuous parameter such as the voltage on a wire or the strength or frequency of flux on a tape. In a recorder, distance along the medium is a further, continuous, analog of time. It does not matter at what point a recording is examined along its length – a value will be found for the recorded signal. That value can itself change with infinite resolution within the physical limits of the system.

Those characteristics are the main weakness of analog signals. Within the allowable bandwidth, *any* waveform is valid. If the speed of the medium is not constant, one valid waveform is changed into another valid waveform; a timebase error cannot be detected in an analog system. In addition, a voltage error simply changes one valid voltage into another; noise cannot be detected in

1

an analog system. We might suspect noise, but how is one to know what proportion of the received signal is noise and what is the original? If the transfer function of a system is not linear, distortion results, but the distorted waveforms are still valid; an analog system cannot detect distortion. Again we might suspect distortion, but how are we to know how much of the energy at a given frequency is due to the distortion and how much was actually present in the original signal?

It is a characteristic of analog systems that degradations cannot be separated from the original signal, so nothing can be done about them. At the end of a system a signal carries the sum of all degradations introduced at each stage through which it passed. This sets a limit to the number of stages through which a signal can be passed before it is useless. Alternatively, if many stages are envisaged, each piece of equipment must be far better than necessary so that the signal is still acceptable at the end. The equipment will naturally be more expensive.

1.2 The characteristics of video signals

Video signals are electrical waveforms which allow moving pictures to be conveyed from one place to another. Observing the real world with the human eye results in a two-dimensional image on the retina. This image changes with time and so the basic information is three dimensional. With two eyes a stereoscopic view can be obtained and stereoscopic television is possible with suitable equipment. However, this is restricted to specialist applications and has not been exploited in broadcasting.

An electrical waveform is two dimensional in that it carries a voltage changing with respect to time. In order to convey three-dimensional picture information down a two-dimensional cable it is necessary to resort to scanning. Instead of attempting to convey the brightness of all parts of a picture at once, scanning conveys the brightness of a single point which moves with time.

The cathode ray tube is not a linear device, but produces light following a power law with an index of about 2.2. This non-linear characteristic is known as *gamma*. In practice an inverse law is applied in the camera so that no non-linear circuitry is needed in the television receiver. Thus recording and processing is performed on compressed signals. Perhaps surprisingly, the presence of the non-linearity makes little difference. One reason for this is the fact that the majority of the energy in a typical picture is concentrated at low frequencies.

In television systems the scan consists of rapid horizontal sweeps combined with a slower vertical sweep so that the image is scanned in lines. At the end of each vertical sweep, or frame, the process recommences. Computer monitors scan in this way, but in most broadcast systems the scanning process is 2:1 interlaced. In an interlaced system the vertical sweep speed is doubled so that spaces open up between the scanned lines. The vertical scan, or field, takes half as long and contains half as many lines. In the second field the areas which were missed in the first field are scanned. Fig. 1.1(a) shows that this is readily achieved by having an odd number of lines, e.g. 525 or 625 in the frame, so that the first field begins with a whole line and ends half-way along a line and the second field begins half-way through a line and ends on a whole line. The lines of the two fields then automatically mesh vertically.

First field begins on a full
line and ends on a half line

Second field begins on a half
line and ends on a full line

Field 1   Field 2

1   2   3   4   5   6   7   8   9   10   11   12   13   14   15

There must be an odd number of lines in a frame

Figure 1.1(a) 2:1 interlace

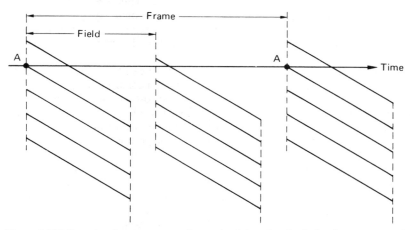

Figure 1.1(b) In an interlaced system, a given point A is only refreshed at frame rate, causing twitter on fine vertical detail

The scanning process converts resolution on the image into the frequency domain. The higher the resolution of the image, the more lines are necessary to resolve the vertical detail. The line rate is increased along with the number of cycles of modulation which need to be carried in each line. If the frame rate remains constant, the bandwidth goes up as the square of the resolution. A 625 line system has a bandwidth of nearly 6 MHz, whereas a 1250 line HDTV system having twice the resolution needs about 30 MHz. The bandwidth required is more than four times higher because HDTV uses a 16:9 aspect ratio instead of 4:3, and so the lines are longer.

In interlaced systems, the field rate is intended to determine the flicker frequency, whereas the frame rate determines the bandwidth needed, which is thus halved along with the information rate. Information theory tells us that halving the information rate must reduce quality, and so the saving in bandwidth is accompanied by a variety of effects. Fig. 1.1(b) shows the spatial/temporal sampling points in a 2:1 interlaced system. If an object has a sharp horizontal edge, it will be present in one field but not in the next. The refresh rate of the edge will be reduced to frame rate, 25 Hz or 30 Hz, and becomes visible as twitter.

Fig. 1.2 shows some of the basic types of analog colour video. Each of these types can, of course, exist in a variety of line standards. Since practical colour cameras generally have three separate sensors, one for each primary colour, an *RGB* system will exist at some stage in the internal workings of the camera, even if it does not emerge in that form. *RGB* consists of three parallel signals each having the same spectrum, and is used where the highest accuracy is needed, often for production of still pictures. Examples of this are paint systems and in computer-aided design (CAD) displays. *RGB* is seldom used for real-time video

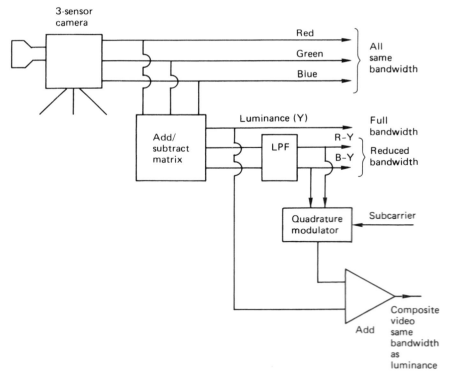

Figure 1.2 The major types of analog video. Red, green and blue signals emerge from the camera sensors, needing full bandwidth. If a luminance signal is obtained by a weighted sum of *R*, *G* and *B*, it will need full bandwidth, but the colour difference signals *R–Y* and *B–Y* need less bandwidth. Combining *R–Y* and *B–Y* into a subcarrier modulation scheme allows colour transmission in the same bandwidth as monochrome

recording because of the high cost. As the red, green and blue signals directly represent part of the image, this approach is known as component video.

Some saving of bandwidth can be obtained by using colour difference working. The human eye relies on brightness to convey detail, and much less resolution is needed in the colour information. R, G and B are matrixed together to form a luminance (and monochrome-compatible) signal Y which has full bandwidth. The eye is not equally sensitive to the three primary colours, as can be seen in Fig. 1.3(a), and so the luminance signal is a weighted sum.

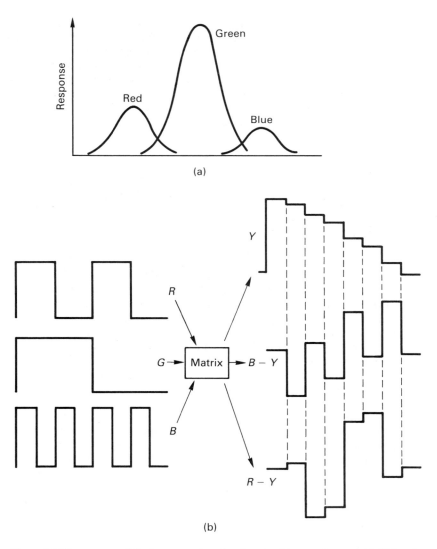

Figure 1.3 The response of the human eye to colour is not uniform as shown at (a). Colour bars originate as three square waves in RGB, but luminance obtained by weighted adding follows an irregular staircase shown at (b)

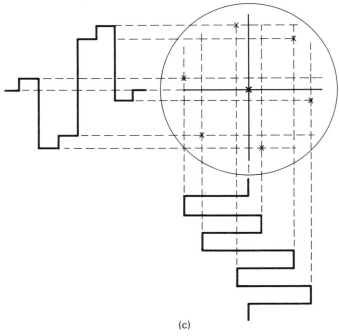

(c)

Figure 1.3 cont Colour difference signals can be shown two-dimensionally on a vectorscope as at (c)

The origin of the common colour bar test signal is shown in Fig. 1.3(b). Binary *RGB* signals are produced, having one, two and four cycles per screen width. When these are added together, an eight-level luminance staircase results because of the unequal weighting. The matrix also produces two colour difference signals, $R-Y$ and $B-Y$, and these are often displayed simultaneously on a vectorscope as shown in Fig. 1.3(c). Note that the white bar and the black bar are not colours and so the colour difference signal is zero in those bars, resulting in a central spot. There are six remaining colours, each of which results in a spot on the perimeter of the vectorscope display.

Colour difference signals do not need the same bandwidth as Y, because the eye's acuity does not extend to colour vision. One-half or one-quarter of the bandwidth will do depending on the application. Chroma keying is more accurate with wide colour difference bandwidth, and so production systems use one-half of the luminance bandwidth for the colour difference signals. The overall bandwidth is then two-thirds that needed by *RGB*. Analog colour difference recorders such as Betacam and M II record the luminance and colour difference signals separately. The D-1, D-5 and Digital Betacam formats record 525/60 or 625/50 colour difference signals digitally. In casual parlance, colour difference formats are often called component formats to distinguish them from composite formats.

For monochrome-compatible colour television broadcast in a single channel, the NTSC, PAL and SECAM systems interleave into the spectrum of a monochrome signal a subcarrier which carries two colour difference signals of restricted bandwidth. The subcarrier is intended to be invisible on the screen of a monochrome television set. A subcarrier-based colour system is generally referred to as composite video, and the modulated subcarrier is called chroma.

PAL and SECAM share the same scanning standard of 625/50, but the methods of conveying the colour are totally incompatible. NTSC scans at 525/59.94, but the colour system has a few things in common with PAL. All three standards use 2:1 interlace. Analog composite recorders include the B and C formats, and the D-2 and D-3 formats record PAL or NTSC digitally.

1.3 What is digital video?

One of the vital concepts to grasp is that digital video is simply an alternative means of carrying a video waveform. An ideal digital video system has the same characteristics as an ideal analog system: both of them are totally transparent and reproduce the original applied waveform without error. One need only compare high-quality analog and digital equipment side by side with the same signals to realize how transparent modern equipment can be. Needless to say, in the real world ideal conditions seldom prevail, so analog and digital equipment both fall short of the ideal. Digital equipment simply falls short of the ideal by a smaller distance than does analog and at lower cost, or, if the designer chooses, it can have the same performance as analog at much lower cost.

Although there are a number of ways in which video waveforms can be represented digitally, there is one system, known as pulse code modulation (PCM) which is in virtually universal use.[2] Fig. 1.4 shows how PCM works. Instead of being continuous, the time axis is represented in a discrete, or

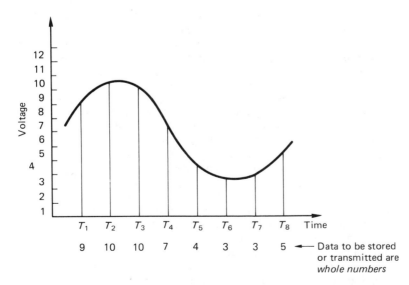

Figure 1.4 In pulse code modulation (PCM) the analog waveform is measured periodically at the sampling rate. The voltage (represented here by the height) of each sample is then described by a whole number. The whole numbers are stored or transmitted rather than the waveform itself

stepwise, manner. The waveform is not carried by continuous representation, but by measurement at regular intervals. This process is called sampling and the frequency with which samples are taken is called the sampling rate or sampling frequency F_s. It should be stressed that sampling is an analog process. Each sample still varies infinitely as the original waveform did. Sampled analog devices are well known in video. The charge-coupled sensor in a television camera is one example. To complete the conversion to PCM, each sample is then represented to finite accuracy by a discrete number in a process known as quantizing.

In television systems the input image which falls on the camera sensor will be continuous in time, and continuous in two spatial dimensions corresponding to the height and width of the sensor. In analog video systems, the time axis is sampled into frames, and the vertical axis is sampled into lines. Digital video simply adds a third sampling process along the lines.

There is a direct connection between the concept of temporal sampling, where the input changes with respect to time at some frequency and is sampled at some other frequency, and spatial sampling, where an image changes a given number of times per unit distance and is sampled at some other number of times per unit distance. The connection between the two is the process of scanning. Temporal frequency can be obtained by multiplying spatial frequency by the speed of the scan. Fig. 1.5 shows a hypothetical image sensor which has 1000 discrete sensors

Figure 1.5 If the above spatial sampling arrangement of 1000 points per centimetre is scanned in 1 millisecond, the sampling rate will become 1 megahertz

across a width of 1 centimetre. The spatial sampling rate of this sensor is thus 1 per centimetre. If the sensors are measured sequentially during a scan which takes millisecond to go across the 1 centimetre width, the result will be a temporal sampling rate of 1 MHz. In the spatial domain we refer to resolution, whereas in the time domain we refer to frequency response. The two are linked by scanning.

Whilst any sampling rate which is high enough could be used for video, it is common to make the sampling rate a whole multiple of the line rate. Samples are then taken in the same place on every line. If this is done, a monochrome digital image is a rectangular array of points at which the brightness is stored as a number. The points are known as picture cells, generally abbreviated to pixels, although sometimes the abbreviation is more savage and they are known as pels. As shown in Fig. 1.6(a), the array will generally be arranged with an even spacing between pixels, which are in rows and columns. By placing the pixels close together, it is hoped that the observer will perceive a continuous image.

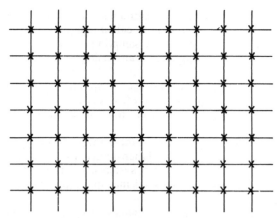

Figure 1.6(a) A picture can be stored digitally by representing the brightness at each of the above points by a binary number. For a colour picture each point becomes a vector and has to describe the brightness, hue and saturation of that part of the picture. Samples are usually but not always formed into regular arrays of rows and columns, and it is most efficient if the horizontal and vertical spacing are the same

Figure 1.6(b) In the case of component video, each pixel site is described by three values and so the pixel becomes a vector quantity

Obviously the finer the pixel spacing, the greater the resolution of the picture will be, but the amount of data needed to store one picture will increase as the square of the resolution, and with it the costs.

If it is desired to convey a coloured image, then it will be seen from Fig. 1.6(b) that each image consists of three superimposed layers of samples, one for each component. The pixel is no longer a single number representing a scalar brightness value, but a vector which describes in some way the brightness, hue and saturation of that point in the picture. In *RGB*, the pixels contain three unipolar numbers representing the proportion of each of the three primary colours at that point in the picture. In colour difference working, each pixel again contains three numbers, but one of these is a unipolar number representing the luminance and the other two are bipolar numbers representing the colour difference values.

In order to produce moving pictures, the current approach is simply to provide a mechanism where the value of every pixel can be updated periodically. This effectively results in a three-dimensional array, where two of the axes are spatial and the third is temporal.

Since it is possible to represent any analog waveform digitally, composite video can also be digitized. Owing to the critical nature of chroma phase, the sampling rate will generally be locked to subcarrier so that it can be readily created from burst. It should be stressed that digital composite is simply another way of conveying composite video, and all of the attributes of composite, such as colour framing sequences, are still present in the resulting data.

At the ADC (Analog-to-Digital Converter), every effort is made to rid the sampling clock of jitter, or time instability, so every sample is taken at an exactly even time step. Clearly if there is any subsequent timebase error, the instants at which samples arrive will be changed and the effect can be detected. If samples arrive at some destination with an irregular timebase, the effect can be eliminated by storing the samples temporarily in a memory and reading them out using a stable, locally generated clock. This process is called timebase correction and all properly engineered digital video systems must use it. Clearly timebase error is not reduced; it is totally eliminated. As a result there is little point measuring the timebase stability of a digital recorder.

Those who are not familiar with digital principles often worry that sampling takes away something from a signal because it is not taking notice of what happened between the samples. This would be true in a system having infinite bandwidth, but no analog signal can have infinite bandwidth. All analog signal sources from cameras, VTRs and so on have a resolution or frequency response limit, as indeed do devices such as CRTs and human vision. When a signal has finite bandwidth, the rate at which it can change is limited, and the way in which it changes becomes predictable. When a waveform can only change between samples in one way, it is then only necessary to convey the samples and the original waveform can be reconstructed from them. A more detailed treatment of the principle will be given in Chapter 3.

As stated, each sample is also discrete, or represented in a stepwise manner. The length of the sample, which will be proportional to the voltage of the video signal, is represented by a whole number. This process is known as quantizing and results in an approximation, but the size of the error can be controlled until it is negligible. If, for example, we were to measure the height of humans to the nearest metre, virtually all adults would register 2 metres high and obvious difficulties would result. These are generally overcome by measuring height to the nearest centimetre. Clearly there is no advantage in going further and expressing our height in a whole number of millimetres or even micrometres. The point is that an appropriate resolution can also be found for video signals, and a higher figure is not beneficial. The link between video quality and sample resolution is explored in Chapter 3. The advantage of using whole numbers is that they are not prone to drift. If a whole number can be carried from one place to another without numerical error, it has not changed at all. By describing video waveforms numerically, the original information has been expressed in a way which is better able to resist unwanted changes.

Essentially, digital video carries the original waveform numerically. The number of the sample is an analog of time, which itself is an analog of position across the screen, and the magnitude of the sample is (in the case of luminance) an analog of the brightness at the appropriate point in the image. In fact the succession of samples in a digital system is actually *an analog* of the original waveform. This sounds like a contradiction and as a result some authorities prefer the term 'numerical video' to 'digital video' and in fact the French word is numérique. The term 'digital' is so well established that it is unlikely to change.

As both axes of the digitally represented waveform are discrete, the waveform can be accurately restored from numbers as if it were being drawn on graph paper. If we require greater accuracy, we simply choose paper with smaller squares. Clearly more numbers are then required and each one could change over a larger range.

In simple terms, the video waveform is conveyed in a digital recorder as if the voltage had been measured at regular intervals with a digital meter and the readings had been written down on a roll of paper. The rate at which the measurements were taken and the accuracy of the meter are the only factors which determine the quality, because once a parameter is expressed as a discrete number, a series of such numbers can be conveyed unchanged. Clearly in this example the handwriting used and the grade of paper have no effect on the information. The quality is determined only by the accuracy of conversion and is independent of the quality of the signal path.

1.4 Why binary?

Humans insist on using numbers expressed to the base of ten, having evolved with that number of digits. Other number bases exist; most people are familiar with the duodecimal system which uses the dozen and the gross. The most minimal system is binary, which has only two digits, 0 and 1. BInary digiTS are universally contracted to bits. These are readily conveyed in switching circuits by an 'on' state and an 'off' state. With only two states, there is little chance of error. Had humans evolved with only one finger, we might have adopted binary more commonly.

In decimal systems, the digits in a number (counting from the right, or least significant end) represent ones, tens, hundreds and thousands, etc. Fig. 1.7 shows that in binary, the bits represent one, two, four, eight, sixteen, etc. A multidigit binary number is commonly called a word, and the number of bits in the word is called the wordlength. The right-hand bit is called the least significant bit (LSB) whereas the bit on the left-hand end of the word is called the most significant bit (MSB). Clearly more digits are required in binary than in decimal, but they are more easily handled. A word of 8 bits is called a byte, which is a contraction of 'by eight'. The capacity of memories and storage media is measured in bytes, but to avoid large numbers, kilobytes, megabytes and gigabytes are often used. As memory addresses are themselves binary numbers, the wordlength limits the address range. The range is found by raising two to the power of the wordlength. Thus a 4 bit word has 16 combinations, and could address a memory having 16 locations. A 10 bit word has 1024 combinations,

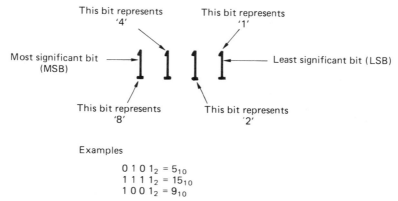

Examples

$$0\ 1\ 0\ 1_2 = 5_{10}$$
$$1\ 1\ 1\ 1_2 = 15_{10}$$
$$1\ 0\ 0\ 1_2 = 9_{10}$$

Figure 1.7 In a binary number, the digits represent increasing powers of two from the LSB. Also defined here are MSB and wordlength. When the wordlength is 8 bits, the word is a byte. Binary numbers are used as memory addresses, and the range is defined by the address wordlength. Some examples are shown here

which is close to 1000. In digital terminology, 1K = 1024, so a kilobyte of memory contains 1024 bytes. A megabyte (1MB) contains 1024 kilobytes and a gigabyte contains 1024 megabytes.

In a digital video system, the whole number representing the length of the sample is expressed in binary. The signals sent have two states, and change at predetermined times according to some stable clock. Fig. 1.8 shows the consequences of this form of transmission. If the binary signal is degraded by noise, this will be rejected by the receiver, which judges the signal solely by whether it is above or below the half-way threshold, a process known as slicing.

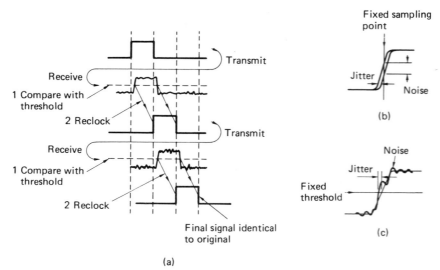

Figure 1.8 (a) A binary signal is compared with a threshold and relocked on receipt; thus the meaning will be unchanged. (b) Jitter on a signal can appear as noise with respect to fixed timing. (c) Noise on a signal can appear as jitter when compared with a fixed threshold

The signal will be carried in a channel with finite bandwidth, and this limits the slew rate of the signal; an ideally upright edge is made to slope. Noise added to a sloping signal can change the time at which the slicer judges that the level passed through the threshold. This effect is also eliminated when the output of the slicer is reclocked. However many stages the binary signal passes through, it still comes out the same, only later.

Video samples which are represented by whole numbers can be reliably carried from one place to another by such a scheme, and if the number is correctly received, there has been no loss of information *en route*.

There are two ways in which binary signals can be used to carry samples and these are shown in Fig. 1.9. When each digit of the binary number is carried on

Figure 1.9 When a signal is carried in numerical form, either parallel or serial, the mechanisms of Fig. 1.8 ensure that the only degradation is in the conversion process

a separate wire this is called parallel transmission. The state of the wires changes at the sampling rate. Using multiple wires is cumbersome, particularly where a long wordlength is in use, and a single wire can be used where successive digits from each sample are sent serially. This is the definition of pulse code modulation. Clearly the clock frequency must now be higher than the sampling rate. Whilst the transmission of video by such a scheme is advantageous in that noise and timebase error have been eliminated, there is a penalty that a high-quality colour difference signal requires around 200 million bits per second. Clearly digital video could only become commonplace when such a data rate could be handled economically. Further applications become possible when means to reduce the data rate become economic.

1.5 Why digital?

There are two main answers to this question, and it is not possible to say which is the most important, as it will depend on one's standpoint.

(1) The quality of reproduction of a well-engineered digital video system is independent of the medium and depends only on the quality of the conversion processes.
(2) The conversion of video to the digital domain allows tremendous opportunities which were denied to analog signals.

Someone who is only interested in picture quality will judge the former the most relevant. If good-quality converters can be obtained, all of the shortcomings of analog recording can be eliminated to great advantage. One's greatest effort is expended in the design of converters, whereas those parts of the system which handle data need only be workmanlike. Timebase error, tape noise, print-through, dropouts, and moiré are all history. When a digital recording is copied, the same numbers appear on the copy: it is not a dub, it is a clone. If the copy is indistinguishable from the original, there has been no generation loss. Digital recordings can be copied indefinitely without loss of quality.

In the real world everything has a cost, and one of the greatest strengths of digital technology is low cost. If copying causes no quality loss, recorders do not need to be far better than necessary in order to withstand generation loss. They need only be adequate on the first generation whose quality is then maintained. There is no need for the great size and extravagant tape consumption of professional analog recorders. When the information to be recorded is discrete numbers, they can be packed densely on the medium without quality loss. Should some bits be in error because of noise or dropout, error correction can restore the original value. Digital recordings take up less space than analog recordings for the same or better quality. Tape costs are far less and storage costs are reduced.

Digital circuitry costs less to manufacture. Switching circuitry which handles binary can be integrated more densely than analog circuitry. More functionality can be put in the same chip. Analog circuits are built from a host of different component types which have a variety of shapes and sizes and are costly to assemble and adjust. Digital circuitry uses standardized component outlines and is easier to assemble on automated equipment. Little if any adjustment is needed.

Once video is in the digital domain, it becomes data, and as such is indistinguishable from any other type of data. Systems and techniques developed in other industries for other purposes can be used for video. Computer equipment is available at low cost because the volume of production is far greater than that of professional audio equipment. Disk drives and memories developed for computers can be put to use in video products. A word processor adapted to handle video samples becomes a workstation. There seems to be little point in waiting for a tape to wind when a disk head can access data in milliseconds.

Communications networks developed to handle data can happily carry digital video and accompanying audio over indefinite distances without quality loss. Digital TV broadcasting makes use of these techniques to eliminate the interference, fading and multipath reception problems of analog broadcasting. At the same time, more efficient use is made of available bandwidth.

Digital equipment can have self-diagnosis programs built in. The machine points out its own failures. The days of chasing a signal with an oscilloscope are over. Even if a faulty component in a digital circuit could be located with such a primitive tool, it is well nigh impossible to replace a chip having 60 pins soldered through a six-layer circuit board. The cost of finding the fault may be more than the board is worth. Routine, mind-numbing adjustment of analog circuits to counteract drift is no longer needed. The cost of maintenance falls. A small operation may not need maintenance staff at all; a service contract is sufficient. A larger organization will still need maintenance staff, but they will be fewer in number and their skills will be oriented more to systems than devices.

As a result of the above, the cost of ownership of digital equipment is less than that of analog. Debates about quality are academic; analog equipment can no longer compete economically, and it will dwindle away as surely as the transistor once replaced the vacuum tube in electronics and the turbine replaced the piston engine in commercial aviation.

1.6 Some digital video processes outlined

Whilst digital video is a large subject, it is not necessarily a difficult one. Every process can be broken down into smaller steps, each of which is relatively easy to follow. The main difficulty with study is to appreciate where the small steps fit in the overall picture. Subsequent chapters of this book will describe the key processes found in digital technology in some detail, whereas this chapter illustrates why these processes are necessary and shows how they are combined in various ways in real equipment. Once the general structure of digital devices is appreciated, the following chapters can be put in perspective.

(a)

(b)

Figure 1.10 In (a) two converters are joined by a serial link. Although simple, this system is deficient because it has no means to prevent noise on the clock lines causing jitter at the receiver. In (b) a phase-locked loop is incorporated, which filters jitter from the clock

Fig. 1.10(a) shows a minimal digital video system. This is no more than a point-to-point link which conveys analog video from one place to another. It consists of a pair of converters and hardware to serialize and deserialize the samples. There is a need for standardization in serial transmission so that various devices can be connected together. These standards for digital interfaces are described in Chapter 7.

Analog video entering the system is converted in the analog-to-digital converter (ADC) to samples which are expressed as binary numbers. A typical sample would have a wordlength of 8 bits. The sample is connected in parallel into an output register which controls the cable drivers. The cable also carries the sampling-rate clock. The data are sent to the other end of the line where a slicer rejects noise picked up on each signal. Sliced data are then loaded into a receiving register by the clock and sent to the digital-to-analog converter (DAC), which converts the sample back to an analog voltage.

Following a casual study one might conclude that if the converters were of transparent quality, the system must be ideal. Unfortunately this is incorrect. As Fig. 1.8 showed, noise can change the timing of a sliced signal. Whilst this system rejects noise which threatens to change the numerical value of the samples, it is powerless to prevent noise from causing jitter in the receipt of the word clock. Noise on the word clock means that samples are not converted with a regular timebase and the impairment caused can be noticeable. Stated another way, analog characteristics of the interconnect are not prevented from affecting the reproduced waveform and so the system is not truly digital.

The jitter problem is overcome in Fig. 1.10(b) by the inclusion of a phase-locked loop which is an oscillator which synchronizes itself to the *average* frequency of the clock but which filters out the instantaneous jitter. The operation of a phase-locked loop is analogous to the function of the flywheel on a piston engine. The samples are then fed to the converter with a regular spacing and the impairment is no longer audible. Chapter 3 shows why the effect occurs and deduces the clock accuracy needed for accurate conversion.

1.7 The frame store

The system of Fig. 1.10 is extended in Fig. 1.11 by the addition of some random access memory (RAM). The operation of RAM is described in Chapter 2. What

Figure 1.11 In the frame store, the recording medium is a random access memory (RAM). Recording time available is short compared with other media, but access to the recording is immediate and flexible as it is controlled by addressing the RAM

the device does is determined by the way in which the RAM address is controlled. If the RAM address increases by one every time a sample from the ADC is stored in the RAM, a recording can be made for a short period until the RAM is full. The recording can be played back by repeating the address sequence at the same clock rate but reading the memory into the DAC. The result is generally called a frame store.[3] If the memory capacity is increased, the device can be used for recording. At a rate of 200 million bits per second, each frame needs a megabyte of memory and so the RAM recorder will be restricted to a fairly short playing time.

Using data reduction, the playing time of a RAM-based recorder can be extended. For predetermined images such as test patterns and station IDs, read only memory (ROM) can be used instead as it is non-volatile.

1.8 The synchronizer

If the RAM is used in a different way, it can be written and read at the same time. The device then becomes a synchronizer which allows video interchange between two systems which are not genlocked. Controlling the relationship between the addresses makes the RAM into a variable delay. The addresses are generated by counters which overflow to zero after they have reached a maximum count at the end of a frame. As a result the memory space appears to be circular as shown in Fig. 1.12. The read and write addresses chase one another

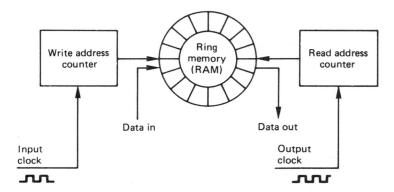

Figure 1.12 If the memory address is arranged to come from a counter which overflows, the memory can be made to appear circular. The write address then rotates endlessly, overwriting previous data once per revolution. The read address can follow the write address by a variable distance (not exceeding one revolution) and so a variable delay takes place between reading and writing

around the circle. If the read address follows close behind the write address, the delay is short. If it just stays ahead of the write address, the maximum delay is reached. If the input and output have an identical frame rate, the address relationship will be constant, but if there is a drift then the address relationship will change slowly. Eventually the addresses will coincide and then cross. Properly handled, this results in a frame being omitted or repeated.

A synchronizer with less than a frame of RAM can be used to remove static timing errors due, for example, to propagation delays in large systems. The finite RAM capacity gives a finite range of timing error which can be accommodated. This is known as the window.

1.9 The DVE

The modern digital video effects (DVE) unit has a large repertoire of manipulations. These can be divided into various categories. Certain effects such as posterization or mosaicing do not move the picture and are quite simple to perform. These simple effects are treated in Chapter 2. More complex effects manipulate the size and position of the picture. Fig. 1.13 shows that these are

Figure 1.13 A DVE manipulates images by transferring from one memory to another but using different read and write addresses

achieved by transferring pixel data from one frame store to another. The read and write addresses are different so that pixel values move across the screen. There are a number of difficulties to overcome, such as the change in pixel spacing when the size is changed, and the solution to this is a form of sampling-rate conversion. Details of the process are considered in Chapter 4 which also considers rotation in perspective and effects where the picture does not remain flat.

1.10 Time compression

When samples are converted, the ADC must run at a constant clock rate and it outputs an unbroken stream of samples during the active line. Following a break during blanking, the sample stream resumes. Time compression allows the sample stream to be broken into blocks for convenient handling.

Fig. 1.14 shows an ADC feeding a pair of RAMs. When one is being written by the ADC, the other can be read, and vice versa. As soon as the first RAM is

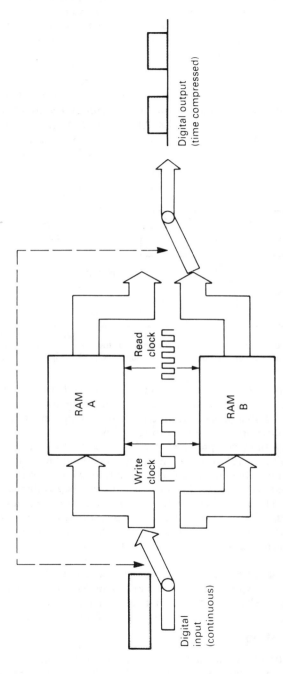

Figure 1.14 In time compression, the unbroken real-time stream of samples from an ADC is broken up into discrete blocks. This is accomplished by the configuration shown here. Samples are written into one RAM at the sampling rate by the write clock. When the first RAM is full, the switches change over, and writing continues into the second RAM whilst the first is read using a higher-frequency clock. The RAM is read faster than it was written and so all of the data will be output before the other RAM is full. This opens spaces in the data flow which are used as described in the text

full, the ADC output switches to the input of the other RAM so that there is no loss of samples. The first RAM can then be read at a higher clock rate than the sampling rate. As a result the RAM is read in less time than it took to write it, and the output from the system then pauses until the second RAM is full. The samples are now time compressed. Instead of being an unbroken stream which is difficult to handle, the samples are now arranged in blocks with convenient pauses in between them. In these pauses numerous processes can take place. A rotary-head recorder might spread the data from a field over several tape tracks; a hard disk might move to another track. In all types of recording, the time compression of the samples allows time for synchronizing patterns, subcode and error-correction words to be recorded.

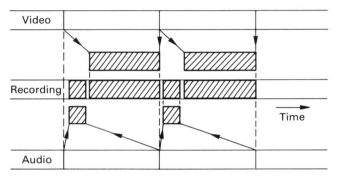

Figure 1.15 Time compression is used to shorten the length of track needed by the video. Heavily time-compressed audio samples can then be recorded on the same track using common circuitry

In digital VTRs, the video data are time compressed so that part of the track is left for audio data. Fig. 1.15 shows that heavy time compression of the audio data raises the data rate up to that of the video data so that the same tracks, heads and much common circuitry can be used to record both.

Subsequently, any time compression can be reversed by time expansion. Samples are written into a RAM at the incoming clock rate, but read out at the standard sampling rate. Unless there is a design fault, time compression is totally undetectable. In a recorder, the time expansion stage can be combined with the timebase-correction stage so that speed variations in the medium can be eliminated at the same time. The use of time compression is universal in digital recording. In general the *instantaneous* data rate at the medium is not the same as the rate at the converters, although clearly the *average* rate must be the same.

Another application of time compression is to allow several channels of audio to be carried along with video on a single cable. This technique is used in the serial digital interface (SDI) which is explained in Chapter 7.

1.11 Synchronization

The issue of signal timing has always been critical in analog video, particularly in composite working, but the adoption of digital routing relaxes the requirements considerably. Analog vision mixers need to be fed by equal-length cables from the router to prevent propagation delay variation. In the digital domain this is no longer an issue as delay is easily obtained and each input of a digital vision mixer can have its own local timebase corrector. Provided signals are received having timing within the window of the inputs, all inputs are retimed to the same phase within the mixer. Chapter 7 deals with synchronizing large systems.

1.12 Error correction and concealment

As anyone familiar with analog recording will know, magnetic tape is an imperfect medium. It suffers from noise and dropouts, which in analog recording are visible. In a digital recording of binary data, a bit is either correct or wrong, with no intermediate stage. Small amounts of noise are rejected, but inevitably, infrequent noise impulses cause some individual bits to be in error. Dropouts cause a larger number of bits in one place to be in error. An error of this kind is called a burst error. Whatever the medium and whatever the nature of the mechanism responsible, data either are recovered correctly, or suffer some combination of bit errors and burst errors. In optical discs, random errors can be caused by imperfections in the moulding process, whereas burst errors are due to contamination or scratching of the disc surface.

The visibility of a bit error depends upon which bit of the sample is involved. If the LSB of one sample was in error in a detailed, contrasty picture, the effect would be totally masked and no-one could detect it. Conversely, if the MSB of one sample was in error in a flat field, no-one could fail to notice the resulting spot. Clearly a means is needed to render errors from the medium inaudible. This is the purpose of error correction.

In binary, a bit has only two states. If it is wrong, it is only necessary to reverse the state and it must be right. Thus the correction process is trivial and perfect. The main difficulty is in identifying the bits which are in error. This is done by coding the data by adding redundant bits. Adding redundancy is not confined to digital technology: airliners have several engines and cars have twin braking systems. Clearly the more failures which have to be handled, the more redundancy is needed. If a four-engined airliner is designed to fly normally with one engine failed, three of the engines have enough power to reach cruise speed, and the fourth one is redundant. The amount of redundancy is equal to the amount of failure which can be handled. In the case of the failure of two engines, the plane can still fly, but it must slow down; this is graceful degradation. Clearly the chances of a two-engine failure on the same flight are remote.

In digital recording, the amount of error which can be corrected is proportional to the amount of redundancy, and it will be shown in Chapter 6 that within this limit, the samples are returned to exactly their original value. Consequently *corrected* samples are indetectable. If the amount of error exceeds the amount of redundancy, correction is not possible, and, in order to allow graceful degradation, concealment will be used. Concealment is a process where the value of a missing sample is estimated from those nearby. The estimated sample value is not necessarily exactly the same as the original, and so under some circumstances concealment can be audible, especially if it is frequent. However, in a well-designed system, concealments occur with negligible frequency unless there is an actual fault or problem.

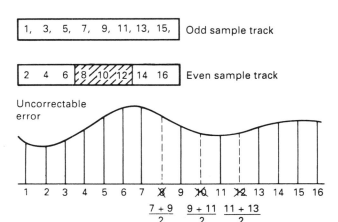

Figure 1.16 In cases where the error correction is inadequate, concealment can be used provided that the samples have been ordered appropriately in the recording. Odd and even samples are recorded in different places as shown here. As a result an uncorrectable error causes incorrect samples to occur singly, between correct samples. In the example shown, sample 8 is incorrect, but samples 7 and 9 are unaffected and an approximation to the value of sample 8 can be had by taking the average value of the two. This interpolated value is substituted for the incorrect value

Concealment is made possible by rearranging the sample sequence prior to recording. This is shown in Fig. 1.16 where odd-numbered samples are separated from even-numbered samples prior to recording. The odd and even sets of samples may be distributed over two tape tracks, so that an uncorrectable burst error only affects one set. On replay, the samples are recombined into their natural sequence, and the error is now split up so that it results in every other sample being lost in a two-dimensional structure. The picture is now described half as often, but can still be reproduced with some loss of accuracy. This is better than not being reproduced at all even if it is not perfect. Almost all digital recorders use such an odd/even distribution for concealment. Clearly if any errors are fully correctable, the distribution is a waste of time; it is only needed if correction is not possible.

The presence of an error-correction system means that the video (and audio) quality is independent of the tape/head quality within limits. There is no point in trying to assess the health of a machine by watching a monitor or listening to the audio, as this will not reveal whether the error rate is normal or within a whisker of failure. The only useful procedure is to monitor the frequency with which errors are being corrected, and to compare it with normal figures. Professional DVTRs have an error rate display for this purpose and in addition most allow the error-correction system to be disabled for testing.

1.13 Product codes

In high-density recorders, more data are lost in a given-sized dropout. Adding redundancy equal to the size of a dropout to every code is inefficient. Fig. 1.17(a)

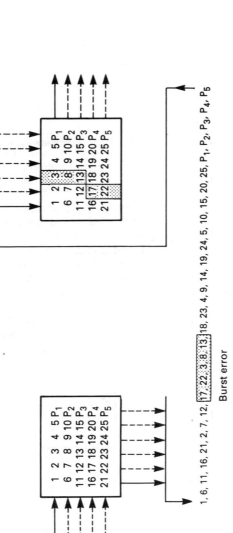

(a)

Figure 1.17(a) Interleaving is essential to make error correction schemes more efficient. Samples written sequentially in rows into a memory have redundancy P added to each row. The memory is then read in columns and the data sent to the recording medium. On replay the non-sequential samples from the medium are de-interleaved to return them to their normal sequence. This breaks up the burst error (shaded) into one error symbol per row in the memory, which can be corrected by the redundancy P

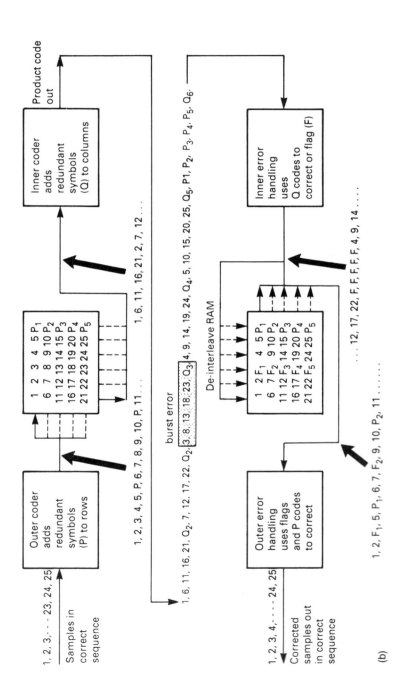

Figure 1.17(b) In addition to the redundancy P on rows, inner redundancy Q is also generated on columns. On replay, the Q code checker will pass on flags F if it finds an error too large to handle itself. The flags pass through the de-interleave process and are used by the outer error correction to identify which symbol in the row needs correcting with P redundancy. The concept of crossing two codes in this way is called a product code

(b)

shows that the efficiency of the system can be raised using interleaving. Following distribution, sequential samples from the ADC are assembled into codes, but these are not recorded in their natural sequence. A number of sequential codes are assembled along rows in a memory. When the memory is full, it is copied to the medium by reading down columns. On replay, the samples need to be de-interleaved to return them to their natural sequence. This is done by writing samples from tape into a memory in columns, and when it is full, the memory is read in rows. Samples read from the memory are now in their original sequence so there is no effect on the recording. However, if a burst error occurs on the medium as is shown shaded on the diagram, it will damage sequential samples in a vertical direction in the de-interleave memory. When the memory is read, a single large error is broken down into a number of small errors whose size is exactly equal to the correcting power of the codes and the correction is performed with maximum efficiency.

An extension of the process of interleave is where the memory array has not only rows made into codewords, but also columns made into codewords by the addition of vertical redundancy. This is known as a product code. Fig. 1.17(b) shows that in a product code the redundancy calculated first and checked last is called the outer code, and the redundancy calculated second and checked first is called the inner code. The inner code is formed along tracks on the medium. Random errors due to noise are corrected by the inner code and do not impair the burst correcting power of the outer code. Burst errors are declared uncorrectable by the inner code which flags the bad samples on the way into the de-interleave memory. The outer code reads the error flags in order to locate the erroneous data. As it does not have to compute the error locations, the outer code can correct more errors.

The interleave, de-interleave, time compression and timebase-correction processes cause delay and this is evident in the timing of the confidence replay output of DVTRs.

1.14 Shuffling

When a product-code-based recording suffers an uncorrectable error the result is a rectangular block of failed sample values which require concealment. Such a regular structure would be visible even after concealment, and an additional process is necessary to reduce the visibility. Fig. 1.18 shows that a shuffle process is performed prior to product coding in which the pixels are moved around the picture in a pseudo-random fashion. The reverse process is used on replay, and the overall effect is nullified. However, if an uncorrectable error occurs, this will only pass through the de-shuffle and so the regular structure of the failed data blocks will be randomized. The errors are spread across the picture as individual failed pixels in an irregular structure. Chapter 9 treats shuffling techniques in more detail.

1.15 Channel coding

In most recorders used for storing digital information, the medium carries a track which reproduces a single waveform. Clearly data words representing video samples contain many bits and so they have to be recorded serially, a bit at a time. Some media, such as disks, only have one active track, so it must be totally self-

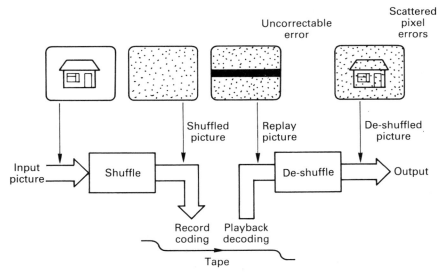

Figure 1.18 The shuffle before recording and the corresponding de-shuffle after playback cancel out as far as the picture is concerned. However, a block of errors due to dropout only experiences the de-shuffle, which spreads the error randomly over the screen. The pixel errors are then easier to correct

contained. DVTRs usually have two or four tracks read or written on simultaneously. At high recording densities, physical tolerances cause phase shifts, or timing errors, between tracks and so it is not possible to read them in parallel. Each track must still be self-contained until the replayed signal has been timebase corrected.

Recording data serially is not as simple as connecting the serial output of a shift register to the head. In digital video, samples may contain strings of identical bits. If a shift register is loaded with such a sample and shifted out serially, the output stays at a constant level for the period of the identical bits, and nothing is recorded on the track. On replay there is nothing to indicate how many bits were present, or even how fast to move the medium. Clearly serialized raw data cannot be recorded directly; they have to be modulated into a waveform which contains an embedded clock irrespective of the values of the bits in the samples. On replay a circuit called a data separator can lock to the embedded clock and use it to separate strings of identical bits.

The process of modulating serial data to make them self-clocking is called channel coding. Channel coding also shapes the spectrum of the serialized waveform to make it more efficient. With a good channel code, more data can be stored on a given medium. Spectrum shaping is used in optical discs to prevent the data from interfering with the focus and tracking servos, and in certain DVTRs to allow re-recording without erase heads.

Channel coding is also needed to broadcast digital television signals where shaping of the spectrum is an obvious requirement to avoid interference with other services. NICAM TV sound and digital audio broadcasting (DAB) rely on it.

All of the techniques of channel coding are covered in detail in Chapter 5.

1.16 Standards conversion

In addition to changing the number of lines in the picture, standards conversion requires new fields to be created on the time axis in between input fields, as shown in Fig. 1.19. Both of these processes are a form of sampling-rate conversion and are performed with logic similar to that contained in a DVE. The field-rate conversion requires interpolation along the time axis using several fields, typically four, as input. Objects which are moving appear in different

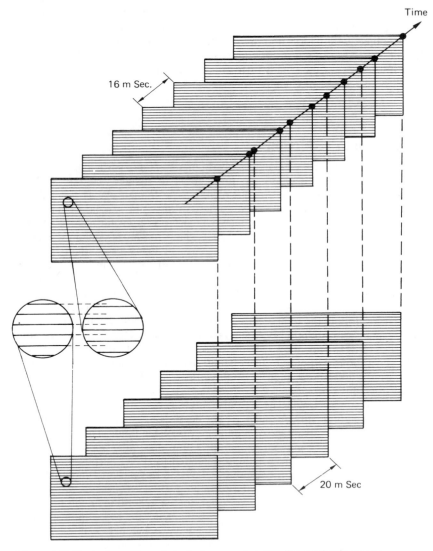

Figure 1.19 The basic problem of standards conversion. The line spacing is easy to accommodate. The field spacing is not

places in each field and with a conventional standards converter the result is judder or double images in the output. Until recently these motion artefacts had to be accepted, but now solutions are available at the cost of some complexity.

Motion estimation is a technique for measuring how objects in a television picture move from one image to another. The movement is expressed as a series of motion vectors which have both direction and magnitude. Motion compensation is a technique which uses the motion vectors to enhance some process. One of the first applications is in motion-compensated standards conversion which identifies moving objects and measures their displacement from field to field. An opposing, or compensating, displacement can then be used in each input field to align each object with its location in the output field. The result is freedom from judder and better resolution of moving objects.

In the future there will be many different devices based on this technology and these will be discussed in Chapter 4.

1.17 Video data reduction

Digital video suffers from an extremely high data rate, particularly in high definition, and one approach to the problem is to reduce that rate without affecting the subjective quality of the picture. The human eye is not equally sensitive to all spatial frequencies, so some coding gain can be obtained by quantizing more coarsely the frequencies which are less visible. Video images typically contain a great deal of redundancy where flat areas contain the same pixel value repeated many times. Furthermore, in many cases there is little difference between one field and the next, and interfield data reduction can be achieved by sending only the differences. Whilst this may achieve considerable reduction, the result is difficult to edit because individual fields can no longer be identified in the data stream. Thus for production purposes, data reduction is restricted to exploiting the redundancy within each field individually. Production DVTRs such as Sony's Digital Betacam and the Ampex DCT use only very mild compression of 2:1. This allows simple algorithms to be used and also permits multiple generations without artefacts being visible. A similar approach is used in disk-based workstations such as Lightworks and AVID. Data reduction is discussed in Chapter 4.

Clearly a consumer DVTR needs only single-generation operation and has simple editing requirements. A much greater degree of compression can then be used, which also takes advantage of redundancy between fields. The same is true for broadcasting, where bandwidth is at a premium. A similar approach may be used in disk-based camcorders which are intended for ENG purposes.

There is now no doubt that the future of television broadcasting (and radio for that matter) lies in data-reduced digital technology.

Data reduction requires an encoder prior to the recording medium and a decoder after it. Unless the correct decoder is available, the recording cannot be played. Interchange of data-reduced material will be hampered unless coding standards are available. Data reduction and the corresponding decoding are complex processes and take time, adding to existing delays in signal paths. Concealment of uncorrectable errors is also more difficult on reduced data.

1.18 Disk based recording

The magnetic disk drive was perfected by the computer industry to allow rapid random access to data, and so it makes an ideal medium for editing. As will be seen in Chapter 10, the heads do not touch the disk, but are supported on a thin air film which gives them a long life but which restricts the recording density. Thus disks cannot compete with tape for lengthy recordings, but for short-duration work such as commercials or animation they have no equal. The data rate of digital video is too high for a single disk head, and so a number of solutions have been explored. One obvious solution is to use data reduction, which cuts the data rate and extends the playing time. Another approach is to use special multiplatter disk drives in which each disk head has its own circuitry allowing parallel transfer. Yet another possibility is to operate a large array of conventional drives in parallel. The highest-capacity magnetic disks are not removable from the drive.

Development of the optical disc was stimulated by the availability of low-cost lasers. Optical discs are available in many different types, some of which can only be recorded once, some of which are erasable. These will be contrasted in Chapter 10. Optical discs have in common the fact that access is generally slower than with magnetic drives and it is difficult to obtain high data rates, but most of them are removable and can act as interchange media.

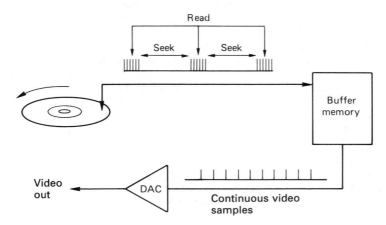

Figure 1.20 In a hard disk recorder, a large-capacity memory is used as a buffer or timebase corrector between the converters and the disk. The memory allows the converters to run constantly despite the interruptions in disk transfer caused by the head moving between tracks

The disk drive suffers from intermittent data transfer owing to the need to reposition the heads. Fig. 1.20 shows that disk-based devices rely on a quantity of RAM acting as a buffer between the real-time video environment and the intermittent data environment.

Fig. 1.21 shows the block diagram of a camcorder based on hard disks and data reduction. The recording time and picture quality will not compete with full-bandwidth tape-based devices, but following acquisition the disks can be used directly in an edit system, allowing a useful time saving in ENG applications.

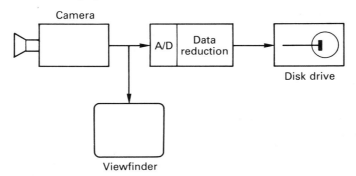

Figure 1.21 In a disk based camcorder, PCM data rate from the camera is too high for direct recording on disk. Data reduction is used to cut the bit rate and extend playing time. If standard file structure is used, disks may be physically transferred to an edit system after recording

1.19 Rotary-head digital recorders

The rotary-head recorder has the advantage that the spinning heads create a high head-to-tape speed offering a high bit rate recording without high tape speed. Whilst mechanically complex, the rotary-head transport has been raised to a high degree of refinement and offers the highest recording density and thus lowest cost per bit of all digital recorders.[4] Rotary-head transports are considered in Chapter 8.

Digital VTRs segment incoming fields into several tape tracks and invisibly reassemble them in memory on replay in order to keep the tracks reasonably short.

Fig. 1.22 shows a representative block diagram of a DVTR. Following the converters, an optional data reduction unit may be found. There will be distribution of odd and even samples and a shuffle process for concealment purposes. An interleaved product code will be formed prior to the channel coding stage which produces the recorded waveform. On replay the data separator decodes the channel code and the inner and outer codes perform correction as in Section 1.11. Following the de-shuffle the data channels are recombined and any necessary concealment will take place. Any data expansion necessary will be performed prior to the output converters. Chapter 9 treats the signal systems of rotary-head recorders in some detail.

1.20 Digital broadcasting

Although it has given good service for many years, analog television broadcasting is extremely inefficient because the transmitted waveform is directly compatible with the CRT display, and nothing is transmitted during the blanking periods whilst the beam retraces. Using time compression, data reduction and digital modulation techniques the same picture quality can be obtained in a fraction of the bandwidth of analog. Pressure on spectrum use from other users such as mobile telephones will only increase and this will ensure that future television and radio broadcasts will be digital.

If high-definition television ever reaches the home it will do so via digital data-reduced transmission as the bandwidth required will otherwise be hopelessly

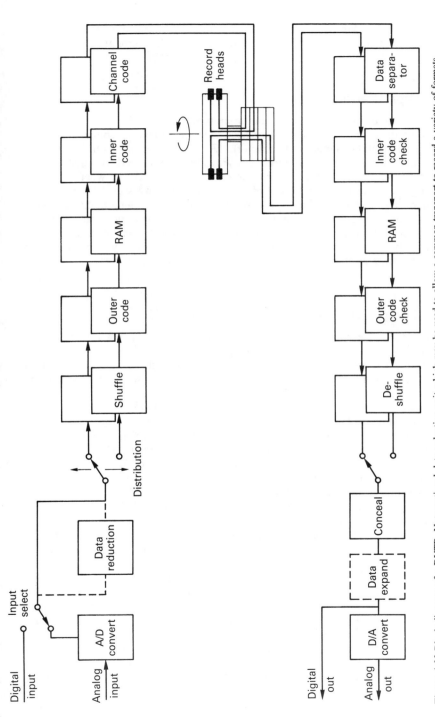

Figure 1.22 Block diagram of a DVTR. Note optional data reduction unit which may be used to allow a common transport to record a variety of formats

uneconomic. In addition to conserving spectrum, digital transmission is resistant to multipath reception and gives consistent picture quality throughout the service area.

1.21 Digital audio

Audio was traditionally the poor relation in television, and the situation was not helped by the characteristics of rotary-head video recorders which had low linear tape speed by audio standards and high flutter. Most of the advantages attributed to digital video also apply to audio, and have recently helped to transform TV sound. Digital audio eliminates wow, flutter and phase errors between channels, and the use of error correction eliminates dropouts. Any signal-to-noise ratio required can be had by choice of a suitable sample wordlength. In fact most DVTRs can record 20 bit audio and thus outperform many audio-only formats. The Compact Disc served to raise the consumer's expectations in audio and this was shortly followed by the NICAM 728 digital transmission system. In view of the importance of audio in today's television productions, the entire contents of Chapter 12 are devoted to it.

1.22 The potential

Digital video does far more than merely compare favourably with analog. Its most exciting aspects are the tremendous possibilities which are denied to analog technology. Error correction, data reduction, motion estimation and interpolation are difficult or impossible in the analog domain, but are straightforward in the digital domain. Once converted, the original picture is just a series of numbers, and these can be stored, conveyed and processed in many and varied ways. The computer industry has spent decades perfecting machines to store, convey and process streams of numbers at high speed and at a cost which continues to fall. Computers can generate artificial images for computer-aided design systems and simulators. Work has been done on the improvement of resolution and the elimination of flicker and other artefacts via oversampling and motion compensation techniques, and broadcast digital video can take full advantage of such techniques. Recordings can be stored on computer disk drives, magnetic or optical, whose radially moving heads allow rapid random access to the information. For animation or editing of video, this is far superior to waiting for tape recorders to shuttle and preroll, although the sheer data rate of digital video prevents current disk-based machines from economically making lengthy recordings. An edit can be effected by reading samples from two sources and fading or switching between them in digital circuitry. The edit can be simulated, so that the outcome can be assessed, and the edit points can be moved around at will until the result is satisfactory. The final edited version can be recorded on a different medium if necessary, leaving the source material intact.

The cable and satellite communications networks around the world are increasingly being used for digital transmission, and a packet of digital video information can pass through as easily as a telex message or a bank transaction. Provided the original numbers are fed in the correct order at the correct rate to the final destination, for conversion to a picture, it does not matter how they have been conveyed.

The worlds of digital video, digital audio, communication and computation are closely related, and that is where the real potential lies. The time when television was a specialist subject which could evolve in isolation from other disciplines has gone; digital technology has made sure of that. Video has now become a branch of data processing.

At one time computers were too slow to handle digital video and special purpose hardware was made for broadcast use at considerable cost. As processing speeds continue to rise, an increasing number of tasks can be undertaken at low cost by general purpose processors with suitable software. Inevitably the very nature of broadcast equipment and the ways in which it is used will change along with the manufacturers who supply it. The computer industry will soon compete with traditional broadcast manufacturers, but they will have the economics of mass production on their side.

References

1. Ginsburg, C.P., Comprehensive description of the Ampex video tape recorder. *SMPTE J.*, **66** 177–182 (1957)
2. Devereux, V.G., Pulse code modulation of video signals: 8 bit coder and decoder. *BBC Res. Dep. Rep.*, **EL-42**, No.25 (1970)
3. Pursell, S. and Newby, H., Digital frame store for television video. *SMPTE J.*, **82**, 402–403 (1973)
4 Baldwin, J.L.E., Digital television recording – history and background. *SMPTE J.*, **95**, 1206–1214 (1986)

Some essential principles

The conversion process expresses the analog input as a numerical code. The choice of code for video will be shown to be governed by the requirements of the processing. Within the digital domain, all signal processing must be performed by arithmetic manipulation of the code values in suitable logic circuits. All of the necessary principles of binary arithmetic and their implementation in logic are shown here. Processes required to implement simple vision mixers and filters are introduced here. Advanced processes are considered in Chapter 4.

2.1 Pure binary code

For digital video use, the prime purpose of binary numbers is to express the values of the samples which represent the original analog video waveform. Fig. 2.1 shows some binary numbers and their equivalent in decimal. The radix point has the same significance in binary: symbols to the right of it represent one-half, one-quarter and so on. Binary is convenient for electronic circuits, which do not get tired, but numbers expressed in binary become very long, and writing them is tedious and error prone. The octal and hexadecimal notations are both used for writing binary since conversion is so simple. Fig. 2.1 also shows that a binary number is split into groups of three or four digits starting at the least significant end, and the groups are individually converted to octal or hexadecimal digits. Since 16 different symbols are required in hex, the letters A–F are used for the numbers above nine.

There will be a fixed number of bits in a PCM video sample, and this number determines the size of the quantizing range. In the 8 bit samples used in much digital video equipment, there are 256 different numbers. Each number represents a different analog signal voltage, and care must be taken during conversion to ensure that the signal does not go outside the converter range, or it will be clipped. In Fig. 2.2(a) it will be seen that in an 8 bit pure binary system, the number range goes from 00 hex, which represents the smallest voltage, through to FF hex, which represents the largest positive voltage. The video waveform must be accommodated within this voltage range, and Fig. 2.2(b) shows how this can be done for a PAL composite signal. A luminance signal is shown in Fig. 2.2(c). As component digital systems only handle the active line, the quantizing range is optimized to suit the gamut of the unblanked luminance. There is a small offset in order to handle slightly misadjusted inputs.

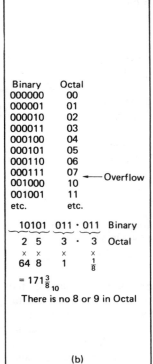

Figure 2.1 (a) Binary and decimal. (b) In octal, groups of 3 bits make one symbol 0–7. (c) In hex, groups of 4 bits make one symbol 0–F. Note how much shorter the number is in hex

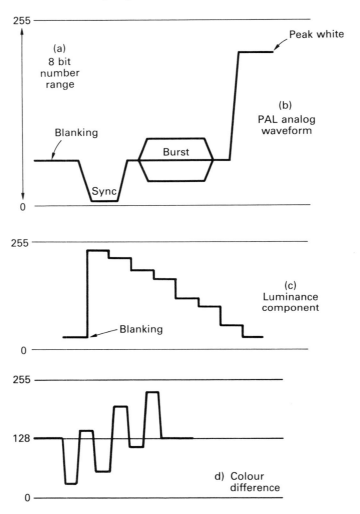

Figure 2.2 The unipolar quantizing range of an 8 bit pure binary system is shown at (a). The analog input must be shifted to fit into the quantizing range, as shown for PAL at (b). In component, sync pulses are not digitized, so the quantizing intervals can be smaller as at (c). An offset of half scale is used for colour difference signals (d)

Colour difference signals are bipolar and so blanking is in the centre of the signal range. In order to accommodate colour difference signals in the quantizing range, the blanking voltage level of the analog waveform has been shifted as in Fig. 2.2(d) so that the positive and negative voltages in a real audio signal can be expressed by binary numbers which are only positive. This approach is called offset binary. Strictly speaking both the composite and luminance signals are also offset binary because the blanking level is part way up the quantizing scale.

Offset binary is perfectly acceptable where the signal has been digitized only for recording or transmission from one place to another, after which it will be

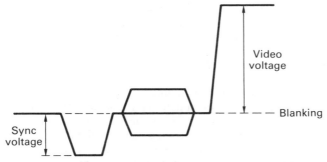

Figure 2.3 All video signal voltages are referred to blanking and must be added with respect to that level

converted directly back to analog. Under these conditions it is not necessary for the quantizing steps to be uniform, provided both ADC and DAC are constructed to the same standard. In practice, it is the requirements of signal processing in the digital domain which make both non-uniform quantizing and offset binary unsuitable.

Fig. 2.3 shows that analog video signal voltages are referred to blanking. The level of the signal is measured by how far the waveform deviates from blanking, and attenuation, gain and mixing all take place around blanking level. Digital vision mixing is achieved by adding sample values from two or more different sources, but unless all of the quantizing intervals are of the same size and there is no offset, the sum of two sample values will not represent the sum of the two original analog voltages. Thus sample values which have been obtained by non-uniform or offset quantizing cannot readily be processed because the binary numbers are not proportional to the signal voltage.

Figure 2.4 The result of an attempted attenuation in pure binary code is an offset. Pure binary cannot be used for digital video processing

If two offset binary sample streams are added together in an attempt to perform digital mixing, the result will be that the offsets are also added and this may lead to an overflow. Similarly, if an attempt is made to attenuate by, say, 6.02 dB by dividing all of the sample values by two, Fig. 2.4 shows that the offset is also divided and the waveform suffers a shifted baseline. This problem can be overcome with digital luminance signals simply by subtracting the offset from each sample before processing as this results in numbers truly proportional to the luminance voltage. This approach is not suitable for colour difference or composite signals because negative numbers would result when the analog voltage goes below blanking and pure binary coding cannot handle them. The problem with offset binary is that it works with reference to one end of the range. What is needed is a numbering system which operates symmetrically with reference to the centre of the range.

2.2 Two's complement

In the two's complement system, the upper half of the pure binary number range has been redefined to represent negative quantities. If a pure binary counter is

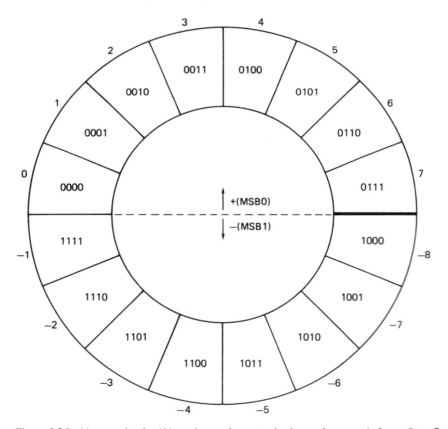

Figure 2.5 In this example of a 4 bit two's complement code, the number range is from −8 to +7. Note that the MSB determines polarity

constantly incremented and allowed to overflow, it will produce all the numbers in the range permitted by the number of available bits, and these are shown for a 4 bit example drawn around the circle in Fig. 2.5. As a circle has no real beginning, it is possible to consider it to start wherever it is convenient. In two's complement, the quantizing range represented by the circle of numbers does not start at zero, but starts on the diametrically opposite side of the circle. Zero is midrange, and all numbers with the MSB (Most Significant Bit) set are considered negative. The MSB is thus the equivalent of a sign bit where 1 = minus. Two's complement notation differs from pure binary in that the MSB is inverted in order to achieve the half circle rotation.

Fig. 2.6 shows how a real ADC is configured to produce two's complement output. At (a) an analog offset voltage equal to one-half the quantizing range is added to the bipolar analog signal in order to make it unipolar as at (b). The ADC produces positive-only numbers at (c) which are proportional to the input voltage. The MSB is then inverted at (d) so that the all-zeros code moves to the centre of the quantizing range. The analog offset is often incorporated in the ADC as is the MSB inversion. Some converters are designed to be used in either pure binary or two's complement mode. In this case the designer must arrange the appropriate DC conditions at the input. The MSB inversion may be selectable by an external logic level. In the digital video interface standards the colour difference signals use offset binary because the codes of all zeros and all ones are at the end of the range and can be reserved for synchronizing. A digital vision

Figure 2.6 A two's complement ADC. At (a) an analog offset voltage equal to one-half the quantizing range is added to the bipolar analog signal in order to make it unipolar as at (b). The ADC produces positive only numbers at (c), but the MSB is then inverted at (d) to give a two's complement output

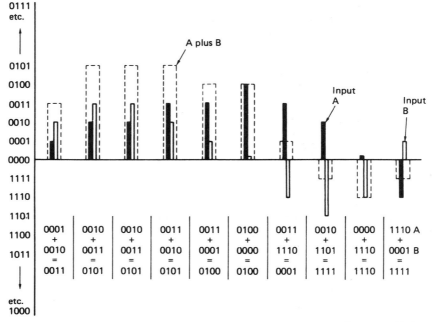

Figure 2.7 Using two's complement arithmetic, single values from two waveforms are added together with respect to midrange to give a correct mixing function

mixer simply inverts the MSB of each colour difference sample to convert it to two's complement.

The two's complement system allows two sample values to be added, or mixed in video parlance, and the result will be referred to the system midrange; this is analogous to adding analog signals in an operational amplifier.

Fig. 2.7 illustrates how adding two's complement samples simulates a bipolar mixing process. The waveform of input A is depicted by solid black samples, and that of B by samples with a solid outline. The result of mixing is the linear sum of the two waveforms obtained by adding pairs of sample values. The dashed lines depict the output values. Beneath each set of samples is the calculation which will be seen to give the correct result. Note that the calculations are pure binary. No special arithmetic is needed to handle two's complement numbers.

It is sometimes necessary to phase-reverse or invert a digital signal. The process of inversion in two's complement is simple. All bits of the sample value are inverted to form the one's complement, and one is added. This can be checked by mentally inverting some of the values in Fig. 2.5. The inversion is transparent and performing a second inversion gives the original sample values.

Using inversion, signal subtraction can be performed using only adding logic. The inverted input is added to perform a subtraction, just as in the analog domain. This permits a significant saving in hardware complexity, since only carry logic is necessary and no borrow mechanism need be supported.

In summary, two's complement notation is the most appropriate scheme for bipolar signals, and allows simple mixing in conventional binary adders. It is in virtually universal use in digital video and audio processing.

Two's complement numbers can have a radix point and bits below it just as pure binary numbers can. It should, however, be noted that in two's complement, if a radix point exists, numbers to the right of it are added. For example, 1100.1 is not −4.5, it is −4 + 0.5 = −3.5.

2.3 Introduction to digital processes

However complex a digital process, it can be broken down into smaller stages until finally one finds that there are really only two basic types of element in use, and these can be combined in some way and supplied with a clock to implement virtually any process. Fig. 2.8 shows that the first type is a *logical* element. This produces an output which is a logical function of the input with minimal delay. The second type is a *storage* element which samples the state of the input(s) when clocked and holds or delays that state. The strength of binary logic is that the signal has only two states, and considerable noise and distortion of the binary

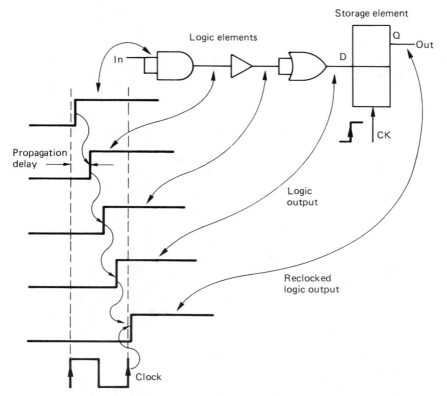

Figure 2.8 Logic elements have a finite propagation delay between input and output and cascading them delays the signal an arbitrary amount. Storage elements sample the input on a clock edge and can return a signal to near coincidence with the system clock. This is known as reclocking. Reclocking eliminates variations in propagation delay in logic elements

waveform can be tolerated before the state becomes uncertain. At every logical element, the signal is compared with a threshold, and can thus pass through any number of stages without being degraded. In addition, the use of a storage element at regular locations throughout logic circuits eliminates time variations or jitter. Fig. 2.8 shows that if the inputs to a logic element change, the output will not change until the *propagation delay* of the element has elapsed. However, if the output of the logic element forms the input to a storage element, the output of that element will not change until the input is sampled *at the next clock edge*. In this way the signal edge is aligned to the system clock and the propagation delay of the logic becomes irrelevant. The process is known as reclocking.

2.4 Logic elements

The two states of the signal when measured with an oscilloscope are simply two voltages, usually referred to as high and low. The actual voltage levels will depend on the type of logic family in use, and on the supply voltage used. Within logic, these levels are not of much consequence, and it is only necessary to know them when interfacing between different logic families or when driving external devices. The pure logic designer is not interested at all in these voltages, only in their meaning. Just as the electrical waveform from a microphone represents sound velocity, so the waveform in a logic circuit represents the truth of some statement. As there are only two states, there can only be *true* or *false* meanings. The true state of the signal can be assigned by the designer to either voltage state. When a high voltage represents a true logic condition and a low voltage represents a false condition, the system is known as *positive logic*, or *high true* logic. This is the usual system, but sometimes the low voltage represents the true condition and the high voltage represents the false condition. This is known as *negative logic* or *low true* logic. Provided that everyone is aware of the logic convention in use, both work equally well.

Negative logic is often found in the TTL (Transistor–Transistor Logic) family, because in this technology it is easier to sink current to ground than to source it from the power supply. Fig. 2.9 shows that if it is necessary to connect several logic elements to a common bus so that any one can communicate with any other, an open-collector system is used, where high levels are provided by pull-up resistors and the logic elements only pull the common line down. If positive logic were used, when no device was operating the pull-up resistors would cause the common line to take on an absurd true state; whereas if negative logic is used, the common line pulls up to a sensible false condition when there is no device using the bus. Whilst the open collector is a simple way of obtaining a shared bus system, it is limited in frequency of operation owing to the time constant of the pull-up resistors charging the bus capacitance. In the so-called tri-state bus systems, there are both active pull-up and pull-down devices connected in the so-called totem-pole output configuration. Both devices can be disabled to a third state, where the output assumes a high impedance, allowing some other driver to determine the bus state.

In logic systems, all logical functions, however complex, can be configured from combinations of a few fundamental logic elements or *gates*. It is not profitable to spend too much time debating which are the truly fundamental ones, since most can be made from combinations of others. Fig. 2.10 shows the important simple gates and their derivatives, and introduces the logical

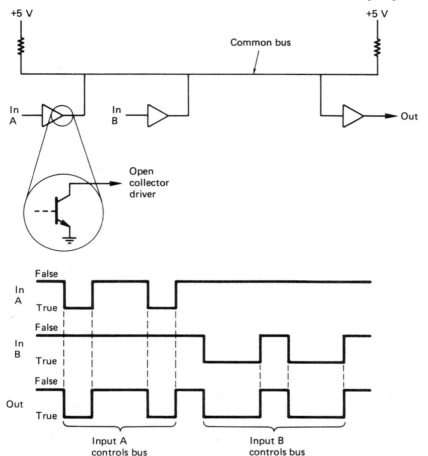

Figure 2.9 Using open-collector drive, several signal sources can share one common bus. If negative logic is used, the bus drivers turn off their output transistors with a false input, allowing another driver to control the bus. This will not happen with positive logic

expressions to describe them, which can be compared with the truth-table notation. The figure also shows the important fact that when negative logic is used, the OR gate function interchanges with that of the AND gate. Sometimes schematics are drawn to reflect which voltage state represents the true condition. In the so-called intentional logic scheme, a negative logic signal always starts and ends at an inverting 'bubble'. If an AND function is required between two negative logic signals, it will be drawn as an AND symbol with bubbles on all the terminals, even though the component used will be a positive logic OR gate. Opinions vary on the merits of intentional logic.

If numerical quantities need to be conveyed down the two-state signal paths described here, then the only appropriate numbering system is binary, which has only two symbols, 0 and 1. Just as positive or negative logic could be used for the truth of a logical binary signal, it can also be used for a numerical binary signal. Normally, a high voltage level will represent a binary 1 and a low voltage

Positive logic name	Boolean expression	Positive logic symbol	Positive logic truth table	Plain English
Inverter or NOT gate	$Q = \overline{A}$		$\begin{array}{c\|c} A & Q \\ \hline 0 & 1 \\ 1 & 0 \end{array}$	Output is opposite of input
AND gate	$Q = A \cdot B$		$\begin{array}{cc\|c} A & B & Q \\ \hline 0 & 0 & 0 \\ 0 & 1 & 0 \\ 1 & 0 & 0 \\ 1 & 1 & 1 \end{array}$	Output true when both inputs are true only
NAND (Not AND) gate	$Q = \overline{A \cdot B}$ $= \overline{A} + \overline{B}$		$\begin{array}{cc\|c} A & B & Q \\ \hline 0 & 0 & 1 \\ 0 & 1 & 1 \\ 1 & 0 & 1 \\ 1 & 1 & 0 \end{array}$	Output false when both inputs are true only
OR gate	$Q = A + B$		$\begin{array}{cc\|c} A & B & Q \\ \hline 0 & 0 & 0 \\ 0 & 1 & 1 \\ 1 & 0 & 1 \\ 1 & 1 & 1 \end{array}$	Output true if either or both inputs true
NOR (Not OR) gate	$Q = \overline{A + B}$ $= \overline{A} \cdot \overline{B}$		$\begin{array}{cc\|c} A & B & Q \\ \hline 0 & 0 & 1 \\ 0 & 1 & 0 \\ 1 & 0 & 0 \\ 1 & 1 & 0 \end{array}$	Output false if either or both inputs true
Exclusive OR (XOR) gate	$Q = A \oplus B$		$\begin{array}{cc\|c} A & B & Q \\ \hline 0 & 0 & 0 \\ 0 & 1 & 1 \\ 1 & 0 & 1 \\ 1 & 1 & 0 \end{array}$	Output true if inputs are different

Figure 2.10 The basic logic gates compared

will represent a binary 0, described as a 'high for a one' system. Clearly a 'low for a one' system is just as feasible. Decimal numbers have several columns, each of which represents a different power of ten; in binary the column position specifies the power of two.

Several binary digits or bits are needed to express the value of a binary video sample. These bits can be conveyed at the same time by several signals to form a parallel system, which is most convenient inside equipment or for short distances because it is inexpensive, or one at a time down a single signal path, which is more complex, but convenient for cables between pieces of equipment because the connectors require fewer pins. When a binary system is used to convey numbers in this way, it can be called a digital system.

2.5 Storage elements

The basic memory element in logic circuits is the latch, which is constructed from two gates as shown in Fig. 2.11(a) and which can be set or reset. A more useful variant is the D-type latch shown at (b) which remembers the state of the input at the time a separate clock either changes state for an edge-triggered device, or after it goes false for a level-triggered device. D-type latches are commonly available with four or eight latches to the chip. A shift register can be made from a series of latches by connecting the Q output of one latch to the D input of the next and connecting all of the clock inputs in parallel. Data are delayed by the number of stages in the register. Shift registers are also useful for converting between serial and parallel data transmissions.

Where large numbers of bits are to be stored, cross-coupled latches are less suitable because they are more complicated to fabricate inside integrated circuits than dynamic memory, and consume more current.

In large random access memories (RAMs), the data bits are stored as the presence or absence of charge in a tiny capacitor as shown in Fig. 2.11(c). The capacitor is formed by a metal electrode, insulated by a layer of silicon dioxide from a semiconductor substrate, hence the term MOS (Metal Oxide Semi-conductor). The charge will suffer leakage, and the value would become indeterminate after a few milliseconds. Where the delay needed is less than this, decay is of no consequence, as data will be read out before they have had a chance to decay. Where longer delays are necessary, such memories must be refreshed periodically by reading the bit value and writing it back to the same place. Most modern MOS RAM chips have suitable circuitry built in. Large RAMs store thousands of bits, and it is clearly impractical to have a connection to each one. Instead, the desired bit has to be addressed before it can be read or written. The size of the chip package restricts the number of pins available, so that large memories use the same address pins more than once. The bits are arranged internally as rows and columns, and the row address and the column address are specified sequentially on the same pins.

2.6 The phase-locked loop

All digital video systems need to be clocked at the appropriate rate in order to function properly. Whilst a clock may be obtained from a fixed-frequency oscillator such as a crystal, many operations in video require *genlocking* or synchronizing the clock to an external source. The phase-locked loop excels at this job, and many others, particularly in connection with recording and transmission.

In phase-locked loops, the oscillator can run at a range of frequencies according to the voltage applied to a control terminal. This is called a voltage-controlled oscillator or VCO. Fig. 2.12 shows that the VCO is driven by a phase error measured between the output and some reference. The error changes the control voltage in such a way that the error is reduced, such that the output eventually has the same frequency as the reference. A low-pass filter is fitted in the control voltage path to prevent the loop becoming unstable. If a divider is placed between the VCO and the phase comparator, as in the figure, the VCO frequency can be made to be a multiple of the reference. This also has the effect

Figure 2.11 Digital semiconductor memory types. In (a), one data bit can be stored in a simple set–reset latch, which has little application because the D-type latch in (b) can store the state of the single data input when the clock occurs. These devices can be implemented with bipolar transistors of FETs, and are called static memories because they can store indefinitely. They consume a lot of power

In (c), a bit is stored as the charge in a potential well in the substrate of a chip. It is accessed by connecting the bit line with the field effect from the word line. The single well where the two lines cross can then be written or read. These devices are called dynamic RAMs because the charge decays, and they must be read and rewritten (refreshed) periodically

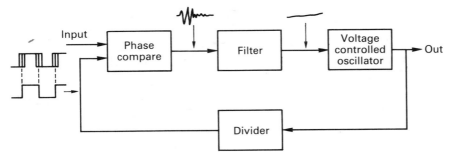

Figure 2.12 A phase-locked loop requires these components as a minimum. The filter in the control voltage serves to reduce clock jitter

Figure 2.13 In order to obtain 13.5 MHz from input syncs, a PLL with an appropriate division ratio is required

of making the loop more heavily damped, so that it is less likely to change frequency if the input is irregular.

In digital video, the frequency multiplication of a phase-locked loop is extremely useful. Fig. 2.13 shows how the 13.5 MHz clock of component digital video is obtained from the sync pulses of an analog reference by such a multiplication process. In composite systems, a phase-locked loop may lock to subcarrier instead.

2.7 Binary adding

The circuitry necessary for adding pure binary or two's complement numbers is shown in Fig. 2.14. Addition in binary requires 2-bits to be taken at a time from the same position in each word, starting at the least significant bit. Should both be ones, the output is zero, and there is a *carry-out* generated. Such a circuit is called a half adder, shown in Fig. 2.14(a), and is suitable for the least significant bit of the calculation. All higher stages will require a circuit which can accept a carry input as well as two data inputs. This is known as a full adder (Fig. 2.14(b)). Multibit full adders are available in chip form, and have carry-in and carry-out terminals to allow them to be cascaded to operate on long wordlengths. Such a device is also convenient for inverting a two's complement number, in

(a)

Data A	Bits B	Carry in	Out	Carry out
0	0	0	0	0
0	0	1	1	0
0	1	0	1	0
0	1	1	0	1
1	0	0	1	0
1	0	1	0	1
1	1	0	0	1
1	1	1	1	1

(b)

A MSB

B MSB

High when
A and B negative
but adder output
positive

High when
A and B positive
but adder output
negative

Adder
MSB

Input A

Two's
complement

Σ

Out

Input B

Maximum
positive
value

Maximum
negative
value

(c)

Figure 2.14 (a) Half adder; (b) full-adder circuit and truth table; (c) comparison of sign bits prevents wraparound on adder overflow by substituting clipping level conjunction with a set of inverters. The adder chip has one set of inputs grounded, and the carry-in permanently held true, such that it adds one to the one's complement number from the inverter.

When mixing by adding sample values, care has to be taken to ensure that if the sum of the two sample values exceeds the number range the result will be

(a)

(b)

Figure 2.15 Two configurations which are common in processing. In (a) the feedback around the adder adds the previous sum to each input to perform accumulation or digital integration. In (b) an inverter allows the difference between successive inputs to be computed. This is differentiation clipping rather than wraparound. In two's complement, the action necessary depends on the polarities of the two signals. Clearly if one positive and one negative number are added, the result cannot exceed the number range. If two positive numbers are added, the symptom of positive overflow is that the most significant bit sets, causing an erroneous negative result, whereas a negative overflow results in the most significant bit clearing. The overflow control circuit will be designed to detect these two conditions and override the adder output. If the MSB of both inputs is zero, the numbers are both positive; thus if the sum has the MSB set, the output is replaced with the maximum positive code (0111 . . .). If the MSB of both inputs is set, the numbers are both negative, and if the sum has no MSB set, the output is replaced with the maximum negative code (1000 . . .). These conditions can also be connected to warning indicators. Fig. 2.14(c) shows this system in hardware. The resultant clipping on overload is sudden, and sometimes a PROM is included which translates values around and beyond maximum to soft-clipped values below or equal to maximum.

A storage element can be combined with an adder to obtain a number of useful functional blocks which will crop up frequently in audio equipment. Fig. 2.15(a) shows that a latch is connected in a feedback loop around an adder. The latch contents are added to the input each time it is clocked. The configuration is known as an accumulator in computation because it adds up or accumulates values fed into it. In filtering, it is known as a discrete-time integrator. If the input is held at some constant value, the output increases by that amount on each clock. The output is thus a sampled ramp.

Fig. 2.15(b) shows that the addition of an inverter allows the difference between successive inputs to be obtained. This is digital differentiation. The output is proportional to the slope of the input.

2.8 Gain control by multiplication

When making a digital recording, the gain of the analog input will usually be adjusted so that the quantizing range is fully exercised in order to make a recording of maximum signal-to-noise ratio. During post production, the recording may be played back and mixed with other signals, and the desired effect can only be achieved if the level of each can be controlled independently. Gain is controlled in the digital domain by multiplying each sample value by a coefficient. If that coefficient is less than one, attenuation will result; if it is greater than one, amplification can be obtained.

Multiplication in binary circuits is difficult. It can be performed by repeated adding, but this is too slow to be of any use. In fast multiplication, one of the inputs will be simultaneously multiplied by one, two, four, etc., by hard-wired bit shifting. Fig. 2.16 shows that the other input bits will determine which of these powers will be added to produce the final sum, and which will be neglected. If multiplying by five, the process is the same as multiplying by four, multiplying by one, and adding the two products. This is achieved by adding the input to itself shifted two places. As the wordlength of such a device increases, the complexity increases exponentially, so this is a natural application for an integrated circuit. It is probably true that digital video would not have been viable without such chips.

Figure 2.16 Structure of fast multiplier: the input A is multiplied by 1, 2, 4, 8, etc., by bit shifting. The digits of the B input then determine which multiples of A should be added together by enabling AND gates between the shifters and the adder. For long wordlengths, the number of gates required becomes enormous, and the device is best implemented in a chip

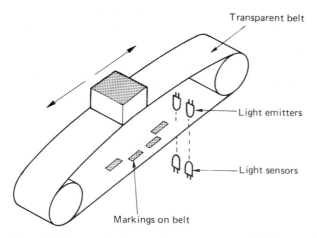

Figure 2.17 An absolute linear fader uses a number of light beams which are interrupted in various combinations according to the position of a grating. A Gray code shown in Figure 2.18 must be used to prevent false codes

2.9 Digital faders and controls

In a digital mixer, the gain coefficients will originate in hand-operated faders, just as in analog. Analog faders may be retained and used to produce a varying voltage which is converted to a digital code or gain coefficient in an ADC, but it is also possible to obtain coefficients directly in digital faders. Digital faders are a form of displacement transducer in which the mechanical position of the

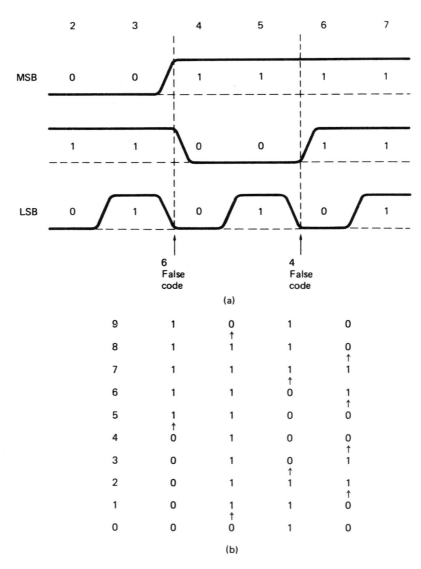

Figure 2.18 (a) Binary cannot be used for position encoders because mechanical tolerances cause false codes to be produced. (b) In Gray code, only one bit (arrowed) changes in between positions, so no false codes can be generated

control is converted directly to a digital code. The position of other controls, such as jog wheels on VTRs or editors, will also need to be digitized. Controls can be linear or rotary, and absolute or relative. In an absolute control, the position of the knob determines the output directly. In a relative control, the knob can be moved to increase or decrease the output, but its absolute position is meaningless.

Fig. 2.17 shows an absolute linear fader. A grating is moved with respect to several light beams, one for each bit of the coefficient required. The interruption

Figure 2.19 The fixed and rotating gratings produce moiré fringes which are detected by two light paths as quadrature sinusoids. The relative phase determines the direction, and the frequency is proportional to speed of rotation

of the beams by the grating determines which photocells are illuminated. It is not possible to use a pure binary pattern on the grating because this results in transient false codes due to mechanical tolerances. Fig. 2.18 shows some examples of these false codes. For example, on moving the fader from 3 to 4, the MSB goes true slightly before the middle bit goes false. This results in a momentary value of $4 + 2 = 6$ between 3 and 4. The solution is to use a code in which only 1 bit ever changes in going from one value to the next. One such code is the Gray code which was devised to overcome timing hazards in relay logic but is now used extensively in position encoders.

Gray code can be converted to binary in a suitable PROM or gate array. These are available as industry-standard components.

Fig. 2.19 shows a rotary incremental encoder. This produces a sequence of pulses whose number is proportional to the angle through which it has been turned. The rotor carries a radial grating over its entire perimeter. This turns over a second, fixed radial grating whose bars are not parallel to those of the first grating. The resultant moiré fringes travel inwards or outwards depending on the direction of rotation. Two suitably positioned light beams falling on photocells will produce outputs in quadrature. The relative phase determines the direction and the frequency is proportional to speed. The encoder outputs can be connected to a counter whose contents will increase or decrease according to the direction the rotor is turned. The counter provides the coefficient output.

The wordlength of the gain coefficients requires some thought as they determine the number of discrete gains available. If the coefficient wordlength is inadequate, the gain control becomes 'steppy' particularly towards the end of a fadeout. A compromise between performance and the expense of high-resolution faders is to insert a digital interpolator having a low-pass characteristic between the fader and the gain control stage. This will compute intermediate gains to higher resolution than the coarse fader scale so that the steps cannot be discerned.

2.10 A simple digital vision mixer

The luminance path of a simple component digital mixer is shown in Fig. 2.20. The CCIR-601 digital input is offset binary in that it has a nominal black level of 16_{10}, and a subtraction has to be made in order that fading will take place with respect to black. On a perfect signal, subtracting 16 would achieve this, but on a slightly out-of-range signal, it would not. Since the digital active line is slightly longer than the analog active line, the first sample should be blanking level, and this will be the value to subtract to obtain pure binary luminance with respect to black. This is the digital equivalent of black-level clamping. The two inputs are then multiplied by their respective coefficients, and added together to achieve the mix. Peak limiting will be required as in Section 2.7, and then, if the output is to be to CCIR-601, 16_{10} must be added to each sample value to establish the correct offset. In some video applications, a crossfade will be needed, and a rearrangement of the crossfading equation allows one multiplier to be used instead of two, as shown in Fig. 2.21.

The colour difference signals are offset binary with an offset of 128_{10}, and again it is necessary to normalize these with respect to blanking level so that proper fading can be carried out. Since colour difference signals can be positive

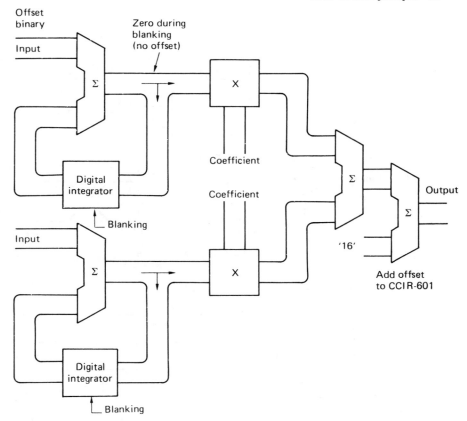

Figure 2.20 A simple digital mixer. Offset binary inputs must have the offset removed. A digital integrator will produce a counter-offset which is subtracted from every input sample. This will increase or reduce until the output of the subtractor is zero during blanking. The offset must be added back after processing if a CCIR-601 output is required

or negative, this process results in two's complement samples. Fig. 2.22 shows some examples.

In this form, the samples can be added with respect to blanking level. Following addition, a limiting stage is used as before, and then, if it is desired to return to CCIR-601 standard, the MSB must be inverted once more in order to convert from two's complement to offset binary.

In practice the same multiplier can be used to process luminance and colour difference signals. Since these will be arriving time multiplexed at 27 MHz, it is only necessary to ensure that the correct coefficients are provided at the right time. Fig. 2.23 shows an example of part of a slow fade. As the co-sited samples C_B, Y and C_R enter, all are multiplied by the same coefficient K_n, but the next sample will be luminance only, so this will be multiplied by K_{n+1}. The next set of co-sited samples will be multiplied by K_{n+2} and so on. Clearly coefficients must be provided which change at 13.5 MHz. The sampling rate of the two inputs must be exactly the same, and in the same phase, or the circuit will not be able

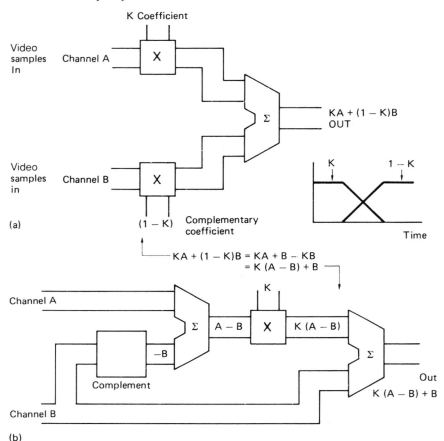

Figure 2.21 Crossfade at (a) requires two multipliers. Reconfiguration at (b) requires only one multiplier

to add on a sample-by-sample basis. If the two inputs have come from different sources, they must be synchronized by the same master clock, and/or timebase correction must be provided on the inputs.

Some thought must be given to the wordlength of the system. If a sample is attenuated, it will develop bits which are below the radix point. For example, if an 8 bit sample is attenuated by 24 dB, the sample value will be shifted four places down. Extra bits must be available within the mixer to accommodate this shift. Digital vision mixers may have an internal wordlength of 16 bits or more. When several attenuated sources are added together to produce the final mix, the result will be a 16 bit sample stream. As the output will generally need to be of the same format as the input, the wordlength must be shortened. Shortening the wordlength of samples effectively makes the quantizing intervals larger and can thus be called requantizing. This must be done very carefully to avoid artefacts and the necessary processes will be treated in Chapter 3.

Figure 2.22 Offset binary colour difference values are converted to two's complement by reversing the state of the first bit. Two's complement values A and B will then add around blanking level

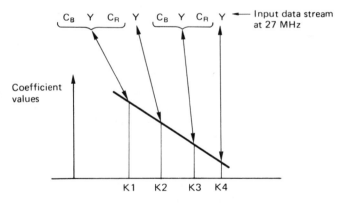

Coefficients produced at 13.5 MHz

Figure 2.23 When using one multiplier to fade both luminance and colour difference in a 27 MHz multiplex 4:2:2 system, one coefficient will be used three times on the co-sited samples, whereas the next coefficient will only be used for a single luminance sample

It is possible to construct a digital composite switcher for NTSC or PAL which operates in much the same way as has been described for a colour difference channel above.

Fig. 2.24 shows that the black level to be subtracted will be numerically larger than for the luminance signal in a component system, and may result in negative sample values which will need to be expressed in two's complement form before processing.

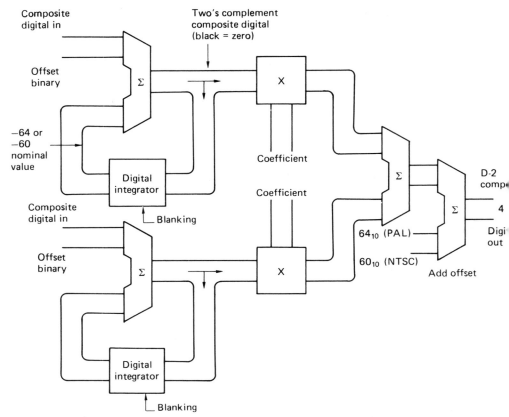

Figure 2.24 In a composite digital switcher, the samples also carry the sub-carrier, and thus have meaning at levels below black. A larger offset, 60 or 64, is used than for components, and when this is subtracted a two's complement system is necessary to convey signals above or below black as positive or negative values which can then be faded without offsets resulting

Clearly the adder which mixes the two channels can only produce a meaningful result if both input values are derived from samples which were taken at precisely the same phase relationship to subcarrier. The critical timing-in process of an analog composite switcher has been removed as far as the digital switcher is concerned, but the need for critical timing accuracy has not been eliminated; it has simply been moved to a different part of the system. A digital timebase corrector can be used to remove timing errors between input channels, but as it can only correct to the nearest sample, which is 90° in a $4F_{sc}$ system, it cannot remove errors due to the sampling clocks of the two channels having a different relationship to subcarrier. If the two channels have such a timing error, it can only be corrected in the digital domain by an interpolator of some complexity. It is necessary to bear in mind that a composite digital recorder must have an input sampling clock which is accurately set to a standardized phase relationship with subcarrier, otherwise the recordings made cannot be mixed with others in the digital domain.

2.11 Concentrators/combiners

A concentrator or combiner is the name given to a special kind of digital switcher which is driven by a number of perspective effects machines. The illusion of a solid object can be created, where each video input represents one face, often of a cube, but other shapes are possible.

Using the principle of transparency, images can be placed on the inside of a solid, and those at the rear can be seen through those at the front.

Transparency requires control of the amplitude of keying signals. Fig. 2.25 shows that a digital mixer is used, where the key signals are processed to become the coefficients for the mixer. The key processing is the most important aspect of the system, because it determines the realism of the final result. It is necessary to specify the priority of the images, that is to say which lies closest to the viewer,

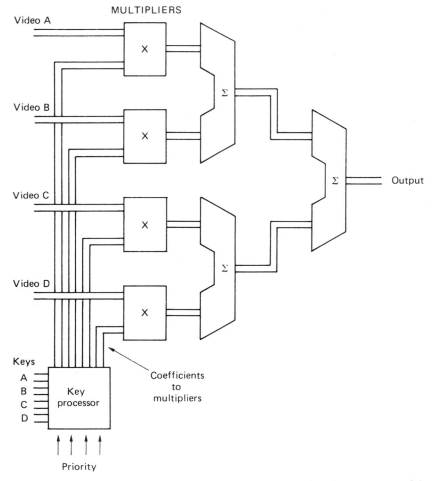

Figure 2.25 Transparency mixing requires one multiplication per input. The transparency of the highest-priority input determines the gain given to lower-priority inputs and so on

in the order A, B, C, D for a four-channel system. The priority determines the order in which the incoming key signals are processed. The goal of the key processor is to produce four coefficients which never sum to more than unity. In this way the output can be prevented from clipping.

On a pixel-by-pixel basis, the key signals are used to compute new coefficients. Suppose that the highest priority, or front, picture A has been given a transparency of 33%. This will result from a two-thirds amplitude key signal accompanying picture A. The key processor produces the A coefficient and also

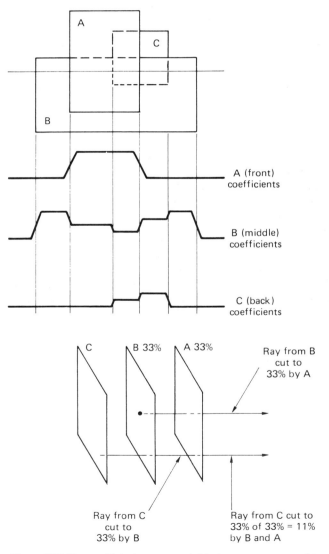

Figure 2.26 How coefficients are computed in transparency processing

passes down to lower-priority circuits the fact that two-thirds of the total permitted sum of coefficients has been used up. The transparency of A is 33%, so only 33% of the brightness of the B picture can be added where A obscures B. Suppose that B also has a transparency of 33%; then light from picture C will be reduced to 33% of its original brightness passing through B, and reduced again by passing through A, so the coefficient needed will be about 11%. The process continues for as many channels of input as are available, plus a background value.

The coefficients then multiply their respective channels, and the products are summed to produce a single digital video stream carrying the final effect. Fig. 2.26 shows the effect on the key coefficients during a single raster line scan across a multilayer effect with transparency.

In some machines it is possible to make pictures in different planes intersect realistically. The position of the two planes in the Z axis is compared, and the picture with the lowest Z at a given pixel position will get priority in the combiner. At the intersection point, priority will pass to the other picture. The transparencies allocated to both pictures will then be used to produce coefficients as before.

2.12 Blanking

It is often necessary to blank the ends of the active line smoothly to prevent out-of-band signals being generated. This is usually the case where an effects machine has cropped the picture to fit inside a coloured border. The border will be generated by supplying constant luminance and colour difference values to the data stream. Blanking consists of sloping off the active line by multiplying the sample values by successively smaller coefficients until blanking is reached. This is easy where the sample values have been normalized so that zero represents black, but where the usual offset of 16_{10} is present, multiplication by descending coefficients will cause a black-level shift. The solution is to use a correction PROM which can be seen in Fig. 2.27. This is addressed by the multiplier coefficient and adds a suitable constant to the multiplier output. If the multiplier

Figure 2.27 In order to fade an offset binary signal, a correction term from a PROM can be added to remove the level shift caused by fading

were to have a gain of one-half, this would shift the black level by eight quantizing intervals, and so the correction PROM would add eight to the output. Where the multiplier has fully blanked, the output will be zero, and the correction PROM has to add 16_{10} to the output.

2.13 Keying

Keying is the process where one video signal can be cut into another to replace part of the picture with a different image. One application of keying is where a switcher can wipe from one input to another using one of a variety of different patterns. Fig. 2.28 shows that an analog switcher performs such an effect by

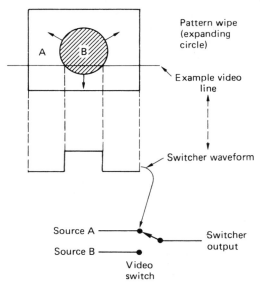

Figure 2.28 In a video switcher a pattern generator produces a switching waveform which changes from line to line and from frame to frame to allow moving pattern wipes between sources

generating a binary switching waveform in a pattern generator. Video switching between inputs actually takes place during the active line. In most analog switchers, the switching waveform is digitally generated, then fed to a DAC, whereas in a digital switcher, the pattern generator outputs become the coefficients supplied to the crossfader, which is sometimes referred to as a cutter. The switching edge must be positioned to an accuracy of a few nanoseconds, much less than the spacing of the pixels, otherwise slow wipes will not appear to move smoothly, and diagonal wipes will have stepped edges, a phenomenon known as ratcheting.

Positioning the switch point to subpixel accuracy is not particularly difficult, as Fig. 2.29 shows. A suitable series of coefficients can position the effective crossover point anywhere. The finite slope of the coefficients results in a brief crossfade from one video signal to the other. This soft keying gives a much more

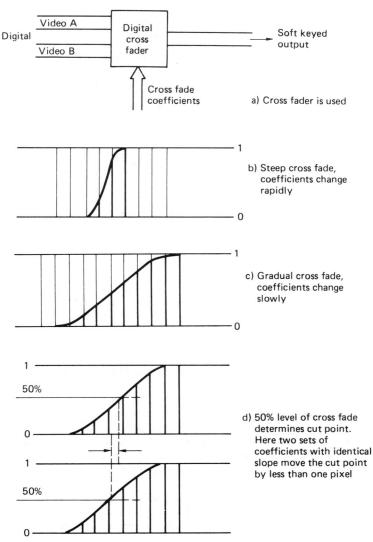

a) Cross fader is used

b) Steep cross fade, coefficients change rapidly

c) Gradual cross fade, coefficients change slowly

d) 50% level of cross fade determines cut point. Here two sets of coefficients with identical slope move the cut point by less than one pixel

Figure 2.29 Soft keying

realistic effect than binary switchers, which often give a 'cut out with scissors' appearance. In some machines the slope of the crossfade can be adjusted to achieve the desired degree of softness.

2.14 Chroma keying

Another application of keying is to derive the switching signal by processing video from a camera in some way. By analysing colour difference signals, it is possible to determine where in a picture a particular colour occurs. When a key

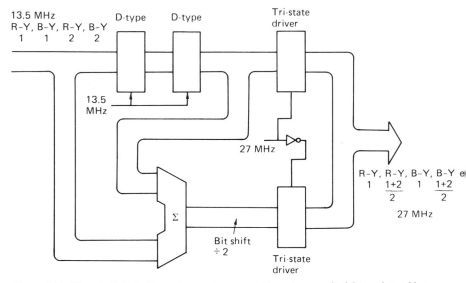

Figure 2.30 Alternate *R–Y*, *B–Y* samples can be averaged by a *two*-sample delay and an adder. Output will then alternate between sample values and averaged sample values at 27 MHz. Demultiplexing the output will give two colour difference signals each at 13.5 MHz so that they can be used to produce coefficients at that rate to key luminance

signal is generated in this way, the process is known as chroma keying, which is the electronic equivalent of matting in film.

In a 4:2:2 component system, it will be necessary to provide coefficients to the luminance crossfader at 13.5 MHz. Chroma samples only occur at half this frequency, so it is necessary to provide a chroma interpolator to raise the chroma sampling rate artificially. For chroma keying a simple linear interpolator is perfectly adequate. Intermediate chroma samples are simply the average of two adjacent samples. Fig. 2.30 shows how a multiplexed C_r, C_b signal can be averaged using a delay of two clocks.

As with analog switchers, chroma keying is also possible with composite digital inputs, but decoding must take place before it is possible to obtain the key signals. The video signals which are being keyed will, however, remain in the composite digital format.

In switcher/keyers, it is necessary to obtain a switching signal which ramps between two states from an input signal which can be any allowable video waveform. Manual controls are provided so that the operator can set thresholds and gains to obtain the desired effect. In the analog domain, these controls distort the transfer function of a video amplifier so that it is no longer linear. A digital keyer will perform the same functions using logic circuits.

Fig. 2.31(a) shows that the effect of a non-linear transfer function is to switch when the input signal passes through a particular level. The transfer function is implemented in a memory in digital systems. The incoming video sample value acts as the memory address, so that the selected memory location is proportional to the video level. At each memory location, the appropriate output level code is stored. If, for example, each memory location stored its own address, the output

Figure 2.31 (a) A non-linear transfer function can be used to produce a keying signal. (b) The non-linear transfer function emphasizes contrast in part of the range but reduces it at other parts. (c) If a RAM is used as a flexible transfer function, it will be necessary to provide multiplexers so that the RAM can be preset with the desired values from the control system

would equal the input, and the device would be transparent. In practice switching is obtained by distorting the transfer function to obtain more gain in one particular range of input levels at the expense of less gain at other input levels. With the transfer function shown in Fig. 2.31(b), an input level change from (a) to (b) causes a smaller output change, whereas the same level change between (c) and (d) causes a considerable output change.

If the memory is RAM, different transfer functions can be loaded in by the control system, and this requires multiplexers in both data and address lines as shown in Fig. 2.31(c).

In practice such a RAM will be installed in Y, C_r and C_b channels, and the results will be combined to obtain the final switching coefficients.

2.15 Simple effects

If a RAM of the type shown in Fig. 2.31 is inserted in a digital luminance path, the result will be *solarizing* which is a form of contrast enhancement. Fig. 2.32 shows that a family of transfer functions can be implemented which control the degree of contrast enhancement. When the transfer function becomes so distorted that the slope reverses, the result is *luminance reversal*, where black and white are effectively interchanged. Solarizing can also be implemented in colour difference channels to obtain *chroma solarizing*. In effects machines, the degree of solarizing may need to change smoothly so that the effect can be gradually introduced. In this case the various transfer functions will be kept in different pages of a PROM, so that the degree of solarization can be selected immediately by changing the page address of the PROM. One page will have a straight transfer function, so the effect can be turned off by selecting that page.

In the digital domain it is easy to introduce various forms of quantizing distortion to obtain special effects. Fig. 2.33 shows that 8 bit luminance allows 256 different brightnesses, which to the naked eye appears to be a continuous range. If some of the low-order bits of the samples are disabled, then a smaller number of brightness values describe the range from black to white. For example, if 6 bits are disabled, only 2 bits remain, and so only four possible brightness levels can be output. This gives an effect known as *contouring* since the visual effect somewhat resembles a relief map.

When the same process is performed with colour difference signals, the result is to limit the number of possible colours in the picture, which gives an effect known as *posterizing*, since the picture appears to have been coloured by paint from pots. Solarizing, contouring and posterizing cannot be performed in the composite digital domain, owing to the presence of the subcarrier in the sample values.

Fig. 2.34 shows a latch in the luminance data which is being clocked at the sampling rate. It is transparent to the signal, but if the clock to the latch is divided down by some factor n, the result will be that the same sample value will be held on the output for n clock periods, giving the video waveform a staircase characteristic. This is the horizontal component of the effect known as *mosaicing*. The vertical component is obtained by feeding the output of the latch into a line memory, which stores one horizontally mosaiced line and then repeats that line m times. As n and m can be independently controlled, the mosaic tiles can be made to be of any size, and rectangular or square at will. Clearly the mosaic circuitry must be implemented simultaneously in luminance and colour

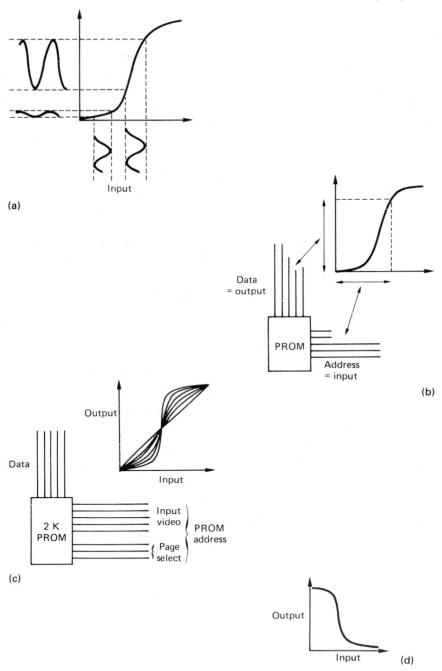

Figure 2.32 Solarization. (a) The non-linear transfer function emphasizes contrast in part of the range but reduces it at other parts. (b) The desired transfer function is implemented in a PROM. Each input sample value is used as the address to select a corresponding output value stored in the PROM. (c) A family of transfer functions can be accommodated in a larger PROM. Page select affects the high-order address bits. (d) Transfer function for luminance reversal

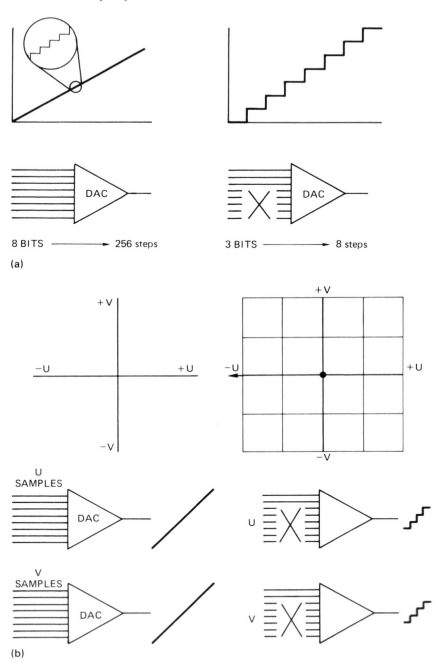

Figure 2.33 (a) In contouring, the least significant bits of the luminance samples are discarded, which reduces the number of possible output levels. (b) At left, the 8 bit colour difference signals allow 2^{16} different colours. At right, eliminating all but 2 bits of each colour difference signals allows only 2^4 different colours

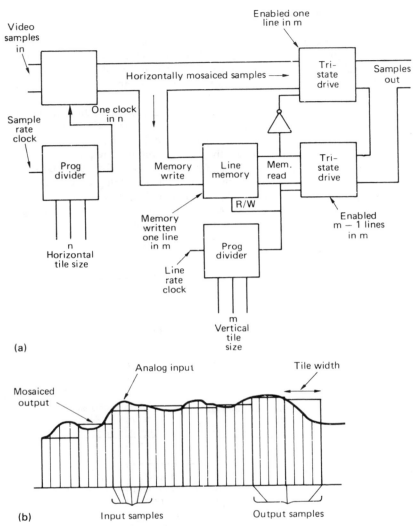

(a)

(b)   Input samples   Output samples

Figure 2.34(a) Simplified diagram of mosaicing system. At left-hand side, horizontal mosaicing is done by intercepting sample clocks. On one line in m, the horizontally mosaiced line becomes the output, and is simultaneously written into a one-line memory. On the remaining $(m-1)$ lines the memory is read to produce several identical successive lines to give the vertical dimensions of the tile. (b) In mosaicing, input samples are neglected, and the output is held constant by failing to clock a latch in the data stream for several sample periods. Heavy vertical lines here correspond to the clock signal occurring. Heavy horizontal line is resultant waveform

difference signal paths. It is not possible to perform mosaicing on a composite digital signal, since it will destroy the subcarrier. It is common to provide a bypass route which allows mosaiced and unmosaiced video to be simultaneously available. Dynamic switching between the two sources controlled by a separate key signal then allows mosaicing to be restricted to certain parts of the picture.

2.16 Timebase manipulation

In Chapter 1 it was stated that a strength of digital technology is the ease with which delay can be provided. Accurate control of delay is the essence of timebase manipulation which is necessary whenever the instantaneous time of arrival or rate from one stage of the system does not match the requirements of the next stage.

Fig. 2.35 shows a number of applications of timebase manipulation in digital video systems. Timebase manipulation is a general term which embraces processes such as time compression and expansion, data buffering and delay.

In many digital video applications, the destination will require perfectly regular sample timing. For example, the sampling rate clock of the final DAC in a system must be jitter free otherwise the quality of the analog output will be degraded. Fig. 2.35(a) shows that a stable reference clock is used to drive the DAC. Timebase correction is the process of aligning jittery samples from storage media or transmission channels with that stable reference.

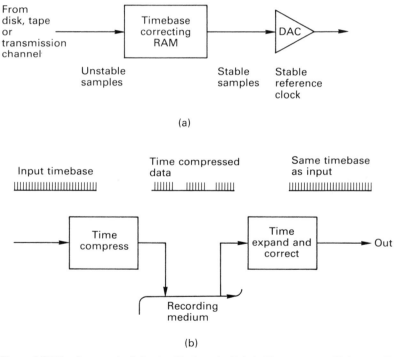

(a)

(b)

Figure 2.35 Timebase manipulation is ubiquitous in digital video processes. Various applications are shown here. At (a), unstable or jittery data from storage or transmission media are time aligned to a stable reference in a timebase correcting memory. At (b) the timebase correction stage doubles as the time expansion process needed to oppose the time compression used on recording. At (c) heavy time compression can be used to raise audio sampling rates up to those used by video. It is then possible to convey audio and video in the same channel, the so called sound-in-syncs technique. At (d) most TBCs are implemented as a memory addressed by a counter which periodically overflows to give a ring structure. The memory allows the read and write sides to be asynchronous

Input video

Input audio
samples

Time compressed
audio

Sound-in-syncs

(c)

Write address
counter

Ring
memory
(RAM)

Read address
counter

Data in

Data out

Input
clock

Output
clock

(d)

Fig. 2.35(b) shows that a further application of timebase correction is where it is used to reverse the time compression applied prior to recording or transmission. As was shown in Section 1.8, digital recorders compress data into blocks to facilitate editing and error correction as well as to permit head switching between blocks in rotary-head machines. Owing to the spaces between blocks, data arrive in bursts on replay, but must be fed to the output converters in an unbroken stream at the sampling rate. The time expansion used in the D-1 recorder to reduce the frequency at the heads is a further example of the use of the principle (see Chapter 8).

When conventional analog video signals are digitized, only the unblanked parts of the analog signals result in useful data, and there will be spare capacity in any continuously running data channel. This capacity can be used for auxiliary data transmission, one application of which is to carry a number of channels of digital audio along with the video. Fig. 2.35(c) shows how a sound-in-syncs system works. Audio samples have longer wordlength than video samples, and so each audio sample must be broken up into smaller sections, typically three. This raises the audio word rate by a factor of three. In order to use the spare capacity of a video link, the audio data are time compressed by a factor in the region of 200:1 so that the audio word rate becomes the same as the video word rate. Audio words can then be multiplexed into the data stream during blanking. At the receiver, the data stream is demultiplexed and a corresponding time expansion stage is required to bring the audio data back to the correct rate once more. The audio samples are also reassembled into words of the correct length.

In digital VTRs, the rotation of the heads is servo locked to the video framing and so it is only necessary to correct relatively small timebase errors. In contrast, hard-disk drives, which are used in, for example, digital video workstations, seldom have synchronized rotation. Instead the data transfer rate of the disk drive is arranged to be greater than that needed by the application. Disk transfers will be suspended periodically to keep the average data rate correct, and a larger amount of buffering is then necessary. On reading such a disk, data from the disk blocks arrive at a reasonably constant rate, but cannot necessarily be accepted at a steady rate by the logic because of competition for the use of buses and memory by the different parts of the system. In this case the data must be buffered by a relative of the timebase corrector which is usually referred to as a silo. Silos are considered in Section 2.17.

Although delay is easily implemented, it is not possible to advance a data stream. Most real machines cause instabilities balanced about the correct timing: the output jitters between too early and too late. Since the information cannot be advanced in the corrector, only delayed, the solution is to run the machine in advance of real time. In this case, correctly timed output signals will need a nominal delay to align them with reference timing. Early output signals will receive more delay, and late output signals will receive less delay.

Section 2.5 showed the principles of digital storage elements which can be used for delay purposes. The shift-register approach and the RAM approach to delay are very similar, as a shift register can be thought of as a memory whose address increases automatically when clocked. The data rate and the maximum delay determine the capacity of the RAM required. Fig. 2.35(d) shows that the addressing of the RAM is by a counter that overflows endlessly from the end of the memory back to the beginning, giving the memory a ring-like structure. The write address is determined by the incoming data, and the read address is determined by the outgoing data. This means that the RAM has to be able to read and write at the same time. The switching between read and write involves not only a data multiplexer but also an address multiplexer. In general the arbitration between read and write will be done by signals from the stable side of the TBC as Fig. 2.36 shows. In the replay case the stable clock will be on the read side. The stable side of the RAM will read a sample when it demands, and the writing will be locked out for that period. The input data cannot be interrupted in many applications, however, so a small buffer silo is installed before the memory, which fills up as the writing is locked out, and empties again as writing is permitted. Alternatively, the memory will be split into blocks as was shown in Chapter 1, such that when one block is reading a different block will be writing and the problem does not arise.

In most digital video applications, the sampling rate exceeds the rate at which economically available RAM chips can operate. The solution is to arrange several video samples into one longer word, known as a superword, and to construct the memory so that it stores superwords in parallel.

Figure 2.36 In a RAM-based TBC, the RAM is reference synchronous, and an arbitrator decides when it will read and when it will write. During reading, asynchronous input data back up in the input silo, asserting a write request to the arbitrator. Arbitrator will then cause a write cycle between read cycles

2.17 FIFO timebase correction

Fig. 2.37 shows the operation of a FIFO chip, colloquially known as a silo because the data are tipped in at the top on delivery and drawn off at the bottom when needed. Each stage of the chip has a data register and a small amount of logic, including a data-valid or V bit. If the input register does not contain data, the first V bit will be reset, and this will cause the chip to assert 'input ready'. If data are presented at the input, and clocked into the first stage, the V bit will set, and the 'input ready' signal will become false. However, the logic associated with the next stage sees the V bit set in the top stage, and if its own V bit is clear, it will clock the data into its own register, set its own V bit, and clear the input V bit, causing 'input ready' to reassert, when another word can be fed in. This process then continues as the word moves down the silo, until it arrives at the last register in the chip. The V bit of the last stage becomes the 'output ready' signal, telling subsequent circuitry that there are data to be read. If this word is not read, the next word entered will ripple down to the stage above. Words thus stack up at the bottom of the silo. When a word is read out, an external signal must be provided which resets the bottom V bit. The 'output ready' signal now goes false, and the logic associated with the last stage now sees valid data above, and loads down the word when it will become ready again. The last register but one will now have no V bit set, and will see data above itself and bring that down. In this way a reset V bit propagates up the chip while the data ripple down, rather like

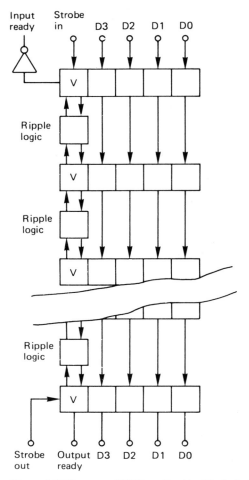

Figure 2.37 Structure of FIFO or silo chip. Ripple logic controls propagation of data down silo

a hole in a semiconductor going the opposite way to the electrons. Silo chips are usually available in 4 bit wordlengths, but can easily be connected in parallel to form superwords. Silo chips are asynchronous, and paralleled chips will not necessarily all work at the same speed. This problem is easily overcome by 'ANDing' together all of the input-ready and output-ready signals and parallel connecting the strobes. Fig. 2.38 shows this mode of operation.

When used in a hard-disk system, a silo will allow data to and from the disk, which is turning at constant speed. When reading the disk, Fig. 2.39(a) shows that the silo starts empty, and if there is bus contention, the silo will start to fill. Where the bus is free, the disk controller will attempt to empty the silo into the memory. The system can take advantage of the interblock gaps on the disk, containing headers, preambles and redundancy, for in these areas there are no data to transfer, and there is some breathing space to empty the silo before the next block. In practice the silo need not be empty at the start of every block,

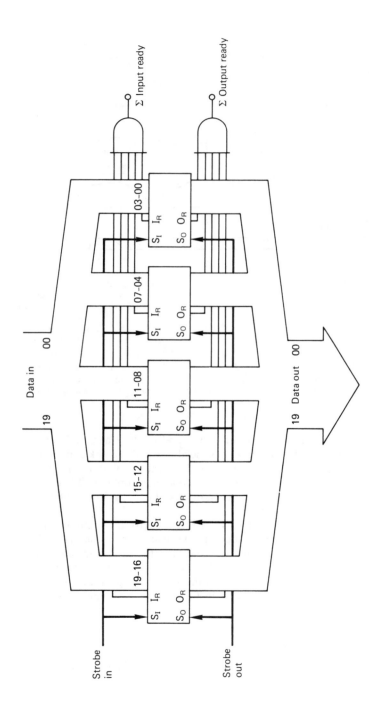

Figure 2.38 In this example, a 20 bit wordlength silo is made from five parallel FIFO chips. The asynchronous ripple action of FIFOs means that it is necessary to 'AND' together the ready signals

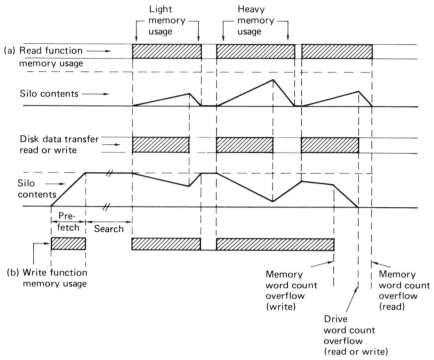

Figure 2.39 The silo contents during read functions (a) appear different from those during write functions (b). In (a), the control logic attempts to keep the silo as empty as possible; in (b) the logic prefills the silo and attempts to keep it full until the memory word count overflows

provided it never becomes full before the end of the transfer. If this happens some data are lost and the function must be aborted. The block containing the silo overflow will generally be re-read on the next revolution. In sophisticated systems, the silo has a kind of dipstick, and can interrupt the CPU if the data get too deep. The CPU can then suspend some bus activity to allow the disk controller more time to empty the silo.

When the disk is to be written, as in Fig. 2.39(b), a continuous data stream must be provided during each block, as the disk cannot stop. The silo will be prefilled before the disk attempts to write, and the disk controller attempts to keep it full. In this case all will be well if the silo does not become empty before the end of the transfer. Fig. 2.40 shows the silo of a typical disk controller with the multiplexers necessary to put it in the read data stream or the write data stream.

2.18 Modulo-*n* arithmetic

Conventional arithmetic which is in everyday use relates to the real world of counting actual objects, and to obtain correct answers the concepts of borrow and carry are necessary in the calculations.

Asynchronous data
to memory bus

(a)

Asynchronous data
from memory

(b)

Figure 2.40 In order to guarantee that the drive can transfer data in real time at regular intervals (determined by disk speed and density) the silo provides buffering to the asynchronous operation of the memory access process. At (a) the silo is configured for a disk read. The same silo is used at (b) for a disk write

There is an alternative type of arithmetic which has no borrow or carry which is known as modulo arithmetic. In modulo-n no number can exceed n. If it does, n or whole multiples of n are subtracted until it does not. Thus 25 modulo-16 is 9 and 12 modulo-5 is 2. The count shown in Fig. 2.5 is from a 4 bit device which overflows when it reaches 1111 because the carry-out is ignored. If a number of clock pulses m are applied from the zero state, the state of the counter will be given by m mod.16. Thus modulo arithmetic is appropriate to systems in which there is a fixed wordlength and this means that the range of values the system can have is restricted by that wordlength. A number range which is restricted in this way is called a finite field.

Figure 2.41 In modulo-2 calculations, there can be no carry or borrow operations and conventional addition and subtraction become identical. The XOR gate is a modulo-2 adder

Modulo-2 is a numbering scheme which is used frequently in digital processes. Fig. 2.41 shows that in modulo-2 the conventional addition and subtraction are replaced by the XOR function such that: $A + B$ mod.2 = A XOR B. When multibit values are added in mod.2, each column is computed quite independently of any other. This makes mod.2 circuitry very fast in operation as it is not necessary to wait for the carries from lower-order bits to ripple up to the high-order bits.

Modulo-2 arithmetic is not the same as conventional arithmetic and takes some getting used to. For example, adding something to itself in mod.2 always gives the answer zero.

2.19 The Galois field

Fig. 2.42 shows a simple circuit consisting of three D-type latches which are clocked simultaneously. They are connected in series to form a shift register. At (a) a feedback connection has been taken from the output to the input and the result is a ring counter where the bits contained will recirculate endlessly. At (b) one XOR gate is added so that the output is fed back to more than one stage. The result is known as a twisted-ring counter and it has some interesting properties. Whenever the circuit is clocked, the left-hand bit moves to the right-hand latch, the centre bit moves to the left-hand latch and the centre latch becomes the XOR of the two outer latches. The figure shows that whatever the starting condition of the 3 bits in the latches, the same state will always be reached again after seven clocks, except if zero is used. The states of the latches form an endless ring of non-sequential numbers called a Galois field after the French mathematical prodigy Evariste Galois who discovered them. The states of the circuit form a maximum length sequence because there are as many states as are permitted by the wordlength. As the states of the sequence have many of the characteristics of random numbers, yet are repeatable, the result can also be called a pseudo-random sequence (prs). As the all-zeros case is disallowed, the length of a maximum length sequence generated by a register of m bits cannot exceed (2^m-1) states. The Galois field, however, includes the zero term. It is useful to explore the bizarre mathematics of Galois fields which use modulo-2 arithmetic.

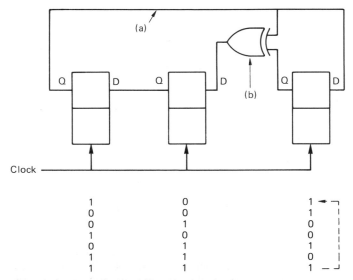

Figure 2.42 The circuit shown is a twisted-ring counter which has an unusual feedback arrangement. Clocking the counter causes it to pass through a series of non-sequential values. See text for details

Familiarity with such manipulations is helpful when studying the error correction, particularly the Reed–Solomon codes used in recorders and treated in Chapter 6. They will also be found in processes which require pseudo-random numbers such as digital dither, treated in Chapter 3, and randomized channel codes used in, for example, NICAM 728 and discussed in Chapters 5 and 7.

The circuit of Fig. 2.42 can be considered as a counter and the four points shown will then be representing different powers of 2 from the MSB on the left to the LSB on the right. The feedback connection from the MSB to the other stages means that whenever the MSB becomes 1, two other powers are also forced to 1 so that the code of 1011 is generated.

Each state of the circuit can be described by combinations of powers of x, such as:

$$x^2 = 100$$

$$x = 010$$

$$x^2 + x = 110, \text{ etc.}$$

The fact that 3 bits have the same state because they are connected together is represented by the mod.2 equation

$$x^3 + x + 1 = 0$$

Let $x = a$, which is a primitive element.
Now:

$$a^3 + a + 1 = 0 \tag{2.1}$$

In modulo-2:

$$a + a = a^2 + a^2 = 0$$

$$a = x = 010$$

$$a^2 = x^2 = 100$$

$$a^3 = a + 1 = 011 \text{ from } (2.1)$$

$$a^4 = a \times a^3 = a(a + 1) = a^2 + a = 110$$

$$a^5 = a^2 + a + 1 = 111$$

$$a^6 = a \times a^5 = a(a^2 + a + 1)$$

$$= a^3 + a^2 + a = a + 1 + a^2 + a$$

$$= a^2 + 1 = 101$$

$$a^7 = a(a^2 + 1) = a^3 + a$$

$$= a + 1 + a = 1 = 001$$

In this way it can be seen that the complete set of elements of the Galois field can be expressed by successive powers of the primitive element. Note that the twisted-ring circuit of Fig. 2.42 simply raises a to higher and higher powers as it is clocked; thus the seemingly complex multibit changes caused by a single clock of the register become simple to calculate using the correct primitive and the appropriate power.

The numbers produced by the twisted-ring counter are not random; they are completely predictable if the equation is known. However, the sequences produced are sufficiently similar to random numbers that in many cases they will be useful. They are thus referred to as pseudo-random sequences. The feedback connection is chosen such that the expression it implements will not factorize. Otherwise a maximum length sequence could not be generated because the circuit might sequence around one or other of the factors depending on the initial

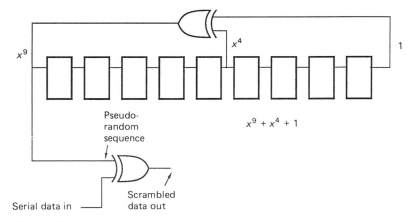

Figure 2.43 In NICAM, randomizing is done by adding the serial data to a polynomial generated by the circuit shown here. The receiver needs an identical system which is synchronous with that of the transmitter

condition. A useful analogy is to compare the operation of a pair of meshed gears. If the gears have a number of teeth which are relatively prime, many revolutions are necessary to make the same pair of teeth touch again. If the number of teeth have a common multiple, far fewer turns are needed.

Fig. 2.43 shows the pseudo-random sequence generator used in NICAM 728. Its purpose is to break up the transmitted spectrum so that the sound carrier does not cause patterning on the TV picture. The sequence length of the circuit shown is 511 because the expression will not factorize. Further details of NICAM 728 can be found in Chapter 7.

2.20 Noise and probability

Probability is a useful concept when dealing with processes which are not completely predictable. Thermal noise in electronic components is random, and although under given conditions the noise power in a system may be constant, this value only determines the heat that would be developed in a resistive load. In digital systems, it is the instantaneous voltage of noise which is of interest, since it is a form of interference which could alter the state of a binary signal if it were large enough. Unfortunately the instantaneous voltage cannot be predicted; indeed if it could the interference could not be called noise. Noise can only be quantified statistically, by measuring or predicting the likelihood of a given noise amplitude.

Fig. 2.44 shows a graph relating the probability of occurrence to the amplitude of noise. The noise amplitude increases away from the origin along the horizontal axis, and for any amplitude of interest, the probability of that noise amplitude occurring can be read from the curve. The shape of the curve is known as a Gaussian distribution, which crops up whenever the overall effect of a large number of independent phenomena is considered. Thermal noise is due to the contributions from countless molecules in the component concerned. Magnetic recording depends on superimposing some average magnetism on vast numbers of magnetic particles.

If it were possible to isolate an individual noise-generating microcosm of a tape or a head on the molecular scale, the noise it could generate would have physical limits because of the finite energy present. The noise distribution might

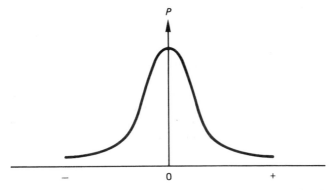

Figure 2.44 White noise in analog circuits generally has the Gaussian amplitude distribution shown

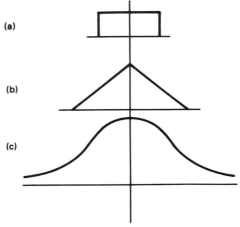

(a)

(b)

(c)

Figure 2.45 At (a) is a rectangular probability; all values are equally likely but between physical limits. At (b) is the sum of two rectangular probabilities, which is triangular, and at (c) is the Gaussian curve which is the sum of an infinite number of rectangular probabilities

then be rectangular as shown in Fig. 2.45(a), where all amplitudes below the physical limit are equally likely. The output of a twisted-ring counter such as that in Fig. 2.42 can have a uniform probability. Each value occurs once per sequence. The outputs are positive only but do not include zero, but every value from 1 up to $2^n - 1$ is then equally likely.

The output of a prs generator can be made into the two's complement form by inverting the MSB. This has the effect of exchanging the missing all-zeros value for a missing fully negative value as can be seen by considering the number ring in Fig. 2.5. In this example, inverting the MSB causes the code of 1000 representing -8 to become 0000. The result is a 4 bit prs generating uniform probability from -7 to $+7$ as shown in Fig. 2.45(a).

If the combined effect of two of these uniform probability processes is considered, clearly the maximum amplitude is now doubled because the two effects can add, but provided the two effects are uncorrelated, they can also subtract, so the probability is no longer rectangular, but becomes triangular as in Fig. 2.45(b). The probability falls to zero at peak amplitude because the chances of two independent mechanisms reaching their peak value with the same polarity at the same time are understandably small.

If the number of mechanisms summed together is now allowed to increase without limit, the result is the Gaussian curve shown in Fig. 2.45(c), where it will be seen that the curve has no amplitude limit, because it is just possible that all mechanisms will simultaneously reach their peak value together, although the chances of this happening are incredibly remote. Thus the Gaussian curve is the overall probability of a large number of uncorrelated uniform processes.

2.21 Filters

Filtering is inseparable from digital video and audio. Analog or digital filters, and sometimes both, are required in ADCs, DACs, in the data channels of digital

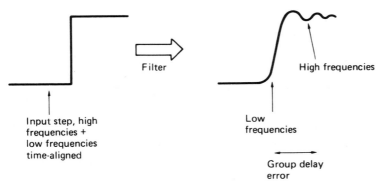

Figure 2.46 Group delay time-displaces signals as a function of frequency

recorders and transmission systems and in sampling-rate converters and equalizers. Optical systems used in disk recorders also act as filters.[1] There are many parallels between analog, digital and optical filters, which this section treats as a common subject. The main difference between analog and digital filters is that in the digital domain very complex architectures can be constructed at low cost in LSI and that arithmetic calculations are not subject to component tolerance or drift.

Filtering may modify the frequency response of a system, and/or the phase response. Every combination of frequency and phase response determines the impulse response in the time domain. Fig. 2.46 shows that impulse response testing tells a great deal about a filter. In a perfect filter, all frequencies should experience the same time delay. If some groups of frequencies experience a different delay to others, there is a group-delay error. As an impulse contains an infinite spectrum, a filter suffering from group-delay error will separate the different frequencies of an impulse along the time axis.

A pure delay will cause a phase shift proportional to frequency, and a filter with this characteristic is said to be phase linear. The impulse response of a phase-linear filter is symmetrical. If a filter suffers from group-delay error it cannot be phase linear. It is almost impossible to make a perfectly phase-linear analog filter, and many filters have a group-delay equalization stage following them which is often as complex as the filter itself. In the digital domain it is straightforward to make a phase-linear filter, and phase equalization becomes unnecessary.

Because of the sampled nature of the signal, whatever the response at low frequencies may be, all digital channels (and sampled analog channels) act as low-pass filters cutting off at the Nyquist limit, or half the sampling frequency.

Fig. 2.47(a) shows a simple *RC* network and its impulse response. This is the familiar exponential decay due to the capacitor discharging through the resistor (in series with the source impedance which is assumed here to be negligible). The figure also shows the response to a square wave at (b). These responses can be calculated because the inputs involved are relatively simple. When the input waveform and the impulse response are complex functions, this approach becomes almost impossible.

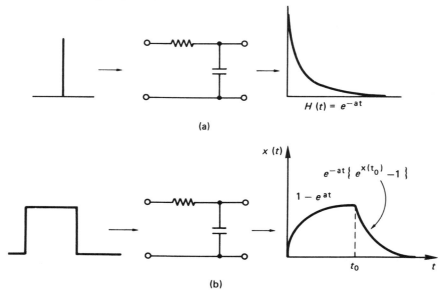

Figure 2.47 (a) The impulse response of a simple RC network is an exponential decay. This can be used to calculate the response to a square wave, as in (b)

In any filter, the time-domain output waveform represents the convolution of the impulse response with the input waveform. Convolution can be followed by reference to a graphic example in Fig. 2.48. Where the impulse response is asymmetrical, the decaying tail occurs *after* the input. As a result it is necessary to reverse the impulse response in time so that it is mirrored prior to sweeping it through the input waveform. The output voltage is proportional to the shaded area shown where the two impulses overlap.

The same process can be performed in the sampled, or discrete, time domain as shown in Fig. 2.49. The impulse and the input are now a set of discrete samples which clearly must have the same sample spacing. The impulse response only has value where impulses coincide. Elsewhere it is zero. The impulse response is therefore stepped through the input one sample period at a time. At each step, the area is still proportional to the output, but as the time steps are of uniform width, the area is proportional to the impulse height and so the output is obtained by adding up the lengths of overlap. In mathematical terms, the output samples represent the convolution of the input and the impulse response by summing the coincident cross-products.

As a digital filter works in this way, perhaps it is not a filter at all, but just a mathematical simulation of an analog filter. This approach is quite useful in visualizing what a digital filter does.

Somewhere between the analog filter and the digital filter is the switched capacitor filter. This uses analog quantities, namely the charges on capacitors, but the time axis is discrete because the various charges are routed using electronic switches which close during various phases of the sampling-rate clock. Switched capacitor filters have the same characteristics as digital filters with infinite precision. They are often used in preference to continuous-time analog filters in

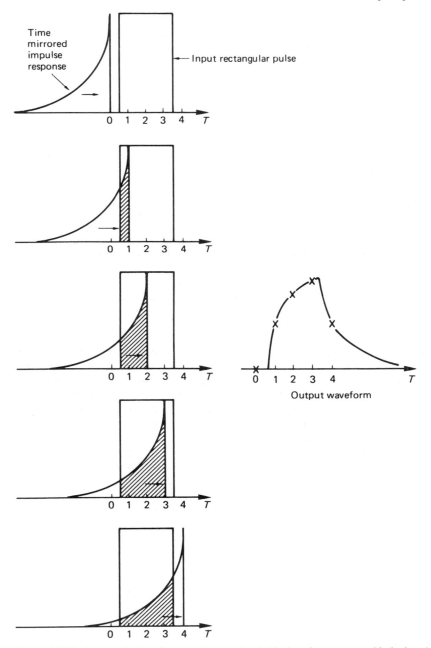

Figure 2.48 In the convolution of two continuous signals (the impulse response with the input), the impulse must be time reversed or mirrored. This is necessary because the impulse will be moved from left to right, and mirroring gives the impulse the correct time-domain response when it is moved past a fixed point. As the impulse response slides continuously through the input waveform, the area where the two overlap determines the instantaneous output amplitude. This is shown for five different times by the crosses on the output waveform

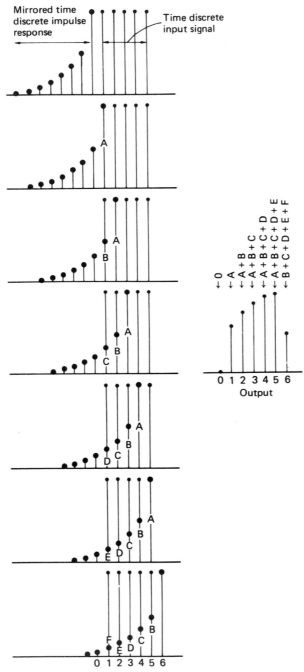

Figure 2.49 In time discrete convolution, the mirrored impulse response is stepped through the input one sample period at a time. At each step, the sum of the cross-products is used to form an output value. As the input in this example is a constant height pulse, the output is simply proportional to the sum of the coincident impulse response samples. This figure should be compared with Figure 2.48

(a)

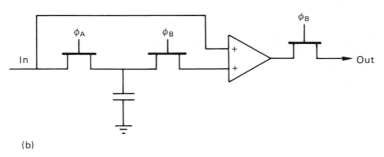

(b)

Figure 2.50 In a switched capacitor delay (a), there are two clock phases, and during the first the input voltage is transferred to the capacitor. During the second phase the capacitor voltage is transferred to the output. (b) A simple switched capacitor filter. The delay causes a phase shift which is dependent on frequency and the resultant frequency response is sinusoidal

integrated circuit converters because they can be implemented with the same integration techniques. Fig. 2.50(a) shows a switched capacitor delay. There are two clock phases and during the first the input voltage is transferred to the capacitor. During the second phase the capacitor voltage is transferred to the output. Combining delay with operational amplifier summation allows frequency-dependent circuitry to be realized. Fig. 2.50(b) shows a simple switched capacitor filter. The delay causes a phase shift which is dependent on frequency. The frequency response is sinusoidal.

2.22 Transforms

Convolution is a lengthy process to perform on paper. It is much easier to work in the frequency domain. Fig. 2.51 shows that if a signal with a spectrum or frequency content a is passed through a filter with a frequency response b the result will be an output spectrum which is simply the product of the two. If the frequency responses are drawn on logarithmic scales (i.e. calibrated in decibels) the two can be simply added because the addition of logs is the same as multiplication. Whilst frequency in video has traditionally meant temporal frequency measured in hertz, frequency in optics can also be spatial and measured in lines per millimetre (mm^{-1}). Multiplying the spectra of the responses is a much simpler process than convolution.

In order to move to the frequency domain or spectrum from the time domain or waveform, it is necessary to use the Fourier transform, or in sampled systems, the discrete Fourier transform (DFT). Fourier analysis holds that any waveform

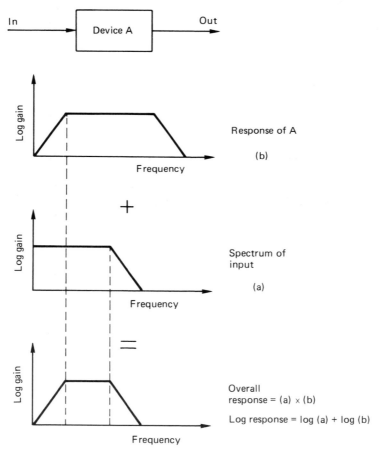

Figure 2.51 In the frequency domain, the response of two series devices is the product of their individual responses at each frequency. On a logarithmic scale the responses are simply added

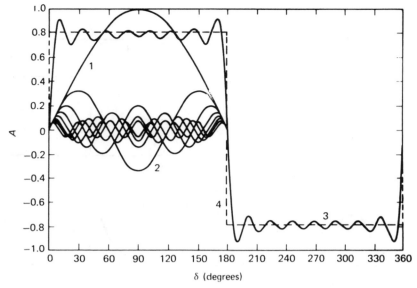

Figure 2.52 Fourier analysis of a square wave into fundamental and harmonics. A, amplitude; δ, phase of fundamental wave in degrees; 1, first harmonic (fundamental); 2, odd harmonics 3–15; 3, sum of harmonics 1–15; 4, ideal square wave

can be reproduced by adding together an arbitrary number of harmonically related sinusoids of various amplitudes and phases. Fig. 2.52 shows how a square wave can be built up of harmonics. The spectrum can be drawn by plotting the amplitude of the harmonics against frequency. It will be seen that this gives a spectrum which is a decaying wave. It passes through zero at all even multiples of the fundamental. The shape of the spectrum is a $\sin x/x$ curve. If a square wave has a $\sin x/x$ spectrum, it follows that a filter with a rectangular impulse response will have a $\sin x/x$ spectrum.

A low-pass filter has a rectangular spectrum, and this has a $\sin x/x$ impulse response. These characteristics are known as a transform pair. In transform pairs, if one domain has one shape of the pair, the other domain will have the other shape. Thus a square wave has a $\sin x/x$ spectrum and a $\sin x/x$ impulse has a square spectrum. Fig. 2.53 shows a number of transform pairs. Note the pulse pair. A time-domain pulse of infinitely short duration has a flat spectrum. Thus a flat waveform, i.e. DC, has only zero in its spectrum. Interestingly the transform of a Gaussian response is still Gaussian. The impulse response of the optics of a laser disc has a $\sin^2 x/x^2$ function, and this is responsible for the triangular falling frequency response of the pickup.

The spectrum of a pseudo-random sequence is not flat because it has a finite sequence length. The rate at which the sequence repeats is visible in the spectrum. Where pseudo-random sequences are to be used in sample manipulation, i.e. where their effects can be visible, it is essential that the sequence length should be long enough to prevent the periodicity being noticed.

Fig. 2.54 shows that the spectrum of a pseudo-random sequence has a $\sin x/x$ characteristic, with nulls at multiples of the clock frequency. A closer inspection

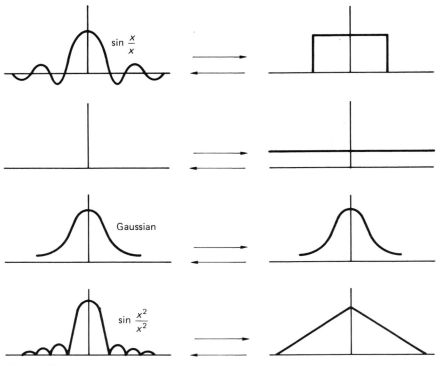

Figure 2.53 The concept of transform pairs illustrates the duality of the frequency (including spatial frequency) and time domains

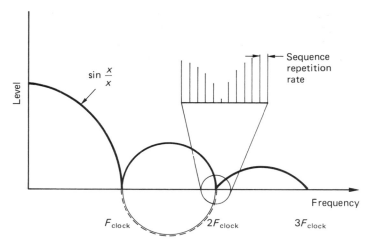

Figure 2.54 The spectrum of a pseudo-random sequence has a sin x/x characteristic, with nulls at multiples of the clock frequency. The spectrum is not continuous, but resembles a comb where the spacing is equal to the repetition rate of the sequence

of the spectrum shows that it is not continuous, but takes the form of a comb where the spacing is equal to the repetition rate of the sequence.

2.23 FIR and IIR filters compared

Filters can be described in two main classes, as shown in Fig. 2.55, according to the nature of the impulse response. Finite-impulse response (FIR) filters are always stable and, as their name suggests, respond to an impulse once, as they have only a forward path. In the temporal domain, the time for which the filter responds to an input is finite, fixed and readily established. The same is therefore true about the distance over which an FIR filter responds in the spatial domain. FIR filters can be made perfectly phase linear if required. Most filters used for sampling-rate conversion and oversampling fall into this category.

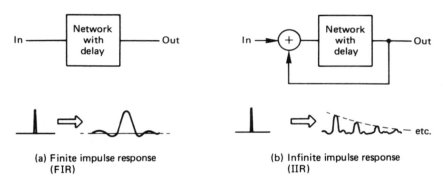

(a) Finite impulse response
(FIR)

(b) Infinite impulse response
(IIR)

Figure 2.55 An FIR filter (a) responds only to an input, whereas the output of an IIR filter (b) continues indefinitely rather like a decaying echo

Infinite-impulse response (IIR) filters respond to an impulse indefinitely and are not necessarily stable, as they have a return path from the output to the input. For this reason they are also called recursive filters. As the impulse response is not symmetrical, IIR filters are not phase linear. Noise reduction units employ recursive filters and will be treated in Chapter 4.

2.24 FIR filters

An FIR filter works by graphically constructing the impulse response for every input sample. It is first necessary to establish the correct impulse response. Fig. 2.56(a) shows an example of a low-pass filter which cuts off at one-quarter of the sampling rate. The impulse response of a perfect low-pass filter is a $\sin x/x$ curve, where the time between the two central zero crossings is the reciprocal of the cut-off frequency. According to the mathematics, the waveform has always existed, and carries on for ever. The peak value of the output coincides with the input impulse. This means that the filter is not causal, because the output has changed before the input is known. Thus in all practical applications it is necessary to truncate the extreme ends of the impulse response, which causes an aperture effect, and to introduce a time delay in the filter equal to half the duration of the

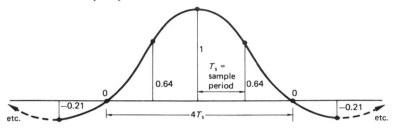

Figure 2.56(a) The impulse response of an LPF is a sin x/x curve which stretches from $-\infty$ to $+\infty$ in time. The ends of the response must be neglected, and a delay introduced to make the filter causal

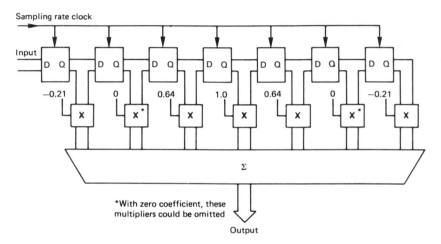

Figure 2.56(b) The structure of an FIR LPF. Input samples shift across the register and at each point are multiplied by different coefficients

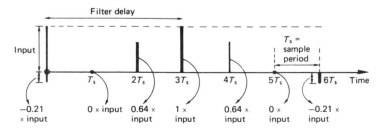

Figure 2.56 (c) When a single unit sample shifts across the circuit of Figure 2.36(b), the impulse response is created at the output as the impulse is multiplied by each cofficient in turn

truncated impulse in order to make the filter causal. As an input impulse is shifted through the series of registers in Fig. 2.56(b), the impulse response is created, because at each point it is multiplied by a coefficient as in Fig. 2.56(c). These coefficients are simply the result of sampling and quantizing the desired impulse response. Clearly the sampling rate used to sample the impulse must be the same as the sampling rate for which the filter is being designed. In practice the coefficients are calculated, rather than attempting to sample an actual impulse response. The coefficient wordlength will be a compromise between cost and performance. Because the input sample shifts across the system registers to create the shape of the impulse response, the configuration is also known as a transversal filter. In operation with real sample streams, there will be several consecutive sample values in the filter registers at any time in order to convolve the input with the impulse response.

Simply truncating the impulse response causes an abrupt transition from input samples which matter and those which do not. Truncating the filter superimposes a rectangular shape on the time-domain impulse response. In the frequency domain the rectangular shape transforms to a $\sin x/x$ characteristic which is superimposed on the desired frequency response as a ripple. One consequence of this is known as Gibb's phenomenon: a tendency for the response to peak just before the cut-off frequency.[2,3] As a result, the length of the impulse which must be considered will depend not only on the frequency response, but also on the amount of ripple which can be tolerated. If the relevant period of the impulse is measured in sample periods, the result will be the number of points or multiplications needed in the filter. Fig. 2.57 compares the performance of filters with different numbers of points. Video filters may use as few as eight points whereas a high-quality digital audio FIR filter may need as many as 96 points.

Figure 2.57 The truncation of the impulse in an FIR filter caused by the use of a finite number of points (N) results in ripple in the response. Shown here are three different numbers of points for the same impulse response. The filter is an LPF which rolls off at 0.4 of the fundamental interval. (Courtesy *Philips Technical Review*)

Rather than simply truncate the impulse response in time, it is better to make a smooth transition from samples which do not count to those that do. This can be done by multiplying the coefficients in the filter by a window function which peaks in the centre of the impulse. Fig. 2.58 shows some different window functions and their responses. The rectangular window is the case of truncation, and the response is shown at I. A linear reduction in weight from the centre of the window to the edges characterizes the Bartlett window II, which trades ripple

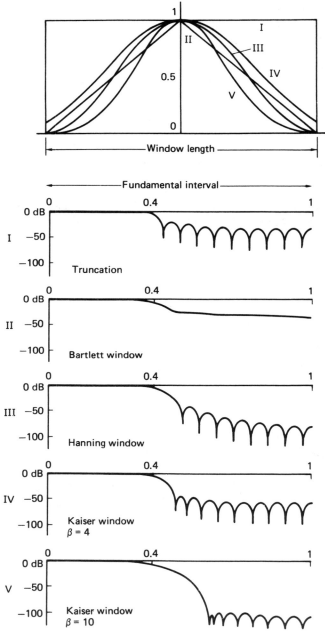

Figure 2.58 The effect of window functions. At top, various window functions are shown in continuous form. Once the number of samples in the window is established, the continuous functions shown here are sampled at the appropriate spacing to obtain window coefficients. These are multiplied by the truncated impulse response coefficients to obtain the actual coefficients used by the filter. The amplitude responses I–V correspond to the window functions illustrated. (Responses courtesy *Philips Technical Review*)

for an increase in transition-region width. At III is shown the Hanning window, which is essentially a raised cosine shape. Not shown is the similar Hamming window, which offers a slightly different trade-off between ripple and the width of the main lobe. The Blackman window introduces an extra cosine term into the Hamming window at half the period of the main cosine period, reducing Gibb's phenomenon and ripple level, but increasing the width of the transition region. The Kaiser window is a family of windows based on the Bessel function, allowing various trade-offs between ripple ratio and main lobe width. Two of these are shown in IV and V. The drawback of the Kaiser windows is that they are complex to implement.

Filter coefficients can be optimized by computer simulation. One of the best known techniques used is the Remez exchange algorithm, which converges on the optimum coefficients after a number of iterations.

In the example of Fig. 2.59, the low-pass filter of Fig. 2.56 is shown with a Bartlett window. Acceptable ripple determines the number of significant sample periods embraced by the impulse. This determines in turn both the number of

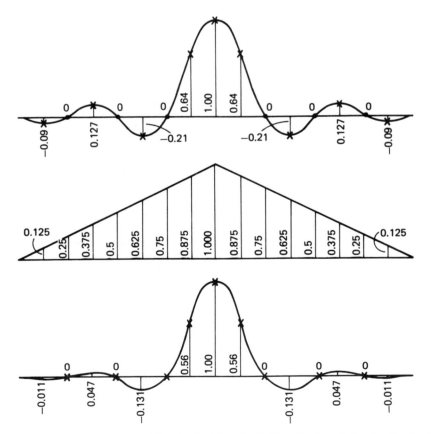

Figure 2.59 A truncated sin x/x impulse (top) is multiplied by a Bartlett window function (centre) to produce the actual coefficients used (bottom)

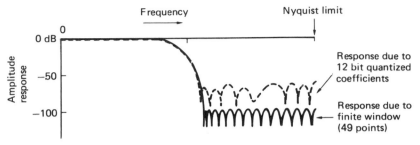

Figure 2.60 Frequency response of a 49 point transversal filter with infinite precision (solid line) shows ripple due to finite window size. Quantizing coefficients to 12 bits reduces attenuation in the stopband. (Responses courtesy *Philips Technical Review*)

points in the filter and the filter delay. As the impulse is symmetrical, the delay will be half the impulse period. The impulse response is a $\sin x/x$ function, and this has been calculated in the figure. The $\sin x/x$ response is next multiplied by the window function to give the windowed impulse response.

If the coefficients are not quantized finely enough, it will be as if they had been calculated inaccurately, and the performance of the filter will be less than expected. Fig. 2.60 shows an example of quantizing coefficients. Conversely, raising the wordlength of the coefficients increases cost.

The FIR structure is inherently phase linear because it is easy to make the impulse response absolutely symmetrical. The individual samples in a digital system do not know in isolation what frequency they represent, and they can only pass through the filter at a rate determined by the clock. Because of this inherent phase linearity, an FIR filter can be designed for a specific impulse response, and the frequency response will follow.

The frequency response of the filter can be changed at will by changing the coefficients. A programmable filter only requires a series of PROMs to supply the coefficients; the address supplied to the PROMs will select the response. The frequency response of a digital filter will also change if the clock rate is changed, so it is often less ambiguous to specify a frequency of interest in a digital filter in terms of a fraction of the fundamental interval rather than in absolute terms. The configuration shown in Fig. 2.56 serves to illustrate the principle. The units used on the diagrams are sample periods and the response is proportional to these periods or spacings, and so it is not necessary to use actual figures.

Where the impulse response is symmetrical, it is often possible to reduce the number of multiplications, because the same product can be used twice, at equal distances before and after the centre of the window. This is known as folding the filter. A folded filter is shown in Fig. 2.61.

2.25 The need for sampling-rate conversion

Sampling-rate conversion or interpolation is an important enabling technology on which a large number of practical digital video devices are based. In digital video, the sampling rate takes on many guises. When analog video is sampled in real time, the sampling rate is temporal, but where pixels form a static array, the sampling rate is a spatial frequency.

Figure 2.61 A seven-point folded filter for a symmetrical impulse response. In this case K1 and K7 will be identical, and so the input sample can be multiplied once, and the product fed into the output shift system in two different places. The centre coefficient K4 appears once. In an even-numbered filter the centre coefficient would also be used twice

Some of the applications of interpolation are set out here:

(1) Standards converters need to change two of the sampling rates of the video they handle, namely the temporal frame rate and the vertical line spacing, which is in fact a spatial sampling frequency. Standards converters working with composite digital signals will also need to change the sampling rate along the line since it will be a multiple of the appropriate subcarrier frequency.

(2) Different sampling rates exist today for different purposes. Most component digital devices sample at 13.5 MHz, using the 4:2:2 format, but other variations are possible, such as 3:1:1. Composite machines sample at a multiple of the subcarrier frequency of their line standard. Rate conversion allows material to be exchanged freely between such formats. For example, the output of a 4:2:2 paint system at 13.5 MHz may be digitally converted to $4F_{sc}$ for use as input to a composite digital recorder.

(3) To take advantage of oversampling converters, an increase in sampling rate is necessary for DACs and a reduction in sampling rate is necessary for ADCs. In oversampling the factors by which the rates are changed are simpler than in other applications.

(4) In effects machines, the size of the picture may be changed without the pixel spacing being changed. This is exactly the converse of the standards converter, which leaves the picture size unchanged and changes the pixel spacing. Alternatively the picture may be shifted with respect to the sampling matrix by any required distance to subpixel accuracy. Similar processes are necessary in motion estimation for standards converters and data reduction.

(5) When a digital VTR is played back at other than the correct speed to achieve some effect or to correct pitch, the sampling rate of the reproduced audio signal changes in proportion. If the playback samples are to be fed to a digital mixing console which works at some standard frequency, audio sampling-rate conversion will be necessary.

   Whilst DVTRs universally use an audio sampling rate of 48 kHz, Compact Disc uses 44.1 kHz and 32 kHz is common for broadcast use (e.g. NICAM 728).

(6) When digital audio is used in conjunction with film or video, difficulties arise because it is not always possible to synchronize the sampling rate with the frame rate. An example of this is where the digital audio recorder uses its internally generated sampling rate, but also records studio timecode. On playback, the timecode can be made the same as on other units, or the sampling rate can be locked, but not both. Sampling-rate conversion allows a recorder to play back an asynchronous recording locked to timecode.

2.26 Categories of rate conversion

There are three basic but related categories of rate conversion, as shown in Fig. 2.62. The most straightforward (a) changes the rate by an integer ratio, up or down. The timing of the system is thus simplified because all samples (input and output) are present on edges of the higher-rate sampling clock. Such a system is generally adopted for oversampling converters; the exact sampling rate

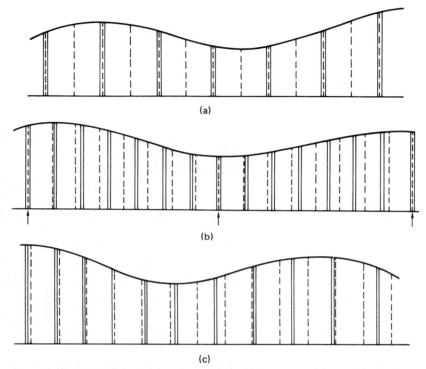

Figure 2.62 Categories of rate conversion. (a) Integer-ratio conversion, where the lower-rate samples are always coincident with those of the higher rate. There are a small number of phases needed. (b) Fractional-ratio conversion, where sample coincidence is periodic. A larger number of phases is required. Example here is conversion from 50.4 kHz to 44.1 kHz (8/7). (c) Variable-ratio conversion, where there is no fixed relationship, and a large number of phases are required

immediately adjacent to the analog domain is not critical, and will be chosen to make the filters easier to implement.

Next in order of difficulty is the category shown at (b) where the rate is changed by the ratio of two small integers. Samples in the input periodically time-align with the output. Such devices can be used for converting from $4 \times F_{sc}$ to $3 \times F_{sc}$, in the vertical processing of standards converters, or between the various rates of CCIR-601.

The most complex rate-conversion category is where there is no simple relationship between input and output sampling rates, and in fact they may vary. This situation, shown at (c), is known as variable-ratio conversion. The temporal or spatial relationship of input and output samples is arbitrary. This problem will be met in effects machines which zoom or rotate images.

2.27 Integer-ratio conversion

The technique of integer-ratio conversion is used in conjunction with over-sampling converters in digital video and audio and in data motion estimation and

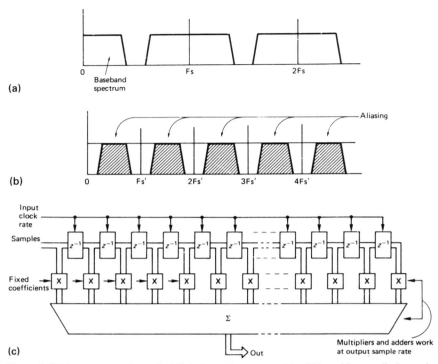

(a)

(b)

(c)

Figure 2.63 The spectrum of a typical digital sample stream at (a) will be subject to aliasing as in (b) if the baseband width is not reduced by an LPF. At (c) an FIR low-pass filter prevents aliasing. Samples are clocked transversely across the filter at the input rate, but the filter only computes at the output sample rate. Clearly this will only work if the two are related by an integer factor

reduction systems where subsampled or reduced-resolution versions of an input image are required. These applications will be detailed in Chapter 4. Sampling-rate reduction by an integer factor is dealt with first.

Fig. 2.63(a) shows the spectrum of a typical sampled system where the sampling rate is a little more than twice the analog bandwidth. Attempts to reduce the sampling rate by simply omitting samples, a process known as decimation, will result in aliasing, as shown in Fig. 2.63(b). Intuitively it is obvious that omitting samples is the same as if the original sampling rate was lower. In order to prevent aliasing, it is necessary to incorporate low-pass filtering into the system where the cut-off frequency reflects the new, lower, sampling rate. An FIR-type low-pass filter could be installed, as described earlier in this chapter, immediately prior to the stage where samples are omitted, but this would be wasteful, because for much of its time the FIR filter would be calculating sample values which are to be discarded. The more effective method is to combine the low-pass filter with the decimator so that the filter only calculates values to be retained in the output sample stream. Fig. 2.63(c) shows how this is done. The filter makes one accumulation for every output sample, but that accumulation is the result of multiplying all relevant input samples in the filter window by an appropriate coefficient. The number of points in the filter is determined by the number of *input* samples in the period of the filter window, but the number of multiplications per second is obtained by multiplying that figure by the *output* rate. If the filter is not integrated with the decimator, the number of points has to be multiplied by the input rate. The larger the rate-reduction factor the more advantageous the decimating filter ought to be, but this is not quite the case, as the greater the reduction in rate, the longer the filter window will need to be to accommodate the broader impulse response.

When the sampling rate is to be increased by an integer factor, additional samples must be created at even spacing between the existing ones. There is no need for the bandwidth of the input samples to be reduced since, if the original sampling rate was adequate, a higher one must also be adequate.

Fig. 2.64 shows that the process of sampling-rate increase can be thought of in two stages. First the correct rate is achieved by inserting samples of zero value at the correct instant, and then the additional samples are given meaningful values by passing the sample stream through a low-pass filter which cuts off at the Nyquist frequency of the original sampling rate. This filter is known as an interpolator, and one of its tasks is to prevent images of the lower input sampling spectrum from appearing in the extended baseband of the higher-rate output spectrum.

How do interpolators work? Remember that, according to sampling theory, all sampled systems have finite bandwidth. An individual digital sample value is obtained by sampling the instantaneous voltage of the original analog waveform, and because it has zero duration, it must contain an infinite spectrum. However, such a sample can never be seen in that form because of the reconstruction

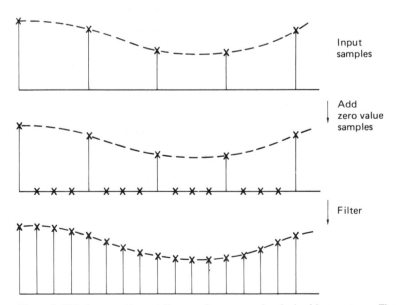

Figure 2.64 In integer-ratio sampling, rate increase can be obtained in two stages. First zero-value samples are inserted to increase the rate, and then filtering is used to give the extra samples real values. The filter necessary will be an LPF with a response which cuts off at the Nyquist frequency of the input samples

process, which limits the spectrum of the impulse to the Nyquist limit. After reconstruction, one infinitely short digital sample ideally represents a $\sin x/x$ pulse whose central peak width is determined by the response of the reconstruction filter, and whose amplitude is proportional to the sample value. This implies that, in reality, one sample value has meaning over a considerable timespan, rather than just at the sample instant. If this were not true, it would be impossible to build an interpolator.

As in rate reduction, performing the steps separately is inefficient. The bandwidth of the information is unchanged when the sampling rate is increased; therefore the original input samples will pass through the filter unchanged, and it is superfluous to compute them. The combination of the two processes into an interpolating filter minimizes the amount of computation.

As the purpose of the system is purely to increase the sampling rate, the filter must be as transparent as possible, and this implies that a linear-phase configuration is mandatory, suggesting the use of an FIR structure. Fig. 2.65 shows that the theoretical impulse response of such a filter is a $\sin x/x$ curve which has zero value at the position of adjacent input samples. In practice this impulse cannot be implemented because it is infinite. The impulse response used will be truncated and windowed as described earlier. To simplify this discussion, assume that a $\sin x/x$ impulse is to be used. There is a strong parallel with the operation of a DAC where the analog voltage is returned to the time-continuous state by summing the analog impulses due to each sample. In a digital interpolating filter, this process is duplicated.[4]

If the sampling rate is to be doubled, new samples must be interpolated exactly half-way between existing samples. The necessary impulse response is shown in Fig. 2.66; it can be sampled at the *output* sample period and quantized to form

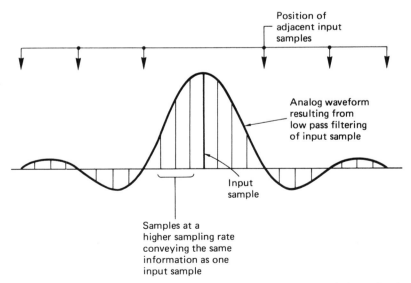

Figure 2.65 A single sample results in a sin x/x waveform after filtering in the analog domain. At a new, higher, sampling rate, the same waveform after filtering will be obtained if the numerous samples of differing size shown here are used. It follows that the values of these new samples can be calculated from the input samples in the digital domain in an FIR filter

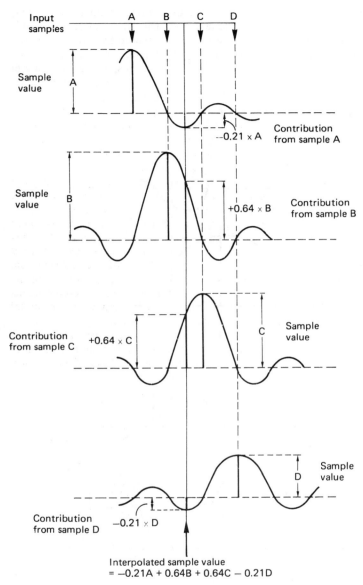

Figure 2.66 A two times oversampling interpolator. To compute an intermediate sample, the input samples are imagined to be sin x/x impulses, and the contributions from each at the point of interest can be calculated. In practice, rather more samples on either side need to be taken into account

coefficients. If a single input sample is multiplied by each of these coefficients in turn, the impulse response of that sample at the new sampling rate will be obtained. Note that every other coefficient is zero, which confirms that no computation is necessary on the existing samples; they are just transferred to the output. The intermediate sample is computed by adding together the impulse responses of every input sample in the window. The figure shows how this mechanism operates. If the sampling rate is to be increased by a factor of four, three sample values must be interpolated between existing input samples. Fig. 2.67 shows that it is only necessary to sample the impulse response at one-quarter

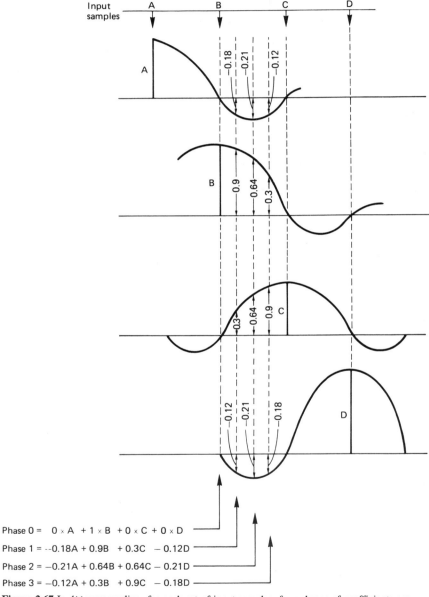

Phase 0 =   0 × A + 1 × B + 0 × C + 0 × D
Phase 1 = --0.18A + 0.9B + 0.3C − 0.12D
Phase 2 = −0.21A + 0.64B + 0.64C − 0.21D
Phase 3 = −0.12A + 0.3B + 0.9C − 0.18D

Figure 2.67 In 4×oversampling, for each set of input samples, four phases of coefficients are necessary, each of which produces one of the oversampled values the period of input samples to obtain three sets of coefficients which will be used in turn. In hardware-implemented filters, the input sample which is passed straight to the output is transferred by using a fourth filter phase where all coefficients are zero except the central one which is unity.

2.28 Fractional-ratio conversion

Fractional-ratio conversion allows interchange between different CCIR-601 rates such as 4:2:2 and 3:1:1. Fractional ratios also occur in the vertical axis of standards converters. Fig. 2.62 showed that when the two sampling rates have a simple fractional relationship m/n, there is a periodicity in the relationship between samples in the two streams. It is possible to have a system clock running

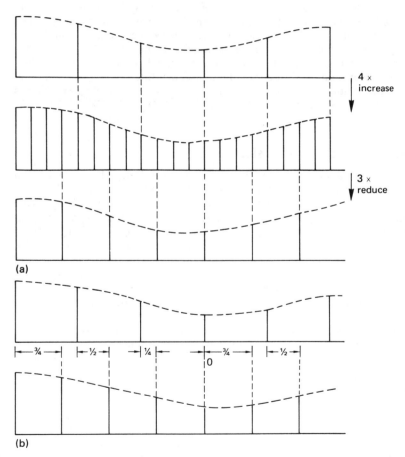

Figure 2.68 At (a), fractional-ratio conversion of ¾ in this sample is by increasing to 4× input prior to reducing by 3×. The inefficiency due to discarding previously computed values is clear. At (b), efficiency is raised since only needed values will be computed. Note how the interpolation phase changes for each output. Fixed coefficients can no longer be used

at the least common multiple frequency which will divide by different integers to give each sampling rate.[5]

The existence of a common clock frequency means that a fractional-ratio converter could be made by arranging two integer-ratio converters in series. This configuration is shown in Fig. 2.68(a). The input sampling rate is multiplied by m in an interpolator, and the result is divided by n in a decimator. Although this system would work, it would be grossly inefficient, because only one in n of the interpolator's outputs would be used. A decimator followed by an interpolator would also offer the correct sampling rate at the output, but the intermediate sampling rate would be so low that the system bandwidth would be quite unacceptable.

As has been seen, a more efficient structure results from combining the processes. The result is exactly the same structure as an integer-ratio interpolator, and requires an FIR filter. The impulse response of the filter is determined by the lower of the two sampling rates, and as before it prevents aliasing when the rate is being reduced, and prevents images when the rate is being increased. The interpolator has sufficient coefficient phases to interpolate m output samples for every input sample, but not all of these values are computed; only interpolations which coincide with an output sample are performed. It will be seen in Fig. 2.68(b) that input samples shift across the transversal filter at the input sampling rate, but interpolations are only performed at the output sample rate. This is possible because a different filter phase will be used at each interpolation.

2.29 Variable-ratio conversion

In the previous examples, the sample rate or spacing of the filter output had a constant relationship to the input, which meant that the two rates had to be phase locked. This is an undesirable constraint in some applications, including image manipulators. In a variable-ratio interpolator, values will exist for the points at which input samples were made, but it is necessary to compute what the sample values would have been at absolutely any point between available samples. The general concept of the interpolator is the same as for the fractional-ratio converter, except that an infinite number of filter phases is ideally necessary. Since a realizable filter will have a finite number of phases, it is necessary to study the degradation this causes. The desired continuous temporal or spatial axis of the interpolator is quantized by the phase spacing, and a sample value needed at a particular point will be replaced by a value for the nearest available filter phase. The number of phases in the filter therefore determines the accuracy of the interpolation. The effects of calculating a value for the wrong point are identical to those of sampling with clock jitter, in that an error occurs proportional to the slope of the signal. The result is program-modulated noise. The higher the noise specification, the greater the desired time accuracy and the greater the number of phases required. The number of phases is equal to the number of sets of coefficients available, and should not be confused with the number of points in the filter, which is equal to the number of coefficients in a set (and the number of multiplications needed to calculate one output value).

The sampling jitter accuracy necessary for 8 bit working is measured in picoseconds. This implies that something like 32 filter phases will be required for adequate performance in an 8 bit sampling-rate converter.

Some essential principles 107

References

1. Ray, S.F., *Applied Photographic Optics*. Oxford: Focal Press, Ch. 17 (1994)
2. van den Enden, A.W.M. and Verhoeckx, N.A.M., Digital signal processing: theoretical background. *Philips Tech. Rev.*, **42**, 110–144 (1985)
3. McClellan, J.H., Parks, T.W. and Rabiner, L.R., A computer program for designing optimum FIR linear-phase digital filters. *IEEE Trans. Audio Electroacoust.* **AU-21**, 506–526 (1973)
4. Crochiere, R.E. and Rabiner, L.R., Interpolation and decimation of digital signals – a tutorial review. *Proc. IEEE*, **69**, 300–331 (1981)
5. Rabiner, L.R., Digital techniques for changing the sampling rate of a signal. In *Digital Audio*, edited by B. Blesser, B. Locanthi and T.G. Stockham Jr, pp.79–89, New York: Audio Engineering Society (1982)

Conversion

The power of digital techniques is in storage without degradation and in complex processing and manipulations. If video is to take advantage of digital techniques, then means must be found to express the colour and movement of a real-life scene as a series of numbers. Once in the digital domain, degradations can be controlled, and so the conversion processes to and from the digital domain become the main sources of degradation. In the interests of quality, these processes deserve a great deal of attention, and will form the main subjects of this chapter.

3.1 Introduction to conversion

There are a number of ways in which a video waveform can be digitally represented, but the most useful and therefore common is pulse code modulation or PCM which was introduced in Chapter 1. The input is a continuous-time, continuous-voltage video waveform, and this is converted into a discrete-time, discrete-voltage format by a combination of sampling and quantizing. As these two processes are orthogonal (a 64 dollar word for at right angles to one another) they are totally independent and can be performed in either order. Fig. 3.1(a) shows an analog sampler preceding a quantizer, whereas (b) shows an asynchronous quantizer preceding a digital sampler. Ideally, both will give the same results; in practice each has different advantages and suffers from different deficiencies. Both approaches will be found in real equipment.

The independence of sampling and quantizing allows each to be discussed quite separately in some detail, prior to combining the processes for a full understanding of conversion.

Whilst sampling an analog video waveform takes place in the time domain in an electrical ADC; this is because the analog waveform is the result of scanning an image. In reality the image has been spatially sampled in two dimensions (lines and pixels) and temporally sampled into fields along a third dimension. Sampling in a single dimension will be considered before moving on to more dimensions.

3.2 Sampling and aliasing

Sampling is no more than periodic measurement, and it will be shown here that there is no theoretical need for sampling to be detectable. Practical television

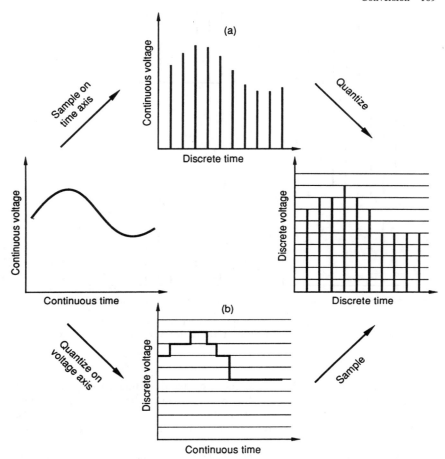

Figure 3.1 Since sampling and quantizing are orthogonal, the order in which they are performed is not important. In (a) sampling is performed first and the samples are quantized. This is common in audio converters. In (b) the analog input is quantized into an asynchronous binary code. Sampling takes place when this code is latched on sampling clock edges. This approach is universal in video converters

equipment is, of course, less than ideal, particularly in the case of temporal sampling.

Video sampling must be regular, because the process of timebase correction prior to conversion back to a conventional analog waveform assumes a regular original process as was shown in Chapter 1. The sampling process originates with a pulse train which is shown in Fig. 3.2(a) to be of constant amplitude and period. The video waveform amplitude-modulates the pulse train in much the same way as the carrier is modulated in an AM radio transmitter. One must be careful to avoid over modulating the pulse train as shown in (b) and this is achieved by applying a DC offset to the analog waveform so that blanking corresponds to a level part-way up the pulses as at (c).

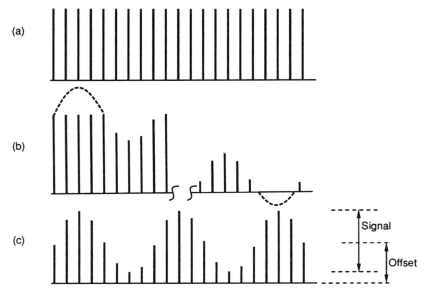

Figure 3.2 The sampling process requires a constant-amplitude pulse train as shown in (a). This is amplitude modulated by the waveform to be sampled. If the input waveform has excessive amplitude or incorrect level, the pulse train clips as shown in (b). For a bipolar waveform, the greatest signal level is possible when an offset of half the pulse amplitude is used to centre the waveform as shown in (c)

In the same way that AM radio produces sidebands or images above and below the carrier, sampling also produces sidebands, although the carrier is now a pulse train and has an infinite series of harmonics as shown in Fig. 3.3(a). The sidebands repeat above and below each harmonic of the sampling rate as shown in (b).

The sampled signal can be returned to the continuous-time domain simply by passing it into a low-pass filter. This filter has a frequency response which prevents the images from passing, and only the baseband signal emerges, completely unchanged. If considered in the frequency domain, this filter can be called an anti-image filter; if considered in the time domain it can be called a reconstruction filter. It can also be considered as a spatial filter if a sampled still image is being returned to a continuous image. Such a filter will be two dimensional.

If an input is supplied having an excessive bandwidth for the sampling rate in use, the sidebands will overlap (Fig. 3.3(c)) and the result is aliasing, where certain output frequencies are not the same as their input frequencies but instead become difference frequencies (Fig. 3.3(d)). It will be seen from Fig. 3.3 that aliasing does not occur when the input frequency is equal to or less than half the sampling rate, and this derives the most fundamental rule of sampling, which is that the sampling rate must be at least twice the highest input frequency. Sampling theory is usually attributed to Shannon[1,2] who applied it to information theory at around the same time as Kotelnikov in Russia. These applications were pre-dated by Whittaker. Despite that it is often referred to as Nyquist's theorem.

Figure 3.3 (a) Spectrum of sampling pulses. (b) Spectrum of samples. (c) Aliasing due to sideband overlap. (d) Beat-frequency production. (e) 4× oversampling

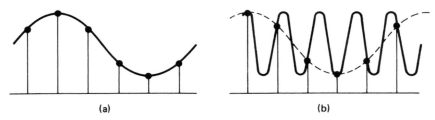

Figure 3.4 In (a), the sampling is adequate to reconstruct the original signal. In (b) the sampling rate is inadequate, and reconstruction produces the wrong waveform (detailed). Aliasing has taken place

Whilst aliasing has been described above in the frequency domain, it can be described equally well in the time domain. In Fig. 3.4(a) the sampling rate is obviously adequate to describe the waveform, but at (b) it is inadequate and aliasing has occurred.

One often has no control over the spectrum of input signals and in practice it is necessary also to have a low-pass filter at the input to prevent aliasing. This anti-aliasing filter prevents frequencies of more than half the sampling rate from reaching the sampling stage. The requirement for an anti-aliasing filter extends to two-dimensional sampling devices such as CCD sensors, as will be seen in Section 3.6.

Whilst electrical or optical anti-aliasing filters are quite feasible, there is no corresponding device which can precede the image sampling at frame or field rate in film or TV cameras and as a result aliasing is commonly seen on television and in the cinema, owing to the relatively low frame rates used. With a frame rate of 24 Hz, a film camera will alias on any object changing at more than 12 Hz. Such objects include the spokes of stagecoach wheels, especially when being chased by Indians. When the spoke-passing frequency reaches 24 Hz the wheels appear to stop, which somewhat confuses the Indians (How?). Temporal aliasing in television is less visible than might be thought because of the way in which the eye perceives motion. This will be discussed further in Section 4.24.

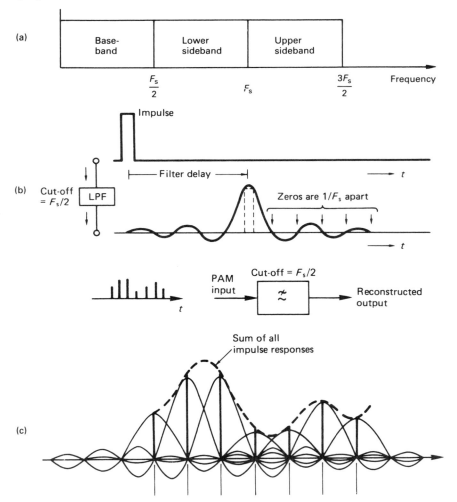

Figure 3.5 If ideal 'brick wall' filters are assumed, the efficient spectrum of (a) results. An ideal low-pass filter has an impulse response shown in (b). The impulse passes through zero at intervals equal to the sampling period. When convolved with a pulse train at the sampling rate, as shown in (c), the voltage at each sample instant is due to that sample alone as the impulses from all other samples pass through zero there

3.3 Reconstruction

If ideal low-pass anti-aliasing and anti-image filters are assumed, having a vertical cut-off slope at half the sampling rate, an ideal spectrum shown in Fig. 3.5(a) is obtained. It was shown in Chapter 2 that the impulse response of a phase-linear ideal low-pass filter is a $\sin x/x$ waveform in the time domain, and this is repeated in Fig. 3.5(b). Such a waveform passes through zero volts periodically. If the cut-off frequency of the filter is one-half of the sampling rate, the impulse passes through zero *at the sites of all other samples*. It can be seen from Fig. 3.5(c) that at the output of such a filter, the voltage at the centre of a sample is due to that sample alone, since the value of *all* other samples is zero at that instant. In other words the continuous-time output waveform must join up the tops of the input samples. In between the sample instants, the output of the filter is the sum of the contributions from many impulses, and the waveform smoothly joins the tops of the samples. If the time domain is being considered, the anti-image filter of the frequency domain can equally well be called the reconstruction filter. It is a consequence of the band limiting of the original anti-aliasing filter that the filtered analog waveform could only travel between the sample points in one way. As the reconstruction filter has the same frequency response, the reconstructed output waveform must be identical to the original band-limited waveform prior to sampling. A rigorous mathematical proof of reconstruction can be found in Betts.[3]

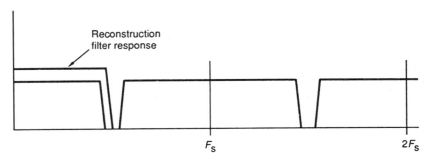

Figure 3.6 As filters with finite slope are needed in practical systems, the sampling rate is raised slightly beyond twice the highest frequency in the baseband

The ideal filter with a vertical 'brick-wall' cut-off slope is difficult to implement. As the slope tends to vertical, the delay caused by the filter goes to infinity. In practice, a filter with a finite slope has to be accepted as shown in Fig. 3.6. The cut-off slope begins at the edge of the required band, and consequently the sampling rate has to be raised a little to drive aliasing products to an acceptably low level. There is no absolute factor by which the sampling rate must be raised; it depends upon the filters which are available and the level of aliasing products which are acceptable. The latter will depend upon the wordlength to which the signal will be quantized.

3.4 Filter design

It is not easy to specify anti-aliasing and reconstruction filters, particularly the amount of stopband rejection needed. The amount of aliasing resulting would depend on, among other things, the amount of out-of-band energy in the input signal. Very little is known about the energy in typical source material outside the usual frequency range. As a further complication, an out-of-band signal will be attenuated by the response of the anti-aliasing filter to that frequency, but the residual signal will then alias, and the reconstruction filter will reject it according to its attenuation at the new frequency to which it has aliased. To take the opposite extreme, if a camera were used which had no response at all above the video band, no anti-aliasing filter would be needed.

It would also be acceptable to bypass one of the filters involved in a copy from one digital machine to another via the analog domain, although a digital transfer is of course to be preferred.

The nature of the filters used has a great bearing on the subjective quality of the system. Entire books have been written about analog filters, and they will only be treated briefly here.

Fig. 3.7 shows the terminology used to describe the common elliptic low-pass filter. These are popular because they can be realized with fewer components than other filters of similar response. It is a characteristic of these elliptic filters that there are ripples in the passband and stopband. In much equipment the anti-aliasing filter and the reconstruction filter will have the same specification, so that the passband ripple is doubled. Sometimes slightly different filters are used to reduce the effect.

Active filters can simulate inductors using op-amp techniques, but they tend to suffer non-linearity at high frequencies where the falling open-loop gain reduces the effect of feedback. Active filters also can contribute noise, but this is not necessarily a bad thing in controlled amounts, since it can act as a dither source.

For video applications, the phase response of such filters must be linear (see Chapter 2). Since a sharp cut-off is generally achieved by cascading many filter

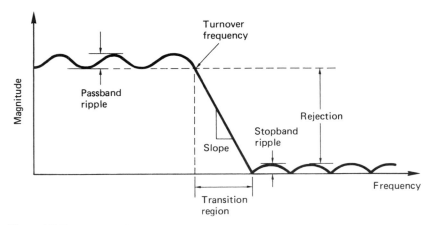

Figure 3.7 The important features and terminology of low-pass filters used for anti-aliasing and reconstruction

sections which cut at a similar frequency, the phase responses of these sections will accumulate. The phase may start to leave linearity at only a half of the passband frequency, and near the cut-off frequency the phase error may be severe. Effective group-delay equalization is necessary.

It is possible to construct a ripple-free phase-linear filter with the required stopband rejection, but it may be expensive due to the amount of design effort needed and the component complexity, and it might drift out of specification as components age. The money may be better spent in avoiding the need for such a filter. Much effort can be saved in analog filter design by using oversampling. Chapter 2 showed that digital filters are inherently phase linear and, using LSI, can be inexpensive to construct. The technical superiority of oversampling converters along with economics means that they will be increasingly used in the future, which is why the subject is more prominent in this volume than the treatment of filter design.

3.5 Aperture effect

The reconstruction process of Fig. 3.5 only operates exactly as shown if the impulses are of negligible duration. In many processes this is not the case, and many real devices keep the analog signal constant for a substantial part of or even all the period. The result is a waveform which is more like a staircase than a pulse train. The case where the pulses have been extended in width to become equal to the sample period is known as a zero-order hold system and has a 100% aperture ratio.

It was shown in Chapter 2 that whereas pulses of negligible width have a uniform spectrum, which is flat within the baseband, pulses of 100% aperture ratio have a $\sin x/x$ spectrum which is shown in Fig. 3.8. The frequency response falls to a null at the sampling rate, and as a result is about 4 dB down at the edge of the baseband. If the pulse width is stable, the reduction of high frequencies is constant and predictable, and an appropriate equalization circuit can render the overall response flat once more. An alternative is to use resampling which is

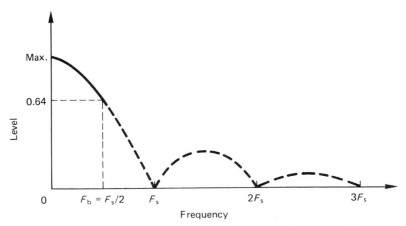

Figure 3.8 Frequency response with 100% aperture nulls at multiples of sampling rate. Area of interest is up to half sampling rate

Figure 3.9 (a) Resampling circuit eliminates transients and reduces aperture ratio. (b) Response of various aperture ratios

shown in Fig. 3.9. Resampling passes the zero-order hold waveform through a further synchronous sampling stage which consists of an analog switch which closes briefly in the centre of each sample period. The output of the switch will be pulses which are narrower than the original. If, for example, the aperture ratio is reduced to 50% of the sample period, the first frequency response null is now at twice the sampling rate, and the loss at the edge of the audio band is reduced. As the figure shows, the frequency response becomes flatter as the aperture ratio falls. The process should not be carried too far, as with very small aperture ratios there is little energy in the pulses and noise can be a problem. A practical limit is around 12.5% where the frequency response is virtually ideal.

The term resampling will also be found in descriptions of sampling-rate converters, where it refers to the process of finding samples at new locations to describe the original waveform. The context usually makes it clear which meaning is intended.

The aperture effect will show up in many aspects of television. Lenses have finite MTF (Modulation Transfer Function), such that a very small object becomes spread in the image. The image sensor will also have a finite aperture function. In tube cameras, the beam will have a finite radius, and will not necessarily have a uniform energy distribution across its diameter. In CCD cameras, the sensor is split into elements which may almost touch in some cases. The element integrates light falling on its surface, and so will have a rectangular aperture. In both cases there will be a roll-off of higher spatial frequencies.

The temporal aperture effect varies according to the equipment used. Tube cameras have a long integration time and thus a wide temporal aperture. Whilst this reduces temporal aliasing, it causes smear on moving objects. CCD cameras do not suffer from lag and as a result their temporal response is better.[4] Some CCD cameras deliberately have a short temporal aperture as the time axis is resampled by a mechanically driven revolving shutter. The intention is to reduce smear (hence the popularity of such devices for sporting events) but there will be more aliasing on certain subjects. The effect of this will be considered in Section 4.24.

The eye has a temporal aperture effect which is known as persistence of vision, and the phosphors of CRTs continue to emit light after the electron beam has passed. These produce further temporal aperture effects in series with those in the camera.

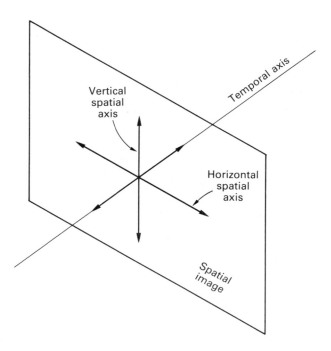

Figure 3.10 The three dimensions in which television signals are sampled. The time domain is the one which causes the greatest difficulty

Current liquid crystal displays do not generate light, but act as a modulator to a separate light source. Their temporal response is rather slow, but there is a possibility to resample by pulsing the light source.

Fig. 3.10 shows the three dimensions available to television signals and shows the possibilities for anti-aliasing, reconstruction and aperture effect in each.

3.6 Two-dimensional sampling spectra

Analog video samples in the time domain and vertically, whereas a two-dimensional still image such as a photograph must be sampled horizontally and

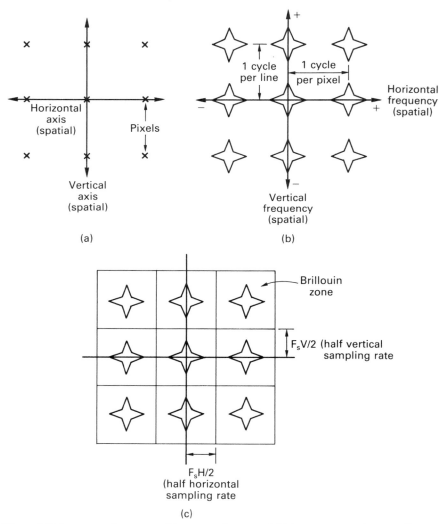

Figure 3.11 Image sampling spectra. The rectangular array of (a) has a spectrum shown at (b) having a rectangular repeating structure. Filtering to return to the baseband requires a two-dimensional filter whose response lies within the Brillouin zone shown at (c).

vertically. In both cases a two-dimensional spectrum will result, one vertical/temporal and one vertical/horizontal.

Fig. 3.11(a) shows a square matrix of sampling sites which has an identical spatial sampling frequency both vertically and horizontally. The corresponding spectrum is shown in Fig. 3.11(b). The baseband spectrum is in the centre of the diagram, and the repeating sampling sideband spectrum extends vertically and horizontally. The star-shaped spectrum results from viewing an image of a man-made object such as a building containing primarily horizontal and vertical elements. A more natural scene such as foliage would result in a more circular or elliptical spectrum.

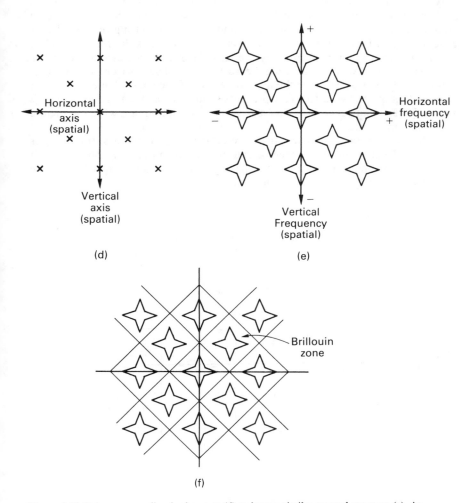

(d)

(e)

(f)

Figure 3.11 Quincunx sampling is shown at (d) to have a similar spectral structure (e). An appropriate Brillouin zone is required as at (f)

In order to return to the baseband image, the sidebands must be filtered out with a two-dimensional spatial filter. The shape of the two-dimensional frequency response shown in Fig. 3.11(c) is known as a Brillouin zone.

Fig. 3.11(d) shows an alternative sampling site matrix known as quincunx sampling because of the similarity to the pattern of five dots on a die. The resultant spectrum has the same characteristic pattern as shown in Fig. 3.11(e). The corresponding Brillouin zones are shown in Fig. 3.11(f). Quincunx sampling offers a better compromise between diagonal and horizontal/vertical resolution but is complex to implement.

It is highly desirable to prevent spatial aliasing, since the result is visually irritating. In tube cameras the spatial aliasing will be in the vertical dimension only, since the horizontal dimension is continuously scanned. Such cameras seldom attempt to prevent vertical aliasing. CCD sensors can, however, alias in both horizontal and vertical dimensions, and so an anti-aliasing optical filter is generally fitted between the lens and the sensor. This takes the form of a plate which diffuses the image formed by the lens. Such a device can never have a sharp cut-off nor will the aperture be rectangular. The aperture of the anti-aliasing plate is in series with the aperture effect of the CCD elements, and the combination of the two effectively prevents spatial aliasing, and generally gives a good balance between horizontal and vertical resolution, allowing the picture a natural appearance.

With a conventional approach, there are effectively two choices. If aliasing is permitted, the theoretical information rate of the system can be approached. If aliasing is prevented, realizable anti-aliasing filters cannot sharp cut, and the information conveyed is below system capacity.

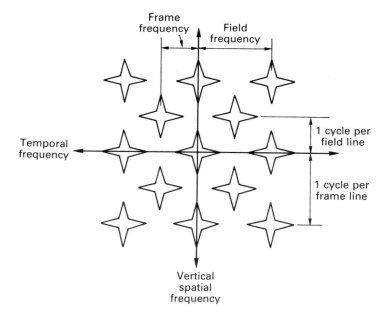

Figure 3.12 The vertical/temporal spectrum of monochrome video due to interlace

These considerations also apply at the television display. The display must filter out spatial frequencies above one-half the sampling rate. In a conventional CRT this means that a vertical optical filter should be fitted in front of the screen to render the raster invisible. Again the aperture of a simply realizable filter would attenuate too much of the wanted spectrum, and so the technique is not used.

Fig. 3.12 shows the spectrum of analog monochrome video (or of an analog component). The use of interlace has a similar effect on the vertical/temporal spectrum as the use of quincunx sampling on the vertical/horizontal spectrum. The concept of the Brillouin zone cannot really be applied to reconstruction in the spatial/temporal domains. This is partly due to there being two different units in which the sampling rates are measured and partly because the temporal sampling process cannot prevent aliasing in real systems.

Three-dimensional (3-D) sampling

3.7.1 3-D spectrum of NTSC

Analog composite video can only be fully described in three dimensions because of the presence of the subcarrier. Digital video samples in three dimensions and also has a three-dimensional spectrum. As such spectra are difficult to illustrate, they are often portrayed in two dimensions at a time.

Fig. 3.13 shows that the structure of the vertical/temporal spectrum of luminance is the same as that of the two colour difference signals because both have the same field and line rates. In NTSC (National Television Systems

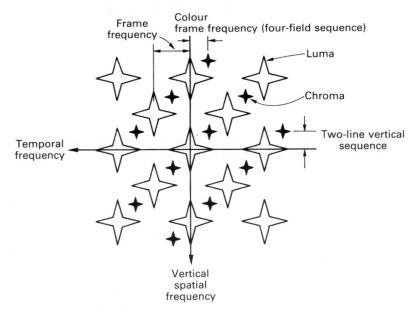

Figure 3.13 The vertical/temporal spectrum of NTSC. Note the one-quarter field rate component responsible for the four-field sequence

Committee), the three signals are encoded into a single channel having the same bandwidth as luminance by exploiting the periodic gaps in the spectrum. The two colour difference signals are used to generate reduced bandwidth signals which alternately phase modulate a subcarrier. The subcarrier is suppressed to produce a chroma signal.

In order to allow the maximum perceived resolution with minimum bandwidth, the chroma phase was shifted slightly with respect to horizontal, so that subcarrier phase demodulation would give a pair of signals known as I and Q (in-phase and quadrature). This placed the Q signal on the colour diagram axis to which the eye is least sensitive.

The chroma is given by:

$$I \sin F_{sc} + Q \cos F_{sc}$$

such that at 90° intervals, the chroma waveform represents I, Q, $-I$, $-Q$ repeatedly. If the receiver samples the chroma at the same intervals, but with the same phase shift, the two baseband colour difference signals can be restored.

The chroma modulation process takes the spectrum of the colour difference signals and produces upper and lower sidebands around the frequency of the subcarrier. Since both colour and luminance signals have gaps in their spectra at multiples of line rate, it follows that the two spectra can be made to interleave and share the same spectrum if an appropriate subcarrier frequency is selected. The subcarrier frequency of NTSC is an odd multiple of half line rate; 227.5 times to be precise. Fig. 3.14 shows that this frequency means that on successive

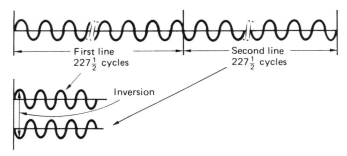

Figure 3.14 The half angle offset in F_{sc} results in a two-line sequence (a) where the first line ends on a half cycle, and the second line chroma will be inverted with respect to the first as at (b)

lines the subcarrier will be phase inverted. There is thus a two-line sequence of subcarrier, responsible for a vertical frequency of half line frequency. The existence of line pairs means that two frames or four fields must elapse before the same relationship between line pairs and frame sync repeats. This is responsible for a temporal frequency component of half the frame rate. These two frequency components can be seen in the vertical/temporal spectrum of Fig. 3.13.

The effect of the chroma added to luminance is to make the luminance alternately too dark or too bright. The phase inversion causes this effect to cancel over pairs of lines, giving compatibility with monochrome receivers. The half frame rate component is responsible for the familiar four-field colour framing sequence. When editing NTSC recordings, this four-field sequence must not be broken. If this rule is not followed, it is possible for a sudden inversion of subcarrier phase to occur at the edit point, which renders the signal unbroadcastable unless it undergoes additional processing.

As the chroma of NTSC is suppressed carrier, it is necessary for the receiver to regenerate the carrier frequency so that it knows when to sample the chroma. This is done by broadcasting a portion of subcarrier, known as the burst, between the sync pulse and the active line. A phase-locked loop in the receiver will freewheel between bursts. The half line offset of NTSC subcarrier means that if an oscilloscope is triggered from H-sync, normal and inverted bursts will appear superimposed on the trace.

Whilst the spectral interleaving of NTSC works fine for the video, there was a problem with the sound carrier. To prevent vision interference with the sound, the sound carrier of the 525/60 monochrome system had itself been placed at an odd multiple of half line rate, and so the addition of the chroma signal meant that chroma and sound could mutually interfere. The audio subcarrier frequency was standardized, and any change would have meant modification to every monochrome television set in the United States on the introduction of colour. The solution adopted was to contract the spectrum of the video slightly by reducing the frame rate to 29.97 Hz. This made the line rate 15 734.25 Hz and the subcarrier frequency 3.5795 MHz. The small disparity between field rate and 60 Hz was of little consequence when it was introduced, but the development of the video recorder revealed a difficulty in synchronizing NTSC recordings to real time, which was alleviated by the invention of drop-frame timecode. This allows a single count to count real-time seconds and NTSC rate frames at the same time by having dropped frames, which do not exist in the video, but which make the seconds count correct. The use of 29 February in the calendar has a similar effect.

The dependence of NTSC on the absolute phase of subcarrier to convey colour accurately led to some difficulties in multipath reception conditions in high-rise districts, and to the somewhat unfair redefinition of the system title as Never Twice the Same Colour. In fact NTSC works well in the majority of other locations.

3.7.2 3-D spectrum of PAL

When the PAL (Phase Alternating Line) system was being developed, it was decided that immunity to received phase errors should be a goal. Fig. 3.15(a) shows how this was achieved. The two colour difference signals (U and V) are used to quadrature-modulate a subcarrier in a similar way as for NTSC, except that the phase of the V signal is reversed on alternate lines. The receiver must then reinvert the V signal in sympathy. If a phase error occurs in transmission, it will cause the phase of V alternately to lead and lag, as shown in Fig. 3.15(b). If the colour difference signals are averaged over two lines, the phase error is eliminated and replaced with a small saturation error which is subjectively much less visible. The receiver needs to know whether or not to invert V on a particular line, and this information is conveyed by swinging the phase of the burst ±135° on alternate lines. A damped PLL in the receiver will run at the average phase, i.e. subcarrier phase, but it will develop a half line rate phase error whose polarity determines the sense of V-switch.

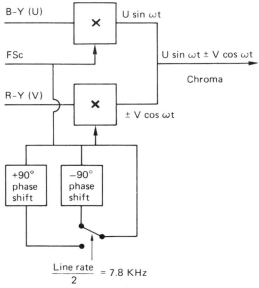

Figure 3.15(a) In PAL the phase of the feed to the V modulator is reversed on alternate lines

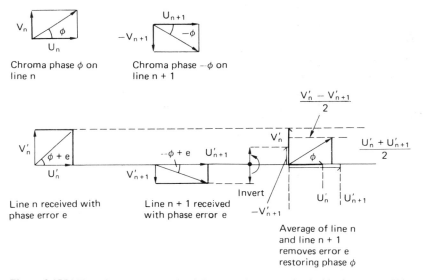

Figure 3.15(b) Top, chroma as transmitted. Bottom, chroma received with phase error. V is reversed on second line and the two lines are averaged, eliminating phase error, and giving a small saturation error

Fig. 3.16(a) shows the vertical temporal spectrum of the U signal, which is identical to that of luminance. However, the inversion of V on alternate lines causes a two-line sequence which is responsible for a vertical frequency component of half line rate. As the two-line sequence does not divide into 625

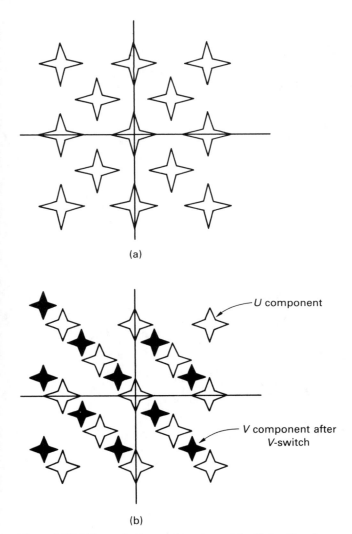

(a)

(b)

Figure 3.16(a) The vertical/temporal spectrum of the U signal has the same structure as luminance. At (b) V-switch has the effect of shifting the spectrum diagonally with respect to U.

lines, two frames elapse before the same relationship between V-switch and the line number repeats. This is responsible for a half frame rate temporal frequency component. Fig. 3.16(b) shows the resultant vertical/temporal spectrum after V-switch and illustrates that the V component has shifted diagonally so that its spectral entries lies half-way between the U component entries. Note that there is an area of the spectrum which appears not to contain signal energy in PAL. This is known as the Fukinuki hole. Spectral interleaving with a half cycle offset of subcarrier frequency as in NTSC will not work, as Fig. 3.16(c) shows. The solution is to adopt a subcarrier frequency with a quarter cycle per line offset.

(c)

(d)

Figure 3.16 (contd.) A half cycle subcarrier offset will not work as (c) shows. Instead a quarter cycle offset is used as at (d)

Multiplying the line rate by 283¾ allows the luminance and chrominance spectra to mesh as in Fig. 3.16(d).

The quarter cycle offset is thus a fundamental consequence of the elimination of phase errors in PAL but it does cause some other effects which raise the complexity of implementation, leading to the retaliatory name of Problems Are Lurking.

The quarter cycle offset means that there are now line quartets instead of line pairs, and this results in a vertical frequency component of one-quarter of line rate which can be seen in the figure. Furthermore four frames or eight fields have to elapse before the same relationship of subcarrier to frame timing repeats. This results in a temporal frequency component of one-quarter of frame rate which is also visible in the figure. This component restricts the way in which PAL recordings can be edited.

The three-quarter cycle offset of subcarrier also means that the line pair cancellation of NTSC is absent, and another means has to be found to achieve visibility reduction. This is done by adding half frame rate to subcarrier frequency, such that an inversion in subcarrier is caused from one field to the next. Since in an interlaced system lines one field apart are adjacent on the screen, cancellation is achieved. The penalty of this approach is that subcarrier phase creeps forward with respect to H-sync at one cycle per frame. The eight-field sequence contains 2500 unique lines all having the subcarrier in a slightly different position. Observing burst on an H-triggered oscilloscope shows a stable envelope with a blurred interior. Measuring the phase of subcarrier with respect to sync requires specialist equipment or a great deal of determination. This is of little consequence for broadcasting, but it does raise the complexity of recorders and timebase correctors.

SECAM (*sequentiel à memoire*) is a composite system which sends the colour difference signals sequentially on alternate lines by *frequency modulating* the subcarrier, which will have one of two different centre frequencies. Although it resists multipath transmission well, it cannot be processed because of the FM chroma. The idiosyncrasies of SECAM have led to the alternative name: *Système Essentiellement Contre les AMericains*.

3.7.3 3-D spectrum of digital luminance

Sampling conventional video along the line to create pixels makes the horizontal axis of the 3-D spectrum repeat at multiples of the sampling rate. Thus combining the 3-D spectrum of analog luminance shown in Fig. 3.13(a) with the sampling spectrum of Fig. 3.3(b) gives the final spectrum shown in Fig. 3.17. Colour difference signals will have a similar structure but often use a lower sampling rate and thereby have less horizontal resolution or bandwidth.

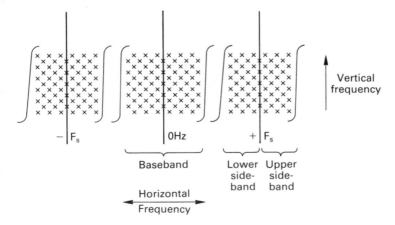

Figure 3.17 Spectrum of digital luminance is the baseband spectrum repeating around multiples of the sampling rate

3.8 Kell effect

As noted, in conventional tube cameras and CRTs the horizontal dimension is continuous, whereas the vertical dimension is sampled. The aperture effect means that the vertical resolution in real systems will be less than sampling theory permits, and to obtain equal horizontal and vertical resolutions a greater number of lines is necessary. The magnitude of the increase is described by the so-called Kell factor[5], although the term factor is a misnomer since it can have a range of values depending on the apertures in use and the methods used to measure resolution.[6] In digital video, sampling takes place in horizontal and vertical dimensions, and the Kell parameter becomes unnecessary. The outputs of digital systems will, however, be displayed on raster scan CRTs, and the Kell parameter of the display will then be effectively in series with the other system constraints.

3.9 Motion perception

The temporal sampling rate, or field rate, of television systems is rather low at 50 or 60 Hz, and as a result temporal frequencies of more than half that will suffer aliasing. High temporal frequencies result from relative movement between the camera and objects in the field of view, as this is a form of scanning. The higher the spatial frequency of the detail in the object, and the faster the scan, the higher the temporal frequencies. It is easy to exceed the temporal frequency response of a television system even with a very slow pan, and yet the result to the viewer is not temporal aliasing. This is because the human eye will follow or track any moving object of sufficient interest. The tracking action renders the object substantially stationary with respect to the retina and so the temporal frequencies in the video spectrum due to motion are brought back to DC. Fig. 3.18 illustrates the concept. In addition the temporal aperture effect of the eye is rendered immaterial and the eye then has its best spatial resolution. Clearly the eye can only track one motion at once; the remainder of the picture will contain relative

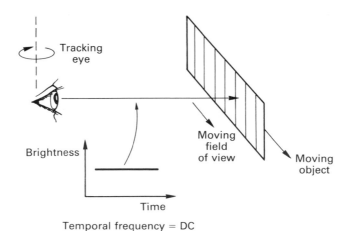

Figure 3.18 When the eye tracks motion there is no relative movement of the image on the retina

motion and will appear to the viewer to have reduced resolution due to the temporal aperture effects of the eye.

In practice the temporal aperture effect of the camera has an effect on the above process. Motion blur is proportional to the length of the temporal aperture, and shuttered CCD cameras will result in better motion portrayal than tube cameras. The effects of motion on a television system can be studied using a moving zone plate.[7]

3.10 Choice of sampling rate – component

If the reason for digitizing a video signal is simply to convey it from one place to another, then the choice of sampling frequency can be determined only by sampling theory and available filters. If, however, processing of the video in the digital domain is contemplated, the choice becomes smaller. In order to produce a two-dimensional array of samples which form rows and vertical columns, the sampling rate has to be an integer multiple of the line rate. This allows for the vertical picture processing necessary in special effects, telecine machines working on various aspect ratios, error concealment in recorders and standards conversion. Whilst the bandwidth needed by 525/59.94 video is less than that of 625/50, and a lower sampling rate might be used, practicality dictated that if a standard sampling rate for video components could be arrived at, then the design of standards converters would be simplified, and digital recorders would operate at a similar data rate even though the frame rates would differ in different standards. This was the goal of CCIR Recommendation 601, which combined the 625/50 input of EBU Docs Tech. 3246 and 3247 and the 525/59.94 input of SMPTE RP 125.

The result is not one sampling rate, but a family of rates based upon the magic frequency of 13.5 MHz.

Using this frequency as a sampling rate produces 858 samples in the line period of 525/59.94 and 864 samples in the line period of 625/50. For lower bandwidths, the rate can be divided by three-quarters, one-half or one-quarter to give sampling rates of 10.125, 6.75 and 3.375 MHz respectively. If the lowest frequency is considered to be 1, then the highest is 4. For maximum quality RGB working, three parallel, identical sample streams would then be required, which would be denoted by 4:4:4. Colour difference signals intended for post production, where a wider colour difference bandwidth is needed, require 4:2:2 sampling for luminance, $R-Y$ and $B-Y$ respectively; 4:2:2 has the advantage that an integer number of colour difference samples also exist in both line standards. Fig. 3.19 shows the spatial arrangement given by 4:2:2 sampling. Luminance samples appear at half the spacing of colour difference samples, and half of the luminance samples are in the same physical position as a pair of colour difference samples, these being called co-sited samples. The D-1, D-5 and Digital Betacam recording formats work with 4:2:2 sampling.

Where the signal is likely to be broadcast as PAL or NTSC, a standard of 4:1:1 is acceptable, since this still delivers a colour difference bandwidth in excess of 1 MHz. Where data rate is at a premium, 3:1:1 can be used, and can still offer just about enough bandwidth for 525 lines. This would not be enough for 625 line working, but would be acceptable for ENG applications. The problem with the factors of three and one is that they do not offer a columnar sampling structure, and so are not appropriate for processing systems.

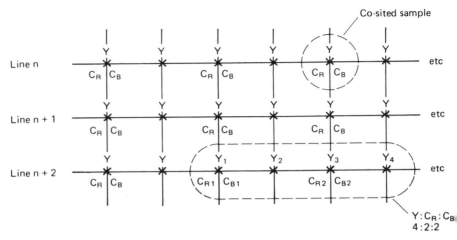

Figure 3.19 In CCIR-601 sampling mode 4:2:2, the line synchronous sampling rate of 13.5 MHz results in samples having the same position in successive lines, so that vertical columns are generated. The sampling rates of the colour difference signals C_R, C_B are one-half of that of luminance, i.e., 6.75 MHz, so that there are alternate Y only samples and co-sited samples which describe Y, C_R and C_B. In a run of four samples, there will be four Y samples, two C_R samples and two C_B samples, hence 4:2:2

Fig. 3.20(a) shows the one-dimensional spectrum which results from sampling 525/59.94 video at 13.5 MHz, and Fig. 3.20(b) shows the result for 625/50 video. Further details of CCIR-601 sampling can be found in Chapter 7.

The conventional TV screen has an aspect ratio of 4:3, whereas in the future an aspect ratio of 16:9 may be adopted. Expressing 4:3 as 12:9 makes it clear that the 16:9 picture is 16/12 or 4/3 times as wide. There are two ways of handling 16:9 pictures in the digital domain. One is to retain the standard sampling rate of 13.5 Mhz, which results in the horizontal resolution falling to three-quarters of its previous value; the other is to increase the sampling rate in proportion to the screen width. This results in a luminance sampling rate of 13.5 × 4/3 MHz or 18.0 MHz.

Figure 3.20 Spectra of video sampled at 13.5 MHz. At (a) the baseband 525/60 signal at left becomes the sidebands of the sampling rate and its harmonics. At (b) the same process for the 625/50 signal results in a smaller gap between baseband and sideband because of the wider bandwidth of the 625 system. The same sampling rate for both standards results in a great deal of commonality between 50 Hz and 60 Hz equipment

3.11 Choice of sampling rate – composite

When composite video is to be digitized, the input will be a single waveform having spectrally interleaved luminance and chroma. Any sampling rate which allows sufficient bandwidth would convey composite video from one point to another. Indeed, 13.5 MHz is successfully used to sample PAL and NTSC, as will be seen in Chapter 5. However, if processing in the digital domain is contemplated, there will be less choice.

In many cases it will be necessary to decode the composite signal which will require some kind of digital filter. Whilst it is possible to construct filters with any desired response, it is a fact that a digital filter whose response is simply related to the sampling rate will be much less complex to implement. This is the reasoning which has led to the near universal use of four times subcarrier sampling rate. Fig. 3.21 shows the spectra of PAL and NTSC sampled at $4 \times F_{sc}$.

Figure 3.21 The spectra of NTSC at (a) and of PAL at (b) where both are sampled at four times the frequency of their respective subcarriers. This high sampling rate is unnecessary to satisfy sampling theory, and so both are oversampled systems. The advantages are in the large spectral gap between baseband and sideband which allows a more gentle filter slope to be employed, and in the relative ease of colour processing at a sampling rate related to subcarrier

It will be evident that there is a considerable space between the edge of the baseband and the lower sideband. This allows the anti-aliasing and reconstruction filters to have a more gradual cut-off, so that ripple in the passband can be reduced. This is particularly important for C-format timebase correctors and for composite digital recorders, since both are digital devices in an analog environment, and signals may have been converted to and from the digital domain many times in the course of production.

3.12 Sampling-clock jitter

The instants at which samples are taken in an ADC and the instants at which DACs make conversions must be evenly spaced, otherwise unwanted signals can be added to the video. Fig. 3.22 shows the effect of sampling-clock jitter on a sloping waveform. Samples are taken at the wrong times. When these samples have passed through a system, the timebase-correction stage prior to the DAC

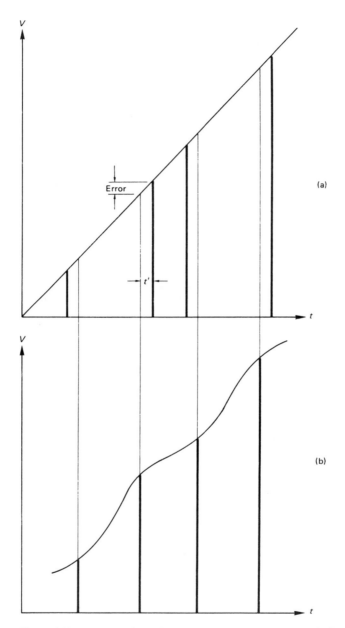

Figure 3.22 The effect of sampling timing jitter on noise. At (a) a sloping signal sampled with jitter has error proportional to the slope. When jitter is removed by reclocking, the result at (b) is noise

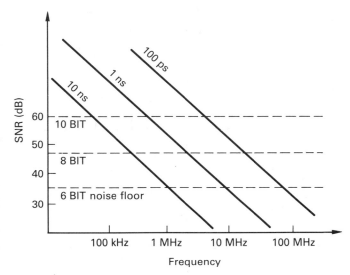

Figure 3.23 The effect of sampling clock jitter on signal-to-noise ratio at various frequencies, compared with the theoretical noise floors with different wordlengths

will remove the jitter, and the result is shown at (b). The magnitude of the unwanted signal is proportional to the slope of the audio waveform and so the amount of jitter which can be tolerated falls at 6 dB per octave. As the resolution of the system is increased by the use of longer sample wordlength, tolerance to jitter is further reduced. The nature of the unwanted signal depends on the spectrum of the jitter. If the jitter is random, the effect is noise-like and relatively benign unless the amplitude is excessive. Fig. 3.23 shows the effect of differing amounts of random jitter with respect to the noise floor of various wordlengths. Note that even small amounts of jitter can degrade a 10 bit converter to the performance of a good 8 bit unit. There is thus no point in upgrading to higher-resolution converters if the clock stability of the system is insufficient to allow their performance to be realized.

Clock jitter is not necessarily random. Fig. 3.24 shows that one source of clock jitter is crosstalk or interference on the clock signal, although a balanced clock line will be more immune to such crosstalk. The unwanted additional signal changes the time at which the sloping clock signal appears to cross the threshold voltage of the clock receiver. This is simply the same phenomenon as that of Fig. 3.22 but in reverse. The threshold itself may be changed by ripple on the clock receiver power supply. There is no reason why these effects should be random; they may be periodic and potentially visible.[8]

The allowable jitter is measured in picoseconds, as shown in Fig. 3.22, and clearly steps must be taken to eliminate it by design. Converter clocks must be generated from clean power supplies which are well decoupled from the power used by the logic because a converter clock must have a signal-to-noise ratio of the same order as that of the signal. Otherwise noise on the clock causes jitter

(a)

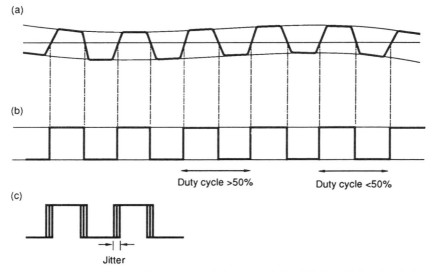

(b)

Duty cycle >50%   Duty cycle <50%

(c)

Jitter

Figure 3.24 Crosstalk in transmission can result in unwanted signals being added to the clock waveform. It can be seen here that a low-frequency interference signal affects the slicing of the clock and causes a periodic jitter

which in turn causes noise in the video. The same effect will be found in digital audio signals, which are perhaps more critical.

3.13 Quantizing

Quantizing is the process of expressing some infinitely variable quantity by discrete or stepped values. Quantizing turns up in a remarkable number of everyday guises. Fig. 3.25 shows that an inclined ramp enables infinitely variable height to be achieved, whereas a step-ladder allows only discrete heights to be had. A step-ladder quantizes height. When accountants round off sums of money to the nearest pound or dollar they are quantizing. Time passes continuously, but the display on a digital clock changes suddenly every minute because the clock is quantizing time.

In video and audio the values to be quantized are infinitely variable voltages from an analog source. Strict quantizing is a process which operates in the

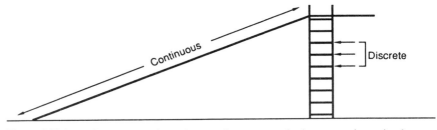

Figure 3.25 An analog parameter is continuous whereas a quantized parameter is restricted to certain values. Here the sloping side of a ramp can be used to obtain any height whereas a ladder only allows discrete heights

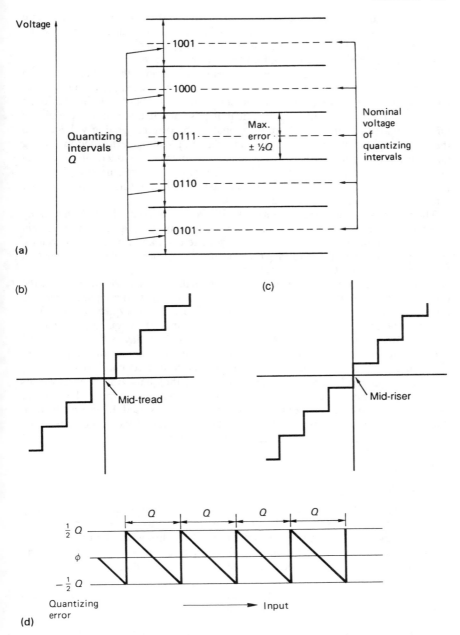

Figure 3.26 Quantizing assigns discrete numbers to variable voltages. All voltages within the same quantizing interval are assigned the same number which causes a DAC to produce the voltage at the centre of the intervals shown by the dashed lines in (a). This is the characteristic of the mid-tread quantizer shown in (b). An alternative system is the mid-riser system shown in (c). Here 0 volts analog falls between two codes and there is no code for zero. Such quantizing cannot be used prior to signal processing because the number is no longer proportional to the voltage. Quantizing error cannot exceed $\pm\frac{1}{2}Q$ as shown in (d)

voltage domain only. For the purpose of studying the quantizing of a single sample, time is assumed to stand still. This is achieved in practice either by the use of a track–hold circuit or the adoption of a quantizer technology such as a flash converter which operates before the sampling stage.

Fig. 3.26(a) shows that the process of quantizing divides the voltage range up into quantizing intervals Q, also referred to as steps S. In applications such as telephony these may advantageously be of differing size, but for digital audio the quantizing intervals are made as identical as possible. If this is done, the binary numbers which result are truly proportional to the original analog voltage, and the digital equivalents of mixing and gain changing can be performed by adding and multiplying sample values. If the quantizing intervals are unequal this cannot be done. When all quantizing intervals are the same, the term uniform quantizing is used. The term linear quantizing will be found, but this is, like military intelligence, a contradiction in terms.

The term LSB (Least Significant Bit) will also be found in place of quantizing interval in some treatments, but this is a poor term because quantizing works in the voltage domain. A bit is not a unit of voltage and can only have two values. In studying quantizing voltages within a quantizing interval will be discussed, but there is no such thing as a fraction of a bit.

Whatever the exact voltage of the input signal, the quantizer will locate the quantizing interval in which it lies. In what may be considered a separate step, the quantizing interval is then allocated a code value which is typically some form of binary number. The information sent is the number of the quantizing interval in which the input voltage lay. Whereabouts that voltage lay within the interval is not conveyed, and this mechanism puts a limit on the accuracy of the quantizer. When the number of the quantizing interval is converted back to the analog domain, it will result in a voltage at the centre of the quantizing interval as this minimizes the magnitude of the error between input and output. The number range is limited by the wordlength of the binary numbers used. In an 8 bit system, 256 different quantizing intervals exist, although in digital video the ones at the extreme ends of the range are reserved for synchronizing.

3.14 Quantizing error

It is possible to draw a transfer function for such an ideal quantizer followed by an ideal DAC, and this is also shown in Fig. 3.26. A transfer function is simply a graph of the output with respect to the input. In audio, when the term linearity is used, this generally means the overall straightness of the transfer function. Linearity is a goal in video and audio, yet it will be seen that an ideal quantizer is anything but linear.

Fig. 3.26(b) shows that the transfer function is somewhat like a staircase, and blanking level is half-way up a quantizing interval, or on the centre of a tread. This is the so-called mid-tread quantizer which is universally used in video and audio. Fig. 3.26(c) shows the alternative mid-riser transfer function which causes difficulty because it does not have a code value at blanking level and as a result the numerical code value is not proportional to the analog signal voltage.

Quantizing causes a voltage error in the audio sample which is given by the difference between the actual staircase transfer function and the ideal straight line. This is shown in Fig. 3.26(d) to be a saw-tooth like function which is periodic in Q. The amplitude cannot exceed $\pm\frac{1}{2}Q$ peak-to-peak unless the input is so large that clipping occurs.

Quantizing error can also be studied in the time domain where it is better to avoid complicating matters with the aperture effect of the DAC. For this reason it is assumed here that output samples are of negligible duration. Then impulses from the DAC can be compared with the original analog waveform and the

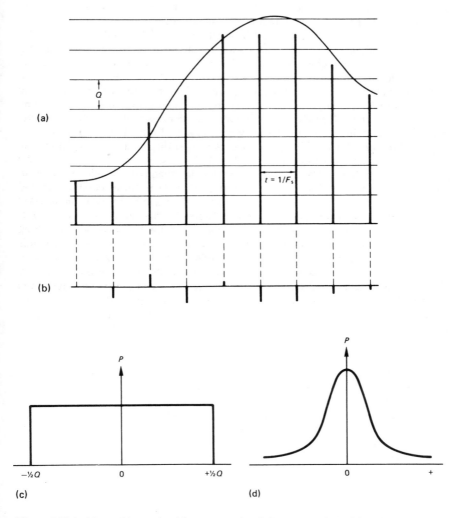

Figure 3.27 At (a) an arbitrary signal is represented to finite accuracy by PAM needles whose peaks are at the centre of the quantizing intervals. The errors caused can be thought of as an unwanted signal (b) added to the original. In (c) the amplitude of a quantizing error needle will be from $-\frac{1}{2}Q$ to $+\frac{1}{2}Q$ with equal probability. Note, however, that white noise in analog circuits generally has Gaussian amplitude distribution, shown in (d)

difference will be impulses representing the quantizing error waveform. This has been done in Fig. 3.27. The horizontal lines in the drawing are the boundaries between the quantizing intervals, and the curve is the input waveform. The vertical bars are the quantized samples which reach to the centre of the quantizing interval. The quantizing error waveform shown at (b) can be thought of as an unwanted signal which the quantizing process adds to the perfect original. If a very small input signal remains within one quantizing interval, the quantizing error *is* the signal.

As the transfer function is non-linear, ideal quantizing can cause distortion. As a result practical digital video equipment deliberately uses non-ideal quantizers to achieve linearity. The quantizing error of an ideal quantizer is a complex function, and it has been researched in great depth.[9-12] It is not intended to go into such depth here. The characteristics of an ideal quantizer will only be pursued far enough to convince the reader that such a device cannot be used in quality video or audio applications.

As the magnitude of the quantizing error is limited, its effect can be minimized by making the signal larger. This will require more quantizing intervals and more bits to express them. The number of quantizing intervals multiplied by their size gives the quantizing range of the converter. A signal outside the range will be clipped. Provided that clipping is avoided, the larger the signal the less will be the effect of the quantizing error.

Where the input signal exercises the whole quantizing range and has a complex waveform (such as from a contrasty, detailed scene), successive samples will have widely varying numerical values and the quantizing error on a given sample will be independent of that on others. In this case the size of the quantizing error will be distributed with equal probability between the limits. Fig. 3.27(c) shows the resultant uniform probability density. In this case the unwanted signal added by quantizing is an additive broadband noise uncorrelated with the signal, and it is appropriate in this case to call it quantizing noise. This is not quite the same as thermal noise which has a Gaussian probability shown in Fig. 3.27(d) (see Chapter 2 for a treatment of statistics). The difference is of no consequence as in the large-signal case the noise is masked by the signal. Under these conditions, a meaningful signal-to-noise ratio can be calculated as follows:

In a system using n bit words, there will be 2^n quantizing intervals. The largest sinusoid which can fit without clipping will have this peak-to-peak amplitude. The peak amplitude will be half as great, i.e. 2^n-1Q and the rms amplitude will be this value divided by $\sqrt{2}$.

The quantizing error has an amplitude of $\frac{1}{2}Q$ peak which is the equivalent of $Q/\sqrt{12}$ rms. The signal-to-noise ratio for the large-signal case is then given by:

$$20 \log_{10} \frac{\sqrt{12} \times 2^{n-1}}{\sqrt{2}} \text{ dB} = 20 \log_{10}(\sqrt{6} \times 2^{n-1}) \text{ dB}$$

$$= 20 \log\left(2^n \times \frac{\sqrt{6}}{2}\right) \text{ dB}$$

$$= 20n \log 2 + 20 \log\left(\frac{\sqrt{6}}{2}\right) \text{ dB}$$

$$= 6.02n + 1.76 \text{ dB} \tag{3.1}$$

By way of example, an 8 bit system will offer very nearly 50 dB SNR.

Whilst the above result is true for a large, complex input waveform, treatments which then assume that quantizing error is *always* noise give results which are at variance with reality. The expression above is only valid if the probability density of the quantizing error is uniform. Unfortunately at low depths of modulation, and particularly with flat fields or simple pictures, this is not the case.

At low modulation depth, quantizing error ceases to be random and becomes a function of the input waveform and the quantizing structure as Fig. 3.27 showed. Once an unwanted signal becomes a deterministic function of the wanted signal, it has to be classed as a distortion rather than a noise. Distortion can also be predicted from the non-linearity, or staircase nature, of the transfer function. With a large signal, there are so many steps involved that we must stand well back, and a staircase with 256 steps appears to be a slope. With a small signal there are few steps and they can no longer be ignored.

The effect can be visualized readily by considering a television camera viewing a uniformly painted wall. The geometry of the lighting and the coverage of the lens means that the brightness is not absolutely uniform, but falls slightly at the ends of the TV lines. After quantizing, the gently sloping waveform is replaced by one which stays at a constant quantizing level for many sampling periods and then suddenly jumps to the next quantizing level. The picture then consists of areas of constant brightness with steps between, resembling nothing more than a contour map; hence the use of the term *contouring* to describe the effect.

Needless to say the occurrence of contouring precludes the use of an ideal quantizer for high-quality work. There is little point in studying the adverse effects further as they should be and can be eliminated completely in practical equipment by the use of dither. The importance of correctly dithering a quantizer cannot be emphasized enough, since failure to dither irrevocably distorts the converted signal: there can be no process which will subsequently remove that distortion.

The signal-to-noise ratio derived above has no relevance to practical applications as it will be modified by the dither.

3.15 Introduction to dither

At high signal levels, quantizing error is effectively noise. As the depth of modulation falls, the quantizing error of an ideal quantizer becomes more strongly correlated with the signal and the result is distortion, visible as contouring. If the quantizing error can be decorrelated from the input in some way, the system can remain linear but noisy. Dither performs the job of decorrelation by making the action of the quantizer unpredictable and gives the system a noise floor like an analog system.[13,14]

In one approach, pseudo-random noise (see Chapter 2) with rectangular probability and a peak-to-peak amplitude of Q was added to the input signal prior to quantizing, but was subtracted after reconversion to analog. This is known as subtractive dither and was investigated by Schuchman[15] and much later by Sherwood.[16] Subtractive dither has the advantages that the dither amplitude is non-critical, the noise has full statistical independence from the signal[11] and has the same level as the quantizing error in the large signal undithered case.[17] Unfortunately, it suffers from practical drawbacks, since the original noise waveform must accompany the samples or must be synchronously recreated at the DAC. This is virtually impossible in a system where the signal may have been edited or where its level has been changed by processing, as the noise needs to remain synchronous and be processed in the same way. All practical digital video systems use non-subtractive dither where the dither signal is added prior to quantization and no attempt is made to remove it at the DAC.[18] The introduction of dither prior to a conventional quantizer inevitably causes a slight reduction in the signal-to-noise ratio attainable, but this reduction is a small price to pay for the elimination of non-linearities.

The ideal (noiseless) quantizer of Fig. 3.26 has fixed quantizing intervals and must always produce the same quantizing error from the same signal. In Fig. 3.28 it can be seen that an ideal quantizer can be dithered by linearly adding a controlled level of noise either to the input signal or to the reference voltage which is used to derive the quantizing intervals. There are several ways of considering how dither works, all of which are equally valid.

The addition of dither means that successive samples effectively find the quantizing intervals in different places on the voltage scale. The quantizing error becomes a function of the dither, rather than a predictable function of the input signal. The quantizing error is not eliminated, but the subjectively unacceptable

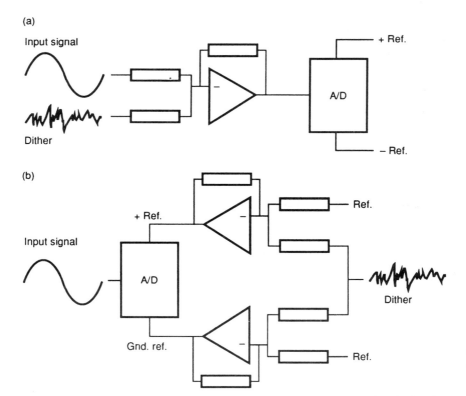

Figure 3.28 Dither can be applied to a quantizer in one of two ways. In (a) the dither is linearly added to the analog input signal, whereas in (b) it is added to the reference voltages of the quantizer

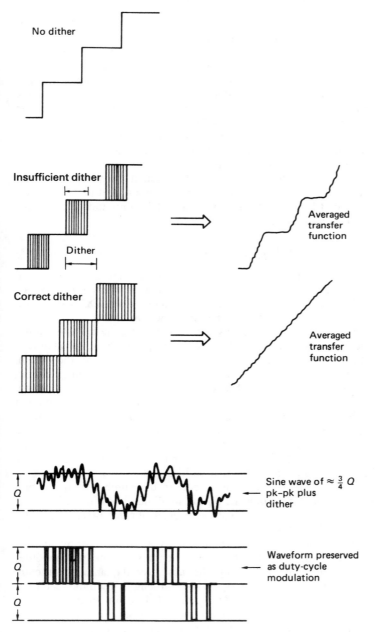

Figure 3.29 Wideband dither of the appropriate level linearizes the transfer function to produce noise instead of distortion. This can be confirmed by spectral analysis. In the voltage domain, dither causes frequent switching between codes and preserves resolution in the duty cycle of the switching

distortion is converted into a broadband noise which is more benign to the ear.

Some alternative ways of looking at dither are shown in Fig. 3.29. Consider the situation where a low-level input signal is changing slowly within a quantizing interval. Without dither, the same numerical code is output for a number of sample periods, and the variations within the interval are lost. Dither has the effect of forcing the quantizer to switch between two or more states. The higher the voltage of the input signal within a given interval, the more probable it becomes that the output code will take on the next higher value. The lower the input voltage within the interval, the more probable it is that the output code will take the next lower value. The dither has resulted in a form of duty cycle modulation, and the resolution of the system has been extended indefinitely instead of being limited by the size of the steps.

Dither can also be understood by considering what it does to the transfer function of the quantizer. This is normally a perfect staircase, but in the presence of dither it is smeared horizontally until with a certain amplitude the average transfer function becomes straight.

3.16 Requantizing and digital dither

Recent ADC technology allows the resolution of video samples to be raised from 8 bits to 10 or even 12 bits. The situation then arises that an existing 8 bit device such as a digital VTR needs to be connected to the output of an ADC with greater wordlength. The words need to be shortened in some way.

Chapter 2 showed that when a sample value is attenuated, the extra low-order bits which come into existence below the radix point preserve the resolution of the signal and the dither in the least significant bit(s) which linearizes the system. The same word extension will occur in any process involving multiplication, such as digital filtering. It will subsequently be necessary to shorten the wordlength. Low-order bits must be removed in order to reduce the resolution whilst keeping the signal magnitude the same. Even if the original conversion was correctly dithered, the random element in the low-order bits will now be some way below the end of the intended word. If the word is simply truncated by discarding the unwanted low-order bits or rounded to the nearest integer the linearizing effect of the original dither will be lost.

Shortening the wordlength of a sample reduces the number of quantizing intervals available without changing the signal amplitude. As Fig. 3.30 shows, the quantizing intervals become larger and the original signal is *requantized* with the new interval structure. This will introduce requantizing distortion having the same characteristics as quantizing distortion in an ADC. It then is obvious that when shortening the wordlength of a 10 bit converter to 8 bits, the two low-order bits must be removed in a way that displays the same overall quantizing structure as if the original converter had been only of 8 bit wordlength. It will be seen from Fig. 3.30 that truncation cannot be used because it does not meet the above requirement but results in signal-dependent offsets because it always rounds in the same direction. Proper numerical rounding is essential in video applications because it accurately simulates analog quantizing to the new interval size. Unfortunately the 10 bit converter will have a dither amplitude appropriate to quantizing intervals one-quarter the size of an 8 bit unit and the result will be highly non-linear.

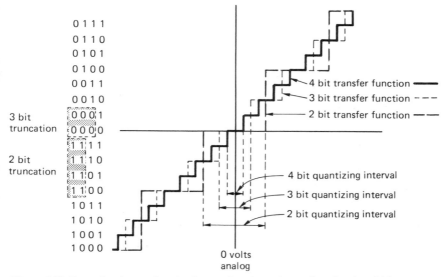

0 volts
analog

Figure 3.30 Shortening the wordlength of a sample reduces the number of codes which can describe the voltage of the waveform. This makes the quantizing steps bigger hence the term requantizing. It can be seen that simple truncation or omission of the bits does not give analogous behaviour. Rounding is necessary to give the same result as if the larger steps had been used in the original conversion

In practice, the wordlength of samples must be shortened in such a way that the requantizing error is converted to noise rather than distortion. One technique which meets this requirement is to use digital dithering[19] prior to rounding. This is directly equivalent to the analog dithering in an ADC.

Digital dither is a pseudo-random sequence of numbers. If it is required to simulate the analog dither signal of Figs. 3.28 and 29, then it is obvious that the noise must be bipolar so that it can have an average voltage of zero. Two's complement coding must be used for the dither values.

Fig. 3.31 shows a simple digital dithering system (i.e. one without noise shaping) for shortening sample wordlength. The output of a two's complement pseudo-random sequence generator (see Chapter 2) of appropriate wordlength is added to input samples prior to rounding. The most significant of the bits to be discarded is examined in order to determine whether the bits to be removed sum to more or less than half a quantizing interval. The dithered sample is either rounded down, i.e. the unwanted bits are simply discarded, or rounded up, i.e. the unwanted bits are discarded but one is added to the value of the new short word. The rounding process is no longer deterministic because of the added dither which provides a linearizing random component.

If this process is compared with that of Fig. 3.28 it will be seen that the principles of analog and digital dither are identical; the processes simply take place in different domains using two's complement numbers which are rounded or voltages which are quantized as appropriate. In fact quantization of an analog dithered waveform is identical to the hypothetical case of rounding after bipolar

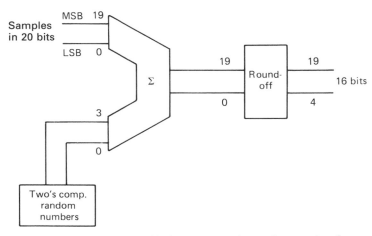

Figure 3.31 In a simple digital dithering system, two's complement values from a random number generator are added to low-order bits of the input. The dithered values are then rounded up or down according to the value of the bits to be removed. The dither linearizes the requantizing

digital dither where the number of bits to be removed is infinite, and remains identical for practical purposes when as few as 8 bits are to be removed. Analog dither may actually be generated from bipolar digital dither (which is no more than random numbers with certain properties) using a DAC.

3.17 Dither techniques

The intention here is to treat the processes of analog and digital dither as identical except where differences need to be noted. The characteristics of the noise used are rather important for optimal performance, although many suboptimal, but nevertheless effective, systems are in use. The main parameters of interest are the peak-to-peak amplitude, the amplitude probability distribution function (pdf) and the spectral content.

The most comprehensive ongoing study of non-subtractive dither has been that of Vanderkooy and Lipshitz[18-20] and the treatment here is based largely upon their work.

3.17.1 Rectangular pdf dither

Chapter 2 showed that the simplest form of dither (and therefore easiest to generate) is a single sequence of random numbers which have uniform or rectangular probability. The amplitude of the dither is critical. Fig. 3.32(a) shows the time-averaged transfer function of one quantizing interval in the presence of various amplitudes of rectangular dither. The linearity is perfect at an amplitude of $1Q$ peak-to-peak and then deteriorates for larger or smaller amplitudes. The same will be true of all levels which are an integer multiple of Q. Thus there is no freedom in the choice of amplitude.

With the use of such dither, the quantizing noise is not constant. Fig. 3.32(b) shows that when the analog input is exactly centred in a quantizing interval (such

Figure 3.32 (a) Use of rectangular probability dither can linearize, but noise modulation (b) results. Triangular p.d.f. dither (c) linearizes, and noise modulation is eliminated as at (d). Gaussian dither (e) can also be used, almost eliminating noise modulation at (f)

that there is no quantizing error), the dither has no effect and the output code is steady. There is no switching between codes and thus no noise. On the other hand when the analog input is exactly at a riser or boundary between intervals, there is the greatest switching between codes and the greatest noise is produced. Mathematically speaking, the first moment, or mean error, is zero but the second moment, which in this case is equal to the variance, is not constant. From an engineering standpoint, the system is linear but suffers noise modulation: the noise floor rises and falls with the signal content and this is audible in the presence of low-frequency signals.

The dither adds an average noise amplitude of $Q/\sqrt{12}$ rms to the quantizing noise of the same level. In order to find the resultant noise level it is necessary to add the powers as the signals are uncorrelated. The total power is given by:

$$2 \times \frac{Q^2}{12} = \frac{Q^2}{6} \tag{3.2}$$

and the rms voltage is $Q/\sqrt{6}$. Another way of looking at the situation is to consider that the noise power doubles and so the rms noise voltage has increased by 3 dB in comparison with the undithered case. Thus for an n bit wordlength, using the same derivation as expression (3.1) above, the signal-to-noise ratio for Q peak-to-peak rectangular dither will be given by:

$$6.02n - 1.24\,\text{dB} \tag{3.3}$$

Unlike the undithered case, this is a true signal-to-noise ratio and linearity is maintained at all signal levels. By way of example, for a 10 bit system nearly 59 dB SNR is achieved.

3.17.2 Triangular pdf dither

The noise modulation due to the use of rectangular probability dither is undesirable. It comes about because the process is too simple. The undithered quantizing error is signal dependent and the dither represents a single uniform probability random process. This is only capable of decorrelating the quantizing error to the extent that its mean value is zero, rendering the system linear. The signal dependence is not eliminated, but is displaced to the next statistical moment. This is the variance and the result is noise modulation. If a further uniform probability random process is introduced into the system, the signal dependence is displaced to the next moment and the second moment or variance becomes constant.

Adding together two statistically independent rectangular probability functions produces a triangular probability function. A signal having this characteristic can be used as the dither source.

Fig. 3.32(c) shows the averaged transfer function for a number of dither amplitudes. Linearity is reached with a peak-to-peak amplitude of $2Q$ and at this level there is no noise modulation. The lack of noise modulation is another way of stating that the noise is constant. The triangular pdf of the dither matches the triangular shape of the quantizing error function.

The dither adds two noise signals with an amplitude of $Q/\sqrt{12}$ rms to the quantizing noise of the same level. In order to find the resultant noise level it is necessary to add the powers as the signals are uncorrelated. The total power is given by:

$$3 \times \frac{Q^2}{12} = \frac{Q^2}{4} \tag{3.4}$$

and the rms voltage is $Q/\sqrt{4}$. Another way of looking at the situation is to consider that the noise power is increased by 50% in comparison to the rectangular dithered case and so the rms noise voltage has increased by 1.76 dB. Thus for an n bit wordlength, using the same derivation as expressions (3.1) and (3.2) above, the signal-to-noise ratio for Q peak-to-peak rectangular dither will be given by:

$$6.02n - 3\,\text{dB} \tag{3.5}$$

Continuing the use of a 10 bit example, an SNR of 57.2 dB is available which is 4.8 dB worse than the SNR of an undithered quantizer in the large-signal case. It is a small price to pay for perfect linearity and an unchanging noise floor.

3.17.3 Gaussian pdf dither

Adding more uniform probability sources to the dither makes the overall probability function progressively more like the Gaussian distribution of analog noise. Fig. 3.32(d) shows the averaged transfer function of a quantizer with various levels of Gaussian dither applied. Linearity is reached with $\frac{1}{2}Q$ rms and at this level noise modulation is negligible. The total noise power is given by:

$$\frac{Q^2}{4} + \frac{Q^2}{12} = \frac{3 \times Q^2}{12} + \frac{Q^2}{12}$$

$$= \frac{Q^2}{3} \tag{3.6}$$

and so the noise level will be $Q/\sqrt{3}$ rms. The noise level of an undithered quantizer in the large signal case is $Q/\sqrt{12}$ and so the noise is higher by a factor of:

$$\frac{Q}{\sqrt{3}} \times \frac{\sqrt{12}}{Q} = \frac{Q}{\sqrt{3}} \times \frac{2\sqrt{3}}{Q} = 2 = 6.02\,\text{dB}$$

Thus the SNR is given by:

$$6.02(n - 1) + 1.76\,\text{dB} \tag{3.7}$$

A 10 bit system with correct Gaussian dither has an SNR of 56 dB.

This is inferior to the figure in expression (3.3) by 1.2 dB. In digital dither applications, triangular probability dither of $2Q$ peak-to-peak is optimum because it gives the best possible combination of nil distortion, freedom from noise modulation and snr. Using dither with more than two rectangular processes added is detrimental. Whilst this result is also true for analog dither, it is not practicable to apply it to a real ADC as all real analog signals contain thermal noise which is Gaussian. If triangular dither is used on a signal containing Gaussian noise, the results derived above are not obtained. ADCs should therefore use Gaussian dither of $Q/2$ rms and performance will be given by expression (3.7).

3.18 Basic digital-to-analog conversion

This direction of conversion will be discussed first, since ADCs often use embedded DACs in feedback loops.

The purpose of a digital-to-analog converter is to take numerical values and reproduce the continuous waveform that they represent. Fig. 3.33 shows the major elements of a conventional conversion subsystem, i.e. one in which oversampling is not employed. The jitter in the clock needs to be removed with a VCO or VCXO. Sample values are buffered in a latch and fed to the converter element which operates on each cycle of the clean clock. The output is then a voltage proportional to the number for at least a part of the sample period. A resampling stage may be found next, in order to remove switching transients, reduce the aperture ratio or allow the use of a converter which takes a substantial part of the sample period to operate. The resampled waveform is then presented to a reconstruction filter which rejects frequencies above the audio band.

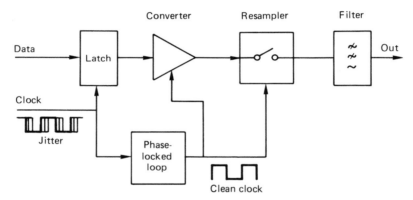

Figure 3.33 The components of a conventional converter. A jitter-free clock drives the voltage conversion, whose output may be resampled prior to reconstruction

This section is primarily concerned with the implementation of the converter element. The most common way of achieving this conversion is to control binary-weighted currents and sum them in a virtual earth. Fig. 3.34 shows the classical R-$2R$ DAC structure. This is relatively simple to construct, but the resistors have to be extremely accurate. To see why this is so, consider the example of Fig. 3.35. At (a) the binary code is about to have a major overflow, and all the low-order currents are flowing. At (b), the binary input has increased by one, and only the most significant current flows. This current must equal the sum of all the others plus one. The accuracy must be such that the step size is within the required limits. In this 8 bit example, if the step size needs to be a rather casual 10% accurate, the necessary accuracy is only one part in 2560, but for a 10 bit system it would become one part in 10 240. This degree of accuracy is difficult to achieve and maintain in the presence of ageing and temperature change.

Figure 3.34 The classical R–$2R$ DAC requires precise resistance values and 'perfect' switches

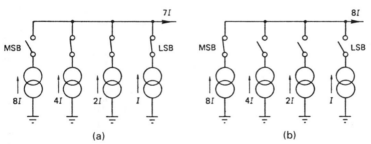

(a)   (b)

Figure 3.35 At (a) current flow with an input of 0111 is shown. At (b) current flow with input code one greater

3.19 Basic analog-to-digital conversion

The general principle of a quantizer is that different quantized voltages are compared with the unknown analog input until the closest quantized voltage is found. The code corresponding to this becomes the output. The comparisons can be made in turn with the minimal amount of hardware, or simultaneously with more hardware.

The flash converter is probably the simplest technique available for PCM video conversion. The principle is shown in Fig. 3.36. The threshold voltage of every quantizing interval is provided by a resistor chain which is fed by a reference voltage. This reference voltage can be varied to determine the sensitivity of the input. There is one voltage comparator connected to every reference voltage, and the other input of all of the comparators is connected to the analog input. A comparator can be considered to be a 1 bit ADC. The input voltage determines how many of the comparators will have a true output. As one

Figure 3.36 The flash converter. In (a) each quantizing interval has its own comparator, resulting in waveforms of (b). A priority encoder is necessary to convert the comparator outputs to a binary code. Shown in (c) is a typical 8 bit flash converter primarily intended for video applications. (Courtesy TRW)

comparator is necessary for each quantizing interval, then, for example, in an 8 bit system there will be 255 binary comparator outputs, and it is necessary to use a priority encoder to convert these to a binary code. Note that the quantizing stage is asynchronous; comparators change state as and when the variations in the input waveform result in a reference voltage being crossed. Sampling takes place when the comparator outputs are clocked into a subsequent latch. This is an example of quantizing before sampling as was illustrated in Fig. 3.1. Although the device is simple in principle, it contains a lot of circuitry and can only be practically implemented on a chip. The analog signal has to drive a lot of inputs, which results in a significant parallel capacitance, and a low-impedance driver is essential to avoid restricting the slewing rate of the input. The extreme speed of a flash converter is a distinct advantage in oversampling. Because computation of all bits is performed simultaneously, no track–hold circuit is required, and droop is eliminated. Fig. 3.36(c) shows a flash converter chip. Note the resistor ladder and the comparators followed by the priority encoder. The MSB can be selectively inverted so that the device can be used either in offset binary or two's complement mode.

The flash converter is ubiquitous in digital video because of the high speed necessary. For audio purposes, many more conversion techniques are available and these are considered in Chapter 12.

3.20 Oversampling

Oversampling means using a sampling rate which is greater (generally substantially greater) than the Nyquist rate. Neither sampling theory nor quantizing theory *requires* oversampling to be used to obtain a given signal quality, but Nyquist rate conversion places extremely high demands on component accuracy when a converter is implemented. Oversampling allows a given signal quality to be reached without requiring very close tolerance, and therefore expensive, components.

Fig. 3.37 shows the main advantages of oversampling. At (a) it will be seen that the use of a sampling rate considerably above the Nyquist rate allows the anti-aliasing and reconstruction filters to be realized with a much more gentle cut-off slope. There is then less likelihood of phase linearity and ripple problems in the passband.

Fig. 3.37(b) shows that information in an analog signal is two dimensional and can be depicted as an area which is the product of bandwidth and the linearly expressed signal-to-noise ratio. The figure also shows that the same amount of information can be conveyed down a channel with an SNR of half as much (6 dB less) if the bandwidth used is doubled, with 12 dB less SNR if the bandwidth is quadrupled, and so on, provided that the modulation scheme used is perfect.

The information in an analog signal can be conveyed using some analog modulation scheme in any combination of bandwidth and SNR which yields the appropriate channel capacity. If bandwidth is replaced by sampling rate and SNR is replaced by a function of wordlength, the same must be true for a digital signal as it is no more than a numerical analog. Thus raising the sampling rate potentially allows the wordlength of each sample to be reduced without information loss.

Information theory predicts that if a signal is spread over a much wider bandwidth by some modulation technique, the SNR of the demodulated signal

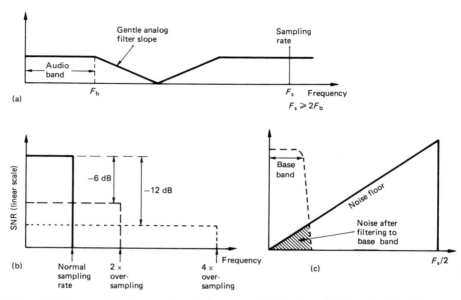

Figure 3.37 Oversampling has a number of advantages. In (a) it allows the slope of analog filters to be relaxed. In (b) it allows the resolution of converters to be extended. In (c) a *noise shaped* converter allows a disproportionate improvement in resolution

can be higher than that of the channel it passes through, and this is also the case in digital systems. The concept is illustrated in Fig. 3.38. At (a) 4 bit samples are delivered at sampling rate F. As 4 bits have 16 combinations, the information rate is $16F$. At (b) the same information rate is obtained with 3 bit samples by raising the sampling rate to $2F$ and at (c) 2 bit samples having four combinations require to be delivered at a rate of $4F$. Whilst the information rate has been maintained, it will be noticed that the bit rate of (c) is twice that of (a). The reason for this is shown in Fig. 3.39. A single binary digit can only have two states; thus it can only convey two pieces of information, perhaps 'yes' or 'no'. Two binary digits together can have four states, and can thus convey four pieces of information, perhaps 'spring summer autumn or winter', which is two pieces of information per bit. Three binary digits grouped together can have eight combinations, and convey eight pieces of information, perhaps 'doh re mi fah so lah te or doh', which is nearly three pieces of information per digit. Clearly the further this principle is taken, the greater the benefit. In a 16 bit system, each bit is worth 4K pieces of information. It is always more efficient, in information-capacity terms, to use the combinations of long binary words than to send single bits for every piece of information. The greatest efficiency is reached when the longest words are sent at the slowest rate which must be the Nyquist rate. This is one reason why PCM recording is more common than delta modulation, despite the simplicity of implementation of the latter type of converter. PCM simply makes more efficient use of the capacity of the binary channel.

As a result, oversampling is confined to converter technology where it gives specific advantages in implementation. The storage or transmission system will

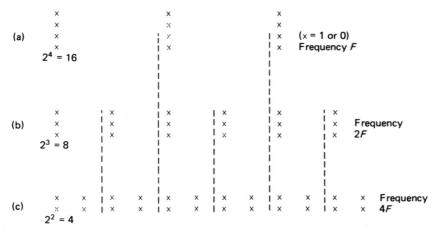

Figure 3.38 Information rate can be held constant when frequency doubles by removing 1 bit from each word. In all cases here it is 16F. Note bit rate of (c) is double that of (a). Data storage in oversampled form is inefficient

					Digital audio sample values
			0000 0	0000	
			0001 1		
			0010 2		
			0011 3		
			0100 4		
			0101 5		
			0110 6		
			0111 7		
		000 do	1000 8		
		001 re	1001 9		
		010 mi	1010 A		
		011 fa	1011 B		
	00 = Spring	100 so	1100 C		
	01 = Summer	101 la	1101 D		
0 = No	10 = Autumn	110 te	1110 E		
1 = Yes	11 = Winter	111 do	1111 F	FFFF	
No of bits 1	2	3	4	16	
Information per word 2	4	8	16	65536	
Information per bit 2	2	≈3	4	4096	

Figure 3.39 The amount of information per bit increases disproportionately as wordlength increases. It is always more efficient to use the longest words possible at the lowest word rate. It will be evident that 16 bit PCM is 2048 times as efficient as delta modulation. Oversampled data are also inefficient for storage

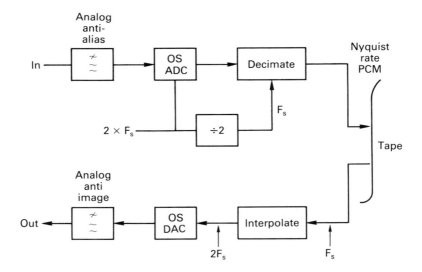

Figure 3.40 An oversampling DVTR. The converters run faster than sampling theory suggests to ease analog filter design. Sampling-rate reduction allows efficient PCM recording on tape

usually employ PCM, where the sampling rate is a little more than twice the input bandwidth. Fig. 3.40 shows a digital VTR using oversampling converters. The ADC runs at n times the Nyquist rate, but once in the digital domain the rate needs to be reduced in a type of digital filter called a *decimator*. The output of this is conventional Nyquist rate PCM, according to the tape format, which is then recorded. On replay the sampling rate is raised once more in a further type of digital filter called an *interpolator*. The system now has the best of both worlds: using oversampling in the converters overcomes the shortcomings of analog anti-aliasing and reconstruction filters and the wordlength of the converter elements is reduced making them easier to construct; the recording is made with Nyquist rate PCM which minimizes tape consumption.

Oversampling is a method of overcoming practical implementation problems by replacing a single critical element or bottleneck by a number of elements whose overall performance is what counts. As Hauser[21] properly observed, oversampling tends to overlap the operations which are quite distinct in a conventional converter. In earlier sections of this chapter, the vital subjects of filtering, sampling, quantizing and dither have been treated almost independently. Fig. 3.41(a) shows that it is possible to construct an ADC of predictable performance by taking a suitable anti-aliasing filter, a sampler, a dither source and a quantizer and assembling them like building bricks. The bricks are effectively in series and so the performance of each stage can only limit the overall performance. In contrast Fig. 3.41(b) shows that with oversampling the overlap of operations allows different processes to augment one another, allowing a synergy which is absent in the conventional approach.

(a)

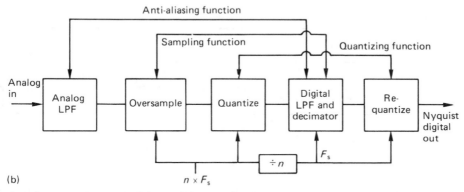

(b) $n \times F_s$

Figure 3.41 A conventional ADC performs each step in an identifiable location as in (a). With oversampling, many of the steps are distributed as shown in (b)

If the oversampling factor is n, the analog input must be bandwidth limited to $nF_s/2$ by the analog anti-aliasing filter. This unit need only have a flat frequency response and phase linearity within the base band. Analog dither of an amplitude compatible with the quantizing interval size is added prior to sampling at nF_s and quantizing.

Next, the anti-aliasing function is completed in the digital domain by a low-pass filter which cuts off at $F_s/2$. Using an appropriate architecture this filter can be absolutely phase linear and implemented to arbitrary accuracy. Such filters were discussed in Chapter 2. The filter can be considered to be the demodulator of Fig. 3.37 where the SNR improves as the bandwidth is reduced. The wordlength can be expected to increase. As Chapter 2 illustrated, the multiplications taking place within the filter extend the wordlength considerably more than the bandwidth reduction alone would indicate. The analog filter serves only to prevent aliasing into the baseband at the oversampling rate; the signal spectrum is determined with greater precision by the digital filter.

With the information spectrum now Nyquist limited, the sampling process is completed when the rate is reduced in the decimator. One sample in n is retained.

The excess wordlength extension due to the anti-aliasing filter arithmetic must then be removed. Digital dither is added, completing the dither process, and the quantizing process is completed by requantizing the dithered samples to the appropriate wordlength which will be greater than the wordlength of the first quantizer. Alternatively noise shaping may be employed.

Fig. 3.42(a) shows the building brick approach of a conventional DAC. The Nyquist rate samples are converted to analog voltages and then a steep-cut analog low-pass filter is needed to reject the sidebands of the sampled spectrum.

(a)

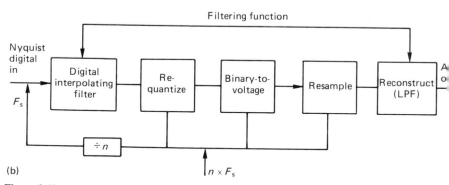

(b)

Figure 3.42 A conventional DAC in (a) is compared with the oversampling implementation in (b)

Fig. 3.42(b) shows the oversampling approach. The sampling rate is raised in an interpolator which contains a low-pass filter which restricts the baseband spectrum to the audio bandwidth shown. A large frequency gap now exists between the baseband and the lower sideband. The multiplications in the interpolator extend the wordlength considerably and this must be reduced within the capacity of the DAC element by the addition of digital dither prior to requantizing.

Oversampling may also be used to considerable benefit in other dimensions. Fig. 3.43 shows how vertical oversampling can be used to increase the resolution of a TV system. A 1250 line camera is used as the input device, but the 1250 line signal is fed to a standards converter which reduces the number of lines to 625. The standards converter must incorporate a vertical low-pass spatial filter to prevent aliasing when the vertical sampling rate is effectively halved. Such a filter was described in Chapter 2. As it is a digital filter, it can have arbitrarily accurate performance, including a flat passband and steep cut-off slope. The combination of the vertical aperture effect of the 1250 line camera and the vertical LPF in the standards converter gives a better spatial frequency response than could be achieved with a 625 line camera. The improvement in subjective quality is quite noticeable in practice.

In the case of display technology, oversampling can also be used, this time to render the raster invisible and to improve the vertical aperture of the display. Once more a standards converter is required, but this now doubles the number of input lines using interpolation. Again the filter can have arbitrary accuracy. The vertical aperture of the 1250 line display does not affect the passband of the input signal because of the use of oversampling.

Oversampling can also be used in the time domain in order to reduce or eliminate display flicker. A different type of standards converter is necessary which doubles the input field rate by interpolation. The standards converter must

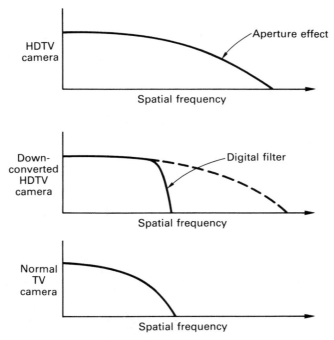

Figure 3.43 Using an HDTV camera with down conversion is a form of oversampling and gives better results than a normal camera because the aperture effect is overcome

use motion compensation, otherwise moving objects will not be correctly positioned in intermediate fields and will suffer from judder. Motion compensation is considered in Chapter 4.

3.21 Factors affecting converter quality

In theory the quality of a digital system comprising an ideal ADC followed by an ideal DAC is determined at the ADC. The ADC parameters such as the sampling rate, the wordlength and any noise shaping used put limits on the quality which can be achieved. Conversely the DAC itself may be transparent, because it only converts data whose quality are already determined back to the analog domain. In other words, the ADC determines the system quality and the DAC does not make things any worse.

In practice both ADCs and DACs can fall short of the ideal, but with modern converter components and attention to detail the theoretical limits can be approached very closely and at reasonable cost. Shortcomings may be the result of an inadequacy in an individual component such as a converter chip, or due to incorporating a high-quality component in a poorly thought out system. Poor system design can destroy the performance of a converter. Whilst oversampling is a powerful technique for realizing high-quality converters, its use depends on digital interpolators and decimators whose quality affects the overall conversion quality.

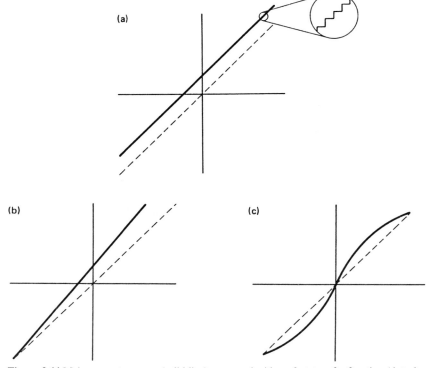

Figure 3.44 Main converter errors (solid line) compared with perfect transfer function (dotted line). These graphs hold for ADCs and DACs, and the axes are interchangeable; if one is chosen to be analog, the other will be digital

ADCs and DACs have the same transfer function, since they are only distinguished by the direction of operation, and therefore the same terminology can be used to classify the possible shortcomings of both.

Fig. 3.44 shows the transfer functions resulting from the main types of converter error:

(1) *Offset error*. A constant appears to have been added to the digital signal. This has a serious effect in video systems because it alters the black level. Offset error is sometimes cancelled by digitally sampling the converter output during blanking and feeding it back to the analog input as a small control voltage.

(2) *Gain error*. The slope of the transfer function is incorrect. Since converters are often referred to one end of the range, gain error causes an offset error. Severe gain error causes clipping.

(3) *Integral linearity*. This is the deviation of the dithered transfer function from a straight line. It has exactly the same significance and consequences as linearity in analog circuits, since if it is inadequate, harmonic distortion will be caused.

(4) *Differential non-linearity* is the amount by which adjacent quantizing intervals differ in size. This is usually expressed as a fraction of a quantizing interval.

(5) *Monotonicity* is a special case of differential non-linearity. Non-monotonicity means that the output does not increase for an increase in input. Fig. 3.35 showed how this can happen in a DAC. With a converter input code of 01111111 (127 decimal), the seven low-order current sources of the converter will be on. The next code is 10000000 (128 decimal), where only the eighth current source is operating. If the current it supplies is in error on the low side, the analog output for 128 may be less than that for 127. In an ADC non-monotonicity can result in missing codes. This means that certain binary combinations within the range cannot be generated by any analog voltage. If a device has better than $\frac{1}{2}Q$ linearity it must be monotonic. It is not possible for a 1 bit converter to be non-monotonic.

(6) *Absolute accuracy.* This is the difference between actual and ideal output for a given input. For video and audio it is rather less important than linearity. For example, if all the current sources in a converter have good thermal tracking, linearity will be maintained, even though the absolute accuracy drifts.

References

1. Shannon, C.E., A mathematical theory of communication. *Bell Syst. Tech. J.*, **27**, 379 (1948)
2. Jerri, A.J., The Shannon sampling theorem – its various extensions and applications: a tutorial review. *Proc. IEEE*, **65**, 1565–1596 (1977)
3. Betts, J.A., *Signal Processing Modulation and Noise*, Ch.6. Sevenoaks: Hodder and Stoughton (1970)
4. Gurley, T. and Haslett, C., Resolution considerations in using CCD imagers in broadcast quality cameras, *SMPTE J.*, **94**, 882–895 (1985)
5. Kell, R., Bedford, A. and Trainer, M.A. An experimental television system, Part 2. *Proc. IRE*, **22**, 1246–1265 (1934)
6. Hsu, S., The Kell factor: past and present. *SMPTE J.*, **95**, 206–214 (1986)
7. Fukinuki, T. and Hirano, Y., The to-and-fro zone plate method for observing frequency characteristics in three dimensions. *SMPTE J.*, **95**, 899–902 (1986)
8. Harris, S., The effects of sampling clock jitter on Nyquist sampling analog to digital converters and on oversampling delta-sigma ADCs. *J. Audio Eng. Soc.*, **38**, 537–542 (1990)
9. Bennett, W.R., Spectra of quantized signals. *Bell Syst. Tech. J.*, **27**, 446–472 (1948)
10. Widrow, B., Statistical analysis of amplitude quantized sampled-data systems. *Trans. AIEE*, Part II, **79**, 555–568 (1961)
11. Lipshitz, S.P., Wannamaker, R.A. and Vanderkooy, J., Quantization and dither: a theoretical survey. *J. Audio Eng. Soc.*, **40**, 355–375 (1992)
12. Maher, R.C., On the nature of granulation noise in uniform quantization systems. *J. Audio Eng. Soc.*, **40**, 12–20 (1992)
13. Goodall, W.M., Television by pulse code modulation. *Bell Syst. Tech. J.*, **30**, 33–49 (1951)
14. Roberts, L.G., Picture coding using pseudo-random noise. *IRE Trans. Inf. Theory*, **IT-8**, 145–154 (1962)
15. Schuchman, L., Dither signals and their effect on quantizing noise. *IEEE Trans. Commun. Technol.*, **COM-12**, 162–165 (1964)
16. Sherwood, D.T., Some theorems on quantization and an example using dither. In *Conf. Rec., 19th Asilomar Conf. on Circuits, Systems and Computers*, (Pacific Grove, CA, 1985)
17. Gerzon, M. and Craven, P.G., Optimal noise shaping and dither of digital signals. Presented at 87th Audio Engineering Society Convention (New York, 1989), preprint 2822 (J-1)
18. Vanderkooy, J. and Lipshitz, S.P., Resolution below the least significant bit in digital systems with dither. *J. Audio Eng. Soc.*, **32**, 106–113 (1984)
19. Vanderkooy, J. and Lipshitz, S.P., Digital dither. Presented at 81st Audio Engineering Society Convention (Los Angeles, 1986), preprint 2412 (C-8)
20. Vanderkooy, J. and Lipshitz, S.P., Digital dither. In *Audio in Digital Times*. New York: Audio Engineering Society (1989)
21. Hauser, M.W., Principles of oversampling A/D conversion. *J. Audio Eng. Soc.*, **39**, 3–26 (1991)

Chapter 4

Advanced digital processing

Chapter 2 showed that the important basics of multiplication, addition and delay form the foundation of all digital filtering. In this chapter, the use of digital filters in a wide range of video applications will be explained. These include composite decoding, standards conversion and special effects. The discrete Fourier transform and the discrete cosine transform are special applications of digital filtering which are normally considered to be quite complex. As the cost of digital processing continues to fall, new applications for these transforms such as motion compensation and data reduction become cost effective and these will also be covered here.

4.1 Luminance/chrominance separation

The ubiquity of composite video results in a frequent need for decoders to return to baseband luminance and colour difference signals. An important part of this process is luminance chrominance separation.

Composite video interleaves the basically similar spectra of chroma and luminance by shifting the chroma spectrum by half a line with respect to luminance as was seen in Chapter 3. They can only be fully separated by using a comb filter or a spatio-temporal filter. There are various requirements for luminance/chrominance separation at different levels of cost and complexity, each appropriate to a given application.

4.2 Simple bandpass filters

This type of filter will be used for minimum cost and complexity, and can be readily described because operation is directly parallel to that of an analog filter.

Fig. 4.1(a) shows that an input signal enters an operational amplifier both directly and through a delay. The phase difference between the ends of the delay is a function of the input frequency, and will be given by:

$$\frac{\text{delay period}}{\text{signal period}} \times 360°$$

The op-amp output is the vector sum of the two inputs:

$$\frac{1}{2}V_{in} + \frac{1}{2}V_{in} \sin T$$

where T is the phase angle between the inputs. When the delay period exceeds the signal period, the phase shift exceeds 360°, and clearly subtracting 360° or

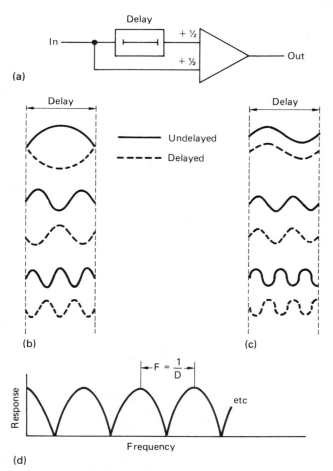

(a)

Delay

(b)

(c)

(d)

Figure 4.1 Simple comb filter at (a) has delay in one input of adder. At some frequencies (b), delay causes cancellation, whereas at others (c) delayed and undelayed signals are in phase. Frequency response shown at (d)

multiples thereof does not change the vector sum. There will thus be a series of signal periods all of which will have the same gain. The frequency response becomes repetitive, hence the term comb filter.

Fig. 4.1(b) shows several frequencies, all of which suffer complete cancellation due to effective inversion by the delay, and Fig. 4.1(c) shows frequencies which give unity gain because the delay is an integer multiple of the signal period. Fig. 4.1(d) shows the overall frequency response, which has a rectified cosine shape. Note that the peak spacing is at the reciprocal of the delay period.

A sharper response peak can be obtained by using two delays, as in Fig. 4.2(a). The op-amp now has three inputs. Fig. 4.2(b) shows the situation where a frequency which suffers a 180° shift in each delay is applied. Since the twice-delayed signal and the input signal will add, they must be given half as much gain

Figure 4.2 Two-delay comb filter at (a). In (b) certain frequencies suffer 360° shift in one delay, but since once-delayed signal has twice the weighting there is cancellation. At (c) is 180° resultant phase shift in one delay, removed by inverting input, permitting unity gain. Response at (d) is cosinusoid

as the signal from the centre tap. The op-amp thus has weighted gains of $+\frac{1}{4}$, $-\frac{1}{2}$ and $+\frac{1}{4}$. The frequency response shown in Fig. 4.2(d) is a cosinusoid, again with the peaks spaced at the reciprocal of the delay.

Fig. 4.3 shows a relative of the two-delay filter of Fig. 4.2. The difference is that the weights and phases of all the inputs are the same at $\frac{1}{3}$. When the input frequency suffers a phase shift of 120°, there will be complete cancellation. Again the system acts as a comb filter with a response shown in Fig. 4.3(b) where the first null is at the reciprocal of the delay.

Transferring to the digital domain, signal voltage is represented by a binary number, delay is achieved using latches or RAM. and the operational amplifier is replaced by an adder. Fig. 4.4 shows the digital equivalent of Fig. 4.2. The constraint in this kind of filter is that the delay periods can only be integer multiples of the sampling period. As the delay period is intimately related to the frequency response, the desired response and the sampling rate largely determine the filter configuration. It is important to remember that there is also an upper limit to the frequency response due to the fact that it is a sampled system.

Figs. 4.2 and 4.4 show filters where a phase shift of 180° is necessary at the null frequency. This phase shift is readily achieved in a $4 \times F_{sc}$ system by using

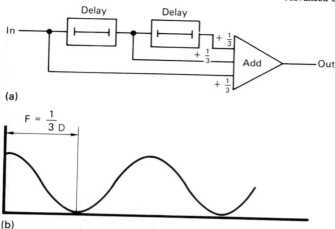

Figure 4.3 Comb filter working on 120° delays to give cancellation. Response at (b). Nulls are 1/3D, 1D, etc

two sample periods of delay. Fig. 4.3 showed a filter which needed 120° of phase shift, and this is readily obtained by a one-sample delay in a $3 \times F_{sc}$ system. Fig. 4.5 shows a digital filter based on this principle. Since division by three is difficult in binary, a close approximation is obtained by multiplying by 85 (64 + 16 + 4 + 1) and dividing by 256, since all of these factors can be obtained by shifting.

The $4 \times F_{sc}$ filter of Fig. 4.4 has a gain peak at subcarrier frequency, and the output will be chroma. To obtain luminance, output values are subtracted from input values, with a compensating delay.

4.3 Line combing composite decoders

The above filters do not offer very good performance and their use is restricted to economy applications. In many broadcast and facility operations, the highest quality is required. In effects units, any change in picture size changes the spectrum of the signal. Where the input is composite, it is paramount that residual chroma in the luminance is minimal before manipulation, so that it does not result in moiré fringes. In component still stores which have composite inputs and outputs, the quality of the decoder is critical. If the decoder is imperfect, it will leave residual subcarrier in the luminance as a *footprint* which is frozen in the stored frame. When the frame is used to drive a composite encoder, the frozen footprint in the frame store will beat with the moving subcarrier of the encoder producing low-frequency flickering of coloured areas.

Section 3.7 evolved the spectra of NTSC and PAL in some detail, and the spectra are repeated in Fig. 4.6(a) and (b). Since the spectral interleave of a composite signal is primarily on multiples of line rate, it follows that delays of one line can be used in a comb filter, so that the frequency response peaks will be at multiples of F_h.

Figure 4.4 Digital *Y/C* separation at $4 \times F_{sc}$ uses pairs of latches to give 180° phase shift at subcarrier frequency. Binary adders and dividers give weighting of $+\frac{1}{4}$, $-\frac{1}{2}$, $+\frac{1}{4}$ to three samples. Chroma output is subtracted from the input to give luminance. There is only one response peak at F_{sc} since Nyquist limit for $4 \times F_{sc}$

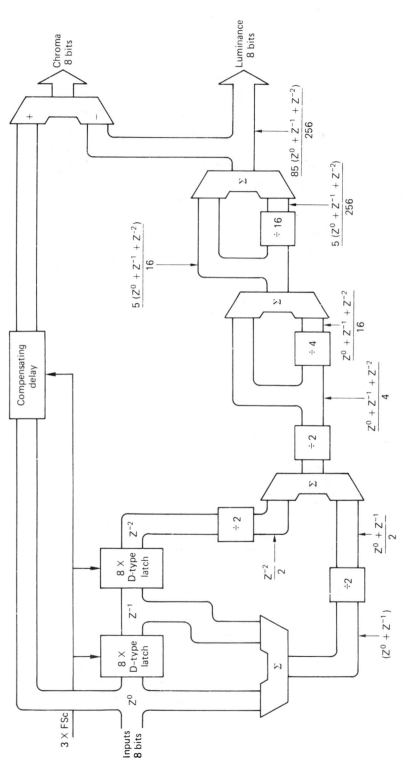

Figure 4.5 $3 \times F_{sc}$ Y/C separation approximates closely to divide by three of Fig. 4.3

(a)

(b)

Figure 4.6 (a) The vertical/temporal spectrum of NTSC. (b) The spectrum of PAL

Fig. 4.7 shows a simple line comb filter. The vertical/horizontal frequency response is shown in Fig. 4.6(c). Although the horizontal spectral response appears ideal for NTSC applications, in fact there are some snags. Firstly the summing junction which is designed to reject chroma is adding together adjacent

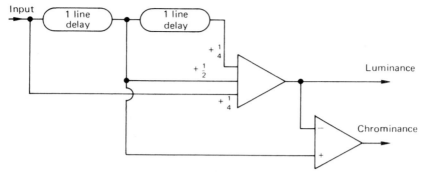

Figure 4.7 Simple line comb filter. Frequency response is ideal, but there are practical shortcomings explained in the text

points on different lines, and is actually reducing the vertical resolution of the picture. Secondly, the filter is working with real chroma, whose phase can change according to picture content, whereas perfect comb response is only achieved when the chroma phase remains consistent over the three points feeding the summing junction. Vertical changes in chroma phase will cause the comb to fail to cancel or *mesh*, and residual chroma will appear in the luminance as a series of white dots at horizontal boundaries between colours.

Some of the vertical resolution can be restored by using a bandpass filter in conjunction with the line comb. Fig. 4.8 shows that incoming video passes through two filters in parallel. One is a low-pass filter which cuts just below chroma frequencies, the other is a band limiting filter. The outputs of the two filters are subtracted to give a bandpass response which contains chroma and high-frequency luminance. This signal is applied to the line comb, which rejects chroma without impairing vertical resolution at frequencies below the bandpass. The high-frequency luminance can then be added back to the low-pass filtered signal to give full bandwidth luminance. Fig. 4.6(d) shows that the vertical/horizontal frequency response is curtailed in the horizontal direction so that only the horizontal frequencies where subcarrier is found are affected. Comb mesh failure can be detected by analysing the chroma signals at the ends of the comb, and if chroma will not be cancelled, the high-frequency luminance is not added back to the main channel, and a low pass-response results.

The line comb gives quite good results in NTSC, as horizontal and vertical resolution are good, but the loss of vertical resolution at high frequency means that diagonal resolution is poor.

Fig. 4.6(e) shows that a line comb filter is at a disadvantage in PAL because of the spreading between U and V components. What is needed is a comb filter having delays of two lines, but this will have an even more severe effect on diagonal frequencies, so PAL comb filters are often found with only single-line delays, a choice influenced by commonality with an NTSC product.

In the special case of still store filtering, where a composite input signal is received from a rostrum camera where no motion takes place, it is possible to use a comb filter with a delay of four fields (PAL) or two fields (NTSC), which takes advantage of the subcarrier inversion which occurs over those periods. Fig. 4.6(f) shows the vertical/temporal frequency response obtained. The time delays are

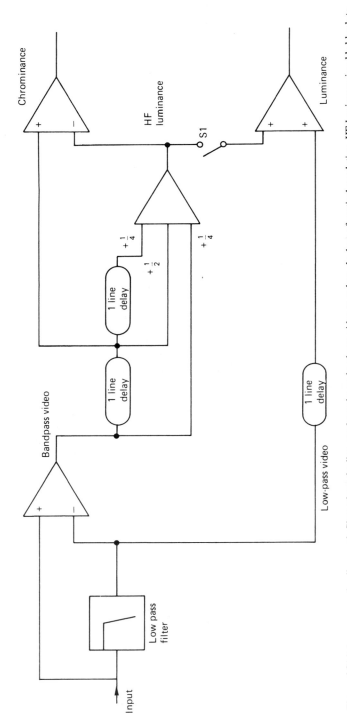

Figure 4.8(a) A more complex line comb filter where the line comb works on bandpass video to reduce the loss of vertical resolution. HF luminance is added back to low-pass signal to restore luminance bandwidth. If comb fails to mesh due to vertical chroma phase change, switch S1 opens to prevent chroma breaking through. Luminance bandwidth is reduced

Figure 4.8(b) Rearranging the filter of Fig. 4.8(a) in this way eliminates a delay line by restoring vertical resolution a different way. Vertical resolution compensation is achieved by taking signals from the top and bottom of the delays and adding them back to luminance via a low-pass filter shown bottom right. In the digital domain, replace operational amplifiers with adders, delays with RAM. Low-pass filters will be FIR types as described

quite long and the slightest motion in the input will cause mesh failure and the system breaks down.

Neither line combing nor field combing alone is really satisfactory, especially for PAL signals, because the diagonal distribution of chroma energy in PAL does not match the horizontal and vertical filtering responses. Equipment has been made which uses both techniques and switches or crossfades between modes as a function of the input motion. The adaptation decision is not easy because reliable motion sensing requires clean luminance which is not yet available. The changeover itself may result in artefacts.

4.4 Spatio-temporal composite decoders

Although the three-dimensional spectrum of PAL is complicated, it is possible to combine elements of both vertical and temporal types of filter to obtain a spatio-temporal response which is closely matched to the characteristics of PAL. Fig. 4.9 shows the vertical/temporal response of such a filter. By following the diagonal structure of the PAL spectrum, the passbands of the signal components are much wider.[1] Comparison with Fig. 4.6(e) shows that the vertical frequency response is around three times better than that of a two-line delay vertical comb

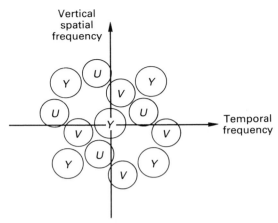

Figure 4.9 Optimum vertical/temporal response for PAL *Y/C* separation

and comparison with Fig. 4.6(f) shows that the temporal frequency response exceeds that of the field-delay-based temporal comb by the same factor. Whilst complex, this approach has the advantage that a fixed response can be used and adaptive circuitry is dispensed with. The absence of adaptation results in the better handling of difficult material.

4.5 Line synchronous digital chroma decoding

Where the goal of a subsystem is to produce 4:2:2 digital component video from a composite NTSC or PAL input, it will be advantageous to sample the composite input at 13.5 MHz,[2] since this will be the sampling rate of the output luminance signal, and the colour difference signals will ultimately be sampled at one half of this rate. The use of 13.5 MHz means that a comb filter using one-line delays will be very easy to implement, and this gives a digital luminance signal at the correct sampling frequency. However, this filter will also produce composite chroma which is also sampled at 13.5 MHz. This can only be decoded to baseband luminance by synchronous demodulation with the original subcarrier. Although the operation of such a system at $4 \times F_{sc}$ is straightforward, it is not easy to visualize how this can be done at 13.5 MHz.

To follow the action of a line synchronous demodulator it is necessary to return to the fundamental way in which the analog equivalent would work, and then to duplicate this action in the digital domain. The operation of a synchronous rectifier in the analog domain is to regenerate a sinusoidal subcarrier signal from burst, and then to multiply the chroma by this signal, which will, after low-pass filtering, produce the $B-Y$ signal. Performing a similar process with a quadrature reference will produce the $R-Y$ signal. In the analog domain all of these signals are continuous, but the same process can be carried out in the sampled domain, whether or not the sampling rate is subcarrier synchronous.

If a subcarrier synchronous system is used, then the samples of the subcarrier will fall at regular positions on the sinusoid, and the coefficients by which the chroma needs to be multiplied become unity and zero, which tremendously

Figure 4.10 A subcarrier of 4.43 MHz sampled at 13.5 MHz. It will be seen that the sample values are variable, and need to be expressed by a multibit sample. Such a sample stream can be used to demodulate composite video which has been sampled at 13.5 MHz

simplifies circuitry. However, if the sampling is asynchronous, it is necessary to create digital values which truly represent a subcarrier sampled in the same instantaneous phase as the input chroma. As Fig. 4.10 shows, this results in values which need to represented by a multibit parameter to give the necessary accuracy. These parameters must then be digitally multiplied by the chroma samples to obtain one of the colour difference signals, which will be rich in subcarrier frequency harmonics. A straightforward low-pass FIR filter can be given a response tailored to the appropriate bandwidth, and can double as the decimator which reduces the sampling rate to 6.75 MHz. A second system which generates samples corresponding to a quadrature subcarrier will yield the other colour difference signal.

The system results in 27 million multiplications per second being necessary, which is rather less than the number which would be necessary to convert the sample rate from $4 \times F_{sc}$ to 13.5 MHz. An application of such a system may be in a DVE which has 4:2:2 internal processing, but which requires to have an analog component input, one example of this being the Ampex ADO 100.

4.6 Converting 625/50 4:2:2 to PAL composite digital

This conversion can be performed in the digital domain quite readily, and since the chroma bandwidth of the component input is greater than that of the composite output, there need be no loss of quality.

The main issues to be addressed are:

(1) Reducing the chroma bandwidth to the 1.3 MHz allowed for composite and handling colours which are legal in component form but not in composite.
(2) Converting the sampling rate of the colour difference signals to $4 \times F_{sc}$ and creating a digital representation of quadrature-modulated subcarrier with V-switch. Steps may also be taken to suppress spectral overlap in the composite signal by prefiltering.
(3) Converting the sampling rate of luminance from 13.5 MHz to $4 \times F_{sc}$ and adding the subcarrier.
(4) Scaling the numerical sample values since quantizing intervals of luminance, colour difference and composite signals are all of different sizes (see Chapter 8).
(5) Generating sync and burst.

The most complex issue in this conversion is clock generation and timing, since the sampling rate of composite digital reflects the 25 Hz offset of PAL subcarrier. One line contains slightly more than 1135 cycles of $4{\times}F_{sc}$ clock, and the clock phase will change from line to line so that an additional four sample periods (one cycle of subcarrier) can be accommodated in one frame. The phase of the interpolations needed will vary not just as a function of the position in the line, as in NTSC, but also as a function of the position in the frame.

The timing system of the converter will need to recreate video timing, and it can do this by regenerating the H-synchronous 27 MHz clock from the parallel or serial digital input, and using the synchronizing patterns to determine the position in the line and frame. Fig. 4.11 shows how the output sampling rate is generated.

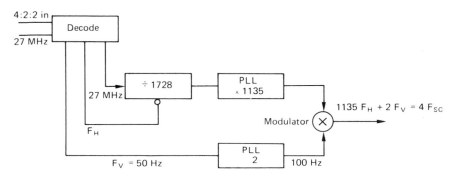

Figure 4.11 Since PAL subcarrier is given by $283\frac{3}{4}F_H + F_{v/2}$, then multiplying this expression by four gives $4F_{sc} = 1135F_H + 2F_v$. Both frequencies are produced from the 4:2:2 decoder and phase-locked loops. Adding in a modular results in $4F_{sc}$

Input 27 MHz is divided down by 1728 to produce line rate, which is synchronized by the SAV signal (see Chapter 7), and this is then used as the input to a phase-locked loop which multiplies by 1135. The resultant frequency is exactly 100 Hz too low, and input field rate will be multiplied by two to obtain 100 Hz. This can conveniently be done by addressing a PROM with a line count in the frame, and storing four cycles of a waveform in the PROM over a range of 625 locations. A modulator can then be used to mix the frequencies and generate $4{\times}F_{sc}$. The ScH phase of the clock is determined by the phase of the 100 Hz component. Alternatively a direct synthesis approach may be used, where a phase accumulator adds the equivalent of the number of degrees of subcarrier in a CCIR-601 sample period at each input clock, and so produces a representation of subcarrier. The $4{\times}F_{sc}$ clock is then divided by four in two different dividers. Combining the output of these dividers in various ways allows the generation of a subcarrier frequency square wave for generation of the U component, and a quadrature square wave for generation of the V component. These waveforms will be phased by presetting the dividers once every eight fields.

There is only one signal in composite digital, which is at a sampling rate of $4{\times}F_{sc}$. Accordingly the sampling rates of the luminance and colour difference signals of the 4:2:2 input must all be raised to this sampling rate by interpolation, before it is possible to create a composite signal.

Reduction of the chroma bandwidth and sampling-rate conversion from 6.75 MHz to $4{\times}F_{sc}$ can be achieved in the same process. Since the new sampling rate is higher than the luminance sampling rate of 13.5 MHz, no bandwidth reduction of luminance is needed.

Three parallel sampling-rate converters will be needed, and these must have a considerable amount of coefficient storage, because the phase of PAL-subcarrier-derived samples constantly slips with respect to the phase of the H-derived 4:2:2 sampling clock. As the colour difference signals have yet to suffer the V-switch inversion, it is only necessary at this stage to consider the relative phases of $4 \times F_{sc}$ and $864 \times F_h$. There will be an integer number of cycles N_{4sc} of $4 \times F_{sc}$ in one frame, given by:

$$N_{4sc} = (625 \times 283.75 \times 4) + 4 = 709\,379$$

In the same period there will also be an integer number of cycles of 13.5 MHz, N_y, given by:

$$N_y = 625 \times 864 = 540\,000$$

It will be possible to determine the relative phase of any cycle of $4 \times F_{sc}$ and any cycle of 13.5 MHz from the position in the frame. A PROM addressed by line count will be able to provide the starting phase for each line, and then a sample count along the line can modify the phase by a constant amount for each interpolation. Fortunately the phase has only to be calculated once, since it can be used by the luminance and both the colour difference interpolators. As the colour difference signals are at half the luminance sampling rate, one interpolator could be multiplexed to process both colour difference signals alternately.

The luminance interpolator will use coefficients which produce a frequency response of 5.75 MHz. There will then be no loss of luminance resolution. The frequency responses of the colour difference interpolators will be much lower, in order to tailor the U and V spectra to that permitted in PAL.

There are now three sample streams, Y, U and V, all running at $4 \times F_{sc}$, and all using offset binary code. Multiplexers are used to insert blanking values outside the active line.

The colour difference signals are next converted to two's complement, and a normal and inverted version of both is made available to a pair of multiplexers. The U and $-U$ multiplexer is switched by the subcarrier rate square wave, and the V and $-V$ multiplexer is switched by a quadrature square wave which is inverted from one line to the next to obtain the characteristic V-switch of PAL. The outputs of the two multiplexers are next added together, and Fig. 4.12 shows that this results in the digital sampled equivalent of chroma, with samples taken at burst phase as the composite digital standard specifies. The slanting vertical lines in the figure show the quarter cycle offset from one line to the next, with U and $\pm V$ superimposed. For each sample period, the relative polarities of U and V are shown. The effect of V-switch can be seen, because although the U signal advances one sample (90°) per line, the inversion of V causes the V signal to lag one sample per line.

The result of this process is not quite digital chroma, because the gain is incorrect. The digital modulation process simply added and subtracted U and V at the sample points, whereas a conventional analog modulator would have produced the sum of Ucos 45 plus Vcos 45 at these points. A further point is that the quantizing intervals of component and composite are a different size.

It is necessary to scale the magnitude of the chroma samples by multiplying by a factor which is cos 45 multiplied by the ratio of the quantizing structures. It is

Figure 4.12 4:2:2 to D-2 PAL conversion requires all three components to be raised to $4F_{sc}$ sampling rate before generating digital chroma with V-switch using selectors running at F_{sc} and quadrative F_{sc} as in (a). Waveforms of the selectors are shown in (b) for two successive lines where effect of V-switch can be seen. Combining U and V in this way results in samples at 45° to vector axes as in (c)

worth remembering that the quantizing intervals of luminance and colour difference are not the same size (see Chapter 7). In this way a maximum value legal colour difference signal will result in maximum amplitude chroma. Ideally steps ought to be taken to check incoming component signals for legality.[3]

The interpolated luminance will also need scaling, since the quantizing intervals are a different size, and the offset value corresponding to blanking level is different between component and composite. Luminance in component ranges from 16_{10} to 235_{10}, whereas PAL luminance ranges from 64_{10} to 211_{10}. Since the scale factor never changes, scaling is most conveniently performed in PROM. The input value forms the PROM address, and the PROM contains the scaled value as data at that address.

The scaled chroma and luminance can now be added numerically. This is easy since they are both sample streams at the same sampling rate. It is only necessary to add syncs digitally, and the output can be either converted to balanced ECL drive and fed to the 25 pin D-type connector, or fed to an SDI interface.

Sync generation is messy in PAL because the sampling rate is not H-coherent. Sync values will change from line to line as the sampling clock slides towards sync by four samples per frame. Since the unit described has a luminance interpolator which is unemployed during blanking, it is probably easiest to regenerate syncs from the H-synchronous 27 MHz input timing, and then pass them through the interpolator to produce syncs at $4F_{sc}$. This needs some care, since the quantizing range of the interpolator only goes from black to white to give the best noise performance, whereas syncs go below black. The simple solution is to generate positive-going syncs for interpolation, and invert them afterwards. The same procedure can be used for burst envelope generation by producing envelope values at 6.75 MHz and passing them through the colour difference interpolators.

4.7 Converting 525/59.94 4:2:2 to NTSC composite digital

This conversion is more straightforward than the PAL conversion, because of the simple subcarrier frequency of NTSC.

The main issues to be addressed are:

(1) Reducing the I and Q bandwidths to the values allowed and handling illegal colours.
(2) Converting the sampling rate of the colour difference signals to $4 \times F_{sc}$ and creating a digital representation of quadrature-modulated subcarrier.
(3) Converting the sampling rate of luminance from 13.5 MHz to $4 \times F_{sc}$ and adding the subcarrier.
(4) Scaling the numerical sample values since quantizing intervals of luminance, colour difference and composite signals are all different (see Chapter 7).
(5) Generating sync and burst, with the burst at a phase shift of 57° to the sampling structure.

The timing system of the converter will need to recreate video timing, and it can do this by regenerating the H-synchronous 27 MHz clock from the parallel or serial digital input, and using the synchronizing patterns to determine the position in the line and frame. Fig. 4.13 shows how the output sampling rate is generated. Input 27 MHz is divided down by 1716 to produce line rate, which is synchronized by the *SAV* signal (see Chapter 7), and this is then used as the input

Figure 4.13 Generating NTSC sampling rate from 4:2:2 digital input requires division to line rate followed by multiplication. This is simpler than for PAL because NTSC subcarrier is line locked. Sine $F_{sc} = 227.5\ F_H$, then $4F_{sc} = 910\ F_H$

to a phase-locked loop which multiplies by 910 to generate $4 \times F_{sc}$. The $4 \times F_{sc}$ clock is then divided by four in two different dividers. Combining the output of these dividers in various ways allows the generation of a subcarrier frequency square wave, for generation of the $R-Y$ component, and a quadrature square wave for generation of the $B-Y$ component. These waveforms will be phased by presetting the dividers once every four fields.

There is only one signal in composite digital, which is at a sampling rate of $4 \times F_{sc}$. Accordingly the sampling rates of the luminance and colour difference signals of the 4:2:2 input must all be raised to this sampling rate by interpolation, before it is possible to create a composite signal.

Reduction of the chroma bandwidth and sampling-rate conversion from 6.75 MHz to $4 \times F_{sc}$ can be achieved in the same process, but even though the new sampling rate is slightly higher than the luminance sampling rate of 13.5 MHz, the bandwidth needed in the interpolator will be that of NTSC.

Three parallel sampling-rate converters will be needed, and the coefficients can be obtained by considering the relative phases of $4 \times F_{sc}$ and $858 \times F_h$. Since both frequencies repeat at line rate, it is only necessary to have one set of coefficients, and these will serve for every line. As the colour difference signals are at half the luminance sampling rate, one interpolator could be multiplexed to process both colour difference signals alternately.

The bandwidths of I and Q in NTSC are different, and the frequency responses of the interpolators can be used to limit them. The $R-Y$ and $B-Y$ signals are matrixed (by multiplication by constants and addition) to convert them to I and Q prior to band limiting and interpolation.

There are now three sample streams, Y, I and Q, all running at $4 \times F_{sc}$, and all using offset binary code. Multiplexers are used to insert blanking values outside the active line, and the colour difference signals can additionally have a burst envelope inserted.

The I and Q signals are next converted to two's complement, and a normal and inverted version of both is made available to a pair of multiplexers. The multiplexer which switches between I and its complement is driven by a subcarrier rate square wave, and the multiplexer which switches between Q and its complement is driven by a quadrature square wave.

The outputs of the two multiplexers are next added together, and Fig. 4.14 shows that this results in the digital sampled equivalent of chroma, with samples

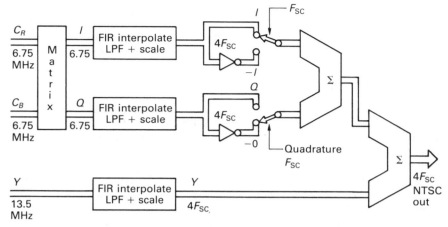

Figure 4.14 4:2:2 to NTSC conversion requires all three components to be raised to $4F_{sc}$ sampling rate. Colour difference signals are matrixed to produce I and Q signals which are filtered to different bandwidths in the rate converters

taken at the correct phase as the composite digital standard specifies. Note that this is not burst phase in NTSC.

The result of this process is not quite digital chroma. The gain is incorrect because the quantizing intervals of component and composite are a different size. It is necessary to scale the magnitude of the chroma samples by multiplying by an appropriate factor. It is worth remembering that the quantizing intervals of luminance and colour difference are not the same size (see Chapter 7). In this way a maximum value colour difference signal will result in maximum amplitude chroma.

The interpolated luminance will also need scaling, since the quantizing intervals are a different size, and the offset value corresponding to blanking level is different between component and composite. Luminance in component ranges from 16_{10} to 235_{10}, whereas NTSC luminance ranges from 60_{10} to 200_{10}. Scaling is most conveniently performed in PROM. The input value forms the PROM address, and the PROM contains the scaled value as data at that address.

The scaled chroma and luminance can now be added numerically. This is easy since they are both sample streams at the same sampling rate. It is only necessary to add syncs digitally, and the output can be either converted to balanced ECL drive and fed to the 25 pin D-type connector or fed to an SDI encoder. Since subcarrier is line synchronous, syncs are easily generated by a PROM addressed by the sample count along the line.

As can be seen in Chapter 7, there is a 57° phase shift between samples and NTSC subcarrier. This requires some caution when generating burst, since NTSC burst is a portion of subcarrier. Burst at any phase can be generated simply by feeding appropriate constants to the I and Q signals prior to modulating, but a more accurate method exists. Since burst has a standard amplitude and phase, and composite digital has standardized quantizing intervals, it follows that burst samples can be calculated allowing for the 57° shift. If a sampling clock is used to generate values of 83_{10}, 74_{10}, 37_{10} and 46_{10} in endless sequence, the result will be correctly phased subcarrier. This will automatically invert from one line to the next, since there are 910 samples per line, which gives a remainder of two when divided by four. Burst values can easily be stored in PROM, along with diminished values to allow the ends of the envelope to be shaped.

4.8 Delays in digital filters

All of the conversion devices described in the preceding paragraphs require phase-linear filters, and these cannot be implemented without causing a delay equal to one-half the window period. In particular, comb filters will delay the video by one or two lines. This makes it difficult to synchronize equipment on both sides of the converter. Where a converter is free standing, one side will have to be the timing reference, and the other side cannot therefore be synchronized. In the case of a component to composite converter, or vice versa, the source will often be a DVTR, whose output timing can be controlled. Fig. 4.15 shows that the converter takes a reference feed on the output side, and synchronizes its output signals to that reference. It then produces an advanced reference which leads the station reference by the processing delay. This advanced reference is fed to the DVTR. The DVTR then provides video ahead of reference, which when delayed by the converter will be synchronous with station reference.

Figure 4.15 Since sampling-rate converters must be phase linear they must have symmetrical impulse responses and will cause a delay to the signal. Practical converters will incorporate an advanced reference generator which advances the source by an amount equal to the converter delay

An alternative solution is to incorporate a frame store in the unit, which will increase the delay from a few lines to an entire frame. Input and output can then be timed together. Where the converter forms part of a DVE, the delay will be added to the overall delay of the effects transforms, which will total an integer number of frames, achieving the same effect.

4.9 Planar digital video effects

One can scarcely watch television nowadays without becoming aware of picture manipulation. Flips, tumbles, spins and page turn effects, perspective rotation, and rolling the picture on to the surface of a solid are all commonly seen. In all but the last mentioned, the picture remains flat, hence the title of this paragraph. Non-planar manipulation requires further complexity which will be treated in due course.

Effects machines which manipulate video pictures are close relatives of the machines which produce computer-generated images.[4] Computer-generated images require enormous processing power, and even with state-of-the-art CPUs the time needed to compute a single frame is several orders of magnitude too long to work with real-time video. Video effects machines, then, represent a significant technical achievement, because they have only a field period to complete the processing before another field comes along. General purpose processors are usually too slow for effects work, and most units incorporate dedicated hardware to obtain sufficient throughput. Owing to the advanced technology used in these machines, the reader should be aware that many of the techniques described here are patented.

4.10 Mapping

The principle of all video manipulators is the same as the technique used by cartographers for centuries. Cartographers are faced with a continual problem in that the earth is round and paper is flat. In order to produce flat maps, it is necessary to project the features of the round original on to a flat surface. Fig. 4.16 shows an example of this. There are a number of different ways of projecting maps, and all of them must by definition produce distortion. The effect of this distortion is that distances measured near the extremities of the map appear further than they actually are. Another effect is that *great circle routes* (the shortest or longest path between two places on a planet) appear curved on a projected map. The type of projection used is usually printed somewhere on the map, a very common system being that due to Mercator. Clearly the process of mapping involves some three-dimensional geometry in order to simulate the paths of light rays from the map so that they appear to have come from the curved surface. Video effects machines work in exactly the same way.

Rounded
surface of
earth

Flat map

Figure 4.16 Map projection is a close relative of video effects units which manipulate the shape of pictures

The distortion of maps means that things are not where they seem. In timesharing computers, every user appears to have their own identical address space in which their program resides, despite the fact that many different programs are simultaneously in the memory. In order to resolve this contradiction, memory management units are constructed which add a constant value to the address which the user thinks they have (the *virtual address*) in order to produce the *physical address*. As long as the unit gives each user a different constant, they can all program in the same virtual address space without one

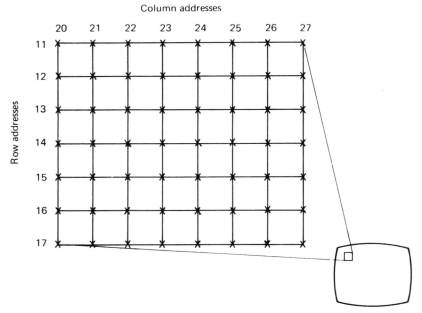

Column addresses

Figure 4.17 The entire TV picture can be broken down into uniquely addressable pixels

corrupting another's programs. Because the program is no longer where it seems to be, the term of mapping was introduced. The address space of a computer is one dimensional, but a video frame expressed as rows and columns of pixels can be considered to have a two-dimensional address as in Fig. 4.17. Video manipulators work by mapping the pixel addresses in two dimensions.

4.11 De-interlacing

All manipulators must begin with an array of pixels, in which the columns must be vertical. This can only be easily obtained if the sampling rate of the incoming video is a multiple of line rate, as is done in CCIR-601. Composite video cannot be used directly, because the phase of the subcarrier would become meaningless after manipulation. If a composite video input is used, it must be decoded to baseband luminance and colour difference, so that in actuality there are three superimposed arrays of samples to be processed, one luminance, and two colour difference. Most modern DVEs use CCIR-601 sampling, so digital signals conforming to this standard could be used directly from, for example, a DVTR or a hard-disk recorder.

There are two main types of effects machines, those which are field based, and those which are frame based. The former are more cost conscious, the latter are more quality conscious.

Fig. 4.18(a) shows an example of a field-based manipulator. In this example, the size of the picture is to be doubled. The information from lines on a given input field will appear on every other output line, and the lines in between will have to be produced by interpolation. In Fig. 4.18(b) a frame-based machine is

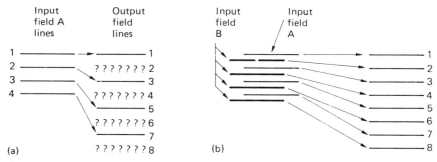

Figure 4.18 (a) In a field-based machine, interpolation becomes necessary when size of the picture is increased. (b) In a frame-based machine, the presence of the second input field allows greater vertical resolution

performing the same operation. Here, the lines necessary for the magnified output field come from the other input field. Clearly there is an improvement in vertical resolution to be gained by using frame-based machines, but it will be seen that there is a considerable increase in complexity.

A frame-based machine must produce a de-interlaced frame from which every output field can choose pixels. Producing frames at field rate sounds rather like getting something for nothing, but this is not exactly what happens. In practice, at a given field time, the lines of that field will be available, and between them will be placed the lines from the previous (most recent) field. Fig. 4.19 shows that at each new field, a new pair of fields will be combined to make a frame. Unfortunately it is not possible to use the information from two different fields directly. Fig. 4.20 shows a scene in which an object is moving. When the second field of the scene leaves the camera, the object will have assumed a different position from the one it had in the first field, and the result of combining the two fields to make a de-interlaced frame will be a double image. This effect can easily be demonstrated on any video recorder which offers a choice of still field or still frame. Stationary objects before a stationary camera, however, can be de-interlaced perfectly. Frame-based machines must use motion sensing so that de-interlacing can be disabled when movement occurs, and interpolation used instead. Motion sensing implies comparison of one picture with the next. If interpolation is only to be used in areas where there is movement, it is necessary to test for motion over the entire frame. Motion can be simply detected by comparing the luminance value of a given pixel with the value of the same pixel two fields earlier. As two fields are to be combined, and motion can occur in

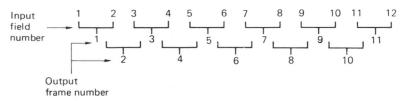

Figure 4.19 Frames are produced at field rate by combining the latest pair of fields

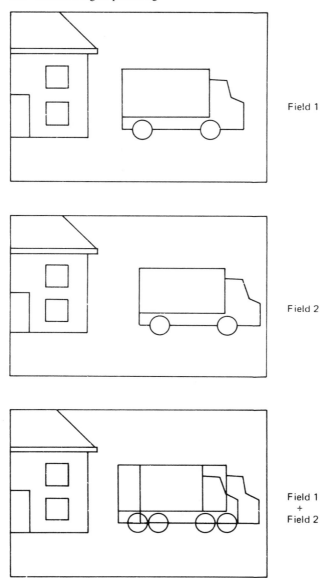

Figure 4.20 Moving object will be in a different place in two successive fields and will produce a double image

either, then the comparison must be made between two odd fields and two even fields. Thus four fields of memory are needed to perform motion sensing correctly. The luminance from four fields requires about a megabyte of storage. In practice the speed of operation required makes it difficult for memories to read and write at once, so that five fields of memory will sometimes be needed, and at any one time, one will be writing a new field, and four will be reading earlier

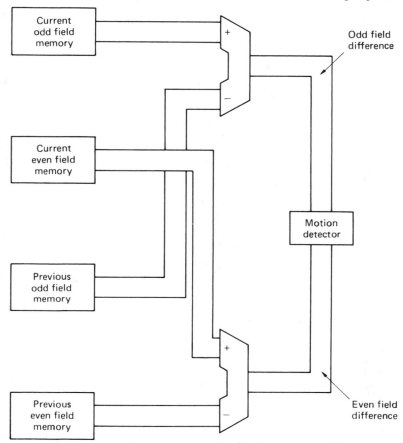

Figure 4.21 The circuit shown here can detect if a double image would result from motion

fields for motion sensing. Fig. 4.21 shows how the motion sensing is performed. One subtractor compares pixels in the most recent odd field with the same pixels in the odd field before that, whereas the other subtractor compares the most recent even field with the even field before that. Clearly, in order to work in real time, the subtractions must each be done at the sampling rate, and so there will be 27 million subtractions per second taking place for the purpose of detecting motion alone. The differences from the subtractors can have many values, from zero with a noise-free still input, to maximum when a cut to black takes place. At some point a decision must be made to abandon pixels from the previous field which are in the wrong place due to motion, and to interpolate them from adjacent lines in the current field. Switching suddenly in this way is visible to the naked eye, and there is a more sophisticated mechanism which can be used. In Fig. 4.22, two fields are shown, separated in time. Interlace can be seen by following lines from pixels in one field, which pass between pixels in the other field. If there is no movement, the fact that the two fields are separated in time is irrelevant, and the two can be superimposed to make a frame array. When there

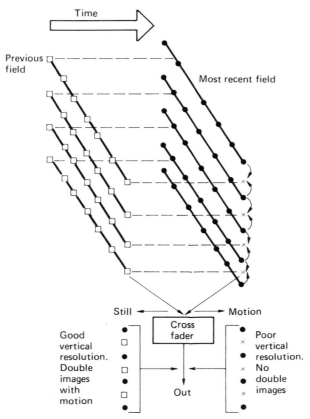

Figure 4.22 Pixels from the most recent field (•) are interpolated spatially to form low vertical resolution pixels (x) which will be used if there is excessive motion; pixels from the previous field (□) will be used to give maximum vertical resolution. The best possible de-interlaced frame results

is motion, pixels from above and below the unknown pixels are added together and divided by two to produce interpolated values. If both of these mechanisms work all the time, a better-quality picture results if a crossfade is made between the two based on the amount of motion. A suitable digital crossfader was shown in Chapter 2. At some motion value, or some magnitude of pixel difference, the loss of resolution due to a double image is equal to the loss of resolution due to interpolation. That amount of motion should result in the crossfader arriving at a 50/50 setting; any less motion will result in a fade towards both fields, any more motion resulting in a fade towards the interpolated values. As the resolution of the eye is much worse for changes in colour than it is for changes in brightness, de-interlacing is not generally necessary for the colour difference signals. More recently frame de-interlacing can be motion compensated so that full resolution remains available in moving areas. Motion compensation is considered later in this chapter. Clearly the additional cost and complexity of a frame-based processor is not trivial, but this is justified for post production work, where the utmost quality is demanded. Where an effects unit is used to increase the range of wipe patterns in an on-air video switcher, a field-based system may be acceptable because a wipe is by definition transient in nature, and there is little opportunity to study the image during the wipe.

The effect of de-interlacing is to produce an array of pixels which are the input data for the processor. In 13.5 MHz systems, the array will be about 750 pixels across, and 600 down for 50 Hz systems (500 down for 60 Hz systems). Most machines are set to strip out VITC or teletext data from the input, so that pixels representing a genuine picture appear surrounded by blanking level.

4.12 Separability and transposition

Every pixel in the frame array has an address. The address is two dimensional, because in order to specify one pixel uniquely, the column address and the row address must be supplied. It is possible to transform a picture by simultaneously addressing in rows and columns, but this is complicated, and very difficult to do in real time. It was discovered some time ago in connection with computer graphics that the two-dimensional problem can be converted with care into two one-dimensional problems.[5] Essentially if a horizontal transform affecting whole rows of pixels independently of other rows is performed on the array, followed by or preceded by a vertical transform which affects entire columns independently of other columns, the effect will be the same as if a two-dimensional transform had been performed. This is the principle of separability. From an academic standpoint, it does not matter which transform is performed first. In a world which is wedded to the horizontally scanned television set, there are practical matters to consider. In order to convert a horizontal raster input into a vertical column format, a memory is needed. These memories already exist in the shape of the motion detection memories. Fig. 4.23 shows a simplified TV standard where there are exactly 750 samples per line. As the first line of a field enters, it will be put into addresses 0 to 749. As the second line of the frame appears, it will be put in addresses 750 to 1499 and so on. If subsequently a small accumulator is arranged to provide addresses which are given by $n \times 750 + k$, where n goes from zero upwards, if $k = 0$ the addresses 0, 750, 1500, 2250, etc., will be generated, which correspond to the first column of pixels. If k is increased to 1, the addresses 1, 751, 1501, 2251, etc., will be generated, which correspond to the second column of pixels. In order to de-interlace two fields A and B, the

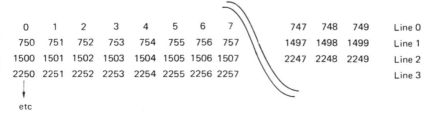

Figure 4.23 Pixels are written into a memory in the order of address counting a line at a time. If the read address is given by $(n \times 750) + k$, for each value of k, a different column will be read by increasing n. For example $k=4$, addresses will be 4, 754, 1504, 2254, etc. This transposes the incoming raster to a vertical scan format

two address accumulators would need to be synchronized so that they alternated. The effect would then be to provide a single column of pixels in the sequence A0, B0, A750, B750, A1500, B1500, etc. Where there is motion, an alternate pixel stream would be selected, which would be A0, A0/2 + A750/2, A750, A750/2 + A1500/2, A2250, etc., which contains no B field data. The average of two successive pixels can be obtained using an adder which has its two inputs connected one at each side of a pixel delay latch.

The process of writing rows and reading columns in a memory is called transposition. Clearly two stages of transposition are necessary to return to a horizontal raster output, as shown in Fig. 4.24. The vertical transform must take place between the two transposes, but the horizontal transform could take place before the first transpose or after the second one. In practice the horizontal transform cannot be placed before the first transpose, because it would interfere with the de-interlace and motion sensing process. The horizontal transform is placed after the second transpose and reads rows from the second transpose memory. As the output of the machine must be a horizontal raster, the horizontal transform can be made to work in synchronism with reference H-sync, so that the digital output samples from the H-transform can be taken direct to a DAC to become analog video with standard structure again. A further advantage is that the real-time horizontal output is one field at a time. The preceding vertical transform need only compute array values which lie in the next field to be needed at the output.

It is not possible to take a complete column from a memory until all of the rows have entered. The presence of the two transposes in a DVE results in an unavoidable delay of one frame in the output image. Some DVEs can manage greater delay. The effect on lip-sync may have to be considered. It is not advisable to cut from the input of a DVE to the output, since a frame will be lost, and on cutting back a frame will be repeated.

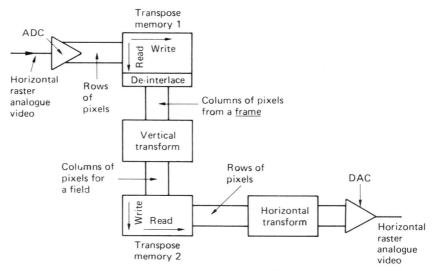

Figure 4.24 Two transposing memories are necessary, one before and one after the vertical transform

In a composite environment, the delay due to effects units has some implications. Video from a colour-framed VTR playing back through an effects machine will appear late relative to timecode, so edits made on it will look different to the same edit made without the effects unit if there is movement in the scene. The delay through an effects unit does not affect colour framing, however, because a decoder is installed before the transforms, and an encoder after. The colour framing of the effects machine output will then be determined entirely by the reference colour black fed to the output encoder.

Because of the decode/encode the VTR does not actually need to be colour framed, provided it is frame synchronized, and if an associated editor has the facility to override the automatic colour framing, then edits can be made to frame accuracy.

4.13 Address generation and interpolation

There are many different manipulations possible, and the approach here will be to begin with the simplest, which require the least processing, and to graduate to the most complex, introducing the necessary processes at each stage.

It has been stated that address mapping is used to perform transforms. Now that rows and columns are processed individually, the mapping process becomes much easier to understand. Fig. 4.25 shows a single row of pixels which are held in a buffer where each can be addressed individually and transferred to another. If a constant is added to the read address, the selected pixel will be to the right of the place where it will be put. This has the effect of moving the picture to the left. If the buffer represented a column of pixels, the picture would be moved vertically. As these two transforms can be controlled independently, the picture could be moved diagonally.

If the read address is multiplied by a constant, say two, the effect is to bring samples from the input closer together on the output, so that the picture size is reduced. Again independent control of the horizontal and vertical transforms is possible, so that the aspect ratio of the picture can be modified. This is very useful for telecine work when cinemascope films are to be broadcast. Clearly the secret of these manipulations is in the constants fed to the address generators. The added constant represents displacement, and the multiplied constant represents magnification. A multiplier constant of less than one will result in the picture getting larger. Fig. 4.25 also shows, however, that there is a problem. If a constant of 0.5 is used, to make the picture twice as big, half of the addresses generated are not integers. A memory does not understand an address of two and a half! If an arbitrary magnification is used, nearly all of the addresses generated are non-integer. A similar problem crops up if a constant of less than one is added to the address in an attempt to move the picture less than the pixel spacing. The solution to the problem is interpolation. Because the input image is spatially sampled, those samples contain enough information to represent the brightness and colour all over the screen. When the address generator comes up with an address of 2.5, it actually means that what is wanted is the value of the signal interpolated half-way between pixel 2 and pixel 3. The output of the address generator will thus be split into two parts. The integer part will become the memory address, and the fractional part is the phase of the necessary interpolation. In order to interpolate pixel values a digital filter is necessary.

(a)

Figure 4.25 Address generation is the fundamental process behind transforms

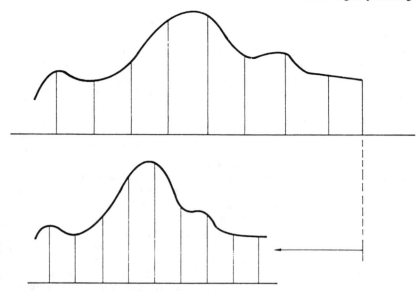

Figure 4.26 It is easy, almost trivial, to reduce the size of a picture by pushing the samples closer together, but this is not often of use, because it changes the sampling rate in proportion to the compression. Where a standard sampling-rate output is needed, interpolation must be used

Fig. 4.26 shows that the input and output of an effects machine must be at standard sampling rates to allow digital interchange with other equipment. When the size of a picture is changed, this causes the pixels in the picture to fail to register with output pixel spacing. The problem is exactly the same as sampling-rate conversion, which produces a differently spaced set of samples which still represent the original waveform. One pixel value actually represents the peak brightness of a two-dimensional intensity function, which is the effect of the modulation transfer function of the system on an infinitely small point. As each dimension can be treated separately, the equivalent in one axis is that the pixel value represents the peak value of an infinitely short impulse which has been low-pass filtered to the system bandwidth. The waveform is that of a $\sin x/x$ curve, which has value everywhere except at the centre of other pixels. In order to compute an interpolated value, it is necessary to add together the contribution from all relevant samples, at the point of interest. Each contribution can be obtained by looking up the value of a unity $\sin x/x$ curve at the distance from the input pixel to the output pixel to obtain a coefficient, and multiplying the input pixel value by that coefficient. The process of taking several pixel values, multiplying each by a different coefficient and summing the products can be performed by the FIR (Finite-Impulse Response) configuration described earlier. The impulse response of the filter necessary depends on the magnification. Where the picture is being enlarged, the impulse response can be the same as at normal size, but as the size is reduced, the impulse response has to become broader (corresponding to a reduced spatial frequency response) so that more input samples are averaged together to prevent aliasing. The coefficient store will need a two-dimensional structure, such that the magnification and the interpolation phase must both be supplied to obtain a set of coefficients. The magnification can easily be obtained by comparing successive outputs from the address generator.

As was seen in Chapter 2, the number of points in the filter is a compromise between cost and performance, eight being a typical number for high quality. As there are two transform processes in series, every output pixel will be the result of 16 multiplications, so there will be 216 million multiplications per second taking place in the luminance channel alone for a 13.5 MHz sampling-rate unit. The quality of the output video also depends on the number of different interpolation phases available between pixels. The address generator may compute fractional addresses to any accuracy, but these will be rounded off to the nearest available phase in the digital filter. The effect is that the output pixel value provided is actually the value a tiny distance away, and has the same result as sampling-clock jitter, which is to produce program-modulated noise. The greater the number of phases provided, the larger will be the size of the coefficient store needed. As the coefficient store is two dimensional, an increase in the number of filter points and phases causes an exponential growth in size and cost. The filter itself can be implemented readily with fast multiplier chips, but one problem is accessing the memory to provide input samples. What the memory must do is to take the integer part of the address generator output and provide simultaneously as many adjacent pixels as there are points in the filter. This problem is usually solved by making the memory from several smaller memories with an interleaved address structure, so that several pixel values can be provided from one address.

Fig. 4.27(a) shows one way in which this can be done. The incoming memory write address is split into two sections. The three low-order bits are decoded successively to enable one out of eight RAMs, which are fed the remainder of the address bits in parallel. The result of this arrangement is that samples 0 through 7 are written into location 0 of successive RAMs, samples 8 through 15 are written in location 1 of the RAMs and so on.

In order to read the memories, a different addressing configuration is used. The read address comes from the address generator and is split into two sections as before. The most significant bits are fed in parallel to all RAMs, but each RAM is furnished with an adder which allows the address to be increased by one. The least significant bits are also treated in a different manner. They decide *how many* of the addresses will be incremented. Fig. 4.27(b) lists the result for a series of input addresses. In each case, providing one *source address* produces eight adjacent sample values simultaneously. The correct sample numbers are produced, but they suffer an end-around rotation of position. As each one is to be fed to one point of a parallel FIR filter, this does not matter, provided that the coefficients fed to the filter are given the same rotation.

4.14 Skew and rotation

It has been seen that adding a constant to the source address produces a displacement. It is not necessary for the displacement constant to be the same throughout the frame. If the horizontal transform is considered, as in Fig. 4.28(a), the effect of making the displacement a function of line address is to cause a skew. Essentially each line is displaced a different amount. The necessary function generator is shown in simplified form in Fig. 4.28(b), although it could equally be realized in a fast CPU with appropriate software.

Figure 4.27(a) The incoming write address is split so that the three least significant bits sequentially enable one of eight parallel RAMs. Then every eighth byte will be written into the same RAM

Figure 4.27(b) The incoming read address is split as before, but now the three least significant bits determine the *number* of carries which will be added to the remainder of the address. In this example two carries are added, so the top two RAMs access an address 8 bytes higher, and the system accesses bytes 18, 19, 20, 21, 22, 23, 24, 25

(a)

(b)

(c)

(d)

Figure 4.28 (a) Skew is achieved by subjecting each line of pixels to a different offset. (b) The hardware necessary to perform a skew where the left-hand accumulator produces the offset which increases every line, and the right-hand accumulator adds it to the address. (c) A z-axis rotate is performed using a pair of skews in succession. The magnification of each transform must also change from unity to cos θ because horizontal and vertical components of distances on the frame reduce as the frame turns. (d) The four modes necessary for a complete z-axis rotation using skews. Switching between modes at the vertical interval allows a skew range of ±45° (outer ring) to embrace a complete revolution in conjunction with memory transposes which exchange rows and columns to give 90° changes

It will be seen that the address generator is really two accumulators in series, where the first operates once per line to calculate a new offset which grows linearly from line to line, and the second operates at pixel rate to calculate source addresses from the required magnification. The initial state of the second accumulator is the offset from the first accumulator.

If two skews, one vertical and one horizontal, are performed in turn on the same frame, the result is a rotation as shown in Fig. 4.28(c). Clearly the skew angle parameters for the two transforms must be in the correct relationship to obtain pure rotation. Additionally the magnification needs to be modified by a cosine function of the rotation angle to counteract the stretching effect of the skews.

In the horizontal process, the offset will change once per line, whereas in the vertical process, the offset will change once per column. For simplicity, the offset generators are referred to as the *slow* address generators, whereas the accumulators which operate at pixel rate are called the *fast* address generators.

Unfortunately skew rotations cannot approach 90°, because the skew parameter goes to infinity, and so a skew rotation is generally restricted to rotations of ±45°. This is not a real restriction, since the apparatus already exists to turn a picture on its side. This can be done readily by failing to transpose in one of the memories. There will no longer be two cancelling transposes, so the picture will be turned through 90° when it emerges. Although the failure to transpose could be at either of the memories if only this effect is required, in practice it cannot be at the second memory, because this would put both transforms in series on the same axis, so that any other manipulation in addition to the rotation could only be done in one axis. The failure to transpose has to be in the input memory, in order to keep the horizontal and vertical transforms at right angles. Using the input memory causes a small problem when motion is detected. When turning the picture 90°, the input memory is read in rows, as it is written, but the readout is treated as a column. In order to de-interlace under these conditions, whole lines must be read from the A and B field memories alternately, and treated as columns by the vertical transform. If there is motion, entire lines must be interpolated from the A memory. The first line would be A0, A1, A2, etc., but the next line would be A0/2 + A750/2, A1/2 + A751/2, A2/2 + A752/2, etc., and the line after that would be A750, A751, A752, etc. This is a different interpolation process to that shown earlier, and the de-interlacer must be told that there has been a failure to transpose. To obtain the correct interpolation, the delay in the pixel averager has to be increased from one pixel to one line.

Fig. 4.28(d) shows how continuous rotation can be obtained. From −45° to +45°, normal skew rotation is used. At 45°, during the vertical interval, the memory transpose is turned off, causing the picture to be flipped 90° and laterally inverted. Reversing the source address sequence cancels the lateral inversion, and at the same time the skew parameters are changed from +45° to −45° In this way the picture passes smoothly through the 45° barrier, and skew parameters continue to change until 135° (90° transpose + 45° skew) is reached. At this point, three things happen, again during the vertical interval. The transpose is switched back on, reorienting the picture, the source addresses are both reversed, which turns the picture upside down, and a skew rotation of −45° is applied, returning the picture to 135° of rotation, from which point motion can continue. The remainder of the rotation takes place along similar lines which can be followed in the diagram.

The rotation described is in the Z axis, i.e. the axis coming out of the source picture at right angles. Rotation about the other axes is rather more difficult, because to perform the effect properly, perspective is needed. In simple machines, there is no perspective, and the effect of rotation is as if viewed from a long way away. These non-perspective pseudo-rotations are achieved by simply changing the magnification in the appropriate axis as a cosine function of the rotation angle.

4.15 Perspective rotation

In order to follow the operation of a true perspective machine, some knowledge of perspective is necessary. Stated briefly, the phenomenon of perspective is due to the angle subtended to the eye by objects being a function not only of their size but also of their distance. Fig. 4.29 shows that the size of an image on the rear wall of a pinhole camera can be increased either by making the object larger or by bringing it closer. In the absence of stereoscopic vision, it is not possible to tell which has happened. The pinhole camera is very useful for the study of perspective, and has indeed been used by artists for that purpose. The clinically precise perspective of Canaletto paintings was achieved through the use of the camera obscura (darkened room in Italian).[6]

Figure 4.29 The image on the rear of the pinhole camera is identical for the two solid objects shown because the size of the object is proportional to distance, and the subtended angle remains the same. The image can be made larger (dotted) by making the object larger or moving it closer

It is sometimes claimed that the focal length of the lens used on a camera changes the perspective of a picture. This is not true: perspective is only a function of the relative positions of the camera and the subject. Fitting a wide-angle lens simply allows the camera to come near enough to keep dramatic perspective within the frame, whereas fitting a long-focus lens allows the camera to be far enough away to display a reasonable-sized image with flat perspective.[7]

Since a single eye cannot tell distance unaided, all current effects machines work by simply producing the correct subtended angles which the brain perceives as a three-dimensional effect. Fig. 4.30 shows that to a single eye, there is no difference between a three-dimensional scene and a two-dimensional image formed where rays traced from features to the eye intersect an imaginary plane.

Figure 4.30 In a planar rotation effect the source plane ABCD is the rectangular input picture. If it is rotated through the angle θ, ray tracing to a single eye at left will produce a trapezoidal image A'B'C'D' on the target. Magnification will now vary with position on the picture

This is exactly the reverse of the map projection shown in Fig. 4.16, and is the principle of all perspective manipulators.

The case of perspective rotation of a plane source will be discussed first. Fig. 4.30 shows that when a plane input frame is rotated about a horizontal axis, the distance from the top of the picture to the eye is no longer the same as the distance from the bottom of the picture to the eye. The result is that the top and bottom edges of the picture subtend different angles to the eye, and where the rays cross the target plane, the image has become trapezoidal. There is now no such thing as the magnification of the picture. The magnification changes continuously from top to bottom of the picture, and if a uniform grid is input, after a perspective rotation it will appear non-linear as the diagram shows.

As the two axes of the picture are transformed consecutively, it can be seen in Fig. 4.31(a) that the first process will be a vertical transform which is non-linear. The address generator produces a function or series of addresses which is curved, which will be seen in Fig. 4.31(b) to produce the desired distortion. The vertical process is followed by the horizontal process where each line or row of pixels has the same magnification, but the magnification changes from one line to the next. The result is the desired trapezoidal shape with the correct non-linearity, which the eye takes to be a rotation of the source, even though the image never leaves the plane of the monitor. Rotation about a vertical axis will now be considered. Again this results in a trapezoidal picture, but now the non-linearity appears in the horizontal transform. Fig. 4.31(c) shows that if the vertical and horizontal transforms are performed in that order, the non-linear horizontal transform causes an unwanted distortion – the edges of the picture become curved. This is a fundamental problem of separating the axes, and some thought is necessary to provide a solution. Fig. 4.31(d) shows that the problem is caused by the vertical process moving a given pixel vertically by what appears to be the correct distance, whereas it should move the pixel so that it will be at the correct vertical position *after* it has been horizontally transformed. In other words, the vertical process must predistort the intermediate image in such a way that the non-linear horizontal process will cancel the predistortion to give the correct overall transform.

The above process implies that the vertical transform must be exactly aware of what the horizontal transform will do. This is no problem because both

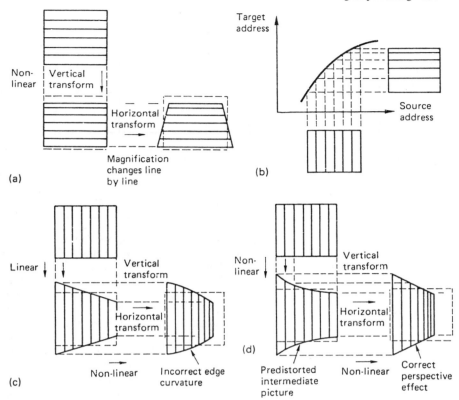

Figure 4.31 (a) A perspective rotation consist of a non-linear vertical transform followed by a horizontal transform where the magnification is linear but changes line by line. (b) Non-linear transforms require a curved relationship between source and target address. (c) How not to perform a rotation about a vertical axis. The non-linear horizontal process distorts the vertical process. (d) In order to give correct manipulation, the vertical process must produce columns which will be the correct length for the position the horizontal process will put them in. This implies that the vertical transform knows what the horizontal transform will do and predistorts accordingly. The non-linear horizontal transform then cancels the distortion

transforms are computed from high-level commands put in to the system by the operator, but it does require some care to supply the transform parameters to the processors at the correct time, because the horizontal transform cannot begin until the vertical transform is completed, due to the presence of the transpose memory. This means that the transform parameters for the horizontal processor will need to be supplied one field later than the parameters for the vertical process. Fig. 4.32 shows how the field shift in the parameters relates to the progress of fields through a machine.

The address generators for perspective operation are necessarily complex, and a careful approach is necessary to produce the complex calculations at the necessary speed.[8] Fig. 4.33 shows a section through a transform where the source plane has been rotated about an axis perpendicular to the page. The mapping or ray tracing process must produce a straight line from every target pixel

Real time field no	n	n + 1	n + 2	n + 3	n + 4
Field being written to input memory	n ∗	n + 1	n + 2	n + 3	n + 4
Vertical transform	n -- 1	n ∗	n + 1	n + 2	n + 3
Horizontal transform	n -- 2	n − 1	n ∗	n + 1	n + 2

Odd field parameters		Vert ∗	Horiz ∗	Vert	Horiz
Even field parameters	Vert	Horiz	Vert	Horiz	

Figure 4.32 Timing chart showing how the transform parameters are supplied at the correct time. For a field which arrives at time n it can be read from input memory at field $n + 1$ where the vertical transform will take place. The horizontal transform will take place in the next field. In order to have matching transform parameters, the vertical parameters must be supplied one field ahead of the horizontal parameters. (Follow asterisk for progress of field n)

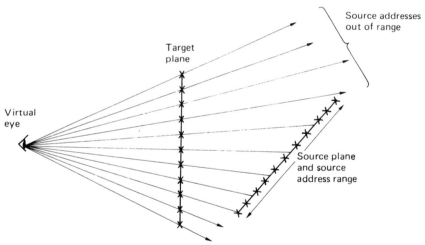

Figure 4.33 A rotation of the source plane along with a movement away from the observer is shown here. The system has to produce pixel values at the spacing demanded by the output. Thus a ray from the eye to each target pixel is produced to locate a source pixel. Since the chances of exactly hitting a source pixel are small, the need for interpolation is clear. If the source plane is missed, this will result in an out-of-range source address, and a background value will be substituted

(corresponding to where an output value is needed) to locate a source address (corresponding to where an input value is available). Moving the source value to the target performs the necessary transform.

Clearly it is possible to compute any source address from the target address and a knowledge of the geometry of the system. This will take several minutes with a pocket calculator, making liberal use of trigonometric functions. The DVE must compute the source address in 75 ns, and few computers can perform the calculation at that speed. The solution is to split the problem into two parts. For a given position of the source plane in space, all of the angles except that of the ray being traced become constants, and therefore the trigonometrical functions of

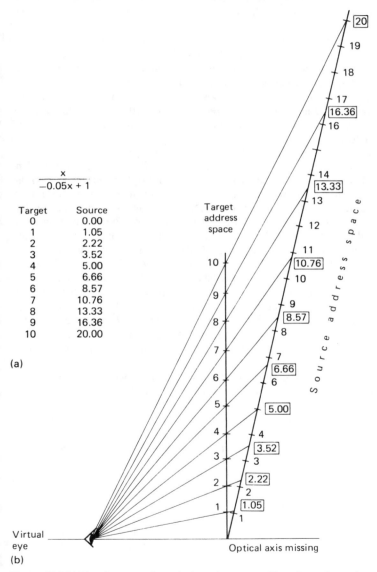

$$\frac{x}{-0.05x + 1}$$

Target	Source
0	0.00
1	1.05
2	2.22
3	3.52
4	5.00
5	6.66
6	8.57
7	10.76
8	13.33
9	16.36
10	20.00

(a)

(b)

Figure 4.34 (a) The above equation calculates the source address for each evenly spaced target address from 0 to 10. All numbers are kept positive for simplicity, so only one side of the picture is represented here. (b) The ray tracing diagram corresponding to the calculations of (a). Following a ray from the virtual eye through any target pixel address will locate the source addresses calculated those angles also become constants. A general purpose computer can work out what the constants are for a given source orientation in less than a field period, and these constants are then used by the slow and fast address generators which execute much simpler equations at line/column and pixel rate.

The derivation of the address generator equations is high-cholesterol mathematics which can be found in Newman and Sproull[5] and in the ADO patent.[8] For the purposes of this chapter, an understanding of the result can be had by considering the example of Fig. 4.34.

In this figure, successive integer values of x have been used in a simple source address calculation equation which contains a division stage. The addresses produced form a non-linear sequence, and will be seen to lie on a rotated source plane. The actual equations necessary for a planar transform are shown in Fig. 4.35 along with the block diagram of one possible implementation. Note that the vertical and horizontal equations are different because of the use of separability. As Fig. 4.31 showed, the vertical transform must predistort if the subsequent horizontal transform is non-linear.

The accumulation stages of the address generator are quite straightforward, as these are simply repeated adders or digital integrators. The difficulty arises with the division. There is no parallel with the fast multiplier. Fast division is impossible, as all divisions are in the form of an experiment to see how many times one number will fit into another. Division can be made easier by calculating the reciprocal of the divisor and multiplying. The calculation of a reciprocal is, admittedly, still a division, but it is a division into a constant, i.e. one, and advantage can be taken of PROMs. For short wordlengths, the reciprocal PROM will be of moderate size, but address wordlengths in DVEs are very large because of the enormous virtual space in which the picture can move, and a more complex solution is necessary. In this approach, the transfer function of the reciprocal is approximated by a piecewise linear graph, as shown in Fig. 4.36. The high-order bits of the number to be inverted now address two PROMs, one to give a coarse reciprocal and one to give the slope of the curve. The low-order bits are multiplied by the slope to give a correction term which is added to the coarse reciprocal.

Where really long wordlengths must be multiplied or divided, the only practicable solution is to use floating point notation. In floating point, the numbers are expressed as a mantissa and an exponent. Only the mantissae need to be multiplied or divided; the exponents are simply added or subtracted. Following the floating point division stage, the addresses must be returned to fixed point. The source address then performs a number of functions as can be seen in Fig. 4.35.

The source address will be compared with limits to see if a ray from target has hit the source picture or missed it. If it has missed, a border or background value must be substituted. The source address also passes to the interpolator memory where it will access a contiguous group of (typically) eight pixels. The low-order bits of the source address below the radix point (the fractional address) determine the position between source samples of the interpolated target pixel, and so these bits control the phase of the interpolator.

All perspective machines must work with dynamic changes in magnification throughout the frame. The situation often arises where at one end of a pixel row the magnification is greater than unity, and the FIR filter has to interpolate between available pixels, whereas at the other end of the row the magnification

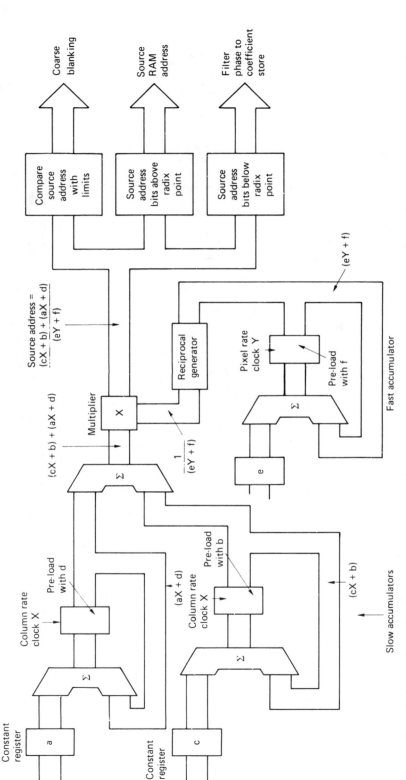

Figure 4.35(a) Hardware block diagram of vertical address generator. Accumulators on left operate once per column. When latch is clocked, preloaded value d (or b) is added to constant a (or c). Each clock X adds a (or c) once more, hence (aX + d) or (cX + b) is calculated. Fast accumulator produces a new denominator by clocking at pixel rate Y. Reciprocal of denominator is multiplied by numerator to give final source address

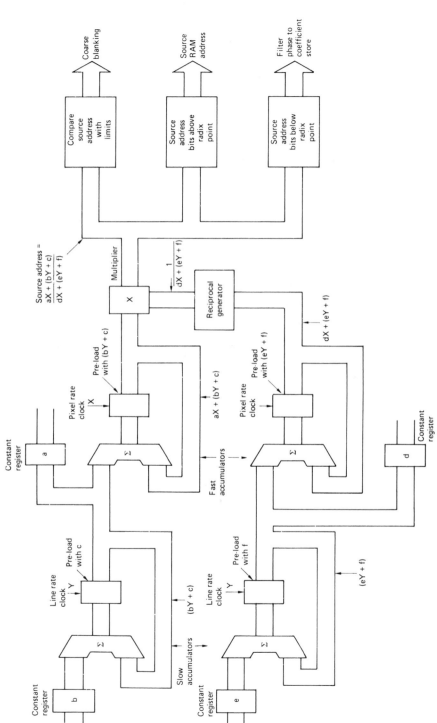

Figure 4.35(b) Hardware block diagram to implement horizontal equation. Slow accumulators are preloaded with constants c and f at the beginning of each field and calculate a new value (bY + c) or (eY + f) every line. Fast accumulators are preloaded with the values from the slow accumulators at the start of every line, then revert to constant registers a, d

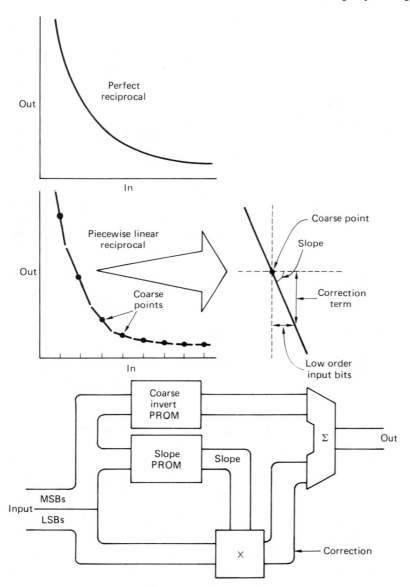

Figure 4.36 Piecewise linear reciprocal calculator

will be less than unity and the FIR filter has to adopt a low pass and decimate mode to eliminate excessive pixels without aliasing. The characteristics of the filter are changed at will by selecting different coefficient sets from pages of memory according to the instantaneous magnification at the centre of the filter window. The magnification can be determined by computing the address slope. This is done by digitally differentiating the output of the address generator, which is to say that the difference between one source address and the next is computed. This produces the address slope, which is inversely proportional to the magnification, and can be used to select the appropriate impulse response width in the interpolator. The interpolator output is then a transformed image.

4.16 DVE backgrounds

When an effects unit reduces the size of the picture, it is necesary to control what happens in the area between the edge of the picture and the edge of the screen. At least, the system must ensure that this area defaults to black, but it is usually possible to insert some kind of plain background instead.

There are two conflicting requirements. The transition between picture and background has to pass through the interpolator so that a smooth edge results. This will be achieved by switching to background values (luminance and colour differences in the respective processing channels) in source space before the interpolator. Fig. 4.37(a) shows the mechanism necessary. When the source memory of the interpolator is loaded from the transpose memory, sample values must pass through a multiplexer which can switch between picture samples and background values from a control system port. The switching points are obtained by comparing the memory addresses with limit addresses which are also provided by a system port. If the memory address falls outside the limits, the multiplexer will switch to background values, and the result will be a column or row of samples in the interpolator memory which has background values at both ends. If the picture is cropped, the limit addresses are simply brought closer, so that more of the source picture is replaced by background.

The transition to background will now be manipulated with the source picture, and can be positioned to subpixel accuracy according to the phase of the interpolator.

This is not, however, the complete solution. Fig. 4.37(b) shows that when the magnification becomes very small, the background area in source space must tend towards infinite size if the screen is to be filled. Clearly this is impossible. In order to allow background generation without a restriction on the magnification which will be used, a further stage is necessary.

The arrangement is shown in Fig. 4.37(c). A further multiplexer inserts an identical background value *after* the interpolator. This device is working in target space, and so can only switch at target pixel spacing, but this is of no consequence provided it operates at the correct time. Several pixels away from the source picture, the interpolator will be outputting background values, and as the result of interpolating a continuous plain area is the same as sampling it, the output of the interpolator will be the same as the background value, and the switch can operate invisibly. The two processes, before and after the interpolator, are called fine and coarse blanking respectively, and should not be confused with the blanking which is necessary to return background values to black level smoothly to prevent out-of-band signals with bright backgrounds. Clearly this is only necessary in the horizontal domain. It is sometimes called smooth blanking to avoid confusion. Fig. 4.37(d) shows the sequence of events in a horizontal line output from a DVE. At the beginning of the line the smooth blanker slowly releases so that a gradual transition to background takes place. The background values have come from the coarse blanker after the interpolatoɪ. As the line proceeds, the output of the transform address generator will fall within the range

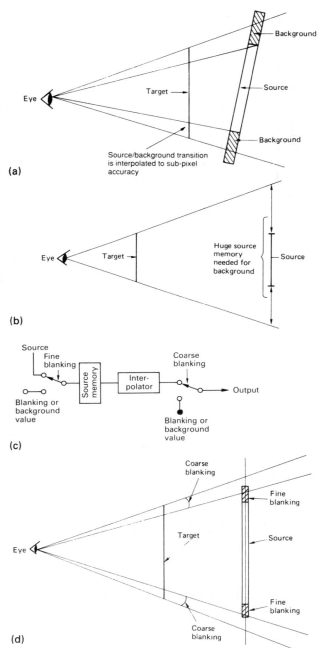

Figure 4.37 (a) Source/background transition is interpolated to subpixel accuracy. (b) At small magnifications the memory needed in source space to hold background values becomes very large. (c) Two multiplexers are necessary to insert background before and after the interpolator. (d) Coarse blanking multiplexer is switched in before the fine blanking in source space runs out at the ends of the address sequence

(e)

Figure 4.37 (*Continued*). (e) The position of the four blanking multiplexers in the vertical and horizontal process, and the position on the screen of the contributions from each when the picture size is greatly reduced

of the interpolator memory, and meaningful samples will begin to come from the interpolator. These will be numerically identical to the coarse blanking value, because they have come from the fine blanking multiplexer via the interpolator. It is now possible to switch invisibly to the interpolator output. The picture/background transition will thus have come through the interpolator. At the opposite edge of the picture, the return transition will be similarly treated. Shortly after this, the interpolator output will again be identical to the coarse blanking value, and a second invisible switch will be made to coarse background. At the end of active line, the smooth blanker will gradually fade the background value to black.

With a reduced size picture it is possible to see the origin of sample values in different parts of the screen (Fig. 4.37(e)), and this is one of the most powerful tools available for locating the position of a failure in a DVE.

4.17 Non-planar effects

The basic approach to perspective rotation of plane pictures has been described, and this can be extended to embrace transforms which make the source picture appear non-planar. Effects in this category include rolling the picture onto the surface of an imaginary solid such as a cylinder or a cone. Fig. 4.38 shows that the ray tracing principle is still used, but that the relationship between source and target addresses has become much more complex. The problem is that when a source picture can be curved, it may be put in such an attitude that one part of the source can be seen through another part. This results in two difficulties. Firstly the source address function needs to be of higher order, and secondly, the target needs to be able to accept and accumulate pixel data from two different source addresses, with weighting given to the one nearer the viewer according to the transparency allocated to the picture. Transparency was discussed in Chapter 2.

The high-order address functions needed for non-planar images cannot be readily implemented in fast hard-wired accumulators, because too much

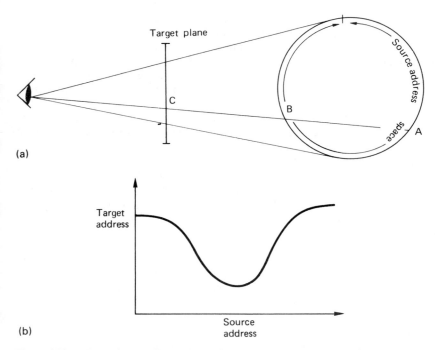

Figure 4.38 (a) To produce a rolled-up image for a given target pixel address C, there will be two source addresses A and B. Pixel data from A and B must be added with weighting dependent on the transparency of the nearer pixel to produce the pixel value to be put on the target plane at C. (b) Transfer function for a rolling-up transform. There are two source addresses for every target address; hence the need for target accumulation

hardware would be needed. A fast CPU will be needed to generate these address sequences in real time. Unfortunately it is not generally possible then to go from high-level operator commands to transform parameters in real time, because the functions are too complex. It is usually necessary to design the effect without seeing it, in high-level language, and then compile the high-level program into machine code which the transform processors can then use as microcode at a later time. Where the picking of source pixels to perform the transform is in a software-driven CPU, accumulation with transparency in target space is relatively easy if the CPU is fast enough, because only a few extra microinstructions will be necessary to include the accumulation, but where dedicated hardware is used to transfer source pixels to target, accumulation is much harder. Dedicated hardware machines, however, are easier to operate because effects can be designed 'hands on' as the compilers will work in real time. For these reasons there is a large jump in cost, complexity and operating difficulty when going from planar perspective manipulators to non-planar machines.

4.18 Controlling effects

The basic mechanism of the transform process has been described, but this is only half of the story, because these transforms have to be controlled. There is a lot of complex geometrical calculation necessary to perform even the simplest effect, and the operator cannot be expected to calculate directly the parameters required for the transforms. All effects machines require a computer of some kind, with which the operator communicates using keyboard entry or joystick/trackball movements at high level. These high-level commands will specify such things as the position of the axis of rotation of the picture relative to the viewer, the position of the axis of rotation relative to the source picture, and the angle of rotation in the three axes.

An essential feature of this kind of effects machines is fluid movement of the source picture as the effect proceeds. If the source picture is to be made to move smoothly, then clearly the transform parameters will be different in each field. The operator cannot be expected to input the source position for every field, because this would be an enormous task. Additionally, storing the effect would require a lot of space. The solution is for the operator to specify the picture position at strategic points during the effect, and then digital filters are used to compute the intermediate positions so that every field will have different parameters.

The specified positions are referred to as knots, nodes or keyframes, the first being the computer graphics term. The operator is free to enter knots anywhere in the effect, and so they will not necessarily be evenly spaced in time, i.e. there may well be different numbers of fields between each knot. In this environment it is not possible to use conventional FIR-type digital filtering, because a fixed-impulse response is inappropriate for irregularly spaced samples.

Interpolation of various orders is used ranging from zero-order hold for special jerky effects through linear interpolation to cubic interpolation for very smooth motion. The algorithms used to perform the interpolation are known as splines, a term which has come down from shipbuilding via computer graphics.[9] When a ship is designed, the draughtsman produces hull cross-sections at intervals along the keel, whereas the shipyard needs to recreate a continuous structure. The solution was a lead-filled bar, known as a spline, which could be formed to join up each cross-section in a smooth curve, and then used as a template to form the hull plating.

The filter which does not ring cannot be made, and so the use of spline algorithms for smooth motion sometimes results in unintentional overshoots of the picture position. This can be overcome by modifying the filtering algorithm. Spline algorithms usually look ahead beyond the next knot in order to compute the degree of curvature in the graph of the parameter against time. If a break is put in that parameter at a given knot, the spline algorithm is prevented from looking ahead, and no overshoot will occur. In practice the effect is created and run without breaks, and then breaks are added later where they are subjectively thought necessary.

It will be seen that there are several levels of control in an effects machine. At the highest level, the operator can create, store and edit knots, and specify the times which elapse between them. The next level is for the knots to be interpolated by spline algorithms to produce parameters for every field in the effect. The field frequency parameters are then used as the inputs to the geometrical computation of transform parameters which the lowest level of the machine will use as microinstructions to act upon the pixel data. Each of these layers will often have a separate processor, not just for speed, but also to allow software to be updated at certain levels without disturbing others.

4.19 Graphics

Although there is no easy definition of a video graphics system which distinguishes it from a graphic art system, for the purposes of discussion it can be said that graphics consists of generating alphanumerics on the screen, whereas graphic art is concerned with generating more general images.

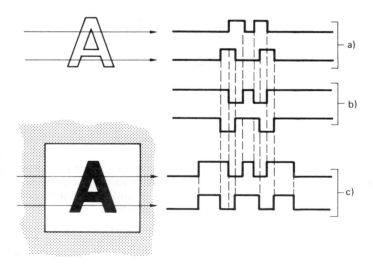

Figure 4.39 Elementary character generation. At (a), white on black waveform for two raster lines passing through letter A. At (b), black on white is simple inversion. At (c), reverse video highlight waveforms

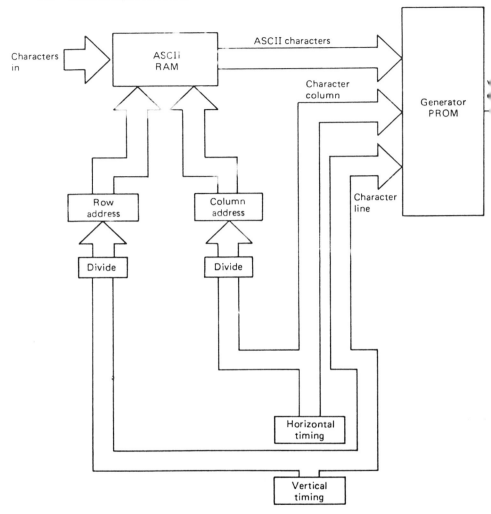

Figure 4.40 Simple character generator produces characters as rows and columns of pixels. See text for details

The simplest form of screen presentation of alphanumerics is the ubiquitous visual display unit (VDU) which is frequently necessary to control computer-based systems. The mechanism used for character generation in such devices is very simple, and thus makes a good introduction to the subject.

In VDUs, there is no grey scale, and the characters are formed by changing the video signal between two levels at the appropriate place in the line. Fig. 4.39 shows how a character is built up in this way, and also illustrates how easy it is to obtain the reversed video used in some word processor displays to simulate dark characters on white paper. Also shown is the method of highlighting single characters or words by using localized reverse video.

Fig. 4.40 is a representative character generator, as might be used in a VDU. The characters to be displayed are stored as ASCII symbols in a RAM, which has one location for each character position on each available text line on the screen. Each character must be used to generate a series of dots on the screen which will extend over several lines. Typically the characters are formed by an array of five dots by nine. In order to convert from the ASCII code to a dot pattern, a ROM is programmed with a conversion. This will be addressed by the ASCII character, and the column and row addresses in the character array, and will output a high or low (bright or dark) output.

As the VDU screen is a raster-scanned device, the display scan will begin at the left-hand end of the top line. The first character in the ASCII RAM will be selected, and this and the first row and column addresses will be sent to the character generator, which outputs the video level for the first pixel. The next column address will then be selected, and the next pixel will be output. As the scan proceeds, it will pass from the top line of the first character to the top line of the second character, so that the ASCII RAM address will need to be incremented. This process continues until the whole video line is completed. The next line on the screen is generated by repeating the selection of characters from the ASCII RAM, but using the second array line as the address to the character generator. This process will repeat until all of the video lines needed to form one row of characters are complete. The next row of characters in the ASCII RAM can then be accessed to create the next line of text on the screen and so on.

The character quality of VDUs is adequate for the application, but is not satisfactory for high-quality broadcast graphics. The characters are monochrome, have a fixed, simple font, fixed size, no grey scale, and the sloping edges of the characters have the usual stepped edges due to the lack of grey scale. This stepping of diagonal edges is sometimes erroneously called aliasing. Since it is not a result of inadequate sampling rate, but a result of quantizing distortion, the use of the term is wholly inappropriate.

In a broadcast graphics unit, the characters will be needed in colour, and in varying size. Different fonts will be necessary, and additional features such as solid lines around characters and drop shadows are desirable. The complexity and cost of the necessary hardware is much greater than in the previous example.

In order to generate a character in a broadcast machine, a font and the character within that font are selected. The characters are actually stored as key signals, because the only difference between one character and another in the

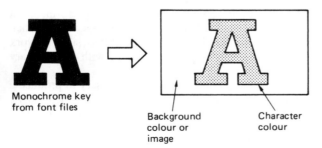

Monochrome key
from font files

Background
colour or
image

Character
colour

Figure 4.41 Font characters only store the shape of the character. This can be used to key any coloured character into a background same font is the shape. A character is generated by specifying a constant background colour and luminance, and a constant character colour and luminance, and using the key signal to cut a hole in the background and insert the character colour. This is illustrated in Fig. 4.41. The problem of stepped diagonal edges is overcome by giving the key signal a grey scale. The grey scale eliminates the quantizing distortion responsible for the stepped edges. The edge of the character now takes the form of a ramp, which has the desirable characteristic of limiting the bandwidth of the character generator output. Early character generators were notorious for producing out-of-band frequencies which drove equipment further down the line to distraction and in some cases would interfere with the sound channel on being broadcast. Fig. 4.42 illustrates how, in a system with grey scale and sloped edges, the edge of a character can be positioned to subpixel resolution, which completely removes the stepped effect on diagonals.

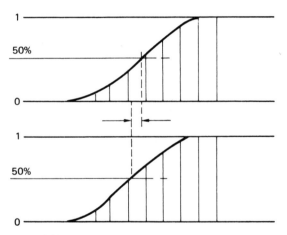

Figure 4.42 When a character has a ramped edge, the edge position can be moved in subpixel steps by changing the pixel values in the ramp

In a powerful system, the number of fonts available will be large, and all of the necessary characters will be stored on disk drives. Some systems allow the user to enter their own fonts using a rostrum camera. A frame grab is performed, but the system can be told to file the image as a font character key signal rather than as a still frame. This approach allows infinite flexibility if it is desired to work in Kanji or Cyrillic, and allows European graphics to be done with all necessary umlauts, tildes and cedillas.

In order to create a character string on the screen, it is necessary to produce a key signal which has been assembled from all of the individual character keys. The keys are usually stored in a large format to give highest quality, and it will be necessary to reduce the size of the characters to fit the available screen area. The size reduction of a key signal in the digital domain is exactly the same as the zoom function of an effects machine, requiring FIR filtering and interpolation, but again, it is not necessary for it to be done in real time, and so less hardware

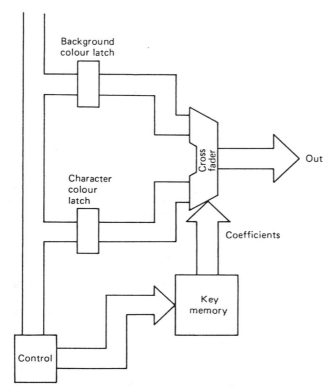

Figure 4.43 Simple character generator using keying. See text for details

can be used. The key source for the generation of the final video output is a RAM which has one location for every screen pixel. The position of the characters on the screen is controlled by changing the addresses in the key RAM into which the size-reduced character keys are written.

The keying system necessary is shown in Fig. 4.43. The character colour and the background colour are produced by latches on the control system bus, which output continuous digital parameters. The grey scale key signal obtained by scanning the key memory is used to provide coefficients for the digital crossfader which cuts between background and character colour to assemble the video signal in real time.

If characters with contrasting edges are required, an extra stage of keying can be used. The steps described above take place, but the background colour is replaced by the desired character edge colour. The size of each character key is then increased slightly, and the new key signal is used to cut the characters and a contrasting border into the final background.

Early character generators were based on a frame store which refreshes the dynamic output video. Recent devices abandon the frame store approach in favour of real-time synthesis.

Fig. 4.44 shows some of the effects which can be achieved. The symbols which make up a word can move on and turn with respect to the plane in which

Independent motion of characters   Text follows irregular outlines

Figure 4.44 The individual characters of a word can be independently controlled, or the entire word can be positioned as a unit in the Alex graphics generator

they reside as a function of time in any way individually or together. Text can also be mapped on to an arbitrarily shaped line. The angle of the characters can follow a tangent to the line, or can remain at a fixed angle regardless of the line angle.

By controlling the size of planes, characters or words can appear to zoom into view from a distance and recede again. Rotation of the character planes off the plane of the screen allows the perspective effects to be seen. Rotating a plane back about a horizontal axis by 90° will reduce it to an edge-on line, but lowering the plane to the bottom of the screen allows the top surface to be seen, receding into the distance like a road. Characters or text strings can then roll off into the distance, getting smaller as they go. In fact the planes do not rotate, but a perspective transform is performed on them.

Since characters can be moved without restriction, it will be possible to make them overlap. Either one can be declared to be at the front, so that it cuts out the other, but if desired the overlapping area can be made a different colour to either of the characters concerned. If this is done with care, the overlapping colour will give the effect of transparency. In fact colour is attributed to characters flexibly so that a character may change colour with respect to time. If this is combined with a movement, the colour will appear to change with position. The background can also be allocated a colour in this way, or the background can be input video. Instead of filling characters with colour on a video background, the characters, or only certain characters, or only the overlapping areas of characters, can be filled with video.

There will be several planes on which characters can move, and these are assigned a priority sequence so that the first one is essentially at the front of the screen and the last one is at the back. Where no character exists, a plane is transparent, and every character on a plane has an 8 bit transparency figure allocated to it. When characters on two different planes are moved until they overlap, the priority system and the transparency parameter decide what will be seen. An opaque front character will obscure any character behind it, whereas using a more transparent parameter will allow a proportion of a character to be seen through one in front of it. Since characters have multibit accuracy, all transparency effects are performed without degradation, and character edges always remain smooth, even at overlaps. Clearly the character planes are not memories or frame stores, because perspective rotation of images held in a frame store in real time in this way would require staggering processing power. Instead, the contents of output fields are computed in real time. Every field is determined individually, so it is scarcely more difficult to animate by making successive fields different.

In a computer a symbol or character exists not as an array of pixels, but as an outline, rather as if a thin wire frame had been made to fit the edge of the symbol. The wire frame is described by a set of mathematical expressions. The operator positions the wire frame in space, and turns it to any angle. The computer then calculates what the wire frame will look like from the viewing position. Effectively the shape of the frame is projected onto a surface which will become the TV screen. The principle is shown in Fig. 4.45, and will be seen to be another example of mapping. If drop or plane shadows are being used, a further projection takes place which determines how the shadow of the wire frame would fall on a second plane. The only difference here between drop and plane shadows is the angle of the plane the shadow falls on. If it is parallel to the symbol frame, the result is a drop shadow. If it is at right angles, the result is a plane shadow.

Figure 4.45 Perspective effects results from mapping or projecting the character outline on to a plane which represents the screen

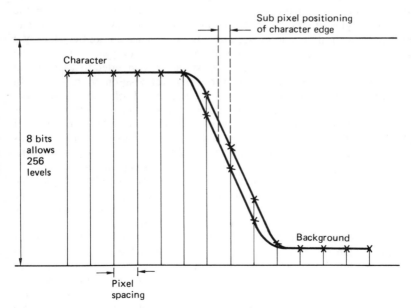

Figure 4.46 The 8 bit resolution of pixels allows the edge of characters to be placed accurately independent of the sampling points. This offers smooth character edges

Since the wire frame can be described by a minimum amount of data, the geometrical calculations needed to project onto the screen and shadow planes are quick, and are repeated for every symbol. This process also reveals where overlaps occur within a plane, since the projected frames will cross each other. This computation takes place for all planes. The positions of the symbol edges are then converted to a pixel array in a field-interlaced raster scan. Because the symbols are described by 8 bit pixels, edges can be positioned to subpixel accuracy. An example is shown in Fig. 4.46. The pixel sequence is now effectively a digital key signal, and the priority and transparency parameters are now used to reduce the amplitude of a given key when it is behind a symbol on a plane of higher priority which has less than 100% transparency.

The key signals then pass to a device known as the filler which is a fast digital mixer which has as inputs the colour of each character, and the background, whether colour or video. On a pixel-by-pixel basis, the filler crossfades between different colours as the video line proceeds. The crossfading is controlled by the key signals. The output is three data streams: red, green and blue. The output board takes the data and converts them to the video standard needed, and the result can then be seen.

4.20 Graphic art/paint systems

In graphic art systems, there is a requirement for disk storage of the generated images, and some art machines incorporate a still store unit, whereas others can be connected to a separate one by an interface. Disk-based stores are discussed in Chapter 10. The essence of an art system is that an artist can draw images which become a video signal directly with no intermediate paper and paint. Central to the operation of most art systems is a digitizing tablet, which is a flat surface over which the operator draws a stylus. The tablet can establish the position of the stylus in vertical and horizontal axes. One way in which this can be done is to launch ultrasonic pulses down the tablet, which are detected by a transducer in the stylus. The time taken to receive the pulse is proportional to the distance to the stylus. The coordinates of the stylus are converted to addresses in the frame store which correspond to the same physical position on the screen. In order to make a simple sketch, the operator specifies a background parameter, perhaps white, which would be loaded into every location in the frame store. A different parameter is then written into every location addressed by movement of the stylus, which results in a line drawing on the screen. The art world uses pens and brushes of different shapes and sizes to obtain a variety of effects, one common example being the rectangular pen nib where the width of the resulting line depends on the angle at which the pen is moved. This can be simulated on art systems, because the address derived from the tablet is processed to produce a range of addresses within a certain screen distance of the stylus. If all of these locations are updated as the stylus moves, a broad stroke results.

If the address range is larger in the horizontal axis than in the vertical axis, for example, the width of the stroke will be a function of the direction of stylus travel. Some systems have a sprung tip on the stylus which connects to a force transducer, so that the system can measure the pressure the operator uses. By making the address range a function of pressure, broader strokes can be obtained simply by pressing harder. In order to simulate a set of colours available on a palette, the operator can select a mode where small areas of each colour are displayed in boxes on the monitor screen. The desired colour is selected by moving a screen cursor over the box using the tablet. The parameter to be written into selected locations in the frame RAM now reflects the chosen colour. In more advanced systems, simulation of airbrushing is possible. In this technique, the transparency of the stroke is great at the edge, where the background can be seen showing through, but transparency reduces to the centre of the stroke. A read–modify–write process is necessary in the frame memory, where background values are read, mixed with paint values with the appropriate transparency, and written back. The position of the stylus effectively determines the centre of a two-dimensional transparency contour, which is convolved with the memory contents as the stylus moves.

4.21 Conventional standards conversion

The interchange of video program material between line standards has been necessary because of the unfortunate number of different broadcast standards in use throughout the world. This section considers conventional standards converters which interpolate along the time axis. Motion-compensated standards conversion is treated later.

Frame- or field-based systems sample the changes of the image with respect to time. The input scene should not then change more often than one cycle per two samples, or aliasing will take place. In practice the camera has no control over the scene, and aliasing is inevitable on fast-moving objects such as helicopter rotors and stagecoach wheels, and for less obvious reasons on slow-moving fine detail. Temporal frequencies due to motion are discussed in Section 4.24.

As was explained in Chapter 3, once a sampled system has aliased, the effects can never be removed, because the alias frequencies cannot be distinguished from genuine information at the same frequency. Conventional standards converters have great difficulty with aliased signals, hence the development of motion compensation.

The bandwidth required by a television signal is obtained by multiplying the number of cycles of resolution in a line by the number of lines in a frame, and then by the frame rate. If similar vertical and horizontal resolution is assumed, bandwidth increases as the square of the resolution for a given frame rate. The adoption of interlace was claimed to allow the apparent picture rate to be higher than the frame rate. The apparent picture rate, or field rate, determines the visibility of flicker. With interlace, sending half the picture twice as often allows the bandwidth to be halved without producing flicker. Since only half of the necessary information is sent, information theory alone will tell us not to expect great things. Interlace is a form of temporal oversampling at the expense of spatial resolution. The presence of interlace makes standards conversion doubly difficult.

Fig. 4.47 shows that a television signal in a certain line standard represents a series of two-dimensional images. A different line standard could have a different number of lines and a different number of frames per second. For colour broadcasts, the modulation method used to carry the colour information could also be different. The task of the standards converter is to transfer the moving image from one signal structure to the other as faithfully as possible.

Conversion from one colour modulation system to another is relatively easy. Another happy chance is that the line periods of 525 and 625 line systems are so

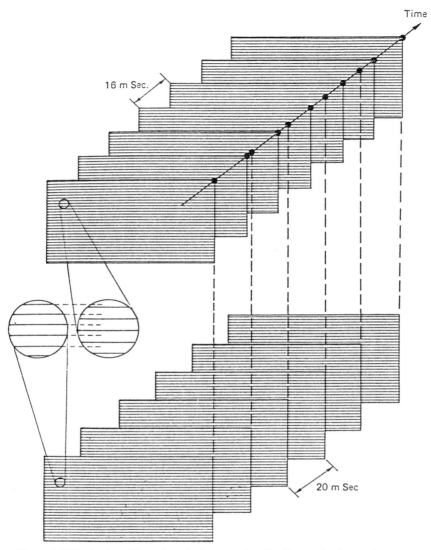

Figure 4.47 The basic problem of standards conversion. The line spacing is easy to accommodate. The field spacing is not

similar that they can be assumed identical. Conversion between different numbers of lines per frame in progressive scan is relatively straightforward, but interlace makes this and conversion between different frame rates very difficult.

The handling of colour information in standards conversion is generally to decode the composite input to form separate luminance and colour difference signal channels. These are then passed to three similar baseband standards converters, although the performance of the colour difference channels would not need to be so high. Following the conversion, the output signals would then be re-encoded into the appropriate composite form if required. This approach is necessary because the transforms needed for spatial and temporal interpolation of the image would destroy the phase and thus the meaning of any subcarrier. The decoding can be considered separately from the conversion process. As there are many different types of colour modulation methods, a multistandard converter will necessarily be complex. The colour decoding and encoding techniques may be analog or digital, and the digital techniques have already been discussed in this chapter. As the composite decoding takes place prior to the standards

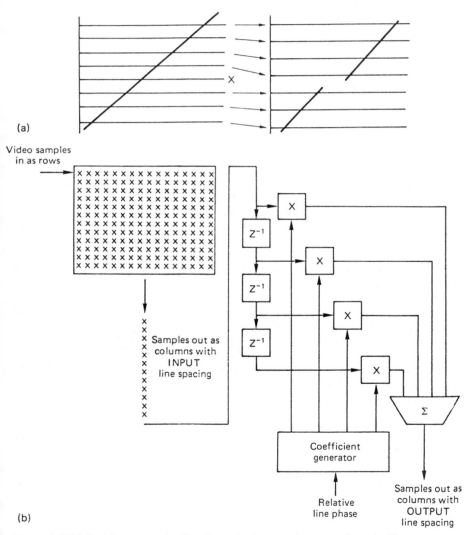

Figure 4.48 (a) Omitting or repeating lines in standards conversion causes discontinuities on diagonal detail. (b) The conversion of line spacing is by vertical FIR filtering on columns of pixels

conversion proper, it is relatively straightforward to insert a digital signal according to CCIR-601 which bypasses the composite decoder and the analog-to-digital converters. It is also feasible to incorporate the composite digital to 4:2:2 decoder described earlier in this chapter to allow the input section to be entirely digital. The digital output of the standards conversion process could then be output according to CCIR-601, but in the alternative line standard. Clearly in this case the internal sampling rate of the machine will need to be 13.5 MHz.

The line period of 625/50 is almost identical to that of 525/60, and the consequence of assuming them to be exactly the same is a minute change of horizontal magnification which can be neglected. The number of lines in a field must be changed, and the number of fields per second must be changed. These processes can be consecutive or simultaneous. The latter may yield hardware economies, the former is easier to visualize, and so the explanation will begin with that approach.

In order to change the number of lines in a field, interpolation is necessary in a vertical direction. The difference in line spacing between PAL and NTSC is such that there are 21 different relationships between the lines. It is not possible to throw away lines or repeat lines, as this results in steps on diagonal edges, as shown in Fig. 4.48. The figure also shows that columns of pixels are fed to a digital filter which has a low-pass response cutting off at the vertical spatial frequency of half the line spatial frequency. The necessary phase-linear characteristic is supplied by using the FIR (Finite-Impulse Response) structure which has been described. Because there are many different line relationships, a different set of coefficients corresponding to a different offset of the impulse is necessary for each phase of interpolation.

In a standards converter, the magnification is fixed by the relationship between the number of active lines in the two standards. Production of the best resolution requires a de-interlaced frame as input but it is not always necessary to de-interlace the incoming fields separately prior to filtering. Fig. 4.49 shows that it is possible to supply alternate points in the FIR filter from columns of pixels in alternate fields. In this case the vertical frequency of the input is doubled, and the impulse response of the filter is sharpened in order to obtain maximum vertical resolution. Unfortunately the presence of movement in the images means that if successive fields are superimposed a double image results. It is necessary to use motion detection by comparing successive frames as has been described. When there is motion in the area of the picture being processed, the pixels from the field farthest away in time are neglected by setting the coefficients fed to every other filter point to zero. The impulse response of the filter must also be broadened to account for the lack of resolution on the input. The coefficient store will thus have a two-dimensional structure, where one dimension is the repeating vertical phase relationship of the lines and the other is the amount of motion detected.[10]

As has been noted, the conversion of field rate is difficult. Fig. 4.50 shows that it is not possible to omit or repeat frames because this results in jerky movement. It is again necessary to interpolate, this time temporally. In temporal interpolation, pixels from the same physical position in several frames form the input to an FIR filter which computes what the pixel value in between frames would have been. The temporal frequency response of the filter must be one-half of the frame rate of the slower standard. Ideally the filter should have a frequency response which is flat, and then falls steeply at the cut-off frequency. In FIR

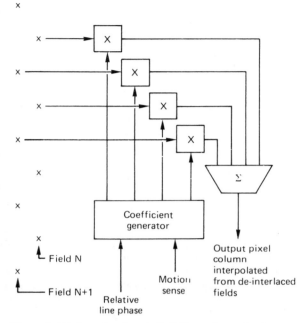

Figure 4.49 Information from both fields can be used to improve vertical resolution when there is little motion. When motion occurs, the filter impulse response must broaden, as samples from one of the fields will be neglected, and vertical resolution falls

Figure 4.50 At (a) a rectangular object is moving smoothly to the right, and seven superimposed fields are shown in the frame in a 60 Hz system. If an attempt is made to convert to 50 Hz by omitting fields, as at (b), there will be jerky movement where the image moves a greater distance due to the omission. This is subjectively highly disturbing

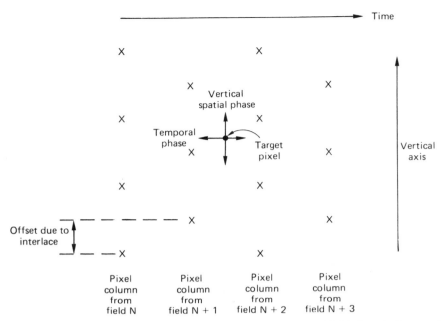

Figure 4.51(a) In a two-dimensional digital filter, columns from several fields form the input, and the target pixel phase vertically and temporally controls the coefficients. The structure of the filter is exactly that of an FIR filter, only the sources of information cause the two-dimensional effect

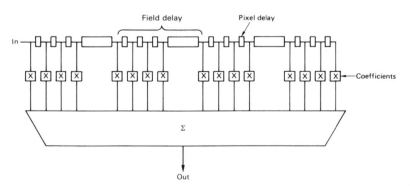

Figure 4.51(b) Rearrangement of 2-D FIR filter into temporal domain illustrates how the impulse response spreads over many fields because of the low temporal frequency response of television systems. Note that input is pixel columns

filters this ideal can only be realized with a large number of filter points, and it must be appreciated that for every point in the filter, there must be a field of video stored in the machine, and an additional fast multiplier. Even the use of four fields, which is increasingly common, is less than perfect, because an FIR filter with such a small number of points must compromise between the conflicting requirements of stopband rejection and rate of roll-off. As the filter is designed to suppress the unwanted field rate in the information spectrum, stopband rejection is important. The symptom of insufficient stopband rejection would be beats between the two field rates modulating the brightness. Since this is highly objectionable, the rate of roll-off is generally sacrificed instead, which means that the temporal frequency response of the converter is impaired.

The use of separate processes for vertical and temporal filtering requires more hardware, such as a further memory to buffer the two processes. It is usual to combine both processes into one, and construct a two-dimensional digital filter. In the analog domain, such a device would be unthinkable; in the digital domain it is much easier to construct than to describe.

Fig. 4.51 shows that the input to a two-dimensional filter can be considered to be pixels in columns whose height represents distance up the tube face, spaced apart by the period between fields. Owing to interlace, the pixels in odd fields have a vertical displacement relative to the pixels in even fields. Assuming a typical value of four filter points in each dimension, four pixels from four fields are combined to produce one output pixel by providing each input pixel with a coefficient by which it is multiplied before adding the products. The output pixel will have a temporal and spatial phase which determines what the coefficients must be.

Fig. 4.52 shows that if the temporal impulse response is considered first, an interpolated pixel value is obtained by computing the time at which the pixel is needed in relation to the time of available fields. In NTSC to PAL conversion, input spacing will be 16.7 milliseconds and output spacing will be 20 milliseconds. The time determines the filter phase, which has the effect of shifting the impulse response of the filter through time to allow a greater contribution from near fields and a smaller contribution from far fields.

The vertical phase of the desired pixel in relation to the available pixels will then determine the vertical phase of the filter. The sum of the four coefficients used in a given field column will equal the (imaginary) coefficient of a one-dimensional temporal filter at that field.

Where the difference between successive frames is very small, this can be assumed to be due to random noise, and broadening the impulse response has the effect of reducing the noise.

It is not practicable to optimize the action of such a device for all material, because good performance on noisy inputs may result in unnatural removal of rain and reflections on water in normal video inputs. It is usual to provide an operator control so that the motion sensing can be made more or less active according to the subject matter.

Where the difference between pixels in successive frames is large, this must be due to motion, and it will be necessary to modify the two-dimensional impulse response to prevent multiple images. Essentially what happens is that the coefficients for fields which contain movement are reduced, so their contribution to the output pixel becomes smaller, and the coefficients fed to remaining fields increase to compensate.

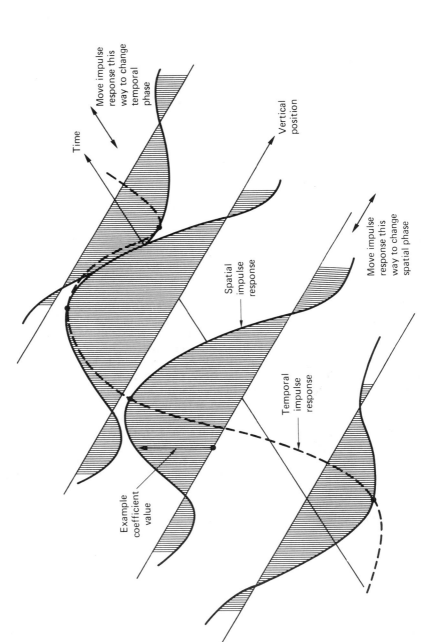

Figure 4.52 Two-dimensional impulse response. See text for details

4.22 The Fourier transform

The Fourier transform is a processing technique which analyses signals changing with respect to time or distance and expresses them in the form of a temporal or spatial spectrum. Any waveform can be broken down into frequency components. Fig. 4.53 shows that if the amplitude and phase of each frequency component is known, linearly adding the resultant components in an inverse transform results in the original waveform.

The Fourier transform may be performed on a continuous analog waveform, in which case a continuous spectrum results. However, in digital systems the waveform is expressed as a number of discrete samples. As a result the Fourier transform analyses the signal into an equal number of discrete frequencies. This is known as a discrete Fourier transform or DFT. The fast Fourier transform is no more than an efficient way of computing the DFT.[11]

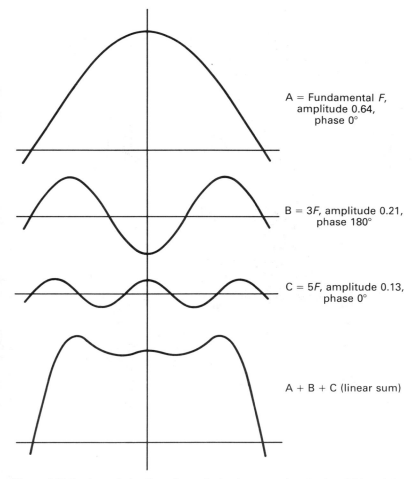

A = Fundamental F, amplitude 0.64, phase 0°

B = 3F, amplitude 0.21, phase 180°

C = 5F, amplitude 0.13, phase 0°

A + B + C (linear sum)

Figure 4.53 Fourier analysis allows the synthesis of any waveform by the addition of discrete frequencies of appropriate amplitude and phase

It will be evident from Fig. 4.53 that knowledge of the phase of the frequency component is vital, as changing the phase of any component will seriously alter the reconstructed waveform. Thus the DFT must accurately analyse the phase of the signal components.

There are a number of ways of expressing phase. Fig. 4.54 shows a point which is rotating about a fixed axis at constant speed. Looked at from the side, the point oscillates up and down at constant frequency. The waveform of that motion is a sine wave, and that is what we would see if the rotating point were to translate along its axis whilst we continued to look from the side.

One way of defining the phase of a waveform is to specify the angle through which the point has rotated at time zero ($T=0$). If a second point is made to revolve at 90° to the first, it would produce a cosine wave when translated. It is

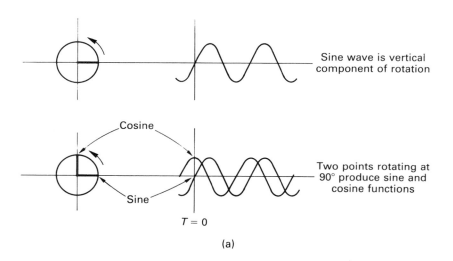

Sine wave is vertical component of rotation

Two points rotating at 90° produce sine and cosine functions

$T = 0$

(a)

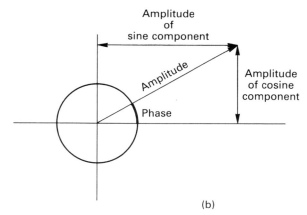

Amplitude of sine component

Amplitude

Amplitude of cosine component

Phase

(b)

Figure 4.54 The origin of sine and cosine waves is to take a particular viewpoint of a rotation. Any phase can be synthesized by adding proportions of sine and cosine waves possible to produce a waveform having arbitrary phase by adding together the sine and cosine waves in various proportions and polarities. For example, adding the sine and cosine waves in equal proportion results in a waveform lagging the sine wave by 45°.

Fig. 4.54 shows that the proportions necessary are respectively the sine and the cosine of the phase angle. Thus the two methods of describing phase can be readily interchanged.

The discrete Fourier transform spectrum-analyses a block of samples by searching separately for each discrete target frequency. It does this by multiplying the input waveform by a sine wave having the target frequency and adding up or integrating the products. Fig. 4.55(a) shows that multiplying by the

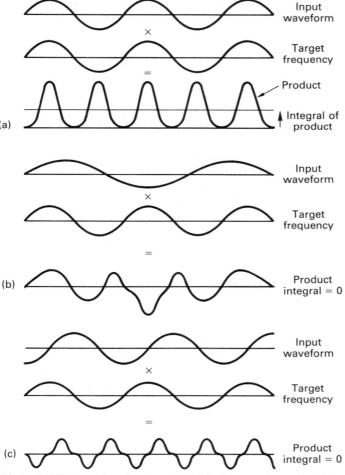

Figure 4.55 The input waveform is multiplied by the target frequency and the result is averaged or integrated. At (a) the target frequency is present and a large integral results. With another input frequency the integral is zero as at (b). The correct frequency will also result in a zero integral shown at (c) if it is at 90° to the phase of the search frequency. This is overcome by making two searches in quadrature

target frequency gives a non-zero integral when the input frequency is the same, whereas Fig. 4.55(b) shows that with a different input frequency (in fact all other different frequencies) the integral is zero showing that no component of the target frequency exists. Thus from a real waveform containing many frequencies, all frequencies except the target frequency are excluded. The magnitude of the integral is proportional to the amplitude of the target component.

Fig. 4.55(c) shows that the target frequency will not be detected if it is phase shifted 90° as the product of quadrature waveforms is always zero. Thus the

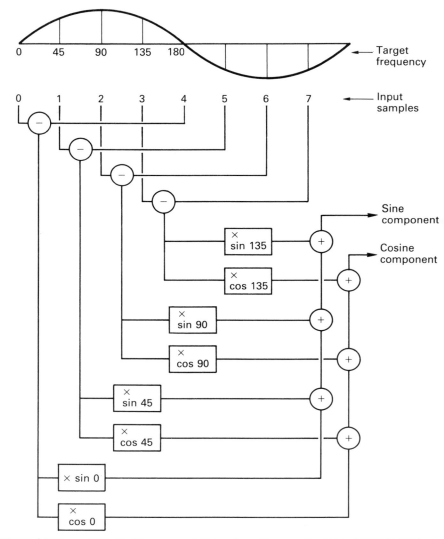

Figure 4.56 An example of a filtering search. Pairs of samples are subtracted and multiplied by sampled sine and cosine waves. The products are added to give the sine and cosine components of the search frequency

discrete Fourier transform must make a further search for the target frequency using a cosine wave. It follows from the arguments above that the relative proportions of the sine and cosine integrals reveal the phase of the input component. Thus each discrete frequency in the spectrum must be the result of a pair of quadrature searches.

Searching for one frequency at a time as above will result in a DFT, but only after considerable computation. However, a lot of the calculations are repeated many times over in different searches. The fast Fourier transform gives the same result with less computation by logically gathering together all of the places where the same calculation is needed and making the calculation once.

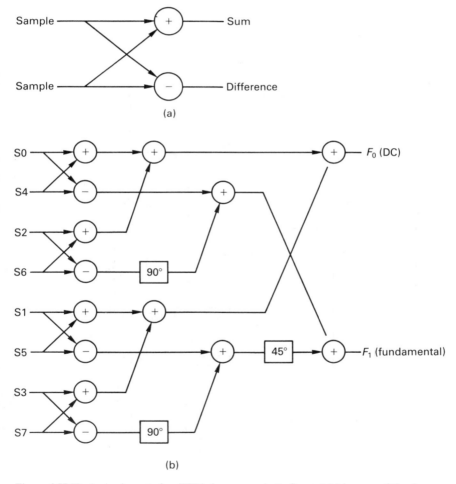

Figure 4.57 The basic element of an FFT is known as a butterfly as at (a) because of the shape of the signal paths in a sum and difference system. The use of butterflies to compute the first two coefficients is shown in (b). An actual example is given in (c) which should be compared with the result of (d) with a quadrature input. At (e) the butterflies for the first two coefficients form the basis of the computation of the third coefficient

The amount of computation can be reduced by performing the sine and cosine component searches together. Another saving is obtained by noting that every 180° the sine and cosine have the same magnitude but are simply inverted in sign. Instead of performing four multiplications on two samples 180° apart and adding the pairs of products, it is more economical to subtract the sample values and multiply twice, once by a sine value and once by a cosine value.

The first coefficient is the geometric mean which is the sum of all of the sample values in the block divided by the number of samples. Fig. 4.56 shows how the search for the lowest frequency in a block is performed. Pairs of samples are subtracted as shown, and each difference is then multiplied by the sine and the cosine of the search frequency. The process shifts one sample period, and a new sample pair are subtracted and multiplied by new sine and cosine factors.

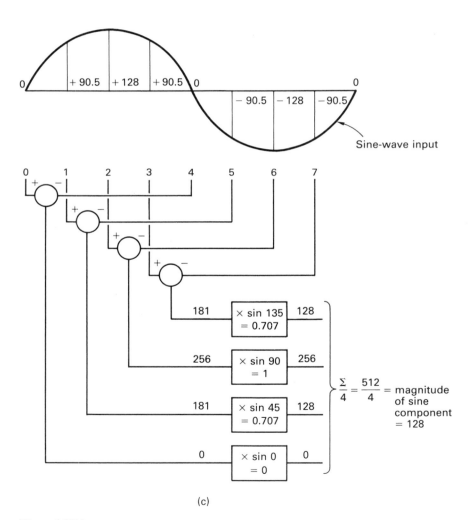

(c)

Figure 4.57(c)

This is repeated until all of the sample pairs have been multiplied. The sine and cosine products are then added to give the value of the sine and cosine coefficients respectively.

It is possible to combine the calculation of the DC component which requires the sum of samples and the calculation of the fundamental which requires sample differences by combining the stages shown in Fig. 4.57(a) which take a pair of samples and add and subtract them. Such a stage is called a butterfly because of the shape of the schematic. Fig. 4.57(b) shows how the first two components are calculated. The phase rotation boxes attribute the input to the sine or cosine component outputs according to the phase angle. As shown the box labelled 90° attributes nothing to the sine output, but unity gain to the cosine output. The 45° box attributes the input equally to both components.

(d)

Figure 4.57 (d)

Fig. 4.57(c) shows a numerical example. If a sine-wave input is considered where 0° coincides with the first sample, this will produce a zero sine coefficient and a non-zero cosine coefficient. Fig. 4.57(d) shows the same input waveform shifted by 90°. Note how the coefficients change over.

Fig. 4.57(e) shows how the next frequency coefficient is computed. Note that exactly the same first-stage butterfly outputs are used, reducing the computation needed.

A similar process may be followed to obtain the sine and cosine coefficients of the remaining frequencies. The full FFT diagram is shown in Fig. 4.58(a). The spectrum this calculates is shown in Fig. 4.58(b). Note that only half of the coefficients are useful in a real band-limited system because the remaining coefficients represent frequencies above one-half of the sampling rate.

The number of frequency coefficients resulting from a DFT is equal to the number of input samples. In the case of digital video, if the input consists of a larger number of samples it must cover a larger area of the screen, but its spectrum will be known more finely. Thus a fundamental characteristic of such transforms is that the more accurately the frequency and phase of a waveform is analysed, the less is known about where such frequencies exist on the screen axis.

(e)

Figure 4.57 (e)

(a)

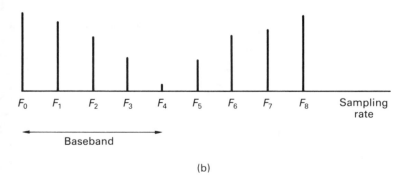

(b)

Figure 4.58 At (a) is the full butterfly diagram for an FFT. The spectrum this computes is shown at (b)

The FFT is used extensively in such applications as phase correlation, where the accuracy with which the phase of signal components can be analysed is essential.

4.23 The discrete cosine transform (DCT)

The DCT is a special case of a discrete Fourier transform in which the sine components of the coefficients have been eliminated leaving a single number. This is actually quite easy. Fig. 4.59(a) shows the input samples to a transform process. By repeating the samples in a time-reversed order and performing a discrete Fourier transform on the double-length sample set a DCT is obtained. The effect of mirroring the input waveform is to turn it into an even function whose sine coefficients are all zero. The result can be understood by considering the effect of individually transforming the input block and the reversed block. Fig. 4.59(b) shows that the phase of all the components of one block is in the

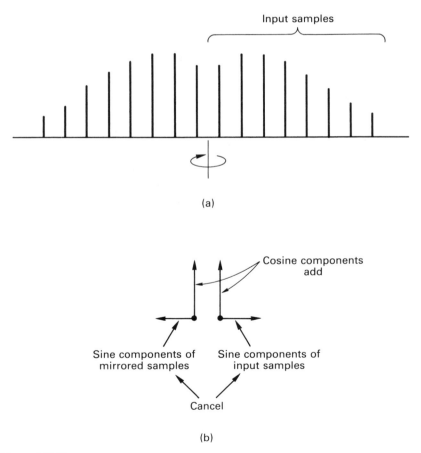

Input samples

(a)

Cosine components add

Sine components of mirrored samples

Sine components of input samples

Cancel

(b)

Figure 4.59 The DCT is obtained by mirroring the input block as shown at (a) prior to an FFT. The mirroring cancels out the sine components as at (b), leaving only cosine coefficients

Figure 4.60 The discrete cosine transform breaks up an image area into discrete frequencies in two dimensions. The lowest frequency can be seen here at the top left corner. Horizontal frequency increases to the right and vertical frequency increases downwards

opposite sense to those in the other. This means that when the components are added to give the transform of the double-length block all of the sine components cancel out, leaving only the cosine coefficients; hence the name of the transform.[12] In practice the sine component calculation is eliminated. Another advantage is that doubling the block length by mirroring doubles the frequency resolution, so that twice as many useful coefficients are produced. In fact a DCT produces as many useful coefficients as input samples.

For image processing two-dimensional transforms are needed. In this case for every horizontal frequency, a search is made for all possible vertical frequencies. A two-dimensional DCT is shown in Fig. 4.60. The DCT is separable (see Section 4.12) in that the two-dimensional DCT can be obtained by computing in each dimension separately. Fast DCT algorithms are available.[13]

The DCT is primarily used in data reduction processing. The DCT itself does not result in any reduction, as there are as many coefficients as samples, but it converts the input video into a form where redundancy can be easily detected and removed.

4.24 Motion and resolution

The human eye resembles a CCD camera in that the retina is covered with a large number of discrete sensors which are used to build up an image. The spacing between the sensors has a similar effect on the resolution of the eye to the number of pixels in a CCD chip. However, the eye acts to a degree as if it were AC coupled so that its response to low spatial frequencies (the average brightness of a scene) falls.

The eye also has a temporal response taking the form of a lag known as persistence of vision. The effect of the lag is that resolution is lost in areas where the image is moving rapidly with respect to the retina. Fig. 4.61 shows the response of the eye in two dimensions: temporal frequency and spatial frequency. The response falls off quite rapidly with temporal frequency, a phenomenon known as motion blur.[14]

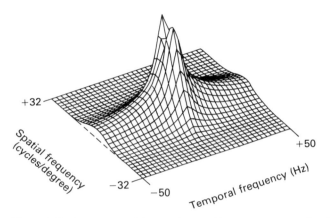

Figure 4.61 The response of the eye shown with respect to temporal and spatial frequencies. Note that even slow relative movement causes a serious loss of resolution. The eye tracks moving objects to prevent this loss

Thus a fixed eye has poor resolution of moving objects but we are not generally aware of this because the eye can move to follow objects of interest. Fig. 4.62 shows the difference this makes. At (a) a detailed object moves past a fixed eye. It does not have to move very fast before the temporal frequency at a fixed point on the retina rises beyond the temporal response of the eye and there is motion blur. At (b) the eye is following the moving object and as a result the temporal frequency at a fixed point on the retina is DC; the full resolution is then available because the image is stationary with respect to the eye. In real life we can see moving objects in some detail unless they move faster than the eye can follow.

Exceptions are in the case of irregular motion which the eye cannot track or rotational motion; the eyeball cannot rotate on the optical axis!

Similar processes occur when watching television. Television viewing is affected both by the motion of the original scene with respect to the camera and by the motion of the eye with respect to the display. The situation is further complicated by the fact that television pictures are not continuous, but are sampled at the field rate.

According to sampling theory, a sampling system cannot properly convey frequencies beyond half the sampling rate. If the sampling rate is considered to be the field rate, then no temporal frequency of more than 25 or 30 Hz can be

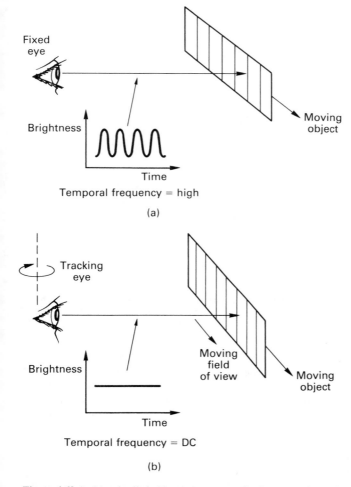

Fixed
eye

Moving
object

Brightness

Time

Temporal frequency = high

(a)

Tracking
eye

Moving
field
of view

Moving
object

Brightness

Time

Temporal frequency = DC

(b)

Figure 4.62 At (a) a detailed object moves past a fixed eye, causing temporal frequencies beyond the response of the eye. This is the cause of motion blur. At (b) the eye tracks the motion and the temporal frequency becomes zero. Motion blur cannot then occur

handled (12 Hz for film). With a stationary camera and scene, temporal frequencies can only result from the brightness of lighting changing, but this will not approach the limit. However, when there is relative movement between camera and scene, detailed areas develop high temporal frequencies, just as was shown in Fig. 4.62 for the eye. This is because relative motion results in a given point on the camera sensor effectively scanning across the scene. The temporal frequencies generated are beyond the limit set by sampling theory, and aliasing should take place.

However, when the resultant pictures are viewed by a human eye, this aliasing is not perceived because, once more, the eye attempts to follow the motion of the scene.[15]

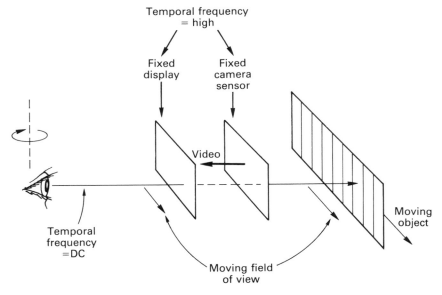

Figure 4.63 An object moves past a camera, and is tracked on a monitor by the eye. The high temporal frequencies cause aliasing in the TV signal, but these are not perceived by the tracking eye as this reduces the temporal frequency to zero. Compare with Fig. 4.62

Fig. 4.63 shows what happens when the eye follows correctly. The original scene and the retina are now stationary with respect to one another, but the camera sensor and display are both moving through the field of view. As a result the temporal frequency at the eye due to the object being followed is brought to zero and no aliasing is perceived by the viewer due to the field-rate sampling.

Whilst the result is highly desirable, we have not actually circumvented sampling theory, because the effect only works if several assumptions are made, including the requirement for the motion to be smooth.

The viewer's impression is not quite the same as if the scene were being viewed through a piece of moving glass, because of the movement of the image relative to the camera sensor and the display. Here, temporal frequencies do exist, and the temporal aperture effect (lag) of both will reduce perceived resolution. This is the reason that shutters are sometimes fitted to CCD cameras used at sporting events. The mechanically rotating shutter allows light onto the CCD sensor for only part of the field period thereby reducing the temporal aperture. The result is obvious from conventional photography in which one naturally uses a short exposure for moving subjects. The shuttered CCD camera effectively has an exposure control.

On the other hand a tube camera displays considerable lag and will not perform as well under these circumstances.

4.25 Motion compensation

The way in which eye tracking avoids aliasing is fundamental to the perceived quality of television pictures. Many processes need to manipulate moving images in the same way in order to avoid the obvious difficulty of processing with respect to a fixed frame of reference. Processes of this kind are referred to as *motion compensated* and rely on a quite separate process which has measured the motion. Motion estimation is literally a process which analyses successive fields and determines how objects move from one to the next. It is an important enabling technology because of the way it parallels the action of the human eye.

In order to see why motion compensation is essential for certain processes, it is necessary to consider the way in which various image-forming systems handle motion. This can be done by showing the position of successive images on the time axis. In fact there is considerable variety in the way in which the time axis is handled, and this leads to some potential incompatibilities.

Fig. 4.64(a) shows the simplest time axis, that of film, where entire frames are simultaneously exposed, or sampled, at typically 24 Hz. The result is that the image is effectively at right angles to the time axis. During filming, some of the frame period is required to transport the film, and the shutter is closed whilst this

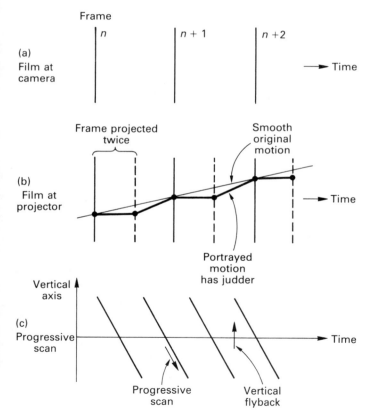

Figure 4.64 (a) The spatio-temporal characteristic of film. Note that each frame is repeated twice on projection. (b) The frame repeating results in motion judder as shown here. (c) The spatio-temporal characteristic of progressive scan TV. Note the characteristic tilt of the image planes.

takes place. The temporal aperture or exposure is thus somewhat shorter than the frame period.

When displayed, each frame of a film is generally projected twice to produce a flicker frequency of 48 Hz. The result with a moving object is that the motion is not properly portrayed and there is judder. Fig. 4.64(b) shows the origin of the judder.

Figure 4.64 (d) The result of interlaced scan. (e) Displaying sampled CCD images on a scanned CRT results in distortion in the presence of motion

Fig. 4.64(c) shows the time axis of progressive scan television cameras (i.e. tube cameras) and CRT displays. The vertical scan takes a substantial part of the frame period and so the image is tilted with respect to the time axis. As both camera and display have the same tilt, the tilt has no effect on motion portrayal.

Fig. 4.64(d) shows the time axis of interlaced progressive scan cameras and displays. The vertical scan is twice as fast and so the tilt is now over a field period. Again as camera and CRT display have the same tilt, the tilt does not affect motion portrayal.

In CCD cameras, the image is sampled at once, like film, and thus the fields are at right angles to the time axis. If displayed on a scanning CRT, the time axis is distorted such that things are displayed later than they should be towards the bottom of the screen. Transversely moving objects have speed-dependent sloping verticals, as shown in Fig. 4.64(e).

The same effect is evident if film is displayed on a CRT via telecine. The film frames are sampled, but the CRT is scanned. In telecine each frame results in two fields in 50 Hz standards and this will result in judder as well. In 60 Hz telecine odd frames result in two fields, even frames result in three fields; the well known 3:2 pulldown. Motion portrayal (or lack of it) in this case is shown in Fig. 4.65. Thus to be pedantic, CCD cameras to some extent and telecines to a great extent are not compatible with scanning (CRT) displays.

The operation of a standards converter can be followed by considering the location of input and output fields on the time axis in the same way as above. The conventional four-field converters shown in Section 4.21 interpolate through time, using pixel data from four input fields in order to compute the likely values of pixels in an intermediate output field. This large temporal aperture is required

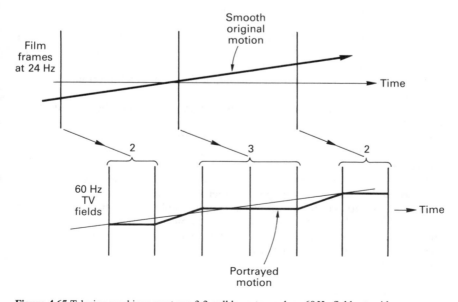

Figure 4.65 Telecine machines must use 3:2 pulldown to produce 60 Hz field rate video

(a)   Fixed camera   (b)   Panning camera

Figure 4.66 (a) Conventional four-field converter with moving object suffers multiple images. (b) If the moving object is panned, the judder moves to the background

to eliminate beat frequencies between the two field rates, but it does not handle motion transparently.

Fig. 4.66(a) shows that if an object is moving, it will be in a different place in successive fields. Interpolating between several fields results in multiple images of the object. The position of the dominant image will not move smoothly, an effect which is perceived as judder. If, however, the camera is panning the moving object, it will be in much the same place in successive fields and Fig. 4.66(b) shows that it will be the background which judders.

This can be overcome by using motion compensation, which can be followed by considering what happens in the spatio-temporal volume. A conventional standards converter interpolates only along the time axis, whereas a motion-compensated standards converter can swivel its interpolation axis off the time axis. Fig. 4.67(a) shows the input fields in which an object is moving. At (b) it will be seen that the interpolation axis is aligned with the trajectory of the moving object.

This has a dramatic effect. An object no longer moves with respect to its own interpolation axis, and so on that axis it no longer generates temporal frequencies due to motion and temporal aliasing cannot occur. Interpolation along the correct axes will then result in a sequence of output fields in which motion is properly portrayed.

Motion compensation is a significant enabling technology because it can be applied to much more than standards conversion. Some examples of motion-compensated processes follow by way of an introduction to the subject.

Noise reduction in video signals works by combining together successive frames on the time axis such that the image content of the signal reinforces strongly whereas the random element in the signal due to noise does not. The noise reduction increases with the number of frames over which the noise is integrated, but image motion prevents simple combining of frames. If motion estimation is available, the image of a moving object in a particular frame can be integrated from the images in several frames which have been superimposed on the same part of the screen by displacements derived from the motion measurement. The result is that greater reduction of noise becomes possible.

In conventional TV displays, the marginal field rates result in flicker. If the rate at which the display is refreshed is, for example, doubled by interpolating extra fields between those in the input signal, the flicker can be eliminated. This

Figure 4.67 (a) Input fields with moving object. (b) Moving the interpolation axis to make it parallel to the trajectory of the object

oversampling technique is a simplified form of standards conversion which requires interpolation on the time axis. Motion compensation is necessary for the same reasons as it is in standards conversion.

Video data reduction relies on removing redundancy from the source signal. Whilst redundancy can be removed from individual images, it will be seen that higher compression factors are only achieved by eliminating data which are common in successive images, so that only data which are different need to be sent. Motion causes the image to move with respect to the sampling grid, causing all the sample values in a moving area to change and preventing effective reduction. With motion estimation the image movement can be cancelled because the comparison can be made along the motion axis rather than the time axis. Greater reduction factors are then possible because it is then only necessary to send the motion parameters and a small number of genuine image differences.

Hierarchical data reduction schemes have been proposed where a picture of different resolution can be decoded from a common data stream according to the available display technology. Subsampling of images is quite easy in progressive scan systems, but where interlace is used, the computation of a half-sized image becomes impossible unless motion compensation is used to cancel interfield movement from the filtering process.

Telecine machines use a medium which has no interlace and in which the entire image is sampled at one instant. Video is displayed with progressive scan and interlace and so there is a considerable disparity between the way the time axis is handled in the two formats. As a result judder on moving parts of the image is inevitable with a direct scanning telecine, particularly when 3:2 pulldown is used to obtain 60 Hz field rate. Proper telecine transfer actually requires a standards conversion process in the time axis which can only be done properly with motion compensation. The result is a reduction in judder.

It will be seen in Chapter 8 that in VTRs which are playing back at other than the correct speed, fields are conventionally repeated or omitted to keep the output field rate correct. This results in judder on moving objects, particularly in slow motion. A dramatic improvement in the slow-motion picture quality can be obtained by using a form of motion-compensated standards converter between the VTR and the viewer in which the input field rate is variable. Such a device is one of the most stringent tests of motion estimation as a large number of fields need to be interpolated between the input fields and each one will have moving objects synthesized in a different place. Inaccuracies in the motion estimation between two source fields would easily be seen as they will be revealed for many output field periods at slow tape speeds. As such a device is intended for use in sport, large interfield motions of 24–30 pixels per field period must be expected and correctly handled.

4.26 Motion estimation techniques

There are three main methods of motion estimation which are to be found in various applications: block matching, gradient matching and phase correlation. Each has its own characteristics which are quite different.

4.26.1 Block matching

This is the simplest technique to follow. In a given picture, a block of pixels is selected and stored as a reference. If the selected block is part of a moving object, a similar block of pixels will exist in the next picture, but not in the same place. As Fig. 4.68 shows, block matching simply moves the reference block around over the second picture looking for matching pixel values. When a match is found, the displacement needed to obtain it is used as a basis for a motion vector.

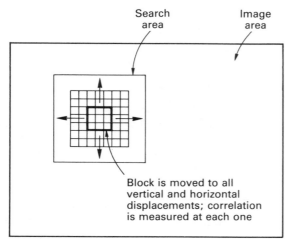

Search area

Image area

Block is moved to all vertical and horizontal displacements; correlation is measured at each one

Figure 4.68 In block matching the search block has to be positioned at all possible relative motions within the search area and a correlation measured at each one

Whilst simple in concept, block matching requires an enormous amount of computation because every possible motion must be tested over the assumed range. Thus if the object is assumed to have moved over a 16 pixel range, then it will be necessary to test 16 different horizontal displacements in each of 16 vertical positions; in excess of 65 000 positions. At each position every pixel in the block must be compared with every pixel in the second picture. In typical video displacements of twice the figure quoted here may be found, particularly in sporting events, and the computation then required becomes enormous.

One way of reducing the amount of computation is to perform the matching in stages, where the first stage is inaccurate but covers a large motion range and the last stage is accurate but covers a small range.[16] The first matching stage is performed on a heavily filtered and subsampled picture which contains far fewer pixels. When a match is found, the displacement is used as a basis for a second stage which is performed with a less heavily filtered picture. Eventually the last stage takes place to any desired accuracy. This hierarchical approach does reduce the computation required, but it suffers from the problem that the filtering of the first stage may make small objects disappear and they can never be found by subsequent stages if they are moving with respect to their background. Many televised sports events contain small, fast-moving objects. As the matching process depends upon finding similar luminance values, this can be confused by objects moving into shade or fades.

Block matching can only measure motion to the nearest pixel, but this is accurate enough for many purposes, including interfield data reduction where it is used extensively.

4.26.2 Gradient matching

At some point in a picture, the function of brightness with respect to distance across the screen will have a certain slope, known as the spatial luminance

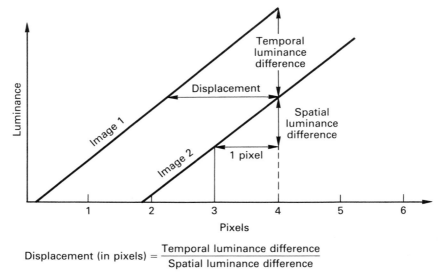

$$\text{Displacement (in pixels)} = \frac{\text{Temporal luminance difference}}{\text{Spatial luminance difference}}$$

Figure 4.69 The principle of gradient matching. The luminance gradient across the screen is compared with that through time

gradient. If the associated picture area is moving, the slope will traverse a fixed point on the screen and the result will be that the brightness now changes with respect to time. This is a temporal luminance gradient. Fig. 4.69 shows the principle. For a given spatial gradient, the temporal gradient becomes steeper as the speed of movement increases. Thus motion speed can be estimated from the ratio of the spatial and temporal gradients.[17]

In practice this is difficult because there are numerous processes which can change the luminance gradient. When an object moves so as to obscure or reveal the background, the spatial gradient will change from field to field even if the motion is constant. Variations in illumination, such as when an object moves into shade, also cause difficulty.

The process can be assisted by recursion, in which the motion is estimated over a larger number of fields, but this will result in problems at cuts.

4.26.3 Phase correlation

Phase correlation works by performing a discrete Fourier transform on two successive fields and then subtracting all of the phases of the spectral components. The phase differences are then subject to a reverse transform which directly reveals peaks whose positions correspond to motions between the fields.[18,19] The nature of the transform domain means that if the distance and direction of the motion are measured accurately, the area of the screen in which they took place is not. Thus in practical systems the phase correlation stage is followed by a matching stage not dissimilar to the block matching process. However, the matching process is steered by the motions from the phase correlation, and so there is no need to attempt to match at all possible motions. By attempting matching on measured motion the overall process is made much more efficient.

One way of considering phase correlation is that by using the Fourier transform to break the picture into its constituent spatial frequencies the hierarchical structure of block matching at various resolutions is in fact performed in parallel. In this way small objects are not missed because they will generate high-frequency components in the transform.

Although the matching process is simplified by adopting phase correlation, the Fourier transforms themselves require complex calculations. The high perform-ance of phase correlation would remain academic if it were too complex to put into practice. However, if realistic values are used for the motion speeds which can be handled, the computation required by block matching actually exceeds that required for phase correlation.

The elimination of amplitude information from the phase correlation process ensures that motion estimation continues to work in the case of fades, objects moving into shade or flashguns firing.

The details of the Fourier transform have been described in Section 4.22. A one-dimensional example of phase correlation will be given here by way of introduction. A line of luminance, which in the digital domain consists of a series of samples, is a function of brightness with respect to distance across the screen. The Fourier transform converts this function into a spectrum of spatial frequencies (units of cycles per picture width) and phases.

All television signals must be handled in linear-phase systems. A linear-phase system is one in which the delay experienced is the same for all frequencies. If video signals pass through a device which does not exhibit linear phase, the various frequency components of edges become displaced across the screen. Fig. 4.70 shows what phase linearity means. If the left-hand end of the frequency axis (DC) is considered to be firmly anchored, but the right-hand end can be rotated to represent a change of position across the screen, it will be seen that as the axis twists evenly the result is phase shift proportional to frequency. A system having this characteristic is said to display linear phase.

In the spatial domain, a phase shift corresponds to a physical movement. Fig. 4.71 shows that if between fields a waveform moves along the line, the lowest

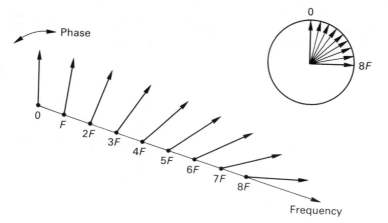

Figure 4.70 The definition of phase linearity is that phase shift is proportional to frequency. In phase-linear systems the waveform is preserved, and simply moves in time or space

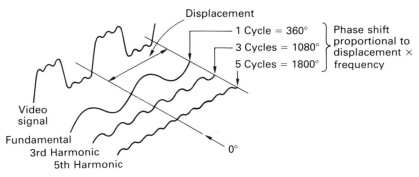

Figure 4.71 In a phase-linear system, shifting the video waveform across the screen causes phase shifts in each component proportional to frequency

frequency in the Fourier transform will suffer a given phase shift, twice that frequency will suffer twice that phase shift and so on. Thus it is potentially possible to measure movement between two successive fields if the phase differences between the Fourier spectra are analysed. This is the basis of phase correlation.

Fig. 4.72 shows how a one-dimensional phase correlator works. The Fourier transforms of two lines from successive fields are computed and expressed in polar (amplitude and phase) notation (see Section 4.22). The phases of one transform are all subtracted from the phases of the same frequencies in the other transform. Any frequency component having significant amplitude is then normalized, or boosted, to full amplitude.

The result is a set of frequency components which all have the same amplitude, but have phases corresponding to the difference between two fields. These coefficients form the input to an inverse transform. Fig. 4.73(a) shows what happens. If the two fields are the same, there are no phase differences between the two, and so all of the frequency components are added with 0° phase to produce a single peak in the centre of the inverse transform. If, however, there was motion between the two fields, such as a pan, all of the components will have phase differences, and this results in a peak shown in Fig. 4.73(b) which is displaced from the centre of the inverse transform by the distance moved. Phase correlation thus actually measures the movement between fields.

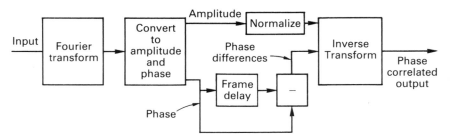

Figure 4.72 The basic components of a phase correlator

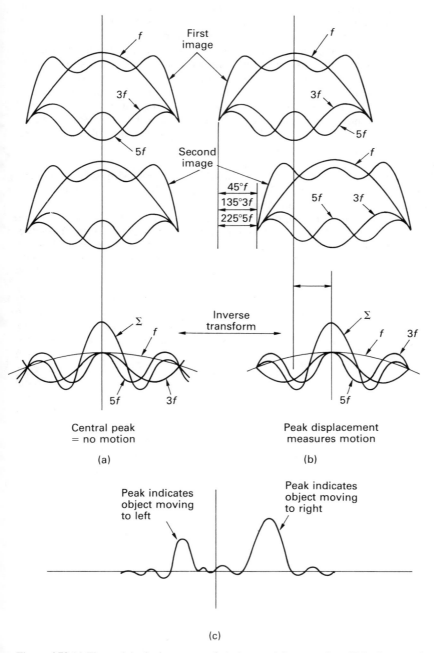

Central peak
= no motion

(a)

Inverse
transform

Peak displacement
measures motion

(b)

Peak indicates
object moving
to left

Peak indicates
object moving
to right

(c)

Figure 4.73 (a) The peak in the inverse transform is central for no motion. (b) In the case of motion, the peak shifts by the distance moved. (c) If there are several motions, each one results in a peak

In the case where the line of video in question intersects objects moving at different speeds, Fig. 4.73(c) shows that the inverse transform would contain one peak corresponding to the distance moved by each object.

Whilst this explanation has used one dimension for simplicity, in practice the entire process is two dimensional. A two-dimensional Fourier transform of each field is computed, the phases are subtracted, and an inverse two-dimensional transform is computed, the output of which is a flat plane out of which three-dimensional peaks rise. This is known as a correlation surface.

Fig. 4.74(a) shows some examples of a correlation surface. At (a) there has been no motion between fields and so there is a single central peak. At (b) there has been a pan and the peak moves across the surface. At (c) the camera has been depressed and the peak moves upwards.

Where more complex motions are involved, perhaps with several objects moving in different directions and/or at different speeds, one peak will appear in the correlation surface for each object.

It is a fundamental strength of phase correlation that it actually measures the direction and speed of moving objects rather than estimating, extrapolating or searching for them. The motion can be measured to subpixel accuracy.

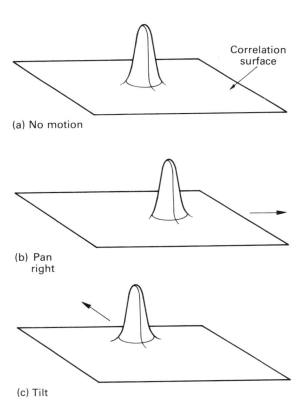

Figure 4.74 (a) A two-dimensional correlation surface has a central peak when there is no motion. (b) In the case of a pan, the peak moves laterally. (c) A camera tilt moves the peak at right angles to the pan

However, it should be understood that accuracy in the transform domain is incompatible with accuracy in the spatial domain. Although phase correlation accurately measures motion speeds and directions, it cannot specify where in the picture these motions are taking place. It is necessary to look for them in a further matching process. The efficiency of this process is dramatically improved by the inputs from the phase correlation stage.

4.27 A phase correlation motion estimation system

This section gives an example of the practical implementation of a motion estimation unit based on phase correlation. In fact the phase correlation stage forms only part of the overall structure.

The input to a motion estimator for most applications consists of interlaced fields. The lines of one field lie between those of the next, making comparisons between them difficult. A further problem is that vertical spatial aliasing may exist in the fields. Preprocessing solves these problems by performing a two-dimensional spatial low-pass filtering operation on input fields. Alternate fields are also interpolated up or down by half a line using the techniques of Section 4.13 so that interlace disappears and all fields subsequently have the same sampling grid. The spatial filtering also cuts down the amount of computation required.

The computation needed to perform a two-dimensional Fourier transform increases dramatically with the size of the block employed, and so no attempt is made to transform the downsampled fields directly. Instead the fields are converted into overlapping blocks by the use of window functions as shown in Fig. 4.75. The size of the window controls the motion speed which can be handled, and so a window size is chosen which allows motion to be detected up to the limit of human judder visibility.

Fig. 4.76 shows a block diagram of a phase-correlated motion estimation system. Following the preprocessing, each windowed block is subject to an FFT, and the output spectrum is converted to the amplitude and phase representation. The phases are subtracted from those of the previous field in each window, and

Point 'A' appears in four
different windows

Figure 4.75 The input fields are converted into overlapping windows. Each window is individually transformed the amplitudes are normalized to eliminate any variations in illumination or the effect of fades from the motion sensing. A reverse transform is performed, which results in a correlation surface. The correlation surface contains peaks whose positions actually measure distances and directions moved by some feature in the window. It is a characteristic of the Fourier transform that the more accurately the spectrum of a signal is known, the less accurately the spatial domain is known. Thus the whereabouts within the window of the moving objects which gave rise to the correlation peaks is not known. Fig. 4.77 illustrates the phenomenon. Two windowed blocks are shown in consecutive fields. Both contain the same objects, moving at the same speed, but from different starting points. The correlation surface will be the same in both cases. The phase correlation process therefore needs to be followed by a further process called image correlation which identifies the picture areas in which the measured motion took place and establishes a level of confidence in the identification. This stage can also be seen in the block diagram of Fig. 4.76.

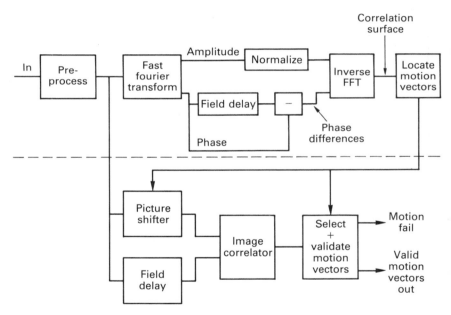

Figure 4.76 The block diagram of a phase correlated motion estimator. See text for details

To employ the terminology of motion estimation, the phase correlation process produces candidate vectors, and the image correlation process assigns the vectors to specific areas of the picture. In many ways the vector assignment process is more difficult than the phase correlation process as the latter is a fixed computation whereas the vector assignment has to respond to infinitely varying picture conditions.

Fig. 4.78 shows the image correlation process which is used to link the candidate vectors from the phase correlator to the picture content. In this example, the correlation surface contains three peaks which define three possible motions between two successive fields. One downsampled field is successively shifted by each of the candidate vectors and compared with the next field a pixel at a time. Similarities or correlations between pixel values indicate that an area with the measured motion has been found. This happens for two of the candidate vectors, and these vectors are then assigned to those areas. However, shifting by the third vector does not result in a meaningful correlation. This is taken to mean that it was a spurious vector, one which was produced in error because of

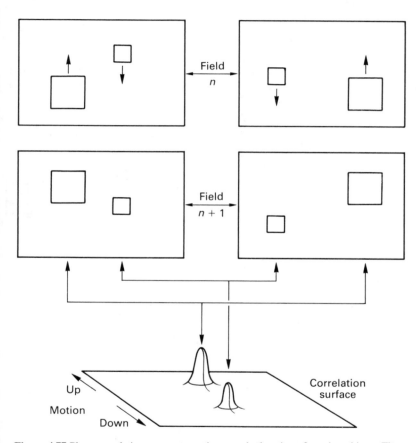

Figure 4.77 Phase correlation measures motion, not the location of moving objects. These two examples give the same correlation surface

difficult program material. The ability to eliminate spurious vectors and establish confidence levels in those which remain is essential to artefact-free conversion.

The phase correlation process produces candidate vectors in each window. The vectors from all windows must be combined to obtain an overall view of the motion in the field before attempting to describe the motion of each pixel individually.

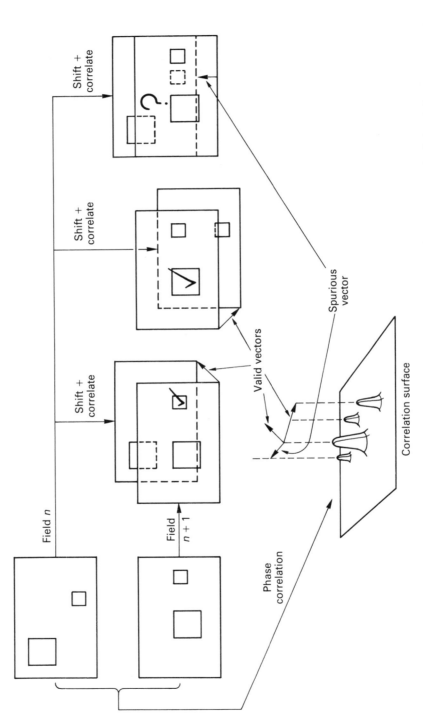

Figure 4.78 Image correlation uses candidate vectors to locate picture areas with the corresponding motion. If no image correlation is found, the vector was spurious and is discounted

Window

(a)

(b)

Figure 4.79 The results of (a) a zoom and (b) a pan on the vectors in various windows in the field

Fig. 4.79(a) shows that if a zoom is in progress, the vectors in the various windows will form a geometric progression becoming longer in proportion to the distance from the axis of the zoom. However, if there is a pan, it will be seen from Fig. 4.79(b) that there will be similar vectors in all of the windows. In practice both motions may occur simultaneously.

An estimate will be made of the speed of a field-wide zoom, or of the speed of picture areas which contain receding or advancing motions which give a zoom-like effect. If the effect of zooming is removed from each window by shifting the peaks by the local zoom magnitude, but in the opposite direction, the position of the peaks will reveal any component due to panning. This can be found by summing all of the windows to create a histogram. Panning results in a dominant peak in the histogram where all windows contain peaks in a similar place which reinforce.

Each window is then processed in turn. Where only a small part of an object overlaps into a window, it will result in a small peak in the correlation surface which might be missed. The windows are deliberately overlapped so that a given pixel may appear in four windows. Thus a moving object will appear in more than one window. If the majority of an object lies within one window, a large peak will be produced from the motion in that window. The resulting vector will be added to the candidate vector list of all adjacent windows. When the vector assignment is performed, image correlations will result if a small overlap occurred, and the vector will be validated. If there was no overlap, the vector will be rejected.

The peaks in each window reflect the degree of correlation between the two fields for different offsets in two dimensions. The volume of the peak corresponds to the amount of the area of the window (i.e. the number of pixels) having that motion. Thus peaks should be selected starting with the largest. However, periodic structures in the input field, such as grilles and striped shirts, will result in partial correlations at incorrect distances which differ from the correct distance by the period of the structure. The effect is that a large peak on the correlation surface will be flanked by smaller peaks at uniform spacing in a straight line. The characteristic pattern of subsidiary peaks can be identified and the vectors invalidated.

One way in which this can be done is to compare the position of the peaks in each window with those estimated by the pan/zoom process. The true peak due to motion will be similar; the false subpeaks due to image periodicity will not be and can be rejected.

Correlations with candidate vectors are then performed. The image in one field is shifted in an interpolator by the amount specified by a candidate vector and the degree of correlation is measured. Note that this interpolation is to subpixel accuracy because phase correlation can accurately measure subpixel motion. High correlation results in vector assignment, low correlation results in the vector being rejected as unreliable.

If all of the peaks are evaluated in this way, then most of the time valid assignments will be made for which there is acceptable confidence from the correlator. Should it not be possible to obtain any correlation with confidence in a window, then the pan/zoom values will be inserted so that that window moves in a similar way to the overall field motion.

4.28 Motion-compensated standards conversion

A conventional standards converter is not transparent to motion portrayal, and the effect is judder and loss of resolution. Fig. 4.80 shows what happens on the time axis in a conversion between 60 Hz and 50 Hz (in either direction). Fields in the two standards appear in different planes cutting through the spatio-temporal volume, and the job of the standards converter is to interpolate along the time axis between input planes in one standard in order to estimate what an

Figure 4.80 The different temporal distribution of input and output fields in a 50/60 Hz converter

intermediate plane in the other standard would look like. With still images, this is easy, because planes can be slid up and down the time axis with no ill effect. Motion compensation is designed to eliminate this undesirable judder.

A conventional standards converter interpolates only along the time axis, whereas a motion-compensated standards converter can swivel its interpolation axis off the time axis. Fig. 4.81(a) shows the input fields in which three objects are moving in a different way. At (b) it will be seen that the interpolation axis is aligned with the path of each moving object in turn.

Each object is no longer moving with respect to its own interpolation axis, and so on that axis it no longer generates temporal frequencies due to motion and

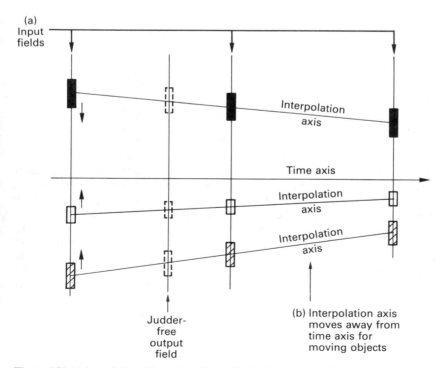

Figure 4.81 (a) Input fields with moving objects. (b) Moving the interpolation axes to make them parallel to the trajectory of each object

temporal aliasing due to motion cannot occur.[20] Interpolation along the correct axes will then result in a sequence of output fields in which motion is properly portrayed. The process requires a standards converter which contains filters which are modified to allow the interpolation axis to move dynamically within each output field. The signals which move the interpolation axis are known as motion vectors. It is the job of the motion estimation system to provide these motion vectors. The overall performance of the converter is determined primarily by the accuracy of the motion vectors. An incorrect vector will result in unrelated pixels from several fields being superimposed and the result is unsatisfactory. Fig. 4.82 shows the sequence of events in a motion-compensated standards converter. The motion estimator measures movements between successive fields. These motions must then be attributed to objects by creating boundaries around sets of pixels having the same motion. The result of this process is a set of motion vectors, hence the term vector assignation. The motion vectors are then input to a modified four-field standards converter in order to deflect the interfield interpolation axis.

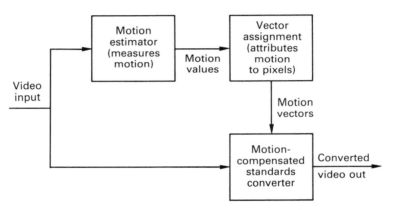

Figure 4.82 The essential stages of a motion-compensated standards converter

The vectors from the motion estimator actually measure the distance moved by an object from one input field to another. What the standards converter requires is the value of motion vectors at an output field. A vector interpolation stage is required which computes where between the input fields A and B the current output field lies, and uses this to proportion the motion vector into two parts. Fig. 4.83(a) shows that the first part is the motion between field A and the output field; the second is the motion between field B and the output field. Clearly the difference between these two vectors is the motion between input fields. These processed vectors are used to displace parts of the input fields so that the axis of interpolation lies along the path of the motion. The moving object is stationary with respect to this axis so interpolation between fields along it will not result in any judder. Whilst a conventional converter only needs to interpolate vertically and temporally, a motion-compensated converter also needs to interpolate horizontally to account for lateral movement in images. Fig. 4.83(b) shows that the motion vector from the motion estimator is resolved into two components, vertical and horizontal. The spatial impulse response of the interpolator is shifted

Figure 4.83 The motion vectors on the input field structure must be interpolated onto the output field structure as in (a). The field to be interpolated is positioned temporally between source fields and the motion vector between them is apportioned according to the location. Motion vectors are two dimensional, and can be transmitted as vertical and horizontal components shown at (b) which control the spatial shifting of input fields

in two dimensions by these components. This shift may be different in each of the fields which contribute to the output field.

When an object in the picture moves, it will obscure its background. The vector interpolator in the standards converter handles this automatically provided the motion estimation has produced correct vectors. Fig. 4.84 shows an example of background handling. The moving object produces a finite vector associated with each pixel, whereas the stationary background produces zero vectors except in the area O–X where the background is being obscured. Vectors converge in the area where the background is being obscured, and diverge where it is being revealed. Image correlation is poor in these areas so no valid vector is assigned.

An output field is located between input fields, and vectors are projected through it to locate the intermediate position of moving objects. These are interpolated along an axis which is parallel to the motion axis. This results in address mapping which locates the moving object in the input field RAMs.

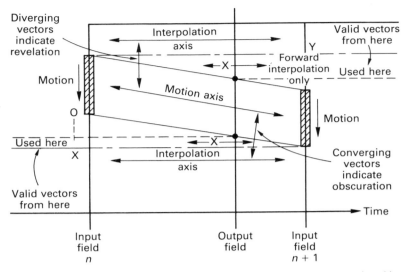

Figure 4.84 Background handling. When a vector for an output pixel near a moving object is not known, the vectors from adjacent background areas are assumed. Converging vectors imply obscuring is taking place which requires that interpolation can only use previous field data. Diverging vectors imply that the background is being revealed and interpolation can only use data from later fields

However, the background is not moving and so the interpolation axis is parallel to the time axis. The pixel immediately below the leading edge of the moving object does not have a valid vector because it is in the area O–X where forward image correlation failed. The solution is for that pixel to assume the motion vector of the background below point X, but only to interpolate in a backwards direction, taking pixel data from previous fields. In a similar way, the pixel immediately behind the trailing edge takes the motion vector for the background above point Y and interpolates only in a forward direction, taking pixel data from future fields. The result is that the moving object is portrayed in the correct place on its trajectory, and the background around it is filled in only from fields which contain useful data.

4.29 Motion-compensated slow-motion system

The provision of video playback at reduced speed has been a useful tool for many years and a great deal of effort has been expended to obtain high quality. Slow motion may be used for artistic effect, or to study a phenomenon more easily. It will be seen in Chapter 8 that the development of the helical-scan video recorder led to machines with automatically deflecting heads which could follow tracks on tape at non-standard speed. In order to maintain the standard output signal structure, the drum speed remained locked to reference video, but to constrain the deflection amplitude, the head would periodically need to jump, repeating one or more fields.[1] Thus the output field rate was correct, but the repeating of fields did not give an accurate portrayal of motion. Fig. 4.85 shows that a moving object would remain in the same place on the screen during field repeats, but jump to a new position as a new field was played. The eye follows a selected moving

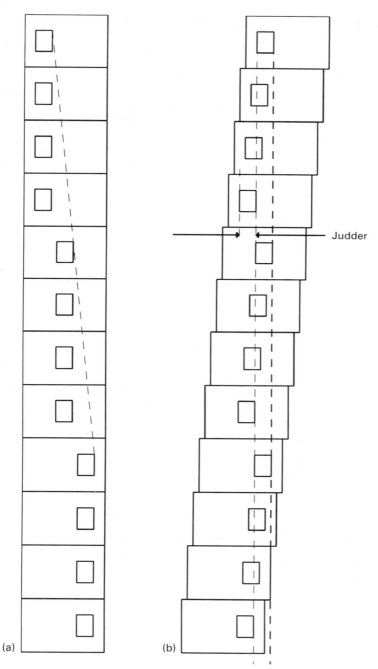

Judder

(a)   (b)

Figure 4.85 Conventional slow motion using field repeating with stationary eye shown at (a).
With tracking eye at (b) the source of judder is seen

object on the screen, attempting to render it stationary on the retina. Fig. 4.85 also shows that the field-repeating process of a conventional VTR causes the location of a moving object to wander with respect to the trajectory of the eye, and this is visible as judder, defined as an apparent variation in the speed of moving picture areas.

Later, specially adapted cameras and video recorders were built which would operate at elevated field rates to make a tape which would play in slow motion on a standard recorder. Whilst the motion portrayal results were better, there remained the problem of cost and the need for advanced knowledge of the requirement.

The current state of the art in slow motion is represented by the Snell and Wilcox/BBC Gazelle slow-motion system which is capable of synthesizing new

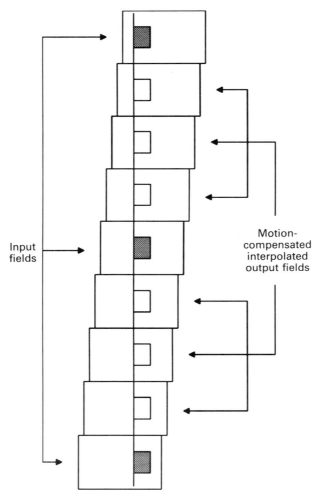

Figure 4.86 In motion-compensated slow motion, output fields are interpolated with moving objects displaying judder-free linear motion between input fields

images which lie between the images from a slow-motion source. Gazelle correctly accounts for the motion of objects between source images by interpolating their position in output fields.

The operation of the Gazelle resembles that of a motion-compensated standards converter, but there is a greater disparity between the input and output field rates. Fig. 4.86 shows that two successive images in the original recording (using DVE terminology, these are source fields) are fed into the unit, which then measures the distance travelled by all moving objects between those images. Using interpolation, intermediate fields (target fields) are computed in which moving objects are positioned so that they lie on the eye trajectory. Using the principles described in Section 4.28, background information is removed as moving objects conceal it, and replaced as the rear of an object reveals it. Judder is thus removed and motion with a fluid quality is obtained. An advantage of the approach is that existing video recordings can be used as it is a process which takes place on playback only.

A block diagram is shown in Fig. 4.87. Input is from a composite VTR having vertical interval timecode. The use of VITC is important because it is tied to individual images on the tape and unlike LTC it remains correct when the machine is in slow-motion mode. By processing the VITC input, Gazelle can determine whether the recorder is repeating fields or has moved to a new one. Repeat fields are ignored, such that in the Gazelle input memory the original source field structure of the recording is recreated, but clearly not in real time.

The composite signal is then decoded into components prior to processing. This is necessary both because the presence of chroma would confuse the motion estimation and because spatial manipulation of composite waveforms destroys the chroma phase information. The motion estimator operates upon two

Figure 4.87 Block diagram of motion-compensated slow-motion units. Performance is critically dependent on accuracy of the motion estimator

successive fields and finds areas of detail which are similar. The movement of such areas is then measured to obtain the motion vectors.

The actual speed of the tape is known, since this reflects in the rate at which new fields, rather than repeat fields, are input from the VTR. Thus it is possible to position source fields on the real-time axis of station reference, as shown in Fig. 4.86. Clearly the slower the VTR moves tape, the less often a new source field will be output, and the more field periods of station reference will occur between source fields. This parameter determines the number of interpolated target fields which must be computed between source fields.

It is then assumed that the motion of all picture areas between the two source fields was linear. Whilst this is an assumption, it should be recalled that with a fixed camera, objects in real life cannot change speed at an unlimited rate, and cameras are equipped with damped mountings to prevent rapid image acceleration due to panning. Thus in practice there is little error due to this assumption.

Fig. 4.87 shows that the motion vectors are linearly interpolated from one source field to the next in order to establish their magnitude at each target field. The direction component of the motion vector is unaffected. Thus at each target field, it is known where moving areas of detail are located. This information is used to synthesize a field in which moving objects are in the correct place. As Fig. 4.86 showed, when the eye follows one of these objects, it becomes stationary with respect to the retina and so judder is not perceived.

4.30 Recursive filtering for noise reduction

The basic principle of all video noise reducers is that there is a certain amount of correlation between the video content of successive frames, whereas there is no correlation between the noise content.

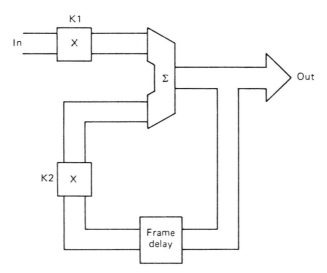

Figure 4.88 A basic recursive device feeds back the output to the input via a frame store which acts as a delay. The characteristics of the device are controlled totally by the values of the two coefficients K1 and K2 which control the multipliers

A basic recursive device is shown in Fig. 4.88. There is a frame store which acts as a delay, and the output of the delay can be fed back to the input through an attenuator, which in the digital domain will be a multiplier. In the case of a still picture, successive frames will be identical, and the recursion will be large. This means that the output video will actually be the average of many frames. If there is movement of the image, it will be necessary to reduce the amount of recursion to prevent the generation of trails or smears. Probably the most famous examples of recursion smear are the television pictures sent back of astronauts walking on the moon. The received pictures were very noisy and needed a lot of averaging to make them viewable. This was fine until the astronaut moved. The technology of the day did not permit motion sensing.

The noise reduction increases with the number of frames over which the noise is integrated, but image motion prevents simple combining of frames. If motion estimation is available, the image of a moving object in a particular frame can be integrated from the images in several frames which have been superimposed on the same part of the screen by displacements derived from the motion measurement. The result is that greater reduction of noise becomes possible.[21]

4.31 Recursive filtering for effects

The principle of recursion can be used for certain special effects, and a suitable frame store is often added at the output of a DVE so that the recursive effects are available superimposed on existing effects, giving a larger range of possibilities.

DVEs often move the source picture around the screen, and in this mode the use of recursion as an effect is the most useful. Adding a decaying trail which follows a moving picture is relatively easy. The presence of a frame store allows the current output frame and the previous output frame to be simultaneously available. A suitable switcher similar to the combiner described in Chapter 3 will allow both to be seen on the screen, with the older image having lower priority, and only visible where the more recent image has moved. The combiner output then becomes the next input to the frame store, so that one frame later, three overlapping images will be seen. This process can continue indefinitely, as the structure used is that of an infinite impulse response filter. In practice the gain of the recursive signals will be less than unity, so that the brightness of the trailing images decays exponentially.

The incorporation of a random number generator allows sparkles to be generated in the recursive data.

It is also possible to use a target frame store to make a collage. The recursion is set to unity gain, and the input to the DVE switches between sources as the image moves rapidly. Each input picture will appear in sequence across the screen.

With unity recursion, the input can be removed, and the output will remain, but if the recursion factor is minutely reduced, the frozen frame will gradually fade.

4.32 Data reduction

The data rates resulting from conventional PCM video are quite high, and although recorders have been developed which store the signals in this form, they will remain exclusively in the professional domain for the foreseeable future. For production purposes, the simplicity of PCM video is attractive because it allows manipulations with the minimum of quality loss. The signals seldom need to travel long distances and the provision of sufficient data rate is not an issue. However, the increasing range of applications of digital video are taking it out of the studio and into the consumer domain. In this case transmission over long distances is required, where the cost is generally proportional to the bit rate. There is then an obvious pressure to reduce the data rate. The running costs of a professional DVTR are reasonable in the context of the overall cost of a television production, but beyond the resources of the individual. If digital video recording is to be made available to the consumer, the running cost and tape consumption will need to be reduced considerably. Digital video recording in this context includes new developments such as interactive video (CD-I) which requires rapid random access to images on optical disc.

As PCM high definition requires about five times the data rate of normal definition then the use of data reduction will be mandatory to deliver the signal to the home and will be considered for production recorders.

The use of data reduction also allows the life of an existing transport and tape design to be extended by raising the apparent data rate. Ampex have used data reduction in order to record 4:2:2 component data on a D-2 type transport; 4:2:2 requires approximately twice the data rate as NTSC sampled at four times subcarrier.

The fundamentals of video data reduction are not new, but the availability of equipment has been hampered until recently by the speed and complexity of the processing required. The cost of implementing coding techniques in VLSI circuitry has now fallen to a level where it is advantageous to use it. The large volume required for consumer applications further lowers the unit cost of such circuitry.

Data reduction is a flexible technology because the degree of coding complexity and the degree of compression used can be varied to suit the application. Video contains redundancy because typical images contain areas which are similar. The actual information in video is known as the entropy, which is the unpredictable or new part of the signal, and the remainder is redundancy, which is a part of the signal which is predictable. The sum of the two is the original data rate. The degree of compression cannot be so severe that the new data rate is less than the entropy, as information must then be lost. In theory, all of the redundancy could be removed, leaving only the entropy, but this would require a perfect algorithm which would be extremely complex. In practice the compression factor will be less than this so that some leeway is available. This allows simpler algorithms to be used and where necessary also permits multiple generations without artefacts being visible. Thus production DVTRs such as Sony's Digital Betacam and the Ampex DCT use only very mild compression of around 2:1.

For production recorders, only redundancy within the field is used, and no advantage is taken of the redundancy between fields as this would compromise editing. Clearly a consumer DVTR needs only single-generation operation and has simple editing requirements. A much greater degree of compression can then be used, which might also take advantage of redundancy between fields. The same is true for broadcasting, where bandwidth is at a premium. There is now no doubt that the future of television broadcasting (and radio for that matter) lies in data-reduced digital technology. Analog simply requires too much bandwidth.

There are thus a number of identifiable and different approaches to data reduction. For production purposes, *intrafield* data reduction is used with a mild compression factor in order to allow maximum editing freedom with negligible occurrence of artefacts. Compression algorithms intended for the transmission of still images in other applications such as wirephotos can be adapted for intrafield video compression. The ISO JPEG (Joint Photographic Experts Group)[22,23] standard is such an algorithm. *Interfield* data reduction allows higher compression factors with infrequent artefacts for the delivery of post-produced material to the consumer. With even higher compression factors, leading to frequent artefacts, non-critical applications such as videophones and games are supported where the data rate has to be as low as possible. The ISO MPEG (Moving Picture Experts Group)[24] standards address these applications.

4.33 Intrafield data reduction

This type of data reduction takes each individual field (or frame in progressive scan standards) and treats it in isolation from any other field or frame. The most common algorithms are based on the discrete cosine transform described in Section 4.23.

Fig. 4.61 showed an example of the different coefficients of a DCT for an 8×8 pixel block, and adding these together in different proportions will give any original pixel block. The top left coefficient conveys the DC component of the block. This one will be a unipolar (positive-only) value in the case of luminance and will typically be the largest value in the block as the spectrum of typical video signals is dominated by the DC component. Moving to the right the coefficients represent increasing horizontal spatial frequencies and moving downwards the coefficients represent increasing vertical spatial frequencies. The bottom right coefficient represents the highest diagonal frequencies in the block. All of these coefficients are bipolar, where the polarity indicates whether the original spatial waveform at that frequency was inverted.

In typical pictures, the coefficients representing the higher two-dimensional spatial frequencies will be zero or of small value in large areas of typical video, due to motion blurring or simply plain undetailed areas before the camera. In general, the further from the top left corner the coefficient is, the smaller will be its magnitude on average. Coding gain (the technical term for reduction in the number of bits needed) is achieved by taking advantage of the zero and low-valued coefficients to cut down on the data necessary. Thus it is not the DCT which compresses the data; it is the subsequent processing. The DCT simply expresses the data in a form which makes the subsequent processing easier. Thus the correct terminology is to say that a compression algorithm is *DCT based*.

Once transformed, there are various techniques which can be used to reduce the data needed to carry the coefficients. These will be based on a knowledge of the signal statistics and the human vision mechanism and will often be combined in practical systems.[25,26]

Possibly the simplest reduction method involves setting a threshold magnitude for coefficients. Only coefficients which exceed the threshold are transmitted, as it is assumed that smaller values make a negligible contribution to the picture block. Fig. 4.89 shows the result, which is that most coefficients then have a value of zero.

95	36	−24	10	0	3	0	0
30	33	−20	8	0	1	2	0
−25	−20	−10	6	0	0	1	0
11	7	2	5	0	0	0	0
0	0	−3	0	0	0	2	0
0	0	0	0	0	0	0	0
0	0	0	3	0	0	0	0
0	0	1	0	0	0	0	0

DCT input

95	36	−24	10	0	3	0	0
30	33	−20	8	0	0	0	0
−25	−20	−10	6	0	0	0	0
11	7	0	5	0	0	0	0
0	0	−3	0	0	0	0	0
0	0	0	0	0	0	0	0
0	3	0	0	0	0	0	0
0	0	0	0	0	0	0	0

DCT output with
threshold > 2

Figure 4.89 After the DCT, a simple way of compressing the data is to transmit only those coefficients which exceed a threshold

Psycho-visual knowledge may also be used to process the coefficients. Omitting a coefficient means that the appropriate frequency component is missing from the reconstructed block. The difference between original and reconstructed blocks is regarded as noise added to the wanted data. The visibility of such noise is far from uniform. Fig. 4.90 shows that the sensitivity of the eye to noise falls with frequency. The maximum sensitivity is at DC and as a result the top left coefficient is often treated as a special case and left unchanged. It may warrant more error protection than other coefficients.

Psycho-visual coding takes advantage of the falling sensitivity to noise by multiplying each coefficient by a different weighting constant as a function of its frequency. This has the effect of reducing the magnitude of each coefficient so that fewer bits are needed to represent it. Another way of looking at this process is that the coefficients are individually requantized with step sizes which increase with frequency. The larger step size increases the quantizing noise at frequencies where it is not visible.

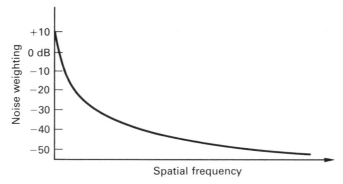

Figure 4.90 The sensitivity of the eye to noise is greatest at low frequencies and drops rapidly with increasing frequency. This can be used to mask quantizing noise caused by the compression process

Knowledge of the signal statistics gained from extensive analysis of real material can be used to describe the probability of a given coefficient having a given value. This is the basis of entropy coding, in which coefficients are described not by fixed wordlength numbers, but by variable-length codes. The shorter codes are allocated to the most probable values and the longer codes to the least probable values. This allows a coding gain on typical signals. One of the best known variable-length codes is the Huffman code.[27]

The main difficulty with variable-length codes is separating the symbols when they are serialized. With fixed wordlength, the bit clock is merely divided by the wordlength to obtain a word clock. With variable-length coding the bit stream coding must be such that the decoder can determine the boundaries between words unaided. Fig. 4.91 shows an example of Huffman coding.

Coefficient	Code	Number of zeros	Code
1	1	1	11
2	001	2	101
3	0111	3	011
4	00001	4	0101
5	01101	5	0011
6	011001	etc.	etc.
7	0000001		
Run-length code	010		

Figure 4.91 In Huffman coding the most probable coefficient values are allocated to the shortest codes. All zero coefficients are coded with run-length coding which counts the number of zeros

When serializing a coefficient block, it is normal to scan in a sequence where the largest coefficient values are scanned first. Clearly such a scan begins in the top left corner and ends in the bottom right corner. Statistical analysis of real program material can be used to determine an optimal scan, but in many cases a regular zig-zag scan shown in Fig. 4.92 will be used with slight loss of performance. The advantage of such a scan is that on typical material the scan finishes with coefficients which are zero valued. Instead of transmitting these zeros, a unique 'end of block' symbol is transmitted instead. Just before the last finite coefficient and the EOB symbol it is likely that some zero-value coefficients will be scanned. The coding enters a different mode whereby it simply transmits a unique prefix called a run-length prefix, followed by a code specifying the number of zeros which follow. This is also shown in Fig. 4.91.

Fig. 4.93(a) shows a block diagram of a representative image data reduction unit. The input image is blocked, and the DCT stage transforms the blocks into a form in which redundancy can be identified. Psycho-visual weighting then reduces coefficient values according to the human visual process. Block scanning and variable-length/run-length coding finish the job. The receiver is shown in Fig. 4.93(b). The input bit stream is deserialized into symbols, and the run-length decoder reassembles the runs of zeros. The variable-length decoder then converts

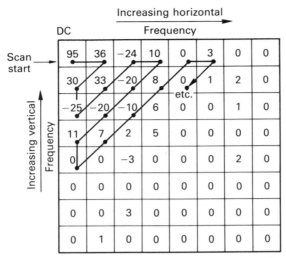

Figure 4.92 The zig-zag scan starting top left orders the coefficients in the best sequence for compression as the later ones will have smaller value

back to constant wordlength coefficients. The psycho-visual weighting is reversed by a division which cancels the original multiplication. An inverse DCT then reconstructs the blocks.

The compression factor of the system of Fig. 4.93 is a function of the input image. A detailed contrasty image will result in more data than a soft image containing self-similar areas. This is not a problem for single image applications like wirephotos, because the result is that on a fixed rate link the transmission time varies slightly from one image to the next, just as it does in a Fax machine.

In a recorder or a real-time transmission system the picture rate is constant and this variable compression is a nuisance because it demands a variable rate link or recorder. The solution is to make the compression factor constant. This is done by using feedback from the output coder which is given a bit budget. If the bit budget is exceeded, the coefficients are requantized to larger steps. If the bit budget is underutilized, the quantization steps are made more accurate. This is an iterative process which converges on an optimally filled output block in a variable time. This variability is undesirable in real-time hardware and instead the coefficients may be requantized by all step sizes in turn. At the end of this fixed time process the best quantization step size is then picked.

Variable quantizing results in variable noise, and it is desirable to reduce the visibility of program-sensitive noise. One way in which this can be done is to combine a number of DCT blocks together into an entropy block. The entropy block is then given a bit budget. In this system, one DCT block having high entropy can use up the bit budget made available by other DCT blocks in the entropy block which have low entropy. Coarse quantization is not then necessary and an improvement in signal-to-noise ratio results. The chances of every DCT block in an entropy block having high entropy are not great, but can be reduced further by shuffling the DCT blocks so that an entropy block is made up from blocks which are distributed around the screen.

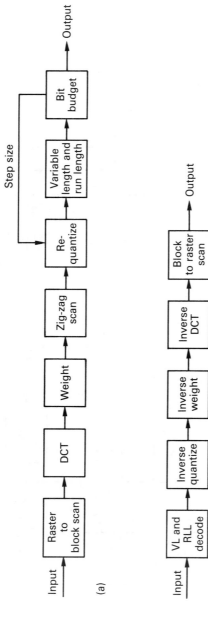

Figure 4.93 An intrafield DCT-based coder at (a) and the corresponding decoder at (b)

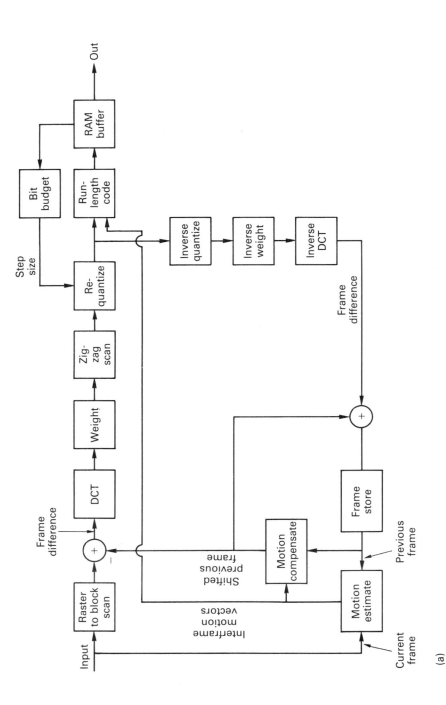

Figure 4.94 An interfield motion-compensated coder at (a) and the corresponding decoder at (b). See text for details

In practice entropy blocks cannot be made arbitrarily large because only an entire block can be properly decoded owing to the use of variable-length coding. In digital VTRs the entropy block length is restricted to the track length which can be recovered in shuttle (see Chapter 8), but a useful noise advantage is still obtained.

4.34 Interfield data reduction

Higher compression factors are easier to obtain if advantage is taken of redundancy between successive images. Only the difference between images need be sent. Clearly with a still picture, successive images will be identical and the difference will be trivial. In practice, movement reduces the similarity between successive images and the difference data increase. One way of increasing the coding gain is to use motion compensation. If the motion of an object between images is known and transmitted, the decoder can use the motion vector to shift the pixel data describing the object in the previous image to the correct position in the current image. The image difference for the object will then be smaller. The differences between images will be compressed by a DCT-based system as described above.

Fig. 4.94 shows a motion-compensated system. Incoming video passes in parallel to the motion estimator and the line scan to block scan converter. The motion estimator compares the incoming frame with the previous one in the frame store in order to measure motion, and sends the motion vectors to the motion compensation unit which shifts objects in the frame store output to their estimated positions in the new frame. This results in a predicted frame, which is

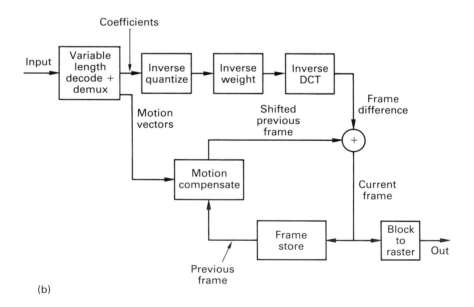

(b)

Figure 4.94 (continued)

subtracted from the input frame in order to obtain the frame difference or prediction error. The result of this process is that the temporal or interframe redundancy and the entropy have been separated. The redundancy is the predictable part of the image as anything which is predictable carries no information. The prediction error is the entropy, the part which could not be predicted. The frame difference is then processed to remove spatial redundancy. This is done with a combination of DCT, weighting and quantizing as was explained in Section 4.33. The spatially reduced frame difference is combined with the motion vectors in order to produce the system output.

It will be seen from Fig. 4.94(a) that there is also a local decoder which consists of an inverse quantizer, inverse weighting stage and an inverse DCT. Adding the locally decoded prediction error (image difference) to the predicted frame must result in the original frame (plus quantizing noise) which updates the frame store. Fig. 4.94(b) shows the decoder. The frame store output is shifted by the transmitted motion vectors and the result is the same predicted frame as was produced in the encoder. The decoded frame error is added to the predicted frame and the original frame results.

The motion estimation process needs to be simple and economical and it does not need to be very accurate as it is inside the error loop. The motion compensator works to pixel accuracy using address mapping only and so there is no point in having subpixel-accurate vectors. If a motion vector is slightly incorrect, the frame difference will correct for it at the expense of a slight increase in data. Block matching is generally adequate for such a motion estimation application and is widely used.

Whilst a system based purely on interfield redundancy will work, it has some weaknesses. One of these is the situation where a moving object reveals background area which was concealed in the previous image. This area cannot be predicted and results in a large error. Data from such an area might just as well be coded on an intrafield basis, and this might be more efficient. Another problem is that the current field is based on the history of many previous fields. The system will take some time to produce a picture from a cold start, and if a transmission error occurs, the result will propagate through a large number of future fields. In practical systems these problems may be overcome by switching between interfield and interframe mode. This may be done on a DCT block basis as required in order to handle obscured and revealed image areas. In addition, a certain proportion of blocks may be forced into intrafield mode in every field. The position of these blocks moves around the field so that within a certain time period, perhaps a second, the entire picture area has been given an absolute reference. This process is known as refreshing, and helps to cut down the effects of error propagation. A further possibility is to transmit a signal structure in which periodically there are fields which are entirely intrafield coded. Fields between are interfield coded as shown in Fig. 4.95.

4.35 Hierarchical coding

In a future digital HDTV broadcasting system it may be advantageous to have a single transmitted signal which supports a variety of decoding resolutions. The entire signal is fully decoded and used to drive large-screen HDTV displays, but a portable small-screen receiver might decode only part of the signal to produce a resolution appropriate to the screen size. The portable receiver should not need

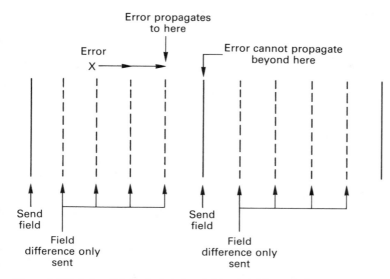

Figure 4.95 It is beneficial to include intrafield coded fields periodically for some applications

to decode the entire transmission in order to select data for display, as this would raise the complexity and cost as well as the power consumption.

Hierarchical coding has been proposed as a solution to this requirement.[28] This takes several forms which will be compared here. Fig. 4.96(a) shows the principle of sub-band coding where the two-dimensional spectrum of the input HDTV picture is divided up before coding. The HDTV input is subject to low-pass filtering and downsampling in both axes to produce a normal definition picture. This is subject to data reduction as described above, and produces a signal which is sufficient to drive a conventional TV set on its own.

The HDTV input is also bandpass filtered to produce a second area of the two-dimensional spectrum which becomes a 'helper' signal which when added to the normal resolution signal results in an HDTV signal once more.

The sub-band technique is not as efficient as it might be. In particular the downsampling process cannot be used on individual fields of an interlaced input as vertical aliasing will result on the normal resolution picture. It is necessary to provide motion-compensated de-interlacing prior to the downsampling. This motion compensation is in addition to the compensation required in the coding stages. A further problem is that the band-splitting filters need to be sharp, otherwise the same frequencies appear in both channels and the compression factor is impaired.

Fig. 4.96(b) shows a pyramidal coding scheme in which the HDTV input is downsampled in two dimensions and fed to the base-level coder which forms the normal resolution output. There is a local decoder for this signal, which is upsampled by interpolation to the HDTV line standard. This signal is then subtracted from the HDTV input to produce the helper signal. The advantage of this structure is that the downsampling filter characteristics no longer affect the coding efficiency. De-interlace is still necessary on interlaced inputs.

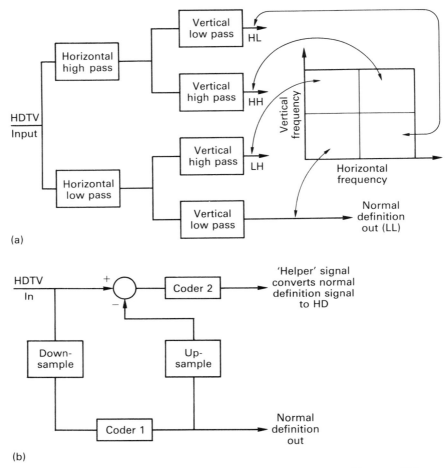

(a)

(b)

Figure 4.96 At (a) a sub-band-based hierarchical coder using prefiltering. At (b) a pyramidal approach is used, whereas at (c) the DCT is used as the band-splitting filter

Fig. 4.96(c) shows a sub-band coding scheme in which the band splitting is performed by the same DCT which is used for the data reduction. Following the input 8×8 DCT, only the top left 16 coefficients are used for the half-resolution picture, the remainder being set to zero. A motion-compensated data reduction process is used to produce the half-resolution output. A local decoder produces a half-resolution coefficient signal which is subtracted from the input coefficients to produce the helper spectrum which is also data reduced.

References

1. Weston, M., Advanced colour decoding techniques. *Record of 18th ITS*, 108–113 (Montreux, 1993)
2. Clarke, C.K.P., High quality decoding for PAL inputs to digital YUV studios. *BBC Res. Dep. Rep.*, RD 1982/12 (1982)

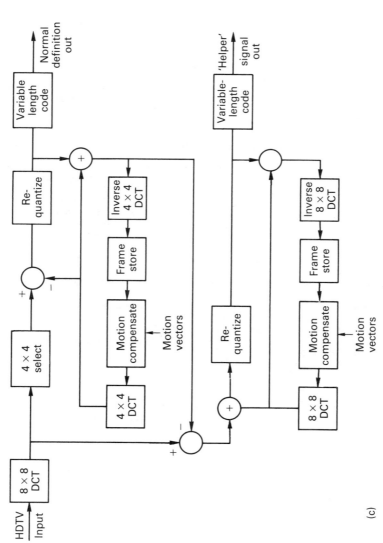

Figure 4.96 (continued)

3. Nicoll, I., *The detection and correction of illegal colour signals*. Presented at 18th ITS (Montreux, 1993)
4. Aird, B., Three dimensional picture synthesis. *Broadcast Syst. Eng.*, **12**, No.3, 34–40 (1986)
5. Newman, W.M. and Sproull, R.F., *Principles of interactive computer graphics*. Tokyo: McGraw-Hill (1979)
6. Gernsheim, H., *A Concise History of Photography*. London: Thames and Hudson, pp. 9–15 (1971)
7. Hedgecoe, J., *The Photographer's Handbook*. London: Ebury Press, pp. 104–105 (1977)
8. Bennett, P., *et al.*, Spatial transformation system including key signal generator. US Patent No. 4,463,372 (1984)
9. de Boor, C., *A Practical Guide to Splines*. Berlin: Springer (1978)
10. Beanland, D., ISIS. *Int. Broadcast Eng.*, **20**, No.229, 40–43 (1989)
11. Kraniauskas, P., *Transforms in Signals and Systems*. Ch. 6, Wokingham: Addison Wesley (1992)
12. Ahmed, N., Natarajan, T. and Rao, K., Discrete cosine transform. *IEEE Trans. Computers*, **C-23**, 90–93 (1974)
13. De With, P.H.N., Data compression techniques for digital video recording. PhD Thesis, Technical University of Delft (1992)
14. Kelly, D.H., Adaptation effects on spatio-temporal sine wave thresholds. *Vision Res.*, **12**, 89–101 (1972)
15. Kelly, D.H., Visual processing of moving stimuli. *J. Opt. Soc. Am.*. **2**, 216–225 (1985)
16. Weiss, P., Christensson, J., Arvidsson, J., Andersson, H., Petrides, G. and Foster, C., Design of an HDTV codec for terrestrial transmission at 25 MBits/sec. *IEE Conf. Publ. No. 358*, 14–17 (1992)
17. Limb, J.O. and Murphy, J.A., Measuring the speed of moving objects from television signals. *IEEE Trans. Commun.*, 474–478 (1975)
18. Thomas, G.A., Television motion measurement for DATV and other applications. *BBC Res. Dep. Rep.*, RD 1987/11 (1987)
19. Pearson, J.J. *et al.*, Video rate image correlation processor. *SPIE*, Vol.119, Application of digital image processing, IOCC (1977)
20. Lau, H. and Lyon, D., Motion compensated processing for enhanced slow motion and standards conversion. *IEE Conf. Publ. No. 358*, 62–66 (1992)
21. Weiss, P. and Christensson, J., Real time implementation of sub-pixel motion estimation for broadcast applications. *IEE Dig.*, 1990/128
22. ISO Joint Photographic Experts Group standard JPEG-8-R8
23. Wallace, G.K., Overview of the JPEG (ISO/CCITT) still image compression standard. ISO/JTC1/SC2/WG8 N932 (1989)
24. Le Gall, MPEG: a video compression standard for multimedia applications. *Commun. ACM*, **34**, No.4, 46–58 (1991)
25. Clarke, R.J., *Transform Coding of Images*. Academic Press (1985)
26. Netravali, A.N. and Haskell, B.G., *Digital Pictures – Representation and Compression*. Plenum Press (1988)
27. Huffman, D.A., A method for the construction of minimum redundancy codes. *Proc. IRE*, **40**, 1098–1101 (1952)
28. Delogne, P., Hierarchical layered coding for digital HDTV/TV broadcasting. *Record of 18th ITS*, 275–290 (Montreux, 1993)

Chapter 5

Digital recording and transmission principles

Recording and transmission are quite different tasks, but they have a great deal in common and have always been regarded as being different applications of the same art. Digital transmission consists of converting data into a waveform suitable for the path along which it is to be sent. Digital recording is basically the process of recording a digital transmission waveform on a suitable medium. Although the physics of the recording or transmission processes is unaffected by the meaning attributed to signals, digital techniques are rather different from those used with analog signals, although often the same phenomenon shows up in a different guise. In this Chapter the fundamentals of digital recording and transmission are introduced along with descriptions of the coding techniques used in practical applications. The parallel subject of error correction is dealt with in the next chapter.

5.1 Introduction to the channel

Data can be recorded on many different media and conveyed using many forms of transmission. The generic term for the path down which the information is sent is the *channel*. In a transmission application, the channel may be no more than a length of cable or an optical fibre. In a recording application the channel will include the record head, the medium and the replay head. In analog systems, the characteristics of the channel affect the signal directly. It is a fundamental strength of digital video that by using pulse code modulation the quality can be made independent of the channel. The dynamic range required by the programme material no longer directly decides the dynamic range of the channel.

In digital circuitry there is a great deal of noise immunity because the signal has only two states, which are widely separated compared with the amplitude of noise. In both digital recording and transmission this is not always the case. In magnetic recording, noise immunity is a function of track width and reduction of the working SNR of a digital track allows the same information to be carried in a smaller area of the medium, improving economy of operation. In broadcasting, the noise immunity is a function of the transmitter power and reduction of working SNR allows lower power to be used with consequent economy. These reductions also increase the random error rate, but, as was seen in Chapter 1, an error-correction system may already be necessary in a practical system and it is simply made to work harder.

In real channels, the signal may *originate* with discrete states which change at discrete times, but the channel will treat it as an analog waveform and so it will not be *received* in the same form. Various loss mechanisms will reduce the amplitude of the signal. These attenuations will not be the same at all frequencies. Noise will be picked up in the channel as a result of stray electric fields or magnetic induction. As a result the voltage received at the end of the channel will have an infinitely varying state along with a degree of uncertainty due to the noise. Different frequencies can propagate at different speeds in the channel; this is the phenomenon of group delay. An alternative way of considering group delay is that there will be frequency-dependent phase shifts in the signal and these will result in uncertainty in the timing of pulses.

In digital circuitry, the signals are generally accompanied by a separate clock signal which reclocks the data to remove jitter as was shown in Chapter 1. In contrast, it is generally not feasible to provide a separate clock in recording and transmission applications. In the transmission case, a separate clock line would not only raise cost, but is impractical because at high frequency it is virtually impossible to ensure that the clock cable propagates signals at the same speed as the data cable except over short distances. In the recording case, provision of a separate clock track is impractical at high density because mechanical tolerances cause phase errors between the tracks. The result is the same: timing differences between parallel channels which are known as skew.

The solution is to use a self-clocking waveform and the generation of this is a further essential function of the coding process. Clearly if data bits are simply clocked serially from a shift register in so-called direct recording or transmission this characteristic will not be obtained. If all the data bits are the same, for example all zeros, there is no clock when they are serialized.

It is not the channel which is digital; instead the term describes the way in which the received signals are *interpreted*. When the receiver makes discrete decisions from the input waveform it attempts to reject the uncertainties in voltage and time. The technique of channel coding is one where transmitted waveforms are restricted to those which still allow the receiver to make discrete decisions despite the degradations caused by the analog nature of the channel.

5.2 Types of transmission channel

Transmission can be by electrical conductors, radio or optical fibre. Although these appear to be completely different, they are in fact just different examples of electromagnetic energy travelling from one place to another. If the energy is made to vary in some way, information can be carried.

Even today electromagnetism is not fully understood, but sufficiently good models, based on experimental results, exist so that practical equipment can be made. It is not actually necessary to understand a process fully in order to harness it; it is only necessary to be able to predict reliably what will happen in given circumstances.

Electromagnetic energy propagates in a manner which is a function of frequency, and our partial understanding requires it to be considered as electrons, waves or photons so that we can predict its behaviour in given circumstances.

At DC and at the low frequencies used for power distribution, electromagnetic energy is called electricity and it is remarkably aimless stuff which needs to be transported completely inside conductors. It has to have a complete circuit to flow in, and the resistance to current flow is determined by the cross-sectional area of the conductor. The insulation around the conductor and the spacing between the conductors has no effect on the ability of the conductor to pass current. At DC an inductor appears to be a short circuit, and a capacitor appears to be an open circuit.

As frequency rises, resistance is exchanged for impedance. Inductors display increasing impedance with frequency, capacitors show falling impedance. Electromagnetic energy becomes increasingly desperate to leave the conductor. The first symptom is that the current flows only in the outside layer of the conductor effectively causing the resistance to rise. This is the skin effect and gives rise to such techniques as Litz wire which has as much surface area as possible per unit cross-section, and to silver-plated conductors in which the surface has lower resistivity than the interior.

As the energy is starting to leave the conductors, the characteristics of the space between them become important. This determines the impedance. A change of impedance causes reflections in the energy flow and some of it heads back towards the source. Constant impedance cables with fixed conductor spacing are necessary, and these must be suitably terminated to prevent reflections. The most important characteristic of the insulation is its thickness as this determines the spacing between the conductors.

As frequency rises still further, the energy travels less in the conductors and more in the insulation between them, and their composition becomes important and they begin to be called dielectrics. A poor dielectric like PVC absorbs high-frequency energy and attenuates the signal. So-called low-loss dielectrics such as PTFE are used, and one way of achieving low loss is to incorporate as much air in the dielectric as possible by making it in the form of a foam or extruding it with voids.

Further rise in frequency causes the energy to start behaving more like waves and less like electron movement. As the wavelength falls it becomes increasingly directional. The transmission line becomes a waveguide and microwaves are sufficiently directional that they can keep going without any conductor at all. Microwaves are simply low-frequency radiant heat, which is itself low-frequency light. All three are reflected well by electrical conductors, and can be refracted at the boundary between media having different propagation speeds. A waveguide is the microwave equivalent of an optical fibre.

This frequency-dependent behaviour is the most important factor in deciding how best to harness electromagnetic energy flow for information transmission. It is obvious that the higher the frequency, the greater the possible information rate, but in general losses increase with frequency, and flat frequency response is elusive. The best that can be managed is that over a narrow band of frequencies, the response can be made reasonably constant with the help of equalization. Unfortunately raw data when serialized have an unconstrained spectrum. Runs of identical bits can produce frequencies much lower than the bit rate would suggest. One of the essential steps in a transmission system is to modify the spectrum of the data into something more suitable.

At moderate bit rates, say a few megabits per second, and with moderate cable lengths, say a few metres, the dominant effect will be the capacitance of the cable due to the geometry of the space between the conductors and the dielectric between. The capacitance behaves under these conditions as if it were a single capacitor connected across the signal. Fig. 5.1 shows the equivalent circuit.

Figure 5.1 With a short cable, the capacitance between the conductors can be lumped as if it were a discrete component. The effect of the parallel capacitor is to slope off the edges of the signal

The effect of the series source resistance and the parallel capacitance is that signal edges or transitions are turned into exponential curves as the capacitance is effectively being charged and discharged through the source impedance. This effect can be observed on the AES/EBU interface with short cables. Although the position where the edges cross the centreline is displaced, the signal eventually reaches the same amplitude as it would at DC.

As cable length increases, the capacitance can no longer be lumped as if it were a single unit; it has to be regarded as being distributed along the cable. With rising frequency, the cable inductance also becomes significant, and it too is distributed.

The cable is now a transmission line and pulses travel down it as current loops which roll along as shown in Fig. 5.2. If the pulse is positive, as it is launched along the line, it will charge the dielectric locally as at (a). As the pulse moves along, it will continue to charge the local dielectric as at (b). When the driver finishes the pulse, the trailing edge of the pulse follows the leading edge along the line. The voltage of the dielectric charged by the leading edge of the pulse is now higher than the voltage on the line, and so the dielectric discharges into the line as at (c). The current flows forward as it is in fact the same current which is flowing into the dielectric at the leading edge. There is thus a loop of current rolling down the line flowing forwards in the 'hot' wire and backwards in the return. The analogy with the tracks of a Caterpillar tractor is quite good. Individual plates in the track find themselves being lowered to the ground at the front and raised again at the back.

The constant to-ing and fro-ing of charge in the dielectric results in the dielectric loss of signal energy. Dielectric loss increases with frequency and so a long transmission line acts as a filter. Thus the term 'low-loss' cable refers primarily to the kind of dielectric used.

Transmission lines which transport energy in this way have a characteristic impedance caused by the interplay of the inductance along the conductors with the parallel capacitance. One consequence of that transmission mode is that correct termination or matching is required between the line and both the driver and the receiver. When a line is correctly matched, the rolling energy rolls

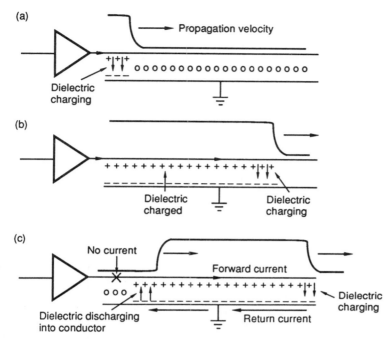

Figure 5.2 A transmission line conveys energy packets which appear with respect to the dielectric. In (a) the driver launches a pulse which charges the dielectric at the beginning of the line. As it propagates the dielectric is charged further along as in (b). When the driver ends the pulse, the charged dielectric discharges into the line. A current loop is formed where the current in the return loop flows in the opposite direction to the current in the 'hot' wire

straight out of the line into the load and the maximum energy is available. If the impedance presented by the load is incorrect, there will be reflections from the mismatch. An open circuit will reflect all of the energy back in the same polarity as the original, whereas a short circuit will reflect all of the energy back in the opposite polarity. Thus impedances above or below the correct value will have a tendency towards reflections whose magnitude depends upon the degree of mismatch and whose polarity depends upon whether the load is too high or too low. In practice it is the need to avoid reflections which is the most important reason to terminate correctly.

Reflections at impedance mismatches have practical applications: electricity companies inject high-frequency pulses into faulty cables and the time taken until the reflection from the break or short returns can be used to locate the source of damage. The same technique can be used to find wiring breaks in large studio complexes.

A perfectly square pulse contains an indefinite series of harmonics, but the higher ones suffer progressively more loss. A square pulse at the driver becomes less and less square with distance as Fig. 5.3 shows. The harmonics are progressively lost until in the extreme case all that is left is the fundamental. A transmitted square wave is received as a sine wave. Fortunately data can still be recovered from the fundamental signal component.

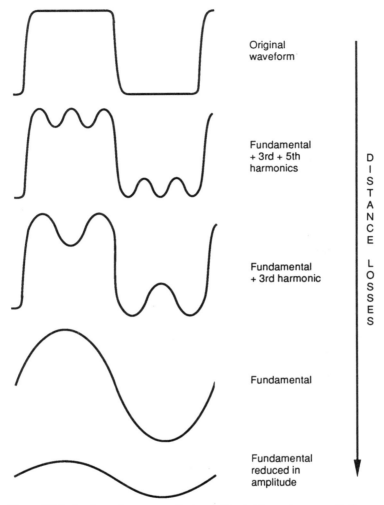

Figure 5.3 A signal may be square at the transmitter, but losses increase with frequency, and as the signal propagates, more of the harmonics are lost until only the fundamental remains. The amplitude of the fundamental then falls with further distance

Once all the harmonics have been lost, further losses cause the amplitude of the fundamental to fall. The effect worsens with distance and it is necessary to ensure that data recovery is still possible from a signal of unpredictable level.

5.3 Types of recording medium

There is considerably more freedom of choice for digital media than was the case for analog signals. Once converted to the digital domain, video and audio are no more than data and can take advantage of the research expended in computer data recording.

Digital media do not need to have linear transfer functions, nor do they need to be noise free or continuous. All they need to do is to allow the player to be able to distinguish the presence or absence of replay events, such as the generation of pulses, with reasonable (rather than perfect) reliability. In a magnetic medium, the event will be a flux change from one direction of magnetization to another. In an optical medium, the event must cause the pickup to perceive a change in the intensity of the light falling on the sensor. In optical discs, the apparent contrast may be obtained by interference or through selective absorption of light by dyes. In magneto-optical disks the recording itself is magnetic, but it is made and read using light.

5.4 Magnetic recording

Magnetic recording relies on the hysteresis of certain magnetic materials. After an applied magnetic field is removed, the material remains magnetized in the same direction. By definition the process is non-linear, and analog magnetic recorders have to use bias to linearize it. Digital recorders are not concerned with the non-linearity, and HF bias is unnecessary.

Fig. 5.4 shows the construction of a typical digital record head, which is not dissimilar to an analog record head. A magnetic circuit carries a coil through which the record current passes and generates flux. A non-magnetic gap forces the flux to leave the magnetic circuit of the head and penetrate the medium. The current through the head must be set to suit the coercivity of the tape, and is arranged almost to saturate the track. The amplitude of the current is constant, and recording is performed by reversing the direction of the current with respect to time. As the track passes the head, this is converted to the reversal of the magnetic field left on the tape with respect to distance. The magnetic recording is therefore bipolar. Fig. 5.5 shows that the recording is actually made just after the trailing pole of the record head where the flux strength from the gap is falling. As in analog recorders, the width of the gap is generally made quite large to ensure that the full thickness of the magnetic coating is recorded, although this cannot be done if the same head is intended to replay.

Figure 5.4 A digital record head is similar in principle to an analog head but uses much narrower tracks

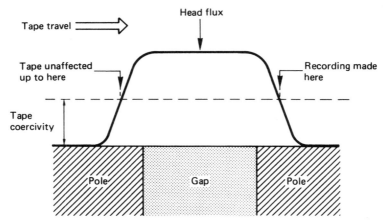

Figure 5.5 The recording is actually made near the trailing pole of the head where the head flux falls below the coercivity of the tape

Fig. 5.6 shows what happens when a conventional inductive head, i.e. one having a normal winding, is used to replay the bipolar track made by reversing the record current. The head output is proportional to the rate of change of flux and so only occurs at flux reversals. In other words, the replay head differentiates the flux on the track. The polarity of the resultant pulses alternates as the flux changes and changes back. A circuit is necessary which locates the peaks of the pulses and outputs a signal corresponding to the original record current waveform. There are two ways in which this can be done.

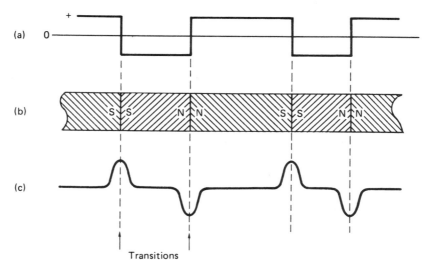

Figure 5.6 Basic digital recording. At (a) the write current in the head is reversed from time to time, leaving a binary magnetization pattern shown at (b). When replayed, the waveform at (c) results because an output is only produced when flux in the head changes. Changes are referred to as transitions

The amplitude of the replay signal is of no consequence and often an AGC system is used to keep the replay signal constant in amplitude. What matters is the time at which the write current, and hence the flux stored on the medium, reverses. This can be determined by locating the peaks of the replay impulses, which can conveniently be done by differentiating the signal and looking for zero crossings. Fig. 5.7 shows that this results in noise between the peaks. This problem is overcome by the gated peak detector, where only zero crossings from a pulse which exceeds the threshold will be counted. The AGC system allows the

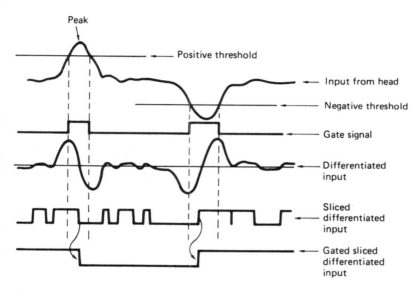

Figure 5.7 Gated peak detection rejects noise by disabling the differentiated output between transitions

thresholds to be fixed. As an alternative, the record waveform can also be restored by integration, which opposes the differentiation of the head as in Fig. 5.8.[1]

The head shown in Fig. 5.4 has a frequency response shown in Fig. 5.9. At DC there is no change of flux and no output. As a result inductive heads are at a disadvantage at very low speeds. The output rises with frequency until the rise is halted by the onset of thickness loss. As the frequency rises, the recorded wavelength falls and flux from the shorter magnetic patterns cannot be picked up so far away. At some point, the wavelength becomes so short that flux from the back of the tape coating cannot reach the head and a decreasing thickness of tape contributes to the replay signal.[2] In digital recorders using short wavelengths to obtain high density, there is no point in using thick coatings. As wavelength further reduces, the familiar gap loss occurs, where the head gap is too big to resolve detail on the track. The construction of the head results in the same action as that of a two-point transversal filter, as the two poles of the head see the tape with a small delay interposed due to the finite gap. As expected, the head response is like a comb filter with the well-known nulls where flux cancellation

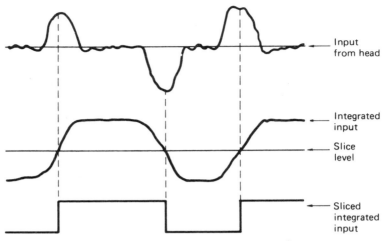

Figure 5.8 Integration method for re-creating write-current waveform

takes place across the gap. Clearly the smaller the gap the shorter the wavelength of the first null. This contradicts the requirement of the record head to have a large gap. In quality analog audio recorders, it is the norm to have different record and replay heads for this reason, and the same will be true in digital machines which have separate record and playback heads. Clearly where the same pair of heads are used for record and play, the head gap size will be determined by the playback requirement.

As can be seen, the frequency response is far from ideal, and steps must be taken to ensure that recorded data waveforms do not contain frequencies which suffer excessive losses.

A more recent development is the magneto-resistive (M-R) head. This is a head which measures the flux on the tape rather than using it to generate a signal

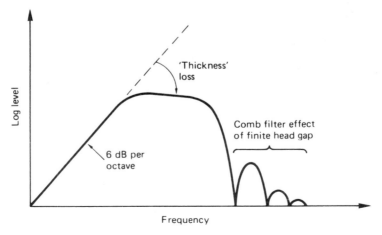

Figure 5.9 The major mechanism defining magnetic channel bandwidth

directly. Flux measurement works down to DC and so offers advantages at low tape speeds. Unfortunately flux-measuring heads are not polarity conscious but sense the modulus of the flux and if used directly they respond to positive and negative flux equally, as shown in Fig. 5.10. This is overcome by using a small extra winding in the head carrying a constant current. This creates a steady bias field which adds to the flux from the tape. The flux seen by the head is now unipolar and changes between two levels and a more useful output waveform results.

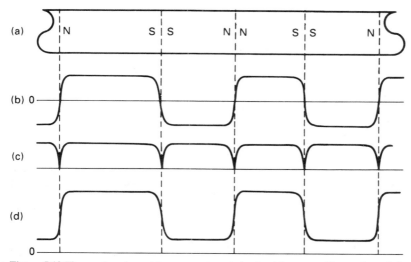

Figure 5.10 The sensing element in a magneto-resistive head is not sensitive to the polarity of the flux, only the magnitude. At (a) the track magnetisation is shown and this causes a bidirectional flux variation in the head as at (b), resulting in the magnitude output at (c). However, if the flux in the head due to the track is biased by an additional field, it can be made unipolar as at (d) and the correct waveform is obtained

M-R heads are advantageous for recorders which have low head-to-medium speed, and so they are not generally found in digital VTRs or magnetic disk drives which use inductive heads.

Heads designed for use with tape work in actual contact with the magnetic coating. The tape is tensioned to pull it against the head. There will be a wear mechanism and need for periodic cleaning.

In the hard disk, the rotational speed is high in order to reduce access time, and the drive must be capable of staying on line for extended periods. In this case the heads do not contact the disk surface, but are supported on a boundary layer of air. The presence of the air film causes spacing loss, which restricts the wavelengths at which the head can replay. This is the penalty of rapid access.

Digital video recorders must operate at high density in order to offer a reasonable playing time. This implies that shortest possible wavelengths will be used. Fig. 5.11 shows that when two flux changes, or transitions, are recorded close together, they affect each other on replay. The amplitude of the composite signal is reduced, and the position of the peaks is pushed outwards. This is known as intersymbol interference, or peak shift distortion, and it occurs in all magnetic media.

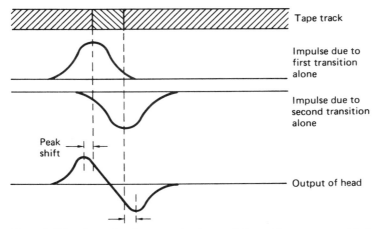

Figure 5.11 Readout pulses from two closely recorded transitions are summed in the head and the effect is that the peaks of the waveform are moved outwards. This is known as peak-shift distortion and equalization is necessary to reduce the effect

The effect is primarily due to high-frequency loss and it can be reduced by equalization on replay, as is done in most tapes, or by precompensation on record as is done in hard disks.

5.5 Azimuth recording and rotary heads

Fig. 5.12(a) shows that in azimuth recording, the transitions are laid down at an angle to the track by using a head which is tilted. Machines using azimuth

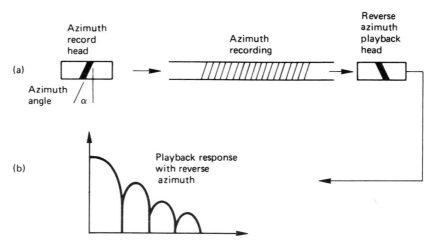

Figure 5.12 In azimuth recording (a), the head gap is tilted. If the track is played with the same head, playback is normal, but the response of the reverse azimuth head is attenuated (b)

recording must always have an even number of heads, so that adjacent tracks can be recorded with opposite azimuth angle. The two track types are usually referred to as A and B. Fig. 5.12(b) shows the effect of playing a track with the wrong type of head. The playback process suffers from an enormous azimuth error. The effect of azimuth error can be understood by imagining the tape track to be made from many identical parallel strips. In the presence of azimuth error, the strips at one edge of the track are played back with a phase shift relative to strips at the other side. At some wavelengths, the phase shift will be 180°, and there will be no output; at other wavelengths, especially long wavelengths, some output will reappear. The effect is rather like that of a comb filter, and serves to attenuate crosstalk due to adjacent tracks so that no guard bands are required. Since no tape is wasted between the tracks, more efficient use is made of the tape. The term guard-band-less recording is often used instead of, or in addition to, the term azimuth recording. The failure of the azimuth effect at long wavelengths is a characteristic of azimuth recording, and it is necessary to ensure that the spectrum of the signal to be recorded has a small low-frequency content. The signal will need to pass through a rotary transformer to reach the heads, and cannot therefore contain a DC component.

In machines such as early D-2 recorders and some digital camcorders there is no separate erase process, and erasure is achieved by overwriting with a new waveform. Overwriting is only successful when there are no long wavelengths in the earlier recording, since these penetrate deeper into the tape, and the short wavelengths in a new recording will not be able to erase them. In this case the ratio between the shortest and longest wavelengths recorded on tape should be limited.

Restricting the spectrum of the code to allow erasure by overwrite also eases the design of the rotary transformer.

5.6 DVTR head construction

Design of a head for DVTRs is not easy, since there are a number of conflicting requirements. The high coercivity of the tape used requires that the head should be able to pass high flux densities into the tape without saturating. The bit rate of digital video is such that eddy current losses in the head are significant.

Ferrite is attractive as a head material because it is a non-conductor and this limits losses. Unfortunately currently available ferrites saturate before 1500 Oe tape can be fully modulated. Metals are available which will carry the required flux density, but they suffer from eddy current losses. One solution to the problem is to make a composite head, where the bulk of the head is made from ferrite, but metal poles are fitted which concentrate the flux from a large cross-section of ferrite into a small track width (see Fig. 5.13).

Another approach to limiting eddy current losses is lamination. Laminated metal heads have been used in stationary-head recorders for many years, but it is difficult to fabricate laminated heads for digital recorders because of the small dimensions involved. Developments in plating technology mean that it is now possible to fabricate laminated heads on an extremely small scale by plating layers of magnetic material alternately with thinly deposited insulating layers. The construction of such a head is shown in Fig. 5.14.

In the amorphous head, particles of metal are sintered under pressure to form the magnetic circuit. The metal allows high flux density, but the magnetic circuit

Azimuth
angle

Figure 5.13 As ferrite will saturate before high coercivity tape, it cannot be used for head poles, but as shown here, it can be used for the bulk of the head, with metal tips to focus the flux to the tip. Eddy current losses in the metal are minimized. Alternatives are laminated or amorphous metal heads

has much higher electrical resistance than solid metal because the metal particles are only joined at their corners. In this way eddy current losses are reduced.

5.7 Optical discs

Optical recorders have the advantage that light can be focused at a distance whereas magnetism cannot. This means that there need be no physical contact between the pickup and the medium and no wear mechanism.

In the same way that the recorded wavelength of a magnetic recording is limited by the gap in the replay head, the density of optical recording is limited by the size of light spot which can be focused on the medium. This is controlled by the wavelength of the light used and by the aperture of the lens. When the light spot is as small as these limits allow, it is said to be diffraction limited. The recorded details on the disc are minute, and could easily be obscured by dust particles. In practice the information layer needs to be protected by a thick transparent coating. Light enters the coating well out of focus over a large area so that it can pass around dust particles, and comes to a focus within the thickness of the coating. Although the number of bits per unit area is high in optical recorders the number of bits per unit volume is not as high as that of tape because of the thickness of the coating.

Fig. 5.14 shows the principle of readout of the Compact Disc which is a read-only disc manufactured by pressing. The track consists of raised bumps separated by flat areas. The entire surface of the disc is metallized, and the bumps are one-quarter of a wavelength in height. The player spot is arranged so that half of its light falls on top of a bump, and half on the surrounding surface. Light returning from the flat surface has travelled half a wavelength further than light returning from the top of the bump, and so there is a phase reversal between the two components of the reflection. This causes destructive interference, and light cannot return to the pickup. It must reflect at angles which are outside the aperture of the lens and be lost. Conversely, when light falls on the flat surface between bumps, the majority of it is reflected back to the pickup. The pickup thus sees a disc *apparently* having alternately good or poor reflectivity. The sensor in

Figure 5.14 CD readout principle and dimensions. The presence of a bump causes destructive interference in the reflected light

the pickup responds to the incident intensity and so the replay signal is unipolar and varies between two levels in a manner similar to the output of an M-R head.

Some discs can be recorded once, but not subsequently erased or re-recorded. These are known as WORM (Write-Once-Read-Mostly) discs. One type of WORM disc uses a thin metal layer which has holes punched in it on recording

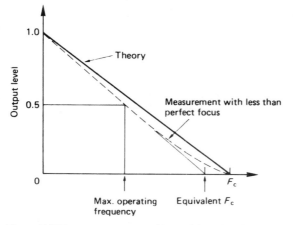

Figure 5.15 Frequency response of laser pickup. Maximum operating frequency is about half of cut-off frequency F_c

by heat from a laser. Others rely on the heat raising blisters in a thin metallic layer by decomposing the plastic material beneath. Yet another alternative is a layer of photochemical dye which darkens when struck by the high-powered recording beam. Whatever the recording principle, light from the pickup is reflected more or less, or absorbed more or less, so that the pickup senses a change in reflectivity.

All optical discs need mechanisms to keep the pickup following the track and sharply focused on it, and these will be discussed in Chapter 10 and need not be treated here.

The frequency response of an optical disc is shown in Fig. 5.15. The response is best at DC and falls steadily to the optical cut-off frequency. Although the optics work down to DC, this cannot be used for the data recording. DC and low frequencies in the data would interfere with the focus and tracking servos and, as will be seen, difficulties arise when attempting to demodulate a unipolar signal. In practice the signal from the pickup is split by a filter. Low frequencies go to the servos, and higher frequencies go to the data circuitry. As a result the optical disc channel has the same inability to handle DC as does a magnetic recorder, and the same techniques are needed to overcome it.

5.8 Magneto-optical discs

When a magnetic material is heated above its Curie temperature, it becomes demagnetized, and on cooling will assume the magnetization of an applied field which would be too weak to influence it normally. This is the principle of magneto-optical recording. The heat is supplied by a finely focused laser, and the field is supplied by a coil which is much larger.

Fig. 5.16 shows that the medium is initially magnetized in one direction only. In order to record, the coil is energized with a current in the opposite direction.

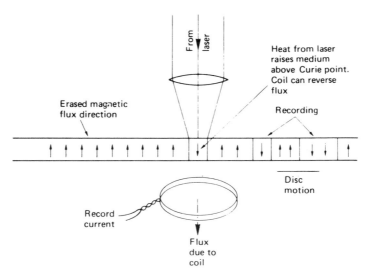

Figure 5.16 The thermomagneto-optical disc uses the heat from a laser to allow magnetic field to record on the disc

This is too weak to influence the medium in its normal state, but when it is heated by the recording laser beam the heated area will take on the magnetism from the coil when it cools. Thus a magnetic recording with very small dimensions can be made even though the magnetic circuit involved is quite large in comparison.

Readout is obtained using the Kerr effect or the Faraday effect, which are phenomena whereby the plane of polarization of light can be rotated by a magnetic field. The angle of rotation is very small and needs a sensitive pickup. The pickup contains a polarizing filter before the sensor. Changes in polarization change the ability of the light to get through the polarizing filter and result in an intensity change which once more produces a unipolar output.

The magneto-optic recording can be erased by reversing the current in the coil and operating the laser continuously as it passes along the track. A new recording can then be made on the erased track.

A disadvantage of magneto-optical recording is that all materials having a Curie point low enough to be useful are highly corrodible by air and need to be kept under an effectively sealed protective layer.

The magneto-optical channel has the same frequency response as that shown in Fig. 5.15.

5.9 Equalization

The characteristics of most channels are that signal loss occurs which increases with frequency. This has the effect of slowing down rise times and thereby sloping off edges. If a signal with sloping edges is sliced, the time at which the waveform crosses the slicing level will be changed, and this causes jitter. Fig. 5.17 shows that slicing a sloping waveform in the presence of baseline wander causes more jitter.

Figure 5.17 A DC offset can cause timing errors

On a long cable, high-frequency roll-off can cause sufficient jitter to move a transition into an adjacent bit period. This is called intersymbol interference and the effect becomes worse in signals which have greater asymmetry, i.e. short pulses alternating with long ones. The effect can be reduced by the application of equalization, which is typically a high-frequency boost, and by choosing a channel code which has restricted asymmetry.

Compensation for peak shift distortion in recording requires equalization of the channel,[3] and this can be done by a network after the replay head, termed an equalizer or pulse sharpener,[4] as in Fig. 5.18(a). This technique uses transversal filtering to oppose the inherent transversal effect of the head. As an alternative, precompensation in the record stage can be used as shown in Fig. 5.18(b).

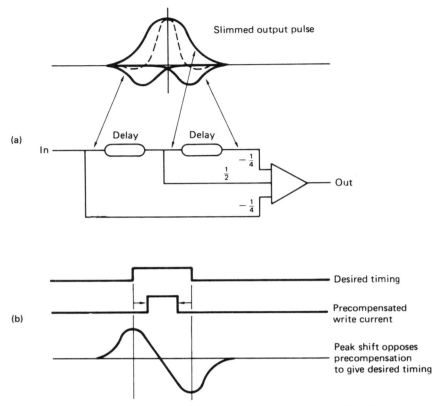

Figure 5.18 Peak-shift distortion is due to the finite width of replay pulses. The effect can be reduced by the pulse slimmer shown in (a) which is basically a transversal filter. The use of a linear operational amplifier emphasizes the analog nature of channels. Instead of replay pulse slimming, transitions can be written with a displacement equal and opposite to the anticipated peak shift as shown in (b)

Transitions are written in such a way that the anticipated peak shift will move the readout peaks to the desired timing.

5.10 Data separation

The important step of information recovery at the receiver or replay circuit is known as data separation. The data separator is rather like an analog-to-digital converter because the two processes of sampling and quantizing are both present. In the time domain, the sampling clock is derived from the clock content of the channel waveform. In the voltage domain, the process of *slicing* converts the analog waveform from the channel back into a binary representation. The slicer is thus a form of quantizer which has only 1 bit resolution. The slicing process makes a discrete decision about the voltage of the incoming signal in order to reject noise. The sampler makes discrete decisions along the time axis in order to reject jitter. These two processes will be described in detail.

5.11 Slicing

The slicer is implemented with a comparator which has analog inputs but a binary output. In a cable receiver, the input waveform can be sliced directly. In an inductive magnetic replay system, the replay waveform is differentiated and must first pass through a peak detector (Fig. 5.7) or an integrator (Fig. 5.8). The signal voltage is compared with the midway voltage, known as the threshold, baseline or slicing level by the comparator. If the signal voltage is above the threshold, the comparator outputs a high level; if below, a low level results.

Fig. 5.19 shows some waveforms associated with a slicer. At (a) the transmitted waveform has an uneven duty cycle. The DC component, or average level, of the signal is received with high amplitude, but the pulse amplitude falls as the pulse gets shorter. Eventually the waveform cannot be sliced.

At (b) the opposite duty cycle is shown. The signal level drifts to the opposite

Figure 5.19 Slicing a signal which has suffered losses works well if the duty cycle is even. If the duty cycle is uneven, as at (a), timing errors will become worse until slicing fails. With the opposite duty cycle, the slicing fails in the opposite direction as at (b). If, however, the signal is DC free, correct slicing can continue even in the presence of serious losses, as (c) shows

polarity and once more slicing is impossible. The phenomenon is called baseline wander and will be observed with any signal whose average voltage is not the same as the slicing level.

At (c) it will be seen that if the transmitted waveform has a relatively constant average voltage, slicing remains possible up to high frequencies even in the presence of serious amplitude loss, because the received waveform remains symmetrical about the baseline.

It is clearly not possible simply to serialize data in a shift register for so-called direct transmission, because successful slicing can only be obtained if the number of ones is equal to the number of zeros; there is little chance of this happening consistently with real data. Instead, a modulation code or channel code is necessary. This converts the data into a waveform which is DC free or nearly so for the purpose of transmission.

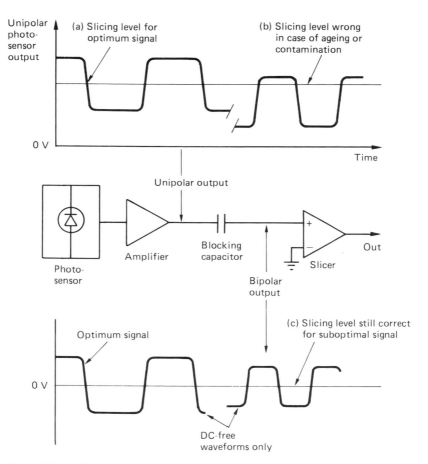

Figure 5.20 (a) Slicing a unipolar signal requires a non-zero threshold. (b) If the signal amplitude changes, the threshold will then be incorrect. (c) If a DC-free code is used, a unipolar waveform can be converted to a bipolar waveform using a series capacitor. A zero threshold can be used and slicing continues with amplitude variations

The slicing threshold level is naturally zero in a bipolar system such as magnetic inductive replay or a cable. When the amplitude falls it does so symmetrically and slicing continues. The same is not true of M-R heads and optical pickups, which both respond to intensity and therefore produce a unipolar output. If the replay signal is sliced directly, the threshold cannot be zero, but must be some level approximately half the amplitude of the signal as shown in Fig. 5.20(a). Unfortunately when the signal level falls it falls towards zero and not towards the slicing level. The threshold will no longer be appropriate for the signal as can be seen at (b). This can be overcome by using a DC-free coded waveform. If a series capacitor is connected to the unipolar signal from an optical pickup, the waveform is rendered bipolar because the capacitor blocks any DC component in the signal. The DC-free channel waveform passes through unaltered. If an amplitude loss is suffered, Fig. 5.20(c) shows that the resultant bipolar signal now reduces in amplitude about the slicing level and slicing can continue.

Whilst cables and optical recording channels need to be DC free, some channel waveforms used in magnetic recording have a reduced DC component, but are

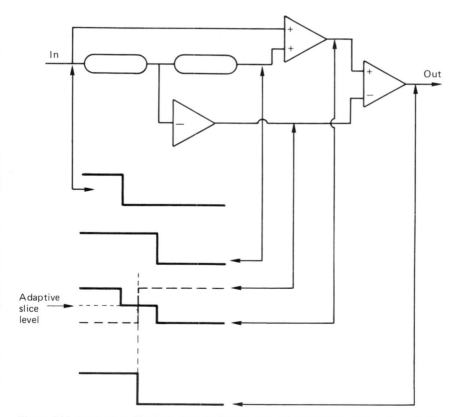

Figure 5.21 An adaptive slicer uses delay lines to produce a threshold from the waveform itself. Correct slicing will then be possible in the presence of baseline wander. Such a slicer can be used with codes which are not DC free

not completely DC free. As a result the received waveform will suffer from baseline wander. If this is moderate, an adaptive slicer which can move its threshold can be used. As Fig. 5.21 shows, the adaptive slicer consists of a pair of delays. If the input and output signals are linearly added together with equal weighting, when a transition passes, the resultant waveform has a plateau which is at the half-amplitude level of the signal and can be used as a threshold voltage for the slicer.

5.12 Jitter rejection

The binary waveform at the output of the slicer will be a replica of the transmitted waveform, except for the addition of jitter or time uncertainty in the position of the edges due to noise, baseline wander, intersymbol interference and imperfect equalization.

Binary circuits reject noise by using discrete voltage levels which are spaced further apart than the uncertainty due to noise. In a similar manner, digital coding combats time uncertainty by making the time axis discrete using events, known as transitions, spaced apart at integer multiples of some basic time period, called a detent, which is larger than the typical time uncertainty. Fig. 5.22 shows how this jitter rejection mechanism works. All that matters is to identify the detent in which the transition occurred. Exactly where it occurred within the detent is of no consequence.

Figure 5.22 A certain amount of jitter can be rejected by changing the signal at multiples of the basic detent period T_d

As ideal transitions occur at multiples of a basic period, an oscilloscope, which is repeatedly triggered on a channel-coded signal carrying random data, will show an eye pattern if connected to the output of the equalizer. Study of the eye pattern reveals how well the coding used suits the channel. In the case of transmission with a short cable, the losses will be small, and the eye opening will be virtually square except for some edge sloping due to cable capacitance. As cable length increases, the harmonics are lost and the remaining fundamental gives the eyes a diamond shape. The same eye pattern will be obtained with a recording channel where it is uneconomic to provide bandwidth much beyond the fundamental.

Noise closes the eyes in a vertical direction, and jitter closes the eyes in a horizontal direction, as in Fig. 5.23. If the eyes remain sensibly open, data separation will be possible. Clearly more jitter can be tolerated if there is less noise, and vice versa. If the equalizer is adjustable, the optimum setting will be where the greatest eye opening is obtained.

In the centre of the eyes, the receiver must make binary decisions at the channel bit rate about the state of the signal, high or low, using the slicer output. As stated, the receiver is sampling the output of the slicer, and it needs to have a sampling clock in order to do that. In order to give the best rejection of noise and jitter, the clock edges which operate the sampler must be in the centre of the eyes.

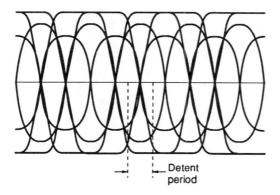

Detent
period

Figure 5.23 A transmitted waveform which is generated according to the principle of Figure 5.21 will appear like this on an oscilloscope as successive parts of the waveform are superimposed on the tube. When the waveform is rounded off by losses, diamond-shaped eyes are left in the centre, spaced apart by the detent period

As has been stated, a separate clock is not practicable in recording or transmission. A fixed-frequency clock at the receiver is of no use as even if it was sufficiently stable, it would not know what phase to run at.

The only way in which the sampling clock can be obtained is to use a phase-locked loop to regenerate it from the clock content of the self-clocking channel-coded waveform. In phase-locked loops, the voltage-controlled oscillator is driven by a phase error measured between the output and some reference, as described in Chapter 2, such that the output eventually has the same frequency as the reference. If a divider is placed between the VCO and the phase comparator, the VCO frequency can be made to be a multiple of the reference. This also has the effect of making the loop more heavily damped. If a channel-coded waveform is used as a reference to a PLL, the loop will be able to make a phase comparison whenever a transition arrives and will run at the channel bit rate. When there are several detents between transitions, the loop will *flywheel* at the last known frequency and phase until it can rephase at a subsequent transition. Thus a continuous clock is recreated from the clock content of the channel waveform. In a recorder, if the speed of the medium should change, the PLL will change frequency to follow. Once the loop is locked, clock edges will be phased with the

Figure 5.24 The clocking system when channel coding is used. The encoder clock runs at the channel bit rate, and any transitions in the channel must coincide with encoder clock edges. The reason for doing this is that, at the data separator, the PLL can lock to the edges of the channel signal, which represent an intermittent clock, and turn it into a continuous clock. The jitter in the edges of the channel signal causes noise in the phase error of the PLL, but the damping acts as a filter and the PLL runs at the average phase of the channel bits, rejecting the jitter

average phase of the jittering edges of the input waveform. If for example, rising edges of the clock are phased to input transitions, then falling edges will be in the centre of the eyes. If these edges are used to clock the sampling process, the maximum jitter and noise can be rejected. The output of the slicer when sampled by the PLL edge at the centre of an eye is the value of a channel bit. Fig. 5.24 shows the complete clocking system of a channel code from encoder to data separator. Clearly data cannot be separated if the PLL is not locked, but it cannot be locked until it has seen transitions for a reasonable period. In recorders, which have discontinuous recorded blocks to allow editing, the solution is to precede each data block with a pattern of transitions whose sole purpose is to provide a timing reference for synchronizing the phase-locked loop. This pattern is known as a preamble. In interfaces, the transmission can be continuous and there is no difficulty remaining in lock indefinitely. There will simply be a short delay on first applying the signal before the receiver locks to it.

One potential problem area which is frequently overlooked is to ensure that the VCO in the receiving PLL is correctly centred. If it is not, it will be running with a static phase error and will not sample the received waveform at the centre of the eyes. The sampled bits will be more prone to noise and jitter errors. VCO centring can simply be checked by displaying the control voltage. This should not change significantly when the input is momentarily interrupted.

5.13 Channel coding

In summary, it is not practicable simply to serialize raw data in a shift register for the purpose of recording or for transmission except over relatively short distances. Practical systems require the use of a modulation scheme, known as a channel code, which expresses the data as waveforms which are self-clocking in order to reject jitter, separate the received bits and to avoid skew on separate clock lines. The coded waveforms should further be DC free or nearly so to enable slicing in the presence of losses and have a narrower spectrum than the raw data to make equalization possible.

Jitter causes uncertainty about the time at which a particular event occurred. The frequency response of the channel then places an overall limit on the spacing of events in the channel. Particular emphasis must be placed on the interplay of bandwidth, jitter and noise, which will be shown here to be the key to the design of a successful channel code.

Fig. 5.25 shows that a channel coder is necessary prior to the record stage, and that a decoder, known as a data separator, is necessary after the replay stage. The output of the channel coder is generally a logic level signal which contains a 'high' state when a transition is to be generated. The waveform generator produces the transitions in a signal whose level and impedance are suitable for driving the medium or channel. The signal may be bipolar or unipolar as appropriate.

Some codes eliminate DC entirely, which is advantageous for optical media and for rotary-head recording. Some codes can reduce the channel bandwidth needed by lowering the upper spectral limit. This permits higher linear density, usually at the expense of jitter rejection. Other codes narrow the spectrum by raising the lower limit. A code with a narrow spectrum has a number of advantages. The reduction in asymmetry will reduce peak shift and data separators can lock more readily because the range of frequencies in the code is

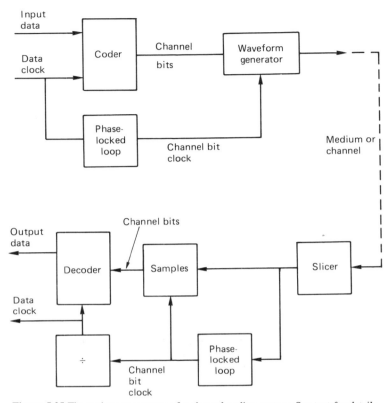

Figure 5.25 The major components of a channel coding system. See text for details

smaller. In theory the narrower the spectrum the less noise will be suffered, but this is only achieved if filtering is employed. Filters can easily cause phase errors which will nullify any gain.

A convenient definition of a channel code (for there are certainly others) is: 'A method of modulating real data such that they can be reliably received despite the shortcomings of a real channel, while making maximum economic use of the channel capacity.'

The basic time periods of a channel-coded waveform are called positions or detents, in which the transmitted voltage will be reversed or stay the same. The symbol used for the units of channel time is T_d.

There are many ways of creating such a waveform, but the most convenient is to convert the raw data bits to a larger number of *channel bits* which are output from a shift register to the waveform generator at the detent rate. The coded waveform will then be high or low according to the state of a channel bit which describes the detent.

Channel coding is the art of converting real data into channel bits. Fig. 5.26 shows that there are two conventions in use relating channel bits to the recorded waveform. The most commonly used convention is one in which a channel bit one represents a voltage (or flux) change, whereas a zero represents no change.

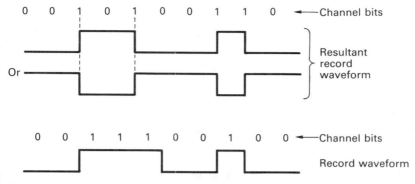

Figure 5.26 The two conventions for channel bit notation. A channel bit one most commonly represents a transition, but some codes use the bit status to describe the direction of the record current

This convention is used because it is possible to assemble sequential groups of channel bits together without worrying about whether the polarity of the end of the last group matches the beginning of the next. The polarity is unimportant in most codes and all that matters is the length of time between transitions. Less common is the convention where the channel bit state directly represents the direction of the recording current. Clearly steps then need to be taken to ensure that the boundary between two groups is properly handled. Such an approach is used in the D-3/D-5 formats and will be explained in Section 5.20.

It should be stressed that channel bits are not recorded. They exist only in a circuit technique used to control the waveform generator. In many media, for example D-3/D-5, the channel bit rate is beyond the frequency response of the channel and so it *cannot* be recorded.

One of the fundamental parameters of a channel code is the density ratio (DR). One definition of density ratio is that it is the worst-case ratio of the number of data bits recorded to the number of transitions in the channel. It can also be thought of as the ratio between the Nyquist rate of the data (one-half the bit rate) and the frequency response required in the channel. The storage density of data recorders has steadily increased due to improvements in medium and transducer technology, but modern storage densities are also a function of improvements in channel coding. Fig. 5.27(a) shows how density ratio has improved as more sophisticated codes have been developed.

As jitter is such an important issue in digital recording and transmission, a parameter has been introduced to quantify the ability of a channel code to reject time instability. This parameter, the jitter margin, also known as the window margin or phase margin (T_w), is defined as the permitted range of time over which a transition can still be received correctly, divided by the data bit-cell period (T).

Since equalization is often difficult in practice, a code which has a large jitter margin will sometimes be used because it resists the effects of intersymbol interference well. Such a code may achieve a better performance in practice than a code with a higher density ratio but poor jitter performance.

A more realistic comparison of code performance will be obtained by taking into account both density ratio and jitter margin. This is the purpose of the figure

Figure 5.27 (a) Comparison of codes by density ratio; (b) comparison of codes by figure of merit. Note how 4/5, 2/3, 8/10 + RNRZ move up because of good jitter performance; HDM-3 moves down because of jitter sensitivity

of merit (FoM), which is defined as DR $\times$ T_w. Fig. 5.27(b) shows a number of codes compared by FoM.

5.14 Recording-oriented codes

Many channel codes are sufficiently versatile that they have been used in recording, electrical or optical cable transmission and radio transmission. Others are more specialized and are intended for only one of these categories. Channel coding has roots in computers, in telemetry and in telex services, but has for some time been considered a single subject. These starting points will be considered here.

In magnetic recording, the first digital recordings were developed for early computers and used very simple techniques. Fig. 5.28(a) shows that in return-to-zero (RZ) recording, the record current has a zero state between bits and flows in one direction to record a one and in the opposite direction to record a zero. Thus every bit contains two flux changes which replay as a pair of pulses, one positive and one negative. The signal is self-clocking because pulses always occur. The order in which they occur determines the state of the bit. RZ recording cannot erase by overwrite because there are times when no record current flows. Additionally the signal amplitude is only one-half of what is possible. These problems were overcome in the non-return-to-zero code shown in Fig. 5.28(b). As the name suggests, the record current does not cease between bits, but flows

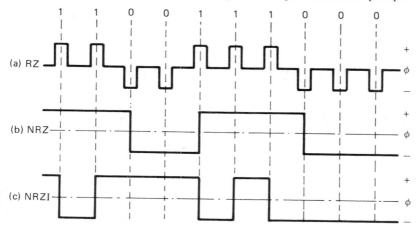

Figure 5.28 Early magnetic recording codes. RZ shown at (a) had poor signal-to-noise ratio and poor overwrite capability. NRZ at (b) overcame these problems but suffered error propagation. NRZI at (c) was the final result where a transition represented a one. NRZI is not self-clocking

at all times in one direction or the other dependent on the state of the bit to be recorded. This results in a replay pulse only when the data bits change from one state to another. As a result if one pulse was missed, the subsequent bits would be inverted. This was avoided by adapting the coding such that the record current would change state or invert whenever a data one occurred, leading to the term non-return-to-zero invert or NRZI shown in Fig. 5.28(c). In NRZI a replay pulse occurs whenever there is a data one. Clearly neither NRZ or NRZI are self-clocking, but require a separate clock track. Skew between tracks can only be avoided by working at low density and so the system cannot be used for digital video. However, virtually all of the codes used for magnetic recording are based on the principle of reversing the record current to produce a transition.

5.15 Transmission-oriented codes

In cable transmission, also known as line signalling, and in telemetry, the starting point was often the speech bandwidth available in existing telephone lines and radio links. There was no DC response, just a range of frequencies available. Fig. 5.29(a) shows that a pair of frequencies can be used, one for each state of a data bit. The result is frequency shift keying (FSK) which is the same as would be obtained from an analog frequency modulator fed with a two-level signal. Clearly FSK is DC free and self-clocking.

Instead of modulating the frequency of the signal, the phase can be modulated or shifted instead, leading to the generic term of phase shift keying or PSK. This method is highly suited to broadcast as it is easily applied to a radio frequency carrier. The simplest technique is selectively to invert the carrier phase according to the data bit as in Fig. 5.29(b). There can be many cycles of carrier in each bit period. This technique is known as phase encoding (PE) and is used in GPS (Global Positioning System) broadcasts. The receiver in a PE system is a well-damped phase-locked loop which runs at the average phase of the transmission. Phase changes will then result in phase errors in the loop and so the phase error is the demodulated signal.

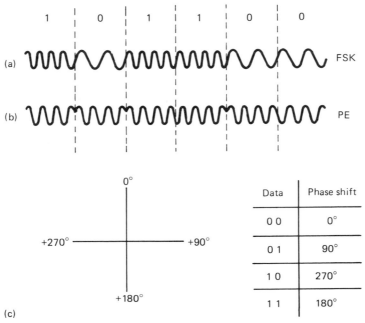

Figure 5.29 Various communications-oriented codes are shown here: at (a) frequency shift keying (FSK), at (b) phase encoding and at (c) differential quadrature phase shift keying (DQPSK)

5.16 General purpose codes

Despite the different origins of codes, there are many similarities between them.

If the two frequencies in an FSK system are one octave apart, the limiting case in which the highest data rate is obtained is when there is one half cycle of the lower frequency or a whole cycle of the high frequency in one bit period. This gives rise to the frequency modulation (FM). In the same way, the limiting case of phase encoding is where there is only one cycle of carrier per bit. In recording, this technique is what is meant by the same term. These can be contrasted in Fig. 5.30.

The FM code, also known as Manchester code or bi-phase mark code, shown in Fig. 5.30(a), was the first practical self-clocking binary code and it is suitable for both transmission and recording. It is DC free and very easy to encode and decode. It is the code specified for the AES/EBU digital audio interconnect standard which will be described in Chapter 7. In the field of recording it remains in use today only where density is not of prime importance, for example in SMPTE/EBU timecode for professional audio and video recorders and in floppy disks.

In FM there is always a transition at the bit-cell boundary which acts as a clock. For a data one, there is an additional transition at the bit-cell centre. Fig. 5.30(a) shows that each data bit can be represented by two channel bits. For a data zero, they will be 10, and for a data one they will be 11. Since the first bit is always one, it conveys no information, and is responsible for the density ratio of only one-half. Since there can be two transitions for each data bit, the jitter

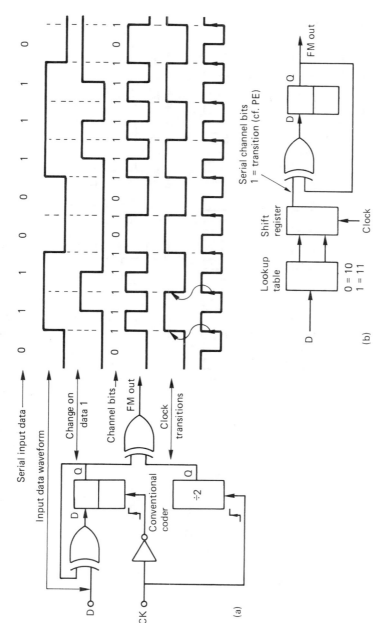

Figure 5.30 FM and PE contrasted. At (a) are the FM waveform and the channel bits which may be used to describe transitions in it. The FM coder is shown at (b). The PE waveform is shown at (c). As PE is polarity conscious, the channel bits must describe the signal level rather than the transitions. The coder is shown at (d)

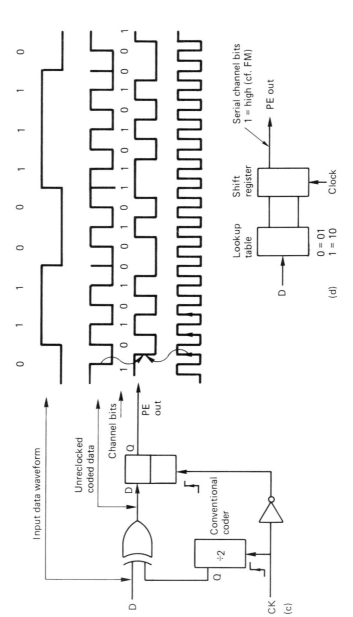

Figure 5.30 (continued)

margin can only be half a bit, and the resulting FoM is only 0.25. The high clock content of FM does, however, mean that data recovery is possible over a wide range of speeds; hence the use for timecode. The lowest frequency in FM is due to a stream of zeros and is equal to half the bit rate. The highest frequency is due to a stream of ones and is equal to the bit rate. Thus the fundamentals of FM are within a band of one octave. Effective equalization is generally possible over such a band. FM is not polarity conscious and can be inverted without changing the data.

Fig. 5.30(b) shows how an FM coder works. Data words are loaded into the input shift register which is clocked at the data bit rate. Each data bit is converted to two channel bits in the codebook or lookup table. These channel bits are loaded into the output register. The output register is clocked twice as fast as the input register because there are twice as many channel bits as data bits. The ratio of the two clocks is called the code rate; in this case it is a rate one-half code. Ones in the serial channel bit output represent transitions whereas zeros represent no change. The channel bits are fed to the waveform generator which is a 1 bit delay, clocked at the channel bit rate, and an exclusive OR gate. This changes state when a channel bit one is input. The result is a coded FM waveform where there is always a transition at the beginning of the data bit period, and a second optional transition whose presence indicates a one.

In PE there is always a transition in the centre of the bit but Fig. 5.30(c) shows that the transition between bits is dependent on the data values. Although its origins were in line coding, phase encoding can be used for optical and magnetic recording as it is DC free and self-clocking. It has the same DR and T_w as FM, and the waveform can also be described using channel bits, but with a different notation. As PE is polarity sensitive, the channel bits determine the level of the encoded signal rather than causing a transition. Fig. 5.30(d) shows that the allowable channel bit patterns are now 10 and 01.

In modified frequency modulation (MFM), also known as Miller code,[5] the highly redundant clock content of FM was reduced by the use of a phase-locked

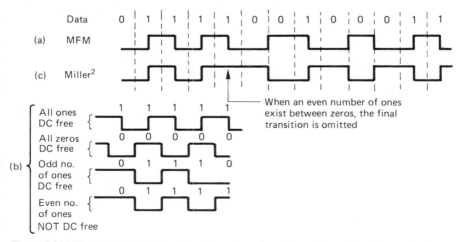

Figure 5.31 MFM or Miller code is generated as shown here. The minimum transition spacing is twice that of FM or PE. MFM is not always DC free as shown at (b). This can be overcome by the modification of (c) which results in the Miller^2 code

loop in the receiver which could flywheel over missing clock transitions. This technique is implicit in all the more advanced codes. Fig. 5.31(a) shows that the bit-cell centre transition on a data one was retained, but the bit-cell boundary transition is now only required between successive zeros. There are still two channel bits for every data bit, but adjacent channel bits will never be one, doubling the minimum time between transitions, and giving a DR of 1. Clearly the coding of the current bit is now influenced by the preceding bit. The maximum number of prior bits which affect the current bit is known as the constraint length L_c, measured in data bit periods. For MFM $L_c = T$. Another way of considering the constraint length is that it assesses the number of data bits which may be corrupted if the receiver misplaces one transition. If L_c is long, all errors will be burst errors.

MFM doubled the density ratio compared with FM and PE without changing the jitter performance; thus the FoM also doubles, becoming 0.5. It was adopted for many rigid disks at the time of its development, and remains in use on double-density floppy disks. It is not, however, DC free. Fig. 5.31(b) shows how MFM can have DC content under certain conditions.

5.17 Miller^2 code

The Miller^2 code is derived from MFM, and Fig. 5.31(c) shows that the DC content is eliminated by a slight increase in complexity.[6,7] Wherever an even number of ones occurs between zeros, the transition at the last one is omitted. This creates two additional, longer run lengths and increases the T_{max} of the code. The decoder can detect these longer run lengths in order to reinsert the suppressed ones. The FoM of Miller^2 is 0.5 as for MFM. Miller^2 is used in high-rate instrumentation recorders and in the D-2 and DCT DVTR formats.

5.18 Group codes

Further improvements in coding rely on converting patterns of real data to patterns of channel bits with more desirable characteristics using a conversion table known as a codebook. If a data symbol of m bits is considered, it can have 2^m different combinations. As it is intended to discard undesirable patterns to improve the code, it follows that the number of channel bits n must be greater than m. The number of patterns which can be discarded is:

$2^n - 2^m$

One name for the principle is group code recording (GCR), and an important parameter is the code rate, defined as:

$$R = \frac{m}{n}$$

It will be evident that the jitter margin T_w is numerically equal to the code rate, and so a code rate near to unity is desirable. The choice of patterns which are used in the codebook will be those which give the desired balance between clock content, bandwidth and DC content.

Fig. 5.32 shows that the upper spectral limit can be made to be some fraction of the channel bit rate according to the minimum distance between ones in the channel bits. This is known as T_{min}, also referred to as the minimum transition

Figure 5.32 A channel code can control its spectrum by placing limits on T_{min} (M) and T_{max} which define upper and lower frequencies. The ratio of T_{max}/T_{min} determines the asymmetry of waveform and predicts DC content and peak shift. Example shown is EFM

parameter M, and in both cases is measured in data bits T. It can be obtained by multiplying the number of channel detent periods between transitions by the code rate. Unfortunately, codes are measured by the number of consecutive zeros in the channel bits, given the symbol d, which is always one less than the number of detent periods. In fact T_{min} is numerically equal to the density ratio:

$$T_{min} = M = DR = \frac{(d + 1) \times m}{n}$$

It will be evident that choosing a low code rate could increase the density ratio, but it will impair the jitter margin. The figure of merit is:

$$FoM = DR \times T_w = \frac{(d + 1) \times m^2}{n^2}$$

since $T_w = m/n$.

Fig. 5.32 also shows that the lower spectral limit is influenced by the maximum distance between transitions T_{max}. This is also obtained by multiplying the maximum number of detent periods between transitions by the code rate. Again, codes are measured by the maximum number of zeros between channel ones, k, and so:

$$T_{max} = \frac{(k + 1) \times m}{n}$$

and the maximum/minimum ratio P is:

$$P = \frac{(k + 1)}{(d + 1)}$$

The length of time between channel transitions is known as the *run length*. Another name for this class is the run-length-limited (RLL) codes.[8] Since m data bits are considered as one symbol, the constraint length L_c will be increased in RLL codes to at least m. It is, however, possible for a code to have run-length limits without it being a group code.

In practice, the junction of two adjacent channel symbols may violate run-length limits, and it may be necessary to create a further codebook of symbol size $2n$ which converts violating code pairs to acceptable patterns. This is known as merging and follows the golden rule that the substitute $2n$ symbol must finish with a pattern which eliminates the possibility of a subsequent violation. These patterns must also differ from all other symbols.

Substitution may also be used to different degrees in the same nominal code in order to allow a choice of maximum run length, e.g. 3PM.[9] The maximum number of symbols involved in a substitution is denoted by r.[10,11] There are many RLL codes and the parameters d, k, m, n and r are a way of comparing them.

Sometimes the code rate forms the name of the code, as in 2/3, 8/10 and EFM; at other times the code may be named after the d,k parameters, as in 2,7 code. Various examples of group codes will be given to illustrate the principles involved.

5.19 2/3 code

Fig. 5.33(a) shows the codebook of an optimized code which illustrates one merging technique. This is a 1,7,2,3,2 code known as 2/3. It is designed to have a good jitter window in order to resist peak shift distortion in disk drives, but it also has a good density ratio.[12] In 2/3 code, pairs of data bits create symbols of three channel bits. For bandwidth reduction, codes having adjacent ones are eliminated so that $d = 1$. This halves the upper spectral limit and the DR is improved accordingly:

Data	Code
0 0	1 0 1
0 1	1 0 0
1 0	0 0 1
1 1	0 1 0

(a)

Data	Illegal code	Substitution
0 0 0 0	1 0 1 1 0 1	1 0 1 0 0 0
0 0 0 1	1 0 1 1 0 0	1 0 0 0 0 0
1 0 0 0	0 0 1 1 0 1	0 0 1 0 0 0
1 0 0 1	0 0 1 1 0 0	0 1 0 0 0 0

(b)

Figure 5.33 2/3 code. At (a) two data bits (m) are expressed as three channel bits (n) without adjacent transitions ($d = 1$). Violations are dealt with by substitution

$$DR = \frac{(d + 1)m}{n} = \frac{2 - 2}{3} = 1.33$$

Adjacent data pairs can break the encoding rule; in these cases substitutions are made, as shown in (b)

$$DR = \frac{(d + 1) \times m}{n} = \frac{2 \times 2}{3} = 1.33$$

In Fig. 5.33(b) it will be seen that some group combinations cause violations. To avoid this, pairs of three channel bit symbols are replaced with a new six channel bit symbol. L_c is thus $4T$, the same as for the 4/5 code. The jitter window is given by:

$$T_w = \frac{m}{n} = \frac{2}{3} T$$

and the FoM is:

$$\frac{2}{3} \times \frac{4}{3} = \frac{8}{9}$$

This is an extremely good figure for an RLL code, and is some 10% better than the FoM of 3PM[13] and 2,7, and as a result 2/3 has been highly successful in Winchester disk drives.

5.20 EFM code in D-3/D-5

The 1/2 inch D-3 and D-5 formats use a group code in which $m = 8$ and $n = 14$, so the code rate is 0.57. The code is called 8,14 after the main parameters. It will be evident that the jitter margin T_w is numerically equal to the code rate, and so for jitter resistance a code rate close to unity is preferable. The choice of patterns which are used in the codebook will be those which give the desired balance between clock content, bandwidth and DC content.

The code used in D-3/D-5 uses the convention in which a channel bit one represents a high in the recorded waveform. In this convention a flux reversal or transition will be written when the channel bits change.

In Fig. 5.34 it is shown that the upper spectral limit can be made to be some fraction of the channel bit rate according to the minimum distance between transitions in the channel bits, which in 8,14 is two channel bits. This is known as T_{min}, also referred to as the minimum transition parameter M, and in both cases is measured in data bits T. It can be obtained by multiplying the number of channel detent periods between transitions by the code rate. In fact T_{min} is numerically equal to the density ratio:

$$T_{min.} = M = DR = \frac{2 \times 8}{14} = 1.14$$

This DR is a little better than the figure of 1 for the codes used in D-1 and D-2.

The figure of merit is:

$$FoM = DR \times T_w = \frac{2 \times 8^2}{14^2} = 0.65$$

since:

$$T_w = \frac{m}{n} = \frac{8}{14}$$

Fig. 5.34 also shows that the lower spectral limit is influenced by the maximum distance between transitions T_{max}, which also determines the

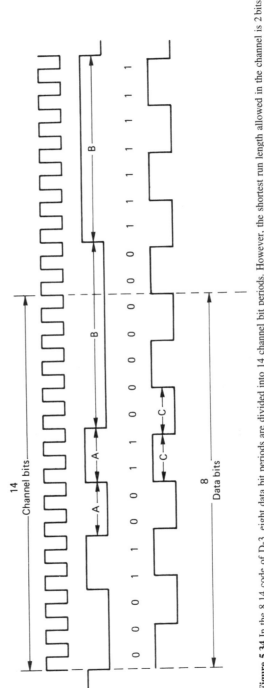

Figure 5.34 In the 8,14 code of D-3, eight data bit periods are divided into 14 channel bit periods. However, the shortest run length allowed in the channel is 2 bits, shown at A. This restriction is obtained by selecting 14 bit patterns from those available. The longest run length in the code is seven channel bits. Note that the shortest run length A is 14% longer than the shortest run length in the raw data C. Thus density ratio DR is 1.14. Using this code 14% more data can be recorded with the same wavelength on tape as a simple code

minimum clock content. This is also obtained by multiplying the maximum number of detent periods between transitions by the code rate. In 8,14 code this is seven channel bits, and so:

$$T_{max} = \frac{7 \times 8}{14} = 4$$

and the maximum/minimum ratio P is:

$$P = \frac{4}{1.14} = 3.51$$

The length of time between channel transitions is known as the run length. Another name for this class is the run-length-limited (RLL) codes.[14] Since eight data bits are considered as one symbol, the constraint length L_c will be increased in this code to at least 8 bits.

In practice, the junction of some adjacent channel symbols may violate coding rules, and it is necessary to extend the codebook so that the original data can be represented by a number of alternative codes at least one of which will be acceptable. This is known as substitution. Owing to the coding convention used, which generates a transition when the channel bits change, transitions will also be generated at the junction of two channel symbols if the adjacent bits are different. It will be seen in Fig. 5.34 that the presence of a junction transition can be controlled by selectively inverting all of the bits in the second channel symbol. Thus for every channel bit pattern in the code, an inverted version also exists.

Fig. 5.35 shows part of the 8,14 code (EFM) used in the D-3 format. As stated, 8 bit data symbols are represented by 14 bit channel symbols. There are 256 combinations of eight data bits, whereas 14 bits have 2^{14} or 16 384 combinations. The initial range of possible codes is reduced by the requirements of the maximum and minimum run-length limits and by a requirement that there shall not be more than five identical bits in the first 6 bits of the code and not more than six in the last 7 bits as shown in Fig. 5.36.

One of the most important parameters of a channel pattern is the code digital sum (CDS) shown in Fig. 5.37. This is the number of channel ones minus the number of channel zeros. As the CDS represents the DC content or average voltage of the channel pattern it is to be kept to a minimum.

There are only 118 codes (and 118 inverse codes) which are DC free (CDS = 0) as well as meeting the other constraints. In order to obtain 256 data combinations, codes with non-zero CDS have to be accepted. The actual codes used in 8,14 have a CDS of 0, ±2 or ±4.

The CDS is a special case of a more general parameter called the digital sum value (DSV). DSV is a useful way of predicting how an analog channel such as a tape/head system will handle a binary waveform. In a stream of bits, a one causes one to be added to the DSV whereas a zero causes one to be subtracted. Thus DSV is a form of running discrete integration. Fig. 5.38(a) shows how the DSV varies along the time axis. The end DSV is the DSV at the end of a string of channel symbols. Clearly CDS is the end DSV of one code pattern in isolation. The next end DSV is the current one plus the CDS of the next symbol as shown in Fig. 5.38(b).

The absolute DSV of a symbol is shown in Fig. 5.38(c). This is obtained by finding the peak DSV. Large absolute DSVs are associated with low frequencies and low clock content.

Data	Code A (begins with 0)	CDS	Code B (begins with 1)	CDS	Code C (begins with 0)	CDS	Code D (begins with 1)	CDS
00								
↑								
42	01100011000111	0	10011100111000	0	01100011000111	0	10011100111000	0
43	01100001111100	0	10011110000011	0	01100001111100	0	10011110000011	0
44	01100001111001	0	10011110000110	0	01100001111001	0	10011110000110	0
45	01100011100011	0	10011110001100	0	01100001110011	0	10011110001100	0
46	01100001100111	0	10011110011000	0	01100001100111	0	10011110011000	0
47	01100000111110	0	10011111000001	0	01100000111110	0	10011111000001	0
48	01100000011111	−2	10011111100000	−4	01100000011111	4	10011111100000	2
49	01111100000001	−2	10000000110011	−4	01111111001100	4	10000001111110	2
50	01111001100000	−2	10000000111001	−4	01111111000110	4	10000110011111	2
51	01111000110000	−2	10000000111100	−4	01111111000011	4	10000111001111	2
52	01111000011000	−2	10000001100011	−4	01111110011100	4	10000111100111	2
53	01111000001100	−2	10000001100110	−4	01111110011001	4	10000111110011	2
54	01111000000110	−2	10000001110001	−4	01111110001001	4	10000111111001	2
55	01111000000011	−2	10000011111000	−4	01111110000111	4	10001111111001	2
56	01110011100000	−2	10000011000011	−4	01111100111100	4	10001100011111	2
57	01110011000001	−2	10000011000110	−4	01111100111001	4	10001100111110	2
↓								
255								

Figure 5.35 Part of the codebook for D-3 EFM code. For every 8 bit data word (left) there are four possible channel bit patterns, two of which begin with 0 and two of which begin with 1. This allows successive symbols to avoid violating the minimum run-length limit (A in Fig. 5.34) at the junction of the two symbols. See Figs 5.36 and 5.37 for further details

Figure 5.36 The selected 14 bit patterns follow the rules that there cannot be more than five consecutive identical bits at the beginning or more than six at the end. In addition the code digital sum (CDS) cannot exceed 4. See Fig. 5.37 for derivation of CDS

When encoding is performed, each 8 bit data symbol selects four locations in the lookup table, each of which contains a 14 bit pattern. The recording is made by selecting the most appropriate one of four candidate channel bit patterns. The decoding process is such that any of the four channel patterns will decode to the same data.

The four possible channel symbols for each data byte are classified according to Fig. 5.35 into types A, B, C or D. Since 8,14 coding requires alternative inverse symbols, two of the candidates are simply bit inversions of the other two. Where codes are not DC free there may be a pair of +2 CDS candidates and their −2 CDS inverses or a +2 CDS and a +4 CDS candidate and their inverses which will of course have −2 and −4 CDS. In the case of all but two of the DC-free

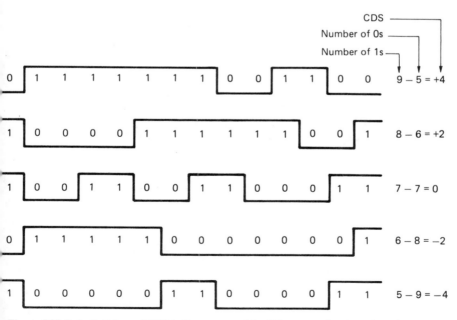

Figure 5.37 Code digital sum (CDS) is the measure of the DC content of a given channel symbol. It is obtained by subtracting the number of zeros in the symbol from the number of ones. Shown above are five actual 14 bit symbols from the D-3 code showing the range of CDS allowed from −4 to +4. Although CDS of zero is optimum, there are not enough patterns with zero CDS to represent all combinations of eight data bits

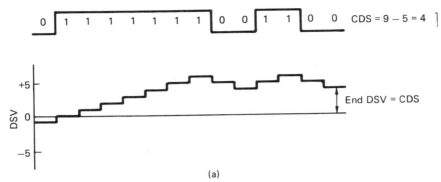

Figure 5.38(a) DSV is obtained by subtracting one for every zero, and adding one for every one which passes during the integration time. Thus DSV changes every channel bit. Note that end DSV = CDS

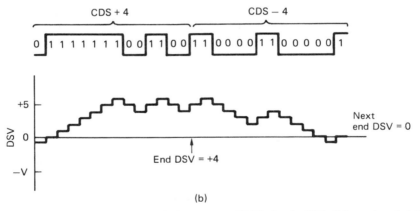

Figure 5.38(b) The next end DSV is the current end DSV plus the CDS of the next symbol. Note how the choice of a CDS −4 symbol after a +4 symbol brings DSV back to zero

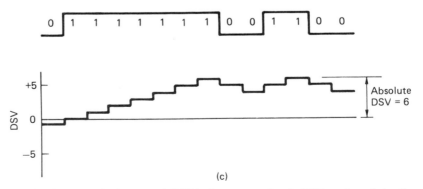

Figure 5.38(c) The absolute or peak DSV is the greatest value the DSV can have during the symbol. As shown here, it can be greater than CDS

codes the two candidates are one and the same code and the four lookup table locations contain two identical codes and two identical inverse codes. As a result of some of the codes being identical, although there are 1024 locations in the table, only 770 different 14 bit patterns are used, representing 4.7% of the total.

Code classes are further subdivided into class numbers, which go from 1 to 5 and specify the number of identical channel bits at the beginning of the symbol, and a priority number which only applies to codes of CDS ±2 and is obtained from the channel bit pattern at the end of the code according to Fig. 5.39.

Clearly the junction of two channel patterns cannot be allowed to violate the run-length limits. As the next code cannot have more than five consecutive identical bits at the beginning, the previous code could end with up to 2 bits in the same state without exceeding the maximum run length of seven. If this limit were to be exceeded by one of the four candidate codes, it would be rejected and one of those having an earlier transition would be chosen instead. Similarly if the previous code ends in 01 or 10, the first bit of the next code must be the same as the last bit of the previous code or the minimum run-length limit will be violated. The run-length limits can always be met because every code has an inverse, so out of the four possible channel symbols available for a given data byte two of them will begin with 0 and two begin with 1. In some cases, such as

+2 end DSV end pattern of channel bits	−2 end DSV end pattern of channel bits	Priority
. . . xxxxx110	. . . xxxxx001	4
. . . xxxx1100	. . . xxxx0011	1
. . . xxx11000	. . . xxx00111	2
. . . xx110000	. . . xx001111	3
. . . x1100000	. . . x0011111	8
. . . xxxxx001	. . . xxxxx110	10
. . . xxxx0011	. . . xxxx1100	5
. . . xxx00111	. . . xxx11000	6
. . . xx001111	. . . xx110000	7
. . . x0011111	. . . x1100000	9
. . . 00111111	. . . 11000000	11

x: Don't care bit

Figure 5.39 Codes having end DSV of ±2 are prioritized according to the above table as part of the selection process where the first code ends in 1100, up to four of the candidates for the next code could meet the run-length limits in some cases. In this case the best candidate will be chosen to optimize some other parameter.

In order to follow how the encoder selects the best channel pattern it is necessary to discuss the criteria that are used. There are a number of these, some of which are compulsory, such as the run-length limits, and others which will be met if possible on a decreasing scale of importance. If a higher criterion cannot be met the decision will still attempt to meet as many of the lower ones as possible.

The overall goal is to meet the run-length limits with a sequence of symbols which has the highest clock content, lowest LF and DC content and the least asymmetry to reduce peak shift. Some channel symbols will be better than others, a phenomenon known as pattern sensitivity. The least optimal patterns are not so

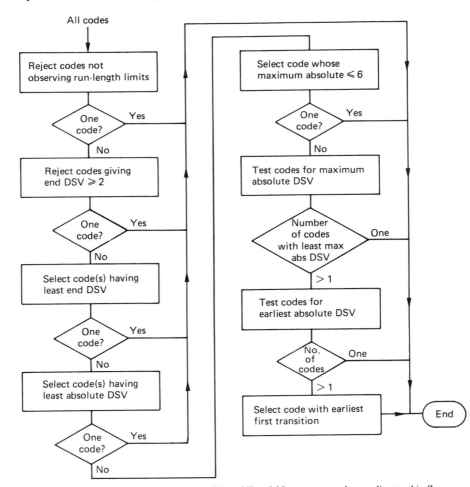

Figure 5.40 The four candidate codes, A,B,C,D, of Fig. 5.35 are compared according to this flow chart to locate the single best code which will represent the data byte. Any of the codes will result in the same decode on replay

bad that they will *cause* errors, but they will be more prone to errors due to other causes. Minimizing the use of sensitive waveforms will enhance the data reliability and is as good as an improvement in the signal-to-noise ratio.

As there are 2^{10} different patterns, there will be 2^{20} different combinations of two patterns. Clearly it is out of the question to create a lookup table to determine how best to merge two patterns. It has to be done algorithmically. The flowchart of the algorithm is shown in Fig. 5.40.

The process begins when a data byte selects four candidate channel symbols. Initially tests are made to eliminate unsuitable patterns, and on some occasions, only one code will emerge from these tests. There are so many combinations, however, that it is possible for several candidate codes to pass the initial tests, and so the flowchart continues to select the best code by further criteria.

The first selection is based on maintaining the run-length limits at the junction between the previous code and the current one and keeping the end DSV as small as possible. If two or more codes give an equal minimum end DSV, the code with the smallest absolute DSV will be selected. If this criterion still results in more than one code being available, a further selection is made to optimize the spectrum due to the junction of the previous and current symbols. The codes are tested to see if any permit six or fewer identical channel bits across the junction. If none of the codes has this characteristic there will be a large run length at the junction and the best code will be one that has a run length of less than 6 bits later. This criterion will also be applied if more than one code passes the junction run-length test.

If a decision still cannot be made, the remaining candidates could have ±2 end DSV or 0 end DSV. In the former case the priority tables are invoked, and the code(s) with the highest priority is selected. In the latter case, or if two codes emerge equal from the priority test, any code(s) which has a run length of less than 6 bits at the end is selected. This makes merging with the next symbol easier. It is possible that no code will pass the end run-length test, or that two or more codes are still equal. In this case some of the criteria cannot be met or are equally met, and the final choice reverts to a further selection of the code with minimum absolute DSV. This test was made much earlier, but some codes with equal minimum values could have been rejected in intermediate tests. If two codes still remain, the one whose absolute DSV appears earliest in the bit stream will be selected. If two codes still remain, the one with the earliest transition is selected.

The complexity of the coding rules in 8,14 is such that it could not have been economically implemented until recently. This illustrates the dependence of advanced recorders on LSI technology.

5.21 Error detection in group codes

In the 8,14 code only 4.7% of the 14 bit patterns are actually recorded, since the others have undesirable characteristics such as excessive DC content or insufficient clock content. In practice reading errors will occur which can corrupt some or all of the channel bits in a symbol. Random noise effects or peak shift could result in a tape transition being shifted along the time axis, or in the wrong number of transitions being detected in a symbol. This will change the channel bit pattern determined by the data separator.

As there are many more channel bit combinations than those which are actually used, it is probable that a random error will convert a channel symbol into one of the patterns which are not used. Thus it is possible for the lookup table which decodes 14 channel bits back to eight data bits to perform an error-detecting function. When an illegal 14 bit code is detected, the lookup table will output an error flag. Clearly this method is not infallible, as it is possible for an error to convert one valid code into a different valid code, which this scheme would not detect. However, the additional detection capability can be used to enhance the power of the error-correction systems which can make use of the error flags produced by the 14,8 decoder. This subject will be discussed in more detail in Chapter 6.

5.22 Tracking signals

Many recorders use track-following systems to help keep the head(s) aligned with the narrow tracks used in digital media. These can operate by sensing low-frequency tones which are recorded along with the data. Whilst this can be done by linearly adding the tones to the coder output, this requires a linear record amplifier. An alternative is to use the DC content group codes. A code is devised where for each data pattern, several code patterns exist having a range of DC components. By choosing groups with a suitable sequence of DC offsets, a low frequency can be added to the coded signal. This can be filtered from the data waveform on replay.

5.23 Randomizing

Randomizing is not a channel code, but a technique which can be used in conjunction with a channel code. Randomizing with NRZI (RNRZI) is used in the D-1 format and in conjunction with partial response (see Section 5.24) in Digital Betacam. It is also used in conjunction with the 8,14 code of D-3/D-5 and in NICAM 728. Fig. 5.41 shows that the randomizing system is arranged outside the channel coder.

NRZ has a DR of 1 and a jitter window of 1 and so has an FoM of 1 which is better than the group codes. It does, however, suffer from an unconstrained spectrum and poor clock content. This can be overcome using randomizing. Fig. 5.42 shows that, at the encoder, a pseudo-random sequence (see Chapter 2) is added modulo-2 to the serial data and the resulting ones generate transitions in the channel. This process drastically reduces T_{max} and reduces DC content. At the

Figure 5.41 The randomizing system of D-3 is arranged outside the EFM channel coder. The pseudo-random sequence added during recording must be generated in a synchronized manner during replay so it can be subtracted. This is done by the EFM sync detector. Note that the sync pattern is not randomized!

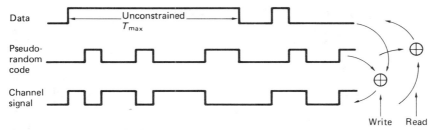

Figure 5.42 Modulo-2 addition with a pseudo-random code removes unconstrained runs in real data. Identical process must be provided on replay

receiver the transitions are converted back to a serial bit stream to which the same pseudo-random sequence is again added modulo-2. As a result the random signal cancels itself out to leave only the serial data, provided that the two pseudo-random sequences are synchronized to bit accuracy.

The 8,14 code displays pattern sensitivity because some waveforms are more sensitive to peak shift distortion than others. Pattern sensitivity is only a problem if a sustained series of sensitive symbols needs to be recorded. Randomizing ensures that this cannot happen because it breaks up any regularity or repetition in the data. The data randomizing is performed by using the exclusive OR function of the data and a pseudo-random sequence as the input to the channel coder. On replay the same sequence is generated, synchronized to bit accuracy, and the exclusive OR of the replay bit stream and the sequence is the original data.

The randomizing polynomial and one way in which it can be implemented are shown in Fig. 5.43. As the polynomial generates a maximum length sequence from an 8 bit wordlength, the sequence length is given by $2^8 - 1 = 255$. The sequence would repeat endlessly but for the fact that it is preset to 80_{16} at the beginning of each sync block immediately after the sync pattern is detected. Fig. 5.44 shows the randomizing sequence starting from 80_{16}.

Clearly the sync pattern cannot be randomized, since this causes a Catch-22 situation where it is not possible to synchronize the sequence for replay until the sync pattern is read, but it is not possible to read the sync pattern until the sequence is synchronized!

The randomizing in D-3 is clearly block based, since this matches the block structure on tape. Where there is no obvious block structure, convolutional or endless randomizing can be used. This is the approach used in the scrambled serial digital video interconnect described in Section 5.26, which allows composite or component video of up to 10 bit wordlength to be sent serially.

5.24 Partial response

It has been stated that a magnetic head acts as a transversal filter, because it has two poles. In addition the output is differentiated, so that the head may be thought of as a $(1-D)$ impulse response system, where D is the delay which is a function of the tape speed and gap size. It is this delay which results in intersymbol interference. Conventional equalizers attempt to oppose this effect, and succeed in raising the noise level in the process of making the frequency response linear. Fig. 5.45 shows that the frequency response necessary to pass data with

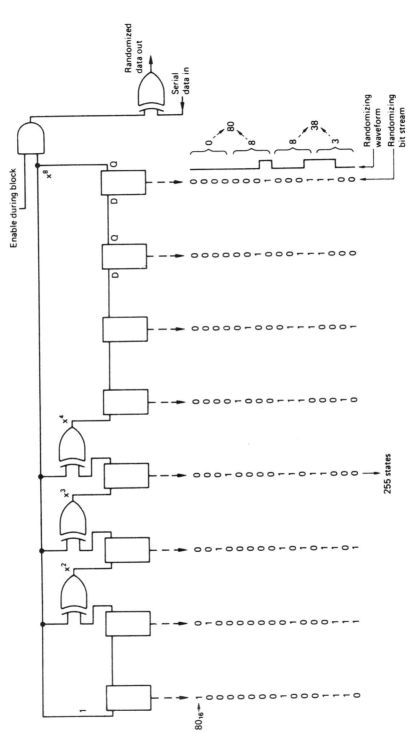

Figure 5.43 The polynomial generator circuit shown here calculates $x^8 + x^4 + x^3 + x^2 + 1$ and is preset to 80_{16} at the beginning of every sync block. When the generator is clocked it will produce a Galois field having 255 states (see Chapter 2). The right-hand bit of each field element becomes the randomizing bit stream and is fed to an exclusive OR gate in the data stream. Randomizing is disabled during preambles and sync patterns. It is also possible to randomize using a counter working at byte rate which addresses a PROM. Eight exclusive OR gates will then be needed to randomize 1 byte at a time

80	38	D2	81	49	76	82	DA	9A	86	6F	AF	8B	B0	F1	9C
D1	12	A5	72	37	EF	97	59	31	B8	EA	53	C8	3F	F4	58
40	1C	E9	C0	24	38	41	6D	4D	C3	B7	D7	45	D8	78	CE
68	89	52	B9	9B	F7	CB	AC	18	5C	F5	29	E4	1F	7A	2C
20	8E	74	60	92	9D	A0	B6	A6	E1	DB	EB	22	6C	3C	67
B4	44	A9	DC	CD	FB	65	56	0C	AE	FA	14	F2	0F	3D	16
10	47	3A	30	C9	4E	50	5B	D3	F0	ED	75	11	36	9E	33
5A	A2	54	EE	E6	FD	32	2B	06	57	7D	0A	F9	87	1E	0B
88	23	1D	98	64	27	A8	AD	69	F8	F6	BA	08	1B	CF	19
2D	51	2A	77	F3	7E	99	15	83	AB	3E	85	FC	43	8F	05
C4	91	0E	4C	B2	13	D4	D6	34	7C	7B	5D	84	8D	E7	8C
96	28	95	BB	79	BF	CC	8A	C1	55	9F	42	FE	A1	C7	02
E2	48	07	D9	09	6A	6B	1A	BE	BD	2E	C2	C6	73	46	
4B	94	CA	DD	BC	5F	66	C5	E0	AA	4F	21	FF	D0	63	01
71	A4	03	93	EC	04	B5	35	0D	DF	5E	17	61	E3	39	A3
25	4A	E5	6E	DE	2F	B3	62	70	D5	A7	90	7F	E8	B1	

Figure 5.44 The sequence which results when the randomizer of Fig. 5.43 is allowed to run

insignificant peak shift is a bandwidth of half the bit rate, which is the Nyquist rate. In Class IV partial response, the frequency response of the system is made to have nulls at DC and at the Nyquist rate. Such a frequency response is particularly advantageous for rotary-head recorders as it is DC free and the low-frequency content is minimal; hence the use in Digital Betacam. The required response is achieved by an overall impulse response of $(1 - D^2)$ where D is now the bit period. There are a number of ways in which this can be done.

If the head gap is made equal to 1 bit, the $(1 - D)$ head response may be converted to the desired response by the use of a $(1 + D)$ filter, as in Fig. 5.46(a).[15] Alternatively, a head of unspecified gapwidth may be connected to an integrator, and equalized flat to reproduce the record current waveform before being fed to a $(1 - D^2)$ filter as in Fig. 5.46(b).[16]

The result of both of these techniques is a ternary signal. The eye pattern has two sets of eyes as in Fig. 5.46(c).[17] When slicing such a signal, a smaller amount of noise will cause an error than in the binary case.

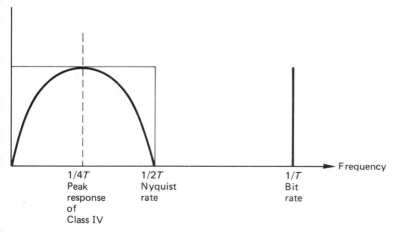

Figure 5.45 Class IV response has spectral nulls at DC and the Nyquist rate, giving a noise advantage, since magnetic replay signal is weak at both frequencies in a high-density channel

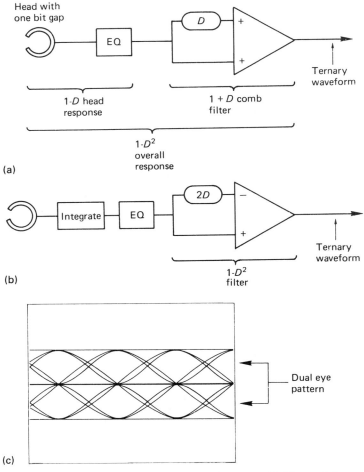

Figure 5.46 (a), (b) Two ways of obtaining partial response. (c) Characteristic eye pattern of ternary signal

The treatment of the signal thus far represents an equalization technique, and not a channel code. However, to take full advantage of Class IV partial response, suitable precoding is necessary prior to recording, which does then constitute a channel coding technique. This precoding is shown in Fig. 5.47(a). Data are added modulo-2 to themselves with a 2 bit delay. The effect of this precoding is that the outer levels of the ternary signals, which represent data ones, alternate in polarity on all odd bits and on all even bits. This is because the precoder acts like two interleaved 1 bit delay circuits, as in Fig. 5.47(b). As this alternation of polarity is a form of redundancy, it can be used to recover the 3 dB SNR loss encountered in slicing a ternary eye pattern. Viterbi decoding[18] can be used for this purpose. In Viterbi decoding, each channel bit is not sliced individually; the slicing decision is made in the context of adjacent decisions. Fig. 5.48 shows a replay waveform which is so noisy that, at the decision point, the signal voltage

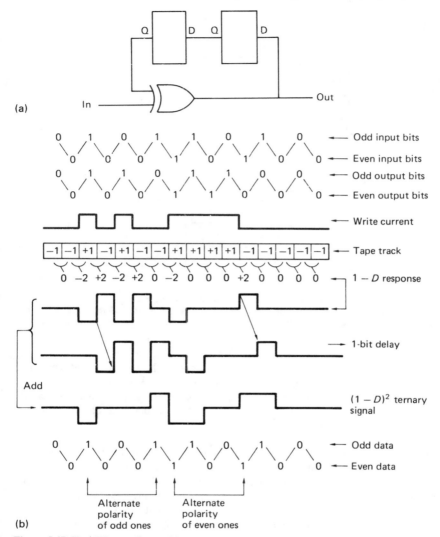

Figure 5.47 Class IV precoding at (a) causes redundancy in replay signal as derived in (b)

crosses the centre of the eye, and the slicer alone cannot tell whether the correct decision is an inner or an outer level. In this case, the decoder essentially allows both decisions to stand, in order to see what happens. A symbol representing indecision is output. It will be seen from the figure that as subsequent bits are received, one of these decisions will result in an absurd situation, which indicates that the other decision was the right one. The decoder can then locate the undecided symbol and set it to the correct value.

Viterbi decoding requires more information about the signal voltage than a simple binary slicer can discern. Fig. 5.49 shows that the replay waveform is sampled and quantized so that it can be processed in digital logic. The sampling

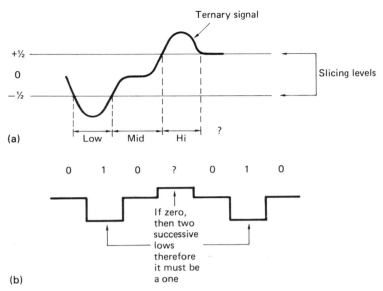

(a)

(b)

Figure 5.48 (a) A ternary signal suffers a noise penalty because there are two slicing levels. (b) The redundancy is used to determine the bit value in the presence of noise. Here the pulse height has been reduced to make it ambiguous 1/0, but only 1 is valid as zero violates the redundancy rules

rate is obtained from the embedded clock content of the replay waveform. The digital Viterbi processing logic must be able to operate at high speed to handle serial signals from a DVTR head. Its application in Digital Betacam is eased somewhat by the adoption of data reduction which reduces the data rate at the heads by a factor of two.

Clearly a ternary signal having a dual eye pattern is more sensitive than a binary signal, and it is important to keep the maximum run length T_{max} small in order to have accurate AGC. The use of pseudo-random coding along with partial response equalization and precoding is a logical combination.[19] There is then considerable overlap between the channel code and the error-correction system. Viterbi decoding is primarily applicable to channels with random errors due to Gaussian statistics, and they cannot cope with burst errors. In a head-noise-

Figure 5.49 A Viterbi decoder is implemented in the digital domain by sampling the replay waveform with a clock locked to the embedded clock of the channel code

limited system, however, the use of a Viterbi detector could increase the power of a separate burst-error-correction system by relieving it of the need to correct random errors due to noise. The error-correction system could then concentrate on correcting burst errors unimpaired. This point will become clearer upon referring to Chapter 6.

5.25 Communications codes

Since the original FSK and PSK codes were developed, advances in circuit techniques have allowed more complex signalling techniques to be used. The common goal of all of these is to minimize the channel bandwidth needed for a given bit rate whilst offering immunity from multipath reception and inter-ference. This is the equivalent of the DR in recording, but is measured in bits/ s/Hz.

In PSK it is possible to use more than two distinct phases. When four phases in quadrature are used, the result is quadrature phase shift keying or QPSK. Each period of the transmitted waveform can have one of four phases and therefore conveys the value of two data bits. In order to resist reflections in broadcasting, QPSK can be modified so that a knowledge of absolute phase is not needed at the receiver. Instead of encoding the signal phase, the data determine the magnitude of a phase shift. This is known as differential quadrature phase shift keying or DQPSK and is the modulation scheme used for NICAM 728 digital TV sound. A DQPSK coder is shown in Fig. 5.50 and as before 2 bits are conveyed for each transmitted period. It will be seen that one bit pattern results in no phase change. If this pattern is sustained the entire transmitter power will be concentrated in the carrier. This can cause patterning on the associated TV pictures. The randomizing technique of Section 5.23 is used to overcome the problem. The effect is to spread the signal energy uniformly throughout the allowable channel bandwidth so that it has less energy at a given frequency. This reduces patterning on the analog video signal in addition to making the signal more resistant to multipath reception which tends to remove notches from the spectrum.

A pseudo-random sequence generator as described in Chapter 2 is used to generate the randomizing sequence used in NICAM. A 9 bit device has a sequence length of 511, and is preset to a standard value of all ones at the beginning of each frame. The serialized data are XORed with the LSB of the Galois field, which randomizes the output which then goes to the modulator. The spectrum of the transmission is now determined by the spectrum of the prs. This was shown in Chapter 2 to have a spikey $\sin x/x$ envelope. The frequencies beyond the first nulls are filtered out at the transmitter, leaving the characteristic 'dead hedgehog' shape seen on a spectrum analyser.

On reception, the derandomizer must contain the identical ring counter which must also be set to the starting condition to bit accuracy. Its output is then added to the data stream from the demodulator. The randomizing will effectively then have been added twice to the data in modulo-2, and as a result is cancelled out leaving the original serial data.

Where an existing wideband channel having a DC response and a good SNR is being used for digital signalling, an increase in data rate can be had using multilevel signalling or *m*-ary coding instead of binary. This is the basis of the sound-in-syncs technique used by broadcasters to convey PCM audio along baseband video routes by inserting data bursts in the analog video sync pulses.

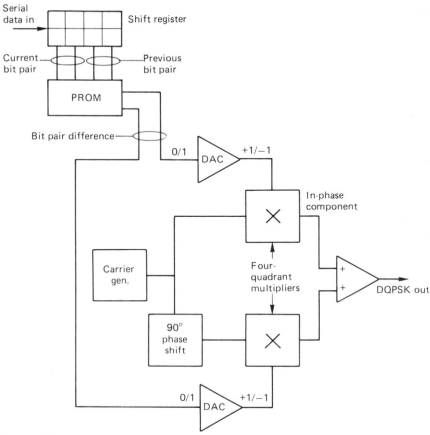

Figure 5.50 A DQPSK coder conveys 2 bits for each modulation period. See text for details

Fig. 5.51 shows the four-level waveform of the UK DSIS (Dual-Channel Sound-in-Syncs) system which is used to carry stereo audio to NICAM-equipped transmitters. Clearly the data separator must have a 2 bit ADC which can resolve the four signal levels. The gain and offset of the signal must be precisely set so that the quantizing levels register precisely with the centres of the eyes.

Where the maximum data rate in a given bandwidth is needed for economic reasons, as in digital audio broadcasting (DAB) or digital television broadcasts, multilevel signalling can be combined with PSK to obtain multilevel quadrature amplitude modulation (QUAM). Fig. 5.52 shows the example of 64-QUAM. Incoming 6 bit data words are split into two 3 bit words and each is used to amplitude-modulate a pair of sinusoidal carriers which are generated in quadrature. The modulators are four-quadrant devices such that 2^3 amplitudes are available, four which are in phase with the carrier and four which are antiphase. The two AM carriers are linearly added and the result is a signal which has 2^6 or 64 combinations of amplitude and phase. There is a great deal of similarity between QUAM and the colour subcarrier used in analog television in which the two colour difference signals are encoded into one amplitude and phase modulated

Figure 5.51 DSIS information within the TV line sync pulse

waveform. On reception, the waveform is sampled twice per cycle in phase with the two original carriers and the result is a pair of eight-level signals.

The data are randomized by addition to a prs before being fed to the modulator. The resultant spectrum has once again the $\sin x/x$ shape with nulls at multiples of the randomizer clock rate. As a result, a large number of carriers can be spaced at multiples of the randomizer clock frequency such that each carrier centre frequency coincides with the nulls of all the adjacent carriers. The result is referred to as COFDM or Coded Orthogonal Frequency Division Multiplexing.[20]

5.26 Convolutional randomizing

The randomizing in NICAM is block based, since this matches the 1 millisecond block structure of the transmission. Where there is no obvious block structure, convolutional or endless randomizing can be used. This is the approach used in the scrambled serial digital video interconnect described in Chapter 7, which allows composite or component video of up to 10 bit wordlength to be sent serially along with digital audio channels.

In convolutional randomizing, the signal sent down the channel is the serial data waveform which has been convolved with the impulse response of a digital filter. On reception the signal is deconvolved to restore the original data. Fig. 5.53(a) shows that the filter is an infinite-impulse response (IIR) filter which has recursive paths from the output back to the input. As it is a 1 bit filter its output cannot decay, and once excited, it runs indefinitely. The filter is followed by a transition generator which consists of a 1 bit delay and an exclusive OR gate. An input 1 results in an output transition on the next clock edge. An input 0 results in no transition.

A result of the infinite-impulse response of the filter is that frequent transitions are generated in the channel which result in sufficient clock content for the phase-locked loop in the receiver.

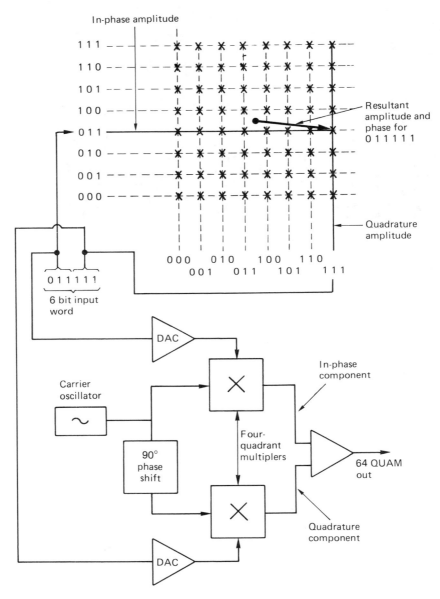

Figure 5.52 In 64-QUAM, two carriers are generated with a quadrature relationship. These are independently amplitude modulated to eight discrete levels in four quadrant multipliers. Adding the signals produces a QUAM signal having 64 unique combinations of amplitude and phase. Decoding requires the waveform to be sampled in quadrature like a colour TV subcarrier

Figure 5.53 (a) Modulo-2 addition with a pseudo-random code removes unconstrained runs in real data. Identical process must be provided on replay. (b) Convolutional randomizing encoder, at top, transmits exclusive OR of 3 bits at a fixed spacing in the data. One bit delay, far right, produces channel transitions from data ones. Decoder, below, has opposing 1 bit delay to return from transitions to data levels, followed by an opposing shift register which exactly reverses the coding process

Transitions are converted back to ones by a differentiator in the receiver. This consists of a 1 bit delay with an exclusive OR gate comparing the input and the output. When a transition passes through the delay, the input and the output will be different and the gate outputs a one which enters the deconvolution circuit.

Fig. 5.53(b) shows that in the deconvolution circuit a data bit is simply the exclusive OR of a number of channel bits at a fixed spacing. The deconvolution is implemented with a shift register having the exclusive OR gates connected in a reverse pattern to that in the encoder. The same effect as block randomizing is obtained, in that long runs are broken up and the DC content is reduced, but it has the advantage over block randomizing that no synchronizing is required to remove the randomizing, although it will still be necessary for deserialization. Clearly the system will take a few clock periods to produce valid data after commencement of transmission; this is no problem on a permanent-wired connection where the transmission is continuous.

5.27 Synchronizing

Once the PLL in the data separator has locked to the clock content of the transmission, a serial channel bit stream and a channel bit clock will emerge from the sampler. In a group code, it is essential to know where a group of channel bits begins in order to assemble groups for decoding to data bit groups. In a randomizing system it is equally vital to know at what point in the serial data stream the words or samples commence. In serial transmission and in recording, channel bit groups or randomized data words are sent one after the other, 1 bit at a time, with no spaces in between, so that although the designer knows that a data block contains, say, 128 bytes, the receiver simply finds 1024 bits in a row. If the exact position of the first bit is not known, then it is not possible to put all the bits in the right places in the right bytes, a process known as deserializing. The effect of sync slippage is devastating, because a 1 bit disparity between the bit count and the bit stream will corrupt every symbol in the block.[21]

The synchronization of the data separator and the synchronization to the block format are two distinct problems which are often solved by the same sync pattern. Deserializing requires a shift register which is fed with serial data and read out once per word. The sync detector is simply a set of logic gates which are arranged to recognize a specific pattern in the register. The sync pattern is either identical for every block or has a restricted number of versions and it will be recognized by the replay circuitry and used to reset the bit count through the

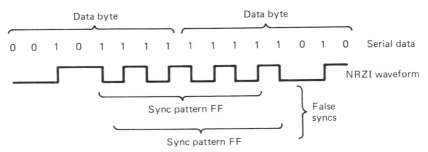

Figure 5.54 Concatenation of two words can result in the accidental generation of a word which is reserved for synchronizing

block. Then by counting channel bits and dividing by the group size, groups can be deserialized and decoded to data groups. In a randomized system, the pseudo-random sequence generator is also reset. Then counting derandomized bits from the sync pattern and dividing by the wordlength enables the replay circuitry to deserialize the data words.

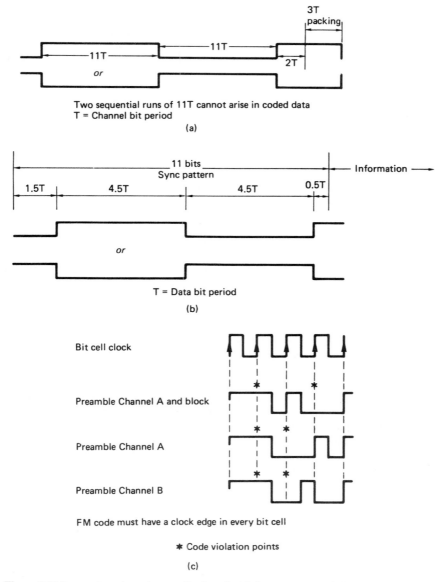

Figure 5.55 Sync patterns in various applications. In (a) the sync pattern of CD violates EFM coding rules, and is uniquely identifiable. In (b) the sync pattern of DASH stays within the run length of HDM-1. In (c) the sync patterns of AES/EBU interconnect

In digital audio the two's complement coding scheme is universal and traditionally no codes have been reserved for synchronizing; they are all available for sample values. It would in any case be impossible to reserve all ones or all zeros as these are in the centre of the range in two's complement. Even if a specific code were excluded from the recorded data so it could be used for synchronizing, this cannot ensure that the same pattern cannot be falsely created at the junction between two allowable data words. Fig. 5.54 shows how false synchronizing can occur due to concatenation. It is thus not practical to use a bit pattern which is a data code value in a simple synchronizing recognizer. The problem is overcome in NICAM 728 by using the fact that sync patterns occur exactly once per millisecond or 728 bits. The sync pattern of NICAM 728 is just a bit pattern and no steps are taken to prevent it from appearing in the randomized data. If the pattern is seen by the recognizer, the recognizer is disabled for the rest of the frame and only enabled when the next sync pattern is expected. If the same pattern recurs every millisecond, a genuine sync condition exists. If it does not, there was a false sync and the recognizer will be enabled again. As a result it will take a few milliseconds before sync is achieved, but once achieved it should not be lost unless the transmission is interrupted. This is fine for the application and no-one objects to the short mute of the NICAM sound during a channel switch. The principle cannot, however, be used for recording because channel interruptions are more frequent due to head switches and dropouts and loss of several blocks of data due to a single dropout is unacceptable.

In run-length-limited codes this is not a problem. The sync pattern is no longer a data bit pattern but is a specific waveform. If the sync waveform contains run lengths which violate the normal coding limits, there is no way that these run lengths can occur in encoded data, nor any possibility that they will be interpreted as data. They can, however, be readily detected by the replay circuitry. The sync patterns of the AES/EBU interface are shown in Fig. 5.55. It will be seen from Fig. 5.30 that the maximum run length in FM-coded data is 1 bit. The sync pattern begins with a run length of one and a half bits which is unique. There are three types of sync pattern in the AES/EBU interface, as will be seen in Chapter 12. These are distinguished by the position of a second pulse after the run-length violation. Note that the sync patterns are also DC free like the FM code.

In a group code there are many more combinations of channel bits than there are combinations of data bits. Thus after all data bit patterns have been allocated group patterns, there are still many unused group patterns which cannot occur in the data. With care, group patterns can be found which cannot occur due to the concatenation of any pair of groups representing data. These are then unique and can be used for synchronizing.

References

1. Deeley, E.M., Integrating and differentiating channels in digital tape recording. *Radio Electron. Eng.*, **56**, 169–173 (1986)
2. Mee, C.D., *The Physics of Magnetic Recording*. Amsterdam and New York: Elsevier–North Holland (1978)
3. Jacoby, G.V., Signal equalization in digital magnetic recording. *IEEE Trans. Magn.*, **MAG-11**, 302–305 (1975)
4. Schneider, R.C., An improved pulse-slimming method for magnetic recording. *IEEE Trans. Magn.*, **MAG-11**, 1240–1241 (1975)

5. Miller, A., US Patent. No. 3, 108, 261
6. Mallinson, J.C. and Miller, J.W., Optimum codes for digital magnetic recording. *Radio Electron. Eng.*, **47**, 172–176 (1977)
7. Miller, J.W., DC-free encoding for data transmission system. US Patent 4, 027, 335 (1977)
8. Tang, D.T., Run-length-limited codes. *IEEE International Symposium on Information Theory* (1969)
9. Cohn, M. and Jacoby, G., Run-length reduction of 3PM code via lookahead technique. *IEEE Trans. Magn.*, **MAG-18**, 1253–1255 (1982)
10. Horiguchi, T. and Morita, K., On optimisation of modulation codes in digital recording. *IEEE Trans. Magn.*, **MAG-12**, 740–742 (1976)
11. Franaszek, P.A., Sequence state methods for run-length limited coding. *IBM J. Res. Dev.*, **14**, 376–383 (1970)
12. Jacoby, G.V. and Kost, R., Binary two-thirds-rate code with full word lookahead. *IEEE Trans. Magn.*, **MAG-20**, 709–714 (1984)
13. Jacoby, G.V., A new lookahead code for increased data density. *IEEE Trans. Magn.*, **13**, 1202–1204 (1977)
14. Uehara, T., Nakayama, T., Minaguchi, H., Shibaya, H., Sekiguchi, T. and Oba, Y., A new 8–14 modulation and its application to small format VTR. *SMPTE Tech. Conf.* (1989)
15. Yokoyama, K., Digital video tape recorder. *NHK Tech. Monogr.*, No.31 (March 1982)
16. Coleman, C.H., *et al.*, High data rate magnetic recording in a single channel. *J. IERE*, **55**, 229–236 (1985)
17. Kobayashi, H., Application of partial response channel coding to magnetic recording systems. *IBM J. Res. Dev.*, **14**, 368–375 (1970)
18. Forney, G.D., Jr, The Viterbi algorithm. *Proc. IEEE*, **61**, 268–278 (1973)
19. Wood, R.W. and Petersen, D.A., Viterbi detection of Class IV partial response on a magnetic recording channel. *IEEE Trans. Commun.*, **34**, 454–461 (1968)
20. Alard, M. and Lasalle, R., Principles of modulation and channel coding for digital broadcasting for mobile receivers. *EBU rev.*, **224**, 168–190 (1987)
21. Griffiths, F.A., A digital audio recording system. Presented at 65th Audio Engineering Society Convention (London, 1980), preprint 1580(C1)

Error correction

The subject of error correction is almost always described in mathematical terms by specialists for the benefit of other specialists. Such mathematical approaches are quite inappropriate for a proper understanding of the concepts of error correction and only become necessary to analyse the quantitative behaviour of a system. The description below will use the minimum possible amount of mathematics, and it will then be seen that error correction is, in fact, quite straightforward.

6.1 Sensitivity of message to error

Before attempting to specify any piece of equipment, it is necessary to quantify the problems to be overcome and how effectively they need to be overcome. For a digital recording system the causes of errors must be studied to quantify the problem, and the sensitivity of the destination to errors must be assessed. In video and audio the sensitivity to errors must be subjective. In PCM, the effect of a single bit in error depends upon the significance of the bit. If the least significant bit of a sample is wrong, the chances are that the effect will be lost in the noise. Advantage is taken of this in NICAM 728 which does not detect low-order bit errors. Conversely, if a high-order bit is in error, a massive transient will be added to the waveform. The use of data reduction complicates the subject. In theory, if redundancy has been removed from a signal, it becomes less tolerant of errors.

Whilst the exact BER (Bit Error Rate) which can be tolerated will depend on the application, digital audio is less tolerant of errors than digital video and more tolerant than computer data.

In all of these cases, if the maximum error rate which the destination can tolerate is likely to be exceeded by the unaided channel, some form of error handling will be necessary.

There are a number of terms which have idiomatic meanings in error correction. The raw BER is the error rate of the medium, whereas the residual or uncorrected BER is the rate at which the error-correction system fails to detect or miscorrects errors. In practical digital systems, the residual BER is negligibly small. If the error correction is turned off, the two figures become the same.

6.2 Error mechanisms

There are many different types of recording and transmission channel and consequently there will be many different mechanisms which may result in errors. As was the case for channel coding, although there are many different applications, the basic principles remain the same.

In magnetic recording, data can be corrupted by mechanical problems such as media dropout and poor tracking or head contact, or Gaussian thermal noise in replay circuits and heads. In optical recording, contamination of the medium interrupts the light beam. Warped discs and birefringent pressings cause defocusing. Inside equipment, data are conveyed on short wires and the noise environment is under the designer's control. With suitable design techniques, errors can be made effectively negligible. In communication systems, there is considerably less control of the electromagnetic environment. In cables, crosstalk and electromagnetic interference occur and can corrupt data, although optical fibres are resistant to interference of this kind. In long-distance cable transmission the effects of lightning and exchange switching noise must be considered. In DAB, multipath reception causes notches in the received spectrum where signal cancellation takes place. In MOS memories the datum is stored in a tiny charge well which acts as a capacitor (see Chapter 2) and natural radioactive decay can cause alpha particles which have enough energy to discharge a well, resulting in a single-bit error. This only happens once every few decades in a single chip, but when large numbers of chips are assembled in computer memories the probability of error rises to one every few minutes.

In Chapter 5 it was seen that when group codes are used, a single defect in a group changes the group symbol and may cause errors up to the size of the group. Single-bit errors are therefore less common in group-coded channels.

Irrespective of the cause, all of these mechanisms cause one of two effects. There are large isolated corruptions, called error bursts, where numerous bits are corrupted all together in an area which is otherwise error free, and there are random errors affecting single bits or symbols. Whatever the mechanism, the result will be that the received data will not be exactly the same as those sent. It is a tremendous advantage of digital audio that the discrete data bits will be each either right or wrong. A bit cannot be off-colour as it can only be interpreted as 0 or 1. Thus the subtle degradations of analog systems are absent from digital recording and transmission channels and will only be found in converters. Equally if a binary digit is known to be wrong, it is only necessary to invert its state and then it must be right and indistinguishable from its original value! Thus error correction itself is trivial; the hard part is working out *which* bits need correcting.

In Chapter 2 the Gaussian nature of noise probability was discussed. Some conclusions can be drawn from the Gaussian distribution of noise.[1] Firstly, it is not possible to make error-free digital recordings, because however high the signal-to-noise ratio of the recording, there is still a small but finite chance that the noise can exceed the signal. Measuring the signal-to-noise ratio of a channel establishes the noise power, which determines the width of the noise distribution curve relative to the signal amplitude. When in a binary system the noise amplitude exceeds the signal amplitude, but with the opposite polarity, a bit error will occur. Knowledge of the shape of the Gaussian curve allows the conversion of signal-to-noise ratio into bit error rate (BER). It can be predicted how many bits will fail due to noise in a given recording, but it is not possible to say *which* bits will be affected. Increasing the SNR of the channel will not eliminate errors; it just reduces their probability. The logical solution is to incorporate an error-correction system.

6.3 Basic error correction

Error correction works by adding some bits to the data which are calculated from the data. This creates an entity called a codeword which spans a greater length of time than 1 bit alone. The statistics of noise means that whilst 1 bit may be lost in a codeword, the loss of the rest of the codeword because of noise is highly improbable. As will be described later in this chapter, codewords are designed to be able to correct totally a finite number of corrupted bits. The greater the timespan over which the coding is performed, or, on a recording medium, the greater area over which the coding is performed, the greater will be the reliability achieved, although this does mean that an encoding delay will be experienced on recording, and a similar or greater decoding delay on reproduction.

Shannon[2] disclosed that a message can be sent to any desired degree of accuracy provided that it is spread over a sufficient timespan. Engineers have to compromise, because an infinite coding delay in the recovery of an error-free signal is not acceptable. Most short digital interfaces do not employ error correction because the build-up of coding delays in large systems is unacceptable.

If error correction is necessary as a practical matter, it is then only a small step to put it to maximum use. All error correction depends on adding bits to the original message, and this of course increases the number of bits to be recorded, although it does not increase the information recorded. It might be imagined that error correction is going to reduce storage capacity, because space has to be found for all the extra bits. Nothing could be further from the truth. Once an error-correction system is used, the signal-to-noise ratio of the channel can be reduced, because the raised BER of the channel will be overcome by the error-correction system. Reduction of the SNR by 3 dB in a magnetic tape track can be achieved by halving the track width, provided that the system is not dominated by head or preamplifier noise. This doubles the recording density, making the storage of the additional bits needed for error correction a trivial matter. In short, error correction is not a nuisance to be tolerated; it is a vital tool needed to maximize the efficiency of recorders. Digital video or audio recording would not be economically viable without it.

6.4 Error handling

Fig. 6.1 shows the broad subdivisions of error handling. The first stage might be called error avoidance and includes such measures as creating bad-block files on hard disks or using verified media. Placing the audio blocks near to the centre of the tape is a further example. The data pass through the channel, which causes whatever corruptions it feels like. On receipt of the data the occurrence of errors is first detected, and this process must be extremely reliable, as it does not matter how effective the correction or how good the concealment algorithm, if it is not known that they are necessary! The detection of an error then results in a course of action being decided.

Figure 6.1 The basic stages of an error-correction system. Of these the most critical is the detection stage, since this controls the subsequent actions

In most cases of digital video or audio replay a retry is not possible because the data are required in real time. However, if a disk-based system is transferring to tape for the purpose of backup, real-time operation is not required. If the disk drive detects an error a retry is easy as the disk is turning at several thousand rpm and will quickly re-present the data. An error due to a dust particle may not occur on the next revolution. Many magnetic tape systems have *read after write*. During recording, offtape data are immediately checked for errors. If an error is detected, the tape will abort the recording, reverse to the beginning of the current block and erase it. The data from that block are then recorded further down the tape. This is the recording equivalent of a retransmission in a communications system.

6.5 Concealment by interpolation

There are some practical differences between data recording for video and the computer data recording application. Although video or audio recorders seldom have time for retries, they have the advantage that there is a certain amount of redundancy in the information conveyed. Thus if an error cannot be corrected, then it can be concealed. If a sample is lost, it is possible to obtain an approximation to it by interpolating between the samples before and after the missing one. Clearly concealment of any kind cannot be used with computer data.

If there is too much corruption for concealment, the only course in video is repeat the previous field or frame in a freeze as it is unlikely that the corrupt picture is watchable.

In general, if use is to be made of concealment on replay, the data must generally be reordered or shuffled prior to recording. To take a simple example, odd-numbered samples are recorded in a different area of the medium from even-numbered samples. On playback, if a gross error occurs on the tape, depending on its position, the result will be either corrupted odd samples or corrupted even samples, but it is most unlikely that both will be lost. Interpolation is then possible if the power of the correction system is exceeded. In practice the shuffle employed in digital video recorders is two dimensional and rather more complex. Further details can be found in section 6.20 and in Chapter 9. The concealment technique described here is only suitable for PCM recording. If data reduction has been employed, different concealment techniques will be needed.

It should be stressed that corrected data are indistinguishable from the original and thus there can be no visible or audible artefacts. In contrast, concealment is only an approximation to the original information and could be detectable. In practical video equipment, concealment occurs infrequently unless there is a defect requiring attention, and its presence is difficult to see.

6.6 Parity

The error-detection and error-correction processes are closely related and will be dealt with together here. The actual correction of an error is simplified tremendously by the adoption of binary. As there are only two symbols, 0 and 1, it is enough to know that a symbol is wrong, and the correct value is obvious. Fig. 6.2 shows a minimal circuit required for correction once the bit in error has been identified. The XOR (exclusive OR) gate shows up extensively in error correction and the figure also shows the truth table. One way of remembering the characteristics of this useful device is that there will be an output when the inputs are different. Inspection of the truth table will show that there is an even number of ones in each row (zero is an even number) and so the device could also be called an even parity gate. The XOR gate is also an adder in modulo-2. (see Chapter 2).

Figure 6.2 Once the position of the error is identified, the correction process in binary is easy

Parity is a fundamental concept in error detection. In Fig. 6.3, the example is given of a 4 bit data word which is to be protected. If an extra bit is added to the word which is calculated in such a way that the total number of ones in the 5 bit word is even, this property can be tested on receipt. The generation of the parity bit in Fig. 6.3 can be performed by a number of the ubiquitous XOR gates configured into what is known as a parity tree. In the figure, if a bit is corrupted, the received message will be seen no longer to have an even number of ones. If 2 bits are corrupted, the failure will be undetected. This example can be used to introduce much of the terminology of error correction. The extra bit added to the message carries no information of its own, since it is calculated from the other bits. It is therefore called a *redundant* bit. The addition of the redundant bit gives the message a special property, i.e. the number of ones is even. A message having some special property *irrespective of the actual data content* is called a *codeword*. All error correction relies on adding redundancy to real data to form codewords for transmission. If any corruption occurs, the intention is that the received message will not have the special property; in other words if the received message is not a codeword there has definitely been an error. The receiver can check for the special property without any prior knowledge of the data content. Thus the same check can be made on all received data. If the received message is a codeword, there probably has not been an error. The word 'probably' must be used because the figure shows that 2 bits in error will cause the received message to be a codeword, which cannot be discerned from an error-

Figure 6.3 Parity checking adds up the number of ones in a word using, in this example, parity trees. One error bit and odd numbers of errors are detected. Even numbers of errors cannot be detected

free message. If it is known that generally the only failure mechanism in the channel in question is loss of a single bit, it is *assumed* that receipt of a codeword means that there has been no error. If there is a probability of two error bits, that becomes very nearly the probability of failing to detect an error, since all odd numbers of errors will be detected, and a 4 bit error is much less likely. It is paramount in all error-correction systems that the protection used should be appropriate for the probability of errors to be encountered. An inadequate error-correction system is actually worse than not having any correction. Error correction works by trading probabilities. Error-free performance with a certain error rate is achieved at the expense of performance at higher error rates. Fig. 6.4 shows the effect of an error-correction system on the residual BER for a given raw BER. It will be seen that there is a characteristic knee in the graph. If the expected raw BER has been misjudged, the consequences can be disastrous. Another result demonstrated by the example is that we can only guarantee to detect the same number of bits in error as there are redundant bits.

Figure 6.4 An error-correction system can only reduce errors at normal error rates at the expense of increasing errors at higher rates. It is most important to keep a system working to the left of the knee in the graph

6.7 Block and convolutional codes

Fig. 6.5(a) shows a strategy known as a crossword code, or product code. The data are formed into a two-dimensional array, in which each location can be a single bit or a multibit symbol. Parity is then generated on both rows and columns. If a single bit or symbol fails, one row parity check and one column parity check will fail, and the failure can be located at the intersection of the two failing checks. Although two symbols in error confuse this simple scheme, using more complex coding in a two-dimensional structure is very powerful, and further examples will be given throughout this chapter.

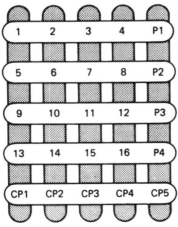

(a)

Figure 6.5 A block code is shown in (a). Each location in the block can be a bit or a word. Horizontal parity checks are made by adding P1, P2, etc., and cross-parity or vertical checks are made by adding CP1, CP2, etc. Any symbol in error will be at the intersection of the two failing codewords. In (b) a convolutional coder is shown. Symbols entering are subject to different delays which result in the codewords in (c) being calculated. These have a vertical part and a diagonal part. A symbol in error will be at the intersection of the diagonal part of one code and the vertical part of another

Figure 6.5 continued

The example of Fig. 6.5(a) assembles the data to be coded into a block of finite size and then each codeword is calculated by taking different sets of symbols. This should be contrasted with the operation of the circuit of Fig. 6.5(b). Here the data are not in a block, but form an endless stream. A shift register allows four symbols to be available simultaneously to the encoder. The action of the encoder depends upon the delays. When symbol 3 emerges from the first delay, it will be added (modulo-2) to symbol 6. When this sum emerges from the second delay, it will be added to symbol 9 and so on. The codeword produced is shown in Fig. 6.5(c) where it will be seen to be bent such that it has a vertical section and a diagonal section. Four symbols later the next codeword will be created one column further over in the data.

This is a convolutional code because the coder always takes parity on the same pattern of symbols which is convolved with the data stream on an endless basis. Fig. 6.5(c) also shows that if an error occurs, it can be located because it will cause parity errors in two codewords. The error will be on the diagonal part of one codeword and on the vertical part of the other so that it can be located uniquely at the intersection and corrected by parity.

Comparison with the block code of Fig. 6.5(a) will show that the convolutional code needs less redundancy for the same single-symbol location and correction performance as only a single redundant symbol is required for every four data symbols. Convolutional codes are computed on an endless basis which makes them inconvenient in recording applications where editing is anticipated. Here the block code is more appropriate as it allows edit gaps to be created between codes. In the case of uncorrectable errors, the convolutional principle causes the syndromes to be affected for some time afterwards and this results in miscorrections of symbols which were not actually in error. This is called error propagation and is a characteristic of convolutional codes. Recording media tend to produce somewhat variant error statistics because media defects and mechanical problems cause errors which do not fit the classical additive noise channel. Convolutional codes can easily be taken beyond their correcting power if used with real recording media.

In transmission and broadcasting, the error statistics are more stable and the editing requirement is absent. As a result convolutional codes are used in digital broadcasting whereas block codes are used in recording. Convolutional codes are not restricted to the simple parity example given here, but can be used in conjunction with more sophisticated redundancy techniques such as the Reed–Solomon codes.

6.8 Hamming code

In a one-dimensional code, the position of the failing bit can be determined by using more parity checks. In Fig. 6.6, the four data bits have been used to compute three redundancy bits, making a 7 bit codeword. The four data bits are examined in turn, and each bit which is a one will cause the corresponding row of a generator matrix to be added to an exclusive OR sum. For example, if the data were 1001, the top and bottom rows of the matrix would be XORed. The matrix used is known as an identity matrix, because the data bits in the codeword are identical to the data bits to be conveyed. This is useful because the original data can be stored unmodified, and the check bits are simply attached to the end to make a so-called systematic codeword. Almost all digital recording equipment

Figure 6.6 (a) The generator and check matrices of a Hamming code. The data and check bits are arranged as shown because this causes the syndrome to be the binary address of the failing bit. (b) An example of Hamming code generation and error correction. (c) Another way of looking at Hamming code is to say that the rows of crosses in this chart are calculated to have even parity. If bit 3 fails, parity check P3 is not affected, but parity checks P1 and P2 both include bit 3 and will fail

uses systematic codes. The way in which the redundancy bits are calculated is simply that they do not all use every data bit. If a data bit has not been included in a parity check, it can fail without affecting the outcome of that check. The position of the error is deduced from the pattern of successful and unsuccessful checks in the check matrix. This pattern is known as a syndrome.

In the figure the example of a failing bit is given. Bit 3 fails, and because this bit is included in only two of the checks, there are two ones in the failure pattern, 011. As some care was taken in designing the matrix pattern for the generation of the check bits, the syndrome, 011, is the address of the failing bit. This is the fundamental feature of the Hamming codes due to Richard Hamming.[3] The performance of this 7 bit codeword can be assessed. In 7 bits there can be 128 combinations, but in four data bits there are only 16 combinations. Thus out of 128 possible received messages, only 16 will be codewords, so if the message is completely trashed by a gross corruption, it will still be possible to detect that this has happened 112 times out of 127, as in these cases the syndrome will be non-zero (the 128th case is the correct data). There is thus only a probability of detecting that all of the message is corrupt. In an idle moment it is possible to work out, in a similar way, the number of false codewords which can result from different numbers of bits being assumed to have failed. For less than 3 bits, the failure will always be detected, because there are three check bits. Returning to the example, if 2 bits fail, there will be a non-zero syndrome, but if this is used to point to a bit in error, a miscorrection will result. From these results can be deduced another important feature of error codes. The power of detection is always greater than the power of correction, which is also fortunate, since if the correcting power is exceeded by an error it will at least be a known problem, and steps can be taken to prevent any undesirable consequences.

The efficiency of the example given is not very high because three check bits are needed for every four data bits. Since the failing bit is located with a binary-split mechanism, it is possible to double the code length by adding a single extra

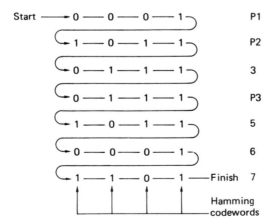

Figure 6.7 The vertical columns of this diagram are all codewords generated by the matrix of Figure 6.6, which can correct a single-bit error. If these words are recorded in the order shown, a burst error of up to 4 bits will result in one single-bit error in each codeword, which is correctable. Interleave and de-interleave require memory, and cause delay

check bit. Thus with 4 bit syndromes there are 15 non-zero codes and so the codeword will be 15 bits long: 4 bits are redundant and 11 are data. Using 5 bits of redundancy, the code can be 31 bits long and contain 26 data bits. Thus provided that the number of errors to be detected stays the same, it is more efficient to use long codewords. Error-correcting memories use typically four or eight data bytes plus redundancy. A drawback of long codes is that if it is desired to change a single memory byte it is necessary to read the entire codeword, modify the desired data byte and re-encode, the so-called read–modify–write process.

The Hamming code shown is limited to single-bit correction, but by the addition of another bit of redundancy it can be made to correct 1 bit and detect 2 bit errors. This is ideal for error-correcting MOS memories where the SECDED (Single-Error-Correcting Double-Error-Detecting) characteristic matches the type of failures experienced.

The correction of 1 bit is of little use in the presence of burst errors, but a Hamming code can be made to correct burst errors by using interleaving. Fig. 6.7 shows that if several codewords are calculated beforehand and woven together as shown before they are sent down the channel, then a burst of errors which corrupts several bits will become a number of single-bit errors in separate codewords upon de-interleaving.

Interleaving is used extensively in digital recording and transmission, and will be discussed in greater detail later in this chapter.

6.9 Hamming distance

It is useful at this point to introduce the concept of Hamming distance. It is not a physical distance but is a specific measure of the difference between two binary numbers. Hamming distance is defined in the general case as the number of bit positions in which a pair of words differ. The Hamming distance of a code is defined as the minimum number of bits that must be changed in any codeword in order to turn it into another codeword. This is an important yardstick because if errors convert one codeword into another, it will have the special characteristic of the code and so the corruption will not even be detected.

Fig. 6.8 shows Hamming distance diagrammatically. A 3 bit codeword is used with two data bits and one parity bit. With 3 bits, a received code could have eight combinations, but only four of these will be codewords. The valid codewords are shown in the centre of each of the disks, and these will be seen to be identical to the rows of the truth table in Fig. 6.2. At the perimeter of the disks are shown the received words which would result from a single-bit error, i.e. they have a Hamming distance of one from codewords. It will be seen that the same received word (on the vertical bars) can be obtained from a different single-bit corruption of any three codewords. It is thus not possible to tell which codeword was corrupted, so although all single-bit errors can be detected, correction is not possible. This diagram should be compared with that of Fig. 6.9, which is a Venn diagram where there is a set in which the MSB is 1 (upper circle), a set in which the middle bit is 1 (lower left circle) and a set in which the LSB is 1 (lower right circle). Note that in crossing any boundary only 1 bit changes, and so each boundary represents a Hamming distance change of one. The four codewords of Fig. 6.8 are repeated here, and it will be seen that single-bit errors in any

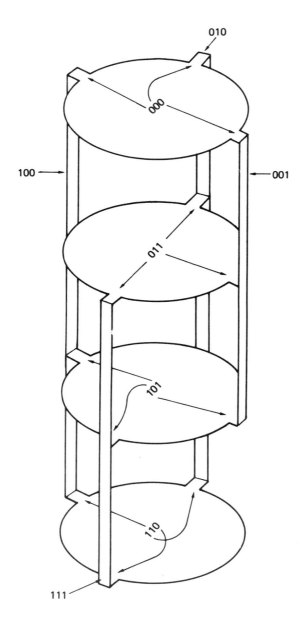

Figure 6.8 Hamming distance of two. The disk centres contain codewords. Corrupting each bit in turn produces the distance 1 values on the vertical members. In order to change one codeword to another, 2 bits must be changed, so the code has a Hamming distance of two

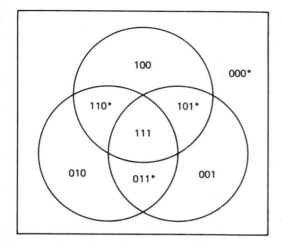

Figure 6.9 Venn diagram shows a 1 bit change crossing any boundary which is a Hamming distance of one. Compare with Figure 6.11. Codewords marked *

codeword produce a non-codeword, and so single-bit errors are always detectable.

Correction is possible if the number of non-codewords is increased by increasing the number of redundant bits. This means that it is possible to spread out the actual codewords in Hamming distance terms.

Fig. 6.10(a) shows a distance 2 code, where there is only one redundancy bit, and so half of the possible words will be codewords. There will be non-codewords at distance 1 which can be produced by altering a single bit in either of two codewords. In this case it is not possible to tell what the original codeword was in the case of a single-bit error.

Fig. 6.10(b) shows a distance 3 code, where there will now be at least two non-codewords between codewords. If a single-bit error occurs in a codeword, the resulting non-codeword will be at distance 1 from the original codeword. This same non-codeword could also have been produced by changing *two* of the bits in a different codeword. If it is known that the failure mechanism is a single bit, it can be *assumed* that the original codeword was the one which is closest in Hamming distance to the received bit pattern, and so correction is possible. If, however, our assumption about the error mechanism proved to be wrong, and in fact a 2 bit error had occurred, this assumption would take us to the wrong codeword, turning the event into a 3 bit error. This is an illustration of the knee in the graph of Fig. 6.4, where if the power of the code is exceeded it makes things worse.

Fig. 6.10(c) shows a distance 4 code. There are now three non-codewords between codewords, and clearly single-bit errors can still be corrected by choosing the nearest codeword. Double-bit errors will be detected, because they result in non-codewords equidistant in Hamming terms from codewords, but it is not possible uniquely to determine what the original codeword was.

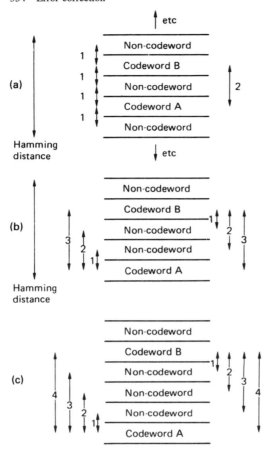

Figure 6.10 (a) Distance 2 code; non-codewords are at distance 1 from two possible codewords so it cannot be deduced what the correct one is. (b) Distance 3 code; non-codewords which have *single-bit errors* can be attributed to the nearest codeword. Breaks down in presence of double-bit errors. (c) Distance 4 code; non-codewords which have single-bit errors can be attributed to the nearest codeword, AND double-bit errors form *different* non-codewords, and can thus be detected but not corrected

6.10 Cyclic codes

The parallel implementation of a Hamming code can be made very fast using parity trees, which is ideal for memory applications where access time is increased by the correction process. However, in digital recording applications, the data are stored serially on a track, and it is desirable to use relatively large data blocks to reduce the amount of the medium devoted to preambles, addressing and synchronizing. Where large data blocks are to be handled, the use of a lookup table or tree has to be abandoned because it would become impossibly large. The principle of codewords having a special characteristic will still be employed, but they will be generated and checked algorithmically by

Figure 6.11 When seven successive bits A–G are clocked into this circuit, the contents of the three latches are shown for each clock. The final result is a parity-check matrix

equations. The syndrome will then be converted to the bit(s) in error not by looking them up, but by solving an equation.

Where data can be accessed serially, simpler circuitry can be used because the same gate will be used for many XOR operations. Unfortunately the reduction in component count is only paralleled by an increase in the difficulty of explaining what takes place.

The circuit of Fig. 6.11 is a kind of shift register, but with a particular feedback arrangement which leads it to be known as a twisted-ring counter. If seven message bits A–G are applied serially to this circuit, and each one of them is clocked, the outcome can be followed in the diagram. As bit A is presented and the system is clocked, bit A will enter the left-hand latch. When bits B and C are presented, A moves across to the right. Both XOR gates will have A on the upper input from the right-hand latch, the left one has D on the lower input and the right one has B on the lower input. When clocked, the left latch will thus be loaded with the XOR of A and D, and the right one with the XOR of A and B. The remainder of the sequence can be followed, bearing in mind that when the same term appears on both inputs of an XOR gate, it goes out, as the exclusive OR of something with itself is nothing. At the end of the process, the latches contain three different expressions. Essentially, the circuit makes three parity checks through the message, leaving the result of each in the three stages of the register. In the figure, these expressions have been used to draw up a check matrix. The significance of these steps can now be explained. The bits A B C and D are four data bits, and the bits E F and G are redundancy. When the redundancy is calculated, bit E is chosen so that there are an even number of ones in bits A B C and E; bit F is chosen such that the same applies to bits B C D and F, and similarly for bit G. Thus the four data bits and the three check bits form a 7 bit codeword. If there is no error in the codeword, when it is fed into the circuit shown, the result of each of the three parity checks will be zero and every stage of the shift register will be cleared. As the register has eight possible states, and one of them is the error-free condition, then there are seven remaining states; hence the 7 bit codeword. If a bit in the codeword is corrupted, there will be a non-zero result. For example, if bit D fails, the check on bits A B D and G will fail, and a one will appear in the left-hand latch. The check on bits B C D F will also fail, and the centre latch will set. The check on bits A B C E will not fail, because D is not involved in it, making the right-hand bit zero. There will be a syndrome of 110 in the register, and this will be seen from the check matrix to correspond to an error in bit D. Whichever bit fails, there will be a different 3 bit syndrome which uniquely identifies the failed bit. As there are only three latches, there can be eight different syndromes. One of these is zero, which is the error-free condition, and so there are seven remaining error syndromes. The length of the codeword cannot exceed 7 bits, or there would not be enough syndromes to correct all of the bits. This can also be made to tie in with the generation of the check matrix. If 14 bits, A to N, were fed into the circuit shown, the result would be that the check matrix repeated twice, and if a syndrome of 101 were to result, it could not be determined whether bit D or bit K failed. Because the check repeats every 7 bits, the code is said to be a cyclic redundancy check (CRC) code.

In Fig. 6.6 an example of a Hamming code was given. Comparison of the check matrix of Fig. 6.11 with that of Fig. 6.6 will show that the only difference is the order of the matrix columns. The two different processes have thus achieved exactly the same results, and the performance of both must be identical. This is not true in general, but a very small cyclic code has been used for simplicity and to allow parallels to be seen. In practice CRC code blocks will be much longer than the blocks used in Hamming codes.

It has been seen that the circuit shown makes a matrix check on a received word to determine if there has been an error, but the same circuit can also be used to generate the check bits. To visualize how this is done, examine what happens if only the data bits A B C and D are known, and the check bits E F and G are set to zero. If this message, ABCD000, is fed into the circuit, the left-hand latch will afterwards contain the XOR of A B C and zero, which is of course what E should be. The centre latch will contain the XOR of B C D and zero, which is what F should be and so on. This process is not quite ideal, however, because it is necessary to wait for three clock periods after entering the data before the check bits are available. Where the data are simultaneously being recorded and fed into the encoder, the delay would prevent the check bits being easily added to the end of the data stream. This problem can be overcome by slightly modifying the encoder circuit as shown in Fig. 6.12. By moving the position of the input to the right, the operation of the circuit is advanced so that the check bits are ready after only four clocks. The process can be followed in the diagram for the four data bits A B C and D. On the first clock, bit A enters the left two latches, whereas on the second clock, bit B will appear on the upper input of the left XOR gate, with bit A on the lower input, causing the centre latch to load the XOR of A and B and so on.

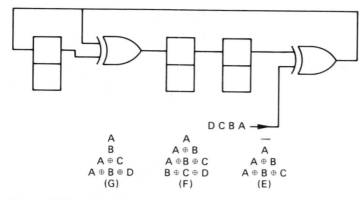

A	A	—
B	A ⊕ B	A
A ⊕ C	A ⊕ B ⊕ C	A ⊕ B
A ⊕ B ⊕ D	B ⊕ C ⊕ D	A ⊕ B ⊕ C
(G)	(F)	(E)

Figure 6.12 By moving the insertion point three places to the right, the calculation of the check bits is completed in only four clock periods and they can follow the data immediately. This is equivalent to premultiplying the data by x^3

The way in which the cyclic codes work has been described in engineering terms, but it can be described mathematically if analysis is contemplated.

Just as the position of a decimal digit in a number determines the power of 10 (whether that digit means one, ten or a hundred), the position of a binary digit determines the power of 2 (whether it means one, two or four). It is possible to rewrite a binary number so that it is expressed as a list of powers of 2. For example, the binary number 1101 means $8 + 4 + 1$, and can be written:

$$2^3 + 2^2 + 2^0$$

In fact, much of the theory of error correction applies to symbols in number bases other than 2, so that the number can also be written more generally as:

$$x^3 + x^2 + 1 \; (2^0 = 1)$$

which also looks much more impressive. This expression, containing as it does various powers, is of course a polynomial, and the circuit of Fig. 6.11 which has been seen to construct a parity-check matrix on a codeword can also be described as calculating the remainder due to dividing the input by a polynomial using modulo-2 arithmetic. In modulo-2 there are no borrows or carries, and addition and subtraction are replaced by the XOR function, which makes hardware implementation very easy. In Fig. 6.13 it will be seen that the circuit of Fig. 6.11 actually divides the codeword by a polynomial which is:

$$x^3 + x + 1 \text{ or } 1011$$

This can be deduced from the fact that the right-hand bit is fed into two lower-order stages of the register at once. Once all the bits of the message have been clocked in, the circuit contains the remainder. In mathematical terms, the special property of a codeword is that it is a polynomial which yields a remainder of zero when divided by the generating polynomial. The receiver will make this division, and the result should be zero in the error-free case. Thus the codeword itself disappears from the division. If an error has occurred it is considered that this is due to an error polynomial which has been added to the codeword polynomial. If a codeword divided by the check polynomial is zero, a non-zero syndrome

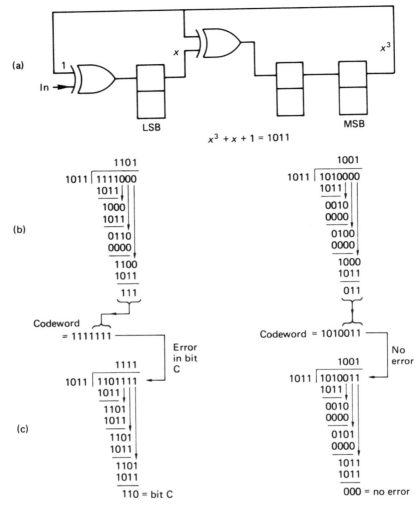

Figure 6.13 Circuit of Figure 6.11 divides by $x^3 + x + 1$ to find remainder. At (b) this is used to calculate check bits. At (c) right, zero syndrome, no error

must represent the error polynomial divided by the check polynomial. Thus if the syndrome is multiplied by the check polynomial, the latter will be cancelled out and the result will be the error polynomial. If this is added modulo-2 to the received word, it will cancel out the error and leave the corrected data.

Some examples of modulo-2 division are given in Fig. 6.13 which can be compared with the parallel computation of parity checks according to the matrix of Fig. 6.11.

The process of generating the codeword from the original data can also be described mathematically. If a codeword has to give zero remainder when divided, it follows that the data can be converted to a codeword by adding the remainder when the data are divided. Generally speaking the remainder would have to be subtracted, but in modulo-2 there is no distinction. This process is also illustrated in Fig. 6.13. The four data bits have three zeros placed on the right-hand end, to make the wordlength equal to that of a codeword, and this word is then divided by the polynomial to calculate the remainder. The remainder is added to the zero-extended data to form a codeword. The modified circuit of Fig. 6.12 can be described as premultiplying the data by x^3 before dividing.

CRC codes are of primary importance for detecting errors, and several have been standardized for use in digital communications. The most common of these are:

$$x^{16} + x^{15} + x^2 + 1 \text{ (CRC-16)}$$

$$x^{16} + x^{12} + x^5 + 1 \text{ (CRC-CCITT)}$$

6.11 Punctured codes

The 16 bit cyclic codes have codewords of length $2^{16} - 1$ or 65 535 bits long. This may be too long for the application. Another problem with very long codes is that with a given raw BER, the longer the code, the more errors will occur in it. There may be enough errors to exceed the power of the code. The solution in both cases is to shorten or *puncture* the code. Fig. 6.14 shows that in a punctured code, only the end of the codeword is used, and the data and redundancy are preceded by a string of zeros. It is not necessary to record these zeros, and of course, errors cannot occur in them. Implementing a punctured code is easy. If a CRC generator starts with the register cleared and is fed with serial zeros, it will not change its state. Thus it is not necessary to provide the zeros; encoding can begin with the first data bit. In the same way, the leading zeros need not be provided during playback. The only precaution needed is that if a syndrome calculates the location of an error, this will be from the beginning of the codeword, not from the beginning of the data. Where codes are used for detection only, this is of no consequence.

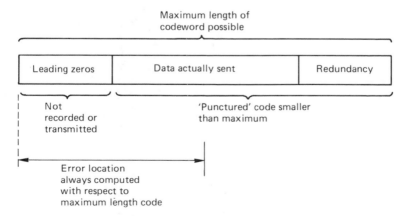

Figure 6.14 Codewords are often shortened, or punctured, which means that only the end of the codeword is actually transmitted. The only precaution to be taken when puncturing codes is that the computed position of an error will be from the beginning of the codeword, not from the beginning of the message

Figure 6.15 The CRCC in the AES/EBU interface is generated by premultiplying the data by x^8 and dividing by $x^8 + x^4 + x^3 + x^2 + 1$. The process can be performed on a serial input by the circuit shown. Premultiplication is achieved by connecting the input at the most significant end of the system. If the output of the right-hand XOR gate is 1 then a 1 is fed back to all of the powers shown, and the polynomial process required is performed. At the end of 23 data bytes, the CRCC will be in the eight latches. At the end of an error-free 24 byte message, the latches will be all zero

6.12 Applications of cyclic codes

The AES/EBU digital audio interface described in Chapter 12 uses an 8 bit cyclic code to protect the channel-status data. The polynomial used and a typical circuit for generating it can be seen in Fig. 6.15. The full codeword length is 255 bits but it is punctured to 192 bits, or 24 bytes, which is the length of the AES/EBU channel-status block. The CRCC is placed in the last byte.

Cyclic codes are also used for signature analysis, which is a reliability testing technique described in Chapter 7. A signature is a parameter similar to a CRCC, but which is used in a slightly different way. Fig. 6.16 shows that the concept of signature analysis is based on dividing data blocks by a polynomial. If a given fixed digital test pattern is produced by the generator of Fig. 6.16, it will result

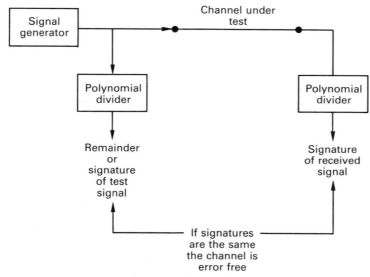

Figure 6.16 In signature analysis a data block is divided by a polynomial to obtain a remainder or signature. If the same signature is obtained elsewhere, the occurrence of an error is remote

in a fixed remainder when divided by a polynomial on the left. The remainder is the signature. If the same signature is reliably obtained when the polynomial divider is moved to the far end of a transmission system, then the transmission system is error free. It is a characteristic of cyclic codes that a single bit in error in a lengthy message will change the signature so that it can be detected. In practice, the data blocks in digital video are quite large and will exceed the length of the codeword. The cyclic code may repeat several times within the block. Thus location of errors is impossible, but this is not a goal of signature analysis as it is not an error-correction process.

6.13 Burst correction

Fig. 6.17 lists all of the possible codewords in the code of Fig. 6.11. Examination will show that it is necessary to change at least 3 bits in one codeword before it

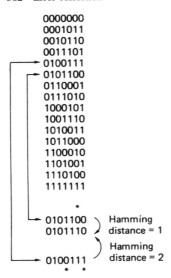

Figure 6.17 All possible codewords of $x^3 + x + 1$ are shown, and the fact that a double error in one codeword can produce the same pattern as a single error in another. Thus double errors cannot be corrected

can be made into another. Thus the code has a Hamming distance of three and cannot detect 3 bit errors. The single-bit error-correction limit can also be deduced from the figure. In the example given, the codeword 0101100 suffers a single-bit error marked * which converts it to a non-codeword at a Hamming distance of one. No other codeword can be turned into this word by a single-bit error; therefore the codeword which is the shortest Hamming distance away must be the correct one. The code can thus reliably correct single-bit errors. However, the codeword 0100111 can be made into the same failure word by a 2 bit error, also marked *, and in this case the original codeword cannot be found by selecting the one which is nearest in Hamming distance. A 2 bit error cannot be corrected and the system will miscorrect if it is attempted.

The concept of Hamming distance can be extended to explain how more than 1 bit can be corrected. In Fig. 6.18 the example of 2 bits in error is given. If a codeword 4 bits long suffers a single-bit error, it could produce one of four different words. If it suffers a 2 bit error, it could produce one of 3 + 2 + 1 different words as shown in the figure (the error bits are underlined). The total number of possible words of Hamming distance 1 or 2 from a 4 bit codeword is thus:

$$4 + 3 + 2 + 1 = 10$$

If the 2 bit error is to be correctable, no other codeword can be allowed to become one of this number of error patterns because of a 2 bit error of its own. Thus every codeword requires space for itself plus all possible error patterns of Hamming distance 2 or 1, which is 11 patterns in this example. Clearly there are only 16 patterns available in a 4 bit code, and thus no data can be conveyed if 2 bit protection is necessary.

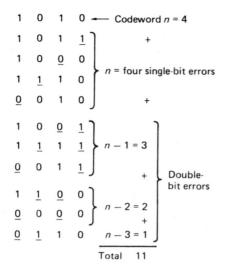

Figure 6.18 Where double-bit errors occur, the number of patterns necessary is $(n-1) + (n-2)$ $+ (n-3) + \ldots$. Total necessary is $1 + n + (n-1) + (n-2) + (n-3) + \ldots$ etc. Example here is of 4 bits, and all possible patterns up to a Hamming distance of two are shown (errors underlined)

The number of different patterns possible in a word of n bits is:

$$1 + n + (n-1) + (n-2) + (n-3) + \ldots$$

and this pattern range has to be shared between the ranges of each codeword without overlap. For example, an 8 bit codeword could result in $1 + 8 + 7 + 6 + 5 + 4 + 3 + 2 + 1 = 37$ patterns. As there are only 256 patterns in 8 bits, it follows that only 256/37 pieces of information can be conveyed. The nearest integer below is six, and the nearest power of 2 below is four, which corresponds to two data bits and six check bits in the 8 bit word. The amount of redundancy necessary to correct *any* 2 bits in error is large, and as the number of bits to be corrected grows, the redundancy necessary becomes enormous and impractical. A further problem is that the more redundancy is added, the greater the probability of an error in a codeword. Fortunately, in practice errors occur in bursts, as has already been described, and it is a happy consequence that the number of patterns that result from the corruption of a codeword by *adjacent* 2 bit errors is much smaller.

It can be deduced that the number of redundant bits necessary to correct a burst error is twice the number of bits in the burst for a perfect code. This is done by working out the number of received messages which could result from corruption of the codeword by bursts of from 1 bit up to the largest burst size allowed, and then making sure that there are enough redundant bits to allow that number of combinations in the received message.

Some codes, such as the Fire code due to Philip Fire,[4] are designed to correct single bursts, whereas later codes such as the B-adjacent code due to Bossen[5] could correct two bursts. The Reed–Solomon codes (Irving Reed and Gustave

Solomon)[6] have the advantage that an arbitrary number of bursts can be corrected by choosing the appropriate amount of redundancy at the design stage.

Whilst the Fire code was discovered at about the same time as the superior Reed–Solomon codes, it was dominant in disk drives for a long time because it was so much easier to implement. Now that LSI technology has advanced, the complexity of Reed–Solomon codes is no longer an issue and Fire code is seldom used.

6.14 Introduction to the Reed–Solomon codes

The Reed–Solomon codes are inherently burst correcting[6] because they work on multibit symbols rather than individual bits. The R–S codes are also extremely flexible in use. One code may be used both to detect and correct errors and the number of bursts which are correctable can be chosen at the design stage by the amount of redundancy. A further advantage of the R–S codes is that they can be used in conjunction with a separate error-detection mechanism in which case they perform only the correction by erasure. R–S codes operate at the theoretical limit of correcting efficiency. In other words, no more efficient code can be found.

In the simple CRC system described in Section 6.11, the effect of the error is detected by ensuring that the codeword can be divided by a polynomial. The CRC codeword was created by adding a redundant symbol to the data. In the Reed–Solomon codes, several errors can be isolated by ensuring that the codeword will divide by a number of polynomials. Clearly if the codeword must divide by, say, two polynomials, it must have two redundant symbols. This is the minimum case of an R–S code. On receiving an R–S coded message there will be two syndromes following the division. In the error-free case, these will both be zero. If both are not zero, there is an error.

It has been stated that the effect of an error is to add an error polynomial to the message polynomial. The number of terms in the error polynomial is the same as the number of errors in the codeword. The codeword divides to zero and the syndromes are a function of the error only. There are two syndromes and two equations. By solving these simultaneous equations it is possible to obtain two unknowns. One of these is the position of the error, known as the *locator*, and the other is the error bit pattern, known as the *corrector*. As the locator is the same size as the code symbol, the length of the codeword is determined by the size of the symbol. A symbol size of 8 bits is commonly used because it fits in conveniently with both 16 bit audio samples and byte-oriented computers. An 8 bit syndrome results in a locator of the same wordlength; 8 bits have 2^8 combinations, but one of these is the error-free condition, so the locator can specify one of only 255 symbols. As each symbol contains 8 bits, the codeword will be $255 \times 8 = 2040$ bits long.

As further examples, 5 bit symbols could be used to form a codeword 31 symbols long, and 3 bit symbols would form a codeword seven symbols long. This latter size is small enough to permit some worked examples, and will be used further here. Fig. 6.19 shows that in the seven-symbol codeword, five symbols of 3 bits each, A–E, are the data, and P and Q are the two redundant symbols. This simple example will locate and correct a single symbol in error. It does not matter, however, how many bits in the symbol are in error.

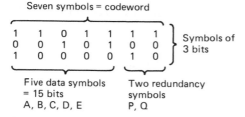

Seven symbols = codeword

1	1	0	1	1	1	1
0	0	1	0	1	0	0
1	0	0	0	0	1	0

Symbols of 3 bits

Five data symbols
= 15 bits
A, B, C, D, E

Two redundancy
symbols
P, Q

Figure 6.19 A Reed–Solomon codeword. As the symbols are of 3 bits, there can only be eight possible syndrome values. One of these is all zeros, the error-free case, and so it is only possible to point to seven errors; hence the codeword length of seven symbols. Two of these are redundant, leaving five data symbols

The two check symbols are solutions to the following equations:

$$A \oplus B \oplus C \oplus D \oplus E \oplus P \oplus Q = 0$$

$$a^7 A \oplus a^6 B \oplus a^5 C \oplus a^4 D \oplus a^3 E \oplus a^2 P \oplus aQ = 0$$

where a is a constant. The original data A–E followed by the redundancy P and Q pass through the channel.

The receiver makes two checks on the message to see if it is a codeword. This is done by calculating syndromes using the following expressions, where the prime implies the received symbol which is not necessarily correct:

$$S_0 = A' \oplus B' \oplus C' \oplus D' \oplus E' \oplus P' \oplus Q'$$

(this is in fact a simple parity check)

$$S_1 = a^7 A' \oplus a^6 B' \oplus a^5 C' \oplus a^4 D' \oplus a^3 E' \oplus a^2 P' \oplus aQ'$$

If two syndromes of all zeros are not obtained, there has been an error. The information carried in the syndromes will be used to correct the error. For the purpose of illustration, let it be considered that D′ has been corrupted before moving to the general case. D′ can be considered to be the result of adding an error of value E to the original value D such that $D' = D \oplus E$

As:

$$A \oplus B \oplus C \oplus D \oplus E \oplus P \oplus Q = 0$$

then:

$$A \oplus B \oplus C \oplus D \oplus E \oplus E \oplus P \oplus Q = E = S_0$$

As:

$$D' = D \oplus E$$

then:

$$D = D' +\oplus E = D' \oplus S_0$$

Thus the value of the corrector is known immediately because it is the same as the parity syndrome S_0. The corrected data symbol is obtained simply by adding S_0 to the incorrect symbol.

At this stage, however, the corrupted symbol has not yet been identified, but this is equally straightforward.

As:

$$a^7 \text{ A} \oplus a^6 \text{ B} \oplus a^5 \text{ C} \oplus a^4 \text{ D} \oplus a^3 \text{ E} \oplus a^2 \text{ P} \oplus a\text{Q} = 0$$

then:

$$a^7 \text{ A} \oplus a^6 \text{ B} \oplus a^5 \text{ C} \oplus a^4 (\text{D} \oplus E) \oplus a^3 \text{ E} \oplus a^2 \text{ P} \oplus a\text{Q}$$
$$= a^4 E = \text{S}_1$$

Thus the syndrome S_1 is the error bit pattern E, but it has been raised to a power of a which is a function of the position of the error symbol in the block. If the position of the error is in symbol k, then k is the locator value and:

$$\text{S}_0 \times a^k = \text{S}_1$$

Hence:

$$a^k = \frac{\text{S}_1}{\text{S}_0}$$

The value of k can be found by multiplying S_0 by various powers of a until the product is the same as S_1. Then the power of a necessary is equal to k. The use of the descending powers of a in the codeword calculation is now clear because the error is then multiplied by a different power of a dependent upon its position. S_1 is known as the locator, because it gives the position of the error. The process of finding the error position by experiment is known as a Chien search.[7]

6.15 R–S calculations

Whilst the expressions above show that the values of P and Q are such that the two syndrome expressions sum to zero, it is not yet clear how P and Q are calculated from the data. Expressions for P and Q can be found by solving the two R–S equations simultaneously. This has been done in Appendix 6.1. The following expressions must be used to calculate P and Q from the data in order to satisfy the codeword equations. These are:

$$\text{P} = a^6 \text{ A} \oplus a\text{B} \oplus a^2 \text{ C} \oplus a^5 \text{ D} \oplus a^3 \text{ E}$$

$$\text{Q} = a^2 \text{ A} \oplus a^3 \text{ B} \oplus a^6 \text{ C} \oplus a^4 \text{ D} \oplus a\text{E}$$

In both the calculation of the redundancy shown here and the calculation of the corrector and the locator it is necessary to perform numerous multiplications and raising to powers. This appears to present a formidable calculation problem at both the encoder and the decoder. This would be the case if the calculations involved were conventionally executed. However, the calculations can be simplified by using logarithms. Instead of multiplying two numbers, their logarithms are added. In order to find the cube of a number, its logarithm is added three times. Division is performed by subtracting the logarithms. Thus all of the manipulations necessary can be achieved with addition or subtraction, which is straightforward in logic circuits.

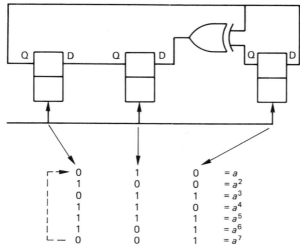

Figure 6.20 The bit patterns of a Galois field expressed as powers of the primitive element a. This diagram can be used as a form of log table in order to multiply binary numbers. Instead of an actual multiplication, the appropriate powers of a are simply added

The success of this approach depends upon simple implementation of log tables. As was seen in Chapter 2, raising a constant, a, known as the *primitive element* to successively higher powers in modulo-2 gives rise to a Galois field. Each element of the field represents a different power n of a. It is a fundamental of the R–S codes that all of the symbols used for data, redundancy and syndromes are considered to be elements of a Galois field. The number of bits in the symbol determines the size of the Galois field, and hence the number of symbols in the codeword.

Fig. 6.20 repeats a Galois field deduced in Chapter 2. The binary values of the elements are shown alongside the power of a they represent. In the R–S codes, symbols are no longer considered simply as binary numbers, but also as equivalent powers of a. In Reed–Solomon coding and decoding, each symbol will be multiplied by some power of a. Thus if the symbol is also known as a power of a it is only necessary to add the two powers. For example, if it is necessary to multiply the data symbol 100 by a^3, the calculation proceeds as follows, referring to Fig. 6.20:

$$100 = a^2 \quad \text{so} \quad 100 \times a^3 = a^{(2\,+\,3)} = a^5 = 111$$

Note that the results of a Galois multiplication are quite different from binary multiplication. Because all products must be elements of the field, sums of powers which exceed seven wrap around by having seven subtracted. For example:

$$a^5 \times a^6 = a^{11} = a^4 = 110$$

Fig. 6.21 shows some examples of circuits which will perform this kind of multiplication. Note that they require a minimum amount of logic.

Fig. 6.22 shows an example of the Reed–Solomon encoding process. The Galois field shown in Fig. 6.20 has been used, having the primitive element $a =$

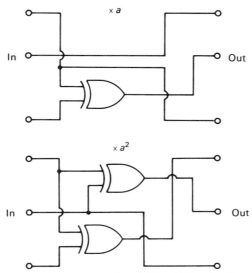

Figure 6.21 Some examples of GF multiplier circuits

010. At the beginning of the calculation of P, the symbol A is multiplied by a^6. This is done by converting A to a power of a. According to Fig. 6.20, $101 = a^6$ and so the product will be $a^{(6 + 6)} = a^{12} = a^5 = 111$. In the same way, B is multiplied by a, and so on, and the products are added modulo-2. A similar process is used to calculate Q.

Fig. 6.23 shows a circuit which can calculate P or Q. The symbols A–E are presented in succession, and the circuit is clocked for each one. On the first

Input data	A	101	a^6 A = 111	a^2 A = 010	
	B	100	a B = 011	a^3 B = 111	
	C	010	a^2 C = 011	a^6 C = 001	
	D	100	a^5 D = 001	a^4 D = 101	
	E	111	a^3 E = 010	a E = 101	
Check symbols	P	100 ◄——————— 100			
	Q	100 ◄————————————— 100			

Codeword	A	101	a^7 A = 101
	B	100	a^6 B = 010
	C	010	a^5 C = 101
	D	100	a^4 D = 101
	E	111	a^3 E = 010
	P	100	a^2 P = 110
	Q	100	a Q = 011
	S_0 = 000		S_1 = 000 ◄——— Both syndromes zero

Figure 6.22 Five data symbols A–E are used as terms in the generator polynomials derived in Appendix 6.1 to calculate two redundant symbols P and Q. An example is shown at the top. Below is the result of using the codeword symbols A–Q as terms in the checking polynomials. As there is no error, both syndromes are zero

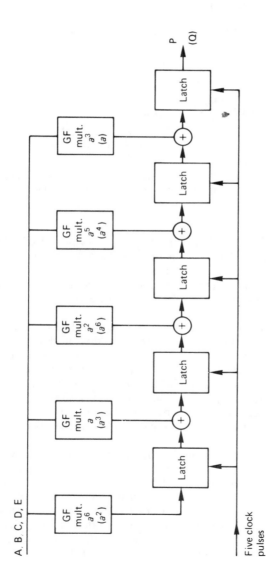

Figure 6.23 If the five data symbols of Figure 6.22 are supplied to this circuit in sequence, after five clocks, one of the check symbols will appear at the output. Terms without brackets will calculate P, bracketed terms calculate Q

7	A	101	$a^7 A = 101$
6	B	100	$a^6 B = 010$
5	C	010	$a^5 C = 101$
4	D'	101	$a^4 D' = 011$
3	E	111	$a^3 E = 010$
2	P	100	$a^2 P = 110$
1	Q	100	$a\ Q = 011$
	$S_0 =$	001	$S_1 = 110$

$$\frac{S_1}{S_0} = \frac{a^4}{1} = a^4$$

$k = 4$

$$D' + S_0 = 101 + 001$$
$$D = 100$$

7	A	101	$a^7 A = 101$
6	B	100	$a^6 B = 010$
5	C'	110	$a^5 C = 100$
4	D	100	$a^4 D = 101$
3	E	111	$a^3 E = 010$
2	P	100	$a^2 P = 110$
1	Q	100	$a\ Q = 011$
	$S_0 =$	100	$S_1 = 001$

$$\frac{S_1}{S_0} = \frac{1}{a^2} = \frac{1}{a^2} \times \frac{a^5}{a^5} = a^5$$

$k = 5$

$$C' + S_0 = 110 + 100$$
$$C = 010$$

7	A'	111	$a^7 A = 111$
6	B	100	$a^6 B = 010$
5	C	010	$a^5 C = 101$
4	D	100	$a^4 D = 101$
3	E	111	$a^3 E = 010$
2	P	100	$a^2 P = 110$
1	Q	100	$a\ Q = 011$
	$S_0 =$	010	$S_1 = 010$

$$\frac{S_1}{S_0} = \frac{a}{a} = 001 = a^7$$

$k = 7$

$$A' + S_0 = 111 + 010$$
$$A = 101$$

Figure 6.24 Three examples of error location and correction. The number of bits in error in a symbol is irrelevant; if all three were wrong, S_0 would be 111, but correction is still possible

clock, $a^6 A$ is stored in the left-hand latch. If B is now provided at the input, the second GF multiplier produces aB and this is added to the output of the first latch and when clocked will be stored in the second latch which now contains $a^6 A + aB$. The process continues in this fashion until the complete expression for P is available in the right-hand latch. The intermediate contents of the right-hand latch are ignored.

The entire codeword now exists, and can be recorded or transmitted. Fig. 6.22 also demonstrates that the codeword satisfies the checking equations. The modulo-2 sum of the seven symbols, S_0, is 000 because each column has an even number of ones. The calculation of S_1 requires multiplication by descending powers of a. The modulo-2 sum of the products is again zero. These calculations confirm that the redundancy calculation was properly carried out.

Fig. 6.24 gives three examples of error correction based on this codeword. The erroneous symbol is marked with a dash. As there has been an error, the syndromes S_0 and S_1 will not be zero.

Fig. 6.25 shows circuits suitable for parallel calculation of the two syndromes at the receiver. The S_0 circuit is a simple parity checker which accumulates the modulo-2 sum of all symbols fed to it. The S_1 circuit is more subtle, because it contains a Galois field (GF) multiplier in a feedback loop, such that early symbols fed in are raised to higher powers than later symbols because they have been recirculated through the GF multiplier more often. It is possible to compare the operation of these circuits with the example of Fig. 6.24 and with subsequent examples to confirm that the same results are obtained.

Figure 6.25 Circuits for parallel calculation of syndromes S_0, S_1. S_0 is a simple parity check. S_1 has a GF multiplication by a in the feedback, so that A is multiplied by a^7, B is multiplied by a^6, etc., and all are summed to give S_1

6.16 Correction by erasure

In the examples of Fig. 6.24, two redundant symbols P and Q have been used to locate and correct one error symbol. If the positions of errors are known by some separate mechanism (see product codes, Section 6.18) the locator need not be calculated. The simultaneous equations may instead be solved for two correctors. In this case the number of symbols which can be corrected is equal to the number of redundant symbols. In Fig. 6.26(a) two errors have taken place, and it is

$$
\begin{array}{llll}
A & 1\bar{0}1 & a^7 A = & 101 \\
B & 100 & a^6 B = & 010 \\
(C \oplus E_C) & 001 & a^5 (C \oplus E_C) & \bar{1}11 \\
(D \oplus E_D) & 0^1 0 & a^4 (D \oplus E_D) & 111 \\
E & 111 & a^3 E = & 010 \\
P & \bar{1}00 & a^2 P = & 110 \\
Q & 1\dot{0}\dot{0} & a\ Q = & 0\underline{11} \\
S_1 = & 10\bar{1} & S_1 = & \overline{000}
\end{array}
$$

$$S_0 = E_C \oplus E_D \qquad S_1 = a^5 E_C \oplus a^4 E_D$$

$$S_1 = a^5 E_C \oplus a^4 (S_0 \ominus E_C)$$

$$= a^5 E_C \oplus a^4 S_0 \oplus a^4 E_C$$

$$\therefore E_C = \frac{S_1 \oplus a^4 S_0}{a^5 \oplus a^4} = \frac{000 \oplus 011}{001} = 011$$

$$C = (C \oplus E_C) \oplus E_C = 001 \oplus 011 = 010$$

$$S_1 = a^5 (S_0 \ominus E_D) \oplus a^4 E_D$$

$$= a^5 S_0 \oplus a^5 E_D \oplus a^4 E_D$$

$$\therefore E_D = \frac{S_1 \oplus a^5 S_0}{a^5 \oplus a^4} = \frac{000 \oplus 110}{001} = 110$$

$$D = (D \oplus E_D) + E_D = 010 \oplus 110 = 1\underline{00} \qquad \textbf{(a)}$$

$$
\begin{array}{llll}
A & 101 & a^7 A = 101 & \\
B & 100 & a^6 B = 010 & S_0 = C \oplus D \\
C & \overline{000} & a^5 C = 000 & \\
D & \overline{000} & a^4 D = 000 & S_1 = a^5 C \oplus a^4 D \\
E & 111 & a^3 E = 010 & \\
P & 100 & a^2 P = 110 & \\
Q & 100 & a\ Q = 011 & \\
S_0 & = 100 & S_1 = 000 &
\end{array}
$$

$$S_1 = a^5 S_0 \oplus a^5 D \oplus a^4 D = a^5 S_0 \oplus D$$

$$\therefore D = S_1 \oplus a^5 S_0 = 000 \oplus 100 = \underline{100}$$

$$S_1 = a^5 C \oplus a^4 C \oplus a^4 S_0 = C \oplus a^4 S_0$$

$$\therefore C = S_1 \oplus a^4 S_0 = 000 \oplus 010 = \underline{010}$$

(b)

Figure 6.26 If the location of errors is known, then the syndromes are a known function of the two errors as shown in (a). It is, however, much simpler to set the incorrect symbols to zero, i.e. to *erase* them as in (b). Then the syndromes are a function of the wanted symbols and correction is easier known that they are in symbols C and D. Since S_0 is a simple parity check, it will reflect the modulo-2 sum of the two errors. Hence:

$$S_0 = E_C \oplus E_D$$

The two errors will have been multiplied by different powers in S_1, such that:

$$S_1 = a^5 E_C \oplus a^4 E_D$$

These two equations can be solved, as shown in the figure, to find E_C and E_D, and the correct value of the symbols will be obtained by adding these correctors to the erroneous values. It is, however, easier to set the values of the symbols in error to zero. In this way the nature of the error is rendered irrelevant and it does not enter the calculation. This setting of symbols to zero gives rise to the term erasure. In this case:

$$S_0 = C \oplus D$$
$$S_1 = a^5C + a^4D$$

Erasing the symbols in error makes the errors equal to the correct symbol values and these are found more simply as shown in Fig. 6.26(b).

Practical systems will be designed to correct more symbols in error than in the simple examples given here. If it is proposed to correct by erasure an arbitrary number of symbols in error given by t, the codeword must be divisible by t different polynomials. Alternatively if the errors must be located and corrected, $2t$ polynomials will be needed. These will be of the form $(x + a^n)$ where n takes all values up to t or $2t$. a is the primitive element discussed in Chapter 2.

Where four symbols are to be corrected by erasure, or two symbols are to be located and corrected, four redundant symbols are necessary, and the codeword polynomial must then be divisible by:

$$(x + a^0)\ (x + a^1)\ (x + a^2)\ (x + a^3)$$

Upon receipt of the message, four syndromes must be calculated, and the four correctors or the two error patterns and their positions are determined by solving four simultaneous equations. This generally requires an iterative procedure, and a number of algorithms have been developed for the purpose.[8-10] Modern DVTR formats use 8 bit R–S codes and erasure extensively. The primitive polynomial commonly used with GF(256) is:

$$x^8 + x^4 + x^3 + x^2 + 1$$

The codeword will be 255 bytes long but will often be shortened by puncturing. The larger Galois fields require less redundancy, but the computational problem increases. LSI chips have been developed specifically for R–S decoding in many high-volume formats.[11]

6.17 Interleaving

The concept of bit interleaving was introduced in connection with a single-bit correcting code to allow it to correct small bursts. With burst-correcting codes such as Reed–Solomon, bit interleave is unnecessary. In most channels, particularly high-density recording channels used for digital video or audio, the

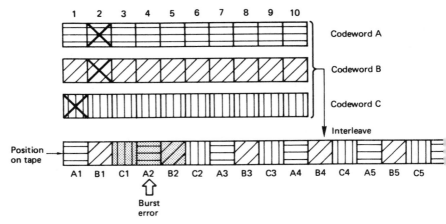

Figure 6.27 The interleave controls the size of burst errors in individual codewords

burst size may be many bytes rather than bits, and to rely on a code alone to correct such errors would require a lot of redundancy. The solution in this case is to employ symbol interleaving, as shown in Fig. 6.27. Several codewords are encoded from input data, but these are not recorded in the order they were input, but are physically reordered in the channel, so that a real burst error is split into smaller bursts in several codewords. The size of the burst seen by each codeword is now determined primarily by the parameters of the interleave, and Fig. 6.28 shows that the probability of occurrence of bursts with respect to the burst length in a given codeword is modified. The number of bits in the interleave word can be made equal to the burst-correcting ability of the code in the knowledge that it will be exceeded only very infrequently.

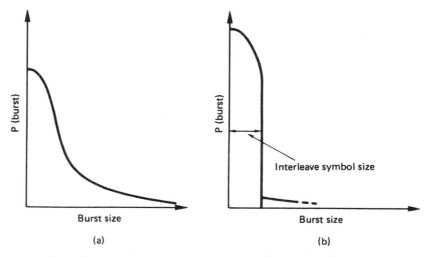

Figure 6.28 (a) The distribution of burst sizes might look like this. (b) Following interleave, the burst size within a codeword is controlled to that of the interleave symbol size, except for gross errors which have low probability

Figure 6.29 In block interleaving, data are scrambled within blocks which are themselves in the correct order

There are a number of different ways in which interleaving can be performed. Fig. 6.29 shows that in block interleaving, words are reordered within blocks which are themselves in the correct order. This approach is attractive for rotary-head recorders, because the scanning process naturally divides the tape up into blocks. The block interleave is achieved by writing samples into a memory in sequential address locations from a counter, and reading the memory with non-sequential addresses from a sequencer. The effect is to convert a one-dimensional sequence of samples into a two-dimensional structure having rows and columns.

Rotary-head recorders naturally interleave spatially on the tape. Fig. 6.30 shows that a single large tape defect becomes a series of small defects owing to the geometry of helical scanning.

The alternative to block interleaving is convolutional interleaving where the interleave process is endless. In Fig. 6.31 symbols are assembled into short blocks and then delayed by an amount proportional to the position in the block. It will be seen from the figure that the delays have the effect of shearing the symbols so that columns on the left side of the diagram become diagonals on the right. When the columns on the right are read, the convolutional interleave will be obtained. Convolutional interleave works well in transmission applications where there is no natural track break. Convolutional interleave has the advantage of requiring less memory to implement than a block code. This is because a block code requires the entire block to be written into the memory before it can be read, whereas a convolutional code requires only enough memory to cause the required delays. Now that RAM is relatively inexpensive, convolutional interleave is less popular.

It is possible to make a convolutional code of finite size by making a loop. Fig. 6.32(a) shows that symbols are written in columns on the outside of a cylinder. The cylinder is then sheared or twisted, and the columns are read. The result is a block-completed convolutional interleave shown at (b). This technique is used in the audio blocks of the Video-8 format.

Figure 6.30 Helical-scan recorders produce a form of mechanical interleaving, because one large defect on the medium becomes distributed over several head sweeps

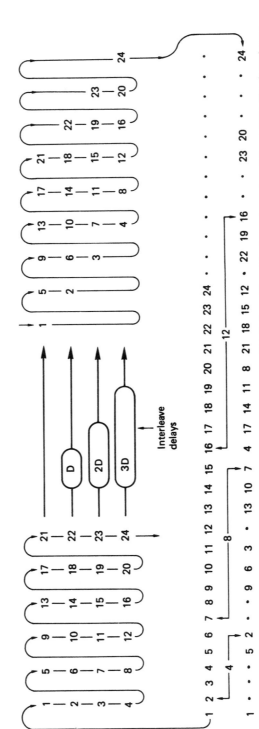

Figure 6.31 In convolutional interleaving, samples are formed into a rectangular array, which is sheared by subjecting each row to a different delay. The sheared array is read in vertical columns to provide the interleaved output. In this example, samples will be found at 4, 8 and 12 places away from their original order

(a)

(b)

Figure 6.32 A block completed convolutional interleave can be considered to be the result of shearing a cylinder as in (a). This results in horizontal and diagonal codewords as shown in (b)

6.18 Product codes

In the presence of burst errors alone, the system of interleaving works very well, but it is known that in most practical channels there are also uncorrelated errors of a few bits due to noise. Fig. 6.33 shows an interleaving system where a

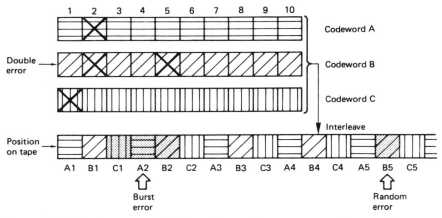

Figure 6.33 The interleave system falls down when a random error occurs adjacent to a burst

dropout-induced burst error has occurred which is at the maximum correctable size. All three codewords involved are working at their limit of one symbol. A random error due to noise in the vicinity of a burst error will cause the correction power of the code to be exceeded. Thus a random error of a single bit causes a further entire symbol to fail. This is a weakness of an interleave solely designed to handle dropout-induced bursts. Practical high-density equipment must address the problem of noise-induced or random errors and burst errors occurring at the same time. This is done by forming codewords both before and after the

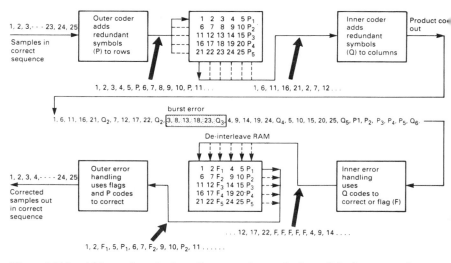

Figure 6.34 In addition to the redundancy P on rows, inner redundancy Q is also generated on columns. On replay, the Q code checker will pass on flags F if it finds an error too large to handle itself. The flags pass through the de-interleave process and are used by the outer error correction to identify which symbol in the row needs correcting with P redundancy. The concept of crossing two codes in this way is called a product code

interleave process. In block interleaving, this results in a *product code*, whereas in the case of convolutional interleave the result is called *cross-interleaving*.

Fig. 6.34 shows that in a product code the redundancy calculated first and checked last is called the outer code, and the redundancy calculated second and checked first is called the inner code. The inner code is formed along tracks on the medium. Random errors due to noise are corrected by the inner code and do not impair the burst-correcting power of the outer code. Burst errors are declared uncorrectable by the inner code which flags the bad samples on the way into the de-interleave memory. The outer code reads the error flags in order to correct the flagged symbols by erasure. The error flags are also known as erasure flags. As it does not have to compute the error locations, the outer code needs half as much redundancy for the same correction power. Thus the inner code redundancy does not raise the code overhead. The combination of codewords with interleaving in several dimensions yields an error-protection strategy which is truly synergistic, in that the end result is more powerful than the sum of the parts. Needless to say, the technique is used extensively in modern DVTR formats.

6.19 Introduction to error correction in DVTR

The interleave and error-correction systems of D-3 will now be discussed by way of a representative example. Details of other formats will be found in Chapter 9. Fig. 6.35 shows a conceptual block diagram of the system which shows that D-3 uses a product code formed by producing Reed–Solomon codewords at right angles across an array. The array is formed in a memory which contains an entire field of data, and the layout used in PAL can be seen in Fig. 6.36. Incoming samples (bytes) are written into the array in columns. Each column is then made into a codeword by the addition of 8 bytes of redundancy. These are the outer codewords. Each row of the array is then formed into eight inner codewords by the addition of 8 bytes of redundancy to each. In order to make a recording, the memory is read in rows, and one inner codeword fits into one sync block along the track. Every sync block in an eight-field sequence is given a unique header address. This process continues until the entire contents of the array has been laid on tape. Owing to the use of segmentation this will require three segments in NTSC and four in PAL.

Writing the memory in columns and reading in rows achieves the necessary interleave.

On replay, a combination of random errors and burst errors will occur. Data will come from tape in the sequence of the inner codewords. The 8,14 channel decoder may provide error flags to assist the inner decoder. In D-3 each inner code has 8 bytes of redundancy, so it would be possible to locate and correct up to 4 bytes in error or correct up to eight flagged errors in the codeword. This, however, is not done, because it is better to limit the correction power and use the remaining redundancy to decrease the probability of miscorrection. In this way,

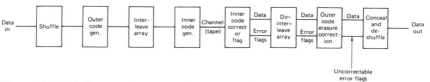

Figure 6.35 Block diagram of error-correction strategy of D-3 DVTR

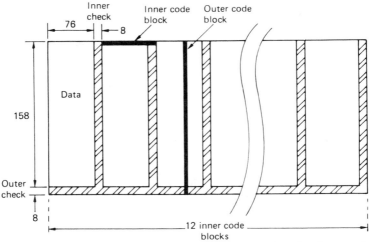

Figure 6.36 The field array of PAL D-3. Incoming data are written in columns and eight R–S bytes are added to make outer codes. The array is split into 12 equal parts, and one row of each part has eight R–S bytes added to make an inner code. There are thus 12 inner code blocks across the array. One inner code is held in one sync block and in practice the codeword is extended to protect the ID pattern

a smaller number of random errors are corrected with a high degree of confidence. Larger errors cause the entire inner codeword to be declared corrupt, and it is written into the appropriate row of the de-interleave array as all zeros, with error flags set. When all of the rows of the array are completed, it is possible to begin processing the columns. A burst error on tape which destroys one or more inner codewords will result in single-byte errors with flags in many different outer codewords. The presence of the error flags means that the outer code does not need to compute the position of the errors, so the full power of the outer code redundancy is available for correction. The eight redundancy bytes of D-3 can correct eight error bytes. The process of using error flags to assist a code is called erasure. It will be evident that enormous damage must be done to the tape track before 4 bytes are corrupted in a single outer codeword, which gives high resistance to dropouts and tape scratches.

6.20 Concealment and shuffle

In the event of a gross error, correction may not be possible, and some bytes may be declared uncorrectable. In this case the errors must be concealed by interpolation from adjacent samples. Owing to the regular structure of the product code block, uncorrectable burst errors would show up as a regular pattern of interpolations on the screen. The eye is extremely good at finding such patterns, so the visibility is higher than might be expected. The solution to this problem is to perform a two-dimensional pseudo-random shuffle on the video samples before generating the product code. The reverse shuffle is performed on replay. The positions of interpolated samples due to an uncorrected error now form a pseudo-random pattern with much decreased visibility.

The details of the shuffle mechanism will be discussed in Chapter 7.

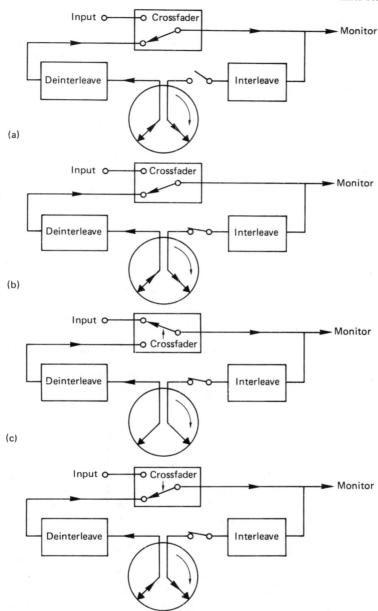

Figure 6.37 In read–modify–write or pre-read editing, there are advanced replay heads on the scanner, which allow editing to be performed on de-interleaved data. An insert sequence is shown. At (a) the replay-head signal is decoded, and fed to the encoder which, after some time, will produce an output representing what is already on the tape. In (b), at a sector boundary, the write circuits are turned on, and the machine begins to re-record. In (c) the crossfade is made to the insert material. At (d) the insert ends with a crossfade back to the signal from the advanced replay heads. After this, the write heads will once again be recording what is already on the tape, and the write circuits can be disabled at a sector boundary. An assemble edit consists of the first three of these steps only

6.21 Editing interleaved recordings

The interleave, de-interleave, time compression and timebase-correction processes cause delay and any data reduction stages will further increase that delay. Confidence replay takes place later than the distance between record and replay heads would indicate.

In analog recording, there is a direct relationship between the distance down the track and the time through the recording. A further consequence of interleaving in digital recorders is that the reordering of samples means that this relationship is lost.

Editing must be undertaken with care. In a block-based interleave, edits can be made at block boundaries so that coded blocks are not damaged, but these blocks may be as big as a field. This is adequate for normal editing using vision cuts, but such blocks are usually too large for accurate audio editing, and editing within the video field to perform crossfades or wipes is impossible.

The only way in which accurate editing can be performed in the presence of interleave is to use a read–modify–write approach, where an entire field is read into memory and de-interleaved to the real-time sample sequence. Any desired part of the field can be replaced with new material before it is re-interleaved and re-recorded. In recorders which can only record or play at one time, an edit of this kind would take a long time because of all of the tape repositioning needed. With extra heads read–modify–write editing can be performed dynamically as shown in Fig. 6.37. The replay head plays back the existing recording, and this is de-interleaved to the normal sample sequence, a process which introduces a delay. The sample stream now passes through a crossfader which at this stage will be set to accept only the offtape signal. The output of the crossfader is then fed to the record interleave stage which introduces further delay. This signal passes to the record heads which must be positioned so that the original recording on the tape reaches them at the same time that the re-encoded signal arrives, despite the encode and decode delays. In a rotary-head recorder this can be done by positioning the record heads at a different height to the replay heads so that they reach the same tracks on different revolutions. With this arrangement it is possible to enable the record heads at the beginning of a frame, and they will then re-record what is already on the tape. Next the crossfader can be operated to fade across to new material, at any desired crossfade speed. Following the interleave stage, the new recording will update only the new samples in the frame and re-record those which do not need changing. After a short time, the recording will only be a function of the new input. If the edit is an insert, it is possible to end the process by crossfading back to the replay signal and allowing the replay data to be re-recorded. Once this re-recording has taken place for a short time, the record process can be terminated at the end of a frame. There is no limit to the crossfade periods which can be employed in this operating technique.

One important point to appreciate about read–modify–write editing is that the physical frames at which the insert begins and ends are independent of the in- and out-points of the audio edit, because the former are in areas where re-recording of the existing data takes place.

Appendix 6.1 Calculation of Reed–Solomon generator polynomials

For a Reed–Solomon codeword over $GF(2^3)$, there will be seven 3 bit symbols. For location and correction of one symbol, there must be two redundant symbols P and Q, leaving A–E for data.

The following expressions must be true, where a is the primitive element of $x^3 \oplus x \oplus 1$ and $\oplus$ is XOR throughout:

$$A \oplus B \oplus C \oplus D \oplus E \oplus P \oplus Q = 0 \tag{1}$$
$$a^7A \oplus a^6B \oplus a^5C \oplus a^4D \oplus a^3E \oplus a^2P \oplus aQ = 0 \tag{2}$$

Dividing Eqn (2) by a:

$$a^6A \oplus a^5B \oplus a^4C \oplus a^3D \oplus a^2E \oplus aP \oplus Q = 0$$
$$= A \oplus B \oplus C \oplus D \oplus E \oplus P \oplus Q$$

Cancelling Q, and collecting terms:

$$(a^6 \oplus 1)A \oplus (a^5 \oplus 1)B \oplus (a^4 \oplus 1)C \oplus (a^3 \oplus 1)D \oplus (a^2 \oplus 1)E$$
$$= (a + 1)P$$

Using Section 2.19 to calculate $(a^n + 1)$, e.g. $a^6 + 1 = 101 + 001 = 100 = a^2$:

$$a^2A \oplus a^4B \oplus a^5C \oplus aD \oplus a^6E = a^3P$$
$$a^6A \oplus aB \oplus a^2C \oplus a^5D \oplus a^3E = P$$

Multiply Eqn (1) by a^2 and equating to eqn (2):

$$a^2A \oplus a^2B \oplus a^2C \oplus a^2D \oplus a^2E \oplus a^2P \oplus a^2Q = 0$$
$$= a^7A \oplus a^6B \oplus a^5C \oplus a^4D \oplus a^3E \oplus a^2P \oplus aQ$$

Cancelling terms a^2P and collecting terms (remember $a^2 \oplus a^2 = 0$):

$$(a^7 \oplus a^2)A \oplus (a^6 \oplus a^2)B \oplus (a^5 \oplus a^2)C \oplus (a^4 \oplus a^2)D \oplus$$
$$(a^3 \oplus a^2)E = (a^2 \oplus a)Q$$

Adding powers according to Section 2.19, e.g.

$$a^7 \oplus a^2 = 001 \oplus 100 = 101 = a^6:$$
$$a^6A \oplus B \oplus a^3C \oplus aD \oplus a^5E = a^4Q$$
$$a^2A \oplus a^3B \oplus a^6C \oplus a^4D \oplus aE = Q$$

References

1 Michaels, S.R., Is it Gaussian? *Electron. World Wireless World*, Jan., 72–73 (1993)
2 Shannon, C.E., A mathematical theory of communication. *Bell Syst. Tech. J.*, **27**, 379 (1948)
3 Hamming, R.W., Error-detecting and error-correcting codes. *Bell Syst. Tech. J.*, **26**, 147–160 (1950)
4 Fire, P., A class of multiple-error correcting codes for non-independent errors. *Sylvania Reconnaissance Systems Lab. Rep.*, RSL-E-2 (1959)
5 Bossen, D.C., B-adjacent error correction. *IBM J. Res. Dev.*, **14**, 402–408 (1970)
6 Reed, I.S. and Solomon, G., Polynomial codes over certain finite fields. *J. Soc. Ind. Appl. Math.*, **8**, 300–304 (1960)
7 Chien, R.T., Cunningham, B.D. and Oldham, I.B., Hybrid methods for finding roots of a polynomial – with application to BCH decoding. *IEEE Trans. Inf. Theory*, **IT-15**, 329–334 (1969)
8 Berlekamp, E.R., *Algebraic Coding Theory.* New York: McGraw-Hill (1967). Reprint edition: Laguna Hills, CA: Aegean Park Press (1983)
9 Sugiyama, Y., *et al.*, An erasures and errors decoding algorithm for Goppa codes. *IEEE Trans. Inf. Theory*, **IT-22**, (1976)
10 Peterson, W.W. and Weldon, E.J., *Error Correcting Codes*, 2nd edn., Cambridge, MA: MIT Press (1972)
11 Onishi, K., Sugiyama, K., Ishida, Y., Kusonoki, Y. and Yamaguchi, T., An LSI for Reed–Solomon encoder/decoder. Presented at 80th Audio Engineering Society Convention (Montreux, 1986), preprint 2316(A-4)

Chapter 7

Digital interfaces and broadcast

Since digital video equipment is supplied by a variety of manufacturers, there is a need for a standardized interconnect so that units may communicate in the digital domain. This chapter discusses the interconnects available for conventional component and composite digital video and for 16:9 aspect ratio and HDTV digital signals. The technology needed for digital television broadcasting is also considered here.

7.1 Introduction

Of all the advantages of digital video the most important of these for production work is the ability to record through multiple generations without quality loss. Effects machines perform transforms on images in the digital domain which remain impossible in the analog domain. For the highest-quality post production work, digital interconnection between such items as switchers, recorders and effects machines is highly desirable to avoid the degradation due to repeated conversion and filtering stages.

In 4:2:2 digital colour difference sampling according to CCIR-601, the luminance is sampled at 13.5 MHz, which is line synchronous to both broadcast line rates, and the two colour difference signals are sampled at one-half that frequency. Composite digital machines sample at four times subcarrier. All of the signals use 8 or 10 bit resolution. Video converters universally use parallel connection, where all bits of the pixel value are applied simultaneously to separate pins. Rotary-head digital recorders lay data on the tape serially, but within the circuitry of the recorder, parallel presentation is in the majority, because it allows slower, and hence cheaper, memory chips to be used for interleaving and timebase correction. The Reed–Solomon error correction depends upon symbols assembled from several bits at once. Digital effects machines and switchers universally operate upon pixel values in parallel using fast multiplier chips.

Bearing all of this in mind, there is a strong argument for parallel connection, because the video naturally appears in the parallel format in typical machines. All that is necessary is a set of suitable driver chips, running at an appropriate sampling rate, to send video down cables having separate conductors for each bit of the sample, and clocks to tell the receiver when to sample the bit values. The cost in electronic components is very small, and for short distances this approach represents the optimum solution. An example would be where it is desired to dub a digital recording from one machine to another standing beside it.

Parallel connection has drawbacks too; these come into play when longer distances are contemplated. A multicore cable is expensive, and the connectors are physically large. It is difficult to provide good screening of a multicore cable without its becoming inflexible. More seriously, there are electronic problems with multicore cables. The propagation speeds of pulses down all of the cores in the cable will not be exactly the same, and so, at the end of a long cable, some bits may still be in transition when the clock arrives, while others may have begun to change to the value in the next pixel. In the presence of crosstalk between the conductors, and reflections due to suboptimal termination, the data integrity eventually becomes marginal.

Where it is proposed to interconnect a large number of units with a router, that device will be extremely complex because of the number of parallel signals to be handled.

The answer to these problems is the serial connection. All of the digital samples are multiplexed into a serial bit stream, and this is encoded to form a self-clocking channel code which can be sent down a single channel. Skew caused by differences in propagation speed cannot then occur. The bit rate necessary is in excess of 200 Mbits/s, but this is easily accommodated by coaxial cable. Provided suitable equalization and termination is used, it may be possible to send such a signal over cables intended for analog video. A similar approach was pioneered in digital audio by the AES/EBU serial interface, which allowed digital audio to be transmitted down existing twisted-pair analog cabling (see Chapter 12).

The cabling savings implicit in such a system are obvious, but the electronic complexity of a serial interconnect is much greater, as high-speed multiplexers or shift registers are necessary at the transmitting end, and a phase-locked loop, data separator and deserializer are needed at the receiver to regenerate the parallel signal needed within the equipment. Although this increased complexity raises cost, it has to be offset against the saving in cabling. The availability of specialized chips will speed the acceptance of serial transmission.

A distinct advantage of serial transmission is that a matrix distribution unit or router is more easily realized. Where numerous pieces of video equipment need to be interconnected in various ways for different purposes, a crosspoint matrix is an obvious solution. With serial signals, only one switching element per signal is needed, whereas in a parallel system, a matrix would be unwieldy. A serial system has a potential disadvantage that the time distribution of bits within the block has to be closely defined, and, once standardized, it is extremely difficult to increase the wordlength if this is found to be necessary. The CCIR 8 bit serial system suffered from this problem, and has been replaced by a new serial standard which incorporates two extension bits which can be transmitted as zero in 8 bit applications, but allows 10 bit use if necessary. In a parallel interconnect, the word extension can be achieved by adding extra conductors alongside the existing bits, which is much easier.

The third interconnect to be considered uses fibre optics. The advantages of this technology are numerous. The bandwidth of an optical fibre is staggering, as it is determined primarily by the response speed of the light source and sensor, and for this reason it has been adopted for a digital HDTV interface. The optical transmission is immune to electromagnetic interference from other sources, nor does it contribute any. This is advantageous for connections between cameras and control units, where a long cable run may be required in outside broadcast applications. The cable can be made completely from insulating materials, so that ground loops cannot occur, although many practical fibre-optic cables include electrical conductors for power and steel strands for mechanical strength.

The drawbacks of fibre optics are few. They do not like too many connectors in a given channel, as the losses at a connection are much greater than with an electrical plug and socket. It is preferable for the only breaks in the fibre to be at the transmitting and receiving points. For similar reasons, fibre optics are less suitable for distribution, where one source feeds many destinations. The familiar loop-through connection of analog video is just not possible. The bidirectional open-collector or tri-state buses of electronic systems cannot be implemented with fibre optics, nor is it easy to build a crosspoint matrix.

7.2 Digital video interfaces

At the time of writing standards or advanced proposals exist for both $4:2:2$ component and $4F_{sc}$ composite digital in both 525/59.94 and 625/50 and in both parallel and serial forms. Interfaces also exist for widescreen and HDTV applications. All digital interfaces require to be standardized in the following areas: connectors, to ensure plugs mate with sockets; pinouts; electrical signal specification, to ensure that the correct voltages and timing are transferred; and protocol, to ensure that the meaning of the data words conveyed is the same to both devices. As digital video of any type is only data, it follows that the same physical and electrical standards can be used for a variety of protocols.

The parallel interface uses common connectors, pinouts and electrical levels for both line standards in both the component and composite versions. The same is true for the serial interfaces. Thus there are only two electrical interfaces: parallel and serial. The type of video being transferred is taken care of in the protocol differences.

7.3 The parallel electrical interface

Composite signals use the same electrical and mechanical interface as is used for $4:2:2$ component working[1,2] This means that it is possible to plug erroneously a component signal into a composite machine. Whilst this cannot possibly work, no harm will be done because the signal levels and pinouts are the same.

Each signal in the interface is carried by a balanced pair using ECL drive levels with a nominal impedance of 110 ohms. As Fig. 7.1 shows, there are eight signal pairs and two optional pairs, so that a 10 bit word can be accommodated. The optional signals are used to add bits at the least significant end of the word. Adding bits in this way extends resolution rather than increasing the magnitude. It will be seen from the figure that the optional bits are called Data -1 and Data -2 where the -1 and -2 refer to the power of 2 represented, i.e. 2^{-1} and 2^{-2}. The 8 bit word ends in a radix point and the extra bits below the radix point represent the half and quarter quantizing intervals. In this way a degree of compatibility exists between 10 and 8 bit systems, as the correct magnitude will always be obtained when changing wordlength, and all that is lost is a degree of resolution in shortening the wordlength when the bits below the radix point are lost. The same numbering scheme can be used for both wordlengths; the longer wordlength simply has a radix point and an extra digit in any number base. Converting to the 8 bit equivalent is then simply a matter of deleting the extra digit and retaining the integer part.

Pin no.	Function	Pin no.	Function
1	Clock +	14	Clock −
2	System ground	15	System ground
3	Data 7 (MSB) +	16	Data 7 (MSB) −
4	Data 6 +	17	Data 6 −
5	Data 5 +	18	Data 5 −
6	Data 4 +	19	Data 4 −
7	Data 3 +	20	Data 3 −
8	Data 2 +	21	Data 2 −
9	Data 1 +	22	Data 1 −
10	Data 0 +	23	Data 0 −
11	Data −1 + ⎫ Ten-bit	24	Data −1 − ⎫ Ten-bit
12	Data −2 + ⎭ systems only	25	Data −2 − ⎭ systems only
13	Cable shield		

Figure 7.1 In the parallel interface there is capacity for 10 bit words plus a clock where each signal is differential. In 8 bit systems 'Data −1' and 'Data −2' are not used. Clock transition takes place in the centre of a data bit cell as shown below

A separate clock signal pair and a number of grounding and shielding pins complete the connection. A 25 pin D-type connector to ISO 2110–1989 is specified. Equipment always has female connectors, cables always have male connectors. Metal or metallized backshells are recommended for optimum shielding. Whilst equipment may produce or accept only 8 bit data, cables must be wired for all 10 bits.

Connector latching is by a pair of 4–40 (an American thread) screws, with suitable posts provided on the female connector. It is important that the screws are used as the multicore cable is quite stiff and can eventually unseat the plug if it is not secured. Some early equipment had slidelocks instead of screw pillars, but these proved to be too flimsy.

Fig. 7.1 also shows the relationship between the clock and the data. A positive-going clock edge is used to sample the signal lines after the level has settled between transitions. In 4:2:2, the clock will be line-locked 27 MHz irrespective of the line standard, whereas in composite digital the clock will be four times the frequency of PAL or NTSC subcarrier.

The parallel interface is suitable for distances of up to 50 metres. Beyond this distance equalization is likely to be necessary and skew or differential delay between signals may become a problem. For longer distances a serial interface is a better option.

7.4 The 4:2:2 parallel interface

It is not necessary to digitize sync in component systems, since the sampling rate is derived from sync. The only useful video data are those sampled during the active line. All other parts of the video waveform can be recreated at a later time.

It is only necessary to standardize the size and position of a digital active line. The position is specified as a given number of sampling-clock periods from the leading edge of sync, and the length is simply a standard number of samples. The component digital active line is 720 luminance samples long. This is slightly longer than the analog active line and allows for some drift in the analog input. Ideally the first and last samples of the digital active line should be at blanking level.

(a)

(b)

Figure 7.2 (a) In 625 line systems to CCIR-601, with 4:2:2 sampling, the sampling rate is exactly 864 times line rate, but only the active line is sampled, 132 sample periods after sync. (b) In 525 line systems to CCIR-601, with 4:2:2 sampling, the sampling rate is exactly 858 times line rate, but only the active line is sampled, 122 sample periods after sync. Note active line contains exactly the same quantity of data as for 50 Hz systems

Fig. 7.2 shows that in 625 line systems[3] the control system waits for 132 sample periods before commencing sampling the line. Then 720 luminance samples and 360 of each type of colour difference sample are taken, 1440 samples in all. A further 12 sample periods will elapse before the next sync edge, making 132 + 720 + 12 = 864 sample periods. In 525 line systems,[2] the analog active line is in a slightly different place and so the controller waits 122 sample periods before taking the same digital active line samples as before. There will then be 16 sample periods before the next sync edge, making 122 + 720 + 16 = 858 sample periods.

Fig. 7.3 shows the luminance signal sampled at 13.5 MHz and two colour difference signals sampled at 6.75 MHz. Three separate signals with different clock rates are inconvenient and so multiplexing can be used. If the colour difference signals are multiplexed into one channel, then two 13.5 MHz channels will be required. If these channels are multiplexed into one, a 27 MHz clock will be required. The word order will be:

C_b, Y, C_r, Y, etc.

In order unambiguously to deserialize the samples, the first sample in the line is always C_b.

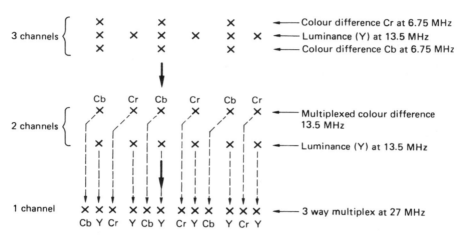

Figure 7.3 The colour difference sampling rate is one-half that of luminance, but there are *two* colour difference signals, C_r and C_b hence the colour difference data rate is equal to the luminance data rate, and a 27 MHz interleaved format is possible in a single channel

In addition to specifying the location of the samples, it is also necessary to standardize the relationship between the absolute analog voltage of the waveform and the digital code value used to express it so that all machines will interpret the numerical data in the same way. These relationships are in the voltage domain and are independent of the line standard used.

Fig. 7.4 shows how the luminance signal fits into the quantizing range of an 8 bit system. Black is at a level of 16_{10} and peak white is at 235_{10} so that there is some tolerance of imperfect analog signals. The sync pulse will clearly go outside the quantizing range, but this is of no consequence as conventional syncs are not transmitted. The visible voltage range fills the quantizing range and this gives the best possible resolution.

The colour difference signals use offset binary, where 128_{10} is the equivalent of blanking voltage. The peak analog limits are reached at 16_{10} and 240_{10} respectively allowing once more some latitude for maladjusted analog inputs.

Note that the code values corresponding to all ones and all zeros, i.e. the two extreme ends of the quantizing range, are not allowed to occur in the active line as they are reserved for synchronizing. Converters must be followed by circuitry which catches these values and forces the LSB to a different value if out-of-range analog inputs are applied.

(a)

(b)

Figure 7.4 (a) The luminance signal fits into the quantizing range with a little allowance for excessive gain. Here black is at 16_{10} and peak white is at 235_{10}. The sync pulse goes outside the quantizing range but this is of no consequence as it is not transmitted. (b) The colour difference signals use offset binary where blanking level is at 128_{10}, and the peaks occur at 16_{10} and 240_{10} respectively

The peak-to-peak amplitude of Y is 220 quantizing intervals, whereas for the colour difference signals it is 225 intervals. There is thus a small gain difference between the signals. This will be cancelled out by the opposing gain difference at any future DAC, but must be borne in mind when digitally converting to other standards.

(a)

Figure 7.5(a) The 4 byte synchronizing pattern which precedes and follows every active line sample block has this structure

(b)

Figure 7.5(b) The relationships between analog video timing and the information in the digital timing reference signals for 625/50 (above) and 525/60 (below)

As conventional syncs are not sent, horizontal and vertical synchronizing is achieved by special bit patterns sent with each line. Immediately before the digital active line location is the *SAV* (Start of Active Video) pattern, and immediately after is the *EAV* (End of Active Video) pattern. These unique patterns occur on every line and continue throughout the vertical interval.

Each sync pattern consists of four symbols. The first is all ones and the next two are all zeros. As these cannot occur in active video, their detection reliably indicates a sync pattern.

The fourth symbol is a data byte which contains three data bits, *H, F* and *V*. These bits are protected by four redundancy bits which form a 7 bit Hamming codeword for the purpose of detecting and correcting errors.

Fig. 7.5(a) shows the structure of the sync pattern. The sync bits have the following meanings:

H is used to distinguish between *SAV*, where it is set to 0, and *EAV* where it is set to 1.

F defines the state of interlace and is 0 during the first field and 1 during the second field. *F* is only allowed to change at *EAV*. In interlaced systems, one field begins at the centre of a line, but there is no sync pattern at that location, so the field bit changes at the end of the line in which the change took place.

V is 1 during vertical blanking and 0 during the active part of the field. It can only change at *EAV*.

Fig. 7.5(b) (top) shows the relationship between the sync pattern bits and 625 line analog timing, whilst below is the relationship for 525 lines. Only the active line is transmitted and this leaves a good deal of spare capacity. The two line standards differ on how this capacity is used. In 625 lines, only the active line period may be used on lines 20 to 22 and 333 to 335.[3] Lines 20 and 333 are reserved for equipment self-testing.

In 525 lines there is considerably more freedom and ancillary data may be inserted anywhere there is no active video, either during horizontal blanking, vertical blanking, or both.[2]

The all-zeros and all-ones codes are reserved for synchronizing and cannot be allowed to appear in ancillary data. In practice only 7 bits of the 8 bit word can be used as data; the eighth bit is redundant and gives the byte odd parity. As all ones and all zeros are even parity, the sync pattern cannot then be generated accidentally.

For 16:9 aspect ratio working, the line and field rate remain the same, but the luminance sampling rate may be raised to 18 MHz and the colour difference sampling rates are raised to 9 MHz. This results in the sampling structure shown for 50 Hz in Fig. 7.6. There are now 960 luminance pixels and 2×480 colour difference pixels. The parallel interface remains the same except that the clock rate rises to 36 MHz.

7.5 HD component parallel interface

The 1250/50 HDTV standard uses a CCIR-601 related sampling rate of 72 MHz for luminance and 36 MHz for colour difference.[4] The HD picture is 16:9 aspect ratio and has twice the resolution of 4:3. Thus the conventional sampling rate of 13.5 MHz is multiplied by $4 \times 4/3$ to give 72 MHz. There are 1920 luminance pixels in the active line. The two colour difference sample streams are

Figure 7.6 In 16:9 working with an 18 MHz sampling rate the sampling structure shown here results

multiplexed to give a second data stream at 72 MHz. Unlike the 4:3 standards, the luminance and colour difference are kept separate to avoid excessive frequencies in the cable. With 10 bit samples and two parallel signals, the data are in a 20 bit parallel format. Transmission is by differential drive with a separate clock. The clock frequency at 36 MHz is exactly half the bit rate. The lower clock frequency reduces losses and allows a longer cable.[5] The signals are all accommodated on a 50 pin D-connector.

7.6 The composite digital parallel interface

Composite digital samples at four times subcarrier frequency, and so there will be major differences between the standards.

Whilst the 4:2:2 interface transmits only active lines and special sync patterns, the composite interfaces carry the entire composite waveform; syncs, burst and all. Although ancillary data may be placed in sync tip, the sync edges must be present. In the absence of ancillary data, the data on the parallel interface are essentially the continuous stream of samples from a converter which is digitizing a normal analog composite signal. Virtually all that is necessary to return to the analog domain is a DAC and a filter. One of the reasons for this different approach is that the sampling clock in composite video is subcarrier based. The sample values during sync can change with ScH phase in NTSC and PAL and change with the position in the frame in PAL due to the 25 Hz component. It is simpler to convey sync sample values on the interface than to go to the trouble of recreating them later.

The instantaneous voltage of composite video can go below blanking on dark saturated colours, and above peak white on bright colours. As a result the quantizing ranges need to be stretched in comparison with 4:2:2 in order to accommodate all possible voltage excursions. Sync tip can be accommodated at the low end and peak white is some way below the end of the scale. It is not so easy to determine when overload clipping will take place in composite as the sample sites are locked to subcarrier. The degree of clipping depends on the chroma phase. When samples are taken either side of a chroma peak, clipping will be less likely to occur than when the sample is taken at the peak. Advantage is taken of this phenomenon in PAL as the peak analog voltage of a 100% yellow bar goes outside the quantizing range. The sampling phase is such that samples are sited either side of the chroma peak and remain within the range.

The PAL and NTSC versions of the composite digital interface will be described separately. The electrical interface is the same for both, and was described in Section 7.3.

7.7 PAL interface

The quantizing range of digital PAL is shown in Fig. 7.7.[6] Blanking level is at 64_{10} or 40 hex and sync tip is the lowest allowable code of 1 as 0 is reserved for digital synchronizing along with 255. Peak white is 211_{10} or D3 hex. As with 4:2:2, two optional bits can be added below the LSB to extend the resolution. In 10 bit working blanking becomes 40.0 hex and peak white becomes D3.0 hex, although some documents will be found which confusingly shift the radix point down in 10 bit mode and denote blanking by 100 hex and peak white by 34C hex.

In PAL, the composite digital interface samples at $4 \times F_{sc}$ with sample phase aligned with burst phase. PAL burst swing results in burst phases of $\pm 135°$, and samples are taken at these phases and at $\pm 45°$, precisely half-way between the U and V axes. This sampling phase is easy to generate from burst and avoids premature clipping of chroma. It is most important that samples are taken exactly at the points specified, since any residual phase error in the sampling clock will cause the equivalent of a chroma phase error when samples from one source are added to samples from a different source in a switcher. A digital switcher can only add together pairs of samples from different inputs, but if these samples were not taken at the same instants with respect to their subcarriers, the samples represent different vectors and cannot be added.

Fig. 7.8 shows how the sampling clock may be derived. The incoming sync is used to derive a burst gate, during which the samples of burst are analysed. If the clock is correctly phased, the sampled burst will give values of 95_{10}, 64_{10}, 32_{10}, 64_{10}, repeated, whereas if a phase error exists, the values at the burst crossings

Figure 7.7 The composite PAL signal fits into the quantizing range as shown here. Note that there is sufficient range to allow the instantaneous voltage to exceed that of peak white in the presence of saturated bright colours. Values shown are decimal equivalents in a 10 or 8 bit system. In a 10 bit system the additional 2 bits increase resolution, not magnitude, so they are below the radix point and the decimal equivalent is unchanged. PAL samples in phase with burst, so that values shown are on the burst peaks and are thus also the values of the envelope

will be above or below 64_{10}. The difference between the sample values and blanking level can be used to drive a DAC which controls the sampling VCO. In this way any phase errors in the ADC are eliminated, because the sampling clock will automatically servo its phase to be identical to digital burst. Burst swing causes the burst peak and burst crossing samples to change places, so a phase comparison is always possible during burst. DC level shifts can be removed by using both positive and negative burst crossings and averaging the results. This also has the effect of reducing the effect of noise.

In PAL, the subcarrier frequency contains a 25 Hz offset, and so $4 \times F_{sc}$ will contain a 100 Hz offset. The sampling rate is not h-coherent, and the sampling structure is not quite orthogonal. As subcarrier is given by:

$$F_{sc} = 283\tfrac{3}{4} \times F_h + F_v/2$$

the sampling rate will be given by:

$$F_s = 1135F_h + 2F_v$$

This results in 709 379 samples per frame, and there will not be a whole number of samples in a line. In practice, 1135 sample periods, numbered 0 to 1134, are defined as one digital line, with an additional four sample periods per frame which are included by having 1137 samples, numbered 0 to 1136, in lines 313 and 625. Fig. 7.9(a) shows the sample numbering scheme for an entire line. Note that the sample numbering begins at 0 at the start of the digital active line so that

Figure 7.8 Obtaining the sample clock in PAL. The values obtained by sampling burst are analysed. When phase is correct, burst will be sampled at zero crossing and sample value will be 64_{10} or blanking level. If phase is wrong, sample will be above or below blanking. Filter must ignore alternate samples at burst peaks and shift one sample every line to allow for burst swing. It also averages over several burst crossings to reduce jitter. Filter output drives DAC and thus controls sampling clock VCO

the horizontal blanking area is near the end of the digital line and the sample numbers will be large. The digital active line is 948 samples long and is longer than the analog active line. This allows the digital active line to move with 25 Hz whilst ensuring the entire analog active line is still conveyed.

Since sampling is not h-coherent, the position of sync pulses will change relative to the sampling points from line to line. The relationship can also be changed by the ScH phase of the analog input. Zero ScH is defined as coincidence between sync and zero degrees of subcarrier phase at line 1 of field 1. Since composite digital samples on burst phase, not on subcarrier phase, the definition of zero ScH will be as shown in Fig. 7.10, where it will be seen that two samples occur at exactly equal distances either side of the 50% sync point.

Figure 7.9 (a) Sample numbering in digital PAL. There are defined to be 1135 sample periods per line of which 948 are the digital active line. This is longer than the analog active line. Two lines per frame have two extra samples to compensate for the 25 Hz offset in subcarrier. NTSC is shown at (b). Here there are 910 samples per line of which 768 are the digital active line

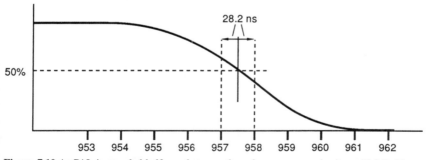

Figure 7.10 As PAL is sampled half-way between the colour axes, sample sites will fall either side of 50% sync at the zero ScH measurement line

If the input is not zero ScH, the samples conveying sync will have different values. Measurement of these values will allow ScH phase to be computed. In a DVTR installation, non-standard ScH is only a problem on the initial conversion from analog because composite DVTRs do not record sync, and will regenerate zero ScH syncs on replay.

7.8 NTSC interface

Although they have some similarities, PAL and NTSC are quite different when analysed at the digital sample level.

Fig. 7.11 shows how the NTSC waveform fits into the quantizing structure.[7] Blanking is at 60_{10} in an 8 bit system, and peak white is at 200_{10}, so that 1 IRE unit is the equivalent of $1.4Q$ which could perhaps be called the DIRE. These different values are due to the different sync/vision ratio of NTSC. PAL is $7:3$ whereas NTSC is $10:4$. As with $4:2:2$ and PAL, two optional extra bits at the LSB end of the sample can extend the resolution.

Subcarrier in NTSC has an exact half-line offset, so there will be an integer number of cycles of subcarrier in two lines. F_{sc} is simply $227.5 \times F_h$, and as sampling is at $4 \times F_{sc}$, there will be $227.5 \times 4 = 910$ samples per line period, and the sampling will be orthogonal. Fig. 7.9(b) shows that the digital active line consists of 768 samples numbered 0 to 767. Horizontal blanking follows the digital active line in sample numbers 768 to 909.

The sampling phase is chosen to facilitate encoding and decoding in the digital domain. In NTSC there is a phase shift of 123° between subcarrier and the I axis. As burst is an inverted piece of the subcarrier waveform, there is a phase shift of 57° between burst and the I axis. Composite digital NTSC does not sample in

Figure 7.11 The composite NTSC signal fits into the quantizing range as shown here. Note that there is sufficient range to allow the instantaneous voltage to exceed peak white in the presence of saturated, bright colours. Values shown are decimal equivalents in an 8 or 10 bit system. In a 10 bit system the additional 2 bits increase resolution, not magnitude, so they are below the radix point and the decimal equivalent is unchanged. *Note that, unlike PAL, NTSC does not sample on burst phase and so values during burst are not shown here. See Fig. 7.12 for burst sample details

Figure 7.12 NTSC ScH phase. Sampling is not performed in phase with burst as in PAL, but on the I and Q axes. Since in NTSC there is a phase angle of 57° between burst and I, this will also be the phase at which burst samples should be taken. If ScH phase is zero, then phase of subcarrier taken at 50% sync will be zero, and the samples will be taken 33° before and 57° after sync; 25 cycles of subcarrier or 100 samples later, during burst, the sample values will be obtained. Note that in NTSC burst is inverted subcarrier, so sample 785 is positive, but sample 885 is negative

phase with burst, but on the I and Q axes at 57°, 147°, 237° and 327° with respect to burst.

Fig. 7.12 shows how this approach works in relation to sync and burst. Zero ScH is defined as 0° of subcarrier at the 50% point on sync, but the 57° sampling phase means that the sync edge is actually sampled 25.6 ns ahead of, and 44.2 ns after, the 50% point. Similarly, when the burst is reached, the phase shift means that burst sample values will be 46_{10}, 83_{10}, 74_{10} and 37_{10} repeating. The phase-locked loop which produces the sampling clock will digitally compare the samples of burst with the values given here. Since it is not sampling burst at a zero crossing, the slope will be slightly less, so the gain of the phase error detector will also be less, and more prone to burst noise than in the PAL process. The phase error can, however, be averaged over several burst samples to overcome this problem.

As in PAL, if the analog input does not have zero ScH phase, the sync pulse values will change, but burst values will not. As in PAL, NTSC DVTRs do not record sync, and will regenerate zero ScH syncs on replay.

7.9 Component serial interface

This obsolescent CCIR-656[8] serial interface was designed to support 4:2:2 component data with 8 bit wordlength as, for example, recorded by the D-1 format. It has no 10 bit or composite variants. Group coding is used to allow transmission over 75 ohm coaxial cable.

Fig. 7.13 shows the major components necessary. The channel coding scheme used is an 8/9 group code. Parallel 4:2:2 input data at 27 MHz according to CCIR-601/RP 125 having 8 bit wordlength are applied to the 8/9 converter. This may be a PROM or gate array which is programmed to output a unique 9 bit pattern for each input data combination. These channel patterns are parallel

Figure 7.13 The major components necessary for a CCIR standard 8 bit serial link. Incoming data bytes are converted to 9 bit symbols which are clocked out of a shift register serially by a 243 MHz clock obtained from input 27 MHz. On reception a 243 MHz PLL locks to the data and produces a clock. When the sync pattern is seen, the divide-by-nine counter is rephased to grab 9 bit symbols correctly from the shift register, which are then reconverted to 8 bits

loaded into a shift register which is clocked at 243 MHz. The clock is obtained by multiplying the input 27 MHz clock by nine in a phase-locked loop. The serial signal from the shift register is sent to a driver stage and then to the cable.

The receiver has a number of tasks. Firstly it must lock to the channel bit rate and generate a local continuous 243 MHz clock from transitions in the serial waveform. The choice of the 9 bit codes is partly determined by their transition content. This is much higher than would be the case with serial raw data. The input waveform is sliced and sampled by the local clock to return it to a bit stream. Secondly the beginning of the 9 bit patterns must be identified so that the serial channel bit stream can be correctly deserialized. Only then can the 9 bit patterns be decoded to the original 8 bit data. This synchronizing step is made possible by the unique 9 bit sync patterns which result from coding the two all-zeros video data bytes which are present in *SAV* and *EAV*. The serialized 9 bit codes produce run lengths of seven channel bits (011111110,100000001) which cannot occur in any data symbol. The combination of the two codes is DC free. The receiver can detect this pattern by a combination of gates which inspect the parallel outputs of a shift register through which the input data pass. When the sync pattern is detected, a reset can be applied to a divide-by-nine counter which runs from the received bit rate and clocks 9 bit parallel patterns from the shift register to the 9/8 decoder. This 27 MHz clock is also the parallel output word clock. The receiver may also check the validity of the Hamming-coded sync data.

7.10 Serial digital interface (SDI)

The interface described here has been developed to allow up to 10 bit samples of component or composite digital video to be communicated serially;[9] 16:9 format component signals with 18 MHz sampling rate can also be handled. The interface allows ancillary data including transparent conveyance of AES/EBU digital audio channels (see Chapter 12).

Scrambling, or pseudo-random coding, uses concepts which were introduced in Chapter 5. The serial interface uses convolutional coding, which is simpler to implement in a cable installation because no separate synchronizing of the randomizing is needed.

The components necessary for a scrambled serial link are shown in Fig. 7.14. Parallel component or composite data having a wordlength of up to 10 bits form the input. These are fed to a 10 bit shift register which is clocked at ten times the input rate, which will be 270 MHz or $40 \times F_{sc}$. If there are only 8 bits in the input words, the missing bits are forced to zero for transmission except for the all-ones condition which will be forced to ten ones. The serial data from the shift register are then passed through the scrambler, in which a given bit is converted to the exclusive OR of itself and 2 bits which are five and nine clocks ahead. This is followed by another stage, which converts channel ones into transitions. The resulting signal can be fed down 75 Ω coaxial cable using BNC connectors.

The scrambling process at the transmitter spreads the signal spectrum and makes that spectrum reasonably constant and independent of the picture content. It is possible to assess the degree of equalization necessary by comparing the energy in a low-frequency band with that in higher frequencies. The greater the disparity, the more equalization is needed. Thus fully automatic cable equalization is easily achieved. The receiver must generate a bit clock at 270 MHz or $40 \times F_{sc}$ from the input signal, and this clock drives the input sampler and slicer which converts the cable waveform back to serial binary. The local bit clock also drives a circuit which simply reverses the scrambling at the transmitter. The first stage returns transitions to ones, and the second stage is a mirror image of the encoder which reverses the exclusive OR calculation to output the original data. Since transmission is serial, it is necessary to obtain word synchronization, so that correct deserialization can take place.

In the component parallel input, the *SAV* and *EAV* sync patterns are present and the all-ones and all-zeros bit patterns these contain can be detected in the shift register and used to reset the deserializer.

In the composite parallel interface signal, there are no equivalents of the 4:2:2 sync patterns and it is necessary to create an equivalent. The timing reference and identification signal (TRS-ID) is added during blanking, and the receiver can detect the patterns which it contains. TRS-ID consists of five words which are inserted just after the leading edge of video sync. Fig. 7.15(a) shows the location of TRS-ID at samples 967–971 in PAL and Fig. 7.15(b) shows the location at samples 790–794 in NTSC.

Out of the five words in TRS-ID, the first four are for synchronizing, and consist of a single word of all ones, followed by three words of all zeros. The fifth word is for identification, and carries the line and field numbering information shown in Fig. 7.16. The field numbering is colour framing information which is useful for editing. In PAL the field numbering will go from zero to seven, whereas in NTSC it will only reach three.

On detection of the synchronizing symbols, a divide-by-ten circuit is reset, and the output of this will clock words out of the shift register at the correct times. This output will also become the output word clock.

It is a characteristic of all randomizing techniques that certain data patterns will interact badly with the randomizing algorithm to produce a channel

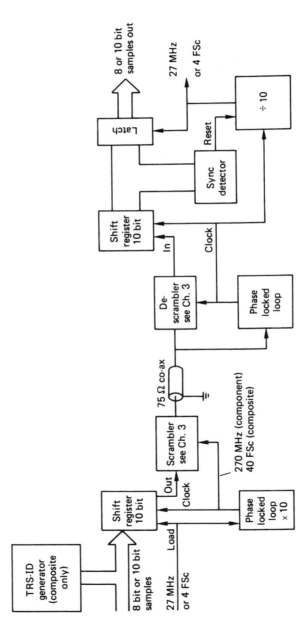

Figure 7.14 Major components of a serial scrambled link. Input samples are converted to serial form in a shift register clocked at ten times the sample rate. The serial data are then scrambled for transmission. On reception, a phase-locked loop recreates the bit rate clock and drives the de-scrambler and serial-to-parallel conversion. On detection of the sync pattern, the divide-by-ten counter is rephased to load parallel samples correctly into the latch. For composite working the bit rate will be 40 times subcarrier, and a sync pattern generator (top left) is needed to inject TRS-ID into the composite data stream. See Fig. 7.16 for TRS-ID detail

(a) PAL

(b) NTSC

Figure 7.15 In composite digital it is necessary to insert a sync pattern during analog sync tip to ensure correct deserialization. The location of TRS-ID is shown at (a) for PAL and at (b) for NTSC

Figure 7.16 The contents of the TRS-ID pattern which is added to the transmission during the horizontal sync pulse just after the leading edge. The field number conveys the composite colour framing field count, and the line number carries a restricted line count intended to give vertical positioning information during the vertical interval. This count saturates at 31 for lines of that number and above

waveform which is low in clock content. These so-called pathological data patterns[10] are extremely rare in real program material, but can be generated in test equipment and used to check the adjustment of the phase-locked loop in a receiver.

7.11 Serial digital routing

Digital routers have the advantage that they need cause no loss of signal quality as they simply pass on a series of numbers. Analog routers inevitably suffer from crosstalk and noise however well made, and this reduces signal quality on every pass.

Routers are available for serial and parallel formats. The parallel video output signal is cheaper to produce as most equipment has parallel format internally. On the other hand a parallel router is potentially complex because of the large number of conductors which need switching for each input.

Serial digital signals are more expensive to output as extra circuitry is required in each device. On the other hand, a serial router is potentially very inexpensive as it is a single-pole device. It can be easier to build than an analog router because the digital signal is more resistant to crosstalk.

As a result, parallel routers are more economical for small installations, whereas the cost rapidly escalates as the router size increases. For large routers, the only logical approach is to use serial, as the economy to be had in the router offsets the requirement for serializers on all contributing equipment.

A digital router can be made using analog switches, so that the input waveform is passed from input to output. This is not the best approach, as the total length of cable which can be used is restricted as the input cable is effectively in series with the output cable and the analog losses in both will add.

A better approach is for each router input to reclock and slice the waveform back to binary. The router itself then routes logic levels and relaunches a clean signal. The cables to and from the router can be maximum length as the router is also a repeater.

It is not necessary to unscramble the serial signal at the router. A phase-locked loop is used to regenerate the bit clock. This rejects jitter on the incoming waveform. The waveform is sliced, and the slicer output is sampled by the local clock. The result is a clean binary waveform, identical to the original driver waveform.

The router is simply a binary bit stream switch, and is not unduly concerned with the meaning or content of the bit stream. It does not matter whether the bit stream is PAL, NTSC or 4:2:2 or whether or not ancillary data are carried, it just passes through.

The only parameter of any consequence is the bit rate: 4:2:2 runs at 270 Mbits/s, PAL runs at 177 Mbits/s and NTSC runs at 143 Mbits/s. 16:9 component video with 18 MHz luminance sampling rate results in 360 Mbits/s.

Some routers require a link or DIP switch to be set in each input in order to centre the VCO at the correct frequency. Otherwise they are standards independent, which allows more flexibility and economy. With a mixed-standard router, it is only necessary to constrain the control software so that inputs of a given standard can only be routed to outputs connected to devices of the same standard, and one router can then handle component and composite signals simultaneously.

7.12 Timing in digital installations

The issue of signal timing has always been critical in analog video, but the adoption of digital routing relaxes the requirements considerably. Analog vision mixers need to be fed by equal-length cables from the router to prevent propagation delay variation. In the digital domain this is no longer an issue as delay is easily obtained and each input of a digital vision mixer can have its own local timebase corrector. Provided signals are received having timing within the window of the inputs, all inputs are retimed to the same phase within the mixer.

Fig. 7.17 shows how a mixing suite can be timed to a large SDI router. Signals to the router are phased so that the router output is aligned to station reference within a microsecond or so. The delay in the router may vary with its configuration but only by a few microseconds. The mixer reference is set with respect to station reference so that local signals arrive towards the beginning of the input windows and signals from the router (which, having come further, will be the latest) arrive towards the end of the windows. Thus all sources can be retimed within the mixer and any signal can be mixed with any other. Clearly the mixer introduces delay, and the signal feedback to the router experiences further delay. In order to send the mix back to the router a frame synchronizer is needed on the output of the suite. This introduces somewhat less than a frame of delay so that by the time the signal has re-emerged from the router it is aligned to station reference once more, but a frame late.

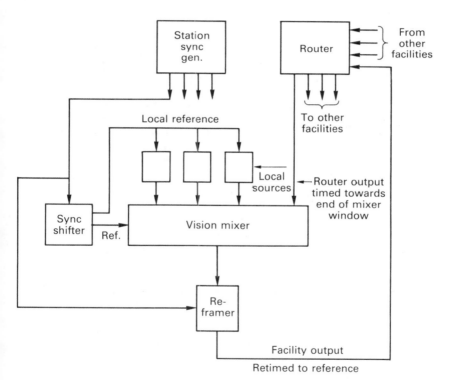

Figure 7.17 In large systems some care is necessary with signal timing as is shown here. See text for details

In an ideal world, every piece of hardware in the station will have component SDI outputs and inputs, and everything is connected by SDI cables. In practice, unless the building is new, this is unlikely. However, there are ways in which SDI can be phased in alongside analog systems. An expensive way of doing this is to fit every composite device with coders and decoders, and every analog device with converters, so that a component SDI router can be used alone. Fig. 7.18

shows an alternative. The SDI router is connected to every piece of digital equipment, using parallel to serial adaptors where necessary. Analog VTRs such as Betacam SP or M-II have digital output options which use the data from the TBC directly. One thing to check with digital output SP and M-II machines is that the *Y/C* timing must be adjusted correctly at the TBC input in the VTR as it cannot be corrected subsequently. These will need DACs to convert SDI signals to analog component inputs. Analog equipment continues to be connected to an analog router, and interconnection paths, called gateways, are created between the two routers. These gateways require converters in each direction, but the number of converters is much less than if every analog device was equipped. The number of gateways will be determined by the number of simultaneous transactions between analog and digital domains.

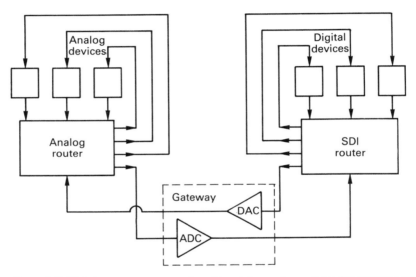

Figure 7.18 Digital routers can operate alongside existing analog routers using gateways as an economical means of introducing digital routing

In many cases the two routers can be made to appear like one large router if appropriate software is available in a common control system. This will only be possible if the SDI router is purchased from the same manufacturer as the existing analog router or if the SDI router manufacturer offers custom software.

Whilst modern DVTRs incorporate the audio data in the SDI signal, adapting older devices to do this, and subsequently demultiplexing the audio, could prove expensive. It may be more cost effective to retain an earlier audio router, or to have a separate AES/EBU digital audio router layer controlled in parallel with the SDI router.

If the analog router handles composite signals, then coders and decoders will be needed in addition to the converters. In this case the use of gateways obviates unnecessary codecs when analog devices are connected together.

7.13 HD fibre-optic interface

High-definition digital video without the use of data reduction needs around five times the data rate of conventional digital video. Whilst a parallel interface keeps down the frequency of individual conductors, the example in Section 7.7 needs a 50 pin connector and is only suitable for distances of a few tens of metres. Serial transmission on electrical cable suffers from skin effect at the extremely high bit rates needed (see Chapter 5). A practical solution to an HD serial interface is to use fibre optics.

Optical fibre has extremely low loss per metre and a nearly constant propagation speed and the only difficulty is the provision of suitable light sources and sensors. The bit rate required is beyond the ability of an LED, and requires a laser.

Lasers are basically unstable (see Chapter 10) and need to be modulated with care. Fig. 7.19 shows that the transfer function of a laser has a threshold which is strongly temperature dependent. If the drive current is allowed to fall below the threshold, transient oscillation may occur when the current is reapplied. Careful biasing is required, using feedback from a local photodetector.

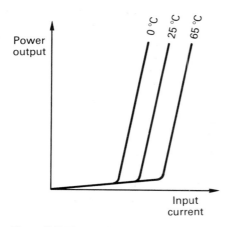

Figure 7.19 The transfer function of a laser shows strong temperature dependency and a threshold

In a fibre-optic serial interface developed for HDTV[11] the same scrambling technique as SDI has been used. Fig. 7.20 shows the modulator. The input is 2×10 bit parallel HDTV at 72 MHz. In order to reduce power consumption, the randomizer is implemented as a 5 bit parallel system, prior to serializing for transmission at 1.44 Gbits/s. The receiving PIN diode is AC coupled to eliminate drift. As the scrambled signal is not DC free, adaptive slicing is needed to eliminate baseline wander. The demodulation system is shown in Fig. 7.21.

7.14 Testing digital video interfaces

Upon installing a new interface it is necessary to test it for data integrity. It is not adequate to see if the picture looks OK. The very nature of digital transmission

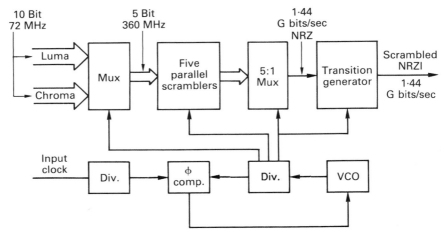

Figure 7.20 The modulator system of an HDTV optical fibre link

Figure 7.21 The demodulation system of the link of Fig. 7.20

gives beneficial resistance to minor noises and cable loss with no effect on the data and thus no visible picture artefacts. The down side of this characteristic is that a digital system can be on the verge of failure and there are no visible symptoms. If one sees a perfect picture on a monitor, it is not possible to say whether the data which produced it were received with a good noise margin which will resist future degradations or whether it was only just received and is likely to fail in the near future. Some more objective testing means is necessary if any confidence is to be had in the long-term reliability of an installation.

It is relatively simple to assess the eye pattern generated by the received waveform. After equalization the eye opening should be clearly visible, and the size of the opening should be consistent with the length and type of cable used. If it is not, the noise and/or jitter margin may be inadequate. Testing the eye pattern on the scrambled serial interface requires a fast oscilloscope, or even a sampling scope. The scope probe cannot be just hooked on to the cable as the impedance mismatch this causes will have a damaging effect on the signal. Equally a coaxial T-piece is ruled out.

One potential problem area which is frequently overlooked is to ensure that the VCO in the receiving phase-locked loop is correctly centred. If it is not, it will be running with a static phase error and will not sample the received waveform at the centre of the eyes. The sampled bits will be more prone to noise and jitter errors. VCO centring can simply be checked by displaying the control voltage. This should not change significantly when the input is momentarily disconnected.

Inspecting the eye pattern is a good technique for establishing that the basic installation is sound and has proper signal levels, termination impedance and equalization, but is not very good at detecting infrequent impulsive noise. Contact noise from electrical power installations such as air conditioners is unlikely to be present for long enough to find with an eye pattern display. The technique of signature analysis is better suited to impulsive noise problems.

Signature analysis requires a stationary test signal to be applied at the transmitting end of the interface. Digitally generated colour bars are suitable. The received data are then processed to generate a value known as a signature. If the transmitted data are always the same, the received signature should always be the same. Any change in the signature indicates that an error has occurred.

The signature generation process expresses an entire frame in component or an entire colour sequence in composite as a single word. A change of a single bit is enough to change the signature. A number of bit errors up to the number of bits in the word will guarantee to change the signature, whereas larger numbers of errors are detected with a high degree of probability.

The signature having these characteristics can be obtained by dividing the received data by a polynomial as was explained in Chapter 6. The remainder after the division is the signature. In error-detection systems, the data to be transmitted are converted to a codeword which gives a remainder or signature of zero when divided by the generating polynomial. Any non-zero remainder, known as a syndrome, indicates an error. Signature analysis is similar except that the transmitted data are not turned into a codeword. This avoids complexity at the transmitting end and the need to reserve word positions in the data. As the transmitted data are not a codeword, the remainder will be non-zero. This does not, however, indicate an error, but is a characteristic or signature of the data. An error is indicated when the signature changes, not by its absolute value.

Signature analysis is a relative detection method, rather than an absolute method. It cannot detect permanent errors, such as a stuck bit in a parallel interface, as the same signature will always be obtained. However, if the signature of the test pattern in use is known, it will be seen that the received signature is permanently different. The test pattern signature can easily be obtained by connecting the generator directly to the signature analyser as well as to the path under test.

Signature analysers can be designed to work on specific parts of the transmission only.[12] If the interface is carrying programme material, the signature will vary from frame to frame. However, the ancillary data slots can still be used for signature analysis.

In component systems, the signature analyser may be set to operate on only one selected component. Some machines can be set to operate only on selected bits in the sample, making stuck bits in parallel systems very easy to find.

7.15 Introduction to digital TV broadcasting

Whilst the use of digital techniques for television broadcasting may be harnessed to provide higher quality, the main benefit is economy. Analog broadcasting is very inefficient and as a result requires a great deal of bandwidth. In the digital domain, techniques such as data reduction are possible, more recently at reasonable cost. Error correction can also be applied to increase tolerance to noise. The result is that less bandwidth is required to deliver the same service. High-definition broadcasting will never become widespread without data reduction because of the enormous basebandwidth required. With a suitable data reduction strategy, different receivers will be able to decode a different degree of resolution from a common data stream, according to the display which is available. This allows HD reception, but compatible display on conventional monitors.

Fig. 7.22 shows a possible digital broadcast system. HD source material is data reduced and protected by the addition of redundancy. A modulation scheme which offers a large number of bits/s/Hz, such as 64-QUAM (see Chapter 5), will be used to minimize bandwidth.

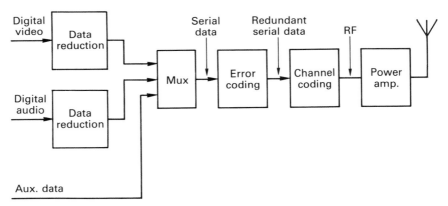

Figure 7.22 A possible digital broadcast system using data reduction, error correction and suitable channel coding

The receiver demodulates the RF signal back to a data stream which is subject to error correction and concealment. Video, audio and data are demultiplexed, and the compressed video data are expanded to the resolution required by the display.

References

1. CCIR Recommendation 656
2. SMPTE 125M, Television – Bit Parallel Digital Interface – Component Video Signal 4:2:2
3. EBU Doc. Tech. 3246
4. Specifications of Eureka 95 digital coding and interfaces, Draft version, Nov. 1992
5. Schiffler, W., The implementation of the European HDTV (HDI) standard in studio equipment. *ITS Montreux Symposium Record*, 354–364 (1993)
6. SMPTE Proposed Standard – Bit parallel digital interface for 625/50 system PAL composite digital video signals

7. SMPTE 244M, Television – System M/NTSC Composite Video Signals – Bit-Parallel Digital Interface
8. EBU Doc. Tech. 3247
9. SMPTE Proposed Standard – 10-bit 4:2:2 Component and 4FSc NTSC Composite Digital Signals – Serial Digital Interface
10. Eguchi, T., Pathological check codes for serial digital interface systems. Presented at SMPTE Conf. (Los Angeles, 1991)
11. Fischer, J. and Jost, J., Sophi-chip set for serial digital HDTV – Basic research. *ITS Montreux Symposium Record*, 365–375 (1993)
12. Elkind, R. and Fibush, D., Proposal for error detection and handling in studio equipment. Presented at 25th SMPTE Television Conf. (Detroit, 1991)

Rotary-head tape transports

There is more to digital video recording than electronics. It depends heavily on mechanical engineering of the highest quality, and several extraordinarily accurate servo systems. This chapter looks at the techniques necessary to build and control a rotary-head transport.

8.1 Why rotary heads?

The helical-scan tape deck has more in common with the helicopter than just the geometrical terminology. The rotary-head recorder is to the fixed-head recorder what the rotary-winged flying machine is to the fixed-wing machine.

In both cases the rotary machine is more complex, more expensive, consumes more power, needs more maintenance and adjustment and makes more noise than its fixed counterpart. If these were our only criteria, this comparison would amount to a condemnation. The truth of the matter is that all of these characteristics have to be accepted in order to obtain one particular attribute which cannot be obtained in any other way. In the case of the helicopter, the ability to stop dead in mid-air is vital for many applications. In the case of the helical recorder, the attribute obtained is the ability to record exceptional bandwidths with high density and the ability to replay at varying speed. If these are the requirements, there is no competition from simpler hardware. The problems have to be overcome by matching each one with the appropriate mechanical design, materials and control systems.

The attractions of the helical recorder are that the head-to-tape speed and hence bandwidth are high, whereas the linear tape speed is not. The space between tracks is determined by the linear tape speed, not by multitrack head technology. Chapter 5 showed how rotary-head machines make better use of the tape area, particularly if azimuth recording is used. The high head speed raises the frequency of offtape signals, and since output is proportional to frequency, playback signals are raised above head noise even with very narrow tracks.

With stationary heads, the offtape frequency is proportional to the linear tape speed and this makes recovery of data at other than the correct speed extremely difficult as data separators tend to work well only over a narrow speed range. In contrast, with rotary heads the scanning speed dominates head-to-tape speed and variations in the linear speed of the tape have a smaller effect. Thus picture-in-shuttle and slow motion are readily accommodated in a rotary-head machine.

8.2 Helical geometry

Fig. 8.1 shows the general arrangement of the two major categories of rotary-head recorder. In transverse-scan recorders, relatively short tracks are recorded almost at right angles to the direction of tape motion by a rotating headwheel containing four or six heads. In helical-scan recorders, the tape is wrapped around the drum in such a way that it enters and leaves in two different positions along the drum axis. This causes the rotating heads to record long slanting tracks. In both approaches, the pitch of the tracks is determined by the linear tape speed. The space between tracks can easily be made much smaller than in stationary-head recorders; in fact it can be zero or even negative.

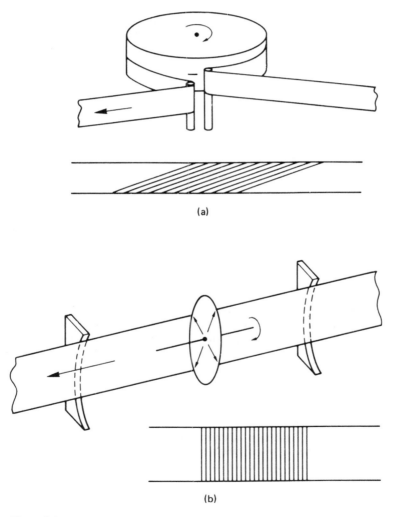

(a)

(b)

Figure 8.1 Types of rotary-head recorder. (a) Helical scan records long diagonal tracks. (b) Transverse scan records short tracks across the tape

The use of rotary heads was instrumental in the development of the first video recorders. As video signals consist of discrete lines and frames, it was possible to conceal the interruptions in the tracks of a rotary-head machine by making them coincident with the time when the CRT was blanked during flyback. The first video recorders developed by Ampex used the transverse-scan approach, with four heads on the rotor; hence the name quadruplex which was given to this system. The tracks were a little shorter than the 2 inch width of the tape, and several sweeps were necessary to build up a video frame. The changeovers between the heads were made during the horizontal synchronizing pulses.

Variable-speed operation in rotary-head machines is obtained by deflecting the playback heads along the drum axis to follow the tape tracks. Periodically the heads will need to jump in order to omit or repeat a field. In transverse scan the number of tracks needed to accommodate one field is high, and the head deflection required to jump fields was virtually impossible to achieve.

In helical scanning, the tracks become longer, so fewer of them are needed to accommodate a field. Fig. 8.2 shows that the head displacement needed is then reduced.

Figure 8.2 Helical scan results in longer tracks so a shorter distance needs to be jumped to miss out or repeat a field

For professional use, the quadruplex format gave way to 1 inch analog C-format, which used helical scan and an almost total wrap to fit an entire field into a slant track about 15 in (380 mm) long. The changeover between tracks was then made in the vertical interval. Field jumps could then be made with a head displacement of single track.

In digital recorders fields are inevitably segmented into between six (NTSC D-2, Digital Betacam) and 16 (D-5) tracks (see Section 8.6), but as the tracks are so much narrower in digital recorders the head displacement required is of the same order as on analog machines.

Fig. 8.3 shows the two fundamental approaches to drum design. In the rotating upper drum system, one or more heads are mounted on the periphery of a revolving drum (also known as the scanner). The fixed base of the drum carries a helical ramp in the form of a step (see inset) or, for greater wear resistance, a hardened band which is suitably attached. Alternatively, both top and bottom of the drum are fixed, and the headwheel turns in a slot between them. Both approaches have advantages and disadvantages. The rotating upper drum approach is simpler to manufacture than the fixed upper drum, because the latter

(a)

(b)

(c)

Figure 8.3 (a) Rotating-top-type scanner. The upper drum is slightly smaller than the lower drum due to the air film it develops. Helical band guides lower edge of tape. (b) Stationary-top scanner, where headwheel rotates in a slot between upper and lower drums. (c) Airflow in stationary-top scanner. Headwheel acts as a centrifugal pump, producing air film between tape and drums requires to be rigidly and accurately cantilevered out over the headwheel. The rotating part of the drum will produce an air film which raises its effective diameter. The rotor will thus need to be made a slightly different diameter to the lower drum, so that the tape sees a constant diameter as it rises up the drum. There will be plenty of space inside the rotor to install individually replaceable heads.

The fixed upper drum approach requires less power, since there is less air resistance. The headwheel acts as a centrifugal pump, and supplies air to the periphery of the slot where it lubricates both upper and lower drums, which are of the same diameter. It is claimed that this approach gives head contact which is more consistent over the length of the track, but it makes the provision of replaceable heads more difficult, and it is generally necessary to replace the entire headwheel as an assembly.

The presence of the air film means that the tape surface is not normally in contact with the cylindrical surface of the drum, but is merely guided by one edge following the helical step. The thickness of the air film is that where the pumping effect of the rotating drum reaches equilibrium with the tape tension. Fig. 8.4 shows that the heads project out of the drum by a distance which must exceed the air film thickness in order to deform the tape slightly. In the absence of such a deformation there would be no contact pressure. The creation and collapse of the deformities in the tape results in appreciable acoustic output, in the form of an irritating buzz.

Figure 8.4 The tape is supported on an air film and the heads must project by a greater distance to achieve contact pressure

Two sets of fixed guides, known as the entry and exit guides, lead the tape to and from the ramp. The tape may wrap around the drum by various amounts. Some early machines used a complete circuit around the drum which led the tape to cross itself in the so-called Alpha wrap. The C-format used almost a complete circuit of the drum where the tape turns sharply around the entrance and exit guides in the shape of an Omega. These techniques were necessary to allow the use of a single head, which avoided banding in analog recording, but the result is a machine which is difficult to lace and cannot use a cassette. In DVTRs the tape passes between half-way and three-quarters of the way around the drum. The total angle of drum rotation for which the heads touch the tape is called the *mechanical wrap angle* or the *head contact angle*. The angle over which a useful recorded track is laid down is always somewhat shorter than the mechanical wrap angle.

It will be evident that as the tape is caused to travel along the drum axis by the ramp, it actually takes on the path of a helix. The head rotates in a circular path, and so will record diagonal tracks across the width of the tape. So it is not really the scanning which is helical, it is the tape path.

In practical machines the tape may travel up the ramp (D-2) or down the ramp (D-3). In addition, the drum can rotate either with (D-3) or against (D-2) the direction of linear tape motion.

If the tape is stationary, as in Fig. 8.5(a) the head will constantly retrace the same track, and the angle of the track can be calculated by measuring the rise of the tape along the drum axis, and the circumferential distance over which this rise takes place. The latter can be obtained from the diameter of the drum and the wrap angle. The tangent of the *helix angle* is given by the rise over the distance.

Figure 8.5(a) and (b) When the tape is moving the track laid down will be at angle which is different from the helix angle, because the tape is in a different place at the end of the scan than at the beginning. Track length can be considered as two components L and w for stationary case, and $L + d$ and w for moving case. Hence:

$$\frac{w}{L} = \tan \hat{H} \text{ and } \frac{w}{L + d} = \hat{T}$$

It can also be obtained by measuring the distance along the ramp corresponding to the wrap angle; this dimension will give the sine of the helix angle.

However, when the tape moves, the angle between the tracks and the edge of the tape will not be the helix angle. Fig. 8.5(b) shows an example in which tape climbs up the drum which rotates against the direction of tape travel (D-2). When the head contact commences, the tape will be at a given location, but when the head contact ceases, the tape will have moved a certain linear distance and the resultant track will be longer.

Fig. 8.5(c) shows what happens when the tape moves down the drum in the same direction as head rotation. In this case the track is shorter.

In order to obtain the *track angle* it is necessary to take into account the tape motion. The length of the track resulting from scanning a stationary tape, which will be at the helix angle, can be resolved into two distances at right angles as shown in Fig. 8.6. One of these is across the tape width, the other is along the length of the tape. The tangent of the helix angle will be the ratio of these lengths. If the length along the tape is corrected by adding or subtracting the distance the tape moves during one scan, depending upon whether tape motion aids or opposes drum rotation; the new ratio of the lengths will be the tangent of the track angle. In practice this process will often be reversed, because it is the track angle which is standardized, and the transport designer has to find a helix angle which will produce it.

It can also be seen from Fig. 8.5 that when a normally recorded tape is stopped, the head must be deflected by a triangular waveform or ramp in order to follow the track. A further consequence of the track angle being different to the helix

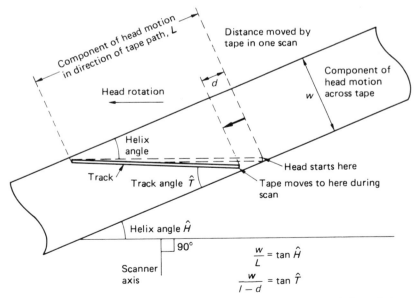

Figure 8.5(c) When the tape moves, the track laid down will not be at the helix angle because the tape is in different places at the beginning and end of the scan. In D-3 the scanner rotates *with* the tape motion, so that the track angle is greater than the helix angle. The diagram is drawn with the observer on the scanner axis looking outwards at the magnetic surface of the tape

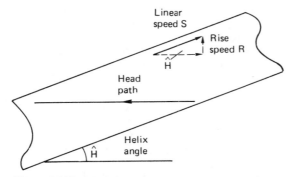

Figure 8.6 The linear speed of the tape S can be resolved into the speed of the tape along the scanner axis which is the rise speed R. $R = S \sin \hat{H}$. Dividing the rise speed by the head passing frequency gives the track pitch. Head passing frequency is simply the number of heads multiplied by the scanner rotational frequency. Thus track pitch is proportional to tape speed

angle is that when azimuth recording is used, the azimuth angles at which the heads are mounted in the drum are not the same as the angles between the transitions and the edge of the track. One of the angles is slightly increased and one is slightly reduced. In D-3 the difference is 0.017°.

The relative direction of drum and tape motion is unimportant, as both configurations work equally well. Often the direction is left undefined until many other parameters have been settled. If the segmentation and coding scheme proposed results in the wavelengths on tape being on the short side, opposite rotation will be chosen, as this lengthens the tracks and with it the wavelength. Sometimes the direction of rotation is a given; in Digital Betacam, playback of analog tapes was a requirement, so the rotation direction had to be the same as in analog Betacam.

Provided that the tape linear speed and drum speed remain the same, the theoretical track angle will remain the same. In practice this will only be the case if the tape tension is constant. Fig. 8.7 shows that if the back tension changes, the effective length of the tape will also change, and with it the track angle, a phenomenon known as *skew*. It will be evident that skew causes a tracking error which increases towards the ends of the track. Tension errors also affect the air

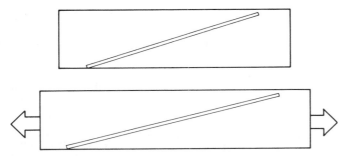

Figure 8.7 Tape is flexible, so change of tension will result in change of length. This causes a change in track angle known as skew shown exaggerated here

film thickness and head contact pressure. All digital rotary-head recorders need some form of tape tension servo to maintain the tape tension around the drum constant irrespective of the size of the pack on the supply hub. In practice tension servos can only control the tension of the tape entering the drum. Since there will be friction between the tape and the drum, the tape tension will gradually increase between the entrance and exit guides, and so the tape will be extended more towards the exit guide. When the tape subsequently relaxes, it will be found that the track is actually curved. The ramp can be made to deviate from a theoretical helix to counteract this effect, or all drums can be built to the same design, so that effectively the track curvature becomes part of the format. Another possibility is to use some form of embedded track-following system, or a system like azimuth recording which tolerates residual tracking errors.

When the tape direction reverses, the sense of the friction in the drum will also reverse, so the back tension has to increase to keep the average tension the same as when going forward.

When verifying the track angle produced by a new design, it is usual to develop a tape which it has recorded with magnetic fluid, and take measurements under a travelling microscope. With the very small track widths of digital recorders, it is usually necessary to compensate for skew by applying standard tension to the tape when it is being measured, or by computing a correction factor for the track angle from the modulus of elasticity of the tape.

8.3 Track and head geometry

The *track pitch* is the distance, measured at right angles to the tracks, from a given place on one track to the same place on the next. The track pitch is a function of the linear tape speed, the head passing frequency and the helix angle. It can be seen in Fig. 8.6 that the linear speed and the helix angle determine the rise rate (or fall rate) with respect to the drum axis, and knowledge of the rotational period of the drum will allow the travel in one revolution to be calculated. If the travel is divided by the number of active heads on the drum, the result will be the track pitch. If everything else remains equal, the track pitch is proportional to the linear tape speed. Note that the track angle will also change with tape speed.

Fig. 8.8(a) shows that in guard-band recording, the track pitch is equal to the width of the track plus the width of the guard band. The track width is determined by the width of the head poles, and the linear tape speed will be high enough so that the desired guard band is obtained. In guard-band recording, the erase head is wider than the record head, which in turn is wider than the replay head, as shown in Fig. 8.9(a). This ensures that despite inevitable misalignments, the entire area to be recorded is erased and the playback head is entirely over a recorded track.

In azimuth recording the situation is different, depending upon whether it is proposed to use flying erase heads. In Fig. 8.8(b) the head width is greater than the track pitch, so that the tape does not rise far enough for one track to clear the previous one. Part of the previous track will be overwritten, so that the track width and the track pitch become identical. As Fig. 8.9(b) shows, this approach guarantees that, when re-recording, previous tracks are fully overwritten as the overlapping heads cover the entire tape area at least once, in places twice. For some purposes, flying erase heads are not then necessary.

(a)

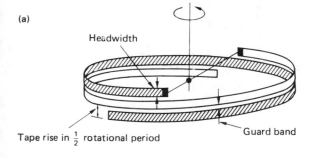

Headwidth

Tape rise in $\frac{1}{2}$ rotational period

Guard band

(b)

Headwidth

Tape rise in $\frac{1}{2}$ rotational period

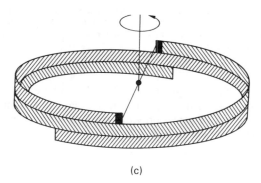

(c)

Figure 8.8 In the absence of azimuth recording, guard bands (a) must be left between the tracks. With azimuth recording, the record head may be wider than (b) or of the same width as (c) the track

(a)

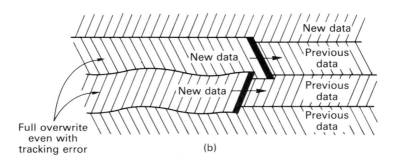

Full overwrite
even with
tracking error

(b)

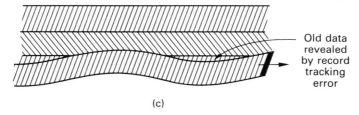

(c)

Figure 8.9 (a) The erase head is wider than the record head in guard-band recording. At (b) If the azimuth record head is wider than the track, full overwrite is obtained even with misalignment. At (c) if the azimuth record head is the same width as the track, misalignment results in failure to overwrite and an erase head becomes necessary

The alternative shown in Fig. 8.8(c) is for the track width to be exactly the same as the track pitch so there is no overlapping. In this case misalignment during re-recording can allow a thin strip of a previous track to survive unless a flying erase head is used. This is shown in Fig. 8.9(c).

8.4 Head configurations

There is some freedom in the positioning of heads in the drum. Fig. 8.10(a) shows a drum which carries four heads spaced evenly around the periphery. All of the heads are at the same height on the drum axis, which means that they would all pass the same point in space as the drum rotates.

One revolution of such a drum would lay down four evenly spaced tracks on the tape, and would play them back equally well. With a wrap angle of 180°, two heads would be in contact with the tape at any one time, and so the data rate of an individual head will be half the total.

If it is necessary to play back at variable speed, each of the heads will need to be movable, and will need to be individually controlled, so the cost of implementation will be rather high. An alternative approach is shown in Fig. 8.10(b) where the heads are mounted in pairs at 180°. The same tape format can

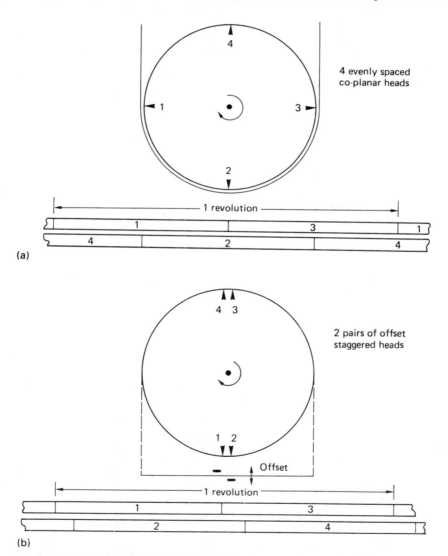

(a)

(b)

Figure 8.10 (a) Evenly spaced heads in a single plane require individual actuators for variable speed. (b) Two of the heads are slid along the tape track to give pairs of offset-staggered heads. Same tape format results if signal timing to heads is suitably modified be recorded, provided that the heads in each pair are mounted in different planes. The separation between the head planes depends on the track pitch and the angular separation between the heads. If this geometry is correct, the same format will result, but the time at which the various tracks are laid down will be different, as the figure shows. The tracks are effectively written in pairs, known as *segments*. No problem will arise provided that the record and reproduce electronics are designed to expect to transfer data at the appropriate time. The main advantage of this approach is that there is now only a requirement for two head positioners, which is a great simplification of the drum.

The physical stagger between the heads is necessary whether the heads are intended for azimuth recording or guard-band recording. In both cases the head is larger than the track it writes, due to the poles being milled away in the area of the gap. It is not possible to put the heads side by side without a large guard band resulting. Fig. 8.11 shows that staggering the heads allows the guard band to be any size, even negative in azimuth applications.

Figure 8.11 Staggering the heads allows any relative track spacing to be used

The heads in the segment are staggered and if the recording waveforms in the two heads are synchronous, diagonal tracks will begin in slightly different places along the tape as is evident in the D-2 format. Alternatively it is possible to delay the record signal to one of the heads so that both tracks begin and end in the same place. This is done in D-3/D-5 and as a result the edit gaps between sectors line up in adjacent tracks allowing the use of a single flying erase head shared between the tracks. The bit error rate from the trailing head of a staggered head pair is generally slightly worse than that of the leading head because it is working in the shock-wave pattern set up by the first head, and flies over any particles of debris which the first head loosens.

The stagger is necessary to allow the two heads physically to overlap, but it also means that the transverse displacement between the two heads is not equal to the track pitch. Fig. 8.12 shows that the longitudinal offset between the heads must take into account the fact that the tape is moving down the drum as the heads pass. By the time the trailing head has reached a given point on a track

Figure 8.12 The movement of the tape causes the track angle to be different from the helix angle of the scanner. Thus the track width T_w is not the same as the head offset. The necessary adjustment to the head spacing along the scanner axis is derived in the text

made by the leading head, that track will be lower on the drum than it was when it was written, and so the trailing head must be positioned lower on the drum to put the next track in the correct place.

It is easy to calculate the adjustment necessary, and an example is given here using the D-3 format. In both PAL and NTSC versions, the tape falls by two track widths in half a rotation of the drum. The correction is obtained by calculating the fall which takes place between the passing of the two heads, or in 6.789° of rotation, which is as follows:

(1) for PAL

$$\text{tape rise} = \frac{18 \times 2 \times 6.789}{180} \, \mu m = 1.36 \, \mu m$$

(2) for NTSC

$$\text{tape rise} = \frac{20 \times 2 \times 6.789}{180} \, \mu m = 1.51 \, \mu m$$

Subtracting these correction factors from the track pitch results in the head displacement along the drum axis which is necessary to produce the standard format. The displacement is 16.7 μm for PAL and 18.5 μm for NTSC.

DVTRs vary considerably in the number of heads installed in the drum. Chapter 6 introduced the concept of read–modify–write or pre-read in which the tape tracks are read by heads prior to the record heads for editing purposes. In many cases, such as D-2 and D-3, the pre-read function is obtained by deflecting the track-following playback heads so that they precede the record heads. Clearly there is then no confidence replay in this editing mode.

In formats which use data reduction, the compression and expansion processes introduce significant additional delay into the read–modify–write loop and the pre-read head must then be physically further advanced. The additional distance required will be beyond the deflection range of the track-following actuator and extra heads will be necessary.

Fig. 8.13(a) shows an early D-2 drum in which two pairs of record heads are mounted opposite one another so that they function alternately with a 180° wrap. The replay-head pairs are mounted at 90° on track-following actuators.

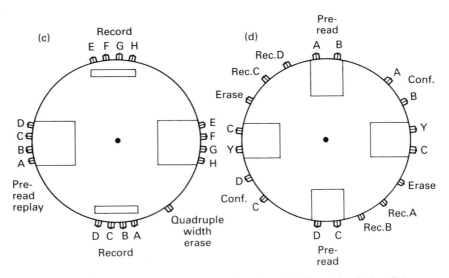

Figure 8.13 Various drum configurations contrasted. At (a) early D-2 recorders had no flying erase. At (b) later D-2 and D-3 drums have flying erase. At (c) D-5 uses four tracks per segment. Two heads of D-5 head base will register with D-3 segments. At (d) analog-compatible Digital Betacam has separate confidence replay heads as well as track-following analog heads

Fig. 8.13(b) shows a D-3 drum which has a pair of flying erase heads in addition to the record and play heads. In D-3 the two tracks in the segment are aligned by delaying the record signals, so one flying erase head functions for two tracks.

The D-5 format is backward compatible with D-3 tapes, but can also record the higher data rate of component digital video by doubling the data throughput of the drum. This is done by having four parallel tracks per segment, requiring four heads on each base. To play a D-3 tape, only two of the heads are used. In order to work in components, the drum speed is unchanged, but the tape linear speed is doubled. Fig. 8.13(c) shows a D-5 drum in which the general arrangement is the same as for D-3, but each base is fitted with four heads.

Fig. 8.13(d) shows the drum of an analog-compatible Digital Betacam. The two tracks in each segment are aligned by delays so that double-width flying erase heads can be used. The erase, record A and record B heads corresponding to one segment can be seen at the bottom right of the diagram, with the same configuration diametrically opposite. Fixed confidence replay heads are arranged nearly at right angles to the record heads. These heads trace the tracks which have just been recorded. At the top and bottom of the diagram can be seen the advanced playback heads which are also used for track following. Finally there are two more track-following actuators which carry pairs of heads which are the width of tracks on analog Betacam tapes.

8.5 Time compression

The length of the track laid on the tape is a function of the drum diameter and the wrap angle. Fig. 8.14 shows a number of ways in which the same length of track can be put on the tape.

A small drum with a large wrap angle works just as well as a large drum with a small wrap angle. If the tape speed, and hence the track rate, is constant, and for the purposes of this comparison the number of heads on the drum remains constant, the heads on the smaller drum will take a longer time to traverse the track than the heads on the larger drum. This has the effect of lowering the frequencies seen by the heads, and is responsible for the 270° wrap of the Sony D-1 recorders.

Changing the wrap angle also means that the helix angle will need to be different so that the same track angle is achieved in all cases. In practice, a larger drum can be used to mount more heads which work in turn, so that the drum speed will then be less than before. Alternatively the space inside the larger drum may be used to incorporate track-following heads. Another advantage of the large drum is that the reduced wrap angle is easier to thread up. A small drum is attractive for a portable machine since it is compact and requires less power. The greater wrap angle has to be accepted.

The different drum sizes in the example of Fig. 8.14 traced standard tracks in different periods of time, as shown in the diagram. In analog recorders such as the C-format and U-matic, the time period had to be one television field so that the television waveform could be directly fed to the heads, and design of the drum was extremely inflexible.

In the digital domain there is more freedom. The video field is expressed by a given number of samples, and as long as these appear on replay in the right sequence, their actual position in the recording or the exact time at which they were recorded is of no consequence. Clearly the record and replay processes must complement one another.

Time compression is used in Digital Betacam in order to play analog tapes. The drum diameter needed for Digital Betacam was larger than for the analog

Figure 8.14 A standard track can be put on tape with a variety of scanners. A large wrap allows the lowest frequencies at the head but increases complexity of threading mechanism and increases tape path friction. The helix angle will be different in each case in order to match the tape rise speed to the head peripheral speed – giving the same track angle

format in order to accommodate the high bit rate with the segmentation chosen. However, the helix angle of a DB transport is such that when analog Betacam tapes are played at the correct linear speed, the track angle matches the head path. Thus the analog heads follow the tracks. As the drum is larger than the original, the head-to-tape speed is too high and the analog Betacam signal is time compressed as it replays. It is expanded in the TBC. The Digital Betacam format has to take the analog-compatible helix angle as a given.

8.6 Segmentation

The number of bits to be recorded for one field will be a direct result of the sampling scheme chosen. The minimum wavelength which can be reliably recorded will then determine the length of track that is necessary.

With 4:2:2 sampling, and allowing for redundancy and the presence of the digital audio, there will be about 4.5 Mbits in one field for 50 Hz, and about 3.75 Mbits for 60 Hz. These figures will be reduced in proportion to the compression factor if data reduction is used. For example, Ampex DCT and Digital Betacam use 2:1 reduction. With $4 \times F_{sc}$ composite sampling, the figures will be about 3 Mbits and 2 Mbits per field respectively.

Since current wavelengths are restricted to about 0.7–0.9 Mm (which records 2 bits) then the total track lengths needed will be between about 1 and 2 metres. Clearly no-one in their right mind is going to design a drum large enough to put the whole of one field on one track. A further consideration is that it is not a good idea to pass all the data through one head. Eddy current losses in the head get worse at high frequencies, and should the single head clog or fail, all of the data are lost.

The solution to both problems is *segmentation* where the data for one field are recorded in a number of head sweeps. With segmentation it is easy to share the data between more than one head, a technique known as distribution. In the D-1 and D-5 formats four heads are necessary, whereas in D-2, D-3 and Digital Betacam, two heads are necessary, and the formats reflect these restrictions.

With segmentation, the contents of a field can be divided into convenient-sized pieces for recording. This allows the width of the tape to be chosen. If the tape is wide, then tracks of a given length can be placed at a greater angle to the edge of the tape, and so the tape will move more slowly for a given track rate. This means that the effective rewinding time will be reduced because a given recording will occupy a shorter length of tape. Taken to extremes, this would result in very wide tape on small reels.

This is not the only criterion, however. A wide tape needs a physically larger drum assembly, and requires greater precision in guidance. It is seldom possible to engineer a tape transport with total precision, so the tape will always be expected to accommodate small inaccuracies by flexing. The stiffness of the tape against bending in its own plane is proportional to the moment of inertia of its cross-section. This rises exponentially with tape width. The selection of a narrower tape will ease transport accuracy requirements slightly. The final factor to be considered is the recording density. A high-density recording requires less tape area per unit time, and so the effective rewinding speed will be proportional to the recording density. Consideration of these factors led to the choice of ¾ inch or ½ inch wide tape for the digital video cassettes. The choice was basically between those widths and 1 inch tape, since choice of a non-standard width would have unnecessarily raised the cost of the medium as existing slitters could not have been used.

Having chosen the tape width, the number of segments per field can be established. A large number of short, steep tracks will give the same overall track length as a smaller number of long, shallow tracks. For normal speed operation, there is little difference between the two approaches, but for variable speed, the smaller the number of segments the better, since the magnitude of head jumps will be reduced.

± 15° azimuth

Audio blocks

D-2

Staggered track start

One segment = two tracks
NTSC field = three segments 90 rps (−0.1%)
PAL field = four segments 100 rps

Guard bands 90° azimuth

Audio blocks

D-1

One segment
50 Hz field = six segments 150 rps
60 Hz field = five segments 150 rps (−0.1%)

Audio blocks

D-3

Edit gaps align in both tracks

One segment = two tracks
NTSC field = three segments 90 rps (−0.1%)
PAL field = four segments 100 rps

±20° azimuth

Audio blocks

D-5

± 20° azimuth

Edit gaps align

One segment = four tracks
50 Hz field = four segments 100 rps
60 Hz field = three segments 90 rps (−0.1%)

± 15° azimuth

Audio blocks

DB

One segment = two tracks
50 Hz field = three segments 75 rps
60 Hz field = three segments 90rps (-0.1%)

The actual segmentation techniques used in the various formats are compared in Fig. 8.15. Composite digital formats use subcarrier-locked sampling rates, so the data rate is substantially higher in PAL than in NTSC and the segmentation changes to reflect the data rate. In component formats the data rate stays the same whether 50 Hz or 60 Hz field rate is used as the same sampling rate is used in both line standards. In this case the segmentation is used to simplify supporting two field rates with as much common hardware as possible.

For these reasons D-2 and D-3, which are both composite digital, use the same segmentation approach. In PAL, data for each field are divided into four segments, each of which requires two tracks, one of each azimuth type. There are thus eight tape tracks per field. In NTSC the data rate is less and three segments suffice, so the field is accommodated in six tracks.

D-1 has a constant segment rate of 300 segments per second. In the case of 50 Hz fields, each contains six segments, whereas 60 Hz fields contain five segments. Once more each segment consists of two tracks.

The Ampex DCT and Sony Digital Betacam formats have a similar data rate to digital NTSC after the reduction process and also require three segments or six tracks per field in the 60 Hz version. However, the 50 Hz version uses four segments or eight tracks per field, so a common segment rate cannot be used because there is no common factor at these lower rates.

8.7 The basic rotary-head transport

Fig. 8.16 shows the important components of a rotary-head helical-scan tape transport. There are four servo systems which must correctly interact to obtain all modes of operation: two reel servos, the drum servo and the capstan servo. The capstan and reel servos together move and tension the tape, and the drum servo

Figure 8.16 The four servos essential for proper operation of a helical-scan DVTR. Cassette-based units will also require loading and threading servos, and for variable speed a track-following servo will be necessary

moves the heads. For variable-speed operation a further servo system will be necessary to deflect the heads.

There are two approaches to capstan drive, those which use a pinch roller and those which do not. In a pinch roller drive, the tape is held against the capstan by pressure from a resilient roller which is normally pulled towards the capstan by a solenoid. The capstan only drives the tape over a narrow speed range, generally the range in which broadcastable pictures are required. Outside this range, the pinch roller retracts, the tape will be driven by reel motors alone, and the reel motors will need to change their operating mode; one becomes a velocity servo whilst the other remains a tension servo.

In a pinch-roller-less transport, the tape is wrapped some way around a relatively large capstan, to give a good area of contact. A drilled capstan connected to a suction pump can also be used to obtain extra adhesion. The tape is always in contact with the capstan, irrespective of operating mode, and so the reel servos never need to change mode. A large capstan has to be used to give sufficient contact area, and to permit high shuttle speed without excessive motor rpm. This means that at play speed it will be turning slowly, and must be accurately controlled and free from cogging. A multipole ironless-rotor pancake-type brush motor is often used, or a sinusoidal-drive brushless motor.

The simplest operating mode to consider is the first recording on a blank tape. In this mode, the capstan will rotate at constant speed, and drive the tape at the linear speed specified for the format. The drum must rotate at a precisely determined speed, so that the correct number of tracks per unit distance will be laid down on the tape. Since in a segmented recording each track will be a constant fraction of a television field, the drum speed must ultimately be determined by the incoming video signal to be recorded. To take the example of a PAL D-2 or D-3 recorder having two record-head pairs, eight tracks or four segments will be necessary to record one field, and so the drum must make exactly two complete revolutions in one field period, requiring it to run at 100 Hz. In the case of NTSC D-2 or D-3, there are six tracks or three segments per field, and so the drum must turn at one and a half times field rate, or a little under 90 Hz. The phase of the drum rotation with respect to input video timing depends upon the time delay necessary to shuffle and interleave the video samples. This time will vary from a minimum of about one segment to more than a field depending on the format.

8.8 Controlling motor speed

In various modes of operation, the capstan and/or the drum will need to have accurate control of their rotational speed. During crash record (a mode in which no attempt is made to lock to a previous recording on the tape) the capstan must run at an exact and constant speed. When the drum is first started, it must be brought to the correct speed before phase lock can be attempted. The principle of speed control commonly used will be examined here.

Fig. 8.17(a) shows that the motor whose speed is to be controlled is fitted with a toothed wheel or slotted disk. For convenience, the number of slots will usually be some power of 2. A sensor, magnetic or optical, will produce one pulse per slot, and these will be counted by a binary divider. A similar counter is driven by a reference frequency. This may often be derived by multiplying the input video

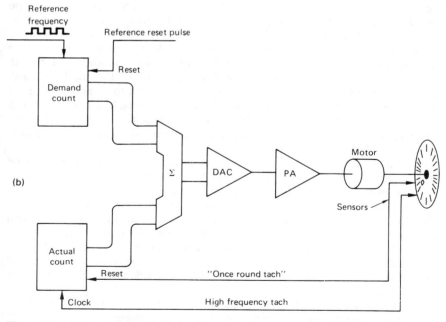

Figure 8.17 (a) Motor speed control using frequency generator on motor shaft. Pulses from FG are compared with pulses from reference to derive servo error. (b) An additional sensor resets the actual count once per revolution, so it counts motor phase angle. Demand count is reset by reference timing. Thus motor phase is locked to reference

field rate in a phase-locked loop. The operation of a phase-locked loop was described in Chapter 2.

The outputs of the two counters are taken to a full adder, whose output drives a DAC which in turn drives the motor. The bias of the motor amplifier is arranged so that a DAC code of one-half of the quantizing range results in zero drive to the motor, and smaller or larger codes will result in forward or reverse drive.

If the count in the tacho divider lags behind the count in the reference divider, the motor will receive increased power, whereas if the count in the tacho divider leads the count in the reference divider, the motor will experience reverse drive, which slows it down. The result is that the speed of the motor is exactly proportional to the reference frequency. In principle the system is a phase-locked loop, where the voltage-controlled oscillator has been replaced by a motor and a frequency-generating wheel.

8.9 Phase-locked servos

In a DVTR the rotational phase of the drum and capstan must be accurately controlled. In the case of the drum, the phase must be controlled so that the heads reach the beginning of a track at a time which is appropriate to the station reference video fed to the machine.

A slightly more complex version of the speed control system of Fig. 8.17(a) is required, as will be seen in Fig. 8.17(b). In addition to a toothed wheel or slotted disk, the motor carries a reference slot which produces a rotational phase reference commonly called *once-round tach*. This reference presets the tacho divider, so that the tach count becomes an accurate binary representation of the actual angle of rotation.

A similar divider is fed by a reference clock as before, and preset at appropriate intervals. The reference clock has the same frequency as the tooth passing frequency of the tacho at normal speed. In a PAL D-2 machine which needs two drum rotations per field, the counter will need to be preset twice per field, or, more elegantly, the counter will have an additional high-order bit which does not go to the adder, and then it can be preset once per field, since disconnection of the upper bit will cause two repeated counts of half a field duration each, with an overflow between.

The adder output will increase or decrease the motor drive until the once-round tach occurs exactly opposite the reference preset pulse, because in this condition the sum of the two inputs to the adder is always zero.

The binary count of the tach counter can be used to address a rotation phase PROM. This will be programmed to generate signals which enable the different sectors of the recorded format to be put in the correct place on the track. For example, if it is desired to edit one audio channel without changing any other part of a recording, the record head must be enabled for a short period at precisely the correct drum angle. The drum phase PROM will provide the timing information needed.

When the tape is playing, the phase of the control track must be locked to reference segment phase in order to achieve accurate tracking.

Fig. 8.18 shows that a similar configuration to the drum servo is used, but there is no once-round tach on the capstan wheel. Instead, the tach counter is reset by the segment pulses obtained by replaying the control track. Since the speed of the

Figure 8.18 If the encoded counter is reset by CTL pulses, it will count linear tape phase, i.e. distance between CTL pulses. Controlling demand counter from reference segment pulses phase locks tape CTL track to segment rate resulting in correct tracking. At an assemble edit the reset is disabled and the capstan servo makes a smooth transition to the velocity control mode of Fig. 8.17(a)

control track is proportional to the capstan speed, resetting the tach count in this way results in a count of control track phase. The reference counter is reset by segment rate pulses, which can be obtained from the drum, and so the capstan motor will be driven in such a way that the phase error between control track pulses and reference pulses is minimized. In this way the rotary heads will accurately track the diagonal tracks.

During an assemble edit, the capstan will phase-lock to control track during the preroll, but must revert to constant speed mode at the in-point, since the control track will be recorded from that point. This transition can be obtained by simply disabling the capstan tach counter reset, which causes the system to revert to the speed control servo of Fig. 8.17.

8.10 Tension servos

It has been shown that tape tension control is critical in helical-scan machines, primarily to ensure interchange and the correct head contact. Tension control will also be necessary for shuttle to ensure correct tape packing.

Fig. 8.19 shows a typical back tension control system. A swinging guide called a tension arm is mounted on a position sensor which can be optical or magnetic. A spring applies a force to the tension arm in a direction which would make the tape path longer. The position sensor output is connected to the supply reel motor amplifier which is biased in such a way that when the sensor is in the centre of

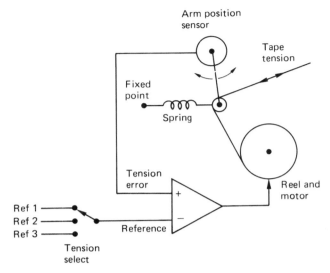

Figure 8.19 Tension servo controls reel motor current so that motor extends sprung arm. Sensor determines extension of spring and thus tape tension

its travel the motor will receive no drive. The polarity of the system is arranged so that the reel motor will be driven in reverse when the spring contracts. The result is that the reel motor will apply a reverse torque which will extend the spring as it attempts to return the tension arm to the neutral position. If the system is given adequate loop gain, a minute deflection of the arm will result in full motor torque, so the arm will be kept in an essentially constant position. This means that the spring will have a constant length, and so the tape tension will be constant. Different tensions can be obtained by switching offsets into the feedback loop, which result in the system null being at a different extension of the spring.

The error in the servo will only be small if the reel can accelerate fast enough to follow tape motion. In a machine with permanent capstan engagement, the capstan can accelerate much faster than the reels can. If not controlled, this would lead to the tension arm moving to one or other end of its travel, resulting in tape stretch, or a slack loop which will subsequently snatch tight with the same results. A fixed acceleration limit on the capstan servo would prevent the problem, but it would have to be set to allow a full reel on a large-size cassette to keep up. The motion of a small cassette with vastly reduced inertia would be made artificially ponderous. The solution is to feed back the displacement of the tension sensors to the capstan servo. If the magnitude of the tension error from either tension arm is excessive, the capstan acceleration is cut back. In this way the reels are accelerated as fast as possible without the tension becoming incorrect.

In a cassette-based recorder, the tension arms usually need to be motorized so that they can fit into the mouth of the cassette for loading, and pull tape out into the threaded position. It is possible to replace the spring which provides tape tension with a steady current through the arm motor. By controlling this current, the tape tension can be programmed.

8.11 Tape-remaining sensing

It is most important in a cassette to prevent the tape running out at speed. The tape is spliced to a heavy leader at each end, and this leader is firmly attached to the reel hub. In an audio cassette, there is sufficient length of this leader to reach to the other reel, and so the impact of a run-off can be withstood. This approach cannot be used with a video cassette, because the heavy leader cannot be allowed to enter the drum, as it would damage the rotating heads.

The transport must compute the tape remaining in order to prevent running off at speed. This may be done by measuring the linear speed of the tape and comparing it with the rotational speed of the reel. The linear speed will be the capstan speed in a permanent capstan drive transport, a timer roller will be necessary in a pinch roller type transport. Alternatively, tape remaining may be computed by comparing the speed of the two reels. The rotational speed of the reels will be obtained from a frequency generator (FG) on the reel motors. Fig. 8.20 shows a simple method of computing the tape remaining. Pulses from the capstan FG cause a counter to increment. When a reel FG pulse occurs, the count will be transferred to a latch, and the counter will be reset. When the reel is full, there will be many capstan FG pulses between reel FG pulses, but as the radius of the tape pack falls, the count transferred to the latch will also fall. It will be possible to determine the limit count from a knowledge of the capstan and reel hub diameters, and the number of teeth on their generators. The latch count is not

Figure 8.20 Tape remaining is calculated by comparing capstan tach with reel tach. If tension arm is moving, tape speed at reel and capstan will be different, so correction term from tension arm sensor is added. Pinch-roller-type transports disengage the capstan in shuttle, and so the timer roller tacho would be used instead

quite the pack radius, because if the tension arm is moving due to an acceleration, the linear speed of the tape at the capstan will not be the same as the linear speed at the reel. To prevent false shutdowns when accelerating near the end of the tape, the tension arm signal may be differentiated to give an arm velocity signal, and this can be digitized and used to produce a correction factor for the radius parameter.

To prevent run-offs, the reel pack radius of the reel which is unwinding profiles the allowable shuttle speed, so that as the pack radius falls, the tape speed falls with it. Thus when the tape finally runs out, it will be travelling at very low speed, and the photoelectric sensor which detects the leader will be able to halt the transport without damage.

8.12 Brushless DC motors

The reliability of digital circuitry is of little consequence if a breakdown is caused by the failure of an associated mechanical component. Video recorders, including digital video recorders, are a complex alliance of mechanical, magnetic and electronic technology, and the electronic wizardry has to be matched by some pretty good mechanical engineering. As the cost of electronics falls, it becomes possible to replace certain mechanical devices cost effectively, and there is an impetus to do this if a wear mechanism can be eliminated. The brushless motor is one such device. The conventional DC brush motor is ubiquitous, and life would be infinitely less convenient without it, for it allows reasonable efficiency, a wide speed range, reversing and relatively compact size. The weak point of all motors of this kind is the brush/commutator system, which serves to distribute current to the windings which are in the best position relative to the field to generate torque. There is a physical wear mechanism, and the best brush material developed will still produce a conductive powder which will be distributed far

Figure 8.21 At (a) a conventional brush motor has rotating windings. Current is fed through stationary bushes and commutation is automatic. At (b) the motor has been turned inside-out, the magnet revolves and the windings are now stationary, so they can be directly connected to an electronic commutating circuit. The rotation sensor on the magnet shaft tells the commutator when to switch

and wide by the need to have airflow through the motor for cooling. The interruption of current in an inductive circuit results in sparking, which can cause electrical interference and erosion of the brushes and commutator. The brushless motor allows all of the benefits of the DC motor, without the drawbacks of commutation.

Fig. 8.21 shows that a brushless motor is not unlike a normal motor turned inside out. In a normal motor, the field magnet is stationary, and the windings rotate. In a brushless motor, the windings are stationary, and the magnet rotates. The stationary windings eliminate the need to supply current to the rotor, and with it the need for brushes. The commutating action is replaced by electronic switches. These need to be told the rotational angle of the shaft, a function which is intrinsic in the conventional commutator. A rotation sensor performs this function.

Figure 8.22 Circuit of a brushless DC motor is basically a three-phase bridge. Six different flux directions can be obtained by switching combinations of FETs. One example is shown

Fig. 8.22 shows the circuit of a typical brushless motor. The three-phase winding is driven by six switching devices, usually power FETs. By switching these on in various combinations, it is possible to produce six resultant field directions in the windings. The switching is synchronized to the rotation of the magnet, such that the magnetic field of the rotor always finds itself at right angles to the field from the windings, and so produces the most torque. In this condition the motor will produce the most back EMF, and the normal way of adjusting the rotation sensor is to allow the motor to run on no load and to adjust the angular sensor position mechanically until the motor consumes minimum current.

The rotating magnet has to be sufficiently powerful to provide the necessary field, and in early brushless motors was heavy, which gave the motor a high inertial time constant. Whilst this was of no consequence in steady speed applications, it caused problems in servos. The brushless servo motor was basically waiting for high-energy permanent magnets, which could produce the necessary field without excessive mass. These rare earth magnets are currently more expensive than the common ferrite magnet, and so the first applications of brushless motors have been in machines where the motor cost is a relatively small proportion of the high overall cost, and where reliability is paramount. Professional recorders come into this category. Down time for brush replacement and labour costs eclipse the cost of the brushes. The drum motor of a video recorder in a modern post production suite has to run at speed hour after hour, day after day, and is a natural application of a brushless motor.

The development of the power FET also facilitated brushless motors, since all DC motors regenerate, which is to say that when the torque opposes the direction of rotation, the current reverses. FETs are not perturbed by current direction, whereas bipolar devices were at best inefficient or would at worst fail in the presence of reverse current. Power FETs can handle currents which would destroy brush gear, and so large transient accelerations are easily obtained, overcoming the inertia of the rotating magnet.

A typical brushless motor appears to the drive amplifier just like a normal DC motor. It has only two power terminals, has back EMF, and will regenerate. The only major difference is the way that reversing is achieved. Brush motors reverse by reversing drive polarity, whereas brushless motors reverse by changing the phase of the commutation.

The number of motor poles directly influences the complexity of the switching circuitry, and brushless motors tend to have relatively few poles. Conventional motors suffer from cogging, or a cyclic variation in torque, and those with few poles suffer most. Whilst it is of little consequence in a drum motor, which runs at high speed and has the inertia of the drum to smooth out rotation, it can be important in direct drive capstan motors, which turn at low speed and have low inertia.

Many transports retain multipole brush motors for the capstan, but it is possible to construct a cogging-free motor. The commutation circuit is no longer switching, but consists of a number of analog amplifiers which will feed the motor with sinusoidal waveforms in fixed phase relationships. In the case of a two-phase motor, this will be two waveforms at 90°; for a three-phase motor, it will be three waveforms at 120°.

The drive signals for the amplifiers are produced by a number of rotation sensors, which directly produce analog sinusoids. These can conveniently be Hall effect sensors which detect the fields from rotating magnets.

8.13 Switched-mode motor amplifiers

The switched-mode motor amplifier has much in common with the switched-mode power supply, since both have the same objectives, namely an increase in electrical efficiency through reduced dissipation, and reduction in size and weight. In studio-based machines reduced dissipation will help to increase reliability, whereas in portable machines the efficiency is paramount since existing battery technology is still a handicap.

The linear amplifier must act as a variable resistance, and so current flowing through it will cause heat to be developed. Linear amplifiers are particularly inefficient for driving tape reel motors, since to obtain fast shuttle speed, the supply voltage must be high, and this means that when the machine plays, the reels are turning slowly and the motor voltage will be very small, so that most of the power supply voltage has to be dropped by the amplifier, which is extremely inefficient. Some transports using linear motor amplifiers will program a switched-mode power supply to provide just enough voltage for the instantaneous requirements, helping to raise efficiency.

The principle of a switched-mode amplifier is quite simple. The current is controlled by an electronic switch which is either fully on or fully off. In both cases dissipation in the switch is minimal. The only difficulty consists of providing a variable output despite the binary switching. This will be done by a combination of duty cycle control and filtering.

Fig. 8.23 shows a typical switched-mode motor amplifier. It consists of a normal bridge configuration with a number of additional components, a pair of inductors and a current sense resistor in series with the motor, and a number of reverse-connected flywheel diodes.

If it is desired to make current flow through the motor from left to right, then field-effect transistors T_1 and T_4 will be turned fully on. Owing to the presence of the inductors, the current through the motor increases gradually, and when the desired current is reached, transistor T_1 is switched off. The current flowing in the inductive circuit must continue flowing, and it will do so through D_3, as shown in (b). Greater efficiency will be obtained if T_3 is then switched on, as the forward drop of the diode is then bypassed. Transistor T_4 is then switched off, and the current loop will be blocked, causing the flux in the inductors to decay, and raising their terminal voltage. This will result in current flowing through D_2 back to the power supply. Greater efficiency will be obtained if T_2 is turned on. The current is now being opposed by the power supply and will decay. After a short time, transistor T_2 must be switched off, and transistor T_4 will be switched on again. In this way, the current rises and falls about the desired value. If the switching rate is made high, the variations in current will be small with respect to the average current. The inertia of the motor will in any case prevent any mechanical response at the switching frequency. It will be noted that during this process current flowed in reverse through two of the transistors, requiring the use of field-effect devices.

Clearly if current flowing from right to left is required, the bridge switching will change over, but the principle remains the same.

The torque generated by the motor is proportional to the current, and torque can be applied with or against rotation. For example, when the transport is in play mode, the take-up motor is turning in the same direction as its torque, whereas the supply motor is providing back tension, and is turning against its torque. In this case, the motor EMF will cause current to flow in the flywheel circuit, and the switching will take energy out of the current flywheel back to the power supply. This is the principle of regenerative braking. If the motor is being turned by the tape, it will generate, and a current will flow as shown in (c). The current will rise gradually owing to the presence of the inductors. When the current reaches the value needed to give the correct back tension, T_3 will be switched off, and the flywheel current will find itself blocked. The result will be a flux collapse causing the inductors to raise their terminal voltage until a current path is found.

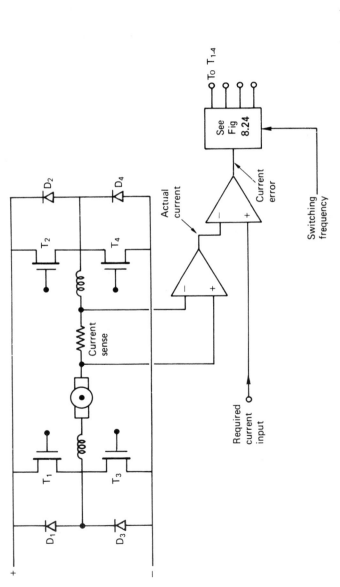

Figure 8.23 General arrangement of switched-mode power amplifier. Devices T_1–T_4 are Power FETs which are on or off. Inductors in series with motor inductance limit rate of change of current

Figure 8.23 continued Switching sequence begins at (a) with current building up, a transitional phase (b) a flywheel phase (c) transitional phase (d) and at (e) the system regenerates, or opposes the power supply. This causes current to fall. System then passes through remaining phases back to (a). To increase current, system spends more time in phase (a), whereas to reduce current, system spends more time in phase (e). Figure 8.24 shows how this is done

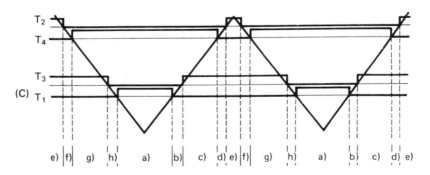

Figure 8.24 The power FETs of Fig. 8.23 are switched by comparing the current error with a sawtooth signal produced from the switching frequency. Four offset voltages are added to the current error, and four comparators are used, one for each power device. The offsets are constant, so all four current errors move together

At (A) above, the current error is zero, so the switching is symmetrical because time period (a) has the same length as time period (e) and the current is neither increased nor reduced. At (B) the current error is negative, and phase (a) is very short whereas phase (e) is much longer; thus current reduces because the motor is regenerating. At (C) the current error is positive and phase (a) is now longer than phase (e), so current increases. If the current error increases further, some phases will no longer take place. An inverse of the error in (C) will result in phase (e) disappearing since (d) and (f) are identical. Further increase will cause (d), (e) and (f) to disappear giving the sequence a, b, c, g, h, . . .

When the voltage exceeds the power supply voltage, current will flow in D_1, back to the supply. Again greater efficiency will be obtained if T1 is switched on, since the diode drop is bypassed. Since the power supply voltage is opposing the motor EMF, the current will fall, and when it has fallen sufficiently, T_1 will be switched off and T_3 will be switched on again.

The switching sequence of the transistors is important, since turning on the wrong pair will short out the power supply! One method of controlling the switching is to produce a current error by comparing the current sensed with the desired current. The current error then changes the DC level of a triangle wave, which is compared with four thresholds, each of which controls one of the transistors. Fig. 8.24 shows the switching sequence which results. Note that when the current error is zero, the system alternates equally between opposing and assisting the current, and so there is no change.

A motor which is producing back tension will return power to the supply, which will be used by the motor which is taking up, and by the drum motor. If the machine is braking from a high shuttle speed, both reel motors may together produce more power than the rest of the machine can use, and the power supply voltage will rise. In AC-powered machines, it is necessary to shunt the supply with a resistor in this condition, whereas in battery-powered machines, the regenerative current simply recharges the battery. Clearly a power failure in shuttle is no problem, for as long as the reels are being decelerated, power is generated. This can be augmented if necessary by decelerating the drum.

8.14 The digital video cassette

The D-1 and D-2 formats use the same mechanical parts and dimensions in their respective ¾ inch cassettes, even though the kind of tape and the track pattern are completely different. The Ampex DCT cassette is the same as a D-2 cassette. D-3 and D-5 use the same ½ inch cassette, and Digital Betacam uses a ½ inch cassette which is identical mechanically to the analog Betacam cassette, but uses different tape.

The main advantages of a cassette are that the medium is better protected from contamination whilst out of the transport, and that an unskilled operator or a mechanical elevator can load the tape.

It is not true that cassettes offer any advantage for storage except for the ease of handling. In fact a cassette takes up more space than a tape reel, because it must contain two such reels, only one of which will be full at any one time. In some cases it is possible to reduce the space needed by using flangeless hubs and guiding liner sheets as is done in the Compact Cassette and RDAT, or pairs of hubs with flanges on opposite sides, as in U-matic. Whilst such approaches are acceptable for consumer and industrial products, they are inappropriate for the digital video cassette, because as a professional unit it will be expected to wind at high speeds in automation and editing systems. Accordingly the digital cassette contains two fully flanged reels side by side. The centre of each hub is fitted with a thrust pad and when the cassette is not in the drive a spring acts on this pad and presses the lower flange of each reel firmly against the body of the cassette to exclude dust. When the cassette is in the machine the relative heights of the reel turntables and the cassette supports are such that the reels seat on the turntables before the cassette comes to rest. This opens a clearance space between the reel flanges and the cassette body by compressing the springs. This should be borne

		D-1	D-2	D-3	D-5	DCT	Digital Betacam
Track pitch (μm)		45	35	18	18	35	26
Tape speed (mm/s)		286·9	131·7	83·2	167·2	131·7	96·7
Play time (min)	S	14/11	32	64/50	32/25	32	40
	M	50/37	104	125/95	62/47	104	–
	L	101/75	208	245/185	123/92	208	124
Data rate (mbits/s)		216	142	142	288	113	126
Density (mbits/cm²)		4	5·8	13	13	5·8	10

Figure 8.25 The D-1/D-2, D-3/D-5, DCT and Digital Betacam tape sizes and playing times contrasted

in mind if a machine is being tested without the cassette elevator as a suitable weight must be placed on the cassette in order to compress the springs.

The use of a cassette means that it is not as easy to provide a range of sizes as it is with open reels. Simply putting smaller reels in a cassette with the same hub spacing does not produce a significantly smaller cassette. The only solution is to specify different hub spacings for different sizes of cassette. This gives the best volumetric efficiency for storage, but it does mean that the transport must be able to reposition the reel drive motors if it is to play more than one size of cassette.

Digital Betacam offers two cassette sizes, whereas the other formats offer three. If the small, medium and large digital video cassettes are placed in a stack with their throats and tape guides in a vertical line, the centres of the hubs will be seen to fall on a pair of diagonal lines going outwards and backwards. This arrangement was chosen to allow the reel motors to travel along a linear track in machines which accept more than one size. The D-1 format has very low recording density by modern standards and is somewhat pushed to get long playing time. The large-size cassette was the largest size which could be accommodated in a transport which would still fit in a 19 inch rack. Fig. 8.25 compares the sizes and capacities of the various digital cassettes.

8.15 The D-1/D-2/DCT cassette

All three sizes of cassette have basically the same structure, and detail differences will be noted. The cassette has a double-door arrangement shown in Fig. 8.26. When the cassette is removed, both sides of the tape in the throat are covered. The inner door is guided by a curved track. The door extends to the edges of the small and medium cassettes, but this is unnecessary on the large cassette. The door has a lock which prevents accidental opening, and this is

Closed

Open

Figure 8.26 When the cassette lid is closed, both sides of the tape are protected by covers. As the outer lid swings up on a pivot, the inner lid is guided around the back of the tape by a curved track

released by a pin when the cassette enters the transport. The lock release mechanism is as near the edge of the small cassette as possible, but it cannot be in the same place on the medium cassette, as it would foul the tape path to the larger reel. Three lock release pins are needed, one for each size, and the larger cassettes need dummy slots which clear the pins used by the smaller sizes.

The cassettes also have hub locks which prevent unwanted rotation in storage or transit. On the larger two sizes, the lock is released by a lever operated by the act of opening the door. There is insufficient room for this mechanism on the small cassette, and so the brake is released by a central post in the transport.

Table 8.1 (a) Manufacturers' coding holes (0 = tab removed). (b) User holes (0 = tab removed)

(a) Holes 1 and 2 shall be used in combination to indicate tape thickness according to the following logic table:	Holes 3 and 4 shall be used to indicate the coercivity of the magnetic recording tape.

Hole Number: 1 2		Hole number: 3 4	
0 0	= 16 μm tape	0 0	= Class 850
0 1	= 13 μm tape	0 1	= Undefined/reserved
1 0	= Undefined/reserved	1 0	= Undefined/reserved
1 1	= Undefined/reserved	1 1	= Undefined/reserved

(b) When a '0' state exists, the user holes shall identify the following conditions:

1. Total record lockout
   (audio/video/cue/time code/control track)
2. Reserved and undefined
3. Reserved and undefined
4. Reserved and undefined

The cassettes are designed for front or side loading, and so have guiding slots running at right angles. Most studio recorders are front loading, whereas most automated machines use side loading. The front-loading guide groove is centrally positioned and the threading throat forms a lead-in to it, helping to centralize the smaller cassettes in a loading slot which will accept a large cassette.

A number of identification holes are provided in the cassettes, which are sensed by switches on the transport. Four of these are coding holes which are in the form of break-off tabs which will be set when the cassette is made, and four of them are resettable user holes, which can be controlled with a screwdriver. Table 8.1 shows the significance of the coding and user holes.

Areas are specified for the positioning of labels, and these are recessed to prevent fouling of elevators or guides. Automated machines will use the end location for a bar code which can be read by the elevator while the cassette is stacked.

8.16 The D-3/D-5 cassette

All three sizes of cassette have basically the same structure, and detail differences will be noted. The cassette has a double-door arrangement shown in Fig. 8.27. The inner door hinges in the top of the outer door. When the cassette is removed, both sides of the tape in the throat are covered. The inner door is guided by a curved track. The door extends to the edges of the S and M cassettes, but this is unnecessary on the L cassette. The door has a lock which prevents accidental opening, and this is released by a pin when the cassette enters the transport. The lock release mechanism is at the edge of the S and M cassettes, and slightly inset on the L cassette. Three lock release pins are needed, one for each size, and the larger cassettes need dummy slots which clear the release pins used by the smaller sizes.

The cassettes also have hub locks which prevent unwanted rotation in storage or transit. On all sizes, the lock is released by a rounded post on the deckplate which enters the cassette as it is lowered. This post contains a light source for the

Figure 8.27 The D-3 cassette has a double door which protects both sides of the front tape run when closed. The inner door (shaded) carries guide pins which run in serpentine tracks in the ends of the cassette. These guide the door around the back of the tape as the cassette closes

BOT/EOT sensors. Light from the post travels across the cassette on a path nearly parallel to the door and if allowed to pass the transparent leader tape emerges through a hole in each end of the cassette which is only revealed when the cassette door is open.

The cassettes are designed for front or side loading, and so have guiding slots running at right angles. The front-loading groove is centrally positioned, whereas the side-loading groove runs across the cassette on the opposite side to the door.

A number of identification holes are provided in the cassettes, which are sensed by switches on the transport. Three of these are coding holes which are in the form of break-off tabs which will be set when the cassette is made, and three of them are resettable user holes, which can be controlled with a screwdriver. Table 8.2 shows the significance of the coding and user holes. It will be seen that the hub diameter of the cassette can be conveyed in the coding holes. The hub of the L

Hole numbers:

(1) = 0 low coercivity		
(1) = 1 high coercivity		
(2)	(3)	
0	0	11 µm tape, small-diameter hub
0	1	11 µm tape, large-diameter hub
1	0	14 µm tape, small-diameter hub
1	1	14 µm tape, large-diameter hub

A '1' in the above table indicates that the indicator tab is removed or open, an undetected state by the record/player sensor mechanism.

When a '0' state exists, the user holes shall identify the following conditions:

(a) Total record lockout (audio/video/cue/timecode/control track)
(b) Video and control-track record lockout
(c) Reserved and undefined

Table 8.2 The cassette has two sets of coding holes. The first of these, labelled 1,2,3, is for cassette recognition. The second, labelled a,b,c, is for user record lockout. Hole significance is shown in the tables below. Holes 1, 2 and 3 shall be used in combination to indicate tape thickness and diameter of hub according to the above logic table cassette is larger in diameter than that of the other sizes. The tape-remaining computation needs to know the hub diameter as well as the tape thickness to work out the remaining time from the reel FGs. It is possible to mix hub sizes and cassette sizes. A large-size hub may be used in a small cassette to increase shuttle speed, reducing access time with the penalty of reduced playing time.

The first user hole is a total record lockout, whereas the second only prevents video and control track recording, and thus allows audio editing. The third user hole is undefined. Two of the user holes are used to align the cassette in the transport. The transport registration pins are fitted with switches.

8.17 Loading the cassette

The sequence of operations when a cassette is inserted in the machine will be followed.

In a studio machine, all cassette sizes can be used without any adjustment. The operator simply pushes the cassette into the aperture in the machine. The smaller sizes are located at the centre of the aperture by sprung guides which are pushed aside when a large-size cassette is used. The presence of the cassette is sensed optically, or by switches, and by the same means the machine can decide which size of cassette has been inserted. The cassette fits into a cage which is driven by a toothed rack so that it can move inwards and down. Alternatively the cassette may be driven by rubber belts. In portable machines and camcorders only the small cassette will be accommodated and the cassette compartment will be closed by hand.

As the hub spacing differs between cassette sizes, the transport automatically moves the sliding reel motors to the correct position. The final part of horizontal travel unlocks the cassette door. The cassette elevator is then driven downwards and the door is opened. The opened cassette is then lowered onto the reel motors, and locating dowels on the transport register the cassette body. The hub brakes are released either by a post entering the cassette as it is lowered or by the act of opening the door. The several guides and tension arms and the pinch roller, where applicable, are positioned so that the throat of the cassette drops over them with the front run of tape between them and the head drum.

8.18 Threading the tape

It is inherent in helical-scan recorders that the tape enters and leaves the head drum at different heights. In open-reel recorders, the reels are simply mounted at different heights, but in a cassette this is not practicable. The tape must be geometrically manipulated in some way. There are several approaches to the geometrical problem:

(1) The drum can be inclined so that the height of the tape is the same at entry and exit.
(2) The drum can be vertical and the tape is manipulated out of the plane of the cassette on both entry and exit sides.
(3) The tape enters the drum in the plane of the cassette and is manipulated on the exit side only.
(4) The tape leaves the drum in the plane of the cassette and is manipulated on the entry side only.

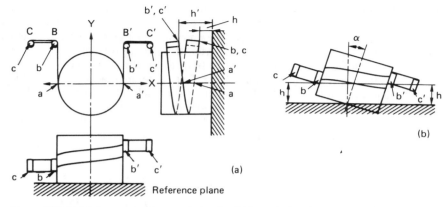

Figure 8.28 At (a) the scanner has a vertical axis which results in a height difference and a twist between the entrance plane BC and the exit plane B' C'

At (b) the scanner has been tilted through an angle α such that points b and b' are both at height h

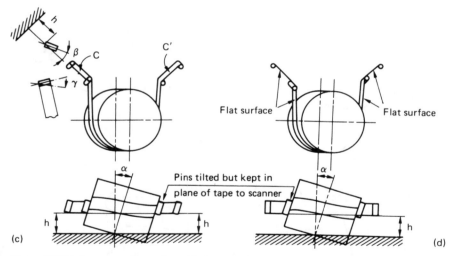

Figure 8.28(c) the wrap angle on the guides nearest the scanner is reduced until the edge of the tape lies in the reference plane. The tape in planes C and C' remains flat. The pins now incline at angle β to the reference surface

At (d) the outer pins can be made vertical if the plane of C and C' is brought perpendicular to the reference surface. This is done by tilting the inner pins but keeping them in the plane of the tape from inner pin to scanner. Tape entry and exit is now coplanar. (Based on drawings courtesy of Sony Broadcast)

In the Sony D-2 transports, the first approach is taken for tape guidance. Fig. 8.28(a) shows tape wrapping a drum, with the usual elevation difference between entrance and exit. In (b) the drum has been tilted so that entrance and exit guides are at the same height. The tape now approaches in the wrong plane. It will be found that if the wrap angle on the entry and exit guides is reduced, an angle can be found where the tape enters and leaves in the plane of the cassette, as shown in (c). At this stage the tape is in the cassette plane, but its surface is not at right angles to that plane, it is leaning over. The entry and exit guides are now tilted in the plane of the tape tangential to the drum until the tape feeding them is at right angles to the cassette plane, as in (d). In this way, the tape is not subjected to any twisting as it always remains planar. The same approach is used in the RDAT transports built by Sony. The coplanar approach allows a very shallow transport construction which is highly suitable for portable operation.

Fig. 8.29 shows the second approach used in the Sony D-1 transport. This uses an extended wrap angle in order to reduce the frequencies at the heads. The

Figure 8.29 In the Sony D-1 transport an extended wrap is used, and guides move on both sides of the scanner to create the wrap. Tape begins the helix below the cassette plane and ends the scan above it. This contrasts with the Ampex approach where the tape begins the helix far below the cassette plane and ends in the cassette plane

previous approach is difficult to use with an extended wrap. The drum axis is vertical and tape is led down from the supply reel to the drum entrance. Tape then climbs up the drum ramp, and is led down once more to the cassette plane.

Fig. 8.30 shows the arrangement of the Panasonic D-3 and D-5 machines which use the third method. Tape stays in the plane of the cassette on the supply side and the drum is angled to receive it. Tape leaving the drum is manipulated back to the cassette plane.

Fig. 8.31 shows arrangement (d) which is used in Ampex D-2 and DCT transports. Here the drum is angled so that tape leaves it in the plane of the take-

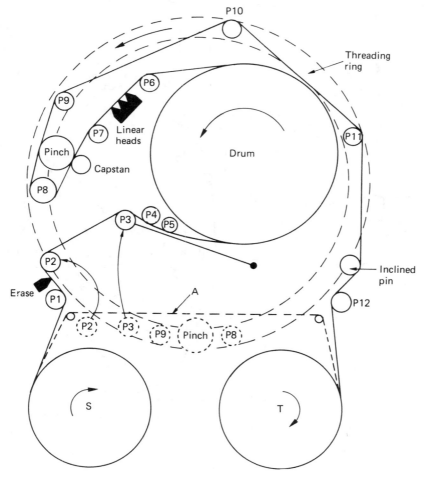

Figure 8.30 Threading sequence of Panasonic D-3 transport. When cassette is first loaded, tape runs straight between the cassette pins (dotted line shown at A) in front of the moving guide pins P2, P3, P9, P8 and the pinch roller. Guides P2 and P3 wrap the entry side by swinging on arms. P3 is in fact the tension arm. The pinch roller and its guides travel anticlockwise on the large threading ring. As the ring rotates P10 and P11 guide the return loop. The inclined pin hinges over the edge of the tape and does not need to be in the cassette mouth at threading start

Figure 8.31 Fixed head guide swings out, and capstan guides swing in. Tension arms extend. Then drum and intermediate guides complete scanner wrap

If the scanner guides are not operated, tape can be transported past stationary heads for timecode striping or prepositioning tape without scanner wear

up reel. All manipulation is then done between the supply reel and the drum entry.

Various methods exist to achieve the helical displacement of the tape. Some VTR transports have used conical posts, but these have the disadvantages that there is a considerable lateral force against the edge of the tape, and that they

Twist   Twist

Guides can
rotate and can
have flanges

(a)

No twist

Guides
cannot rotate
cannot have
flanges

(b)

Figure 8.32 The contradictions of shifting the tape plane in helical scan. If the tape is twisted, the guides can rotate. If it is not, they cannot. Long gentle twist is good, but not compact enough for portable use

cannot be allowed to revolve or the tape would climb off them. Angled pins do not suffer side force, but again cannot be allowed to revolve. The friction caused by non-rotating pins can be reduced by air lubrication from a compressor, as used in Ampex transports, or by vibrating them ultrasonically with a piezoelectric actuator, as is done in certain Sony transports.

In the Ampex D-2 and DCT transports, the tape in the plane of the cassette is slightly twisted on a long run, and then passes around a conventional guide which causes it to leave the cassette plane at an angle. The twist is too small to approach the elastic limit of the tape, which is quite unharmed. A second guide set at the same angle as the drum axis passes the tape to the drum.[1] Fig. 8.32 contrasts the tape twist and angled guide methods.

The threading process will be considered using two different transports as examples.

In the Panasonic D-3/D-5 transports, as with any VCR, the guides start inside the cassette and move to various positions as threading proceeds. The sequence can be followed in Fig. 8.30. The entry side threading is performed by guide P2 which swings anticlockwise on an arm to wrap the tape onto fixed guide P1 and the full-width erase head and by the tension arm guide P3 which swings clockwise to bring the tape across the drum entry guides P4 and P5. The drum wrapping and exit side threading are performed by guides which move in a circular path on a threading ring which rotates around the drum and capstan. When the cassette is initially lowered, guide P8, the pinch roller and guide P9 are inside the front run of tape. As the threading ring turns anticlockwise, these guides take a loop of tape from the cassette and begin to wrap it around the drum. As the threading ring proceeds further, guide P10 and then guide P11 come into contact with the return loop, and the leading guide completes the wrap of the drum and wraps fixed exit guide P6, the fixed heads, fixed capstan guide P7 and the capstan. The pinch roller completes its travel by locating in a cage which is operated by the pinch solenoid. It is no longer supported by the threading ring.

The Ampex ¾ inch transport is designed for rapid threading and unthreading without tape damage, and particular care was taken to ensure that the tape path geometry is perfect, not just when threaded, but at all times during the threading process. The threading sequence can be followed in Fig. 8.33 and Fig. 8.29.

The permanently engaged capstan fits inside the cassette throat. A short movement of the tape guides allows the tape to wrap the capstan and the stationary timecode/erase head. This is known as coplanar mode, which means that the tape path is still entirely in the plane of the tape reels. In this mode tape can be shuttled at high speed, and it is possible to erase and timecode-stripe without causing wear to the rotary-head assembly. Timecode can also be read to position a tape without rotary-head wear.

For functions involving the rotary heads, the threading process proceeds further. There are two guides which primarily control threading the tape around the drum. The drum guide moves in a circular path on a threading ring which rotates concentric with the drum. This guide begins its motion on the wrong side of the tape, but as the threading ring turns, the guide pops up and engages the back of the tape. Then as the threading ring rotates further, the guide is slowly lowered along the drum axis at the correct rate by a cam, such that the tape is laid onto the drum at the helix angle. When the drum guide reaches the end of its travel, its supporting shaft comes up against a fixed vee-block which positions it repeatably. It is held in contact with the block by a solenoid.

The intermediate guide is designed to move away from the cassette as the drum guide proceeds around the threading ring, and the tilt angle of this guide, which imparts the tape twist, is changed as it moves so that a cylindrical wrap is always maintained. This guide is mounted on three vee-shaped rollers which are

Figure 8.33 Ampex D-2 transport with cassette just lowered on to drive hubs. Note permanently engaged capstan in cassette throat

preloaded outwards and ride in a matching slot in the deckplate. The tilt of the guide is controlled by a spherical roller on an extension of the guide shaft, which bears against a cam profile below the guide track. The principle is shown in Fig. 8.34. All of the cam profiles which achieve these operations were computer generated.

Since the total guide wrap angle of cassette transports inevitably amounts to several revolutions, tension build-up is often a problem. In this transport, all tape guides are lubricated by compressed air, except for the tilting threading guide, which is a roller. The drum guide has to travel a long distance, and it is difficult to provide a permanent air supply. The air feed is through the solenoid locking arm, so that air supply becomes available when the tape is fully threaded.

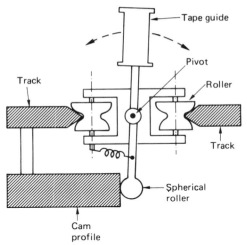

Figure 8.34 The spherical roller and cam profile tilt the tape guide axis to the correct angle as threading proceeds. Tape geometry can then be perfect at all points in the threading

8.19 Operating modes of a digital recorder

The digital video recorder is expected to do much more than record and replay in a modern installation. The main operating modes will be examined here, followed by the more obscure modes.

In *crash record* the tape is either blank or is considered to be blank, and no reference will be made to any previous information on the tape. As with analog video recorders, if a crash recording is made in the middle of an existing recording, the playback will lose lock at the transition.

In this mode the full-width erase head will be active, and the entire tape format will be laid down, including audio blocks and control track.

There are a fixed number of segments in a field, and so the drum speed will be locked to incoming video. The drum phase will be determined by the delay needed to shuffle and encode the data in a segment. Owing to the encoding delay, the recording heads on the drum will begin tracing a segment some time after the beginning of the input field. The capstan will simply rotate at constant speed, driving the tape at the speed specified in the format. As the rotating heads begin a diagonal track, a segment pulse will be recorded in the control track. Once per field, the segment pulse will be accompanied by a field pulse. There will also be a colour frame pulse recorded at appropriate intervals.

8.20 Colour-framed playback

In colour framed playback, the number of frames played from the tape will be equal to the number of station reference frames. Ordinary framing requires that the segmentation on tape is properly undone, so that all of the segments in one field are assembled together, and that the interlace sequence is synchronous with reference, so that an odd field comes from tape when there is an odd field in the station reference. In colour framing, the offtape field must also be the same type of field in the four- or eight-field sequence as exists in the reference.

The error-correction and de-interleaving processes on replay require a finite time in which to operate, and so the transport must play back segments ahead of real time, in the same way that analog machines play back ahead of real time for timebase-correction purposes. The drum speed will be synchronous with reference, and the drum phase will be determined by the decoding delay.

The capstan system will be responsible for tracking and framing, and will need to vary the speed of the tape until framing is achieved. It will then vary the phase of the tape to optimize tracking.

The capstan and tape form part of a phase-locked loop where the phase of the control track pulses is compared with reference pulses. In order to achieve colour framing, the phase comparison must be between reference colour frame pulses and offtape colour frame pulses. In this way the linear motion of the tape is phased such that reference and offtape framing are the same. The capstan speed must vary during this part of the lock-up sequence, and the picture may be temporarily degraded unless the machine has provision for operating at non-normal speed.

Once framing is achieved, the capstan will switch to a different mode in order to obtain accurate tracking. The phase comparison will now be between offtape segment pulses and pulses generated by the rotation of the drum. If the phase error between these is used to modify the capstan drive, the error can be eliminated, since the capstan drives the tape which produces the control track segment pulses. Eliminating this timing error results in the rotating heads following the tape tracks properly. Artificially delaying or advancing the reference pulses from the drum will result in a tracking adjustment.

8.21 Assembly editing

In an assemble edit, new material is appended to an existing recording in such a way that the video timing structure continues unbroken over the edit point. In a composite recording, the subcarrier phase will also need to be continuous.

The recording will begin at a vertical interval, and it will be necessary to have a preroll in order to synchronize tape and drum motion to the signal to be recorded. The procedure during the preroll is similar to that of framed playback, except that the input video timing is used. The goal of the preroll process is to ensure that the record head is at the beginning of the first segment in a field exactly one encode delay after the beginning of the desired field in the input video signal. At this point the record head will be turned on. After the assemble point, there will not necessarily be a control track, and the capstan must smoothly enter constant speed mode without a disturbance to tape motion. The control track will begin to record in a continuation of the phase of the existing control track. This process will then continue indefinitely until halted.

8.22 Insert editing

An insert differs from an assemble in that a short part of a recording is replaced by new material somewhere in the centre. An insert can only be made on a tape which has a continuous control track, because the in- and out-point edits must both be synchronous. The preroll will be exactly as for an assemble edit, and the video record process will be exactly the same, but the capstan control will be achieved by playing back the control track at all times, so that the new video tracks are laid down in exactly the same place as the previous recording. At the out-point, the record heads will be turned off at the end of the last segment in a field.

As the tracks used in DVTRs are so narrow, some thought has to be given to the results of mechanical tolerances when edits are performed. In transports with no flying erase, the record-head width is typically 10% larger than the track width, to ensure full overwrite. As a result a correctly aligned insert edit leaves a track which is slightly narrower than normal at the out-point. This is not a serious problem as the result of a narrow track is that the signal-to-noise ratio is a little less, so the error-correction system works harder.

There is, however, a potential problem if repeated edits are made in the same area of a recording. Fig. 8.35(a) shows the effect of making a second insert edit on top of an earlier edit at the same frame addresses. The second edit is performed with a small tracking error. At the beginning of the insert, the effect is to make the last track of the previous recording slightly less than its normal width, but this is not a problem. However, at the end of the insert, the previous last track is not completely overwritten, and an unwanted *sliver track* of the same azimuth type as the wanted track is left. This will cause a serious reduction in signal quality on playback. The problem is overcome in studio transports by making the record heads the same width as the track pitch and using a flying

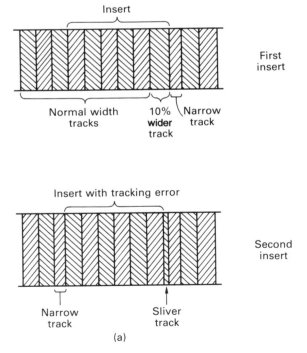

(a)

Figure 8.35 (a) Inaccurate insert edit leaves sliver of previous track which causes errors erase head which is slightly wider than the recorded segment. Fig. 8.35(b) shows that in D-3 the flying erase head is physically positioned in advance of the record heads by virtue of a higher elevation in the scanner and an angular advance of about 210°. Thus the erase head for a particular record-head pair is on the opposite side of the scanner. The timing of the erase current must be shifted by the 210° advance angle so that erasing begins in the correct place on the tape.

The use of the erase head results in a guard band being created before the first segment of the insert and after the last segment, as in Fig. 8.35(c), but not between segments as would happen if the erase head were immediately in front of the record head. The erase head is slightly wider than the width of two tracks or one segment.

The result of the guard bands is that slight mispositioning during an edit now results in the slight noise from an erased guard band being read instead of a coherent signal. Mispositioning during a repeat insert edit merely increases the width of the guard band at one end of the insert.

The flying erase heads will also be used for a short period at the beginning of an assemble edit until the tape erased by the full-width stationary erase head has reached the scanner.

Figure 8.35 continued Rotary erase head at (b) is positioned to leave 2 μm guard band at beginning and end of insert as shown at (c). Guard band partially erases sliver track, reducing error rate

8.23 Tape speed override

One of the most useful features of a production recorder is the ability to operate at variable speed. The variable-speed modes variously available are TSO (Tape Speed Override), slow motion/jog and shuttle.

In TSO, the speed is only changed by a maximum of 15% from normal in order to trim a programme to fit a broadcast time slot. Clearly the audio must be fully recovered, and so no replay-head jumping is permissible. The speed of the entire transport is changed by changing the transport timing reference with respect to station reference. The drum and the capstan change speed in proportion so that the heads still follow the helical tracks properly. All of the audio blocks are recovered, and full-quality digital audio is output. Owing to the speed change, the audio sampling rate will not be exactly 48 kHz, and a digital pitch changer or sampling-rate converter can be used if necessary. Clearly the offtape field rate will no longer match reference, and the difference is accommodated by a frame store/timebase corrector, which is written at offtape speed and read at reference speed. Fields will occasionally be skipped or repeated as TBC addresses lap one another.

In slow motion or jog, it is not normal to recover the audio fully, since it will only be needed for cueing, and so the track-following head system comes into operation. Where audio is recovered, it will contain discontinuities.

8.24 Variable-speed replay

The variable-speed range of analog machines has essentially become the yardstick by which competing formats will be measured. It is important for the success of DVTRs that at least an equal speed range is available and the means to obtain this will be discussed here. Although the problem of variable speed is defined by the format, the solutions adopted by various manufacturers are quite different and will be contrasted.

It was seen in Section 8.3 that the movement of the tape results in the tracks having an angle different from the helix angle. The rotary head will only be able to follow the track properly if the tape travels at the correct speed. At all other speeds, the head will move at an angle to the tracks. If the head is able to move along the drum axis as it turns, it will be possible to follow whole tracks at certain speeds by moving the head as a function of the rotational angle of the drum. The necessary function can be appreciated by considering the situation when the tape is stopped. The tape track will, of course, be at the track angle, but the head will rotate at the helix angle. The head can be made to follow a stationary track by deflecting it at constant rate by one segment pitch per sweep. In other words, a ramp or triangle waveform is necessary to deflect the head. The slope of the ramp is proportional to the speed *difference*, since at normal speed the difference is zero and no deflection is needed. Clearly the deflection cannot continue to grow for ever, because the head will run out of travel, and it must then jump to miss out some tracks and reduce the deflection.

There are a number of issues to be addressed in providing a track following system. The use of segmented formats means that head jumps necessary to omit or repeat one or more fields must jump over several segments. This requires a mechanical head-positioning system which has the necessary travel and will work reliably despite the enormous acceleration experienced at the perimeter of

Figure 8.36 Head deflection waveform for PAL D-3 at +3× normal speed. This requires a jump of two fields between every field played, and this corresponds to eight tracks. Since head pairs trace the tape alternately, the head has half a revolution in which to jump, so the actual jump is only six tracks. However, the vertical position of the above waveform is subject to an uncertainty of plus or minus two tracks because capstan phase is random during variable speed

the drum. As there are generally two head bases, two such systems are needed, and they must be independently controlled since they are mounted in opposition on the drum and contact the tape alternately. Also required is a control system which will ensure that jumps only take place at the end of a field to prevent a picture from two different fields being displayed.

The degree of accuracy required is much higher than in analog formats because the tracks are much narrower.

When the tape speed is close to three times normal, most of the time a two-field jump will be necessary at the end of every field. Fig. 8.36 shows the resulting ramp deflection waveform (for one head pair only). Since the control track phase is random, an offset of up to ±½ field will be superimposed on the deflection, so that if a two-field jump must always be possible, a total deflection of three fields must be available. This, along with the segmentation employed, determines the mechanical travel of the heads.

8.25 The actuator

In Sony and Panasonic machines, the actuator used for head deflection is based on piezoelectric elements as used in numerous previous products. Fig. 8.37 shows the construction of the Sony dynamic tracking head. A pair of parallel piezoelectric bimorphs are used, to ensure that head zenith is affected as little as possible by deflection. The basic principle of the actuator is that an applied voltage causes the barium titanate crystal to shrink. If two thin plates are bonded together to create a bimorph, the shrinkage of one of them will result in bending. A stale sandwich displays the same effect. Application of a voltage to one or other of the elements allows deflection in either direction, although care must be taken to prevent reverse voltage being applied to an element since this will destroy the inherent electric field. In view of the high-g environment, which attempts to restore the actuator to the neutral position, high deflection voltages are necessary. The deflection amplifiers are usually static, and feed the drum via slip rings which are often fitted on the top of the drum. When worn, these can spark and increase the error rate. Piezoelectric actuators display hysteresis, and some form of position feedback is necessary to allow a linear system. This is obtained by strain gauges which are attached to one of the bimorphs, and can be seen in the figure. When power is first applied to the transport, the actuator is

Figure 8.37 The dynamic tracking head of a Sony D-2 transport uses a pair of parallel bimorphs to maintain head zenith angle. Note use of strain gauges for feedback. (Courtesy Sony Broadcast)

supplied with a gradually decaying sinusoidal drive signal, which removes any unwanted set from the bimorph.

In Ampex D-2 and DCT machines, the piezoelectric actuator was not considered adequate for the larger travel demanded in a segmented format,[2] and a moving-coil actuator has been developed. These had been used experimentally in certain analog recorders, but gave way to piezoelectric actuators in the C-format. Now that rare earth magnets are available, which offer high field strength with low mass, the moving-coil actuator becomes attractive again, because it allows a low-mass cantilever which has higher resonant frequencies and requires less force to deflect. The moving coil is inherently a low-impedance device requiring a current drive which is easier to provide than the high voltages needed by piezoelectric devices.

Fig. 8.38(a) shows the concept of the moving-coil head and Fig. 8.38(b) shows the appearance of the actual unit used in D-2. The cantilever is folded from thin sheet metal which is perforated to assist the folding process. The resulting structure is basically a torsion box supported on a wide flexural pivot. This means that it can bend up and down, but it cannot twist, since twisting would introduce unwanted azimuth errors. The cantilever carries the actuator coil, and is supported in a metal shoe which carries the magnet.

Positional feedback of the cantilever deflection is obtained by a photoelectric system. This has one light source and two sensors between which moves a blade

Figure 8.38 (a) Showing the concept of moving-coil head deflection. The cantilever is flexurally pivoted at the opposite end to the heads, and position feedback is obtained from a vane on the cantilever which differentially varies the light falling on two photosensors. (b) The appearance of an actual replaceable AST head assembly. (Courtesy Ampex)

which is integral with the cantilever. When the cantilever deflects, a differential signal results from the sensors. The photoelectric sensor is mounted inside the top of the drum, and automatically aligns with the moving blade when the top is fitted.

For the DCT format a similar actuator was developed, but having a parallel action to maintain constant head zenith angle.

Whichever of these actuators is used, the combination of actuator, drive amplifier and position feedback gives a subassembly which will deflect the head in proportion to an applied voltage. It is then necessary to provide suitable drive signals to ensure that the deflection makes the head follow the track.

8.26 Detecting the tracking error

Track following is a means of actively controlling the relationship between the replay head and the track so that the track is traced more accurately than it would be by purely mechanical means.

This can be applied to systems operating at normal speed, in order to allow interchange in adverse conditions as is done in Digital Betacam, but in many formats track following is an option, and satisfactory interchange can be achieved without it.

The tracking error will be used on two different levels. Firstly, the DC component of the tracking error will be used to set the average elevation of the head about which the ramp deflection will take place. Secondly, variations of tracking error during the track can be used to compensate for tracks which are not straight, due to some relative misalignment between the machine which recorded the tape and the player. The tracking-error-detection systems differ between manufacturers and these differences will be noted.

Fig. 8.39 shows three relationships of the head to the track, and the corresponding signal output. The waveforms in Fig. 8.39 correspond to the RF envelope of the channel-coded signal. Case (a) and case (c) display the same

Figure 8.39 Effect of tracking error on playback signal. Signal amplitude in (a) and (c) is identical, despite sense of tracking error. Maximum signal occurs with correct alignment as in (b)

output, although the tracking error has the opposite sense. Simple processing of the RF level only gives the magnitude of the error, not the sense.

In order to extract the sense of the tracking error, it is necessary to move the tracking head, to see if the error becomes greater or smaller. The process of manually tuning an AM radio is very similar.

In the Sony machines, the head elevation is changed by small steps between segments, and if the steps cause the average RF level to fall, the direction of the steps is reversed. This process is known colloquially as 'bump and look', and was originally developed for the Betacam products.

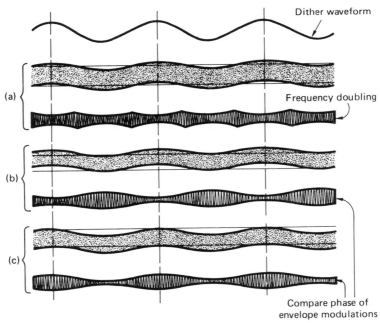

Figure 8.40 Top, dither waveform which causes head to oscillate across track. At (a) is optimum alignment, showing frequency doubling in RF envelope. With head above track centre, as in (b), RF amplitude increases as head reaches lowest point, whereas reverse applies in case (c)

In the Ampex machines, the head is subject to a sinusoidal oscillation or dither, as was done in C-format machines. One field scan contains many cycles of dither. The effect on the RF envelope, as shown in Fig. 8.40, is an amplitude modulation of the carrier, which has little effect on the video, owing to the insensitivity of the digital recording system to amplitude effects. Fig. 8.40(a) shows that the effect of dither on a correctly aligned head is a frequency doubling in the RF envelope. Figs.8.40(b) and (c) show the effect of the head off track. Both cases appear similar, but the phase of the envelope modulation is different, and can be used to extract the sense of the tracking error.

Each cantilever carries two heads, one of each azimuth type, and the RF levels from the two heads are averaged together. This gives a 3 dB improvement in signal-to-noise ratio, as well as accommodating manufacturing tolerances in the elevation of the video tips. Only one detector or synchronous rectifier is then required per cantilever.

Dither cannot be used with analog VTRs employing azimuth recording because the transverse head motion interacts with the azimuth angle to give the effect of rising and falling head-to-tape speed. In FM recording, this introduces an unwanted signal into the video, which is why Sony developed the bump and look system for Betacam. The effect is still present in a digital recorder, but the result is that the instantaneous offtape data rate rises and falls slightly. This is accommodated by the phase-locked loop in the data separator, and has no effect

Figure 8.41 The tracking error is extracted from the RF envelope by a phase-sensitive rectifier

on the data. A harmless dither component will be observed in the VCO control voltage, and the speed variation in the discrete data is completely removed in the timebase correction.

In Fig. 8.41 the RF is detected to obtain a level which is fed to a phase-sensitive rectifier whose reference is the dither drive signal. The output of the phase-sensitive rectifier is a tracking error signal which contains both magnitude and sense and rather a lot of harmonics of dither. Careful choice of the dither frequency allows easier cancelling of the dither harmonics. In the VPR-300, there are five and a half cycles of dither per segment, or 11 cycles per revolution. Both heads are dithered by the same waveform, which means that the dither on odd segments will be phase reversed with respect to even segments. A dither frequency of 1100 Hz results in PAL, whereas in NTSC it is 990 Hz.

The tracking error is averaged over a pair of segments to cancel the harmonics and to produce an elevation error. The tracking error will also be sampled at several points down the track to see if there is a consistent curvature in the tracking. This can be reduced by adding a correction curve to the deflection waveform which will adjust itself until the best envelope is obtained over the whole track length.

Figure 8.42 In the Sony D-2 DT system the tracking error is detected by comparing the times at which sync patterns are detected by the two heads on each arm. Owing to the use of azimuth recording a component of transverse movement results in a movement of the effective position of the head along the track

A different approach to measuring track curvature is used in Sony and Panasonic transports. As has been stated, deflecting a head which uses azimuth recording causes timing changes. If a pair of heads of opposite azimuth are tracing the appropriate tracks, tracking error will result in differential timing changes. This can be measured by comparing the time at which sync patterns are detected in the two channels. Fig. 8.42 illustrates the principle. This system will detect tracking errors due to track distortion. Unfortunately, manufacturing tolerances in the physical stagger between the heads on both the machine which made the recording and the player will combine to put a permanent offset in the tracking error derived using this principle. It is necessary to calibrate the system each time it is used. The bump and look system maximizes the RF level at the beginning of the track, and the control system then inserts a changing offset into the sync timing comparator until it too gives zero tracking error at the beginning of the track. The offset is then held at that value. This process removes the static deflection and allows the tracking error to be used to deflect the heads within the track.

8.27 The ramp generator

The positional feedback generated by the observation of the dithered RF envelope or the sync pattern phase is not sufficiently accurate to follow the tracks unassisted except at normal speed where it can be used as an interchange aid. In variable speed the deflection of the head is predicted to produce a feedforward signal which adds to the head deflection. The feedback then only has to correct for the difference between the feedforward and the actuality. When the tape travels at the wrong speed, the track angle changes, and so the head needs to deflect by a distance proportional to the angle it has rotated in order to follow the track. The deflection signal will be in the form of a ramp, which becomes steeper as the tape speed deviates more from normal. The actual speed of the capstan can be used to generate the slope of the ramp. One possible implementation of this is shown in Fig. 8.43. A counter has count-up and count-down inputs. The first of these is driven by the capstan tacho disk, and the second is driven by a clock whose frequency is exactly equal to that generated by the capstan tacho at normal speed. When the capstan runs at normal speed, the counter receives as many up clocks as down clocks, and remains unchanged. However, if the capstan speed is raised, the counter will begin to count up at a rate proportional to the speed difference. The counter drives a DAC which produces the deflection ramp. The RF amplitude detector will generate pulses which are also fed into the counter so that the elevation correction can be made. It is also possible to predict the average or static deflection of the heads from the control track phase. The capstan frequency generator can be used to measure control track phase. The capstan FG wheel will be designed so that a known number of FG pulses are generated when the capstan transports the tape by the distance between control track segment pulses. The FG pulses are fed to a counter which is reset by segment pulses from the control track head. The counter then produces control track phase which can be used to establish head elevation.

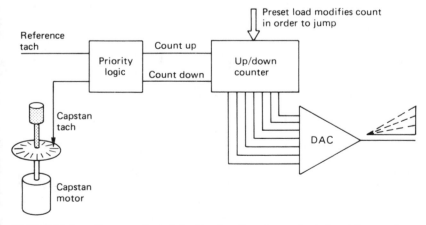

Figure 8.43 An up/down counter is fed with pulses from the capstan tach and from a reference whose frequency is precisely that of capstan tach at normal speed. The counter will thus integrate speed deviation from unity, and the DAC will produce a ramp whose slope is proportional to speed difference. This is the feedforward signal which drives the head deflection system

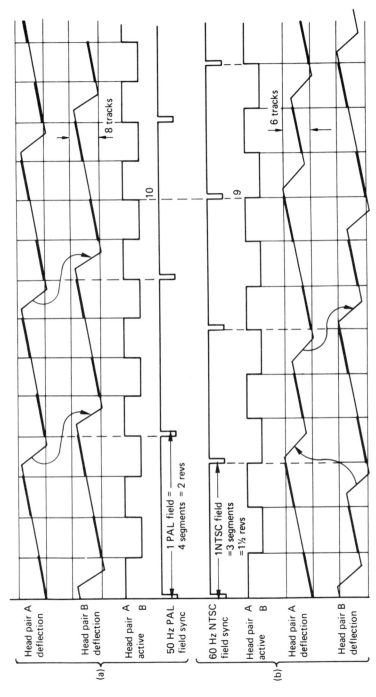

Figure 8.44 The timing and deflections necessary at a speed of +2× in D-2 for (a) PAL and (b) NTSC. Note the segment ratio of 9:10 between the two formats, which is also the ratio of scanner speeds. In order to play entire fields, jumps must take place about the field boundary, so that if one head pair jumps, the other must follow (serpentine arrow). In NTSC there are three segments per field, so the jumping follows a two-field sequence, where the head fails to jump in one field, but jumps twice in the next

The same deflection ramp slope will be fed to both head pairs so that they will read alternate segments for an entire field. At some point it will be necessary to jump the heads to reduce the deflection, and this requires some care. The heads are 180° opposed, and contact the tape alternately. The jump takes place while the head is out of contact with the tape. The two head pairs will have to jump at different times, half a drum revolution apart. Clearly if one head jumps, the second head must also jump, otherwise the resulting picture will have come from two fields. As the jumps are half a revolution apart, it follows that the decision to jump must be made half a drum revolution *before* the end of the current field. The decision is made by extrapolating the deflection ramp forward to see what the deflection *will be* when the end of the field is reached. If the deflection will exceed half a field, it can be reduced by jumping one field. If the deflection will exceed one field, it can be reduced by jumping two fields. The jump can be executed by adding or subtracting a number of pulses in the ramp counter.

Tape tension changes can cause the track width to vary minutely. This is normally of no consequence, but when taken over all of the tracks in a segment the error may be significant. It is possible to compare the tracking error before and after a jump, and if the error becomes greater, the jump distance was inappropriate for the tape being played. It is possible to modify the distance jumped simply by changing the number of pulses fed to the ramp counter during the jump command. In this way the jump distance can optimize itself for the tape being played.

Fig. 8.44(a) shows the ramping action for the two moving heads in PAL D-2 or D-3 with the tape moving at twice normal speed. It will be seen that when one head jumps, the other one will also jump, so both heads always play the same field. The timing shift due to the heads being separated by half a revolution can be seen. As there are four segments per field in PAL, corresponding to two drum revolutions, all fields will contain the same sequence. Fig. 8.44(b) shows the equivalent sequence of events for NTSC. As there are three segments per field and two moving heads, the action differs between odd fields and even fields. During one field, a given head may jump twice, but in the next field it will not jump at all.

8.28 Track-following block diagram

Fig. 8.45 shows an Ampex D-2/DCT track-following system. There is an inner feedback loop which consists of the head actuator, the position feedback sensor and an amplifier. This loop is a position servo which makes the head deflection proportional to the input voltage. Like any position servo it is provided with compensation to prevent oscillation and maximize frequency response. The inner loop is driven by the sum of four signals. These are:

(1) The dither signal, which is a sinusoid designed to wobble the head either side of its average elevation.
(2) The elevation correction obtained by averaging the tracking error over the entire track.
(3) The track curvature compensation which is a segment rate curve obtained by sampling the tracking error at several points along the track.
(4) The feedforward ramp and jump signal. The slope is obtained from capstan speed difference and the jumps are initiated by analysing the deflection.

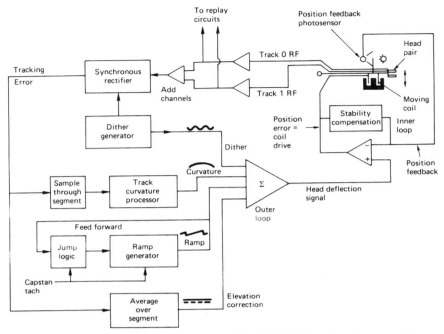

Figure 8.45 Ampex D-2 track-following system. Position feedback in an inner loop around the head positioner linearizes and damps positioner so that mechanical deflection is proportional to head deflection signal from outer loop. Dither generator wobbles the head and drives synchronous receiver to obtain tracking error which is used to correct the head elevation and to compensate for track curvature. Feedforward system generates ramps

Fig. 8.46 shows the track-following system used by Sony and Panasonic. The capstan FG and control track are used together for elevation prediction, and capstan FG is used alone for ramp slope prediction. The bump and look system is controlled by the RF detector, which is also used to calibrate the differential sync pattern timing detector.

In both types of machine, there are two moving heads and so two of these systems are necessary. They are largely independent except for a common jump control system which ensures that when one head jumps during the last segment of a field the other head will follow once it has played that segment.

When a head jumps, it will move to a track which began at a different place along the tape, and so the timing in that track will not be the same as in the track which the head left. In a segmented format, the effect is magnified by the number of tracks in a field. To support a speed range from $-1\times$ to $+3\times$, it has been seen that an overall head travel of three fields is necessary. From the start of a given segment to the start of the same segment three fields away is nearly 8 mm in PAL D-2, and over 6.5 mm in NTSC D-2. The wrap of the scanner must be extended to allow tape contact over a greater angle, and the replay circuitry must be able to accommodate the timing uncertainty which amounts to about 5% of the segment period. Clearly the timing error can be eliminated by the timebase-correction processes within the playback system.

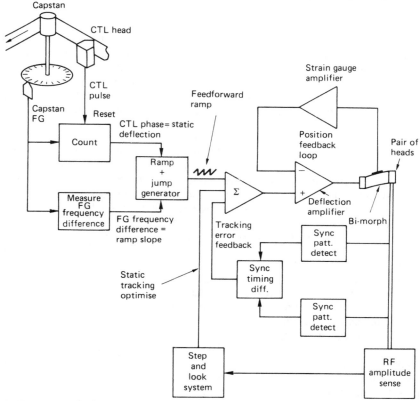

Figure 8.46 The DT system used by Sony D-2 machines combines ramp feedforward from the capstan speed and control track with tracking feedback from the differential sync detection of Fig. 8.42. In addition the bump and look system slightly offsets the heads by a different amount each scan and assesses the RF amplitude to find an optimum static deflection. This is really a slow dither process. Note that this is a conceptual diagram. In practice many of these stages are carried out by microprocessor

8.29 Camcorder transports

One of the greatest difficulties in designing a digital camcorder is obtaining sufficient battery life without excessive weight. A camcorder is impracticable with ¾ inch tape, but quite possible with the ½ inch formats. Most camcorders will be designed to accept only the smallest or perhaps the two smaller sizes of cassette, as this reduces the size of the transport and sufficient battery life is unlikely to be available to record the longest tape.

Compressed-air lubricated or ultrasonic guides are impractical and extensive use will be made of rolling element bearings, where possible, and fixed slant posts. Shuttle speed will be restricted in order to save power and to reduce tape tension.

As the main purpose of a camcorder is signal acquisition, features not essential to this function can be omitted. Simple backspace assembly editing is adequate, and flying erase heads can be dispensed with, reducing noise and power consumption.

8.30 Aligning for interchange

One of the most important aspects of DVTR maintenance is to ensure that tapes made on a particular machine meet the specifications laid down in the format. If they do, then it will be possible to play those tapes on any other properly aligned machine. In this section the important steps necessary to achieve interchange between transports will be outlined. Regular cleaning, particularly of the drum step, is necessary to maintain interchange, and no interchange adjustment should be attempted until it has been verified that the machine is clean.

When the cassette is lowered into the transport it seats on pillars which hold it level. The tape hubs seat on the reel turntables. The first step in aligning the transport is to ensure that the reel hubs and all of the guides the tape runs past on its way to and from the drum are at the correct height. The guides are generally threaded so that they can be screwed up and down. In the correct position, the tape will stay in the cassette plane and distortion will be avoided. The height of the cassette pillars can be adjusted to ensure that the spools inside the cassette are lifted free of the cassette body at the end of the elevator travel. If this is not done the spools will rub against the cassette body, causing debris and tension errors.

Once the tape can be passed through the machine without damage, the basic transport functions can be checked. Since tape tension affects the track angle and the head contact pressure, verifying the correct tension is essential before attempting any adjustments at the drum. This is done with a tape tension gauge. Many tension gauges change their reading as a result of tape motion and it may be necessary to calibrate the gauge whilst moving the tape and calibration weight at approximately the correct speed for the format. The tension can then be checked in various transport and shuttle modes. Since the drum friction is in the opposite sense when the tape is reversed, the back tension must be higher than for forward mode to keep the average drum tension constant. In some transports the tension-sensing arm is not statically balanced, and the tape tension becomes a function of the orientation of the machine. In this case the adjustment must be made with the machine in the attitude in which it is to be used.

The track spacing on record is determined by the capstan speed, which must be checked. As the capstan speed will be controlled by a frequency-generating wheel on the capstan shaft, it is generally only necessary to check that the capstan FG frequency is correct in record mode. A scratch tape will be used for this check.

Helical interchange can now be considered. Tape passing around the drum is guided in three ways. On the approach, the tape is steered by the entrance guide, which continues to affect the first part of the drum wrap. The centre part of the drum wrap is guided by the machined step on the drum base. Finally the last part of the wrap is steered by the exit guide. Helical interchange is obtained by adjusting the entrance and exit guide heights so that the tape passes smoothly between the three regions.

As tape is flexible, it will distort as it passes round the drum if the entrance and exit guides are not correctly set. The state of alignment can be assessed by working out the effect of misalignments on the ability of the replay head to follow tape tracks. Fig. 8.47(a) shows an example of the entrance guide being too low. The tape is forced to climb up to reach the drum step, and then it has to bend down again to run along the step. If straight tracks were originally recorded on

Figure 8.47 The effects of guide misalignment shown exaggerated for clarity. At (a) the entrance guide is too low and forces the tape to flex as it enters the scanner. At (b) the tape relaxes to produce a bent track. At (c) an alignment tape is being played and the transport has bent the tracks. The RF envelope will show different disturbances as the tracking is offset above or below optimum. A correctly aligned transport has an envelope which collapses uniformly as the tracking is offset

the tape, they will no longer be straight when the tape is distorted in this way. Fig. 8.47(b) shows what happens to the track. Since in an azimuth recording machine the head is larger than the track, small distortions of this kind will be undetectable. It is necessary to offset the tracking deliberately so that the effect of the misalignment can be seen. If the head is offset upwards, then the effect will be that the RF signal grows in level briefly at the beginning of the track, giving the envelope an onion-like appearance on an oscilloscope. If the head is offset downwards, the distortion will take the track away from the head path and the RF envelope will be waisted. If the misalignment is in the exit guide, then the envelope disturbances will appear at the right-hand end of the RF envelope. The height of both the entrance and exit guides is adjusted until no disturbance of the RF envelope rectangularity is apparent whatever tracking error is applied. A rough alignment can be performed with a tape previously recorded on a trustworthy machine, but final alignment requires the use of a reference tape.

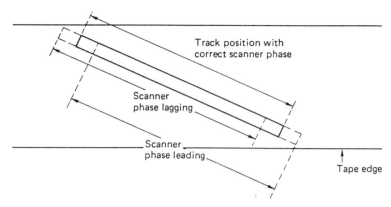

Figure 8.48 Even with correct tape path geometry, a machine can record data in the wrong place along the track if the scanner phase is misadjusted. The scanner pulse generator signal is rephased or delayed in order to make the adjustment

Once the mechanical geometry of the transport is set up, straight tracks on tape will appear straight to the drum, and it is then possible to set up the automatic track-following system so that optimum tracking occurs when the tracking error is zero. This is done by observing the RF level on playback and offsetting the tracking adjustment to each side until two points are found where the level begins to fall. The adjustment is then placed half-way between these points. If the machine has a front panel tracking adjustment, it should be set to zero whilst the internal adjustment is made.

The final interchange adjustment is to ensure that the drum timing is correct. Even with correct geometry, the tracks can be laid down at the correct angle and spacing, but at the wrong height on the tape, as Fig. 8.48 shows. A recording made with this adjustment incorrect may still play, but would cause serious difficulty if insert editing is attempted, particularly of the audio blocks.

The point where recording commences is determined by the sensor which generates a pulse once per revolution of the drum. The correct timing can be obtained either by physically moving the sensor around the drum axis, or by adjusting a variable delay in series with an artificially early fixed sensor. A timing reference tape is necessary that has an observable event in the RF waveform. The tape is played, and the sensor or delay is adjusted to give the specified relative timing between the event on the reference tape and the sensor pulse. When this is correct, the machine will record tracks in the right place along the helical sweep.

References

1. Ryan, D.M., Mechanical considerations in the design of a digital video cassette recorder. Presented at International Broadcasting Convention (Brighton, 1988) *IEE Conf. Publ. No. 293*, 387–390 (1988)
2. Oldershaw, R., Design of an automatic scan tracking system for a D-2 recorder. *IEE Conf. Publ. No. 293*, 395–398 (1988)

The DVTR signal system

The mechanical aspects of the rotary-head DVTR were considered in Chapter 8. The transport simply guides the heads repeatedly along tape tracks so that waveforms can be recorded and replayed. The signal system is responsible for recording and reproducing those waveforms as digital video and audio.

9.1 Introduction

The signal system of a DVTR lies between the signal input/output connectors and the heads, and in production machines is divided into separate record and replay sections so that both processes can take place at the same time.

The data to be recorded are subject to some variation as Fig. 9.1 shows. The input may be composite or component, and data reduction may or may not be

Standard	Lines/field	Pixels/line	Pixels/field	Bit rate
4:2:2 50 Hz	300	720 Y 360 C_r 360 C_b	432 000	173 M bits/s (8 bit) 216 M bits/s (10 bit)
4:2:2 60 Hz	250	720 Y 360 C_r 360 C_b	360 000	173 M bits/s (8 bit) 216 M bits/s (10 bit)
16:9 50 Hz	300	960 Y 480 C_r 480 C_b	576 000	230 M bits/s (8 bit) 288 M bits/s (10 bit)
16:9 60 Hz	250	960 Y 480 C_r 480 C_b	480 000	230 M bits/s (8 bit) 288 M bits/s (10 bit)
$4F_{sc}$ PAL	304	948	288 192	115 M bits/s (8 bit) 144 M bits/s (10 bit)
$4F_{sc}$ NTSC	255	768	195 840	94 M bits/s (8 bit) 117 M bits/s (10 bit)

Figure 9.1 The data to be recorded in DVTR formats are subject to a great deal of variation as shown here

employed. The various DVTR formats largely employ the same processing stages, but there are considerable differences in the order in which these are applied. It is proposed first to define here the processes and then to contrast the formats by the way in which they are applied.

Distribution is shown in Fig. 9.2(a). This is a process of sharing the input bit rate over two or more signal paths so that the bit rate recorded in each is reduced. The data are subsequently recombined on playback. Each signal path requires its own tape track and head. The parallel tracks which result form a *segment*.

Segmentation is shown in Fig. 9.2(b). This is the process of sharing the data resulting from one video field over several segments. The replay system must have some means to ensure that associated segments are reassembled into the original field. This is generally a function of the control track.

Fig. 9.2(c) shows a product code. Data to be recorded are protected by two error-correcting codeword systems at right angles: the inner code and the outer code (see Chapter 6). When it is working within its capacity the error-correction

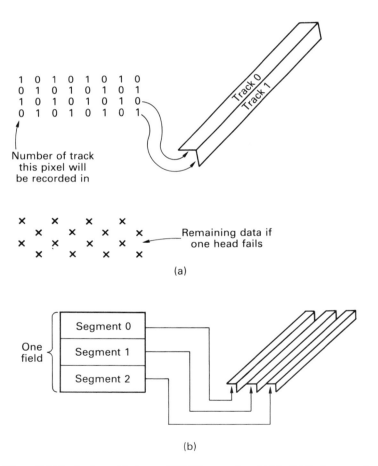

(a)

(b)

Figure 9.2 The fundamental stages of DVTR processing. At (a), distribution spreads data over more than one track to make concealment easier and to reduce the data rate per head

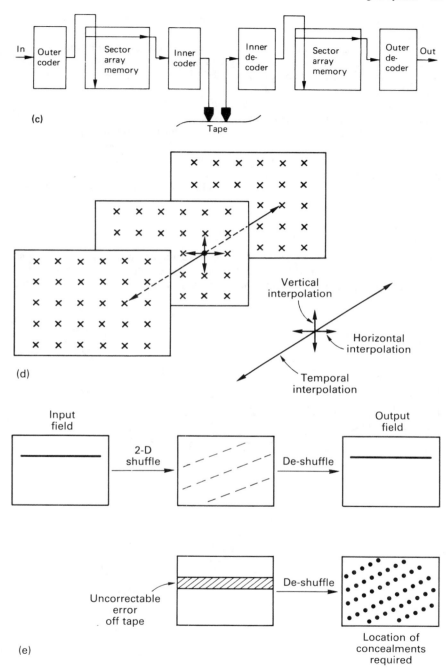

Figure 9.2 continued At (b) segmentation breaks video fields into manageable track lengths. Product codes (c) correct mixture of random and burst errors. Correction failure requires concealment which may be in three dimensions as shown in (d). Irregular shuffle (e) makes concealments less visible

system returns corrupt data to their original value and its operation is undetectable.

If errors are too great for the correction system, concealment will be employed. Concealment is the *estimation* of missing data values from surviving data nearby. Nearby means data on vertical, horizontal or time axes as shown in Fig. 9.2(d). Concealment relies upon distribution, as all tracks of a segment are unlikely to be simultaneously lost, and upon the *shuffle* shown in Fig. 9.2(e). Shuffling reorders the pixels prior to recording and is reversed on replay. The result is that uncorrectable errors due to dropouts are not concentrated, but are spread out by the de-shuffle, making concealment easier. A different approach is required where data reduction is used because the data recorded are not pixels representing a point, but coefficients representing an area of the image. In this case it is the DCT blocks (typically eight pixels across) which must be shuffled.

9.2 Product codes and segmentation

There are two approaches to error correction in segmented recordings. In D-1 and D-2 the approach shown in Fig. 9.3(a) is used. Here, following distribution the input field is segmented first, and then each segment becomes an independent

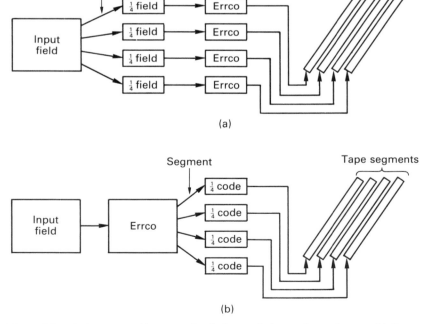

Figure 9.3 Early formats would segment data before producing product codes as at (a). Later formats perform product coding first, and then segment for recording as at (b). This gives more robust performance

shuffled product code. This requires less RAM to implement, but it means that from an error-correction standpoint each tape track is self-contained and must deal alone with any errors encountered.

Later formats, beginning with D-3, use the approach shown in Fig. 9.3(b). Here, following distribution the entire field is used to produce one large shuffled product code in each channel. The product code is then segmented for recording on tape. Although more RAM is required to assemble the large product code, the result is that outer codewords on tape spread across several tracks and redundancy in one track can compensate for errors in another. The result is that the size of a single burst error which can be fully corrected is increased. As RAM is now cheaper than when the first formats were designed, this approach is becoming more common.

9.3 The data to be recorded

The input data rate of a component digital machine can be directly deduced from the CCIR-601 standard. In every active line, 720 luminance samples and 360 of each type of colour difference sample are produced, making a total of 1440 samples per line (see Chapter 7). In 625/50, lines 11–310 and lines 324–623 are recorded, making 300 lines per field, or 1500 lines per second. The D-1 format records these data directly. In 525/60, lines 14–263 and lines 276–525 are recorded, making 250 lines per field, which results in the same data rate of 1500 lines per second.

In both cases the video data rate will be 1500×1440 samples per second, or 2.16 million samples per second. If 18 MHz sampling is used, the data rate will be correspondingly higher.

The actual bit rate recorded will be in excess of the video data rate to take into account the redundancy, the audio and identification codes. Further track space will be required to accommodate preambles and synchronizing patterns.

As the fields in the two line standards contain 300 and 250 lines, it makes a good deal of sense for each segment or track pair to record the highest common multiple, 50 lines, such that a field will comprise either six or five segments. The segment rate will then be 300 Hz in both standards, and since the scanner in a typical transport has two pairs of heads, it will turn at 150 revolutions per second. The transport can be mechanically identical in the two line standards. It should be appreciated that in fact the field rate of the 525 line system is 59.94 Hz, and so the scanner speed (and hence the capstan speed) will be 0.1% slower in the 525 line version. This is of no real consequence to the format, except for some very small dimensional changes, and for simplicity will not be mentioned again in this chapter.

In composite formats the situation becomes more complex. It has been seen from Chapters 3 and 7 that in both line standards, the sampling clock is precisely derived from subcarrier. The very existence of the samples indicates the phase of subcarrier, and so it is not necessary to record the burst. The subcarrier has a mathematical relationship with sync, which can readily be reconstructed on replay, and so it is not necessary to record syncs either.

Accordingly, D-2 and D-3 only record the active line, along with sufficient positioning information so that syncs and burst can be regenerated on replay.

As a result, if a non-standard ScH signal is fed into a composite recorder, standard ScH will be automatically generated on playback.

Both D-2 and D-3 in PAL record 948 samples symmetrically disposed around the unblanked active line, and in NTSC record 768 samples similarly. In each case, sample 0 is defined as the first sample to be recorded in each line. Since not all of the line period is recorded, it then becomes important to ensure that sampling commences in a consistent place on each line of each frame, and that the first sample has a consistent relationship to subcarrier. Clearly the position of the first sample in a line must be on one cycle or another of the sampling clock, and, as has been seen, this is derived from input burst. The edge of the picture is, however, defined by the sync pulse leading edge, and the input stage has to resolve the conflict of sampling at a fixed relationship to H-sync in order to keep the edge of the picture straight with the need to sample coherently with subcarrier. In NTSC this is relatively easy, owing to the simple relationship between subcarrier and sync. It is only necessary to wait a fixed number of sample periods after sync, and the first sample of the active line will be consistently located.

In the PAL system it becomes more complex because of the 25 Hz component of subcarrier. In the absence of 25 Hz, there would be exactly 283¾ cycles per line and exactly 1135 sample clocks per line. Instead, there will be an additional four sample clocks in one frame period.

The H-modulator in the colour framer (see Section 9.14) allows the ScH phase of the input to be established, and this can be used to ensure that the first sample period of line 1 of the eight-field sequence is identified. From then on, the beginning of subsequent lines is deemed to occur 1135 sample periods later. This means that at the end of the frame, the virtual beginning of a line will be a whole cycle of subcarrier early. During the vertical interval, the line count of one line is modified to 1139, and the error is removed for the beginning of the next frame. The first sample of the active line is obtained by counting a whole number of cycles of sampling clock from the virtual beginning of the line.

Using the above mechanisms, samples can be put into memory in a consistent way. Because H-sync was displaced to align it with subcarrier, the picture on tape will be slightly rhombic, but this is of no consequence, because identical circuitry, including an H-modulator, is necessary on the replay side of the machine to generate a read clock from reference subcarrier and to generate a subcarrier coherent read start pulse from reference sync. The picture distortion caused by H-modulating the input sync is cancelled by H-modulating output sync. Fig. 9.4 shows that the unblanked picture lies within the rhombic outline of the recorded area.

In either standard, if the ScH phase of the input changes, the sync pulse will move with respect to the sampling structure, but the system will continue to select the same cycle of subcarrier with which to start the sampling by adapting the measured ScH phase value. If subcarrier phase drifts so much that it inverts, the colour framer cannot reframe if the machine is recording, since this would result in a discontinuous control track. It will be necessary to stay with the same subcarrier cycle which results in a drift of the picture position. If drift continues for an entire cycle, the input stage will need to dump four samples to prevent the picture winding across the screen. This will cause a picture shift.

Not all lines of the field are recorded, and in fact the lines which are recorded vary from one field to the next. This is necessary to allow picture-in-shuttle. The recording is composite and contains an embedded chroma signal. Colour processing is necessary in shuttle to change the phase of the offtape signal to that

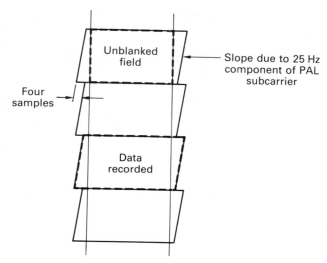

Figure 9.4 In PAL, the data to be recorded are subcarrier locked and result in a rhombic field. The sloping sides are in video blanking and have no ill effect

of reference. When tracks are crossed in shuttle, sync blocks are picked up at random, and a frame store is updated by information which has come from several different fields. This is only possible if samples off tape can be colour processed. The necessary interleave and shuffle processes in a DVTR mean that each sync block contains samples which have come from various places within a field segment. When a frame store is updated in shuttle, successive samples in a given line could have come from a different colour line type, and they would no longer represent the modulation of a continuous subcarrier. The colour processor would not be able to operate.

The solution adopted in D-2 is to record more lines than necessary, so that the first line of each field recorded can change over a four- or eight-field sequence as shown in Fig. 9.5. The choice of the first line to be recorded is made by the input colour framer. This ensures that all fields on tape have the same chroma phase at the same line number, and (in PAL only) to change the position of the first sample recorded in those lines. The choice of the first sample in a field to be recorded is made by the input colour framer. In NTSC, there is only the subcarrier inversion from line to line to consider, and so sampling will begin one line later in alternate frames.

At normal speed and in slow motion, the recorded lines are put back into the correct position in the reference fields, and the normal chroma sequences result, but in shuttle, the colour processor now only needs to know the line number of recovered pixels and they can be correctly processed without knowing the number of the field from which they came. The offset of the line start causes a loss of vertical resolution in shuttle (four lines in PAL, two in NTSC).

D-3 uses the same technique in NTSC, but achieves the same goal in a slightly different way in PAL. Instead of moving the starting line over four lines, a range of two lines is used to handle changes in V-switch in conjunction with a two-pixel horizontal shift which opposes the subcarrier inversion between line pairs. Fig.

9.6(a) shows how the sampling structure results in every field beginning with a $(U–V)$ sample.

The offset of the line start causes a loss of vertical resolution in shuttle of two lines in NTSC and PAL along with a loss of horizontal resolution of two pixels in PAL only, but this is acceptable since resolution falls in shuttle anyway due to movement in the picture.

The raw video data rate which must be sustained by a composite digital recorder can now be derived. For PAL, 948 samples in 304 lines at 50 Hz result in 14 409 600 samples per second, whereas for NTSC, 768 samples in 255 lines at 59.94 Hz result in 11 738 650 samples per second. Each sample is of 8 bit resolution in D-2 and D-3.

Figure 9.5(a) Each field recorded contains 304 lines in PAL D-2, but the actual lines recorded change from field to field so that the fields always begin with the same line type in the PAL sequence. This eases the production of picture-in-shuttle since the colour processor then only needs to know the position in the field, since all fields offtape appear identical

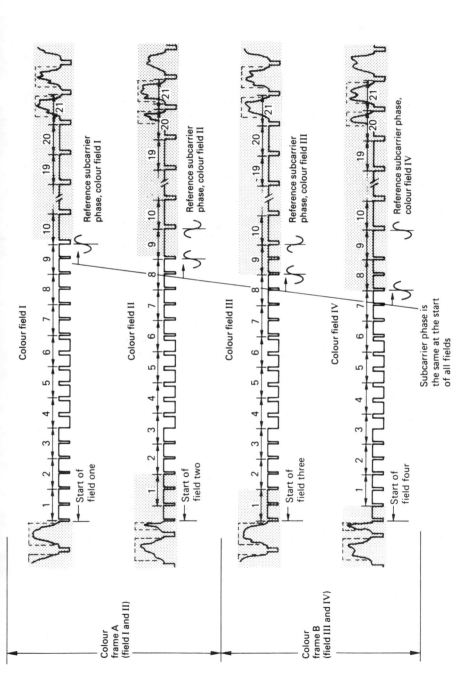

Figure 9.5(b) The recorded lines in NTSC D-2 are shown shaded here. The starting point in each field is chosen so that the subcarrier-phase is the same at the beginning of all fields on tape

Field number	(a) PAL	(b) NTSC
1	Line 8 Sample 1133	Line 9 Sample 0
2	Line 320 Sample 0	Line 8 Sample 0
3	Line 7 Sample 1133	Line 9 Sample 2
4	Line 321 Sample 1133	Line 8 Sample 2
5	Line 8 Sample 0	
6	Line 320 Sample 1133	
7	Line 7 Sample 0	
8	Line 321 Sample 0	

Figure 9.6 Composite sampling requires the first recorded sample to move from field to field to enable picture-in-shuttle with constant colour framing off tape

At (a) combinations of two sample shifts to invert chroma and one line shift to reverse V-switch allow every field on tape to begin with $U - V$ sample in PAL

At (b) NTSC requires only two sample shifts to compensate for inversion of subcarrier from line to line

In practice, these figures will need to be increased somewhat to allow for an error-correction overhead, the presence of addressing or identification codes and for the recording of four audio channels. Additionally, a proportion of each track will be used up with the preambles and sync patterns necessary to the operation of the channel coding, and tolerance gaps needed to allow independent editing of audio and video.

9.4 Distribution

Component formats require three signal components to be recorded in parallel. These components must be distributed between the number of signal channels used. In D-1 and D-5 no data reduction is employed and four signal channels are required. The distribution strategy is based on the requirement for concealment of uncorrected errors. This requires samples from all three video components to be distributed over all four recording channels. If this is done the loss of a channel causes an equal loss to each video component rather than a greater loss concentrated in one component.

Fig. 9.7(a) shows the distribution strategy of D-1 in which the data are distributed over four channels.[1] The distribution is complicated by the fact that the video data consist of pixels which are alternately co-sited Y, C_r, C_b samples and Y-only samples. The goal of the distribution strategy is to permit the best concealment possible in the case of lost sectors, and Fig. 9.7(b) also shows the samples which will be lost if one sector is unrecoverable. Horizontal or vertical interpolation is possible to conceal the missing samples. Fig. 9.7(c) shows the result if two sectors are lost. Samples of both luminance and colour difference are

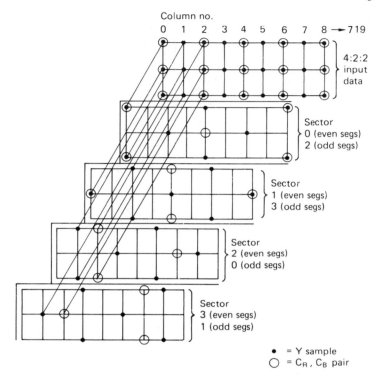

Figure 9.7(a) Distribution of the input 4:2:2 data over four parallel channels is performed as shown here. The criterion is the best concealment ability in case of the loss of one or more channels

Figure 9.7(b) The result of combining the channels when data from sector 1 are lost. Spatial interpolation can be used to restore picture content

Figure 9.7(c) When sectors 0 and 1 are both lost both Y and C_R, C_B are still available at half the normal sampling rate and so effective concealment is still possible

Figure 9.8 D-2 distribution, showing the track number (0 or 1) in which a given sample will be recorded. In PAL (left) there is an even number of lines in the segment so they are all the same. In NTSC there is an odd number, so the distribution reverses from segment to segment in order to maintain the pattern across segment boundaries

still available at one-half of the original sampling rates of each, and so a reduced bandwidth picture can still be produced.

In composite digital formats, data to be recorded are distributed between the two heads which are active at any one time. Fig. 9.8 shows the segmented distribution scheme for D-2 and Fig. 9.9 shows the same scheme applied to D-3 but over entire fields. In both cases the distribution ensures that in both the rows and columns of a field, alternate samples are recorded by a different head. If samples from a given head are lost for any reason, each lost sample is surrounded on four sides by samples from the other head. In the case of complete loss of signal from one head, due perhaps to clogging, it is still possible to produce a picture of reasonable quality from the remaining head because the quality will be as if the picture had originally been sampled at $2 \times F_{sc}$.

Where data reduction is employed, the reduction process takes place directly on the input signal and produces blocks of coefficients. It is these blocks which enter the distribution process. The contents of the DCT blocks cannot be divided because of the requirement of picture-in-shuttle. When a single sync block is recovered in shuttle, it must have all of the coefficients of the DCT blocks it

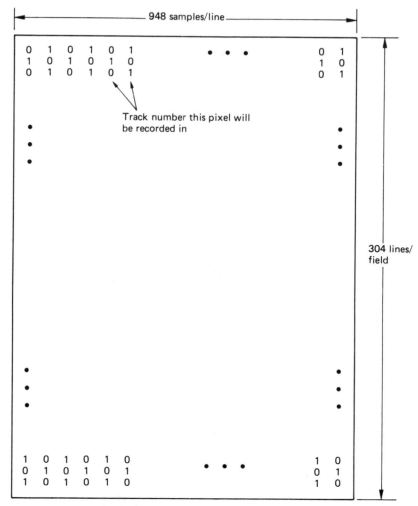

Figure 9.9 Distribution scheme for PAL D-3 (NTSC similar) shows that alternate pixels in two dimensions are recorded by alternate heads. Loss of one head signal allows interpolation from the remaining data

contains, otherwise the pixel data cannot be recreated in that screen area. Thus the distribution and shuffle processes take the DCT block as the minimum unit of data.

9.5 Video mapping

In binary PCM systems, the samples consist of a number of bits, in this case eight, which each determine whether a particular power of 2 should be present in the output level. An 8 bit system has 256 quantizing intervals, and an error in the least significant bit of a sample results in an error of one of these levels, whereas

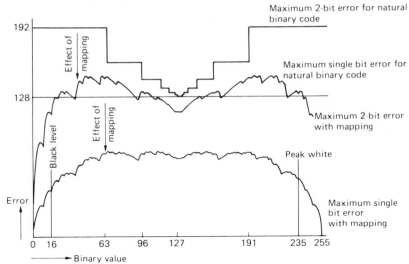

Figure 9.10(a) A single-bit error will cause a maximum deviation of 128Q in natural binary, but this is reduced to the lower line by mapping. A double-bit error will cause a maximum deviation of $128 + 64 = 192Q$, and the effect of mapping on this magnitude of error is also shown

		Least significant four bits														
Input	0	1	2	3	4	5	6	7	8	9	A	B	C	D	E	F
0	00	80	40	20	10	08	04	02	01	C0	A0	90	88	84	82	81
1	60	50	48	44	42	41	30	28	24	22	21	18	14	12	11	0C
2	0A	09	06	05	03	E0	D0	C8	C4	C2	C1	B0	A8	A4	A2	A1
3	98	94	92	91	8C	8A	89	86	85	83	70	68	64	62	61	58
4	54	52	51	4C	4A	49	46	45	43	38	34	32	31	2C	2A	29
5	26	25	23	1C	1A	19	16	15	13	0E	0D	0B	07	F0	E8	E4
6	E2	E1	D8	D4	D2	D1	CC	CA	C9	C6	C5	C3	**B8**	B4	B2	B1
7	AC	AA	A9	A6	A5	A3	9C	9A	99	96	95	93	8E	8D	8B	87
8	78	74	72	71	6C	6A	69	66	65	63	5C	5A	59	56	55	53
9	4E	4D	4B	47	3C	3A	39	36	35	33	2E	2D	2B	27	1E	1D
A	1B	17	0F	F8	F4	F2	F1	EC	EA	E9	E6	E5	E3	DC	DA	D9
B	D6	D5	D3	CE	CD	CB	C7	BC	BA	B9	B6	B5	B3	AE	AD	AB
C	A7	9E	9D	9B	97	8F	7C	7A	79	76	75	73	6E	6D	6B	67
D	5E	5D	5B	57	4F	3E	3D	3B	37	2F	1F	FC	FA	F9	F6	F5
E	F3	EE	ED	EB	E7	DE	DD	DB	D7	CF	BE	BD	BB	B7	AF	9F
F	7E	7D	7B	77	6F	5F	3F	FE	FD	FB	F7	EF	DF	BF	7F	FF

Most significant four bits

Figure 9.10(b) The mapping table. This will need to be reversed on playback an error in the most significant bit results in an error of 128 levels, or half of the signal range. If the two most significant bits are considered, the maximum possible error will be 192 levels, but the largest errors will result if the sample value is near the end of the range, as shown in Fig. 9.10(a).

Essentially some bits are more important than others in PCM systems. An uncorrected least significant bit would probably go unnoticed on real program material, whereas an uncorrected most significant bit would result in an obvious dot contrasting with the surrounding picture area. The eye is most sensitive to such errors where the background is dark, i.e. the numerical values of the samples involved are small, and yet it is in exactly this region that the double-bit error is the greatest.[2]

Mapping is a process which is designed to reduce the dominance of the most significant bits. Incoming video samples to be recorded are fed to a lookup table which translates each 8 bit value to a different 8 bit value. The reverse process takes place on replay, and in the absence of errors, the original data are restored perfectly. However, if 1 or 2 bits of the mapped sample are wrong, the incorrect value which results from the reverse mapping process will have an error which is considerably smaller.

Fig. 9.10(a) shows that the result of mapping is to reduce the actual error magnitude when bit errors occur. If the error-correction system is working properly, this is of no consequence, but it was included in D-1 because it was felt that portable machines might be made which had full record circuitry, but which had confidence replay without error correction to reduce power consumption and size. In this case, mapping would result in a real improvement in subjective quality. Developments in LSI technology mean that full error correction is now possible even in portable machines, so this feature is in fact unnecessary, and it has no parallel in later formats.

The mapping table is shown in Fig. 9.10(b). This is most commonly implemented in a PROM. An example is shown to illustrate the reduction in error magnitude achieved. Only active line video samples are mapped.

9.6 The shuffle strategy

Error correction in DVTRs is more complex than in other forms of recording because of the number of conflicting requirements. Chapter 6 showed that interleave is necessary to break up burst errors, and that a product code gives an efficient and reliable system. Unfortunately the product code produces a regular structure of rows and columns, and if such a system is overwhelmed, regular patterns of uncorrected errors are produced, and the effectiveness of concealment is reduced because the eye can still perceive the regular structure.

An irregular interleave, or *shuffle*, can be designed to disperse contiguous errors on the tape track over two dimensions on the screen, and the concealment is then more effective. For the best concealment, the shuffle should work over the entire field and this will also help the provision of picture-in-shuttle.

In shuttle the track-following process breaks down, and the heads cross tracks randomly so that the recovery of entire segments is impossible. A picture of some sort is needed in shuttle, in order to assist in the location of wanted material, but the quality does not need to be as high as in other modes.

Fig. 9.11 shows that in shuttle, the path of the head crosses tape tracks obliquely. The use of azimuth recording allows the replay head to be about 50%

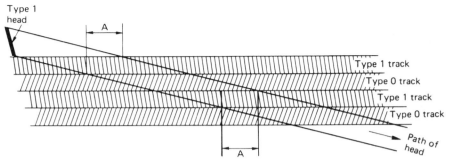

Figure 9.11 During shuttle, the heads cross tracks randomly as shown here (exaggerated). Owing to the use of azimuth recording, a head can only play a track of its own type (0 or 1) but as the head is typically 50% wider than the track (see Section 5.5) it is possible to recover normal signal for the periods above marked A. If sync blocks are shorter than this period, they can be picked up intact. In fact a slightly longer pickup will be possible because the replay system may tolerate a less-than-perfect signal. In any case the final decision is made by checking that the sync block recovered contains valid or correctable codewords

wider than the track, and so a useful replay signal results for a reasonable proportion of the head path, at the times where the head is near the centreline of a track of the same azimuth type, interrupted by noise when the heads cross tracks of the wrong azimuth type. The sectors are broken into short elements called *sync blocks* which are smaller than the length of track which can be recovered at typical shuttle speeds. Each sync block contains a Reed–Solomon codeword, and so it is possible to tell if the sync block was correctly recovered or not, without reference to any other part of the recording.

If a sync block is read properly, it is used to update a frame store which refreshes the picture monitor. Sync blocks which are not read correctly will not update the frame store, and so if concealment cannot be used, data from an earlier field will be used to refresh the display.

Using this mechanism, picture-in-shuttle is composed of data from different segments of many offtape fields. A problem with segmented recordings is that at certain tape speeds beating occurs between the passage of tracks and the scanner rotation so that some parts of the segments are never recovered and the picture has to be refreshed with stale data which are no longer representative of the recording. There are two solutions to the problem. The use of a field-based shuffle helps because one offtape sync block then contains samples from all over the screen. A field-based shuffle is complex to implement and D-3 was the first format to use it. In the earlier D-1 and D-2 formats the shuffle was restricted to operate only over one segment of the field.

The beating effect is mechanical and results in certain parts of a track being inaccessible. If the data within successive tracks are ordered differently, beating will cause loss from all over the picture once more. Thus in a segment-based shuffle, each track in the field will use a different shuffle. In a field-based shuffle the two channels will use different shuffles. In composite formats the data in successive fields of the colour frame sequence may be rotated by differing amounts.

Obtaining a shuttle picture is easier if the shuffle is random, but a random shuffle is less effective for concealment, because it can result in variable density of uncorrected errors, which are harder to conceal than the constant error density resulting from a maximum distance shuffle.

Essentially the field of data to be shuffled is considered to be a two-dimensional memory, and the shuffle is achieved by address mapping in each dimension. The address generator used should not be unnecessarily complicated and it will be simpler if the rows and columns of the memory are mapped in turn. Clearly the shuffle process on recording has to be exactly reversed on replay.

In address mapping, samples in each channel of a segment are at addresses which are initially sequential. The samples are selected non-sequentially by generating a suitable address sequence. When data reduction is used, individual pixels cannot be shuffled, but instead it is the addresses of DCT blocks which are mapped.

In principle, the address sequence could be arbitrarily generated from a lookup table, but the memory arrays are large, and this approach would be extremely expensive to implement. It is desirable that the address generation should be algorithmic to reduce cost, but an algorithm must be found which gives irregular results.

The solution adopted in DVTR formats is to obtain a pseudo-random address sequence by using address multiplication by a prime number in modulo arithmetic for one of the mapping axes. This is easier than it sounds, as the simple example of Fig. 9.12(a) shows. In this example, 16 pixels are to be shuffled. The pixel addresses are multiplied by 11, which is relatively prime to 16, and the result is expressed modulo-16, which is to say that if the product exceeds an

Address A	A × 11		A × 11 mod 16
0	0		0
1	11		11
2	22	(−16)	6
3	33	(−32)	1
4	44	(−32)	12
5	55	(−48)	7
6	66	(−64)	2
7	77	(−64)	13
8	88	(−80)	8
9	99	(−96)	3
10	110	(−96)	14
11	121	(−112)	9
12	132	(−128)	4
13	143	(−128)	15
14	154	(−144)	10
15	165	(−160)	5

Figure 9.12(a) The permuted addresses for a shuffle can be obtained by multiplication of the addresses by a number relatively prime to the modulo base

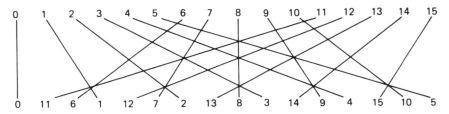

Figure 9.12(b) The shuffle which results from the calculation in Fig. 9.12(a)

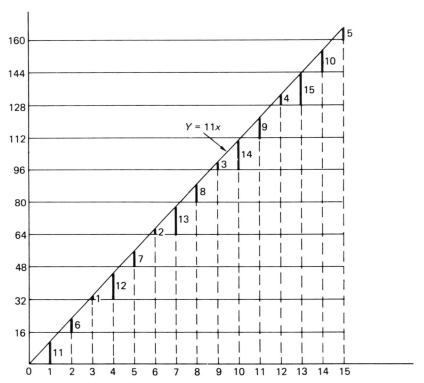

Figure 9.12(c) Modulo arithmetic is rather similar to quantizing. The results of Fig. 9.12(a) can be obtained by quantizing the graph of $y = 11x$ with the quantizing intervals of 16 units

integer multiple of 16, that integer multiple is subtracted. It will be seen from the Fig. 9.12(b) that an effective shuffle is created. Modulo arithmetic has a similar effect to quantizing; in fact a number expressed modulo is the quantizing error due to quantizing in steps equal to the modulo base as Fig. 9.12(c) shows. When the input has a large range, the quantizing error becomes random.

Generating a randomizing effect with modulo arithmetic depends upon the terms in the expression being relatively prime so that repeats are not found in the resulting shuffle, and this constrains the dimensions which can be used for the codewords.

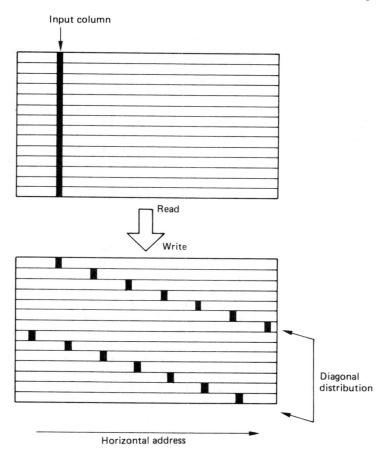

Figure 9.13 The second dimension of the shuffle is obtained by offsetting the horizontal address during transfer from one array to another. This results in a diagonal shuffle if the offset increases by a constant from one line to the next

A calculation of the type described will shuffle samples or DCT blocks in a pseudo-random manner in one dimension, but in the other dimension of the memory a pseudo-random shuffle is undesirable as this would result in a variable-distance shuffle. A straightforward interleave is used in the other dimension to give a maximum distance shuffle. Fig. 9.13 shows a conceptual example. When samples are read in rows for recording they retain the same horizontal sequence but there is an offset in the starting address which is a simple function of the row number. This turns a column into a series of diagonals. The combination of these two processes results in the two-dimensional shuffle. The effect of the shuffle can be seen by turning off the correction and concealment circuits on a machine and searching for a large dropout with the jog control. This will reveal the irregular diagonal structure.

9.7 The product code

The product code of a DVTR may extend over a segment, as in D-1 and D-2, or over the entire field, as in D-3. Fig. 9.14(a) shows the field array of D-3 PAL, and Fig. 9.14(b) shows the equivalent in NTSC. Outer codes are vertical columns and three of these are necessary to contain the samples from one TV line after distribution. Data are recorded on tape by passing horizontally across the array to form inner codewords which are placed sequentially along the track. The inner codeword will correct random errors, but if its correction power is exceeded the inner code declares the entire block bad, and the outer code must correct by erasure. If the inner code were too large, this would effectively magnify burst errors to the size of the codeword. A further consideration is that if each sector were to be one long data block, loss of synchronization in the data separator due to a dropout would result in the loss of the rest of the sector, again magnifying the error.

Instead, one row of the segment array is made into 12 inner code blocks in PAL and nine in NTSC, and this reduces error magnification due to small bursts. Each array will be recorded on four different tracks for PAL, three for NTSC. Two arrays are needed to record one field. Each array is recorded in tracks of the same azimuth type. The outer redundancy is distributed evenly over the tracks. Since the outer codes contain eight redundancy symbols, each can correct eight symbols by erasure. This corresponds to 8 bytes per column of the field array. The largest data loss which can be handled will be when this damage is experienced in every column of the array, so the maximum correctable burst-error size is given by multiplying the number of columns in the sector array by eight. The resulting figures are $912 \times 8 = 7296$ data bytes for PAL and $765 \times 8 = 6120$ data bytes for NTSC. These figures are for video data only; the actual size of the burst will be larger because the length of the track involved also contains sync and ID patterns and inner redundancy.

As the field array in D-3 is spread over several tracks, the length of a correctable tape defect along the track depends upon the number of tracks over which the defect spreads. Fig. 9.15 shows that if the error is due to a helical scratch or a particle of debris passing under the head, it will be restricted to one track only and the correctable track length will be a maximum. If the defect is a linear tape scratch affecting all tracks, the correctable length of the defect is given by dividing the field array correction power by the number of tracks in which the array is recorded (three or four). Note that this is only possible because the product code spreads over the whole field.

The maximum correctable single-track burst corresponds to about 19 mm of track length, or a longitudinal tape scratch of about 1.6 mm width.

If these conditions are exceeded, total correction is no longer possible, and rows of flagged erroneous data will appear in the field array. Concealment will become necessary and the concealment patterns are made irregular by using shuffling.

In shuttle, sync blocks will be recovered at random, and the shuffle means that when a sync block is successfully read, the pixels it contains are spread over the field, so the frame store will be updated all over instead of just in certain areas. The twinkling effect on the picture-in-shuttle is caused by the shuffle.

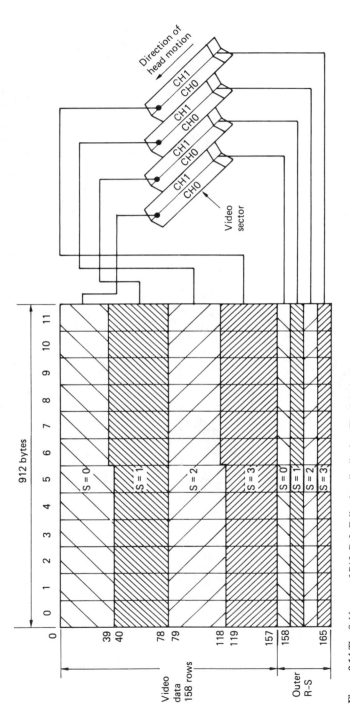

Figure 9.14 The field array of PAL D-3. Following distribution (Fig. 9.9) the 948 samples per line become 474 samples per channel. Three columns of the array shown here hold 474 samples. Eight redundancy bytes are added to each column to form outer codes. The rows of the array are split into 12 parts and each has an ID pattern and redundancy added to make an inner code which occupies one sync block. The array is recorded on one of the tracks of four segments. The second array is recorded on the other tracks. Outer redundancy is recorded first in each track

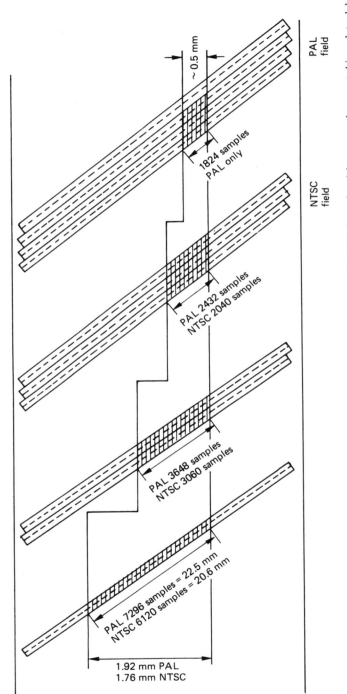

Figure 9.15 Error-correcting performance of D-3. For a single-segment helical scratch, reference to Fig. 9.14 shows that eight rows can be corrected in each track by outer codes. This corresponds to 8 × 912 = 7296 samples (PAL) or 8 × 765 = 6120 samples (NTSC). In the case of a scratch along the tape, the maximum correction per field array must be divided by the number of tracks affected. In NTSC there are six tracks per field so a sustained scratch of 2040 samples can be corrected. In PAL there are eight tracks per field so a sustained scratch of 1824 samples can be corrected. This could be up to about 0.5 mm wide

9.8 Implementing the product code and shuffle – D-1

An example of a segment-based shuffle used in D-1 will be given. The shuffle within the segment is designed primarily with dispersion in mind to give good concealment. If all sectors were the same, at certain tape speeds, parts of the track would never be read and stale samples would be read from the frame store. However, the shuffle is not constant; it changes between odd sectors and even sectors, and from field to field over a four-field sequence. This changing shuffle pattern generates the necessary spatial variability to reduce the probability of stale data in shuttle.

Figure 9.16(a) Shuffle address generator of D-1. The two least significant bits of the column count bypass the column map PROM so that sets of four columns are permuted to keep co-sited samples adjacent. The row counter is loaded with a starting count from the row start PROM. When the two least significant bits of the column count are one, this corresponds to the last column of the set of four. This condition is detected by the AND gate which modifies the row start PROM address to shuffle the luminance-only pixel in the last column relative to the co-sited samples in the other three columns

Fig. 9.16(a) shows the address generator which is used in the D-1 shuffle.[1] On recording, this device generates the read addresses to shuffle the sector array before it is written to tape. On playback, the same configuration determines the write addresses, so that offtape data are automatically subjected to a reverse shuffle as the sector array is written.

The column counter is cleared at the beginning of the sector, and produces a column count from 0 to 599. The columns in the sector array are arranged into groups of four, so that the co-sited samples will still be in the same inner codewords after group permutation. There are thus 150 group addresses, and these are shuffled by multiplying them by 41, which is relatively prime to 150, and expressing the product modulo-150. This is performed by the column map PROM, and it will be seen that the two least significant bits of the column address bypass the PROM so that groups of four columns are permuted together. This process results in the horizontal dimension of the shuffle.

The vertical dimension of the shuffle is obtained by performing a vertical address permutation on each column in the sector array, where the starting address of the process is also permuted.

Considering a horizontal row through a group of four columns, the left-hand three samples are the components of a co-sited pixel. The right-hand sample is a luminance-only sample. The row permutations must be the same for the first three columns of the group, again to maintain the presence of all components of a co-sited pixel in an inner codeword, but the luminance-only pixel in the fourth column is physically near on the screen, and concealment would be better if it were in a different inner codeword. Accordingly, the row start count permutation stays the same for columns 0, 1 and 2, but an AND gate detects a column value of 3 which adds a constant to the row start address in the fourth column of the group. The column count is multiplied by 30, and expressed modulo-32 to give the starting address except when the last column of the group is encountered, when 5 is added to the product before being expressed modulo-32.

The row start count is loaded into the row counter which is clocked at sample rate. The row count runs from 0 to 31 since there are 32 symbols in an outer codeword and hence 32 rows in the sector array. The row count is multiplied by

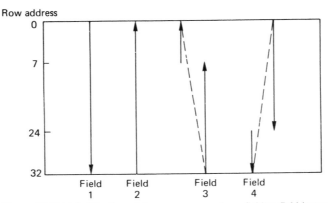

Figure 9.16(b) Modification of the row sequence from field to field improves randomness of shuffle for better shuttle picture. Field 1 reads forward from 0, field 2 reads reverse from 32, field 3 reads reverse from 7 and field 4 reads forward from 24

7, which is relatively prime to 32, and the product is expressed modulo-32 to produce a permuted row address.

The pixels within a sector are now shuffled, but all sectors are not shuffled the same. The shuttle picture is improved by changing the shuffle over a four-field sequence, and this is shown in Fig. 9.16(b).

Since two heads work in parallel, a linear tape scratch could cause damage at the same place in two sector arrays, and could therefore damage the concealment distribution strategy. This is prevented by rotating the row address by 16 between sectors written by adjacent heads, and is simply implemented by inverting the MSB of the row address. Then in different fields, the row address is rotated by differing amounts.

9.9 Implementing the product code and shuffle – D-3

The two-dimensional shuffle of PAL D-3 is obtained using two one-dimensional shuffles, one each side of the outer redundancy coder. The outer check bytes are not, however, shuffled, but are kept together so that they can be recorded at the beginning of the sectors.

There are two virtually identical channels running in parallel, one for each head, so the input to each process consists of half the samples from each of 304 lines. Each distributed line contains 474 samples, and these will be clocked into the process at $2 \times F_{sc}$.

Fig. 9.17 shows one possible implementation of the shuffle process. Each TV line is split into a set of three outer blocks (Oblk). One outer block forms a column in the product code array, so there are three times as many columns as there are TV lines recorded ($304 \times 3 = 912$).

The incoming clock drives a divide-by-three counter which produces the parameter Oblk. As the outer block count changes between samples, successive samples in the input sequence will be distributed around the set of three outer blocks. As there is a two-channel distribution in addition to this process, samples in a given block will be six samples apart on the TV line.

The carry output of the divide-by-three stage drives an accumulator which adds 59 on each clock. The clock is also divided by 158 to provide a pulse once per line to reset the accumulator and clock the line counter.

The parameter Oblk is multiplied by 72, the line count is multiplied by 82 and these values are added to the accumulator output and the sum is expressed modulo-158. The result is a pseudo-random permuted row address where the incoming sample at that instant will be stored. This produces the vertical component of the shuffle. In order to produce a two-dimensional maximum distance shuffle, the column address is also permuted, but the horizontal shift stays the same for each TV line.

As an incoming line is distributed over three blocks, the parameter Oblk also needs to control the column address to put sequential input samples into three different columns. It will be seen from the figure that the line address and Oblk generate the column address. For a given TV line, the line address is constant, and the sequencing of Oblk will place samples in three complete columns.

Once the columns of the memory have been filled, the outer error-correction coder can generate outer redundancy terms. Each column contains 158 samples, and 8 bytes of redundancy are added to make the column 166 symbols high.

The contents of the field array are written to four tape tracks by reading the

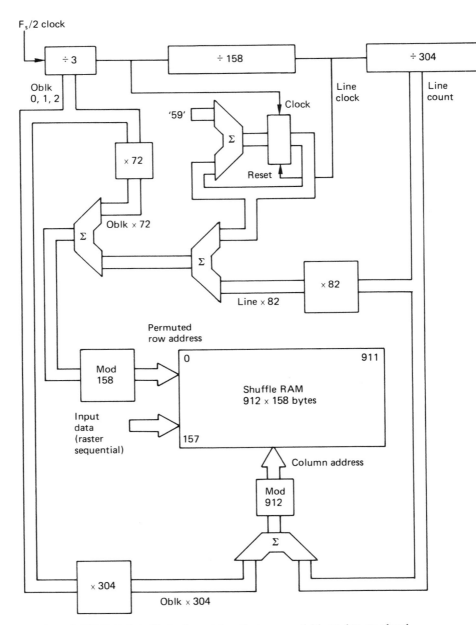

Figure 9.17 PAL D-3 shuffle implementation. Raster sequential input data are placed non-sequentially in the shuffle RAM by permuting row and column addresses to give a two-dimensional shuffle. See text for details

array in rows and adding redundancy to produce inner codewords which occupy tape sync blocks. The 912 column array is split into 12 subarrays of 76 columns each. Reading across one subarray at a time produces 76 byte blocks to which 8 bytes of redundancy are added to make inner codewords. The addition of a sync pattern and ID code makes the codeword into a sync block. As there are 166 rows in the array and 12 sync blocks per row, there are a total of 1992 sync blocks to be recorded; 1896 of these are data and 96 are outer check symbols. As the outer redundancy is shared equally among the tracks, each records 498 sync blocks, 474 being data and 24 being outer code.

It will be seen from Fig. 9.14 that the sync blocks are numbered beginning with 0 at top left in the field array and proceeding along rows.

The redundancy is recorded at the beginning of each track by selecting an appropriate sync block address in the memory which is a function of the segment address. In segment 0, the address will be 1896, the beginning of the outer check symbols. As there are 24 outer check sync patterns in each track, the next segment will begin with address 1896 + 24 = 1920 and the one after that with 1896 + 48 and so on.

Following the recording of the outer check sync blocks at the beginning of the track, one-quarter of the data sync blocks (474) are recorded in the rest of the track. The starting sync block address is obtained by adding 474 times the segment address. The address is further modified by adding 711 for an odd track so that adjacent data in a track pair are non-adjacent on the screen. The starting address is further modified by the field number in the colour framing sequence in order to reduce the probability of stale data in shuttle.

As the 76 byte data contents of each sync block are read from the array memory, they are sent via the inner coder circuit which adds 8 bytes of inner check symbols. The inner coder is shared with the audio data.

9.10 The sync block

The inner codes in product codes are designed to correct random errors and to detect the presence of burst errors by declaring the whole inner block bad. There is an optimum size for an inner code: too small and the redundancy factor rises; too large and burst errors are magnified, as are errors due to losing sync.

When the product code becomes large, one row will be too long to be one inner code, and so in D-3, for example, it is split into 12 or nine inner code blocks. The dimensions of these are chosen to give adequate correction performance. One sync block contains one inner codeword and an ID code; 12 or nine sync blocks then form one complete row of the sector array.

Fig. 9.18(a) shows a PAL D-3 sync block. A 2 byte synchronizing pattern serves to phase the data separator and the deserializer. Following this is a 2 byte ID code which uniquely identifies this sync block in an eight-field sequence. The data block of 76 bytes then follows, and the 8 bytes of inner redundancy are calculated over the ID code as well as the data, so a random error in the ID can be corrected. The codeword is thus 86 bytes long. The entire sync block occupies about a quarter of a millimetre of track.

Fig. 9.18(b) shows an NTSC D-3 sync block. A 2 byte synchronizing pattern serves to phase the data separator and the deserializer. Following this is a 2 byte ID code which uniquely identifies this sync block in a four-field sequence. The data block of 85 bytes then follows, and the 8 bytes of inner redundancy are

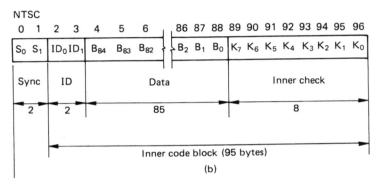

Figure 9.18 D-3 sync blocks (a) PAL and (b) NTSC. Each begins with the sync pattern 97F1 which is not randomized. The 2 byte ID, the data and the 8 bytes of inner check symbols are all randomized prior to EFM coding. The same block structure is used in both audio and video sectors

calculated over the ID code as well as the data, so a random error in the ID can be corrected. The codeword is thus 95 bytes long.

Whilst the size of the inner codeword is related to correction power, it is not essential for each inner code to have its own ID. In fact individually identifying each inner code would raise the recording overheads. In shuttle, a geometric calculation reveals the shortest length of track which will be recovered at maximum tape speed, and this determines that in D-2, for example, it is not necessary to identify every inner codeword. Accordingly one sync block contains two inner codewords, but only one ID code. Three sync blocks then form one complete row of the sector array.

Fig. 9.19(a) shows a PAL D-2 sync block. A 2 byte synchronizing pattern serves to phase the data separator and the deserializer. Following this is a 2 byte ID code which uniquely identifies this sync block in an eight field sequence. The first data block of 76 bytes then follows, and the 8 bytes of inner redundancy are calculated over the ID code as well as the data, so a random error in the ID can be corrected. The first codeword is thus 86 bytes long. The second inner code block is 2 bytes shorter because it contains no ID. The entire sync block occupies just over half a millimetre of track.

Figure 9.19 The sync blocks of D-2 contain two codewords but only one ID code which forms part of the first codeword. As a result, the first code block is 2 bytes longer than the second

Fig. 9.19(b) shows an NTSC D-2 sync block. A 2 byte synchronizing pattern serves to phase the data separator and the deserializer. Following this is a 2 byte ID code which uniquely identifies this sync block in a four-field sequence. The first data block of 85 bytes then follows, and the 8 bytes of inner redundancy are calculated over the ID code as well as the data, so a random error in the ID can be corrected. The first codeword is thus 95 bytes long. The second inner code block is 2 bytes shorter because it contains no ID. The entire sync block occupies nearly two-thirds of a millimetre of track.

9.11 Synchronization and identification

Each sync block contains one or two inner codewords, depending on the format, and is the smallest quantum of data on the track with which the playback channel can synchronize independently. Synchronization takes place on three levels: to the bit, to the symbol and to the sync block.

The recording density in DVTRs is such that it is not possible mechanically to position the heads with sufficient accuracy to locate an individual bit. The heads are rotated with reasonable accuracy, and the replay signal is accepted as and when it arrives. A phase-locked loop in the data separator must lock to the bit rate and phase of the recording. At the beginning of the track a reference for the phase-locked loop known as a track preamble is recorded. This serves to set the frequency of the PLL the same as the offtape bit rate. Once the loop is locked, it can stay in synchronism by phase comparing the data transitions with its own. However, if synchronism is lost due to a dropout, it cannot be regained until the next synchronizing pattern is seen. This is one reason that the tracks are broken into short sync blocks.

Once bit synchronism has been achieved at the preamble, the serial data have to be correctly divided up into symbols, or deserialized, in order to decode the original samples. This requires word synchronization, and is achieved by the unique pattern which occurs at the beginning of every sync block. Detection of this pattern resets the counter which deserializes the data by dividing by the wordlength. If randomizing is used, as in D-1, D-3/D-5 and Digital Betacam, sync detection will also be used to preset the derandomizer to the correct starting value. The sync pattern should differ from itself shifted by as many bits as possible to reduce the possibility of false sync generation. Within a sector, sync patterns occur at regular spacing, so it is possible for the replay circuitry to predict the arrival of the sync pattern in a time window.

Once symbol synchronizing is achieved, it is then possible to read the inner code blocks, particularly the 2 bytes which contain the ID code as this reveals which sync block has been recovered. In normal play this will be the one after the previous one, but in shuttle, the sequence will be unpredictable.

In shuttle, samples from any sync block properly recovered can be put in the correct place in a frame store by reference to the ID code.

Fig. 9.20(a) shows the ID structure of D-3 which is very similar to that of D-2. The information recorded in the ID code is split into two parts. The first byte and bit 0 of the second is the 9 bit sync block number in the track, the remaining 7 bits of the second byte identify the sector. The V/A bit specifies whether the block is audio or video. The segment bits determine which segment out of four for PAL and three for NTSC is present, and the field bits specify the position in the eight- or four-field sequences to help colour framing.

Fig. 9.20(b) shows the sync block numbering within the segment for PAL, and Fig. 9.20(c) shows the equivalent for NTSC.

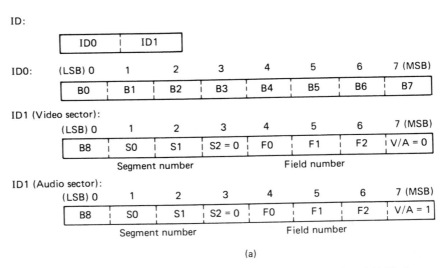

(a)

Figure 9.20(a) D-3 ID pattern consists of 2 bytes. ID0 and bit 0 of ID1 form a 9-bit block address. Bit 7 of ID1 is the video/audio flag and determines the type of sector. Remainder of the data carries field number (0–3 NTSC, 0–7 PAL) and segment number (0–2 NTSC, 0–3 PAL). Segment number requires only 2-bit code; thus S2 = 0

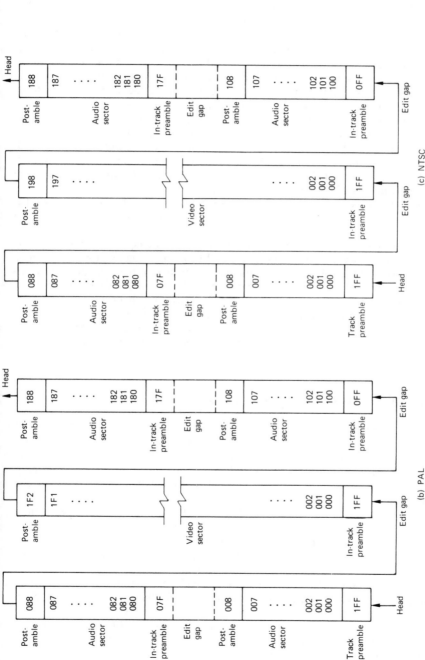

Figure 9.20(b) Showing ID code numbering to identify individually every sync block in the track. PAL video sector has more sync blocks and reaches higher count than that of NTSC at (c)

9.12 Gaps, preambles and postambles

Each slant track is subdivided into sectors. In D-1, D-5, DCT and Digital Betacam there is a video sector at each end and four audio sectors in the middle. In D-2 and D-3 there are two audio sectors at each end and one video sector in the centre. It is necessary to be able to edit any or all of the audio channels independently of the video. For this reason short spaces are left between the sectors to allow write current to turn on and off away from wanted data. Since the write current can only turn off at the end of a sector, it follows that the smallest quantum of data which can be written in the track at one time is a whole sector, although the smallest quantum which can be read is a sync block.

A preamble is necessary before the first sync block in a sector to allow the phase-locked loop in the data separator to lock. The preamble also contains a sync pattern and ID code so that the machine can confirm the position of the head before entering the sector proper. At the end of the sector a postamble containing an ID code is written before the write current is turned off. The pre- and postamble details of D-3 can be seen in Fig. 9.21.

The space between two adjacent sectors is known as an edit gap, and it will be seen in Fig. 9.21 to begin with the postamble of the previous sector and end with the preamble of the next sector. Editing may result in a discontinuity nominally in the middle of the gap. There is some latitude, but the new recording must not begin so early that the postamble at the end of the previous sector is damaged, and at least 20 bytes of preamble must be written before the sync pattern at the beginning of the next sector, because it will not be possible to maintain continuity of bit phase at an edit, and the PLL must resynchronize.

In practice the length of the postamble, gap and preamble combined will be made exactly equal to the length of one or two sync blocks according to the format. This simplifies the design of the sequencer which controls the track recording.

9.13 Colour framing and colour processing

Although the recording technique used in composite formats is digital, it is vital to remember at all times that the data which are recorded are no more than a numerical representation of a composite video waveform. All of the characteristics of composite video remain, including the requirement for a colour framing system to synchronize the four- or eight-field sequences embedded in the subcarrier.

No description of a composite digital VTR can be complete without a discussion of the techniques necessary to handle colour framing and the intimately related ScH phase, and colour processing needed for variable-speed replay. There are considerable differences between the subcarriers of PAL and NTSC, and so there will be corresponding differences between the approaches to colour framing and between the data rates which result from digitizing the two standards. As a result D-2 and D-3 are each two formats which leave different tape footprints, but which nevertheless have a lot in common in order to use the same circuitry and mechanical parts as much as possible. Since colour framing has such a far reaching effect on composite recording, it will be necessary to treat the subject first so that the implications for following topics become clear.

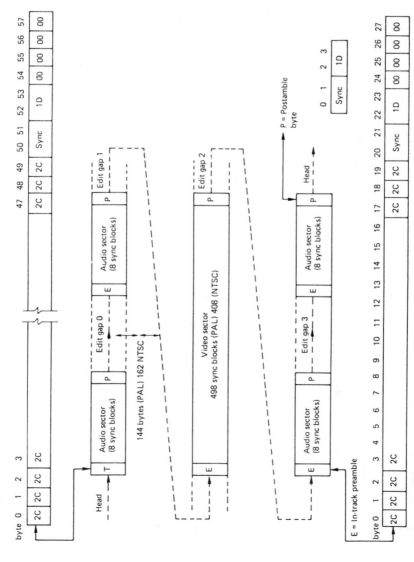

Figure 9.21 All separately recordable areas begin with a preamble E except for the first sector which has a longer track preamble T. Edit gaps are the same size as two sync blocks and begin with the postamble P of the previous sector and end with the preamble E of the next sector

9.14 Colour framing in PAL

In PAL, the eight-field sequence comes about because of the quarter cycle offset of subcarrier against line rate. There are 283¾ cycles of subcarrier in one line, which means that four lines must pass before the same relationship occurs between subcarrier and horizontal sync. The odd number of lines in a frame necessary for interlace mean that four frames must elapse before the four-line sequence assumes the same relationship with vertical. Unlike NTSC which has a half cycle offset, PAL does not naturally have good cancellation of chroma on the screen. This is achieved by the addition of 25 Hz to the subcarrier frequency, which causes chroma on a given line to be antiphase with chroma on the line in the next field which will be physically adjacent on the interlaced display. Although this 25 Hz component achieves its goal, it also complicates the colour framer because instead of having four different relationships of subcarrier to horizontal there are now 2500!

Since composite digital samples using burst as a phase reference, it is necessary to follow what the burst does with respect to horizontal. Owing to the quarter cycle offset, subcarrier phase advances by 90° from line to line, but the

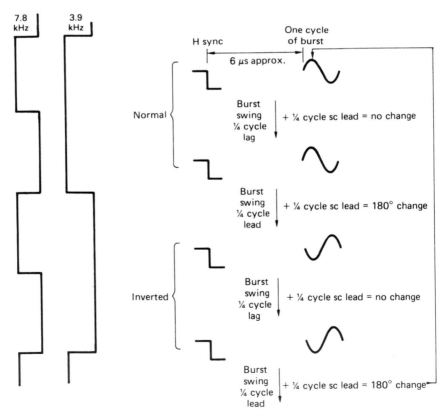

Figure 9.22 Quarter cycle subcarrier/H relationship and burst swing combine to give four-line sequence

burst swings forward 90° on one line and back 90° on the next to convey the state of V-switch. This means that the burst swing will alternately cancel or double the subcarrier phase advance, giving two lines with the same burst to sync relationship followed by two lines with an inverted burst to sync relationship. Fig. 9.22 shows that these four lines repeat at 3.9 kHz and contain two complete cycles of V-switch which runs at 7.8 kHz. Once every four frames, line 1 of the frame will be the first of the four line types, and this fact will be indicated by the colour framing flag on the control track. It is the job of the record colour framer to determine when to produce that colour framing flag. Fig. 9.23(a) shows the record colour framing process.

On replay, a second colour framer examines the reference input to determine when the start of the colour framing sequence occurs. Fig. 9.23(b) shows that the

Figure 9.23 At (a) the presence of field 1 on the input is denoted by a colour frame flag on the control track. The field sequence is also written in the rotary tracks. At (b), on replay the capstan speed will be changed until offtape colour frame flags coincide with reference field 1 identification. Replay video will then be colour framed to reference

phase difference between the reference colour frame flag and the replay colour frame pulse from the control track controls the capstan speed until the pulse and the flag coincide. When this is achieved, the tape playback is said to be colour framed, and the lines from the tape will be of exactly the same type as the lines in the reference signal. The offtape samples can be fed directly to the machine output. In all other replay modes, a colour processor will be necessary to convert the offtape line type to the reference line type. Since the control track phase is meaningless at anything other than the correct speed, D-3 machines record identification codes on the helical tracks which uniquely locate a segment within the eight-field sequence. In some machines there is only one colour framing circuit, and it is simply switched to the input or the reference according to whether the machine is recording or playing back.

As was seen in Chapters 3 and 7, the sampling clock in PAL uses burst as a phase reference. The colour framer must use sample values obtained by digitizing the leading edge of sync with a burst phased sampling clock.

The first stage in colour framing is to determine the phase of burst swing. This process is integral with the operation of the sampling-clock phase-locked loop. The phase-locked loop includes the video ADC so that chroma phase errors are minimized. The ADC runs constantly, and digitizes the entire video signal. Control of the VCO is achieved by examining the numerical value of samples taken during the burst.

Figure 9.24 shows one possible implementation. Owing to PAL burst swing, burst phase can have one of two values, 90° apart, so both of them will have the same phase relationship to $4 \times F_{sc}$. A two-phase divider running from the VCO produces a pair of quadrature square waves at subcarrier frequency. These are used on alternate lines to synchronize the numerical processing of sampled burst.

Figure 9.24 Two quadrature clocks are derived from $4F_{sc}$ whose crossings are at 45° phase in PAL. These two clocks are used on alternate lines, where they predict the position and direction of a burst crossing. If it is a downward crossing, the phase error needs to be inverted. If the odd/even sequence gets out of step, the clock moves forward a quadrant when an incoming burst moves back a quadrant, so the burst is perceived as inverted. The phase error alternates at half line rate and can be used to reset the 7.8 kHz divider

In the first quadrant, A, there should be a positive burst crossing, and blanking level, or 64 is subtracted from the sample value to give a phase error measurement. In the next quadrant, B, a positive burst value above 64 should be obtained. In the third quadrant, C, there should be a negative burst crossing; 64 will be subtracted from the sample value, and the result inverted to give a phase error value. The phase error values for several cycles of burst are numerically averaged and fed to a DAC which produces the VCO control voltage. Upon first applying an input, the alternate selection of the quadrature control signals will have a random phase which may be right or wrong. If by chance it is correct, the above sequence of events will hold true for all lines. However, if the selection is in the wrong phase, the timing will lag by a quadrant when burst leads by a quadrant and vice versa. This will make the burst invert with respect to the measurement timing on alternate lines, and a negative peak value below 64 will be obtained instead of a positive peak value above 64 in quadrant B. This condition is easily detected, and is used to reset the phase of the line frequency divider. This divider will now be truly reflecting the input burst swing, and an accurate phase comparison can be made between burst and sampling clock on every line. The line frequency divider is now producing 7.8 kHz.

By numerically analysing the ADC output, it is easy to detect the sync pulses, and using programmable counters it is possible to detect both vertical and horizontal syncs from their duration. In this way a gate can be opened during the first line of each frame. During the gate, the state of 7.8 kHz is examined, and this will only be true on alternate frames, and allows four-field colour framing to be achieved. The burst swing (7.8 kHz) derived colour framing cannot tell whether it has found field 1 or field 5, and this can only be resolved by looking at the 3.9 kHz relationship between burst and sync.

The problems involved in determining the colour frame are summarized below, prior to the somewhat involved solutions.

Since sampling is subcarrier locked, it is necessary to consider how sync pulses move with respect to subcarrier rather than the other way round. The quarter cycle offset means that the position of a sync edge will move forward by one quadrant of subcarrier per line.

The presence of the 25 Hz offset causes sync edges to slide back constantly with respect to the sampling clock by four cycles or 225 ns per frame. The absolute position of the sync edge depends on the ScH phase of the input signal which can drift.

Assessment of ScH phase according to the definition can only be made once every eight fields, and reliance on a single measurement is prone to noise. Techniques must be found to allow a colour framer to make a continuous assessment of framing so that a faster, more reliable lock is achieved.

Fig. 9.25(a) shows how the phase of sync with respect to subcarrier can be found for any line in the eight-field sequence. The presence of the 25 Hz component is responsible for the diagonal slippage. Since phase only has meaning with respect to a cycle, it is possible to redraw Fig. 9.25(a) to produce (b). The timing of sync with respect to subcarrier now takes on the appearance of a frame rate sawtooth. The sync edge has a finite slope, and so several samples will be taken during the transition. Fig. 9.25(c) shows how the phase of the instant when the 50% level of sync is crossed can be computed to a fraction of a subcarrier cycle. Since this position moves by a fixed amount per line (0.36 ns) it is possible to subtract a time which is obtained by multiplying the line number

Figure 9.25(a) The position of sync with respect to subcarrier can be found for any line in an eight-field sequence using this chart. The quarter cycle offset causes sync to move forward one quadrant per line over a four-line sequence, but the addition of 25 Hz causes sync to slip back towards subcarrier by one cycle per frame

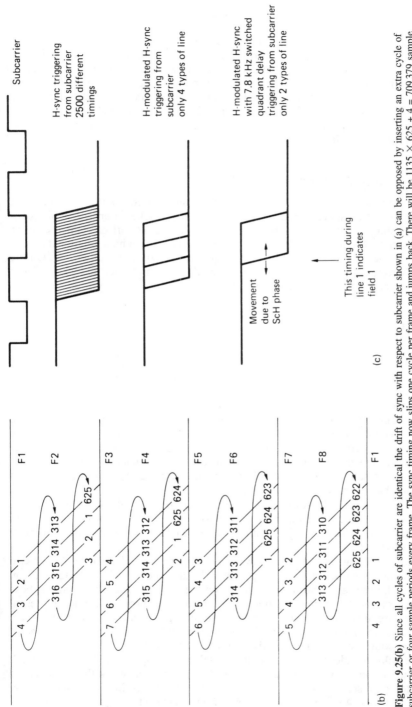

Figure 9.25(b) Since all cycles of subcarrier are identical the drift of sync with respect to subcarrier shown in (a) can be opposed by inserting an extra cycle of subcarrier or four sample periods every frame. The sync timing now slips one cycle per frame and jumps back. There will be $1135 \times 625 + 4 = 709\,379$ sample periods in a frame exactly. By modulating the position of sync by 0.36 ns per line, it can be made to have a constant relationship to subcarrier over a four-line period. (c) Horizontal modulation gives four types of line by cancelling the effect of 25 Hz. Using 7.8 kHz from Fig.9.24 to insert or remove delays of one sample period results in two relationships. Sampling during line 1 will determine whether field 1 or field 5 is present

in the frame by 0.36 ns. This process is called horizontal modulation, and results in a modulated sync edge which appears to have four phases which are stationary with respect to subcarrier. The four phases are due to the quarter cycle offset. A further offset of one sample period is subtracted on alternate lines according to the state of 7.8 kHz, giving modulated sync edges which now have two phases. During the colour frame, the sync edge will be in phase with subcarrier; during frame 3 it will be antiphase. The colour frame is thus uniquely identified. If the input is not exactly EBU ScH phase, there will be a fixed phase error in the sync timing, and the system must pick the sync edge which is most nearly in phase with subcarrier to identify frame 1.

9.15 Colour framing in NTSC

The four-field sequence of NTSC arises because of the half cycle offset of subcarrier with respect to line frequency. The phase-locked loop which produces the sampling clock synchronizes to burst, but with a 57° offset so that samples are taken on the $R-Y$ and $B-Y$ axes. The standard ScH phase relationship will occur on the first line of the four-field sequence, and on every other line. On the lines between, the sync edge will be located two sample periods away. These lines are easily detected and so the colour frame flag is readily produced.

9.16 Colour processing

When variable speed is used, the transport cannot change its scanner speed, because this determines field rate. If the tape speed is too low, some fields on tape have to be repeated to maintain field rate, whereas if tape speed is too high, some will need to be skipped. The effect of a head jump is that the subcarrier sequence is randomly broken. If variable speed is to be used, then it is necessary to decode the discontinuous incoming subcarrier, and re-encode it to continuous reference phase. The unit which does this job is called the colour processor. In NTSC there are only two line types, and the colour processor simply has to invert the subcarrier selectively before adding it back to the luminance. A digital filter is necessary to separate the chroma from the luminance, and the operation of such a device has been described in Chapter 4.

In PAL, as usual, the solution is more complex because of the use of V-switch. Chroma is filtered from luminance as before, but then the chroma signal will have to be re-encoded not just with the correct phase, but also with the correct sense of V-switch.

Fig. 9.26(a) shows that from line to line, the phase of U advances 90° due to the quarter cycle offset, and the phase of V alternately leads and lags U. Fig. 9.26(b) shows that if chroma is sampled on the U and V axes the result of these two effects is that from one line to the next, the chroma samples represent different sequences of U and V. The shift to the right of the U sample due to the quarter cycle offset can be seen. It is not immediately obvious how one line of chroma could be made into another with this approach.

The solution adopted in composite digital is to sample at 45° to the U and V axes, i.e. in phase with the burst. Fig. 9.26(c) shows that when this is done, the samples represent $U \times \cos 45 + V \times \cos 45$ etc. If everything is normalized by dividing by $\cos 45$, the samples become $U+V$, $-U+V$, etc.

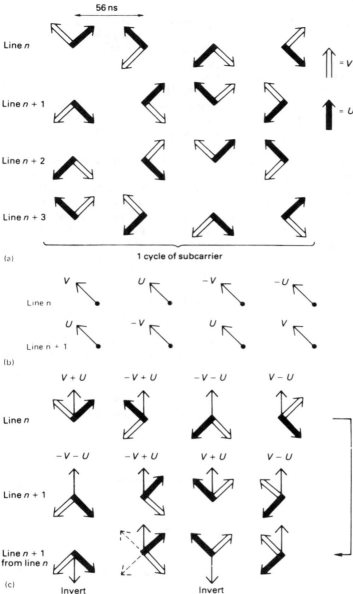

Figure 9.26 (a) The combined effects of V-switch and quarter cycle offset in PAL cause the above relative phases of U and V from line to line, in a four-line sequence which only repeats after four frames. (b) If a sampling system takes samples on the U and V axes, it results in the samples having the values shown here. It is not then possible to convert from one line type to the next because, for example, V cannot be processed to become U and so on. (c) If sampling is performed with sample phase between U and V axes (thin arrow) the samples represent sums and differences of the two signals (cosine term neglected). It will be seen that line n can be made into line $n + 1$ by inverting the samples when U and V have the same sign. When the sample is made, phase information is lost and only amplitude is known. For this reason, the non-inverted samples phase-mirror (dotted arrow) because the phase is determined in the context of adjacent samples

If it is required to convert a line into the next line type, having the opposite sense of V-switch, this can be done by inverting the samples where U and V have different polarities, but not where they have the same polarity.

If the difference is two lines, the only requirement is to invert the whole chroma waveform, as V-switch is the same after two lines, and there have been two quarter cycle offsets of subcarrier making 180°.

If the difference is three lines, an inversion combined with V-switch reversal and a quadrature shift is needed, and this can simply be done by inverting samples where U and V have the same polarity and not where the polarity is different.

The type of line required on the output is available from the reference colour framer, and the type of line played back is determined from the ID codes in variable speed and from the line address in shuttle. By comparing the two line types, the conversion to be performed by the colour processor can be determined. Once chroma and luminance are separated, a digital chroma gain control can be incorporated simply by passing the chroma samples through a multiplier.

Owing to the use of interlace, the head jumps may result in an odd field being played when an even field is needed, and vice versa. The vertical picture movement which results from outputting the wrong field can be completely removed by vertical interpolation.

The output raster and the input raster are shifted slightly so that neither input field aligns with either output field. By using memory to produce three delays of one line each, samples representing four points in a vertical line on the input field are simultaneously available to a four-point FIR filter. If the output field is to be the same as the input field, the phase of the interpolator will be such that the sample value for a line one-quarter of the way down from an input line will be computed. If the opposite type of field is required, the order of the coefficients to the FIR filter will be reversed such that a line three-quarters of the way down from an input line will be computed. Fig. 9.27 illustrates how this process results

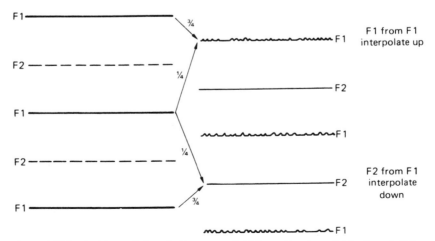

Figure 9.27 Vertical interpolation of either output field from either input field using a half line shift means that output resolution is not changed whether the VTR is interlaced or not, and vertical movement is eliminated

in the image staying at the same vertical position on the screen irrespective of the relation of input and output fields.

The luminance conveys the subjective resolution, and so the vertical chroma interpolation can be done with a simpler filter having only one line of delay to give two points. In this way the output picture in slow motion has the same bandwidth as in colour framed operation, and there are no other artefacts to show that the picture has been processed.

9.17 The D-1 format

D-1 was the first production DVTR format and records 4:2:2 component data using ¾ inch 850 oersted tape. Fig. 9.28(a) shows the track layout. Azimuth recording is not used; instead guard bands are placed between the tracks. These tracks consist of pairs of sectors containing the video data, and the four audio channels are carried in smaller sectors between them. The audio is then in the centre of the tape, where the better data reliability compensates for the fact that the audio blocks must be interleaved over a smaller area. As a further measure, all audio sectors are recorded twice with a different head and in a different sector location for each version. Fig. 9.28(a) also shows that there are three linear tracks in addition to the slant tracks.

A control track is used to drive the capstan in replay and in the various edit modes as was explained in Chapter 8. As this is a segmented format, the control track contains pulses which occur every two segments as in Fig. 9.28(b). This is the equivalent of once per scanner rotation in a four-headed machine, and so these will be at 150 Hz at normal speed. The segment is considered to begin after the audio blocks at the centre of the track; in fact the servo pulse coincides with the end of the preamble on the video sector.

Once per frame, a second pulse is recorded. The frame pulse accompanies every sixth servo pulse for 625 lines, every fifth servo pulse for 525 lines. There is no field pulse, since in 525 line working it would have to occur in between the servo pulses.

It will be seen in Chapter 12 that interaction between the audio sampling rate and the 525 line frame rate produces a five-frame sequence, and this is recorded in a third control track pulse. Finally, if the component input has come from a decoded composite signal, the colour framing flag of that composite signal can optionally be recorded. If a residual subcarrier footprint exists in the component recording, it can be cancelled out if the coder/decoder combination is reversible (see Chapter 4) and if the recording is colour framed to a subsequent composite modulator.

The cue audio track is designed to permit audio to be heard over a wide speed range, when the slant tracks are not accessible. The recording is analog with conventional bias, and is not intended to be of high quality.

The timecode track is essentially identical to the existing EBU/SMPTE timecodes used on other video products.

The segment begins after the audio blocks, with sectors 0 and 1, and continues on the next pair of tracks with sectors 2 and 3. This arrangement ensures that in a four-headed machine data from each segment are distributed over all four heads. Fig. 9.29 shows the relationship between sector number and head number. Heads 0 and 1 begin the track by playing sectors 2 and 3 of an odd segment, and continue through the audio sectors to play sectors 0 and 1 of the next segment.

A	Time-code track lower edge	0.2	±0.1
B	Time-code track upper edge	0.7	±0.1
C	Control track lower edge	1.0	±0.1
D	Control track upper edge	1.5	±0.05
E	Lower edge of programme area	1.8	(derived)
F*	Programme area width	16.00	(derived)
G	Cue audio track lower edge	18.1	±0.15
H	Cue audio track upper edge	18.8	±0.2
I	Programme track width	0.040	±0/-0.005
J	Programme track pitch	0.045	basic
K	Video sector length	77.78	(derived)
M	Audio sector length	2.56	(derived)
N*	Programme track total length	170.00	(derived)
W	Tape width	19.010	0.015

*For 525/60; F: 16.00/1.001, N: 170.00/1.001

X_1	Location of start of segment	0	±0.1
X_2	Location of start of audio sector 3	3.4	±0.1
X_3	Location of start of audio sector 2	6.8	±0.1
X_4	Location of start of audio sector 1	10.2	±0.1
X_5	Location of start of audio sector 0	13.6	±0.1
X_6	Location of start of lower video sector	92.2	±0.1
Y	Programme track reference location	10.490	basic

All dimensions in mm

Figure 9.28(a) The track dimensions of D-1. Note that the segment begins at X_1 after the audio blocks

If head 1 should clog, sector 1 will be lost in even-numbered segments, whereas sector 3 will be lost in odd-numbered segments. Similarly if head 2 clogs, sector 2 in even-numbered segments and sector 0 in odd-numbered segments will be lost. It will be seen that this alternation between odd and even segments is reflected in the data distribution over the four sectors.

Fig. 9.30(a) shows the sample sequence from the sector distributor shown in Fig. 9.7. If samples in this sequence were made into an outer code and written in the sector array as a column, the effect would be as shown in Fig. 9.30(b). Samples relating to one pixel would appear in three different inner codewords,

Figure 9.28(b) The arrangement of the D-1 control track. Servo pulses coincide with the beginning of an even segment after the audio blocks. The next segment has no control track pulse, and so the pulses repeat at drum rotation rate for a four-headed machine. Additional pulses locate the top segment in a frame and record optional colour framing (see text). The value T is $\frac{1}{64}$ the time taken for four tracks to pass. Values shown are for 625/50, with 525/60 values in brackets; 525/50 also has audio frame pulse described in Chapter 12

Figure 9.29 Sector distribution within a segment. In even segments, sector number equals head number, whereas in odd segments (shown shaded) head 0 exchanges with head 2 and head 1 exchanges with head 3. If, for example, head 1 were to clog, sector 1 would be lost in even segments whereas sector 3 would be lost in odd segments. In the absence of this arrangement, a clogged head would lose half of every other segment, which would be harder to conceal

and so it would not be possible to update pixels properly if a single sync block is recovered in shuttle. The sector array has done an excellent job of interleaving the samples; unfortunately it has done too well, and it is necessary to oppose some of the sector array interleave with a reverse interleave prior to the generation of outer codewords in order to get all samples relating to a pixel into one sync block.

Fig. 9.30(c) shows that the samples from the distributor are split into three blocks of one-third of a line which each contain 120 samples. These blocks are then subjected to a four-way interleave which produces four 30 byte blocks to which 2 bytes of Reed–Solomon redundancy are added to produce outer codewords. It will be seen from Fig. 9.30(c) that each codeword is formed entirely from the same type of sample. When these outer codewords become adjacent columns of the sector array, it will be seen from Fig. 9.30(d) that all three samples relating to a given pixel will be in the same row of the array, and so will be recorded in the same sync block, permitting frame store updating in shuttle.[1]

The process must be repeated three times to deal with the whole line, and this will result in 12 outer code blocks which occupy 12 adjacent columns in the sector array. As there are 50 lines in the segment, the sector array will need $12 \times 50 = 600$ columns.

Fig. 9.31(a) shows a typical block diagram of the record section of a D-1 machine, where the inputs will be component video and four audio channels. Audio and video inputs can be either analog or digital, and machines can

Horizontal Index $\longrightarrow$	0	1	2	3	4	5	6	7	8	//	356	357	358	359
Type of symbol $\longrightarrow$	CB_0	Y_0	CR_0	Y_1	CB_2	Y_2	CR_2	Y_3	CB_4	//	CB_{178}	Y_{178}	CR_{178}	Y_{179}

Figure 9.30(a) The output of the four-channel distributor is a sequence of this kind in each channel. There will be 360 bytes in each line

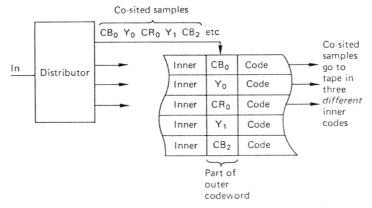

Figure 9.30(b) The result of interleaving the sample sequence of (a) is that co-sited samples appear in different inner codes and cannot be recovered in shuttle

incorporate converters which will be bypassed if a direct digital input is available. Whichever input form is used, the input video will always control the timing of the recording circuitry. In the case of a digital video input, the 27 MHz clock accompanying the data will be used to derive the symbol clock for much of the recorder. In the case of an analog input, the sync pulses will be fed to a phase-locked loop which produces a line-locked sampling rate which then will be used for the symbol clock.

The video data are distributed over four logical channels as was shown in Fig. 9.7. Only one of these is shown in full since they differ only in detail.

Figure 9.30(c) The line of (a) is split into three parts. Each is then made into four interleaved codewords as shown here. Each outer code has 30 data bytes and two redundancy bytes. Twelve such outer codes are needed to complete the line. Each code is formed from the same type of sample

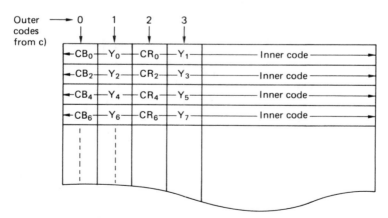

Figure 9.30(d) When the outer codes of (c) are used to form columns in a sector array as shown here, the inner codes will contain co-sited pixels due to the reverse interleave which was performed prior to generating the outer codes. Inner codes picked up at random in shuttle now can be used to update a frame store

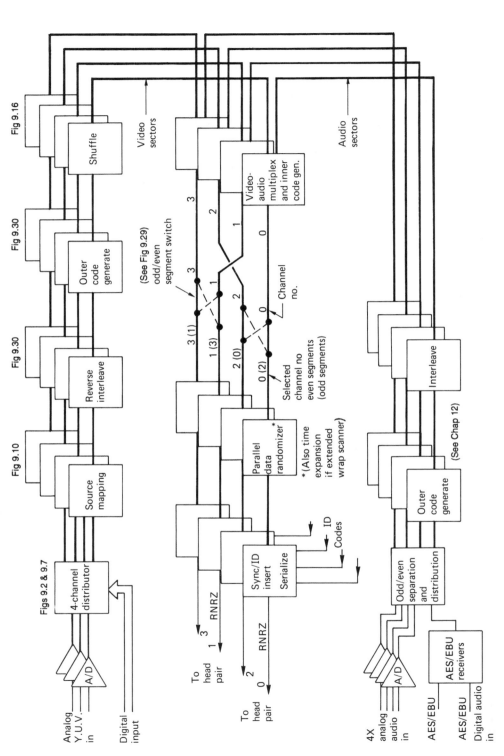

Figure 9.31(a) The essential stages in a D-1 record system described in the text. Note that the odd/even segment switching can be performed using a more complex

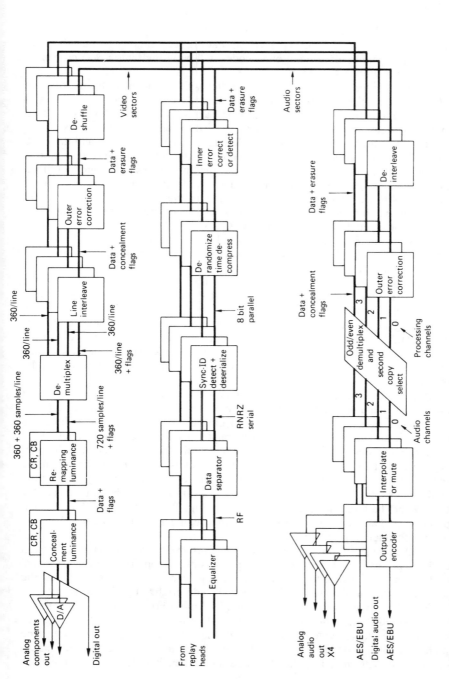

Figure 9.31(b) D-1 replay system. Note time decompression stage to allow data read in one head sweep to be processed in the time taken for the scanner to complete one revolution

Following distribution, the mapping process of Fig. 9.10 is performed. The reverse interleave of Fig. 9.30 then takes place, and these data blocks then have two redundancy bytes added to make outer codes which are written into a sector array in columns. When the sector array is full, it is transferred to a second array memory, but the read addresses are sequential, whereas the write addresses are generated by the shuffler of Fig. 9.16, so that the second array is then shuffled. While this is taking place input outer codes will be written into a second pair of arrays which work alternately.

The audio processing takes place in parallel with the video, with a distribution scheme which spreads samples from all channels over all four heads. This is explained more fully in Chapter 12. Since audio is not two dimensional, no shuffle is necessary, and a regular array is used to form a product block.

The audio samples have longer wordlength than video samples, and there are no details such as co-sited samples to handle, so the outer coding of the audio is somewhat different to that of the video, but the dimensions of the product block are designed so that the audio inner codes are identical in size to video inner codes. In this way, the inner code generation, randomizing, ID generation and serializing are common to both audio and video, which effectively share the same circuitry, heads and tracks in a time multiplex.

At the beginning of a track, the audio and video data to be recorded have been interleaved and shuffled and are held in RAM so they can be made available at the appropriate time.

Input to the serializer will be from the ID generator which produces the preamble and the sync/ID pattern of the first sync block. The serializer input is then switched to the data path.

Reading along a row of the shuffled video sector array then produces two inner blocks, and four bytes of redundancy are added to each to make inner codewords which are randomized and recorded in the sync block. The ID generator then produces the next sync/ID pattern, and the process repeats 160 times until the sector is completed.

At the end of the sector the postamble is written followed by the edit gap and the preamble and sync/ID for the audio sector. The multiplexer on the input to the inner coder switched to the audio RAM during the gap, and now audio inner blocks are turned into inner codewords, randomized and recorded as before.

Five sync blocks are needed to record one audio sector, and then another gap is generated. This process continues until the track is completed at the end of the second video sector with a postamble. Since the logical segment begins after the audio blocks, the inner coder must switch to a different distribution channel for the second half of the track, as shown in Fig. 9.29. There are four logical processing channels, but only two tracks in a segment, so the need to select one of two channels for each track is clear.

Fig. 9.31(b) shows the replay system. The offtape signal is equalized, and fed to the data separator which contains a phase-locked loop. This will synchronize to the bit clock. Sync patterns and IDs are recognized and used to synchronize the derandomizer and the shift register needed to deserialize the data stream.

The inner code processor corrects single-symbol errors with high reliability since four R–S equations agree on the single error.[3] Two symbols or more in error are used to generate erasure flags for the outer codes. Every symbol in the inner code is flagged bad. Inner blocks are then written into a sector array, audio or video as determined by the ID code, and when it is full, the contents are transferred to a second array. This time the read address comes from the shuffle generator, and the write address is sequential. The data are thus de-shuffled, and any burst errors are now dotted around the sector array.

The outer correction now uses the erasure flags which have come from the inner detection system. Two error symbols in each outer code can be corrected. If there are more, correction is not possible, and uncorrectable flags accompany the samples forward.

The reverse interleave is then opposed, and the four channels are combined. The recombination must reflect the changing relationship between head number and sector number. The video mapping is then reversed to restore the original sample values. Samples and uncorrectable flags now pass to the concealment system which can interpolate over different distances and in different directions dependent on the nature of the errors to be concealed.

The samples are now in their original sequence, and can be output digitally or fed to converters.

The audio samples are corrected by inner and outer codes in the same way, and as there are two copies of all audio data, any error-free data will be used to reassemble the output samples. The distribution of audio samples over all channels makes the audio demultiplexer more complex because it has to select any audio channel from any processing channel, and in the case of an uncorrectable error, it must select the second copy from a different channel.

9.18 The D-2 format

The D-2 format was the first production composite digital recorder. It used the same ¾ inch cassette shell as D-1, but the tape was replaced with a 1600 Oe metal particle formulation. A further increase in density was achieved by incorporating azimuth recording. This became standard on all later formats. The basics of the D-2 format are shown in Fig. 9.32. The audio blocks are placed at the ends of the tracks, and the fields begin and end with whole tracks. In a typical

Figure 9.32 Track layout of D-2. Type 0 track has clockwise azimuth rotation, type 1 track has anticlockwise azimuth rotation. Note video outer redundancy at beginning of video sector. This can be omitted in some modes to give the heads more time to settle on track. Audio channels are in separate sectors with gaps so they can be independently edited. Note second copy of audio on opposite side of tape and on different head

Figure 9.33 (a) PAL segmentation in D-2. Four segments of 76 lines are necessary to record one field. The numbering scheme needed to re-create correctly framed pictures is shown here. The field number reflects the 8-field sequence of PAL. Audio blocks are omitted for clarity

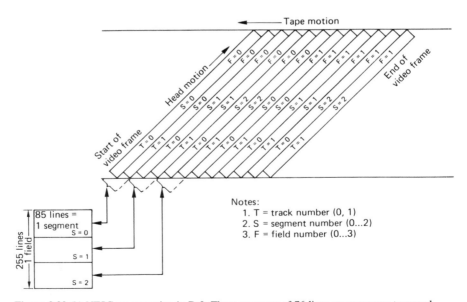

Figure 9.33 (b) NTSC segmentation in D-2. Three segments of 76 lines are necessary to record one field. The numbering scheme needed to recreate correctly framed pictures is shown here. The field number reflects the four-field sequence of NTSC. Audio blocks are omitted for clarity

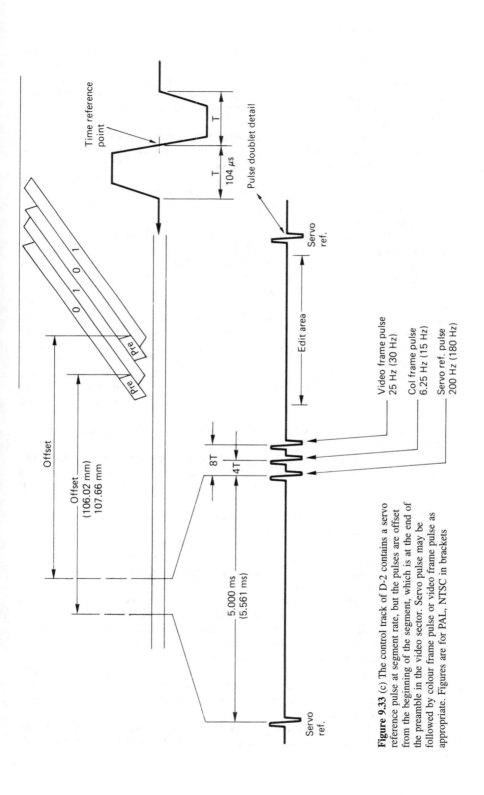

Figure 9.33 (c) The control track of D-2 contains a servo reference pulse at segment rate, but the pulses are offset from the beginning of the segment, which is at the end of the preamble in the video sector. Servo pulse may be followed by colour frame pulse or video frame pulse as appropriate. Figures are for PAL, NTSC in brackets

Time reference point

Pulse doublet detail

T

T

104 µs

Servo ref.

Edit area

Video frame pulse 25 Hz (30 Hz)

Col frame pulse 6.25 Hz (15 Hz)

Servo ref. pulse 200 Hz (180 Hz)

8T

4T

5.000 ms (5.561 ms)

Servo ref.

Offset

Offset (106.02 mm) 107.66 mm

Pre

Pre

0 1 0 1

transport, two pairs of heads are positioned at 180° apart on a scanner which uses a wrap of just over half a turn. The head pairs trace the tape alternately, so each has almost half a revolution in which to jump. As the tape speed increases, the audio will no longer be necessary, and the heads can begin to jump in the audio blocks at the end of the track, and continue to settle during the audio blocks at the beginning of the track.

The wide disparity between the subcarrier frequencies of NTSC and PAL leads to different segmentation being used in each case. The fundamental unit in the D-2 format is the segment, which consists of a pair of tracks, 0 and 1, one of each azimuth type. The first recorded track in a field is always a type 0 track, in which the azimuth is rotated clockwise by 14.97° from perpendicular when looking at the magnetic coating side of the tape. In a type 1 track, the azimuth is rotated 15.03° anticlockwise.

Fig. 9.33(a) shows that in PAL, four segments of 76 lines each record a total of 304 lines per field,[4] whereas in NTSC, shown in Fig. 9.33(b), three segments of 85 lines each record a total of 255 lines per field.[5] The segment and track numbering is also shown. The control track necessary for segmented operation must convey segment, colour frame and frame information. Fig. 9.33(c) shows that there is an event in the control track once per segment, and there are three positions in which a control track pulse can occur. A pulse is always present in the first position, and is used to control the capstan servo so that the segments will be properly traced on replay. The second pulse will occur once per colour frame, and the third pulse will occur once per frame. When tape travel initially starts, the capstan speed will slip until a control track colour frame pulse coincides with a pulse from the reference colour framer. At this point the capstan phase-locked loop will be closed, and the chroma phase of the replay signal will match that of the reference. The frame pulses allow the picture to be reassembled from segments correctly when playback is not colour framed, for example in TSO (Tape Speed Override) mode.

In a scanner of the type normally used, having opposing pairs of heads, two rotations per field will be needed in PAL, and one and a half rotations per field will be necessary in NTSC, giving scanner speeds of 100 Hz and 90/1.001 Hz respectively.

The tape speed does not differ between the formats, so that the laying time remains the same for both. The different scanner speeds result in the two formats having different track angles. The track widths are in inverse proportion to the scanner speeds, so the PAL track is 90% of the width of the NTSC track. A common transport can be used, having one helix angle, but the heads fitted will need to be specific to the format.

Fig. 9.34 shows a typical block diagram of the record section of a D-2 machine, where the inputs will be composite video and four audio channels. Audio and video can be analog or digital, and most machines incorporate converters which can be bypassed if a digital input is available. Whichever input is used, the input video will always control the timing of the recording circuitry. In the case of a digital input, the $4 \times F_{sc}$ clock accompanying the data will be used to derive the symbol clock for much of the recorder. In the case of an analog input, the video burst will be fed to a phase-locked loop which generates the sampling clock locally.

The video data are distributed over two logical channels as was shown in Fig. 9.8. The distribution process results in each logical channel having half of the

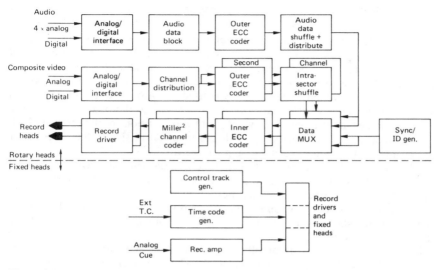

Figure 9.34 D-2 record section showing major stages. Note particularly the distribution of video over two channels, and the merging of the audio and video data into common inner coding circuits

original number of samples in each line: 474 in PAL and 384 in NTSC. Each of these lines will be interleaved into six outer codewords, such that samples in the same codeword are six samples apart in the channel, and 12 samples apart on the television line. This is done by calculating the sample address along the line as a function of the block number and the byte number within the block. The first stage of the shuffle is obtained by changing the address calculation from line to line so that samples in the same place in an outer block on an adjacent line will have come from a different position along the line. This interleave/shuffle process results in blocks of 79 samples in PAL and 64 samples in NTSC. Four bytes of Reed–Solomon redundancy are calculated on each block to make it into a codeword. The size of the outer codewords is equal to the height of the sector array memory, and outer codewords form columns in the sector array. Adjacent outer blocks do not form adjacent columns due to the second stage of the shuffle. In this, the column number is a function of the line number as well as the block number.

Eventually the sector array will be filled with columns of outer codewords, and it is then read in rows which are used to form inner codewords.

Each row results in six inner codewords, and two inner codewords are used in each sync block. The first codeword in the sync block is extended to protect the ID code and so it is 2 bytes longer than the second codeword.

There will be 249 video sync blocks in a PAL track and 204 video sync blocks in an NTSC track. In both channels, the reading of the sector array begins at the bottom, so that the four rows of outer code redundancy are placed at the beginning of the track. In the case of channel 0, readout continues in descending row order, but the memory readout sequence is modified for channel 1 so that a linear tape scratch crossing both tracks in the same place does not result in an identical corruption pattern in the two channels and so that a more random shuffle is effected in shuttle.

The audio processing is shown in parallel with the video processing, and uses a distribution scheme to spread samples in all channels over both heads and double recording to compensate for the fact that the audio blocks are small. This is explained more fully in Chapter 12. Since audio is not two dimensional, no shuffle is necessary, and a regular array is used to form a product block. Audio samples have longer wordlength than video samples, so the outer coding of the audio is somewhat different to the video, but the dimensions of the product block are such that the audio inner codewords are identical in size to the video inner codewords, so that common processing can be used.

The inner code generation, ID generation, serializing and Miller^2 channel coding are common to both audio and video, which effectively share the same circuitry, heads and tracks in a time multiplex.

At the beginning of a segment, the audio and video to be recorded have been interleaved and shuffled and are held in RAM so that they can be made available at the appropriate time.

Input to the serializer will initially be from the sync generator which produces the preamble at the beginning of the track. The serializer input then receives audio sync blocks until the end of the first audio sector, when the edit gap will be written. Following the preamble at the end of the edit gap, the second audio sector will be written, followed by another edit gap. After this edit gap, video sync blocks will be written, followed by a second edit gap and the second pair of audio sectors.

Fig. 9.35 shows the replay system. Following the channel decoder, the sync detector phases the shift register in the deserializer so that the serial bit stream is correctly assembled into a parallel byte stream.

Figure 9.35 D-2 replay section. Two replay channels handle both audio and video as far as inner code error correction, and the data router then splits the audio and video to separate outer code processing

Inner blocks are checked by the inner decoder, which therefore also checks the ID code in the first inner block of a sync block. With 8 bytes of redundancy, the inner decoder could correct up to four random errors, but this would be at the expense of too many miscorrections. Accordingly, the inner code corrects up to three random errors, and a larger number are handled by declaring the entire inner code to be corrupt. An error flag is attached to every symbol in the block. Inner blocks are written into the sector array and de-shuffled, and any burst errors are converted to single-byte errors dotted around the array. These are accompanied by the error flags from the inner decoder, and so the 4 bytes of redundancy in the outer codes can correct four errors by erasure. If there are more than four error flags in an outer code, the symbols will be flagged as uncorrectable, and concealment must be used. When the two channels are combined the concealment process takes place.

The samples are now in their original sequence and can be output digitally or fed to a converter.

The audio samples are corrected by the inner and outer codes as for video, but as there are two copies of all audio data, any error-free data will be used to reassemble output samples.

9.19 The Ampex DCT format

The Ampex DCT (Digital Component Technology) format records data-reduced 8 bit 4:2:2 component video on a development of the D-2 transport. The intrafield data reduction system is based on the discrete Cosine transform having 8 pixel by 4 pixel blocks and uses approximately 2:1 reduction. The DCT transport is designed to be dual standard, which means that it can be configured from the control system menu to record either 525/60 or 625/50 signals. The same segmentation as D-2 is used, i.e. three segments per field for 60 Hz resulting in a drum speed of 90 Hz, and four segments per field for 50 Hz resulting in a drum speed of 100 Hz. It will be recalled that in D-2 the linear tape speed is independent of input standard and this required different track widths and heads. As DCT has a dual-standard transport, a common head width must be used and this is the same as in NTSC D-2. With 60 Hz input the same tape speed as D-2 is obtained, but with 50 Hz input the higher drum speed means that the linear speed will be higher and the playing time is slightly reduced.

The track layout differs from D-2 in that the audio blocks are moved to the centre of the track between divided video blocks. As the data to be recorded have been data reduced, the error-correction system is correspondingly more powerful.

Whilst details of the format were not available at the time of writing, from a conceptual standpoint the block diagram of the machine is broadly similar to that of Digital Betacam.

9.20 The D-3 and D-5 formats

The D-3 format is a composite digital format which records the same data as D-2, and dubs can be made between the two formats using the composite digital interface described in Chapter 7. Whilst the data to be recorded are the same, there is otherwise little in common as D-3 uses ½ inch tape. The fundamental unit in the D-3 format is the segment, which consists of a pair of tracks, 0 and 1, one

Figure 9.36 D-3 uses segmented recording where one video field is recorded on several tracks. At (a) the PAL format requires four segments on eight tracks for one field, whereas at (b) NTSC requires only three segments because the lower subcarrier frequency results in less data per line and there are fewer lines per field

of each azimuth type. These can be seen in Fig. 9.36. Note that the tracks are slanted the opposite way to D-2 because the tape descends the drum and is brought back to the cassette plane on the exit side. In D-2 the tape is taken below the cassette plane on the entry side and climbs the drum.

The first recorded track in a field is always a type 1 track, in which the azimuth is rotated anticlockwise by 19.983° from perpendicular when looking at the magnetic coating side of the tape. In a type 0 track, the azimuth is rotated 20.017° clockwise.

Fig. 9.36(a) shows that in D-3 PAL, four segments holding the equivalent of 76 lines each record a total of 304 lines per field, whereas in D-3 NTSC, shown in Fig. 9.36(b), three segments holding the equivalent of 85 lines each record a total of 255 lines per field.

A D-5 recorder handles component digital signals with 13.5 MHz samples resolved to 10 bit wordlength or 18 MHz samples to 8 bit wordlength. Data reduction is not used and the resultant data rate is approximately twice that of the composite standard. A D-5 transport is basically a double-rate D-3 machine which can replay D-3 format tapes if fitted with an optional circuit board. For component recording, the scanner speed stays the same, but linear tape speed is doubled and extra heads on the scanner come into use, recording four tracks per segment as shown in Fig. 9.37.

In 625/50 D-5, shown in Fig. 9.37(a), four segments of 75 lines form one field whereas in 525/60, shown in (b), three segments of 85 lines are necessary. The segment and track numbering is also shown. It should be stressed that the data contained in a field are shuffled prior to segmentation, so the contents of a given segment could have come from anywhere in the field.

The control track necessary for segmented operation must convey segment, colour frame and frame information. Fig. 9.38 also shows that the control track

Cue track

Video sector 1

Audio sector 3

Audio sector 2

Audio sector 1

Audio sector 0

Video sector 0

Control track

Time code track

Figure 9.37 The D-5 format has four tracks per segment. Note edit gap alignment as per D-3 which allows quadruple-width erase head

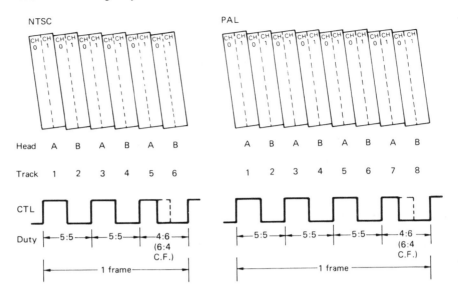

Figure 9.38 The D-3 control track uses one flux change per segment (or one cycle per scanner revolution). Normally the CTL duty cycle is 5:5 but at the end of every frame the duty cycle becomes 4:6 so that the segments can be put back in the correct frames. At the end of a colour frame, every two frames in NTSC or every four frames in PAL, CTL duty cycle changes to 6:4 to denote the colour frame flag

in PAL uses a 100 Hz waveform where the rising edge should occur coincident with a given scanner angle to allow capstan phase control. There are, however, three duty cycles which can be used in the control track waveform. A 50% duty cycle indicates a segment pulse, whereas a 40% cycle indicates a frame pulse every eight segments, so that the segmentation can be properly reversed on replay. A 60% duty cycle indicates a colour frame pulse every four frames. In NTSC the frequency will be 90/1.001 Hz, frame pulses will be every six segments and the colour frame pulse will be every two frames.

When tape travel initially starts, the capstan speed will slip until a control track colour frame pulse coincides with a pulse from the reference colour framer. At this point the capstan phase-locked loop will be closed, and the chroma phase of the replay signal will match that of the reference. The frame pulses allow the picture to be reassembled from segments correctly when playback is not colour framed, for example in TSO (Tape Speed Override) mode.

Fig. 9.39 shows a typical block diagram of the record section of a D-3 machine,[6] where the inputs will be composite video and four audio channels. Audio and video can be analog or digital, and most machines incorporate converters which can be bypassed if a digital input is available. Whichever input is used, the input video will always control the timing of the recording circuitry. In the case of a digital input, the $4 \times F_{sc}$ clock accompanying the data will be used to derive the symbol clock for much of the recorder. In the case of an analog input, the video burst will be fed to a phase-locked loop which generates the sampling clock locally.

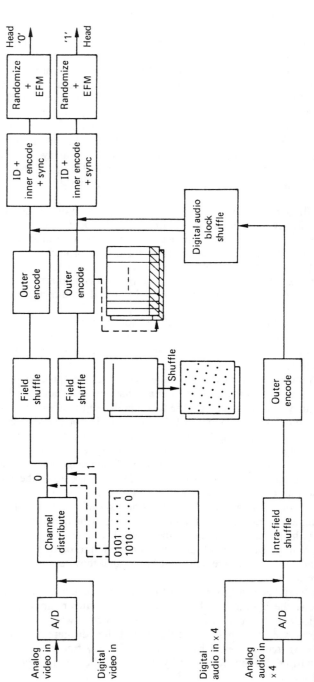

Figure 9.39 Block diagram of record section of D-3 showing conversion, shuffling and outer code generation separately for audio and video. Inner code, ID and sync generation, randomizing and EFM coding are common to video and audio

The video data are distributed over two logical channels as was shown in Fig. 9.9.

The distribution process results in each logical channel having half of the original number of samples in each line: 474 in PAL and 384 in NTSC. Each of these lines will be interleaved into three outer codewords, such that samples in the same codeword are six samples apart on the television line. The first stage of the shuffle is obtained by changing the address calculation from line to line so that samples in the same place in an outer block on an adjacent line will have come from a different position along the line. This interleave/shuffle process results in blocks of 158 samples in PAL and 128 samples in NTSC. Eight bytes of Reed–Solomon redundancy are calculated on each block to make it into a codeword. The size of the outer codewords is equal to the height of the field array memory, and outer codewords form columns in the field array. Adjacent outer blocks do not form adjacent columns due to the second stage of the shuffle. In this, the column number is a function of the line number as well as the block number.

Eventually the sector array will be filled with columns of outer codewords, and it is then read in rows which are used to form inner codewords.

Each row results in 12 or nine inner codewords, and one inner codeword is used in each sync block. The codeword is extended to protect the ID code.

There will be 498 video sync blocks in a PAL track and 408 video sync blocks in an NTSC track. In both channels, the reading of the field array begins at the bottom, so that the outer code redundancy is placed at the beginning of the track.

The memory readout sequence is modified for channel 1 so that a linear tape scratch crossing both tracks in the same place does not result in an identical corruption pattern in the two channels and so that a more random shuffle is effected in shuttle.

The audio processing is shown in parallel with the video processing, and uses a distribution scheme to spread samples in all channels over both heads and over 100% redundancy to compensate for the fact that the audio blocks are small. This is explained more fully in Chapter 12. Since audio is not two dimensional, no shuffle is necessary, and a regular array is used to form a product block. Audio samples have longer wordlength than video samples, so the outer coding of the audio is somewhat different to the video, but the dimensions of the product block are such that the audio inner codewords are identical in size to the video inner codewords, so that common processing can be used.

The inner code generation, ID generation, serializing, randomizing and channel coding are common to both audio and video, which effectively share the same circuitry, heads and tracks in a time multiplex.

At the beginning of a segment, the audio and video to be recorded have been interleaved and shuffled and are held in RAM so that they can be made available at the appropriate time.

Input to the serializer will initially be from the sync generator which produces the preamble at the beginning of the track. The serializer input then receives audio sync blocks until the end of the first audio sector, when the edit gap will be written. Following the preamble at the end of the edit gap, the second audio sector will be written, followed by another edit gap. After this edit gap, video sync blocks will be written, followed by a second edit gap and the second pair of audio sectors.

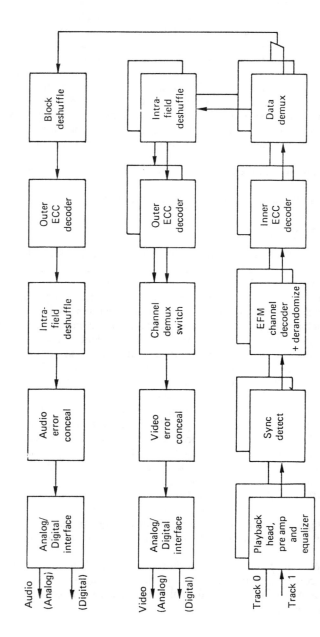

Figure 9.40 Replay block of D-3. Common circuitry is used for audio and video EFM demodulation and inner error correction. Data are then demultiplexed to separate audio and video signal paths

Fig. 9.40 shows the replay system. The sync detector phases the shift register in the deserializer so that the serial bit stream is correctly assembled into 14 bit channel symbols for 14–8 decoding and phases the derandomizer.

Inner blocks are checked by the inner decoder, which therefore also checks the ID code. The 14–8 decoder can also generate error flags if a 14 bit channel pattern is detected which is not in the codebook. With 8 bytes of redundancy, the inner decoder could correct up to four random errors, but this would be at the expense of too many miscorrections. Using flags from the channel decoder helps to make the inner code more reliable. If the inner code correcting power is exceeded, this will be handled by declaring the entire inner code to be corrupt. An error flag is attached to every symbol in the block. Inner blocks are written into the field array and de-shuffled, and any burst errors are converted to single-byte errors dotted around the array. These are accompanied by the error flags from the inner decoder, and so the 8 bytes of redundancy in the outer codes can correct eight errors by erasure. If there are more than eight error flags in an outer code, the symbols will be flagged as uncorrectable, and concealment must be used. When the two channels are combined the concealment process takes place.

The samples are now in their original sequence and can be output digitally or fed to a converter.

The audio samples are corrected by the inner and outer codes as for video.

9.21 Digital Betacam

Digital Betacam (DB) is a component format which accepts 8 or 10 bit 4:2:2 data with 720 luminance samples per active line and four channels of 48 kHz digital audio having up to 20 bit wordlength. Video data reduction based on the Discrete Cosine Transform is employed, with a compression factor of almost two to one (assuming 8 bit input). The audio data are uncompressed. The cassette shell of the ½ inch analog Betacam format is retained, but contains 14 micrometre metal particle tape. The digital cassette contains an identification hole which allows the transport to identify the tape type. Unlike the other digital formats, only two cassette sizes are available. The large cassette offers 124 minutes of playing time; the small cassette plays for 40 minutes.

Owing to the trade off between SNR and bandwidth, which is a characteristic of digital recording, the tracks must be longer than in the analog Betacam format, but narrower. The drum diameter of the DB transport is 81.4 mm which is designed to produce tracks of the required length for digital recording. The helix angle of the digital drum is designed such that when an analog Betacam tape is driven past at the correct speed, the track angle is correct. Certain DB machines are fitted with analog heads which can trace the tracks of an analog tape. As the drum size is different, the analog playback signal is time compressed by about 9%, but this is easily dealt with in the timebase-correction process.[7] The fixed heads are compatible with the analog Betacam positioning. The reverse compatibility is for playback only; the digital machine cannot record on analog cassettes.

Fig. 9.41 shows the track pattern for 625/50 Betacam. The four digital audio channels are recorded in separate sectors of the slant tracks, and so one of the linear audio channels of the analog format is dispensed with, leaving one linear audio track for cueing.

Figure 9.41 The track pattern of Digital Betacam. Control and timecode tracks are identical in location to the analog format, as is the single analog audio cue track. Note the use of a small guard band between segments

Azimuth recording is employed, with two tracks being recorded simultaneously by adjacent heads. Electronic delays are used to align the position of the edit gaps in the two tracks of a segment, allowing double-width flying erase heads to be used. Three segments are needed to record one field, requiring one and a half drum revolutions. Thus the drum speed is three times that of the analog format. However, the track pitch is less than one-third that of the analog format, so the linear speed of the digital tape is actually slower. The track width is 24 micrometres, with a 4 micrometre guard band between segments making the effective track pitch 26 micrometres, compared with 18 for D-3/D-5 and 39 for D-2/DCT.

There is a linear timecode track whose structure is identical to the analog Betacam timecode and a control track shown in Fig. 9.42 having a fundamental

Figure 9.42 The control track of Digital Betacam uses duty cycle modulation for colour framing purposes

frequency of 50 Hz. Ordinarily the duty cycle is 50%, but this changes to 65/35 in field 1 and 35/65 in field 5. The rising edge of the CTL signal coincides with the first segment of a field, and the duty cycle variations allow four- or eight-field colour framing if decoded composite sources are used. As the drum speed is 75 Hz, CTL and drum phase coincide every three revolutions.

Fig. 9.43 shows the track layout in more detail. Unlike other digital formats, DB incorporates tracking pilot tones recorded between the audio and video sectors. The first tone has a frequency of approximately 4 MHz and appears once per drum revolution. The second is recorded at approximately 400 kHz and appears twice per drum revolution. The pilot tones are recorded when a recording is first made on a blank tape, and will be re-recorded following an assemble edit, but during an insert edit the tracking pilots are not re-recorded, but used as a guide to the insertion of the new tracks.

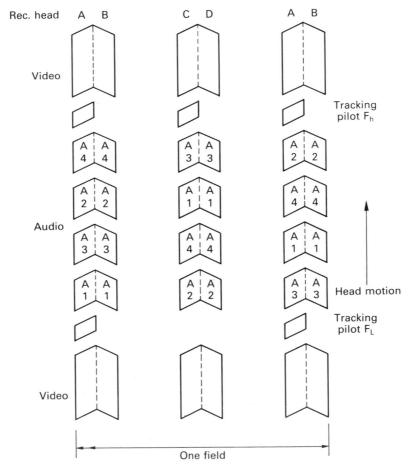

Figure 9.43 The sector structure of Digital Betacam. Note the tracking tones between the audio and video sectors which are played back for alignment purposes during insert edits

The amplitude of the pilot signal is a function of the head tracking. The replay heads are somewhat wider than the tracks, and so a considerable tracking error will have to be present before a loss of amplitude is noted. This is partly offset by the use of a very long-wavelength pilot tone in which fringing fields increase the effective track width. The low-frequency tones are used for automatic playback tracking.

With the tape moving at normal speed, the capstan phase is changed by steps in one direction and then the other as the pilot tone amplitude is monitored. The phase which results in the largest amplitude will be retained. During the edit preroll the record heads play back the high-frequency pilot tone and capstan phase is set for largest amplitude. The record heads are the same width as the tracks and a short-wavelength pilot tone is used such that any mistracking will cause immediate amplitude loss. This is an edit optimize process and results in new tracks being inserted in the same location as the originals. As the pilot tones are played back in insert editing, there will be no tolerance build-up in the case of multiple inserts.

The data reduction of DB[8] works on an intrafield basis to allow complete editing freedom and uses processes described in Chapter 4.

Fig. 9.44 shows a block diagram of the record section of DB. Analog component inputs are sampled at 13.5 and 6.75 MHz. Alternatively the input may be SDI at 270 Mbits/s which is deserialized and demultiplexed to separate components. The raster scan input is first converted to blocks which are 8 pixels wide by 4 pixels high in the luminance channel and 4 pixels by 4 in the two colour difference channels. When two fields are combined on the screen, the result is effectively an interlaced 8 × 8 luminance block with colour difference pixels having twice the horizontal luminance pixel spacing. The pixel blocks are then subject to a field shuffle. A shuffle based on individual pixels is impossible because it would raise the high-frequency content of the image and destroy the power of the data reduction process. Instead the block shuffle helps the data reduction by making the average entropy of the image more constant. This happens because the shuffle exchanges blocks from flat areas of the image with blocks from highly detailed areas. The shuffle algorithm also has to consider the requirements of picture-in-shuttle. The blocking and shuffle take place when the read addresses of the input memory are permuted with respect to the write addresses.

Following the input shuffle the blocks are associated into sets of ten in each component and are then subject to the discrete cosine transform. The resulting coefficients are then subject to an iterative requantizing process followed by variable-length coding. The iteration adjusts the size of the quantizing step until the overall length of the ten coefficient sets is equal to the constant capacity of an entropy block which is 364 bytes. Within that entropy block the amount of data representing each individual DCT block may vary considerably, but the overall block size stays the same.

The DCT process results in coefficients whose wordlength exceeds the input wordlength. As a result it does not matter if the input wordlength is 8 bits or 10 bits; the requantizer simply adapts to make the output data rate constant. Thus the compression is greater with 10 bit input, corresponding to about 2.4 to 1.

The next step is the generation of product codes as shown in Fig. 9.45(a). Each entropy block is divided into two halves of 162 bytes each and loaded into the rows of the outer code RAM which holds 114 such rows, corresponding to one-

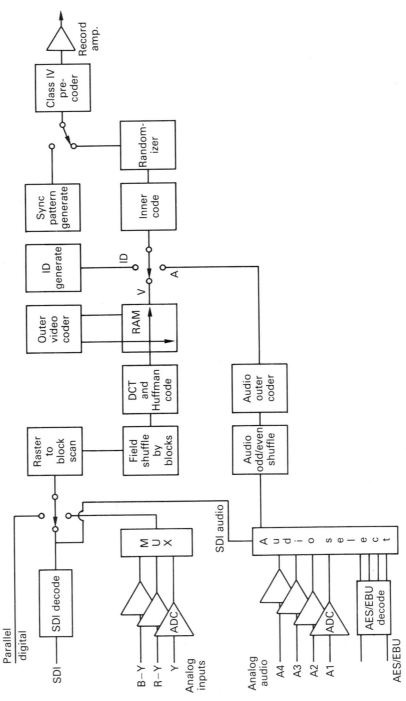

Figure 9.44 Block diagram of Digital Betacam record channel. Note that the use of data reduction makes this rather different to the block layout of full-bit formats

twelfth of a field. When the RAM is full, it is read in columns by address mapping and 12 bytes of outer Reed–Solomon redundancy are added to every column, increasing the number of rows to 126.

The outer code RAM is read out in rows once more, but this time all 126 rows are read in turn. To the contents of each row is added a 2 byte ID code and then the data plus ID bytes are turned into an inner code by the addition of 14 bytes of Reed–Solomon redundancy.

Inner codewords pass through the randomizer and are then converted to serial form for Class IV partial response precoding. With the addition of a sync pattern of 2 bytes, each inner codeword becomes a sync block as shown in Fig. 9.45(c). Each video block contains 126 sync blocks, preceded by a preamble and followed by a postamble. One field of video data requires 12 such blocks. Pairs of blocks are recorded simultaneously by the parallel heads of a segment. Two

(a) Video . . . 12 ECC blocks/field (2 ECC blocks/track)

(b) Audio . . . 2 ECC blocks/ (CH. × field)

(c) Sync block

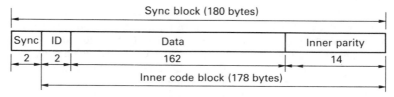

Figure 9.45 Video product codes of Digital Betacam are shown at (a); 12 of these are needed to record one field. Audio product codes are shown at (b); two of these record samples corresponding to one field period. Sync blocks are common to audio and video as shown at (c). The ID code discriminates between video and audio channels

video blocks are recorded at the beginning of the track, and two more are recorded after the audio and tracking tones.

The audio data for each channel are separated into odd and even samples for concealment purposes and assembled in RAM into two blocks corresponding to one field period. Two 20 bit samples are stored in 5 bytes. Fig. 9.45(b) shows that each block consists of 1458 bytes including auxiliary data from the AES/EBU interface, arranged as a block of 162 × 9 bytes. Outer code redundancy of 100% is obtained by adding 9 bytes of Reed–Solomon check bytes to each column of the blocks.

The inner codes for the audio blocks are produced by the same circuitry as the video inner codes on a time-shared basis. The resulting sync blocks are identical in size and differ only in the provision of different ID codes. The randomizer and precoder are also shared. It will be seen from Fig. 9.43 that there are three segments in a field and that the position of an audio sector corresponding to a particular audio channel is different in each segment. This means that damage due to a linear tape scratch is distributed over three audio channels instead of being concentrated in one.

Each audio product block results in 18 sync blocks. These are accommodated in audio sectors of six sync blocks each in three segments. The audio sectors are preceded by preambles and followed by postambles. Between these are edit gaps which allow each audio channel to be independently edited.

By spreading the outer codes over three different audio sectors the correction power is much improved because data from two sectors can be used to correct errors in the third.

Fig. 9.46 shows the replay channel of DB. The RF signal picked up by the replay head passes first to the Class IV partial response playback circuit in which it becomes a three-level signal as was shown in Chapter 5. The three level signal is passed to an ADC which converts it into a digitally represented form so that the Viterbi detection can be carried out in logic circuitry. The sync detector identifies the synchronizing pattern at the beginning of each sync block and resets the block bit count. This allows the entire inner codeword of the sync block to be deserialized into bytes and passed to the inner error checker. Random errors will be corrected here, whereas burst errors will result in the block being flagged as in error.

Sync blocks are written into the de-interleave RAM with error flags where appropriate. At the end of each video sector the product code RAM will be filled, and outer code correction can be performed by reading the RAM at right angles and using the error flags to initiate correction by erasure. Following outer code correction the RAM will contain corrected data or uncorrectable error flags which will later be used to initiate concealment.

The sync blocks can now be read from memory and assembled in pairs into entropy blocks. The entropy block is of fixed size, but contains coefficient blocks of variable length. The next step is to identify the individual coefficients and separate the luminance and colour difference coefficients by decoding the Huffman-coded sequence. Following the assembly of coefficient sets the inverse DCT will result in pixel blocks in three components once more.

The pixel blocks are de-shuffled by mapping the write address of a field memory. When all of the tracks of a field have been decoded, the memory will contain a de-shuffled field containing either correct sample data or correction flags. By reading the memory without address mapping the de-shuffled data are

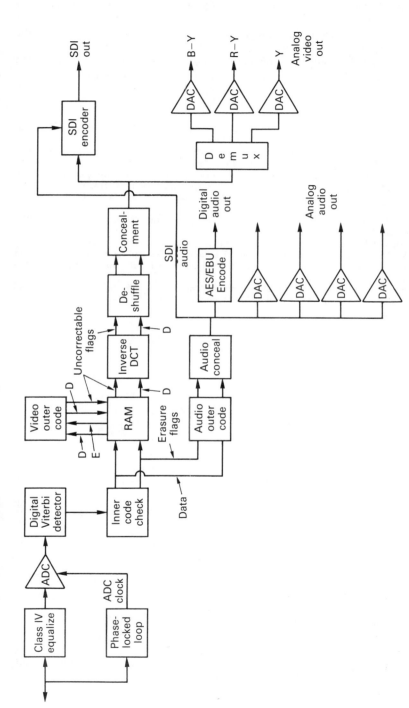

Figure 9.46 The replay channel of Digital Betacam. This differs from a full-bit system primarily in the requirement to deserialize variable-length coefficient blocks prior to the inverse DCT

then passed through the concealment circuit where flagged data are concealed by data from nearby in the same field or from a previous field. The memory readout process is buffered from the offtape timing by the RAM and as a result the timebase-correction stage is inherent in the replay process. Following concealment the data can be output as conventional raster scan video either formatted to parallel or serial digital standards or converted to analog components.

References

1. Brush, R., Video data shuffling for the 4:2:2 DVTR. Presented at 20th SMPTE Television Conf. (Chicago, 1986), *SMPTE J.*, **95**, 1009–1016 (1986)
2. Slavin, K.R. and Wells, N.D., The effects of random bit errors on YUV component video signals – II, *BBC Res. Dep. Tech. Memo.*, No. ER-1526 (1985)
3. Wilkinson, J.H., The SMPTE type D-1 digital television tape recorder – error control. Presented at 20th SMPTE Television Conf. (Chicago, 1986), *SMPTE J.*, **95**, 1144–1149 (1986)
4. Brush, R., Design considerations for the D-2 PAL composite DVTR. *IERE Conf. Publ. No. 79*, 141–148 (1988)
5. Brush, R., Design considerations for the D-2 NTSC composite DVTR. Presented at SMPTE Technical Conf. (Los Angeles, 1987).
6. AJ-D350 1/2" Digital Studio VTR Technical Guide. Panasonic (1991)
7. Huckfield, D., Sato, N. and Sato, I., Digital Betacam - The application of state of the art technology to the development of an affordable component DVTR. *Record of 18th ITS*, 180–199 (Montreux, 1993)
8. Creed, D. and Kaminaga, K., Digital compression strategies for video tape recorders in studio applications. *Record of 18th ITS*, 291–301 (Montreux, 1993)

Chapter 10

Disk drives in digital video

Disk drives came into being as random access file-storage devices for digital computers. The explosion in personal computers has fuelled demand for low-cost high-density disk drives and the rapid access offered is increasingly finding applications in digital video. After lengthy development, optical discs are also emerging in digital video applications. This Chapter discusses the technology behind all types of disk storage.

10.1 Types of disk

Once the operating speed of computers began to take strides forward, it became evident that a single processor could be made to jump between several different programs so fast that they all appeared to be executing simultaneously, a process known as multiprogramming. Computer memory remains more expensive than other types of mass storage, and so it has never been practicable to store every program or data file necessary within the computer memory. In practice some kind of storage medium is necessary where only programs which are running or are about to run are in the memory, and the remainder are stored on the medium. Punched cards, paper tape and magnetic tape are all computer media, but suffer from the same disadvantage of slow access. The disk drive was developed specifically to offer rapid random access to stored data. Fig. 10.1 shows that, in a disk drive, the data are recorded on a circular track. In floppy disks, the magnetic medium is flexible, and the head touches it. This restricts the rotational speed. In hard-disk drives, the disk rotates at several thousand rpm so that the head-to-disk speed is of the order of 100 miles per hour. At this speed no contact

Figure 10.1 The rotating store concept. Data on the rotating circular track are repeatedly presented to the head

can be tolerated, and the head flies on a boundary layer of air turning with the disk at a height measured in microinches. The longest time it is necessary to wait to access a given data block is a few milliseconds. To increase the storage capacity of the drive without a proportional increase in cost, many concentric tracks are recorded on the disk surface, and the head is mounted on a positioner which can rapidly bring the head to any desired track. Such a machine is termed a moving-head disk drive. An increase in capacity could be obtained by assembling many disks on a common spindle to make a disk pack. The small size of magnetic heads allows the disks to be placed close together. The positioner is usually designed so that it can remove the heads away from the disk completely, so that it can be exchanged. The exchangeable-pack moving-head disk drive became the standard for mainframe computers and minicomputers for a long time, and usually at least two were furnished so that important data could be 'backed up' or copied to a second disk for safe keeping.

Later came the so-called Winchester technology disks, where the disk and positioner formed a compact sealed unit which allowed increased storage capacity but precluded exchange of the disk pack alone. This led to the development of high-speed tape drives which could be used as security backup storage.

Disk drive development has been phenomenally rapid. The first flying-head disks were about 3 feet across. Subsequently disk sizes of 14, 8, 5¼, 3½ and 1⅞ inches were developed. Despite the reduction in size, the storage capacity is not compromised because the recording density has increased and continues to increase. In fact there is an advantage in making a drive smaller because the moving parts are then lighter and travel a shorter distance, improving access time.

There are numerous types of optical disc, which have different characteristics.[1] There are, however, three broad groups which can be usefully compared.

(1) The Compact Disc and LaserVision are examples of a read-only laser disc, which is designed for mass duplication by stamping. They cannot be recorded.
(2) Some laser discs can be recorded, but once a recording has been made, it cannot be changed or erased. These are usually referred to as write-once-read-mostly (WORM) discs. The general principle is that the disc contains a thin layer of metal; on recording, a powerful laser melts holes in the layer. Clearly once a pattern of holes has been made, it is permanent.
(3) Erasable optical discs have essentially the same characteristic as magnetic disks, in that new and different recordings can be made in the same track indefinitely, but there is usually a separate erase cycle needed before a new recording can be made since overwrite is not always possible.

Fig. 10.2 introduces the essential subsystems of a disk drive which will be discussed here. Magnetic drives and optical drives are similar in that both have a spindle drive mechanism to revolve the disk, and a positioner to give radial access across the disk surface. In the optical drive, the positioner has to carry a collection of lasers, lenses, prisms, gratings and so on, and will be rather larger than a magnetic head. The heavier pickup cannot be accelerated as fast as a magnetic drive positioner, and access time is slower. A large number of pickups on one positioner makes matters worse. For this reason and because of the larger spacing needed between the discs, multiplatter optical discs are uncommon.

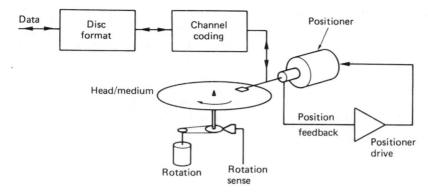

Figure 10.2 The main subsystems of a typical disk drive

Instead 'juke box' mechanisms have been developed to allow a large library of optical discs to be mechanically accessed by one or more drives.[2] Access time is sometimes reduced by having more than one positioner per disc, a technique adopted rarely in magnetic drives. A penalty of the very small track pitch possible in laser discs, which gives the enormous storage capacity, is that very accurate track following is needed, and it takes some time to lock on to a track. For this reason tracks on laser discs are usually made as a continuous spiral, rather than the concentric rings of magnetic disks. In this way, a continuous data transfer involves no more than track following once the beginning of the file is located.

10.2 Structure of disk

The floppy disk is actually made using tape technology, and will be discussed later. Rigid disks are made from aluminium alloy. Magnetic oxide types use an aluminium oxide substrate, or undercoat, giving a flat surface to which the oxide binder can adhere. Later metallic disks having higher coercivity are electroplated with the magnetic medium. In both cases the surface finish must be extremely good owing to the very small flying height of the head. As the head-to-disk speed and recording density are functions of track radius, the data are confined to the outer areas of the disks to minimize the change in these parameters. As a result, the centre of the pack is often an empty well. In fixed (i.e. non-interchangeable) disks the drive motor is often installed in the centre well.

The information layer of optical discs may be made of a variety of substances, depending on the working principle. This layer is invariably protected beneath a thick transparent layer of glass or polycarbonate.

Exchangeable optical and magnetic disks are usually fitted in protective cartridges. These have various shutters which retract on insertion in the drive to allow access by the drive spindle and heads. Removable packs usually seat on a taper to ensure concentricity and are held to the spindle by a permanent magnet. A lever mechanism may be incorporated in the cartridge to assist their removal.

10.3 Magnetic disk terminology

In all technologies there are specialist terms, and those relating to magnetic disks will be explained here. Fig. 10.3 shows a typical multiplatter magnetic disk pack in conceptual form. Given a particular set of coordinates (cylinder, head, sector), known as a disk physical address, one unique data block is defined. A common block capacity is 512 bytes. The subdivision into sectors is sometimes omitted for special applications. A disk drive can be randomly accessed, because any block address can follow any other, but unlike a RAM, at each address a large block of data is stored, rather than a single word.

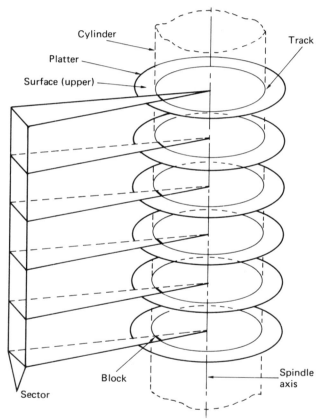

Figure 10.3 Disk terminology. Surface: one side of a platter. Track: path described on a surface by a fixed head. Cylinder: imaginary shape intersecting all surfaces at tracks of the same radius. Sector: angular subdivision of pack. Block: that part of a track within one sector. Each block has a unique cylinder, head and sector address

10.4 Principle of flying head

Magnetic disk drives permanently sacrifice storage density in order to offer rapid access. The use of a flying head with a deliberate air gap between it and the medium is necessary because of the high medium speed, but this causes a severe separation loss which restricts the linear density available. The air gap must be accurately maintained, and consequently the head is of low mass and is mounted flexibly.

The aerohydrodynamic part of the head is known as the slipper; it is designed to provide lift from the boundary layer which changes rapidly with changes in flying height. It is not initially obvious that the difficulty with disk heads is not making them fly, but making them fly close enough to the disk surface. The boundary layer travelling at the disk surface has the same speed as the disk, but as height increases, it slows down due to drag from the surrounding air. As the lift is a function of relative air speed, the closer the slipper comes to the disk, the greater the lift will be. The slipper is therefore mounted at the end of a rigid cantilever sprung towards the medium. The force with which the head is pressed towards the disk by the spring is equal to the lift at the designed flying height.

(a)

(b)

(c)

Figure 10.4 (a) Winchester head construction showing large air bleed grooves. (b) Close-up of slipper showing magnetic circuit on trailing edge. (c) Thin film head is fabricated on the end of the slipper using microcircuit technology

Because of the spring, the head may rise and fall over small warps in the disk. It would be virtually impossible to manufacture disks flat enough to dispense with this feature. As the slipper negotiates a warp it will pitch and roll in addition to rising and falling, but it must be prevented from yawing, as this would cause an azimuth error. Downthrust is applied to the aerodynamic centre by a spherical thrust button, and the required degrees of freedom are supplied by a thin flexible gimbal. The slipper has to bleed away surplus air in order to approach close enough to the disk, and holes or grooves are usually provided for this purpose in the same way that pinch rollers on some tape decks have grooves to prevent tape slip.

In exchangeable-pack drives, there will be a ramp on the side of the cantilever which engages a fixed block when the heads are retracted in order to lift them away from the disk surface.

10.5 Magnetic reading and writing

Fig. 10.4 shows how disk heads are made. The magnetic circuit of disk heads was originally assembled from discrete magnetic elements. As the gap and flying height became smaller to increase linear recording density, the slipper was made from ferrite, and became part of the magnetic circuit. This was completed by a small C-shaped ferrite piece which carried the coil. Ferrite heads were restricted in the coercivity of disk they could write without saturating. In thin-film heads, the magnetic circuit and coil are both formed by deposition on a substrate which becomes the rear of the slipper.

In a moving-head device it is not practicable to position separate erase, record and playback heads accurately. Erase is by overwriting, and reading and writing are carried out by the same head. The presence of the air film causes severe separation loss, and peak shift distortion is a major problem. The flying height of the head varies with the radius of the disk track, and it is difficult to provide accurate equalization of the replay channel because of this. The write current is often controlled as a function of track radius so that the changing reluctance of the air gap does not change the resulting record flux. Automatic gain control (AGC) is used on replay to compensate for changes in signal amplitude from the head.

Equalization may be used on recording in the form of precompensation, which moves recorded transitions in such a way as to oppose the effects of peak shift in addition to any replay equalization used. This was discussed in Chapter 5, which also introduced digital channel coding.

Early disks used FM coding, which was easy to decode, but had a poor density ratio. The invention of MFM revolutionized hard disks, and was at one time universal. Further progress led to run-length-limited codes such as 2/3 and 2/7 which had a high density ratio without sacrificing the large jitter window necessary to reject peak shift distortion. Partial response is also suited to disks, but is not yet in common use.

Typical drives have several heads, but with the exception of special purpose parallel-transfer machines, only one head will be active at any one time, which means that the read and write circuitry can be shared between the heads. Fig. 10.5 shows that in one approach the centre-tapped heads are isolated by connecting the centre tap to a negative voltage, which reverse biases the matrix diodes. The centre tap of the selected head is made positive. When reading, a small current flows through both halves of the head winding, as the diodes are forward biased. Opposing currents in the head cancel, but read signals due to transitions on the medium can pass through the forward-biased diodes to become differential signals on the matrix bus. During writing, the current from the write generator passes alternately through the two halves of the head coil. Further isolation is necessary to prevent the write-current-induced voltages from destroying the read preamplifier input. Alternatively, FET analog switches may be used for head selection.

The read channel usually incorporates AGC, which will be overridden by the control logic between data blocks in order to search for address marks, which are short unmodulated areas of track. As a block preamble is entered, the AGC will be enabled to allow a rapid gain adjustment.

The high bit rates of disk drives, due to the speed of the medium, mean that peak detection in the replay channel is usually by differentiation. The detected peaks are then fed to the data separator.

10.6 Moving the heads

The servo system required to move the heads rapidly between tracks, and yet hold them in place accurately for data transfer, is a fascinating and complex piece of engineering.

In exchangeable-pack drives, the disk positioner moves on a straight axis which passes through the spindle. The head carriage will usually have preloaded

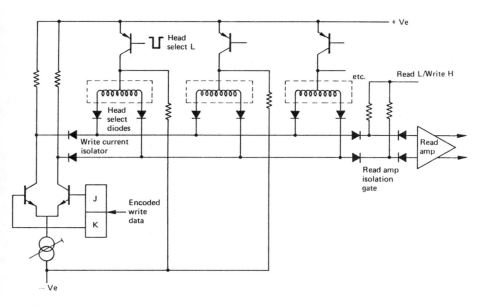

Figure 10.5 representative head matrix

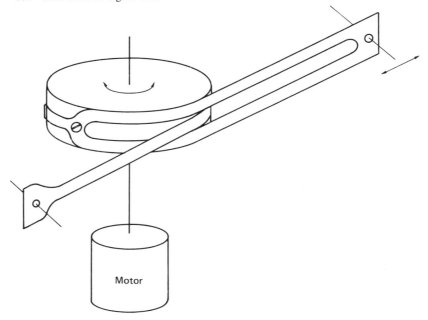

Figure 10.6 A low-cost linear positioner can be obtained using a drum and split-band drive, shown here, or with flexible wire. The ends of the band are fixed to the carriage

ball races which run on rails mounted on the bed of the machine, although some drives use plain sintered bushes sliding on polished rods.

Motive power on early disk drives was hydraulic, but this soon gave way to moving-coil drive, because of the small moving mass which this technique permits. Lower-cost units use a conventional electric motor, as shown in Fig. 10.6, which drives the carriage through steel wires wound around it, or via a split metal band which is shaped to allow both ends to be fixed to the carriage despite the centre making a full turn around the motor shaft. The final possibility is a coarse-threaded shaft or leadscrew which engages with a nut on the carriage. In very low-cost drives, the motor will be a stepping motor, and the positions of the tracks will be determined by the natural detents of the stepping motor. This has an advantage for portable drives, because a stepping motor will remain detented without power. Moving-coil actuators require power to stay on track.

When a drive is track following, it is said to be detented, in fine mode or in linear mode depending on the manufacturer. When a drive is seeking from one track to another, it can be described as being in coarse mode or velocity mode. These are the two major operating modes of the servo.

With the exception of stepping-motor-driven carriages, the servo system needs positional feedback of some kind. The purpose of the feedback will be one or more of the following:

(1) to count the number of cylinders crossed during a seek
(2) to generate a signal proportional to carriage velocity
(3) to generate a position error proportional to the distance from the centre of the desired track.

Magnetic and optical drives obtain these feedback signals in different ways, which will be discussed individually. Many drives incorporate a tacho which may be a magnetic moving-coil type or its complementary equivalent, the moving-magnet type. Both generate a voltage proportional to velocity, and can give no positional information.

A seek is a process where the positioner moves from one cylinder to another. The speed with which a seek can be completed is a major factor in determining the access time of the drive. The main parameter controlling the carriage during a seek is the cylinder difference, which is obtained by subtracting the current cylinder address from the desired cylinder address. The cylinder difference will be a signed binary number representing the number of cylinders to be crossed to reach the target, direction being indicated by the sign. The cylinder difference is loaded into a counter which is decremented each time a cylinder is crossed. The counter drives a DAC which generates an analog voltage proportional to the cylinder difference. As Fig. 10.7 shows, this voltage, known as the scheduled

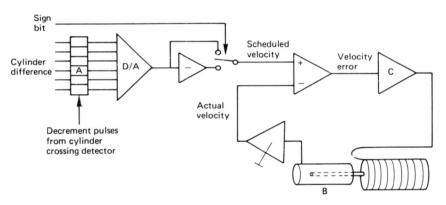

Figure 10.7 Control of carriage velocity by cylinder difference. The cylinder difference is loaded into the difference counter A. A digital-to-analog converter generates an analog voltage from the cylinder difference, known as the scheduled velocity. This is compared with the actual velocity from the transducer B in order to generate the velocity error which drives the servo amplifier C

velocity, is compared with the output of the carriage-velocity tacho. Any difference between the two results in a velocity error which drives the carriage to cancel the error. As the carriage approaches the target cylinder, the cylinder difference becomes smaller, with the result that the run-in to the target is critically damped to eliminate overshoot.

Fig. 10.8(a) shows graphs of scheduled velocity, actual velocity and motor current with respect to cylinder difference during a seek. In the first half of the seek, the actual velocity is less than the scheduled velocity, causing a large velocity error which saturates the amplifier and provides maximum carriage acceleration. In the second half of the graphs, the scheduled velocity is falling below the actual velocity, generating a negative velocity error which drives a reverse current through the motor to slow the carriage down. The scheduled deceleration slope can clearly not be steeper than the saturated acceleration slope. Areas A and B on the graph will be about equal, as the kinetic energy put into

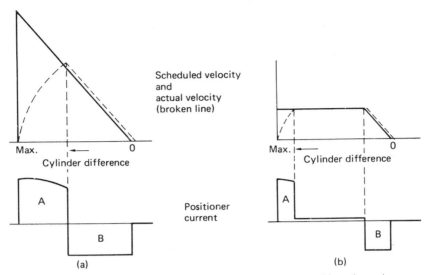

Figure 10.8 In the simple arrangement at (a) the dissipation in the positioner is continuous, causing a heating problem. The effect of limiting the scheduled velocity above a certain cylinder difference is apparent in (b) where heavy positioner current only flows during acceleration and deceleration. During the plateau of the velocity profile, only enough current to overcome friction is necessary. The curvature of the acceleration slope is due to the back EMF of the positioner motor

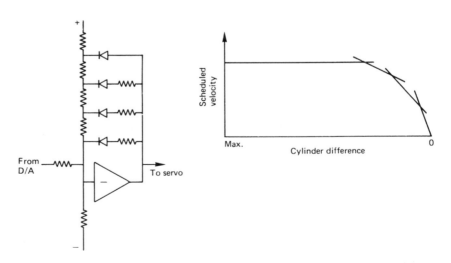

Figure 10.9 The use of voltage-dependent feedback around an operational amplifier permits a piecewise linear approximation to a curved velocity profile. This has the effect of speeding up short seeks without causing a dissipation problem on long seeks. The circuit is referred to as a shaper

the carriage has to be taken out. The current through the motor is continuous, and would result in a heating problem, so to counter this, the DAC is made non-linear so that above a certain cylinder difference no increase in scheduled velocity will occur. This results in the graph of Fig. 10.8(b). The actual velocity graph is called a velocity profile. It consists of three regions: acceleration, where the system is saturated; a constant velocity plateau, where the only power needed is to overcome friction; and the scheduled run-in to the desired cylinder. Dissipation is only significant in the first and last regions.

A consequence of the critically damped run-in to the target cylinder is that short seeks are slow. Sometimes further non-linearity is introduced into the velocity scheduler to speed up short seeks. The velocity profile becomes a piecewise linear approximation to a curve by using non-linear feedback. Fig. 10.9 shows the principle of an analog shaper or profile generator. Later machines will compute the curve in microprocessor sofware or use a PROM lookup table.

In small disk drives the amplifier may be linear in all modes of operation, resembling an audio power amplifier. Larger units may employ pulse-width-modulated drive to reduce dissipation, or even switched-mode amplifiers with inductive flywheel circuits. These switching systems can generate appreciable electromagnetic radiation, but this is of no consequence as they are only active during a seek. In track-following mode, the amplifier reverts to linear mode; hence the use of the term linear to mean track-following mode.

The input of the servo amplifier normally has a number of analog switches which select the appropriate drive and feedback signals according to the mode of the servo. A typical system is shown in Fig. 10.10.

Figure 10.10 A typical servo-amplifier input stage. In velocity mode the shaper and the velocity transducer drive the error amp. In track-following mode the position error is the only input

10.7 Rotation

The rotation subsystems of disk drives will now be covered. The track-following accuracy of a drive positioner will be impaired if there is bearing run-out, and so the spindle bearings are made to a high degree of precision. Most modern drives incorporate brushless DC motors with integral speed control (see Chapter 8). In exchangeable-pack drives, some form of braking is usually provided to slow down the pack for convenient removal.

In order to control reading and writing, the drive control circuitry needs to know which cylinder the heads are on, and which sector is currently under the head. Sector information used to be obtained from a sensor which detects holes or slots cut in the hub of the disk. Modern drives will obtain this information from the disk surface as will be seen. The result is that a sector counter in the control logic remains in step with the physical rotation of the disk. The desired sector address is loaded into a register, which is compared with the sector counter. When the two match, the desired sector has been found. This process is referred to as a search, and usually takes place after a seek. Having found the correct physical place on the disk, the next step is to read the header associated with the data block to confirm that the disk address contained there is the same as the desired address.

10.8 Cooling and filtration

Rotation of a disk pack at speed results in heat build-up through air resistance. This heat must be carried away. A further important factor with exchangeable-pack magnetic drives is to keep the disk area free from contaminants which might lodge between the head and the disk and cause the destructive phenomenon known as a head crash, where debris builds up on the head until it ploughs the disk surface. Optical drives have a larger separation between the pickup and the disc, but contamination can block the light beam and cause errors.

The cooling and filtration systems are usually combined. Air is drawn through an absolute filter, passed around the disk, and exhausted, sometimes cooling the positioner motor and circuitry on the way. This full-flow system is fine for environmentally controlled computer rooms, but for the office or studio environment, a closed-circuit filtration system can be used, where the same air goes round the pack and through the blower and filter endlessly. This results in extended filter life in adverse environments, but may require a heat exchanger in the loop to carry away the heat developed by disk rotation. In many drives, particularly the smaller units, the disk rotation itself is used as the source of airflow.

10.9 Servo-surface disks

One of the major problems to be overcome in the development of high-density disk drives was that of keeping the heads on track despite changes of temperature. The very narrow tracks used in digital recording have similar dimensions to the amount a disk will expand as it warms up. The cantilevers and the drive base all expand and contract, conspiring with thermal drift in the cylinder transducer to limit track pitch. The breakthrough in disk density came with the introduction of the servo-surface drive. The position error in a servo-

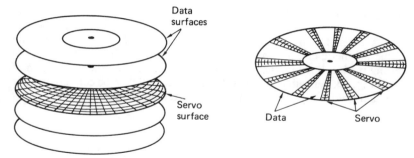

Figure 10.11 In a multiplatter disk pack, one surface is dedicated to servo information. In a single platter, the servo information is embedded in the data on the same surfaces

surface drive is derived from a head reading the disk itself. This virtually eliminates thermal effects on head positioning and allows great increases in storage density.

In a multiplatter drive, one surface of the pack holds servo information which is read by the servo head. In a ten-platter pack this means that 5% of the medium area is lost, but this is unimportant since the increase in density allowed is enormous. Using one side of a single-platter cartridge for servo information would be unacceptable as it represents 50% of the medium area, so in this case the servo information can be interleaved with sectors on the data surfaces. This is known as an embedded-servo technique. These two approaches are contrasted in Fig. 10.11.

The servo surface is written at the time of disk pack manufacture, and the disk drive can only read it. Writing the servo surface has nothing to do with disk formatting, which affects the data storage areas only.

The key to the operation of the servo surface is the special magnetic pattern recorded on it. In a typical servo surface, recorded pairs of transitions, known as dibits, are separated by a space. Fig. 10.12 shows that there are two kinds of

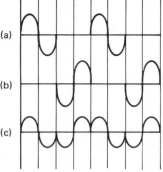

Figure 10.12 The servo surface is divided into two types of track, A and B, which are out of phase by 180° and are recorded with reverse polarity with respect to one another. Waveform (a) results when the servo head is entirely above a type A track, and waveform (b) results from reading solely a type B track. When the servo head is correctly positioned with one-half of its magnetic circuit over each track, the waveform of (c) results

track. On an A track, the first transition of the pair will cause a positive pulse on reading, whereas on a B track, the first pulse will be negative. In addition the A-track dibits are shifted by one half cycle with respect to the B-track dibits. The width of the magnetic circuit in the servo head is equal to the width of a servo track. During track following, the correct position for the servo head is with half of each type of track beneath it. The read/write heads will then be centred on their respective data tracks. Fig. 10.13 illustrates this relationship.

Figure 10.13 When the servo head is straddling two servo tracks, the data heads are correctly aligned with their respective tracks

The amplitude of dibits from A tracks with respect to the amplitude of dibits from B tracks depends on the relative areas of the servo head which are exposed to the respective tracks. As the servo head has only one magnetic circuit, it will generate a composite signal whose components will change differentially as the position of the servo head changes. Fig. 10.14 shows several composite waveforms obtained at different positions of the servo head. The composite waveform is processed by using the first positive and negative pulses to generate a clock. From this clock are derived sampling signals which permit only the second positive and second negative pulses to pass. The resultant waveform has a DC component which after filtering gives a voltage proportional to the distance from the centre of the data tracks. The position error reaches a maximum when the servo head is entirely above one type of servo track, and further movement causes it to fall. The next time the position error falls to zero will be at the centreline of the adjacent cylinder.

Cylinders with even addresses (LSB = 0) will be those where the servo head is detented between an A track and a B track. Cylinders with odd addresses will be those where the head is between a B track and an A track. It can be seen from Fig. 10.14 that the sense of the position error becomes reversed on every other cylinder. Accordingly, an inverter has to be switched into the track-following feedback loop in order to detent on odd cylinders. This inversion is controlled by the LSB of the desired cylinder address supplied at the beginning of a seek, such that the sense of the feedback will be correct when the heads arrive at the target cylinder.

Seeking across the servo surface results in the position-error signal rising and falling in a sawtooth. This waveform can be used to count down the cylinder difference counter which controls the seek. As with any cyclic transducer there is the problem of finding the absolute position. This difficulty is overcome by

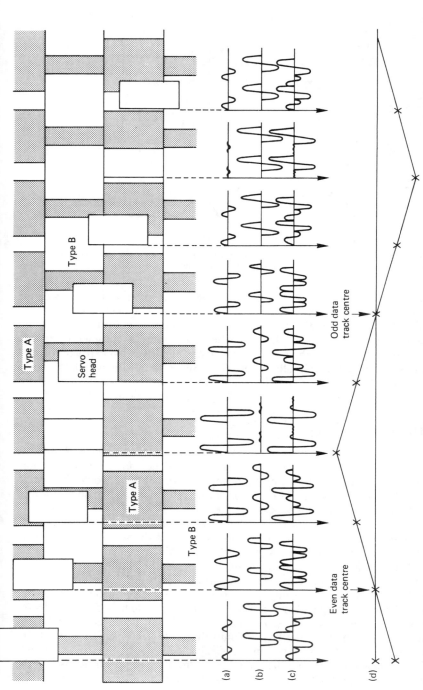

Figure 10.14 Waveforms resulting from several positions of the servo head with respect to the disk. At (a) and (b) are the two components of the waveforms, whose relative amplitudes are controlled by the relative areas of the servo head exposed to the two types of servo track. Because the servo head has only one magnetic circuit, these waveforms are not observed in practice, but are summed together, resulting in the composite waveforms shown at (c). By comparing the magnitudes of the second positive and second negative peaks in the composite waveforms, a position error signal is generated, as shown at (d)

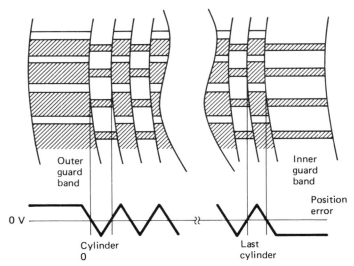

Figure 10.15 The working area of the servo surface is defined by the inner and outer guard bands, in which the position error reaches its maximum value

making all servo tracks outside cylinder 0 type A, and all servo tracks inside the innermost cylinder type B. These areas of identical track are called guard bands, and Fig. 10.15 shows the relationship between the position error and the guard bands. During a head load, the servo head generates a constant maximum positive position error in the outer guard band. This drives the carriage forward until the position error first falls to zero. This, by definition, is cylinder 0. Some drives, however, load by driving the heads across the surface until the inner guard band is found, and then perform a full-length reverse seek to cylinder 0.

10.10 Soft sectoring

It has been seen that a position error and a cylinder count can be derived from the servo surface, eliminating the cylinder transducer. The carriage velocity could also be derived from the slope of the position error, but there would then be no velocity feedback in the guard bands or during retraction, and so some form of velocity transducer is still necessary.

As there are exactly the same number of dibits or tribits on every track, it is possible to describe the rotational position of the disk simply by counting them. All that is needed is a unique pattern of missing dibits once per revolution to act as an index point, and the sector transducer can also be eliminated.

Unlike the read-data circuits, the servo-head circuits are active during a seek as well as when track following, and have to be protected against interference from switched-mode positioner drivers. The main problem is detecting index, where noise could cause a 'missing' dibit to be masked. There are two solutions available: a preamplifier can be built into the servo-head cantilever, or driver switching can be inhibited when index is expected.

The advantage of deriving the sector count from the servo surface is that the number of sectors on the disk can be varied. Any number of sectors can be accommodated by feeding the dibit-rate signal through a programmable divider, so the same disk and drive can be used in numerous different applications.

In a non-servo-surface disk, the write clock is usually derived from a crystal oscillator. As the disk speed can vary owing to supply fluctuations, a tolerance gap has to be left at the end of each block to cater for the highest anticipated speed, to prevent overrun into the next block on a write. In a servo-surface drive, the write clock is obtained by multiplying the dibit-rate signal with a phase-locked loop. The write clock is then always proportional to disk speed, and recording density will be constant.

Most servo-surface drives have an offset facility, where a register written by the controller drives a DAC which injects a small voltage into the track-following loop. The action of the servo is such that the heads move off track until the position error is equal and opposite to the injected voltage. The position of the heads above the track can thus be program controlled. Offset is only employed on reading if it is suspected that the pack in the drive has been written by a different drive with non-standard alignment. A write function will cancel the offset.

10.11 Embedded-servo drives

In drives with a small number of platters, the use of an entire surface for servo information gives an excessive loss of data recording area. In the embedded-servo drive, servo information is interleaved with data on the same surface, causing a smaller loss of storage area.

The embedded-servo drive heads will be reading data at some times and alignment information at others as the disk rotates. A sector transducer is required to generate a pulse which is true when the head is over servo information. Fig. 10.16 and Fig. 10.17 show the principle. On all disk drives, the width of the head pole is less than the track pitch to prevent crosstalk. As the servo head is also the read/write head in an embedded-servo drive, it is slightly narrower than the servo-information pitch. This has the harmless effect of rounding off the peaks of the position-error waveform. During the pulse from the sector transducer, the head sees alignment information, and develops a position

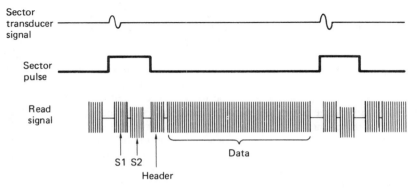

Figure 10.16 The same head is used on the embedded servo drive for both servo information and read/write data. During a sector pulse, the read signal is treated as servo information

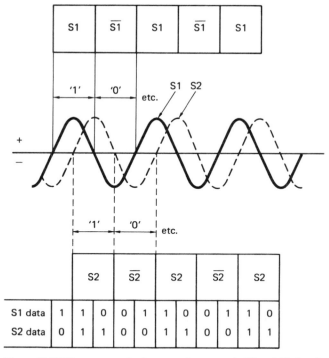

Figure 10.17 There are two basic types of servo track, S1 and S2, but these are recorded at two different places, in a staggered fashion. During S1 time, a position error is generated from the relative areas of the two types of track under the head as in the conventional servo-surface drive. This position error is maintained with sample-and-hold circuitry. For track counting, the position error is compared with 0 V to generate a data bit. At S2 time another position-error and another data bit are generated. The four possible combinations of the 2 bits are shown here in relation to the two position errors

error in much the same way as any servo drive. Within the servo area are two sets of patterns, the second giving a position error of zero when the first is a maximum, i.e. there is a 90° phase shift between them. The two bursts of information are known as S1 and S2. Sample-and-hold circuitry is used to carry over the position errors whilst the head is reading and writing in the data area.

The discontinuous nature of the servo information means that cylinder crossings cannot be counted directly during a seek as the positioner is fast enough to cross several tracks between bursts. With reference to Fig. 10.18, this problem is overcome as follows. During the S1 period, the position error is compared with zero volts to produce a single data bit, whose state depends upon whether the head was inside or outside the track centre. A similar process takes place for the S2 period, and the position of the head relative to the track centre is then described to the accuracy of one-fourth of the track pitch by the 2 bits. These bits are stored, and at the next servo burst, two further bits are computed, describing the new position of the head. Fig. 10.18 shows that there can be many cases which can satisfy the same initial and final conditions. The only difference between the cases is the carriage velocity, so the output of the velocity transducer

Figure 10.18 For the same initial and subsequent data bits, there can be several possible head trajectories. The ambiguity is resolved by using the carriage velocity in digital form

is digitized and used to resolve the ambiguity. At every sector pulse, 2 bits from the previous burst, 2 bits from the current burst and the digitized velocity are fed into a ROM which is preprogrammed to return the number of cylinders which must have been crossed for all combinations of inputs. This number is then subtracted from the cylinder-difference counter which is controlling the seek. The calculation will only be valid for one disk rotational speed, and so the disk motor requires close control. This is conveniently done by counting cycles of a reference clock between sector pulses to produce a speed error. As the cylinder count is deductive, there will be the odd occasion where the count is in error and the positioner comes to the wrong cylinder. In a conventional disk drive this would result in a mispositioning error which would warrant maintenance. In the embedded-servo drive, however, the condition is handled differently. Fig. 10.19 shows a flowchart for control of the drive, which has no absolute cylinder-address register, and in which all seeks are relative. The system only knows where the heads are by reading headers. In order to reach a particular cylinder, the program has to read the first header it sees on the current cylinder, and calculate the cylinder difference needed. This is used to perform a deductive seek. When this is complete, a further header will be read. Most of the time this

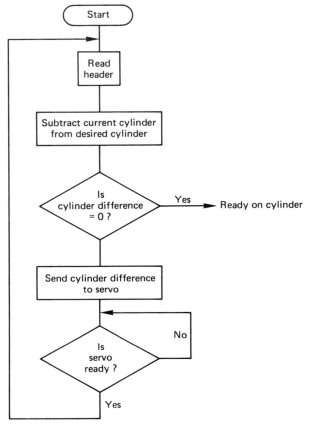

Figure 10.19 Flowchart for the control of an embedded-servo positioner. All seeks are relative, and seek errors are transparent, as they simply cause an extra execution of the loop

will indicate the correct cylinder, but in the occasional condition where the positioning was in error, the program simply loops and calculates a new cylinder difference until the correct cylinder is finally reached.

Since each surface has its own alignment information, some exchangeable-pack drives using this principle need no head alignment during manufacture at all. When switching between heads, a repositioning cycle will be necessary because all of the heads will not necessarily be on the same cylinder. In fact the definition of a cylinder is indistinct in such drives.

Alternatively a multiplatter disk may combine a servo surface with embedded servos on each of the data surfaces. The servo surface provides write clock, sector timing and tacho functions, along with coarse positioning during a seek, and the embedded servo allows the individual heads to track accurately despite discrepancies in temperature and adjustment of the individual platters and heads in the stack.

10.12 Winchester technology

In order to offer extremely high capacity per spindle, which reduces the cost per bit, a disk drive must have very narrow tracks placed close together, and must use very short recorded wavelengths, which implies that the flying height of the heads must be small. The so-called Winchester technology is one approach to high storage density. The technology was developed by IBM, and the name came about because the model number of the development drive was the same as that of the famous rifle.

Reduction in flying height magnifies the problem of providing a contaminant-free environment. A conventional disk is well protected whilst inside the drive, but outside the drive the effects of contamination become intolerable.

In exchangeable-pack drives, there is a real limit to the track pitch that can be achieved because of the difficulty or cost of engineering head-alignment mechanisms to make the necessary minute adjustments to give interchange compatibility.

The essence of Winchester technology is that each disk pack has its own set of read/write and servo heads, with an integral positioner. The whole is protected by a dust-free enclosure, and the unit is referred to as a head disk assembly, or HDA.

As the HDA contains its own heads, compatibility problems do not exist, and no head alignment is necessary or provided for. It is thus possible to reduce track pitch considerably compared with exchangeable-pack drives. The sealed environment ensures complete cleanliness which permits a reduction in flying height without loss of reliability, and hence leads to an increased linear density. If the rotational speed is maintained, this can also result in an increase in data transfer rate.

The HDA is completely sealed, but some have a small filtered port to equalize pressure. Into this sealed volume of air, the drive motor delivers the majority of its power output. The resulting heat is dissipated by fins on the HDA casing. Some HDAs are filled with helium which significantly reduces drag and heat build-up.

An exchangeable-pack drive must retract the heads to facilitate pack removal. With Winchester technology this is not necessary. An area of the disk surface is reserved as a landing strip for the heads. The disk surface is lubricated, and the heads are designed to withstand landing and take-off without damage. Winchester heads have very large air-bleed grooves to allow low flying height with a much smaller downthrust from the cantilever, and so they exert less force on the disk surface during contact. When the term *parking* is used in the context of Winchester technology, it refers to the positioning of the heads over the landing area.

Disk rotation must be started and stopped quickly to minimize the length of time the heads slide over the medium. A powerful motor will accelerate the pack quickly. Eddy current braking cannot be used, since a power failure would allow the unbraked disk to stop only after a prolonged head contact period. A failsafe mechanical brake is used, which is applied by a spring and released with a solenoid.

A major advantage of contact start/stop is that more than one head can be used on each surface if retraction is not needed. This leads to two gains: first, the travel of the positioner is reduced in proportion to the number of heads per surface,

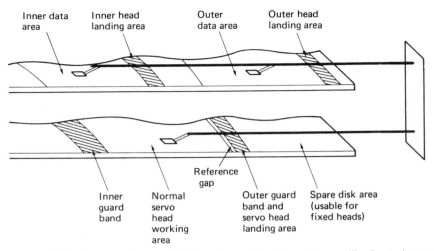

Figure 10.20 When more than one head is used per surface, the positioner still only requires one servo head. This is often arranged to be equidistant from the read/write heads for thermal stability

reducing access time; and, second, more data can be transferred at a given detented carriage position before a seek to the next cylinder becomes necessary. This increases the speed of long transfers. Fig. 10.20 illustrates the relationships of the heads in such a system.

10.13 Servo-surface Winchester drives

With contact start/stop, the servo head is always on the servo surface, and it can be used for all of the transducer functions needed by the drive. Fig. 10.21 shows the position-error signal during a seek. The signal rises and falls as servo tracks are crossed, and the slope of the signal is proportional to positioner velocity. The position-error signal is differentiated and rectified to give a velocity feedback

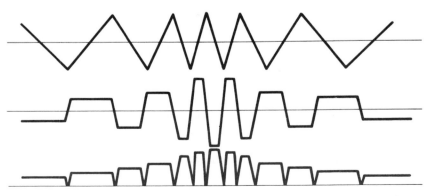

Figure 10.21 To generate a velocity signal, the position error from the servo head is differentiated and rectified

signal. Owing to the cyclic nature of the position-error signal, the velocity signal derived from it has troughs where the derivative becomes zero at the peaks. These cannot be filtered out, as the signal is in a servo loop, and the filter would introduce an additional lag. The troughs would, however, be interpreted by the servo driver as massive momentary velocity errors which might overload the amplifier. The solution which can be adopted is to use a signal obtained by integrating the positioner motor current which is selected when there is a trough in the differentiated position-error signal.

In order to make velocity feedback available over the entire servo surface, the conventional guard-band approach cannot be used since it results in steady position errors in the guard bands. In contact start/stop drives, the servo head must be capable of detenting in a guard band for the purpose of landing on shutdown.

A modification to the usual servo surface is used in Winchester drives, one implementation of which is shown in Fig. 10.22, where it will be seen that there

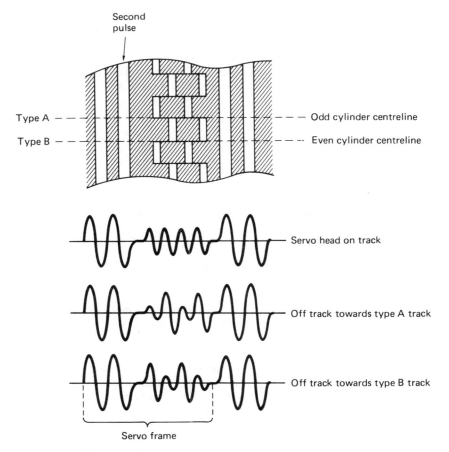

Figure 10.22 This type of servo-surface pattern has a second pulse which may be omitted to act as a data bit. This is used to detect the guard bands and index

are extra transitions, identical in both types of track, along with the familiar dibits. The repeating set of transitions is known as a frame, in which the first dibit is used for synchronization, and a phase-locked oscillator is made to run at a multiple of the sync signal rate. The PLO is used as a reference for the write clock, as well as to generate sampling pulses to extract a position error from the composite waveform and to provide a window for the second dibit in the frame, which may or may not be present. Each frame thus contains one data bit, and successive frames are read to build up a pattern in a shift register. The parallel output of the shift register is examined by a decoder which recognizes a number of unique patterns. In the guard bands, the decoder will repeatedly recognize the guard-band code as the disk revolves. An index is generated in the same way, by recognizing a different pattern. In a contact start/stop drive, the frequency of index detection is used to monitor pack speed in order to dispense with a separate transducer. This does mean, however, that it must be possible to detect index everywhere, and for this reason, index is still recorded in the guard bands by replacing the guard-band code with index code once per revolution.

A consequence of deriving velocity information from the servo surface is that the location of cylinder 0 is made more difficult, as there is no longer a continuous maximum position error in the guard band. A common solution is to adopt a much smaller area of continuous position error known as a reference gap; this is typically three servo tracks wide. In the reference gap and for several tracks outside it, there is a unique reference gap code recorded in the frame data bits. Fig. 10.23 shows the position error which is generated as the positioner

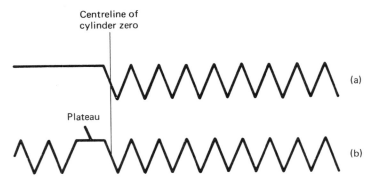

Figure 10.23 (a) Conventional guard band. (b) Winchester guard band, showing the plateau in the position error, known as the reference gap, which is used to locate cylinder 0

crosses this area of the disk, and shows the plateau in the position-error signal due to the reference gap. During head loading, which in this context means positioning from the parking area to cylinder 0, the heads move slowly inwards. When the reference code is detected, positioner velocity is reduced, and the position error is sampled. When successive position-error samples are the same, the head must be on the position-error plateau, and if the servo is put into track-following mode, it will automatically detent on cylinder 0, since this is the first place that the position error falls to zero.

10.14 Rotary positioners

Fig. 10.24 shows that rotary positioners are feasible in Winchester drives; they cannot be used in exchangeable-pack drives because of interchange problems. There are some advantages to a rotary positioner. It can be placed in the corner of a compact HDA allowing smaller overall size. The manufacturing cost will be less than a linear positioner because fewer bearings and precision bars are needed. Significantly, a rotary positioner can be made faster since its inertia is smaller. With a linear positioner all parts move at the same speed. In a rotary positioner, only the heads move at full speed, as the parts closer to the shaft must

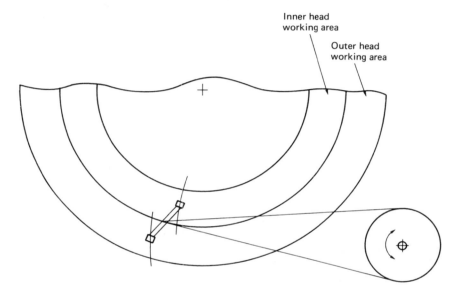

Figure 10.24 A rotary positioner with two heads per surface. The tolerances involved in the spacing between the heads and the axis of rotation mean that each arm records data in a unique position. Those data can only be read back by the same heads, which rules out the use of a rotary positioner in exchangeable-pack drives. In a head disk assembly the problem of compatibility does not arise

move more slowly. Fig. 10.25 shows a typical HDA with a rotary positioner. The principle of many rotary positioners is exactly that of a moving-coil ammeter, where current is converted directly into torque. Alternatively various configurations of electric motor or stepping motor can be used with band or wire drive.

One disadvantage of rotary positioners is that there is a component of windage on the heads which tends to pull the positioner in towards the spindle. In linear positioners windage is at right angles to motion and can be neglected. Windage can be overcome in rotary positioners by feeding the current cylinder address to a ROM which sends a code to a DAC. This produces an offset voltage which is fed to the positioner driver to generate a torque which balances the windage whatever the position of the heads.

When extremely small track spacing is contemplated, it cannot be assumed that all the heads will track the servo head due to temperature gradients. In this

Breather filter

Figure 10.25 Head disk assembly with a rotary positioner. The adoption of this technique allows a very compact structure

case the embedded-servo approach must be used, where each head has its own alignment patterns. The servo surface is often retained in such drives to allow coarse positioning, velocity feedback and index and write clock generation, in addition to locating the guard bands for landing the heads.

Winchester drives have been made with massive capacity, but the problem of backup is then magnified, and the general trend has been for the physical size of the drive to come down as the storage density increases in order to improve access time. Very small Winchester disk drives are now available which plug into standard integrated circuit sockets. These are competing with RAM for memory applications where non-volatility is important.

10.15 Floppy disks

Floppy disks are the result of a search for a fast yet cheap non-volatile memory for the programmable control store of a processor under development at IBM in the late 1960s. Both magnetic tape and hard disk were ruled out on grounds of cost since only intermittent duty was required. The device designed to fulfil these requirements – the floppy disk drive – incorporated both magnetic tape and disk technologies.

The floppy concept was so cost effective that it transcended its original application to become a standard in industry as an online data-storage device. The original floppy disk, or diskette as it is sometimes called, was 8 in in diameter, but a 5¼ in diameter disk was launched to suit more compact applications. More recently Sony introduced the 3½ in floppy disk which has a

One-quarter revolution

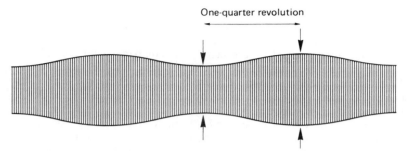

Figure 10.26 Sinusoidal amplitude modulation of floppy-disk output due to anisotropy of medium

rigid shell with sliding covers over the head access holes to reduce the likelihood of contamination.

Strictly speaking the floppy is a disk, since it rotates and repeatedly presents the data on any track to the heads, and it has a positioner to give fast two-dimensional access, but it also resembles a tape drive in that the magnetic medium is carried on a flexible substrate which deforms when the read/write head is pressed against it.

Floppy disks are stamped from wide, thick tape, and are anisotropic, because the oxide becomes oriented during manufacture. On many disks this can be seen by the eye as parallel striations on the disk surface. A more serious symptom is the presence of sinusoidal amplitude modulation of the replay signal at twice the rotational frequency of the disk, as illustrated in Fig. 10.26.

Floppy disks have radial apertures in their protective envelopes to allow access by the head. A further aperture allows a photoelectric index sensor to detect a small hole in the disk once per revolution.

Fig. 10.27 shows that the disk is inserted into the drive edge-first, and slides between an upper and a lower hub assembly. One of these has a fixed bearing

Figure 10.27 The mechanism of a floppy-disk drive

which transmits the drive; the other is spring loaded and mates with the drive hub when the door is closed, causing the disk to be centred and gripped firmly. The moving hub is usually tapered to assist centring. To avoid frictional heating and prolong life, the spindle speed is restricted when compared with that of hard disks. Recent drives almost universally use direct-drive brushless DC motors. Since the rotational latency is so great, there is little point in providing a fast positioner, and the use of leadscrews driven by a stepping motor is universal. The permanent magnets in the stepping motor provide the necessary detenting, and to seek it is only necessary to provide a suitable number of drive pulses to the motor. As the drive is incremental, some form of reference is needed to determine the position of cylinder 0. At the rearward limit of carriage travel, a light beam is interrupted which resets the cylinder count. Upon power-up, the drive has to reverse-seek until this limit is found in order to calibrate the positioner. The grinding noise this makes is a characteristic of most PCs on power-up.

One of the less endearing features of plastics materials is a lack of dimensional stability. Temperature and humidity changes affect plastics much more than metals. The effect on the anisotropic disk substrate is to distort the circular tracks into a shape resembling a dog bone. For this reason, the track width and pitch have to be generous.

The read/write head of a single-sided floppy disk operates on the lower surface only, and is rigidly fixed to the carriage. Contact with the medium is achieved with the help of a spring-loaded pressure pad applied to the top surface of the disk opposite the head. Early drives retracted the pressure pad with a solenoid when not actually transferring data; later drives simply stop the disk. In double-sided drives, the pressure pad is replaced by a second sprung head.

Because of the indifferent stability of the medium, side trim or tunnel erasing is used, because it can withstand considerable misregistration.

Fig. 10.28 shows the construction of a typical side-trimming head, which has erase poles at each side of the magnetic circuit. When such a head writes, the

Figure 10.28 The poor dimensional stability of the plastic diskette means that tunnel erase or side trim has to be used. The extra erase poles can be seen here

erase poles are energized and erase a narrow strip of the disk either side of the new data track. If the recording is made with misregistration, the side trim prevents traces of the previous recording from being played back as well (Fig. 10.29).

As the floppy-disk drive was intended to be a low-cost item, sophisticated channel codes are only found on later products. Single-density drives use FM and double-density drives use MFM, with a trend towards RLL codes. As the recording density becomes higher at the inner tracks, the write current is sometimes programmed to reduce with inward positioner travel.

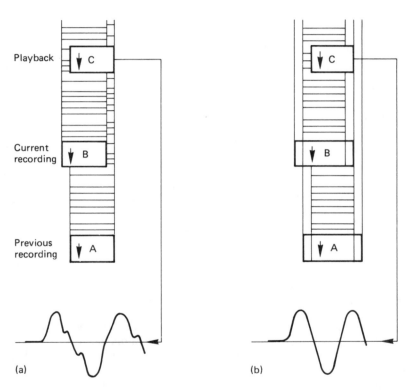

Figure 10.29 The effect of side trim is to prevent the traces of a previous recording from interfering with the latest recording: (a) without side trim; (b) with side trim

The capacity of floppy disks is in the range of hundreds of kilobytes to a few megabytes. This virtually precludes their use for digital video recording. Recording time can be increased by the use of data reduction, but this is currently quite expensive and contradicts the low cost of the floppy. Floppy disks find almost universal application in edit-list storage, console set-up storage, and as a software-loading medium for computer-based equipment.

10.16 Optical disc principles

In order to record MO discs or replay any optical disc, a source of monochromatic light is required. The light source must have low noise otherwise the variations in intensity due to the noise of the source will mask the variations due to reading the disc. The requirement for a low-noise monochromatic light source is economically met using a semiconductor laser.

The semiconductor laser is a relative of the light-emitting diode (LED). Both operate by raising the energy of electrons to move them from one valence band to another conduction band. Electrons which fall back to the valence band emit a quantum of energy as a photon whose frequency is proportional to the energy difference between the bands. The process is described by Planck's law:

Energy difference $E = H \times f$

Where H = Planck's constant

$= 6.6262 \times 10^{-34}$ joules/hertz

For gallium arsenide, the energy difference is about $1.6\,eV$, where $1\,eV$ is 1.6×10^{-19} joules.

Using Planck's Law, the frequency of emission will be:

$$f = \frac{1.6 \times 1.6 \times 10^{-19}}{6.6262 \times 10^{-34}} \text{ Hz}$$

The wavelength will be c/f where:

c = the velocity of light = 3×10^8 m/s

$$\text{wavelength} = \frac{3 \times 10^8 \times 6.6262 \times 10^{-34}}{2.56 \times 10^{-19}} \text{ m/s}$$

$$= 780 \text{ nanometres}$$

In the LED, electrons fall back to the valence band randomly, and the light produced is incoherent. In the laser, the ends of the semiconductor are optically flat mirrors, which produce an optically resonant cavity. One photon can bounce to and fro, exciting others in synchronism, to produce coherent light. This is known as light amplification by stimulated emission of radiation, mercifully abbreviated to LASER, and can result in a runaway condition, where all available energy is used up in one flash. In injection lasers, an equilibrium is reached between energy input and light output, allowing continuous operation. The equilibrium is delicate, and such devices are usually fed from a current source. To avoid runaway when a temperature change disturbs the equilibrium, a photosensor is often fed back to the current source. Such lasers have a finite life, and become steadily less efficient. The feedback will maintain output, and it is possible to anticipate the failure of the laser by monitoring the drive voltage needed to give the correct output.

Fig. 10.30(a) shows that there are two main types of WORM discs. In the first, the disc contains a thin layer of metal; on recording, a powerful laser melts spots on the layer. Surface tension causes a hole to form in the metal, with a thickened rim around the hole. Subsequently a low-power laser can read the disc because the metal reflects light, but the hole passes it through. Computer WORM discs work on this principle. In the second, the layer of metal is extremely thin, and the

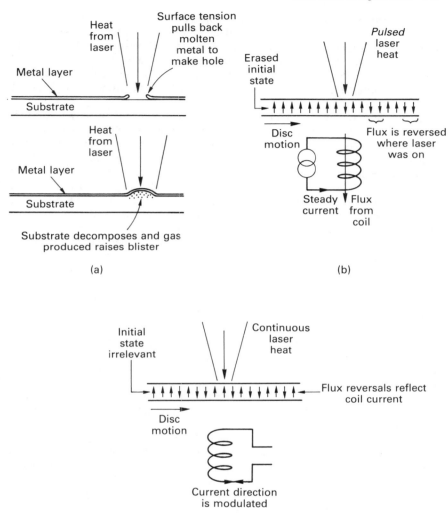

Figure 10.30 At (a) the two main types of WORM (Write-Once-Read-Mostly) disc. MO discs can be written by modulating the laser (b) or the magnetic field (c). See text for differences

heat from the laser heats the material below it to the point of decomposition. This causes gassing which raises a blister or bubble in the metal layer. Clearly once such a pattern of holes or blisters has been made, it is permanent.

Re-recordable or erasable optical discs rely on magneto-optics,[3] also known more fully as thermomagneto-optics. Writing in such a device makes use of a thermomagnetic property possessed by all magnetic materials, which is that above a certain temperature, known as the Curie temperature, their coercive force becomes zero. This means that they become magnetically very soft, and take on the flux direction of any externally applied field. On cooling, this field orientation will be frozen in the material, and the coercivity will oppose attempts to change it. Although many materials possess this property, there are relatively few which have a suitably low Curie temperature. Compounds of terbium and gadolinium have been used, and one of the major problems to be overcome is that almost all suitable materials from a magnetic viewpoint corrode very quickly in air.

There are two ways in which magneto-optic (MO) discs can be written. Fig. 10.30(b) shows the first system, in which the intensity of the laser is modulated with the waveform to be recorded. If the disc is considered to be initially magnetized along its axis of rotation with the north pole upwards, it is rotated in a field of the opposite sense, produced by a steady current flowing in a coil which is weaker than the room-temperature coercivity of the medium. The field will therefore have no effect. A laser beam is focused on the medium as it turns, and a pulse from the laser will momentarily heat a very small area of the medium past its Curie temperature, whereby it will take on a reversed flux due to the presence of the field coils. This reversed-flux direction will be retained indefinitely as the medium cools.

Alternatively the waveform to be recorded modulates the magnetic field from the coils as shown in Fig. 10.30(c). In this approach, the laser is operating continuously in order to raise the track beneath the beam above the Curie temperature, but the magnetic field recorded is determined by the current in the coil at the instant the track cools.

In both of these cases, the storage medium is clearly magnetic, but the writing mechanism is the heat produced by light from a laser; hence the term thermomagneto-optics. The advantage of this writing mechanism is that there is no physical contact between the writing head and the medium. The distance can be several millimetres, some of which is taken up with a protective layer to prevent corrosion. In prototypes, this layer is glass, but commercially available discs use plastics.

The laser beam will supply a relatively high power for writing, since it is supplying heat energy. For reading, the laser power is reduced, such that it cannot heat the medium past the Curie temperature, and it is left on continuously. Readout depends on the so-called Kerr effect, which describes a rotation of the plane of polarization of light due to a magnetic field. The magnetic areas written on the disc will rotate the plane of polarization of incident polarized light to two different planes, and it is possible to detect the change in rotation with a suitable pickup.

10.17 Optical pickups

Whatever the type of disc being read, it must be illuminated by the laser beam. Some of the light reflected back from the disc re-enters the aperture of the objective lens. The pickup must be capable of separating the reflected light from the incident light. Fig. 10.31 shows two systems. In (a) an intensity beam splitter consisting of a semisilvered mirror is inserted in the optical path and reflects some of the returning light into the photosensor. This is not very efficient, as half of the replay signal is lost by transmission straight on. In the example in (b) separation is by polarization.

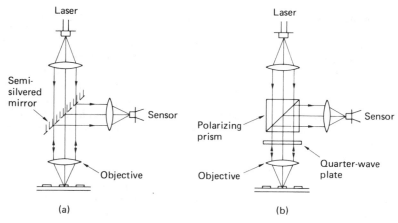

Figure 10.31 (a) Reflected light from the disc is directed to the sensor by a semisilvered mirror. (b) A combination of polarizing prism and quarter-wave plate separate incident and reflected light

In natural light, the electric field component will be in many planes. Light is said to be polarized when the electric field direction is constrained. The wave can be considered as made up from two orthogonal components. When these are in phase, the polarization is said to be linear. When there is a phase shift between the components, the polarization is said to be elliptical, with a special case at 90° called circular polarization. These types of polarization are contrasted in Fig. 10.32.

In order to create polarized light, anisotropic materials are necessary. Polaroid material, invented by Edwin Land, is vinyl which is made anisotropic by stretching it while hot. This causes the long polymer molecules to line up along the axis of stretching. If the material is soaked in iodine, the molecules are rendered conductive, and short out any electric field component along

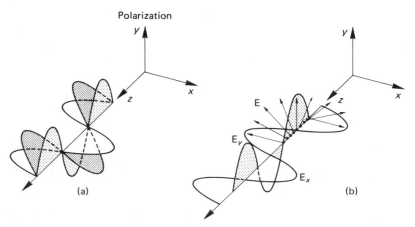

Figure 10.32 (a) Linear polarization: orthogonal components are in phase. (b) Circular polarization: orthogonal components are in phase quadrature

themselves. Electric fields at right angles are unaffected; thus the transmission plane is at right angles to the stretching axis.

Stretching plastics can also result in anisotropy of refractive index; this effect is known as birefringence. If a linearly polarized wavefront enters such a medium, the two orthogonal components propagate at different velocities, causing a relative phase difference proportional to the distance travelled. The plane of polarization of the light is rotated. Where the thickness of the material is such that a 90° phase change is caused, the device is known as a quarter-wave plate. The action of such a device is shown in Fig. 10.33. If the plane of

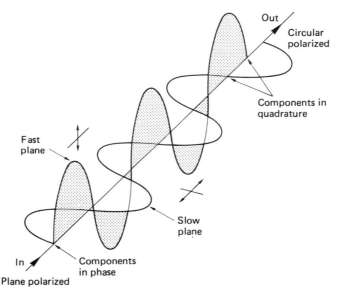

Figure 10.33 Different speed of light in different planes rotates the plane of polarization in a quarter-wave plate to give a circularly polarized output

polarization of the incident light is at 45° to the planes of greatest and least refractive index, the two orthogonal components of the light will be of equal magnitude, and this results in circular polarization. Similarly, circularly-polarized light can be returned to the linearly-polarized state by a further quarter-wave plate. Rotation of the plane of polarization is a useful method of separating incident and reflected light in a laser pickup. Using a quarter-wave plate, the plane of polarization of light leaving the pickup will have been turned 45°, and on return it will be rotated a further 45°, so that it is now at right angles to the plane of polarization of light from the source. The two can easily be separated by a polarizing prism, which acts as a transparent block to light in one plane, but as a prism to light in the other plane, such that reflected light is directed towards the sensor.

In LaserVision or WORM disc drives, the sensor is concerned only with the intensity of the light falling on it. When playing MO discs, the intensity does not change, but the magnetic recording on the disc rotates the plane of polarization

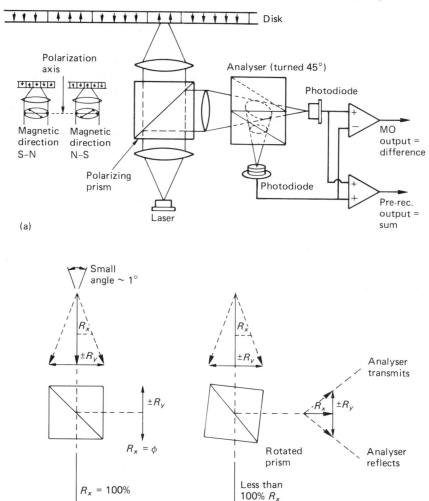

Figure 10.34 A pickup suitable for the replay of magneto-optic disks must respond to very small rotations of the plane of polarization

one way or the other depending on the direction of the vertical magnetization. MO discs cannot be read with circularly polarized light. Light incident on the medium must be plane polarized and so the quarter-wave plate of the CD pickup cannot be used. Fig. 10.34(a) shows that a polarizing prism is still required to linearly polarize the light from the laser on its way to the disc. Light returning from the disc has had its plane of polarization rotated by approximately ±1°. This is an extremely small rotation. Fig. 10.34(b) shows that the returning rotated light can be considered to be comprised of two orthogonal components. R_x is the component which is in the same plane as the illumination and is called the *ordinary* component, and R_y is the component due to the Kerr effect rotation and is known as the *magneto-optic* component. A polarizing beam splitter mounted squarely would reflect the magneto-optic component R_y very well because it is at right angles to the transmission plane of the prism, but the ordinary component would pass straight on in the direction of the laser. By rotating the prism slightly a small amount of the ordinary component is also reflected. Fig. 10.34(c) shows that when combined with the magneto-optic component, the angle of rotation has increased.[4] Detecting this rotation requires a further polarizing prism or analyser as shown in Fig. 10.34(a). The prism is twisted such that the transmission plane is at 45° to the planes of R_x and R_y. Thus with an unmagnetized disc, half of the light is transmitted by the prism and half is reflected. If the magnetic field of the disk turns the plane of polarization towards the transmission plane of the prism, more light is transmitted and less is reflected. Conversely if the plane of polarization is rotated away from the transmission plane, less light is transmitted and more is reflected. If two sensors are used, one for transmitted light and one for reflected light, the difference between the two sensor outputs will be a waveform representing the angle of polarization and thus the recording on the disc. This differential analyser eliminates common mode noise in the reflected beam.[5]

High-density recording implies short wavelengths. Using a laser focused on the disc from a distance allows short-wavelength recordings to be played back without physical contact, whereas conventional magnetic recording requires

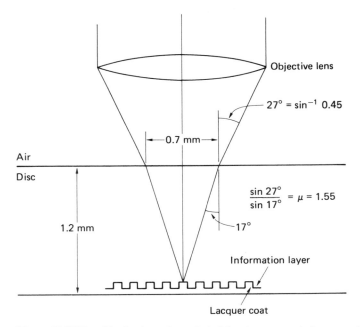

Figure 10.35 The objective lens of a typical pickup has a numerical aperture (NA) of 0.45; thus the outermost rays will be inclined at approximately 27° to the normal. Refraction at the air/disc interface changes this to approximately 17° within the disc. Thus light focused to a spot on the information layer has entered the disc through a 0.7 mm diameter circle, giving good resistance to surface contamination

intimate contact and implies a wear mechanism, the need for periodic cleaning, and susceptibility to contamination.

The information layer is read through the thickness of the disc. Fig. 10.35 shows that this approach causes the readout beam to enter and leave the disc surface through the largest possible area. Typical dimensions involved are shown in the figure. Despite the minute spot size of about 1.2 µm diameter, light enters and leaves through a 0.7 mm diameter circle. As a result, surface debris has to be three orders of magnitude larger than the readout spot before the beam is obscured. This approach has the further advantage in MO drives that the magnetic head, on the opposite side to the laser pickup, is then closer to the magnetic layer in the disc.

The bending of light at the disc surface is due to refraction of the wavefronts arriving from the objective lens. The wave theory of light suggests that a wavefront advances because an infinite number of point sources can be considered to emit spherical waves which will only add when they are all in the same phase. This can only occur in the plane of the wavefront. Fig. 10.36 shows that at all other angles, interference between spherical waves is destructive.

When such a wavefront arrives at an interface with a denser medium, such as the surface of an optical disc, the velocity of propagation is reduced; therefore the wavelength in the medium becomes shorter, causing the wavefront to leave the interface at a different angle (Fig. 10.37). This is known as refraction. The ratio of velocity *in vacuo* to velocity in the medium is known as the refractive index of that medium; it determines the relationship between the angles of the incident and refracted wavefronts. Reflected light, however, leaves at the same angle to the normal as the incident light. If the speed of light in the medium varies with wavelength, dispersion takes place, where incident white light will be split into

Figure 10.36 Plane-wave propagation considered as infinite numbers of spherical waves

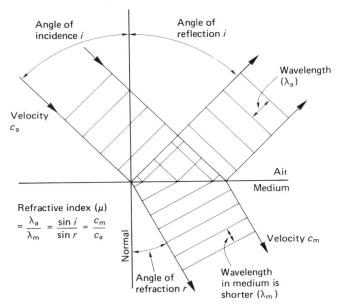

Figure 10.37 Reflection and refraction, showing the effect of the velocity of light in a medium

a rainbow-like spectrum leaving the interface at different angles. Glass used for chandeliers and cut glass is chosen to be highly dispersive, whereas glass for optical instruments will be chosen to have a refractive index which is as constant as possible with changing wavelength. The use of monochromatic light in optical discs allows low-cost optics to be used as they only need to be corrected for a single wavelength.

The size of the entry circle in Fig. 10.35 is a function of the refractive index of the disc material, the numerical aperture of the objective lens and the thickness of the disc.

10.18 The density limit

The smaller the spot of light which can be created, the smaller can be the details carrying the information, and so more information per unit area (known in the art as the superficial recording density) can be stored. Development of a successful high-density optical recorder requires an intimate knowledge of the behaviour of light focused into small spots.

If it is attempted to focus a uniform beam of light to an infinitely small spot on a surface normal to the optical axis, it will be found that it is not possible. This is probably just as well as an infinitely small spot would have infinite intensity and any matter it fell on would not survive. Instead the result of such an attempt is a distribution of light in the area of the focal point which has no sharply defined boundary. This is called the Airy distribution[6] (sometimes pattern or disk) after Lord Airy (1835) the then Astronomer Royal. If a line is considered to pass across the focal plane, through the theoretical focal point, and the intensity of the light is plotted on a graph as a function of the distance along that

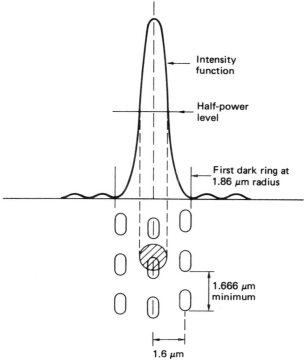

Figure 10.38 The structure of a maximum frequency recording is shown here, related to the intensity function of an objective of 0.45NA with 780 μm light. Note that track spacing puts adjacent tracks in the dark rings, reducing crosstalk. Note also that as the spot has an intensity function it is meaningless to specify the spot diameter without some reference such as an intensity level

line, the result is the intensity function shown in Fig. 10.38. It will be seen that this contains a central sloping peak surrounded by alternating dark rings and light rings of diminishing intensity. These rings will in theory reach to infinity before their intensity becomes zero. The intensity distribution or function described by Airy is due to diffraction effects across the finite aperture of the objective. For a given wavelength, as the aperture of the objective is increased, so the diameter of the features of the Airy pattern reduces. The Airy pattern vanishes to a singularity of infinite intensity with a lens of infinite aperture which of course cannot be made. The approximation of geometric optics is quite unable to predict the occurrence of the Airy pattern.

An intensity function does not have a diameter, but for practical purposes an effective diameter typically quoted is that at which the intensity has fallen to some convenient fraction of that at the peak. Thus one could state, for example, the half-power diameter.

Since light paths in optical instruments are generally reversible, it is possible to see an interesting corollary which gives a useful insight into the readout principle. Considering light radiating from a phase structure, as in Fig. 10.39, the

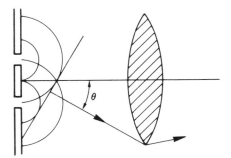

Figure 10.39 Fine detail in an object can only be resolved if the diffracted wavefront due to the highest spatial frequency is collected by the lens. Numerical aperture (NA) = sin θ, and as θ is the diffraction angle it follows that, for a given wavelength, NA determines resolution

more closely spaced the features of the phase structure, i.e. the higher the spatial frequency, the more oblique the direction of the wavefronts in the diffraction pattern which results and the larger the aperture of the lens needed to collect the light if the resolution is not to be lost. The corollary of this is that the smaller the Airy distribution it is wished to create, the larger must be the aperture of the lens. Spatial frequency is measured in lines per millimetre and as it increases, the wavefronts of the resultant diffraction pattern become more oblique. With a fixed objective aperture, as the tangential diffraction pattern becomes more oblique, less light passes the aperture and the depth of modulation transmitted by the lens falls. At some spatial frequency, all of the diffracted light falls outside the aperture and the modulation depth transmitted by the lens falls to zero. This is known as the spatial cut-off frequency. Thus a graph of depth of modulation versus spatial frequency can be drawn and which is known as the modulation transfer function (MTF). This is a straight line commencing at unity at zero spatial frequency (no detail) and falling to zero at the cut-off spatial frequency (finest detail). Thus one could describe a lens of finite aperture as a form of spatial low-pass filter. The Airy function is no more than the spatial impulse response of the lens, and the concentric rings of the Airy function are the spatial analog of the symmetrical ringing in a phase-linear electrical filter. The Airy function and the triangular frequency response form a transform pair[7].

When an objective lens is used in a conventional microscope, the MTF will allow the resolution to be predicted in lines per millimetre. However, in a scanning microscope the spatial frequency of the detail in the object is multiplied by the scanning velocity to give a temporal frequency measured in Hertz. Thus lines per millimetre multiplied by millimetres per second gives lines per second. Instead of a straight line MTF falling to the spatial cut-off frequency, a scanning microscope has a temporal frequency response falling to zero at the optical cut-off frequency. Whilst this concept requires a number of idiomatic terms to be assimilated at once, the point can be made clear by a simple analogy. Imagine the evenly spaced iron railings outside a schoolyard. These are permanently fixed, and can have no temporal frequency, yet they have a spatial frequency which is the number of railings per unit distance. A small boy with a stick takes great delight in running along the railings so that his stick hits each one in turn and

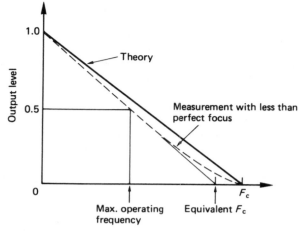

Figure 10.40 Frequency response of laser pickup. Maximum operating frequency is about half of cut-off frequency F_c

makes a great noise. The rate at which his stick hits the railings is the temporal frequency which results from their being scanned. This rate would increase if the boy ran faster, but it would also increase if the rails were closer together. As a consequence it can be seen that the temporal frequency is proportional to the spatial frequency multiplied by the scanning speed. Put more technically, the frequency response of an optical recorder is the Fourier transform of the Airy distribution of the readout spot multiplied by the track velocity. Fig. 10.40 shows that the frequency response falls progressively from DC to the optical cut-off frequency which is given by:

$$F_c = \frac{2NA}{wavelength} \times velocity$$

Measurements reveal that the optical response of practical devices is only a little worse than the theory predicts. This characteristic has a large bearing on the type of modulation schemes which can be successfully employed. Clearly, to obtain any noise immunity, the maximum operating frequency must be rather less than the cut-off frequency.

Lasers do not produce a beam of uniform intensity. It is more intense in the centre than it is at the edges, and this has the effect of slightly increasing the half-power diameter of the intensity function. The effect is analogous to the effect of window functions in FIR filters (see Chapter 2). The intensity function can also be enlarged if the lens used suffers from optical aberrations. This was studied by Maréchal[8] who established criteria for the accuracy to which the optical surfaces of the lens should be made to allow the ideal Airy distribution to be obtained. Pick-up lenses must meet the Maréchal criterion. With such a lens, the diameter of the distribution function is determined solely by the combination of numerical aperture (NA) and the wavelength. When the size of the spot is as small as the NA and wavelength allow, the optical system is said to be diffraction limited.

Fig. 10.39 showed how numerical aperture is defined, and illustrates that the smaller the spot needed, the larger must be the NA. Unfortunately the larger the NA the more obliquely to the normal the light arrives at the focal plane and the smaller the depth of focus will be. This was investigated by Hopkins,[9] who established the depth of focus available for a given NA. Optical disc pickups typically use an NA of around 0.45 which is a compromise between a small spot and an impossibly small depth of focus.[1]

The intensity function will also be distorted and grossly enlarged if the optical axis is not normal to the medium. The initial effect is that the energy in the first bright ring increases strongly in one place and results in a secondary peak adjacent to the central peak. This is known as coma and its effect is extremely serious as the enlargement of the spot restricts the recording density. The larger the NA the smaller becomes the allowable tilt of the optical axis with respect to the medium before coma becomes a problem. With a typical NA this angle is less than a degree.[1]

Numerical aperture is defined as the cosine of the angle between the optical axis and rays converging from the perimeter of the lens. It will be apparent that there are many combinations of lens diameter and focal length which will have the same NA. As the difficulty of manufacture, and consequently the cost, of a lens meeting the Maréchal criterion increases disproportionately with size, it is advantageous to use a small lens of short focal length, mounted close to the medium and held precisely perpendicular to the medium to prevent coma. As the lens needs to be driven along its axis by a servo to maintain focus, the smaller lens will facilitate the design of the servo by reducing the mass to be driven. It is extremely difficult to make a lens which meets the Maréchal criterion over a range of wavelengths because of dispersion. The use of monochromatic light eases the lens design as it has only to be correct for one wavelength.

At high recording densities, there is literally only one scanning mechanism with which all of the optical criteria can be met and this is the approach known from the scanning microscope. The optical pickup is mounted in a carriage which can move it parallel to the medium in such a way that the optical axis remains at all times parallel to the axis of rotation of the medium. The latter rotates as the pickup is driven away from the axis of rotation in such a way that a spiral track on the disc is followed. The pickup contains a short focal length lens of small diameter which must therefore be close to the disc surface to allow a large NA. All high-density optical recorders operate on this principle in which the readout of the carrier is optical but the scanning is actually mechanical.

10.19 Focus systems

The frequency response of the laser pickup and the amount of crosstalk are both a function of the spot size and care must be taken to keep the beam focused on the information layer. If the spot on the disc becomes too large, it will be unable to discern the smaller features of the track, and can also be affected by the adjacent track. Disc warp and thickness irregularities will cause focal plane movement beyond the depth of focus of the optical system, and a focus servo system will be needed. The depth of field is related to the numerical aperture, which is defined, and the accuracy of the servo must be sufficient to keep the focal plane within that depth, which is typically ± 1 µm.

Figure 10.41 Moving-coil-focus servo can be coaxial with the light beam as shown

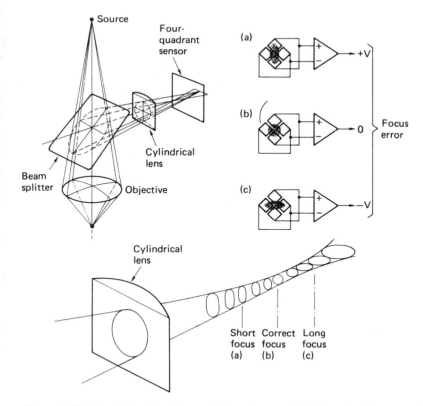

Figure 10.42 The cylindrical lens focus method produces an elliptical spot on the sensor whose aspect ratio is detected by a four-quadrant sensor to produce a focus error

The focus servo moves a lens along the optical axis in order to keep the spot in focus. Since dynamic focus changes are largely due to warps, the focus system must have a frequency response in excess of the rotational speed. A moving-coil actuator is often used owing to the small moving mass which this permits. Fig. 10.41 shows that a cylindrical magnet assembly almost identical to that of a loudspeaker can be used, coaxial with the light beam. Alternatively a moving-magnet design can be used. A rare earth magnet allows a sufficiently strong magnetic field without excessive weight.

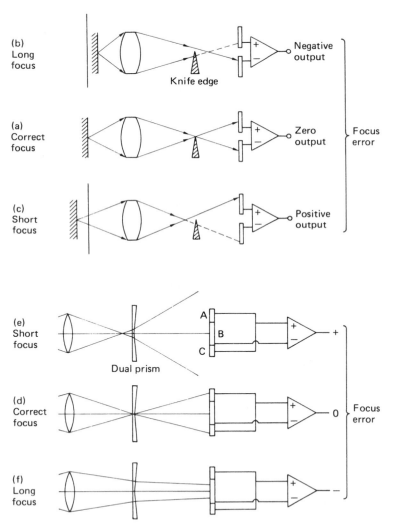

Figure 10.43 (a)–(c) Knife-edge focus-method requires only two sensors, but is critically dependent on knife-edge position. (d)–(f) Twin-prism method requires three sensors (A, B, C), where focus error is $(A + C) - B$. Prism alignment reduces sensitivity without causing focus offset

A focus-error system is necessary to drive the lens. There are a number of ways in which this can be derived, the most common of which will be described here.

In Fig. 10.42 a cylindrical lens is installed between the beam splitter and the photosensor. The effect of this lens is that the beam has no focal point on the sensor. In one plane, the cylindrical lens appears parallel sided, and has negligible effect on the focal length of the main system, whereas in the other plane, the lens shortens the focal length. The image will be an ellipse whose aspect ratio changes as a function of the state of focus. Between the two foci, the image will be circular. The aspect ratio of the ellipse, and hence the focus error, can be found by dividing the sensor into quadrants. When these are connected as shown, the focus-error signal is generated. The data readout signal is the sum of the quadrant outputs.

Fig. 10.43 shows the knife-edge method of determining focus. A split sensor is also required. At (a) the focal point is coincident with the knife edge, so it has little effect on the beam. At (b) the focal point is to the right of the knife edge, and rising rays are interrupted, reducing the output of the upper sensor. At (c) the focal point is to the left of the knife edge, and descending rays are interrupted, reducing the output of the lower sensor. The focus error is derived by comparing the outputs of the two halves of the sensor. A drawback of the knife-edge system is that the lateral position of the knife edge is critical, and adjustment is necessary. To overcome this problem, the knife edge can be replaced by a pair of prisms, as shown in Fig. 10.43(d)–(f). Mechanical tolerances then only affect the sensitivity, without causing a focus offset.

The cylindrical lens method is compared with the knife-edge/prism method in Fig. 10.44, which shows that the cylindrical lens method has a much smaller capture range. A focus–search mechanism will be required, which moves the

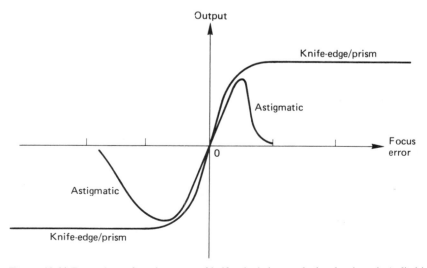

Figure 10.44 Comparison of captive range of knife-edge/prism method and astigmatic (cylindrical lens) system. Knife edge may have range of 1mm, whereas astigmatic may only have a range of 40 micrometres, requiring a focus-search mechanism

focus servo over its entire travel, looking for a zero crossing. At this time the feedback loop will be completed, and the sensor will remain on the linear part of its characteristic. The spiral track of many optical discs starts at the inside and works outwards. This was deliberately arranged because there is less vertical run-out near the hub, and initial focusing will be easier.

10.20 Tracking systems

The track pitch of a typical optical disc is of the order of a micrometre, and this is much smaller than the accuracy to which the player chuck or the disc centre hole can be made; on a typical player, run-out will swing several tracks past a fixed pickup. The non-contact readout means that there is no inherent mechanical guidance of the pickup. In addition, a warped disc will not present its surface at 90° to the beam, but will constantly change the angle of incidence during two whole cycles per revolution. Owing to the change of refractive index at the disc surface, the tilt will change the apparent position of the track to the pickup, and Fig. 10.45 shows that this makes it appear wavy. Warp also results in coma of the readout spot. The disc format specifies a maximum warp amplitude to keep these effects under control. Finally, vibrations induced in the player from outside, particularly in portable and automotive players, will tend to disturb tracking. A track-following servo is necessary to keep the spot centralized on the track in the presence of these difficulties. There are several ways in which a tracking error can be derived.

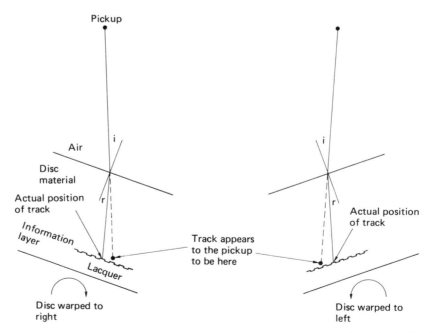

Figure 10.45 Owing to refraction, the angle of incidence (i) is greater than the angle of refraction (r). Disc warp causes the apparent position of the track (dotted line) to move, requiring the tracking servo to correct

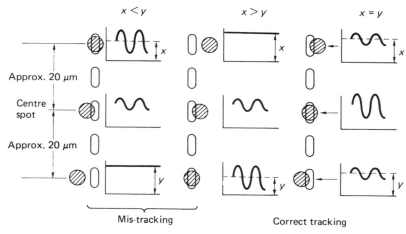

Figure 10.46 Three-spot method of producing tracking error compares average level of side-spot signals. Side spots are produced by a diffraction grating and require their own sensors

In the three-spot method, two additional light beams are focused on the disc track, one offset to each side of the track centreline. Fig. 10.46 shows that, as one side spot moves away from the track into the mirror area, there is less destructive interference and more reflection. This causes the average amplitude of the side spots to change differentially with tracking error. The laser head contains a diffraction grating which produces the side spots, and two extra photosensors onto which the reflections of the side spots will fall. The side spots feed a differential amplifier, which has a low-pass filter to reject the channel code information and retain the average brightness difference. Some players use a delay line in one of the side-spot signals whose period is equal to the time taken for the disc to travel between the side spots. This helps the differential amplifier to cancel the channel code.

The side spots are generated as follows. When a wavefront reaches an aperture which is small compared with the wavelength, the aperture acts as a point source, and the process of diffraction can be observed as a spherical wavefront leaving the aperture as in Fig. 10.47. Where the wavefront passes through a regular structure, known as a diffraction grating, light on the far side will form new wavefronts wherever radiation is in phase, and Fig. 10.48 shows that these will be at an angle to the normal depending on the spacing of the structure and the wavelength of the light. A diffraction grating illuminated by white light will produce a dispersed spectrum at each side of the normal. To obtain a fixed angle of diffraction, monochromatic light is necessary.

The alternative approach to tracking error detection is to analyse the diffraction pattern of the reflected beam. The effect of an off-centre spot is to rotate the radial diffraction pattern about an axis along the track. Fig. 10.49 shows that, if a split sensor is used, one-half will see greater modulation than the other when off track. Such a system may be prone to develop an offset due either to drift or to contamination of the optics, although the capture range is large. A further tracking mechanism is often added to obviate the need for periodic

Figure 10.47 Diffraction as a plane wave reaches a small aperture

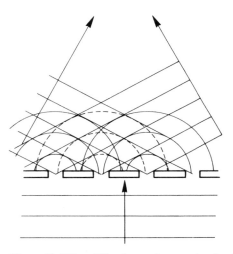

Figure 10.48 In a diffraction grating, constructive interference can take place at more than one angle for a single wavelength

Figure 10.49 Split-sensor method of producing tracking error focuses image of spot onto sensor. One side of spot will have more modulation when off track

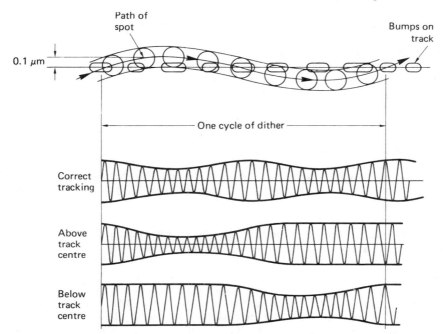

Figure 10.50 Dither applied to readout spot modulates the readout envelope. A tracking error can be derived

adjustment. Fig. 10.50 shows this dither-based system, which resembles in many respects the track-following method used in C-format professional video tape recorders. A sinusoidal drive is fed to the tracking servo, causing a radial oscillation of spot position of about ±50 nm. This results in modulation of the envelope of the readout signal, which can be synchronously detected to obtain the sense of the error. The dither can be produced by vibrating a mirror in the light path, which enables a high frequency to be used, or by oscillating the whole pickup at a lower frequency.

Alternatively, the disc track may be produced with a wobble so that the same effect can be had with a fixed pickup. This has the advantage that the wobble frequency can be used to measure the speed of the track.

10.21 The disk controller

A disk controller is a unit which is interposed between the drives and the rest of the system. It consists of two main parts: that which issues control signals to and obtains status from the drives, and that which handles the data to be stored and retrieved. Both parts are synchronized by the control sequencer. The essentials of a disk controller are determined by the characteristics of drives and the functions needed, and so they do not vary greatly. It is desirable for economic reasons to use a commercially available disk controller intended for computers. Such controllers are adequate for still store applications, but cannot support the data rate required for real-time moving video unless data reduction is employed. Disk drives are generally built to interface to a standard controller interface, such as the SCSI bus. The disk controller will then be a unit which interfaces the drive bus to the host computer system.

The execution of a function by a disk subsystem requires a complex series of steps, and decisions must be made between the steps to decide what the next will be. There is a parallel with computation, where the function is the equivalent of an instruction, and the sequencer steps needed are the equivalent of the microinstructions needed to execute the instruction. The major failing in this analogy is that the sequence in a disk drive must be accurately synchronized to the rotation of the disk.

Most disk controllers use direct memory access, which means that they have the ability to transfer disk data in and out of the associated memory without the assistance of the processor. In order to cause a file transfer, the disk controller must be told the physical disk address (cylinder, sector, track), the physical memory address where the file begins, the size of the file and the direction of transfer (read or write). The controller will then position the disk heads, address the memory, and transfer the samples. One disk transfer may consist of many contiguous disk blocks, and the controller will automatically increment the disk-address registers as each block is completed. As the disk turns, the sector address increases until the end of the track is reached. The track or head address will then be incremented and the sector address reset so that transfer continues at the beginning of the next track. This process continues until all of the heads have been used in turn. In this case both the head address and sector address will be reset, and the cylinder address will be incremented, which causes a seek. A seek which takes place because of a data transfer is called an implied seek, because it is not necessary formally to instruct the system to perform it. As disk drives are block-structured devices, and the error correction is codeword based, the controller will always complete a block even if the size of the file is less than a whole number of blocks. This is done by packing the last block with zeros.

The status system allows the controller to find out about the operation of the drive, both as a feedback mechanism for the control process and to handle any errors. Upon completion of a function, it is the status system which interrupts the control processor to tell it that another function can be undertaken.

In a system where there are several drives connected to the controller via a common bus, it is possible for non-data transfer functions such as seeks to take place in some drives simultaneously with a data transfer in another.

Before a data transfer can take place, the selected drive must physically access the desired block, and confirm this by reading the block header. Following a seek to the required cylinder, the positioner will confirm that the heads are on track and settled. The desired head will be selected, and then a search for the correct sector begins. This is done by comparing the desired sector with the current sector register, which is typically incremented by dividing down servo-surface pulses. When the two counts are equal, the head is about to enter the desired block. Fig. 10.51 shows the structure of a typical magnetic disk track. In between blocks are placed address marks, which are areas without transitions which the read circuits can detect. Following detection of the address mark, the sequencer is roughly synchronized to begin handling the block. As the block is entered, the data separator locks to the preamble, and in due course the sync pattern will be found. This sets to zero a counter which divides the data bit rate by eight, allowing the serial recording to be correctly assembled into bytes, and also

Figure 10.51 The format of a typical disk block related to the count process which is used to establish where in the block the head is at any time. During a read the count is derived from the actual data read, but during a write, the count is derived from the write clock

allowing the sequencer to count the position of the head through the block in order to perform all the necessary steps at the right time.

The first header word is usually the cylinder address, and this is compared with the contents of the desired cylinder register. The second header word will contain the sector and track address of the block, and these will also be compared with the desired addresses. There may also be bad-block flags and/or defect-skipping information. At the end of the header is a CRCC which will be used to ensure that the header was read correctly. Fig. 10.52 shows a flowchart of the position verification, after which a data transfer can proceed. The header reading is completely automatic. The only time it is necessary formally to command a header to be read is when checking that a disk has been formatted correctly.

During the read of a data block, the sequencer is employed again. The sync pattern at the beginning of the data is detected as before, following which the actual data arrive. These bits are converted to byte or sample parallel, and sent to the memory by DMA. When the sequencer has counted the last data byte off the track, the redundancy for the error-correction system will be following.

During a write function, the header-check function will also take place as it is perhaps even more important not to write in the wrong place on a disk. Once the header has been checked and found to be correct, the write process for the associated data block can begin. The preambles, sync pattern, data block, redundancy and postamble have all to be written contiguously. This is taken care of by the sequencer, which is obtaining timing information from the servo surface to lock the block structure to the angular position of the disk. This should be contrasted with the read function, where the timing comes directly from the data.

When video samples are fed into a disk-based system, from a digital interface or from an ADC, they will be placed in a memory, from which the disk controller will read them by DMA. The continuous input sample stream will be split up into disk blocks for disk storage.

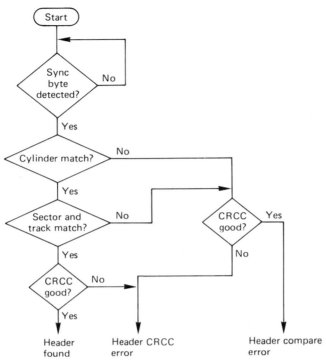

Figure 10.52 The vital process of position confirmation is carried out in accordance with the above flowchart. The appropriate words from the header are compared in turn with the contents of the disk-address registers in the subsystem. Only if the correct header has been found and read properly will the data transfer take place

The disk transfers must by definition be intermittent, because there are headers between contiguous sectors. Once all the sectors on a particular cylinder have been used, it will be necessary to seek to the next cylinder, which will cause a further interruption to the data transfer. If a bad block is encountered, the sequence will be interrupted until it has passed. The instantaneous data rate of a parallel transfer drive is made higher than the continuous video data rate, so that there is time for the positioner to move whilst the video output is supplied from the FIFO memory. In replay, the drive controller attempts to keep the FIFO as full as possible by issuing a read command as soon as one block space appears in the FIFO. This allows the maximum time for a seek to take place before reading must resume. Fig. 10.53 shows the action of the FIFO during reading. Whilst recording, the drive controller attempts to keep the FIFO as empty as possible by issuing write commands as soon as a block of data is present, as in Fig. 10.54. In this way the amount of time available to seek is maximized in the presence of a continuous video sample input.

10.22 Defect handling

The protection of data recorded on disks differs considerably from the approach used on other media in digital video. This has much to do with the intolerance of

Figure 10.53 During a video replay sequence, silo is constantly emptied to provide samples, and is refilled in blocks by the drive

Figure 10.54 During video recording, the input samples constantly fill the silo, and the drive attempts to keep it empty by reading from it

data processors to errors when compared with video data. In particular, it is not possible to interpolate to conceal errors in a computer program or a data file.

In the same way that magnetic tape is subject to dropouts, magnetic disks suffer from surface defects whose effect is to corrupt data. The shorter wavelengths employed as disk densities increase are affected more by a given size of defect. Attempting to make a perfect disk is subject to a law of diminishing returns, and eventually a state is reached where it becomes more cost effective to invest in a defect-handling system.

There are four main methods of handling media defects in magnetic media, and further techniques needed in WORM laser disc, whose common goal is to make their presence transparent to the data. These methods vary in complexity and cost of implementation, and can often be combined in a particular system.

10.23 Bad-block files

In the construction of bad-block files, a brand new disk is tested by the operating system. Known patterns are written everywhere on the disk, and these are read back and verified. Following this the system gives the disk a volume name, and creates on it a directory structure which keeps records of the position and size of every file subsequently written. The physical disk address of every block which fails to verify is allocated to a file which has an entry in the disk directory. In this way, when genuine data files come to be written, the bad blocks appear to the system to be in use storing a fictitious file, and no attempt will be made to write there. Some disks have dedicated tracks where defect information can be written during manufacture or by subsequent verification programs, and these permit a speedy construction of the system bad-block file.

In association with the bad-block file, many drives allocate bits in each header to indicate that the associated block is bad. If a data transfer is attempted at such a block, the presence of these bits causes the function to be aborted. The bad-block file system gives very reliable protection against defects, but can result in a lot of disk space being wasted. Systems often use several disk blocks to store convenient units of data called clusters, which will all be written or read together. Fig. 10.55 shows how a bit map is searched to find free space, and illustrates how the presence of one bad block can write off a whole cluster.

	1	1	1	1	1	1	i	1	1	1	1	0	0	0	0	0	A
A	0	0	0	0	0	0	1	1	1	1	1	1	1	1	1	1	
	1	1	1	1	1	1	1	1	1	1	1	1	1	1	1	1	
	1	1	1	1	1	1	1	0	0	0	0	1	0	0	0	0	B
	0	0	1	1	1	1	1	1	1	1	1	1	1	0	0	0	
	0	0	0	0	0	0	0	0	e	tc.							

Figure 10.55 A disk-block-usage bit map in 16 bit memory for a cluster size of 11 blocks. Before writing on the disk, the system searches the bit map for contiguous free space equal to or larger than the cluster size. The first available space is the second cluster shown at A above, but the next space is unusable because the presence of a bad block B destroys the contiguity of the cluster. Thus one bad block causes the loss of a cluster

10.24 Sector skipping

In sector skipping, space is made at the end of every track for a spare data block, which is not normally accessible to the system. Where a track is found to contain a defect, the affected block becomes a skip sector. In this block, the regular defect flags will be set, but in addition, a bit known as the skip-sector flag is set in this and every subsequent block in the track. When the skip-sector flag is encountered, the effect is to add one to the desired sector address for the rest of the track, as in Fig. 10.56. In this way the bad block is unused, and the track format following the bad block is effectively slid along by one block to bring into use the spare block at the end of the track. Using this approach, the presence of single bad blocks does not cause the loss of clusters, but requires slightly greater control complexity. If two bad blocks exist in a track, the second will be added to the bad-block file as usual.

Figure 10.56 Skip sectoring. The bad block in this example has a physical sector address of 28. By setting the skip-sector flags in the header, this and subsequent logical blocks have one added to their sector addresses, and the spare block is brought into use

10.25 Defect skipping

The two techniques described so far have treated the block as the smallest element. In practice, the effect of a typical defect is to corrupt only a few bytes. The principle of defect skipping is that media defects can be skipped over within the block so that a block containing a defect is made usable. The header of each block contains the location of the first defect in bytes away from the end of the header, and the number of bytes from the first defect to the second defect, and so on up to the maximum of four shown in the example of Fig. 10.57. Each defect is overwritten with a fixed number of bytes of preamble code and a sync pattern. The skip is positioned so that there is sufficient undamaged preamble after the defect for the data separator to regain lock. Each defect lengthens the block, causing the format of the track to slip round. A space is left at the end of each

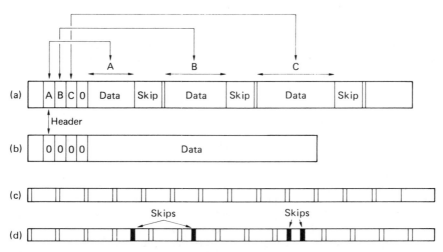

Figure 10.57 Defect skipping. (a) A block containing three defects. The header contains up to four parameters which specify how much data is to be written before each skip. In this example only three entries are needed. (b) An error-free block for comparison with (a); the presence of the skips lengthens in the block. To allow for this lengthening, the track contains spare space at the end, as shown in (c), which is an error-free track. (d) A track containing the maximum of four skips, which have caused the spare space to be used up

Figure 10.58 The purpose of the track descriptor record (TDR) is to keep a record of defects independent of disk format. The positions of the defects stored in the TDR (a) are used by the formatter to establish the positions relative to the format used. With the format (b), the first defect appears in sector 5, but the same defect would be in sector 4 for format (c). The second defect falls where a header would be written in (b) so the header is displaced for sector 10. The same defect falls in the data area of sector 8 in (c)

track to allow a reasonable number of skips to be accommodated. Often a track descriptor is written at the beginning of each track which contains the physical position of defects relative to index. The disk format needed for a particular system can then be rapidly arrived at by reading the descriptor and translating the physical defect locations into locations relative to the chosen sector format. Fig. 10.58 shows how a soft-sectoring drive can have two different formats around the same defects using this principle.

In the case where there are too many defects in a track for the skipping to handle, the system bad-block file will be used. This is rarely necessary in practice, and the disk appears to be a contiguous, error-free, logical and physical space. Defect skipping requires fast processing to deal with events in real time as the disk rotates. Bit-slice microsequencers are one approach, as a typical microprocessor would be too slow.

10.26 Revectoring

A refinement of sector skipping which permits the handling of more than one bad block per track without the loss of a cluster is revectoring. A bad block caused by a surface defect may only have a few defective bytes, so it is possible to record highly redundant information in the bad block. On a revectored disk, a bad block will contain in the data area repeated records pointing to the address where data displaced by the defect can be found. The spare block at the end of the track will be the first such place, and can be read within the same disk revolution, but out of sequence, which puts extra demands on the controller. In the less frequent case of more than one defect in a track, the second and subsequent bad blocks revector to spare blocks available in an area dedicated to that purpose. The principle is illustrated in Fig. 10.59. In this case a seek will be necessary to locate the replacement block. The low probability of this means that access time is not significantly affected.

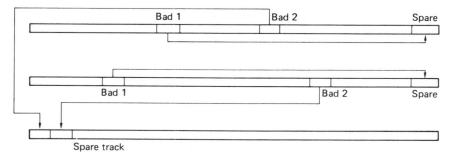

Figure 10.59 Revectoring. The first bad block in each track is revectored to the spare block at the end of the track. Unlike skip sectoring, subsequent good blocks are unaffected, and the replacement of block is read out of sequence. The second bad block on any one track is revectored to one of a number of spare tracks kept on the disk for this purpose

10.27 Error correction

The steps outlined above are the first line of defence against errors in disk drives, and serve to ensure that, by and large, the errors due to obvious surface defects are eliminated. There are other error mechanisms in action, such as noise and jitter, which can result in random errors, and it is necessary to protect disk data against these also. The error-correction mechanisms described in Chapter 6 will be employed. In general each data block is made into a codeword by the addition of redundancy at the end. The error-correcting code used in disks was, for a long time, Fire code, because it allowed correction with the minimum circuit complexity. It could, however, only correct one error burst per block, and it had a probability of miscorrection which was marginal for some applications. The advances in complex logic chips meant that the adoption of a Reed–Solomon code was a logical step, since these have the ability to correct multiple error bursts. As the larger burst errors in disk drives are taken care of by verifying the medium, interleaving in the error-correction sense is not generally needed. When interleaving is used in the context of disks, it usually means that the sectors along a track are interleaved so that reading them in numerical order requires two revolutions. This will slow down the data transfer rate where the drive is too fast for the associated circuitry.

In some systems, the occurrence of errors is monitored to see if they are truly random, or if an error persistently occurs in the same physical block. If this is the case, and the error is small, and well within the correction power of the code, the block will continue in use. If, however, the error is larger than some threshold, the data will be read, corrected and rewritten elsewhere, and the block will then be added to the bad-block file so that it will not be used again.

In erasable optical discs, formatting is possible to map out defects in the same way as for magnetic disks, but in WORM discs, it is not possible to verify the medium because it can only be written once. The presence of a defect cannot be detected until an attempt has been made to write on the disc. The data written can then be read back and checked for error. If there is an error in the verification, the block concerned will be rewritten, usually in the next block along the track. This verification process slows down the recording operation, but some drives have a complex optical system which allows a low-powered laser to read the track in between pulses of the writing laser, and can verify the recording as it is being made.

10.28 A disk based still store

Fig. 10.60 shows a video still store based on disk drives. The incoming video from a slide scanner or rostrum camera is generally decoded into Y, U, V or R, G, B, depending on the application, before it is written into a frame store in real time. In frame stores which are intended primarily for still pictures, advantage can be taken of the phase change of subcarrier from field to field to cancel subcarrier in luminance and vice versa. The frame store can be used as a delay line to make a comb filter which combs over four fields (PAL). As subcarrier inverts after four fields, digital addition of these fields results in luminance only.

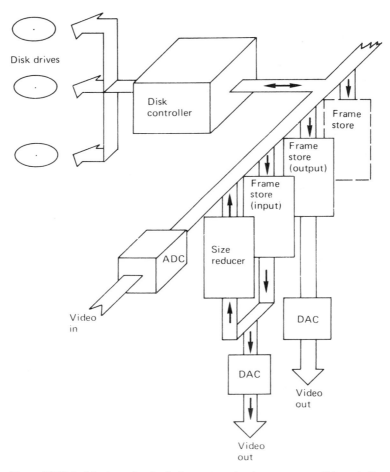

Figure 10.60 Architecture of a simple frame store showing converters, disk controller and the size reducer needed to generate browsing files

Subtraction results in chroma only. Where it is necessary to grab from moving video, a lower-performance mode will be adopted.

Once the frame is in memory it can be repeatedly accessed and sent to a DAC which will produce a continuous video signal suitable for viewing on a monitor. The monitor image can be assessed for suitability, and if necessary the capture can be repeated with a slight repositioning of the camera, for example. If the image in the frame store is suitable for storage, the operator will key in a command to the control processor to file the image to disk. The operator must assign a name or code to the image, and the system will then add that name to the directory of known images. A suitable vacant area on the disk will also be determined, and the disk addresses used will be added to the directory entry so that the image can be retrieved in the future. The disk controller will then be told the disk address to use and the location of the data within the frame stores. The appropriate frame store will then be accessed by the disk controller. The disk controller will read the array of pixels which form the image, and will reformat the data into the block structure used on the disk. The selected disk drive will have its heads positioned to the correct block, and data transfer will commence. The transfer rate of a conventional disk drive will be slower than the data rate of real-time digital video, and the data flow will be discontinuous because of the discrete sector structure of the disk surface. This is not a problem because the image is fixed in the frame store, and can be accessed at leisure. The only necessity is that the frame store must be fast enough to interleave read requests from two sources, so that the displayed monitor image can be refreshed from the memory at the same time as the disk controller is reading it.

10.29 Browsing files

Once a large library of stills has been assembled on a disk database, it is not humanly possible to remember what each still looked like. It is necessary to have a facility to browse through the images to select appropriate material by eye. The fact that the disk drive works at rather less than real time means that retrieving many images for browsing is a lengthy process. One way of accelerating this process is to create browsing files when the disk is written. In addition to the regular image, a reduced-size image is also stored. If, for example, the image is reduced by a linear factor of four, this results in one-sixteenth the storage requirement. In other words, 16 reduced images can be stored in one regular image disk file. The ability to access many images at once dramatically increases the speed with which browsing can be undertaken, since the reduced-size images need only be written into different places in a frame store and many can then be displayed at once on the monitor. The size reducer can be seen in Fig. 10.60. The full-size image is accessed by the size reducer via the lower bus, and reduced in size by FIR filtering using the principles of manipulation dealt with in Chapter 4. The hardware needed will differ from that of a real-time effects machine, since much more time is available to carry out the transform. The number of fast multipliers needed can be drastically reduced. A further asset is that the size reduction is by an integer factor, so no fancy work with coefficient phases is needed. Essentially the size reduction performs FIR filtering and decimation along each line of the image, but places the decimated lines into a recirculating memory so that several decimated lines then become available in parallel for the vertical decimator to operate on. The output of the size reduction process is then written back into spare space in the frame store, so that it can be accessed by the disc controller. The directory will now contain a further entry specifying where on the disk the browse (reduced-size) file can be found. Browsing files are the disk drives' equivalent of pictures-in-shuttle in VTRs.

A large still collection on disk will need facilities for simultaneous access in a broadcast environment. More than one user might want to retrieve stills at once, perhaps one user is using captions on air, whereas another is retrieving images to be incorporated in a post production. Yet another user may be busy adding new images to the database. Such an application can be accommodated by adding more frame stores to the central unit. Requests for files are then dealt with in turn by the disk controller. In some cases, each user may require two frame stores and two DACs, since in an on-air application, one will be producing the live output and the other will be producing a preview of the next still, or be used for browsing to locate the next one. A small complication is that identical timing of video signals from such disparate sources as transmission and post production cannot be guaranteed, so each DAC and frame store is generally configured to use timing from a different reference signal.

10.30 Real-time disk recording

Real-time recording requires a high-enough sustained data rate and sufficient overall capacity. In magnetic disks, the data rate is limited by the head which will suffer increasing losses due to eddy currents with rising frequency. There is also a self-resonance of the head inductance with the stray capacitance of the winding to consider. Current head technology does not allow the recording of full data rate digital video on a single head. There are several solutions to the problem. One of these is to use so-called parallel transfer drives in which each head is fitted with its own read/write circuitry so that the data rate rises in proportion to the number of heads which are simultaneously operating. Whilst this makes the disk drives more expensive as they are no longer a standard computer industry component, it may be a logical solution for a disk-based system in which a relatively short recording time is required. An example may be in an animation system where frames are created individually before a real-time playback.

An alternative is to use a large array of low-cost standard disk drives. This is more suitable where extended playing time is required. The data flow is divided between many drives, each of which has a different access time owing to the data sequence being interrupted by bad blocks. Memory buffering is required to time-align the data from each drive, along with suitable control logic.

Finally data reduction may be employed to reduce both the data rate and the capacity required. As was seen in Chapter 4, data reduction can be interfield or intrafield. Interfield (MPEG) data reduction will allow the greatest compression factors, but causes difficulty in editing. Intrafield (JPEG) compression is a good compromise for production recorders because editing is unrestricted.

In optical discs, bandwidth is limited by laser noise. The wider the bandwidth of the sensor, the more laser noise is admitted. Thus optical discs are also unable to reproduce full data rate digital video with a single pickup, although a composite digital machine has been made using two parallel pickups.[2]

Magnetic and optical disk drives have been made with more than one positioner or pickup operating on the same disk. This is not designed to increase transfer rate, but to allow increased throughput by eliminating time wasted by seeking. While one head transfers data, the other will seek to the beginning of the next block required. At the end of the first block, instead of a seek an instantaneous head switch will allow transfer to continue. This technique can be used to allow real-time editing with a single disk. The drives are, however, expensive because there is little demand for them in the computer mass market.

During execution of an edit, a conventional disk drive has to provide files from two different places on the disk almost simultaneously, and so it has to work much harder than for a simple playback. If there are many close-spaced edits, the drive may be hard pressed to keep ahead of real time, especially if there are long dissolves or wipes, because during such a transition the source data rate is twice as great as during replay. A large buffer memory helps this situation because the drive can fill the memory with files before the edit actually begins, and thus the instantaneous sample rate can be met by the memory's emptying during disk-intensive periods.

Disk formats which handle defects dynamically, such as defect skipping, will also be superior to bad-block files when throughput is important. Some drives rotate the sector addressing from one cylinder to the next so that the drive does not lose a revolution when it moves to the next cylinder. Disk-editor performance is usually specified in terms of peak editing activity which can be achieved, but with a recovery period between edits. If an unusually severe editing task is necessary where the drive just cannot access files fast enough, it will be necessary to rearrange the files on the disk surface so that files which will be needed at the same time are on nearby cylinders. Spare cylinders called caching areas will be spread throughout the disk so that the drive can get data from the cache after a very short seek if it is deduced that there is not time to get it from the original file. An alternative is to spread the material between more drives so that overlapped seeks are possible.

Where synchronized spindle drives are used, an increase in speed can be had by intelligent layout of the data on disk. The disk block becomes the equivalent of a sync block on tape, and each track becomes the equivalent of a segment. The use of revectoring or defect skipping becomes almost mandatory to avoid the structure being upset by a bad block. Chapter 11 will treat editing in more detail.

References

1. Bouwhuis, G., *et al., Principles of Optical Disc Systems*. Bristol: Adam Hilger (1985)
2. Itoi, S., *et al.*, Development of the PAL digital MO disc recorder. *Montreux ITS Record*, 545 (1993)
3. Mee, C.D. and Daniel, E.D. (Eds), *Magnetic Recording Vol.III*, Ch. 6. New York: McGraw-Hill (1988)
4. Connell, G.A.N., Measurement of the magneto-optical constants of reactive metals. *Appl. Opt.*, **22**, 3155 (1983)
5. Goldberg, N., A high density magneto-optic memory. *IEEE Trans. Magn.*, MAG-3, 605 (1967)
6. Airy, G.B., *Trans. Cambridge Philos. Soc.*, **5**, 283 (1835)
7. Ray, S.F., *Applied Photographic Optics*, Ch. 17. Oxford: Focal Press (1988)
8. Maréchal, A., *Rev. Opt.*, **26**, 257 (1947)
9. Hopkins, H.H., Diffraction theory of laser read-out systems for optical video discs. *J. Opt. Soc. Am.*, **69**, 4 (1979)

Chapter 11

Digital video editing

Digital editing takes advantage of the freedom to store data in any suitable medium and the signal processing techniques developed in computation. This Chapter shows how the edit process is achieved using combinations of storage media, processing and control systems.

11.1 Introduction

The term editing covers a multitude of possibilities in video production. Simple video editors work in two basic ways: by assembling or by inserting sections of material comprising a whole number of frames to build the finished work. Assembly begins with a blank master recording. The beginning of the work is copied from the source, and new material is successively appended to the end of the previous material. Fig. 11.1 shows how a master recording is made up by assembly from source recordings. Insert editing begins with an existing recording in which a section is replaced by the edit process.

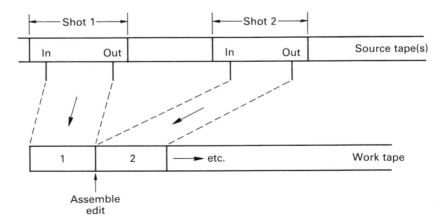

Figure 11.1 Assembly is the most basic form of editing where source clips are sequentially added to the end of a recording

610

At its most general, editing is subdivided into horizontal editing, which refers to any changes with respect to the time axis, and vertical editing,[1] which is the generic term for processes which take place on an imaginary z axis running back into the screen. These include keying, dissolves, wipes, layering and so on.[2] DVEs may also be used for editing, where a page turn or rotate effect reveals a new take.

In all types of editing the goal is the appropriate sequence of material at the appropriate time. The first type of picture editing was by physically cutting and splicing film, in order mechanically to assemble the finished work. This approach was copied on early quadruplex video recorders, a difficult and laborious process. This gave way to electronic editing on VTRs where lengths of source tape were copied to the master.

When this was the only way of editing, it did not need a qualifying name. Now that video is stored as data, alternative storage media have become available which allow editors to reach the same goal but using different techniques. Whilst digital VTR formats copy their analog predecessors and support field-accurate editing on the tape itself, in all other digital editing samples from various sources are brought from the storage media to various pages of RAM. The edit is performed by selectively processing two (or more) sample streams retrieved from RAM and subsequently rewriting on the output medium. Thus the nature of the storage medium does not affect the form of the edit in any way except the amount of time needed to execute it.

Tapes only allow serial access to data, whereas disks and RAM allow random access and so can be much faster. Editing using random access storage devices is very powerful as the shuttling of tape reels is avoided. The technique is sometimes called non-linear editing. This is not a very helpful name, as in these systems the editing itself is performed in RAM in the same way as before. In fact it is only the time axis of the storage medium which is non-linear.

11.2 Timecode

Timecode is essential to editing, as many different processes occur during an edit, and each one is programmed beforehand to take place at a given timecode value. Provision of a timecode reference effectively synchronizes the processes.

SMPTE standard timecode for 525/60 use is shown in Fig. 11.2. EBU timecode is basically similar to SMPTE except that the frame count will reach a lower value in each second. These store hours, minutes, seconds and frames as binary-coded decimal (BCD) numbers, which are serially encoded along with user bits into an FM channel code (see Chapter 5) which is recorded on one of the linear audio tracks of the tape. The user bits are not specified in the standard, but a common use is to record the take or session number. Disks also use timecode for synchronization, but the timecode forms part of the access mechanism so that samples are retrieved by specifying the required timecode.

11.3 Editing on recording media

Digital recording media vary in their principle of operation, but all have in common the use of error correction. This requires an interleave, or reordering, of

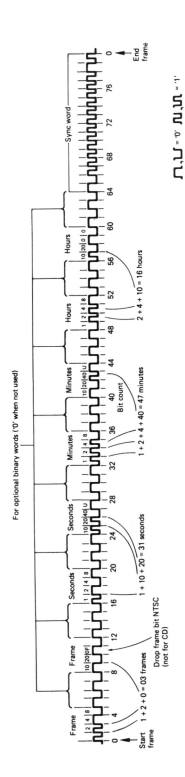

Figure 11.2 In SMPTE standard timecode, the frame number and time are stored as eight BCD symbols. There is also space for 32 user-defined bits. The code repeats every frame. Note the asymmetrical sync word which allows the direction of tape movement to be determined

samples to reduce the impact of large errors, and the assembling of many samples into an error-correcting codeword. Codewords are recorded in constant-sized blocks on the medium. In DVTRs this will be a segment or even a field. Vertical editing requires the modification of source material within the field to pixel accuracy. This contradicts the large interleaved block-based codes of real media.

Editing to pixel accuracy simply cannot be performed directly on real media. Even if an individual pixel could be located in a block, replacing it would destroy the codeword structure and render the block uncorrectable.

The only solution is to ensure that the medium itself is only edited at block boundaries so that entire error-correction codewords are written down. In order to obtain greater editing accuracy, blocks must be read from the medium and de-interleaved into RAM, modified there and re-interleaved for writing back on the medium, the so-called *read–modify–write* process.

In disks, blocks are often associated into clusters which consist of a fixed number of blocks in order to increase data throughput. When clustering is used, editing on the disk can only take place by rewriting entire clusters.

11.4 A digital tape editor

The digital tape editor consists of three main areas. Firstly, the various contributory recordings must enter the processing stage at the right time with respect to the master recording. This will be achieved using a combination of timecode, transport synchronization and RAM timebase correction. The synchronizer will take control of the various transports during an edit so that one section reaches its out-point just as another reaches its in-point.

Secondly the video signal path of the editor must take the appropriate action, under timecode control, such as a dissolve or wipe, at the edit point. This requires some digital processing circuitry except in the case of the simplest editor which merely switches sources during the vertical interval.

Thirdly the editing operation must be supervised by a control system which coordinates the operation of the transports and the signal processing to achieve the desired result.

Fig. 11.3 shows a block diagram of an editor. Each source transport must produce timecode locked to the data. The synchronizer section of the control system uses the timecode to determine the relative timing of sources and sends remote control signals to the transport(s) to make the timing correct. The master recorder is also fed with timecode in such a way that it can make a contiguous timecode track when performing assembly edits. The control system also generates a master video reference to which contributing devices must genlock in order to feed data into the edit process.

If vertical edits such as dissolves or wipes are contemplated, the master recorder must be a DVTR which has a pre-read function. Data from the pre-read heads are routed to the vision mixer and the mixer output is fed to the record input of the master recorder. The signal processor takes contributing sources and mixes or vertically edits them as instructed by the control system. The mix is then routed to the recorder.

Fig. 11.4 shows the sequence of events during an edit where there is a wipe transition from the end of the previous clip on the master to the beginning of the

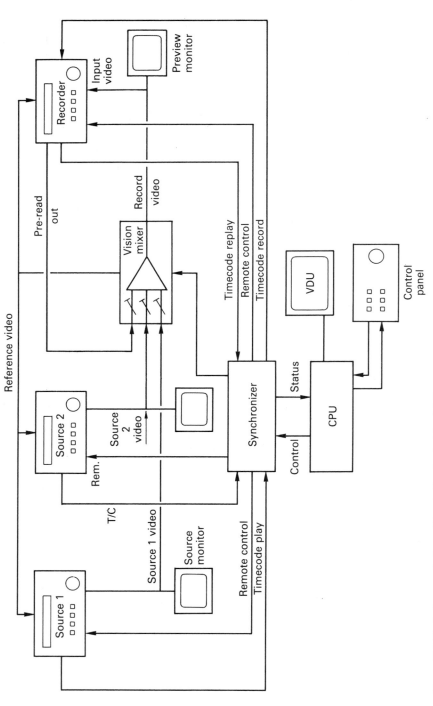

Figure 11.3 Block diagram of a tape edit controller. See text for details

next. Both the master recorder and the source machine will reverse away from their respective edit points by the same number of frames, typically a few seconds. Both transports then roll and lock to reference video. If the correct timecode relationship is not obtained, the source machine will be frame slipped faster or slower until both will reach their edit points simultaneously. Initially the master recorder is simply playing back with the pre-read heads, and sending data to the vision mixer. The vision mixer is switched to the master recorder input and so the end of the first clip is seen on the monitor. When the appropriate timecode is reached, the master recorder begins recording at a field boundary. As the record input is simply the pre-read output, the tape is re-recorded with the existing data. However, once recording has commenced, the vision mixer transitions from the master pre-read signal to the source machine signal. This transition may take as long as required. In the middle of the transition the output fields will contain data from both tapes. At the end of the transition the vision mixer is outputting data

Figure 11.4 The sequence of events during an edit having a wipe between the clips

from the source machine only, and the two machines are now dubbing. This will continue for as long as required.

A preview of the edit can be obtained by performing all of the above steps with the exception of the master recorder entering record mode. The preview can be repeated as often as required and the edit points and the transition period can be changed until the desired effect is obtained without committing anything to tape.

In component DVTRs, any frame relationship betwen the two tapes may be used, but in the case of composite working, the edit must be constrained by the requirement for colour framing which was described in Chapter 9.

If a DVTR with three sets of heads and two playback signal paths is used, the edit can be monitored offtape on the master recorder confidence replay channel.

11.5 The structure of a workstation

Fig. 11.5 shows the general arrangement of a hard-disk based workstation. The VDU in such devices has a screen which is a montage of many different signals, each of which appear in windows. In addition to the video windows there will be a number of alphanumeric and graphic display areas required by the control

Figure 11.5 A hard-disk-based workstation. Note the screen which can display numerous clips at the same time

system. There will also be a cursor which can be positioned by a trackball or mouse. The screen is refreshed by a frame store which is read at the screen refresh rate. The frame store can be simultaneously written by various processes to produce a windowed image. In addition to the VDU, there may be a second screen which reproduces full-size images for preview purposes.

A master timing generator provides reference signals to synchronize the internal processes. This also produces an external reference to which source devices such as VTRs can lock. The timing generator may free-run in a stand-alone system, or genlock to station reference to allow playout to air.

Digital inputs and outputs are provided, along with optional converters to allow working in an analog environment. In many workstations, data reduction is employed, and the appropriate coding and decoding logic will be required adjacent to the inputs and outputs. With mild compression, the video output of the machine may be used directly for some purposes. This is known as *online* editing. Alternatively a high compression factor may be used, and the editor is then used only to create an edit decision list (EDL). This is known as *offline* editing. The EDL is then used to control automatic editing of the full-bandwidth source material, probably on tape.

Disk based workstations fall into two categories depending on the relative emphasis of the vertical or horizontal aspects of the process. High end post production emphasizes the vertical aspect of the editing as a large number of layers may be used to create the output image. The length of such productions is generally quite short and so disk capacity is not an issue and data reduction will not be employed. In contrast a general purpose editor used for program production will emphasize the horizontal aspect of the task. Extended recording ability will be needed, and data reduction is more likely.

The machine will be based around a high data rate bus, connecting the I/O, RAM, disk subsystem and the processor. If magnetic disks are used, these will be Winchester types, because they offer the largest capacity. Exchangeable magneto-optic discs may also be supported.

Before any editing can be performed, it is necessary to have source material on line. If the source material exists on MO discs with the appropriate file structure, these may be used directly. Otherwise it will be necessary to input the material in real time and record it on magnetic disks via the data reduction system. In addition to recording the data-reduced source video, reduced-size versions of each field may also be recorded which are suitable for the screen windows.

11.6 Locating the edit point

Digital editors must simulate the 'rock and roll' process of edit-point location in VTRs where the tape is moved to and fro by the action of a jog wheel or joystick. Whilst DVTRs with track-following systems can work in this way, disks cannot. Disk drives transfer data intermittently and not necessarily in real time. The solution is to transfer the recording in the area of the edit point to RAM in the editor. RAM access can take place at any speed or direction and the precise edit point can then be conveniently found by monitoring signals from the RAM. In a window-based display, a source recording is attributed to a particular window, and will be reproduced within that window, with timecode displayed adjacently.

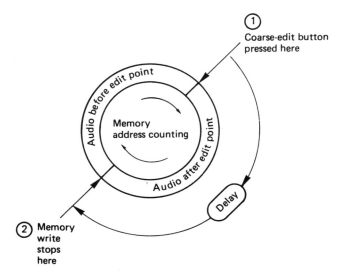

Figure 11.6 The use of a ring memory which overwrites allows storage of samples before and after the coarse edit point

Fig. 11.6 shows how the area of the edit point is transferred to the memory. The source device is commanded to play, and the operator watches the replay in the selected window. The same samples are continuously written into a memory within the editor. This memory is addressed by a counter which repeatedly overflows to give the memory a ring-like structure rather like that of a timebase corrector, but somewhat larger. When the operator sees the rough area in which the edit is required, he or she will press a button. This action stops the memory writing, not immediately, but one-half of the memory contents later. The effect is then that the memory contains an equal number of samples before and after the rough edit point.

Once the recording is in the memory, it can be accessed at leisure, and the constraints of the source device play no further part in the edit-point location.

There are a number of ways in which the memory can be read. If the field address in memory is supplied by a counter which is clocked at the appropriate rate, the edit area can be replayed at normal speed, or at some fraction of normal speed repeatedly. In order to simulate the analog method of finding an edit point, the operator is provided with a *scrub wheel* or rotor, and the memory field address will change at a rate proportional to the speed with which the rotor is turned, and in the same direction. Thus the recording can be seen forward or backward at any speed, and the effect is exactly that of manually jogging an analog tape. The operation of a jog wheel encoder was shown in Section 2.9.

If the position of the jog address pointer through the memory is compared with the addresses of the ends of the memory, it will be possible to anticipate that the pointer is about to reach the end of the memory. A disk transfer can be performed to fetch new data further up the time axis, so that it is possible to jog an indefinite distance along the source recording.

Samples which will be used to make the master recording need never pass through these processes; they are solely to assist in the location of the edit points.

The act of pressing the coarse edit-point button stores the timecode of the source at that point, which is frame accurate. As the rotor is turned, the memory address is monitored and used to update the timecode.

Before the edit can be performed, two edit points must be determined, the out-point at the end of the previously recorded signal, and the in-point at the beginning of the new signal. The second edit point can be determined by moving the cursor to a different screen window in which video from a different source is displayed. The jog wheel will now roll this material to locate the second edit point while the first source video remains frozen in the deselected window. The editor's microprocessor stores these in an edit decision list (EDL) in order to control the automatic assemble process.

It is also possible to locate a rough edit point by typing in a previously noted timecode, and the image in the window will automatically jump to that time. In some systems, in addition to recording video and audio, there may also be text files locked to timecode which contain the dialog. Using these systems one can allocate a textual dialog display to a further window and scroll down the dialog or search for a key phrase as in a word processor. Unlike a word processor, the timecode pointer from the text access is used to jog the video window. As a result an edit point can be located in the video if the actor's lines at the desired point are known.

11.7 Editing with disk drives

Using one or other of the above methods, an edit list can be made which contains an in-point, an out-point and a filename for each of the segments of video which need to be assembled to make the final work, along with a timecode-referenced transition command and period for the vision mixer. This edit list will also be stored on the disk. When a preview of the edited work is required, the edit list is used to determine what files will be necessary and when, and this information drives the disk controller.

Fig. 11.7 shows the events during an edit between two files. The edit list causes the relevant blocks from the first file to be transferred from disk to memory, and these will be read by the signal processor to produce the preview output. As the edit point approaches, the disk controller will also place blocks from the incoming file into the memory. In different areas of the memory there will be simultaneously the end of the outgoing recording and the beginning of the incoming recording. Before the edit point, only pixels from the outgoing recording are accessed, but as the transition begins, pixels from the incoming recording are also accessed, and for a time both data streams will be input to the vision mixer according to the transition period required. The output of the signal processor becomes the edited preview material, which can be checked for the required subjective effect. If necessary the in- or out-points can be trimmed, or the crossfade period changed, simply by modifying the edit-list file. The preview can be repeated as often as needed, until the desired effect is obtained. At this stage the edited work does not exist as a file, but is recreated each time by a further execution of the EDL. Thus a lengthy editing session need not fill up the disks.

Figure 11.7 Sequence of events for a hard-disk edit. See text for details

It is important to realize that at no time during the edit process were the original files modified in any way. The editing was done solely by reading the files. The power of this approach is that if an edit list is created wrongly, the original recording is not damaged, and the problem can be put right simply by correcting the edit list. The advantage of a disk-based system for such work is that location of edit points, previews and reviews are all performed almost instantaneously, because of the random access of the disk. This can reduce the time taken to edit a program to a fraction of that needed with a tape machine.

During an edit, the disk controller has to provide data from two different files simultaneously, and so it has to work much harder than for a simple playback. If there are many close-spaced edits, the controller and drives may be hard pressed to keep ahead of real time, especially if there are long transitions, because during a transition a vertical edit is taking place between two video signals and the source data rate is twice as great as during replay. A large buffer memory helps this situation because the drive can fill the memory with files before the edit actually begins, and thus the instantaneous sample rate can be met by allowing the memory to empty during disk-intensive periods.

Disk formats which handle defects dynamically, such as defect skipping, will also be superior to bad-block files when throughput is important. Some drives rotate the sector addressing from one cylinder to the next so that the drive does not lose a revolution when it moves to the next cylinder. Disk-editor performance is usually specified in terms of peak editing activity which can be achieved, but with a recovery period between edits. If an unusually severe editing task is necessary where the drive just cannot access files fast enough, it will be necessary to rearrange the files on the disk surface so that files which will be needed at the same time are on nearby cylinders.[2] An alternative is to spread the material between two or more drives so that overlapped seeks are possible.

Once the editing is finished, it will generally be necessary to transfer the edited material to form a contiguous recording so that the source files can make way for new work. If the source files already exist on tape the disk files can simply be erased. If the disks hold original recordings they will need to be backed up to tape if they will be required again. In large broadcast systems, the edited work can be broadcast directly from the disk file server. In smaller systems it will be necessary to output to some removable medium, since the Winchester drives in the editor have fixed media.

11.8 The future

Technology will continue to advance, and as a result recording densities of all media will continue to increase, along with improvements in transfer rate. The relative merits of different media will stay the same: disks will always be faster than tape, tape will always be cheaper. Whilst the disk-based workstation has the advantage of rapid access to material, this is only obtained when the material is present on the disks. If Winchester disks are used these are irremovable and the data must come in from another source via an interface. This takes time. One solution is the magneto-optical disc which is exchangeable.[3] However, the recording density of an MO disc is limited by the resolution of the optics of the pickup, and this is governed by the wave nature of light. The only way to increase the density is to use shorter wavelengths, causing increasing difficulty in construction of the laser (and cost). Magnetic tape and disk do not suffer from such a limitation, and it may be that these media will develop further than MO media in the long term.

An alternative to exchangeable disks is to have tape and disk drives which can transfer faster than real-time in order to speed up the process. Whilst these may evolve in the future, the definition of television is also set to increase, and perhaps the higher media data rates will be used up by the high-definition signals.

The density of tape recording has a great bearing on the cost per bit. One limiting factor is the track width. In current DVTR formats, the track width is much greater than theoretically necessary because of the difficulty of mechanically tracking with the heads. This is compounded by the current insistence on editing to field accuracy on the tape itself. This is a convention inherited from analog VTRs, and it is unnecessary in digital machines. Digital VTRs employ read–modify–write, and this makes the edit precision in the data independent of the block size on tape. Future DVTRs may only be able to edit once per second, by employing edit gaps. This allows the tracks to be much narrower and the density rises. Field-accurate editing requires the block to be read intact, edited elsewhere, and written back in its entirety. The obvious way to do this is on a disk. Thus a future approach to workstations is to integrate the DVTR with the workstation and give it a format that it could not use as a standalone unit.

References

1. Rubin, M., The emergence of the desktop: Implications to offline editing. *Record of 18th ITS*, 384–389 (Montreux, 1993)
2. Trottier, L., Digital video compositing on the desktop. *Record of 18th ITS*, 564–570 (Montreux, 1993)
3. Lamaa, F., Open media framework interchange. *Record of 18th ITS*, 571–597 (Montreux, 1993)

Digital audio with video

Television without sound would not be television, but for a long time the sound aspects of television were considered unimportant, and the audio quality of the average television set was mediocre, not just because of its own performance, but also because the quality of the signal reaching it was undistinguished. Fortunately this picture is changing. The advent of the Compact Disc made high-quality audio extremely affordable and raised the expectations of the consumer. Rented video cassettes with stereo soundtracks, CD–Video discs, and the advent of stereo sound with terrestrial and satellite television have all served to raise the profile of audio in the television context. Digital technology made inroads into audio a little before it transformed video, and much of that technology has been absorbed into video equipment.

12.1 Typical digital audio equipment

Once audio has been converted to the digital domain, it becomes data which do not differ in principle from any other. The major difference is that a high-quality digital audio channel will require only 1 megabit per second, which is considerably less than the data rates which have been seen in video. Although the frequency range of audio is much less than that of video, the dynamic range is much greater, and sample wordlengths between 14 and 20 bits will be found. Whilst the sampling and quantizing theory discussed in Chapter 3 is just as valid for audio signals, video converter technology is inadequate for audio word-lengths, and different techniques have evolved for audio which will be described here.

Since data can be stored in many ways, digital audio recorders have been made using many technologies. Early units known as PCM adaptors converted the digital audio data to a black-and-white checkerboard video-like signal which could be recorded on a VCR. Later, direct digital rotary-head recorders such as RDAT[1] appeared. Disk drives have also been successfully employed for audio, because the low data rate compared with video allows a realistic recording time yet with rapid access for editing.

Many of these machines incorporate timecode facilities so that synchronization with video recorders is possible. This is, however, a complex subject which will also be treated here.

As was seen in Chapters 8 and 9, digital video recorders have rotary heads in order to support the substantial data rate. The presence of several channels of digital audio causes an increase in data rate of only a few per cent, and it is common to record the audio with the same heads as the video by allocating small audio blocks at specified places along the main recorded tracks. This simplifies the construction of the machine tremendously, since there are no separate audio heads, and the same RF and coding circuitry is timeshared between audio and video, along with part of the error-correction circuitry.

Standards exist for the interconnection of audio machines in the digital domain, not the least important being the AES/EBU interface which has found wide acceptance and is fully detailed here.

Although most broadcast television sound is analog, and is thus outside the scope of this book, there is a major exception in the shape of the NICAM 728 digital stereo system, itself a close relative of the MAC/packet system developed for satellite work. A full description of NICAM 728 will also be found here.

12.2 What can we hear?

The acuity of the human ear is astonishing. It can detect tiny amounts of distortion, and will accept an enormous dynamic range. The only criterion for quality that we have is that if the ear cannot detect impairments in properly conducted tests, we must say that the reproduced sound is perfect. Thus quality is completely subjective and can only be checked by listening tests. However, any characteristic of a signal which can be heard can also be measured by a suitable instrument. The subjective tests can tell us how sensitive the instrument should be. Then the objective readings from the instrument give an indication of how acceptable a signal is in respect of that characteristic. Fielder[2] has properly suggested that audio converter design should be based on psycho-acoustics.

New technologies tend to solve existing impairments at the same time as introducing more subtle ones, and new measurements and even new instruments are then required to quantify the performance. The introduction of the Class B transistorized power amplifier brought with it the menace of crossover distortion which becomes worse at low levels. Tests at high power which were more suitable for detecting distortion in vacuum-tube amplifiers operating in Class A failed to detect crossover distortion and new tests were required. Unlike Class A analog signal circuits which become more linear at low level, digital audio can become more distorted at low level. Once more early testers failed to appreciate the problem.

The sense we call hearing results from acoustic, mechanical, nervous and mental processes in the ear/brain combination, leading to the term psycho-acoustics. It is only possible briefly to introduce the subject here, but the interested reader is also referred to Moore[3] for an excellent treatment.

Usually, people's ears are at their most sensitive between about 2 kHz and 5 kHz, and although some people can detect 20 kHz at high level, there is much evidence to suggest that most listeners cannot tell if the upper frequency limit of sound is 20 kHz or 16 kHz.[4,5] For a long time it was thought that frequencies below about 40 Hz were unimportant, but it is becoming clear that reproduction of frequencies down to 20 Hz improves reality and ambience.[6] A digital system can deliver a response down to DC and although this is not necessary for audio, it may be advantageous for instrumentation applications. The dynamic range of the ear is obtained by a logarithmic response, and certainly exceeds 100 dB. At the extremes of this range, the ear is either straining to hear or in pain. Neither of these cases can be described as pleasurable or entertaining, and it is hardly necessary to produce recordings of this dynamic range for the consumer since, among other things, he or she is unlikely to have anywhere sufficiently quiet to listen to them. On the other hand extended listening to music which has been excessively compressed is fatiguing.

Before digital techniques were used for high-quality audio, it was thought that the principles of digitizing were adequately understood, but the disappointing results of some early digital audio machines showed that this was not so. The ear could detect the minute imperfections of filters and converters, which could be neglected in, for example, instrumentation applications. The distortions due to quantizing without dither were found to be subjectively unacceptable. A more rigorous study of digitization was soon applied, and the essentials of it can be found here along with a treatment of the essential dithering techniques. The important topic of oversampling is also shown here to be soundly based on information theory, and its significant inherent advantages for audio, particularly when used with noise shaping, are discussed.

12.3 Choice of sampling rate for audio

Sampling theory is only the beginning of the process which must be followed to arrive at a suitable sampling rate. The finite slope of realizable filters will compel designers to raise the sampling rate. For consumer products, the lower the sampling rate the better, since the cost of the medium is directly proportional to the sampling rate: thus sampling rates near to twice 20 kHz are to be expected. For professional products, there is a need to operate at variable speed for pitch correction. When the speed of a digital recorder is reduced, the offtape sampling rate falls, and Fig. 12.1 shows that with a minimal sampling rate the first image frequency can become low enough to pass the reconstruction filter. If the sampling frequency is raised without changing the response of the filters, the speed can be reduced without this problem.

In the early days of digital audio research, the necessary bandwidth of about 1 megabit per second per audio channel was difficult to store. Disk drives had the bandwidth but not the capacity for long recording time, so attention turned to video recorders. These were adapted to store audio samples by creating a pseudo-video waveform which could convey binary as black-and-white levels. The sampling rate of such a system is constrained to relate simply to the field rate and field structure of the television standard used, so that an integer number of samples can be stored on each usable TV line in the field. Such a recording can be made on a monochrome recorder, and these recordings are made in two standards: 525 lines at 60 Hz and 625 lines at 50 Hz. Thus it is possible to find a frequency which is a common multiple of the two and also suitable for use as a sampling rate.

The allowable sampling rates in a pseudo-video system can be deduced by multiplying the field rate by the number of active lines in a field (blanked lines cannot be used) and again by the number of samples in a line. By careful choice of parameters it is possible to use either 525/60 or 625/50 video with a sampling rate of 44.1 kHz.

In 60 Hz video, there are 35 blanked lines, leaving 490 lines per frame, or 245 lines per field for samples. If three samples are stored per line, the sampling rate becomes:

Figure 12.1 At normal speed, the reconstruction filter correctly prevents images entering the baseband, as at (a). When speed is reduced, the sampling rate falls, and a fixed filter will allow part of the lower sideband of the sampling frequency to pass. If the sampling rate of the machine is raised, but the filter characteristic remains the same, the problem can be avoided, as at (c)

$$60 \times 245 \times 3 = 44.1 \, \text{kHz}$$

In 50 Hz video, there are 37 lines of blanking, leaving 588 active lines per frame, or 294 per field, so the same sampling rate is given by:

$$50.00 \times 294 \times 3 = 44.1 \, \text{kHz}$$

The sampling rate of 44.1 kHz came to be that of the Compact Disc. Even though CD has no video circuitry, the equipment used to make CD masters is video based and determines the sampling rate.

For landlines to FM stereo broadcast transmitters having a 15 kHz audio bandwidth, the sampling rate of 32 kHz is more than adequate, and has been in use for some time in the United Kingdom and Japan. This frequency is also in use in the NICAM 728 stereo TV sound system and in DAB. It is also used for the Sony NT format mini-cassette. The professional sampling rate of 48 kHz was proposed as having a simple relationship to 32 kHz, being far enough above 40 kHz for variable-speed operation.

Although in a perfect world the adoption of a single sampling rate might have had virtues, for practical and economic reasons digital audio now has essentially three rates to support: 32 kHz for broadcast, 44.1 kHz for CD and its mastering equipment, and 48 kHz for 'professional' use.[7] In fact the use of 48 kHz is not as common as its title would indicate. The runaway success of CD has meant that much equipment is run at 44.1 kHz to suit CD. With the advent of digital filters, which can track the sampling rate, a higher sampling rate is no longer necessary for pitch changing; 48 kHz is primarily used in television where it can be synchronized to both line standards relatively easily. The currently available DVTR formats offer only 48 kHz audio sampling. A number of formats can operate at more than one sampling rate. Both RDAT and DASH formats are specified for all three rates, although not all available hardware implements every possibility. Most hard-disk recorders will operate at a range of rates.

12.4 Basic digital-to-analog conversion

This direction of conversion will be discussed first, since ADCs often use embedded DACs in feedback loops.

The purpose of a digital-to-analog converter is to take numerical values and reproduce the continuous waveform that they represent. Fig. 12.2 shows the major elements of a conventional conversion subsystem, i.e. one in which oversampling is not employed. The jitter in the clock needs to be removed with a VCO or VCXO. Sample values are buffered in a latch and fed to the converter element which operates on each cycle of the clean clock. The output is then a voltage proportional to the number for at least a part of the sample period. A resampling stage may be found next, in order to remove switching transients, reduce the aperture ratio or allow the use of a converter which takes a substantial

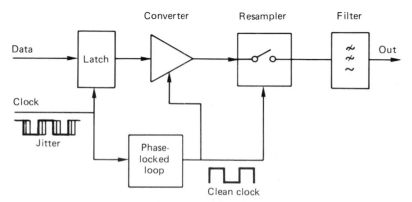

Figure 12.2 The components of a conventional converter. A jitter-free clock drives the voltage conversion, whose output may be resampled prior to reconstruction

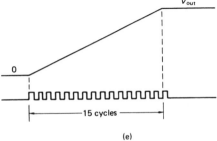

Figure 12.3 Elementary conversion: (a) weighted current DAC; (b) timed integrator DAC; (c) current flow with 0111 input; (d) current flow with 1000 input; (e) integrator ramps up for 15 cycles of clock for input 1111

Figure 12.4 Dynamic element matching. (a) Each resistor spends half its time in each current path. (b) Average current of both paths will be identical if duty cycle is accurately 50%. (c) Typical monolithic implementation. Note clock frequency is arbitrary

part of the sample period to operate. The resampled waveform is then presented to a reconstruction filter which rejects frequencies above the audio band.

This section is primarily concerned with the implementation of the converter element. There are two main ways of obtaining an analog signal from PCM data. One is to control binary-weighted currents and sum them; the other is to control the length of time a fixed current flows into an integrator. The two methods are contrasted in Fig. 12.3. They appear simple, but are of no use for audio in these forms because of practical limitations. In Fig. 12.3(c), the binary code is about to have a major overflow, and all the low-order currents are flowing. In Fig. 12.3(d), the binary input has increased by one, and only the most significant current flows. This current must equal the sum of all the others plus one. The accuracy must be such that the step size is within the required limits. In this simple 4 bit example, if the step size needs to be a rather casual 10% accurate, the necessary accuracy is only one part in 160, but for a 16 bit system it would become one part in 655 360, or about 2 ppm. This degree of accuracy is almost impossible to achieve, let alone maintain in the presence of ageing and temperature change.

The integrator-type converter in this 4 bit example is shown in Fig. 12.3(e); it requires a clock for the counter which allows it to count up to the maximum in less than one sample period. This will be more than 16 times the sampling rate. However, in a 16 bit system, the clock rate would need to be 65 536 times the sampling rate, or about 3 GHz. Whilst there may be a market for a CD player which can defrost a chicken, clearly some refinements are necessary to allow either of these converter types to be used in audio applications.

One method of producing currents of high relative accuracy is *dynamic element matching*.[8,9] Fig. 12.4 shows a current source feeding a pair of nominally equal resistors. The two will not be the same owing to manufacturing tolerances

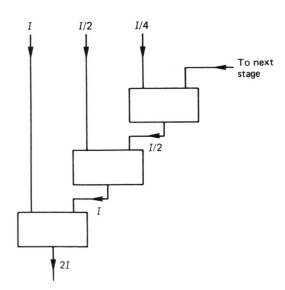

Figure 12.5 Cascading the current dividers of Figure 3.31 produces a binary-weighted series of currents

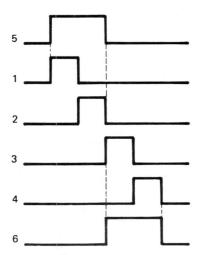

Figure 12.6 More complex dynamic element-matching system. Four drive signals (1, 2, 3, 4) of 25% duty cycle close switches of corresponding number. Tow signals (5, 6) have 50% duty cycle, resulting in two current shares going to right-hand output. Division is thus into 1:1:2

and drift, and thus the current is only approximately divided between them. A pair of changeover switches places each resistor in series with each output. The average current in each output will then be identical, provided that the duty cycle of the switches is exactly 50%. This is readily achieved in a divide-by-two circuit. The accuracy criterion has been transferred from the resistors to the time domain in which accuracy is more readily achieved. Current averaging is performed by a pair of capacitors which do not need to be of any special quality. By cascading these divide-by-two stages, a binary-weighted series of currents can be obtained, as in Fig. 12.5. In practice, a reduction in the number of stages can be obtained by using a more complex switching arrangement. This generates currents of ratio $1:1:2$ by dividing the current into four paths and feeding two of them to one output, as shown in Fig. 12.6. A major advantage of this approach is that no trimming is needed in manufacture, making it attractive for mass production. Freedom from drift is a further advantage.

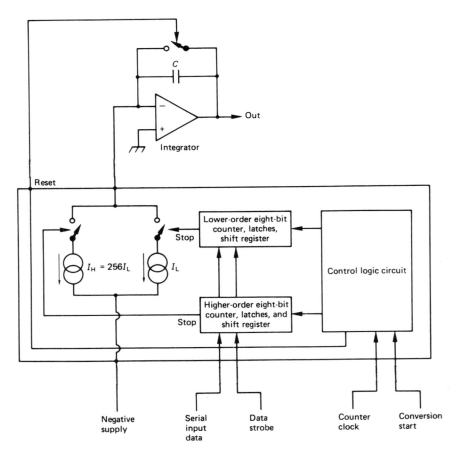

Figure 12.7 Simplified diagram of Sony CX-20017. The high-order and low-order current sources (I_H and I_L) and associated timing circuits can be seen. The necessary integrator is external

To prevent interaction between the stages in weighted-current converters, the currents must be switched to ground or into the virtual earth by changeover switches. The on-resistance of these switches is a source of error, particularly the MSB, which passes most current. A solution in monolithic converters is to fabricate switches whose area is proportional to the weighted current, so that the voltage drops of all the switches are the same. The error can then be removed with a suitable offset. The layout of such a device is dominated by the MSB switch since, by definition, it is as big as all the others put together.

The practical approach to the integrator converter is shown in Fig. 12.7 and Fig. 12.8 where two current sources whose ratio is 256:1 are used; the larger is timed by the high byte of the sample and the smaller is timed by the low byte.

Figure 12.8 In an integrator converter, the output level is only stable when the ramp finishes. An analog switch is necessary to isolate the ramp from subsequent circuits. The switch can also be used to produce a PAM (Pulse Amplitude Modulated) signal which has a flatter frequency response than a zero-order hold (staircase) signal

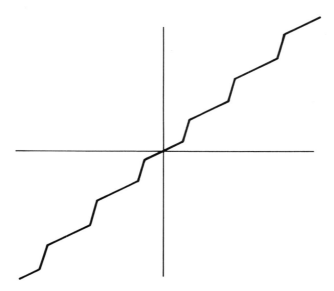

Figure 12.9 Imprecise tracking in a dual-slope converter results in the transfer function shown here

The necessary clock frequency is reduced by a factor of 256. Any inaccuracy in the current ratio will cause one quantizing step in every 256 to be of the wrong size as shown in Fig. 12.9, but current tracking is easier to achieve in a monolithic device. The integrator capacitor must have low dielectric leakage and relaxation, and the operational amplifier must have low bias current as this will have the same effect as leakage.

The output of the integrator will remain constant once the current sources are turned off, and the resampling switch will be closed during the voltage plateau to produce the pulse-amplitude-modulated output. Clearly this device cannot produce a zero-order hold output without an additional sample–hold stage, so it is naturally complemented by resampling. Once the output pulse has been gated to the reconstruction filter, the capacitor is discharged with a further switch in preparation for the next conversion. The conversion count must take place in rather less than one sample period to permit the resampling and discharge phases. A clock frequency of about $20\,\mu Hz$ is adequate for a 16 bit 48 kHz unit, which permits the ramp to complete in $12.8\,\mu s$, leaving $8\,\mu s$ for resampling and reset.

12.5 Basic analog-to-digital conversion

A conventional analog-to-digital subsystem is shown in Fig. 12.10. Following the anti-aliasing filter there will be a sampling process. Many of the ADCs described here will need a finite time to operate, whereas an instantaneous sample must be

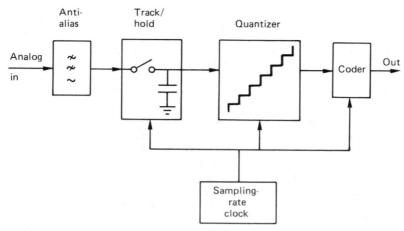

Figure 12.10 A conventional analog-to-digital subsystem. Following the anti-aliasing filter there will be a sampling process, which may include a track–hold circuit. Following quantizing, the number of the quantized level is then converted to a binary code, typically two's complement

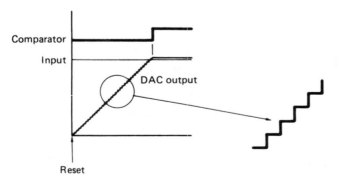

Figure 12.11 Simple ramp ADC compares output of DAC with input. Count is stopped when DAC output just exceeds input. This method, although potentially accurate, is much too slow for digital audio

taken from the input. The solution is to use a track/hold circuit. Following sampling the sample voltage is quantized. The number of the quantized level is then converted to a binary code, typically two's complement. This section is concerned primarily with the implementation of the quantizing step.

The flash converter is probably the simplest technique available for PCM and DPCM conversion. The principle was shown in Chapter 3. Although the device is simple in principle, it contains a lot of circuitry and can only be practicably implemented on a chip. A 16 bit device would need a ridiculous 65 535 comparators, and thus these converters are not practicable for direct audio conversion, although they will be used to advantage in the DPCM and oversampling converters described later in this chapter. The analog signal has to drive a lot of inputs, which results in a significant parallel capacitance, and a low-impedance driver is essential to avoid restricting the slewing rate of the input. The extreme speed of a flash converter is a distinct advantage in oversampling. Because computation of all bits is performed simultaneously, no track/hold circuit is required, and droop is eliminated.

Reduction in component complexity can be achieved by quantizing serially. The most primitive method of generating different quantized voltages is to connect a counter to a DAC as in Fig. 12.11. The resulting staircase voltage is

Figure 12.12 Successive approximation tests each bit in turn, starting with the most significant. The DAC output is compared with the input. If the DAC output is below the input ($\checkmark$) the bit is made 1; if the DAC output is above the input ($\times$) the bit is made zero

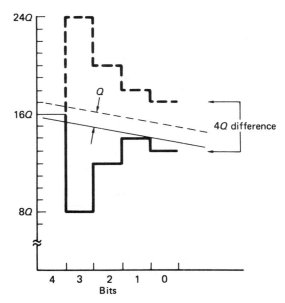

Figure 12.13 Two drooping track–hold signals (solid and dashed lines) which differ by one quantizing interval Q are shown here to result in conversions which are $4Q$ apart. Thus droop can destroy the monotonicity of a converter. Low-level signals (near the midrange of the number system) are especially vulnerable

compared with the input and used to stop the clock to the counter when the DAC output has just exceeded the input. This method is painfully slow, and is not used, as a much faster method exists which is only slightly more complex. Using successive approximation, each bit is tested in turn, starting with the MSB. If the input is greater than half range, the MSB will be retained and used as a base to test the next bit, which will be retained if the input exceeds three-quarters range and so on. The number of decisions is equal to the number of bits in the word, in contrast to the number of quantizing intervals which was the case in the previous example. A drawback of the successive approximation converter is that the least significant bits are computed last, when droop is at its worst. Fig. 12.12 and Fig. 12.13 show that droop can cause a successive approximation converter to make a significant error under certain circumstances.

Analog-to-digital conversion can also be performed using the dual-current-source-type DAC principle in a feedback system; the major difference is that the two current sources must work sequentially rather than concurrently. Fig. 12.14 shows a 16 bit application in which the capacitor of the track/hold circuit is also used as the ramp integrator. The system operates as follows. When the track/hold FET switches off, the capacitor C will be holding the sample voltage. Two currents of ratio $128:1$ are capable of discharging the capacitor. Owing to this ratio, the smaller current will be used to determine the seven least significant bits, and the larger current will determine the nine most significant bits. The currents

Figure 12.14 Dual-ramp ADC using track–hold capacitor as integrator

are provided by current sources of ratio 127:1. When both run together, the current produced is 128 times that from the smaller source alone. This approach means that the current can be changed simply by turning off the larger source, rather than by attempting a changeover.

With both current sources enabled, the high-order counter counts up until the capacitor voltage has fallen below the reference of $-128Q$ supplied to comparator 1. At the next clock edge, the larger current source is turned off. Waiting for the next clock edge is important, because it ensures that the larger source can only run for entire clock periods, which will discharge the integrator by integer multiples of $128Q$. The integrator voltage will overshoot the $128Q$ reference, and the remaining voltage on the integrator will be less than $128Q$ and will be measured by counting the number of clocks for which the smaller current source runs before the integrator voltage reaches zero. This process is termed residual expansion. The break in the slope of the integrator voltage gives rise to the alternative title of gear-change converter. Following ramping to ground in the conversion process, the track/hold circuit must settle in time for the next conversion. In this 16 bit example, the high-order conversion needs a maximum count of 512, and the low order needs 128, a total of 640. Allowing 25% of the sample period for the track/hold circuit to operate, a 48 kHz converter would need to be clocked at some 40 MHz. This is rather faster than the clock needed for the DAC using the same technology.

12.6 Alternative converters

Although PCM audio is universal because of the ease with which it can be recorded and processed numerically, there are several alternative related methods of converting an analog waveform to a bit stream. The output of these converter types is not Nyquist rate PCM, but this can be obtained from them by appropriate digital processing. In advanced conversion systems it is possible to adopt an alternative converter technique specifically to take advantage of a particular characteristic. The output is then digitally converted to Nyquist rate PCM in order to obtain the advantages of both.

Conventional PCM has already been introduced. In PCM, the amplitude of the signal only depends on the number range of the quantizer, and is independent of the frequency of the input. Similarly, the amplitude of the unwanted signals introduced by the quantizing process is also largely independent of input frequency.

Fig. 12.15 introduces the alternative converter structures. The top half of the diagram shows converters which are differential. In differential coding the value of the output code represents the difference between the current sample voltage and that of the previous sample. The lower half of the diagram shows converters which are PCM. In addition, the left side of the diagram shows single-bit converters, whereas the right side shows multibit converters.

In differential pulse code modulation (DPCM), shown at top right, the difference between the previous absolute sample value and the current one is quantized into a multibit binary code. It is possible to produce a DPCM signal from a PCM signal simply by subtracting successive samples; this is digital differentiation. Similarly the reverse process is possible by using an accumulator or digital integrator (see Chapter 2) to compute sample values from the differences received. The problem with this approach is that it is very easy to lose the baseline of the signal if it commences at some arbitrary time. A digital high-pass filter can be used to prevent unwanted offsets.

Differential converters do not have an absolute amplitude limit. Instead there is a limit to the maximum rate at which the input signal voltage can change. They are said to be slew rate limited, and thus the permissible signal amplitude falls at 6 dB per octave. As the quantizing steps are still uniform, the quantizing error amplitude has the same limits as PCM. As input frequency rises, ultimately the signal amplitude available will fall down to it.

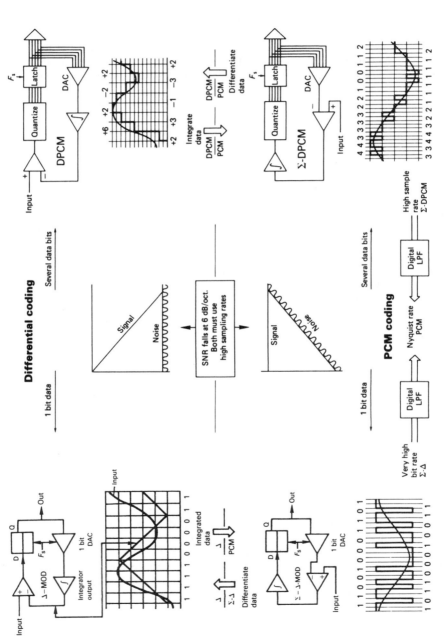

Figure 12.15 The four main alternatives to simple PCM conversion are compared here. Delta modulation is a 1 bit case of differential PCM, and conveys the slope of the signal. The digital output of both can be integrated to give PCM. Σ–Δ (sigma–delta) is a 1 bit case of Σ-DPCM. The application of integrator before differentiator makes the output true PCM, but tilts the noise floor; hence these can be referred to as 'noise-shaping' converters

If DPCM is taken to the extreme case where only a binary output signal is available then the process is described as delta modulation (top left in Fig. 12.15). The meaning of the binary output signal is that the current analog input is above or below the accumulation of all previous bits. The characteristics of the system show the same trends as DPCM, except that there is severe limiting of the rate of change of the input signal. A DPCM decoder must accumulate all the difference bits to provide a PCM output for conversion to analog, but with a 1 bit signal the function of the accumulator can be performed by an analog integrator.

If an integrator is placed in the input to a delta modulator, the integrator's amplitude response loss of 6 dB per octave parallels the converter's amplitude limit of 6 dB per octave; thus the system amplitude limit becomes independent of frequency. This integration is responsible for the term sigma-delta modulation, since in mathematics sigma is used to denote summation. The input integrator can be combined with the integrator already present in a delta modulator by a slight rearrangement of the components (bottom left in Fig. 12.15). The transmitted signal is now the amplitude of the input, not the slope; thus the receiving integrator can be dispensed with, and all that is necessary after the DAC is an LPF to smooth the bits. The removal of the integration stage at the decoder now means that the quantizing error amplitude rises at 6 dB per octave, ultimately meeting the level of the wanted signal.

The principle of using an input integrator can also be applied to a true DPCM system and the result should perhaps be called sigma DPCM (bottom right in Fig. 12.15). The dynamic range improvement over delta-sigma modulation is 6 dB for every extra bit in the code. Because the level of the quantizing error signal rises at 6 dB per octave in both delta-sigma modulation and sigma DPCM, these systems are sometimes referred to as 'noise-shaping' converters, although the word 'noise' must be used with some caution. The output of a sigma DPCM system is again PCM, and a DAC will be needed to receive it, because it is a binary code.

As the differential group of systems suffer from a wanted signal that converges with the unwanted signal as frequency rises, they must all use very high sampling rates.[10] It is possible to convert from sigma DPCM to conventional PCM by reducing the sampling rate digitally. When the sampling rate is reduced in this way, the reduction of bandwidth excludes a disproportionate amount of noise because the noise shaping concentrated it at frequencies beyond the audio band. The use of noise shaping and oversampling is the key to the high resolution obtained in advanced converters.

12.7 Oversampling

Oversampling means using a sampling rate which is greater (generally substantially greater) than the Nyquist rate. Neither sampling theory nor quantizing theory *requires* oversampling to be used to obtain a given signal quality, but Nyquist rate conversion places extremely high demands on component accuracy when a converter is implemented. Oversampling allows a given signal quality to be reached without requiring very close tolerance, and therefore expensive, components. Although it can be used alone, the advantages of oversampling are better realized when it is used in conjunction with noise shaping. Thus in practice the two processes are generally used together and the terms are often seen used in the loose sense as if they were synonymous. For a detailed and quantitative analysis of oversampling having exhaustive references the serious reader is referred to Hauser.[11]

In Section 12.4, where dynamic element matching was described, it was seen that component accuracy was traded for accuracy in the time domain. Oversampling is another example of the same principle.

Fig. 3.37 shows the main advantages of oversampling. These are equally applicable to audio, and the reader is referred to Section 3.20.

Oversampling permits the use of a converter element of shorter wordlength, making it possible to use a flash converter. The flash converter is capable of working at very high frequency and so large oversampling factors are easily realized. The flash converter needs no track/hold system as it works instantaneously. The drawbacks of track/hold set out in Section 12.5 are thus eliminated. If the sigma DPCM converter structure of Fig. 12.15 is realized with a flash converter element, it can be used with a high oversampling factor. This class of converter has a rising noise floor. If the highly oversampled output is fed to a digital low-pass filter which has the same frequency response as an analog anti-aliasing filter used for Nyquist rate sampling, the result is a disproportionate reduction in noise because the majority of the noise was outside the audio band. A high-resolution converter can be obtained using this technology without requiring unattainable component tolerances.

12.8 Oversampling without noise shaping

If an oversampling converter is considered which makes no attempt to shape the noise spectrum, it will be clear that if it contains a perfect quantizer, no amount

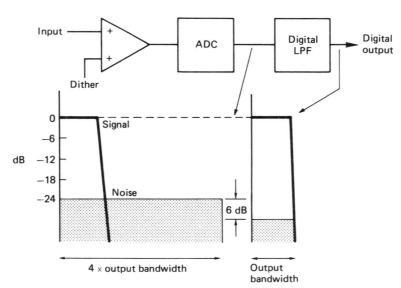

Figure 12.16 In this simple oversampled converter, 4× oversampling is used. When the converter output is low-pass filtered, the noise power is reduced to one-quarter, which in voltage terms is 6 dB. This is a suboptimal method and is not used

of oversampling will increase the resolution of the system, since a perfect quantizer is blind to all changes of input within one quantizing interval, and looking more often is of no help. It was shown earlier that the use of dither would linearize a quantizer, so that input changes much smaller than the quantizing interval would be reflected in the output and this remains true for this class of converter.

Fig. 12.16 shows the example of a white-noise-dithered quantizer, over-sampled by a factor of four. Since dither is correctly employed, it is valid to speak of the unwanted signal as noise. The noise power extends over the whole baseband up to the Nyquist limit. If the basebandwidth is reduced by the oversampling factor of four back to the bandwidth of the original analog input, the noise bandwidth will also be reduced by a factor of four, and the noise power will be one-quarter of that produced at the quantizer. One-quarter noise power implies one-half the noise voltage, so the SNR of this example has been increased by 6 dB, the equivalent of one extra bit in the quantizer. Information theory predicts that an oversampling factor of four would allow an extension by 2 bits. This method is suboptimal in that very large oversampling factors would be needed to obtain useful resolution extension, but it would still realize some advantages, particularly the elimination of the steep-cut analog filter.

The division of the noise by a larger factor is the only route left open, since all the other parameters are fixed by the signal bandwidth required. The reduction of noise power resulting from a reduction in bandwidth is only proportional if the noise is white, i.e. it has uniform power spectral density (PSD). If the noise from the quantizer is made spectrally non-uniform, the oversampling factor will no longer be the factor by which the noise power is reduced. The goal is to concentrate noise power at high frequencies, so that after low-pass filtering in the digital domain down to the audio input bandwidth, the noise power will be reduced by more than the oversampling factor.

12.9 Noise shaping

Noise shaping dates from the work of Cutler[12] in the 1950s. It is a feedback technique applicable to quantizers and requantizers in which the quantizing process of the current sample is modified in some way by the quantizing error of the previous sample.

When used with requantizing, noise shaping is an entirely digital process which is used, for example, following word extension due to the arithmetic in digital mixers or filters in order to return to the required wordlength. It will be found in this form in oversampling DACs. When used with quantizing, part of the noise-shaping circuitry will be analog. As the feedback loop is placed around an ADC it must contain a DAC. When used in converters, noise shaping is primarily an implementation technology. It allows processes which are conveniently available in integrated circuits to be put to use in audio conversion. Once integrated circuits can be employed, complexity ceases to be a drawback and low-cost mass production is possible.

Chapter 2 showed that all analog processes such as mixing, attenuation or integration all have exact numerical parallels. It has been demonstrated that digitally dithered requantizing is no more than a digital simulation of analog quantizing.In this section noise shaping will be treated in the same way. Noise

(a)

(b)

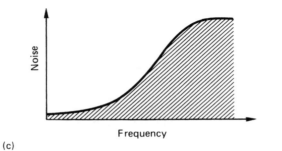

(c)

Figure 12.17 (a) A simple requantizer which feeds back the quantizing error to reduce the error of subsequent samples. The one-sample delay causes the quantizing error to see the equivalent circuit shown in (b) which results in a sinusoidal quantizing error spectrum shown in (c) shaping can be performed by manipulating analog voltages or numbers representing them or both. If the reader is content to make a conceptual switch between the two, many obstacles to understanding fall, not just in this topic, but in digital audio in general.

The term noise shaping is idiomatic and in some respects unsatisfactory because not all devices which are called noise shapers produce true noise. The caution which was given when treating quantizing error as noise is also relevant in this context. Whilst 'quantizing-error-spectrum shaping' is a bit of a mouthful, it is useful to keep in mind that noise shaping means just that in order to avoid some pitfalls. Some noise-shaper architectures do not produce a signal decorrelated quantizing error and need to be dithered.

Fig. 12.17(a) shows a requantizer using a simple form of noise shaping. The low-order bits which are lost in requantizing are the quantizing error. If the value of these bits is added to the next sample before it is requantized, the quantizing error will be reduced. The process is somewhat like the use of negative feedback in an operational amplifier except that it is not instantaneous, but encounters a one-sample delay. With a constant input, the mean or average quantizing error will be brought to zero over a number of samples, achieving one of the goals of additive dither. The more rapidly the input changes, the greater the effect of the delay and the less effective the error feedback will be. Fig. 12.17(b) shows the equivalent circuit seen by the quantizing error, which is created at the requantizer and subtracted from itself one sample period later. As a result the quantizing error spectrum is not uniform, but has the shape of a raised sine wave shown at (c); hence the term noise shaping. The noise is very small at DC and rises with frequency, peaking at the Nyquist frequency at a level determined by the size of the quantizing step. If used with oversampling, the noise peak can be moved outside the audio band.

Figure 12.18 By adding the error caused by truncation to the next value, the resolution of the lost bits is maintained in the duty cycle of the output. Here, truncation of 011 by 2 bits would give continuous zeros, but the system repeats 0111, 0111, which, after filtering, will produce a level of three-quarters of a bit

Fig. 12.18 shows a simple example in which two low-order bits need to be removed from each sample. The accumulated error is controlled by using the bits which were neglected in the truncation, and adding them to the next sample. In this example, with a steady input, the roundoff mechanism will produce an output of 01110111 .... If this is low-pass filtered, the three ones and one zero result in a level of three-quarters of a quantizing interval, which is precisely the level which would have been obtained by direct conversion of the full digital input. Thus the resolution is maintained even though 2 bits have been removed.

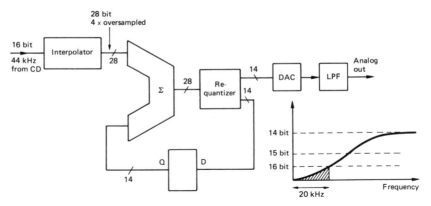

Figure 12.19 The noise-shaping system of the first generation of Philips CD players

The noise-shaping technique was used in the first generation of Philips CD players which oversampled by a factor of four. Starting with 16 bit PCM from the disc, the 4× oversampling will in theory permit the use of an ideal 14 bit converter, but only if the wordlength is reduced optimally. The oversampling DAC system used is shown in Fig. 12.19.[13] The interpolator arithmetic extends the wordlength to 28 bits, and this is reduced to 14 bits using the error feedback loop of Fig. 12.17. The noise floor rises slightly towards the edge of the audio band, but remains below the noise level of a conventional 16 bit DAC which is shown for comparison.

The 14 bit samples then drive a DAC using dynamic element matching. The aperture effect in the DAC is used as part of the reconstruction filter response, in conjunction with a third-order Bessel filter which has a response 3 dB down at 30 kHz. Equalization of the aperture effect within the audio passband is achieved by giving the digital filter which produces the oversampled data a rising response. The use of a digital interpolator as part of the reconstruction filter results in extremely good phase linearity.

Noise shaping can also be used without oversampling. In this case the noise cannot be pushed outside the audio band. Instead the noise floor is shaped or weighted to complement the unequal spectral sensitivity of the ear to noise.[2,14,15] Unless we wish to violate Shannon's theory, this psycho-acoustically optimal noise shaping can only reduce the noise power at certain frequencies by increasing it at others. Thus the average log PSD over the audio band remains the same, although it may be raised slightly by noise induced by imperfect processing.

Fig. 12.20 shows noise shaping applied to a digitally dithered requantizer. The input to the dithered requantizer is subtracted from the output to give the error due to requantizing. This error is filtered (and inevitably delayed) before being subtracted from the system input. The filter is not designed to be the exact inverse of the perceptual weighting curve because this would cause extreme noise levels at the ends of the band. Instead the perceptual curve is levelled off[16] such that it cannot fall more than, for example, 40 dB below the peak.

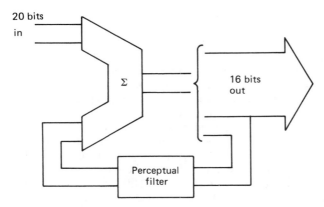

Figure 12.20 Perceptual filtering in a requantizer gives a subjectively improved SNR

Psycho-acoustically optimal noise shaping can offer nearly 3 bits of increased dynamic range when compared with optimal spectrally flat dither.

12.10 Noise-shaping ADCs

The sigma DPCM converter introduced in Fig. 12.15 has a natural application here and is shown in more detail in Fig. 12.21. The current digital sample from the quantizer is converted back to analog in the embedded DAC. The DAC output differs from the ADC input by the quantizing error. The DAC output is subtracted from the analog input to produce an error which is integrated to drive the quantizer in such a way that the error is reduced. With a constant input voltage the average error will be zero because the loop gain is infinite at DC. If

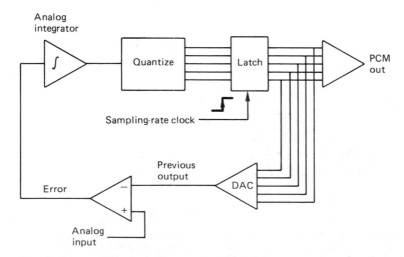

Figure 12.21 The sigma DPCM converter of Figure 12.15 is shown here in more detail

the average error is zero, the mean or average of the DAC outputs must be equal to the analog input. The instantaneous output will deviate from the average in what is called an idling pattern. The presence of the integrator in the error feedback loop makes the loop gain fall with rising frequency. With the feedback falling at 6 dB per octave, the noise floor will rise at the same rate.

Fig. 12.22 shows a simple oversampling system using a sigma DPCM converter and an oversampling factor of only four. The sampling spectrum shows that the noise is concentrated at frequencies outside the audio part of the oversampling baseband. Since the scale used here means that noise power is represented by the area under the graph, the area left under the graph after the filter shows the noise-power reduction. Using the relative areas of similar triangles shows that the reduction has been by a factor of 16. The corresponding noise-voltage reduction would be a factor of four, or 12 dB, which corresponds to an additional 2 bits in wordlength. These bits will be available in the wordlength extension which takes place in the decimating filter. Owing to the rise of 6 dB per octave in the PSD of the noise, the SNR will be 3 dB worse at the edge of the audio band.

One way in which the operation of the system can be understood is to consider that the coarse DAC in the loop defines fixed points in the audio transfer function. The time averaging which takes place in the decimator then allows the transfer function to be interpolated between the fixed points. True signal-independent noise of sufficient amplitude will allow this to be done to infinite

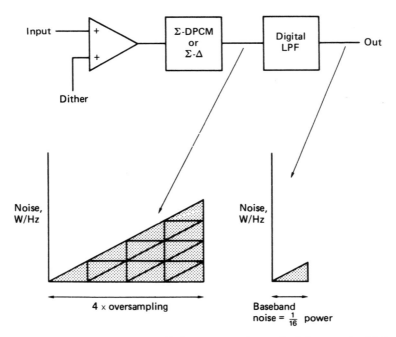

Figure 12.22 In a sigma-DPCM or Σ–Δ converter, noise amplitude increases by 6 dB/octave, noise power by 12dB/octave. In this 4× oversampling converter, the digital filter reduces bandwidth by four, but noise power is reduced by a factor of 16. Noise voltage falls by a factor of four or 12 dB

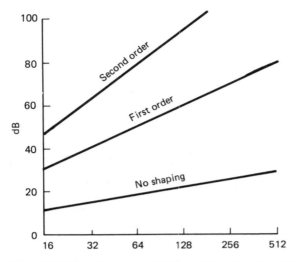

Figure 12.23 The enhancement of SNR possible with various filter orders and oversampling factors in noise-shaping converters

resolution, but by making the noise primarily outside the audio band the resolution is maintained but the audio band signal-to-noise ratio can be extended. A first-order noise-shaping ADC of the kind shown can produce signal-dependent quantizing error and requires analog dither. However, this can be outside the audio band and so need not reduce the SNR achieved.

A greater improvement in dynamic range can be obtained if the integrator is supplanted to realize a higher-order filter.[17] The filter is in the feedback loop and so the noise will have the opposite response to the filter and will therefore rise more steeply to allow a greater SNR enhancement after decimation. Fig. 12.23 shows the theoretical SNR enhancement possible for various loop filter orders and oversampling factors. A further advantage of high-order loop filters is that the quantizing noise can be decorrelated from the signal making dither

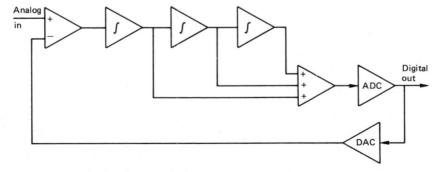

Figure 12.24 Stabilizing the loop filter in a noise-shaping converter can be assisted by the incorporation of feedforward paths as shown here

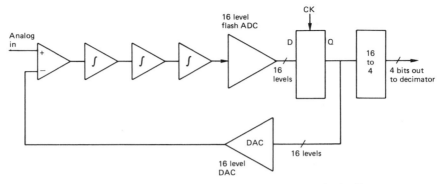

Figure 12.25 An example of a high-order noise-shaping ADC. See text for details

unnecessary. High-order loop filters were at one time thought to be impossible to stabilize, but this is no longer the case, although care is necessary. One technique which may be used is to include some feedforward paths as shown in Fig. 12.24.

An ADC with high-order noise shaping was disclosed by Adams[18] and a simplified diagram is shown in Fig. 12.25. The comparator outputs of the 128 times oversampled 4 bit flash ADC are directly fed to the DAC which consists of 15 equal resistors fed by CMOS switches. As with all feedback loops, the transfer characteristic cannot be more accurate than the feedback, and in this case the feedback accuracy is determined by the precision of the DAC.[19] Driving the DAC directly from the ADC comparators is more accurate because each input has equal weighting. The stringent MSB tolerance of the conventional binary-weighted DAC is then avoided. The comparators also drive a 16 to 4 priority encoder to provide the 4 bit PCM output to the decimator. The DAC output is subtracted from the analog input at the integrator. The integrator is followed by a pair of conventional analog operational amplifiers having frequency-dependent feedback and a passive network which gives the loop a fourth-order response overall. The noise floor is thus shaped to rise at 24 dB per octave beyond the audio band. The time constants of the loop filter are optimized to minimize the amplitude of the idling pattern as this is an indicator of the loop stability. The 4 bit PCM output is low-pass filtered and decimated to the Nyquist frequency. The high oversampling factor and high-order noise shaping extend the dynamic range of the 4 bit flash ADC to 108 dB at the output.

12.11 A 1 bit DAC

It might be thought that the waveform from a 1 bit DAC is simply the same as the digital input waveform. In practice this is not the case. The input signal is a logic signal which need only be above or below a threshold for its binary value to be correctly received. It may have a variety of waveform distortions and a duty cycle offset. The area under the pulses can vary enormously. In the DAC output the amplitude needs to be extremely accurate. A 1 bit DAC uses only the binary information from the input, but reclocks to produce accurate timing and uses a reference voltage to produce accurate levels. The area of pulses produced is then constant. Thus 1 bit DACs will be found in noise-shaping ADCs as well as in the more obvious application of producing analog audio.

Fig. 12.26(a) shows a 1 bit DAC which is implemented with MOS field-effect switches and a pair of capacitors. Quanta of charge are driven into or out of a virtual earth amplifier configured as an integrator by the switched capacitor action. Fig. 12.26(b) shows the associated waveforms. Each data bit period is divided into two equal portions: that for which the clock is high, and that for which it is low. During the first half of the bit period, pulse P+ is generated if the data bit is a 1, or pulse P− is generated if the data bit is a 0. The reference input is a clean voltage corresponding to the gain required.

C1 is *discharged* during the second half of every cycle by the switches driven from the complemented clock. If the next bit is a 1, during the next high period of the clock the capacitor will be connected between the reference and the virtual earth. Current will flow into the virtual earth until the capacitor is charged. If the next bit is not a 1, the current through C1 will flow to ground.

C2 is *charged* to reference voltage during the second half of every cycle by the switches driven from the complemented clock. On the next high period of the clock, the reference end of C2 will be grounded, and so the op-amp end will assume a negative reference voltage. If the next bit is a 0, this negative reference will be switched into the virtual earth; if not the capacitor will be discharged.

(a)

(b)

Figure 12.26 In (a) the operation of a 1 bit DAC relies on switched capacitors. The switching waveforms are shown in (b)

Thus on every cycle of the clock, a quantum of charge is either pumped into the integrator by C1 or pumped out by C2. The analog output therefore precisely reflects the ratio of ones to zeros.

12.12 The 1 bit noise-shaping ADC

In order to overcome the DAC accuracy constraint of the sigma DPCM converter, the sigma-delta converter can be used as it has only 1 bit internal resolution. A 1 bit DAC cannot be non-linear by definition as it defines only two points on a transfer function. It can, however, suffer from other deficiencies such as DC offset and gain error, although these are less offensive in audio. The 1 bit ADC is a comparator.

As the sigma-delta converter is only a 1 bit device, clearly it must use a high oversampling factor and high-order noise shaping in order to have sufficiently good SNR for audio.[20] In practice the oversampling factor is limited not so much by the converter technology as by the difficulty of computation in the decimator. A sigma-delta converter has the advantage that the filter input 'words' are 1 bit long and this simplifies the filter design as multiplications can be replaced by the selection of constants.

Conventional analysis of loops falls down heavily in the 1 bit case. In particular the gain of a comparator is difficult to quantify, and the loop is highly non-linear so that considering the quantizing error as additive white noise in order to use a linear loop model gives rather optimistic results. In the absence of an accurate mathematical model, progress has been made empirically, with listening tests and by using simulation.

Single-bit sigma-delta converters are prone to long idling patterns because the low resolution in the voltage domain requires more bits in the time domain to be integrated to cancel the error. Clearly the longer the period of an idling pattern the more likely it is to enter the audio band as an objectionable whistle or 'birdie'. They also exhibit threshold effects or deadbands where the output fails to react to an input change at certain levels. The problem is reduced by the order of the filter and the wordlength of the embedded DAC. Second- and third-order feedback loops are still prone to audible idling patterns and threshold effect.[21] The traditional approach to linearizing sigma-delta converters is to use dither. Unlike conventional quantizers, the dither used was of a frequency outside the audio band and of considerable level. Square-wave dither has been used and it is advantageous to choose a frequency which is a multiple of the final output sampling rate as then the harmonics will coincide with the troughs in the stopband ripple of the decimator. Unfortunately the level of dither needed to linearize the converter is high enough to cause premature clipping of high-level signals, reducing the dynamic range. This problem is overcome by using in-band white-noise dither at low level.[22]

An advantage of the 1 bit approach is that in the 1 bit DAC, precision components are replaced by precise timing in switched capacitor networks. The same approach can be used to implement the loop filter in an ADC. Fig. 12.27 shows a third-order sigma-delta modulator incorporating a DAC based on the principle of Fig. 12.26. The loop filter is also implemented with switched capacitors.

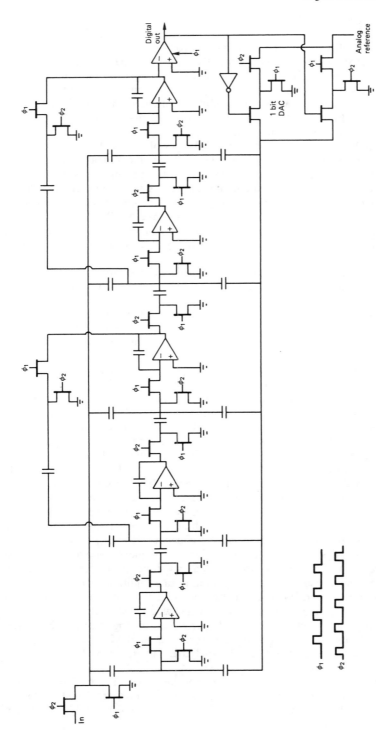

Figure 12.27 A third-order Σ–Δ modulator using a switched capacitor loop jitter

12.13 Factors affecting converter quality

In theory the quality of a digital audio system comprising an ideal ADC followed by an ideal DAC is determined at the ADC. The ADC parameters such as the sampling rate, the wordlength and any noise shaping used put limits on the quality which can be achieved. Conversely the DAC itself may be transparent, because it only converts data whose quality are already determined back to the analog domain. In other words, the ADC determines the system quality and the DAC does not make things any worse.

In practice both ADCs and DACs can fall short of the ideal, but with modern converter components and attention to detail the theoretical limits can be approached very closely and at reasonable cost. Shortcomings may be the result of an inadequacy in an individual component such as a converter chip, or due to incorporating a high-quality component in a poorly thought-out system. Poor system design can destroy the performance of a converter. Whilst oversampling is a powerful technique for realizing high-quality converters, its use depends on digital interpolators and decimators whose quality affects the overall conversion quality.[23]

The shortcomings of converters were considered in Chapter 3 in connection with video. The same considerations hold for audio except that greater accuracy is needed.

Clocks which are free of jitter are a critical requirement in converters as was shown in Section 3.12. The effects of clock jitter are proportional to the slewing rate of the audio signal rather than depending on the sampling rate, and as a result oversampling converters are no more prone to jitter than conventional converters.[24] Clock jitter is a form of frequency modulation with a small modulation index. Sinusoidal jitter produces sidebands which may be audible. Random jitter raises the noise floor which is more benign but still undesirable. As clock jitter produces artefacts proportional to the audio slew rate, it is quite easy to detect. A spectrum analyser is connected to the converter output and a low audio frequency signal is input. The test is then repeated with a high audio frequency. If the noise floor changes, there is clock jitter. If the noise floor rises but remains substantially flat, the jitter is random. If there are discrete frequencies in the spectrum, the jitter is periodic. The spacing of the discrete frequencies from the input frequency will reveal the frequencies in the jitter.

Aliasing of audio frequencies is not generally a problem, especially if oversampling is used. However, the nature of aliasing is such that it works in the frequency domain only and translates frequencies to new values without changing amplitudes. Aliasing can occur for any frequency above one-half the sampling rate. The frequency to which it aliases will be the difference frequency between the input and the nearest sampling-rate multiple. Thus in a non-oversampling converter, *all* frequencies above half the sampling rate alias into the audio band. This includes radio frequencies which have entered via audio or power wiring or directly. RF can leapfrog an analog anti-aliasing filter capacitively. Thus good RF screening is necessary around ADCs, and the manner of entry of cables to equipment must be such that RF energy on them is directed to earth.

Oversampling converters respond to RF on the input in a different manner. Although all frequencies above half the sampling rate are folded into the baseband, only those which fold into the audio band will be audible. Thus an unscreened oversampling converter will be sensitive to RF energy on the input at frequencies within ±20 kHz of integer multiples of the sampling rate. Fortunately interference from the digital circuitry at exactly the sampling rate will alias to DC and be inaudible.

Converters are also sensitive to unwanted signals superimposed on the references. In fact the multiplicative nature of a converter means that reference noise amplitude-modulates the audio to create sidebands. Power supply ripple on the reference due to inadequate regulation or decoupling causes sidebands 50, 60, 100 or 120 Hz away from the audio frequencies, yet do not raise the noise floor when the input is quiescent. The multiplicative effect reveals how to test for it. Once more a spectrum analyser is connected to the converter output. An audio frequency tone is input, and the level is changed. If the noise floor changes with the input signal level, there is reference noise. RF interference on a converter reference is more insidious, particularly in the case of noise-shaped devices. Noise-shaped converters operate with signals which must contain a great deal of high-frequency noise just beyond the audio band. RF on the reference amplitude-modulates this noise and the sidebands can enter the audio band, raising the noise floor or causing discrete tones depending on the nature of the pickup.

Noise-shaped converters are particularly sensitive to a signal of half the sampling rate on the reference. When a small DC offset is present on the input, the bit density at the quantizer must change slightly from 50%. This results in idle patterns whose spectrum may contain discrete frequencies. Ordinarily these are designed to occur near half the sampling rate so that they are beyond the audio band. In the presence of half-sampling-rate interference on the reference, these tones may be demodulated into the audio band.

Although the faithful reproduction of the audio band is the goal, the nature of sampling is such that converter design must respect RF engineering principles if quality is not to be lost. Clean references, analog inputs, outputs and clocks are all required, despite the potential radiation from digital circuitry within the equipment and uncontrolled electromagnetic interference outside.

Unwanted signals may be induced directly by ground currents, or indirectly by capacitive or magnetic coupling. It is good practice to separate grounds for analog and digital circuitry, connecting them in one place only.

Capacitive coupling uses stray capacitance between the signal source and the point where the interference is picked up. Increasing the distance or conductive screening helps. Coupling is proportional to frequency and the impedance of the receiving point. Lowering the impedance at the interfering frequency will reduce the pickup. If this is done with capacitors to ground, it need not reduce the impedance at the frequency of wanted signals.

Magnetic or inductive coupling relies upon a magnetic field due to the source current flow inducing voltages in a loop. Reduction in inductive coupling requires the size of any loops to be minimized. Digital circuitry should always have ground planes in which return currents for the logic signals can flow. At high frequency, return currents flow in the ground plane directly below the signal tracks and this minimizes the area of the transmitting loop. Similarly ground planes in the analog circuitry minimize the receiving loop whilst having no effect on baseband audio. A further weapon against inductive coupling is to use ground fill between all traces on the circuit board. Ground fill will act like a shorted turn to alternating magnetic fields. Ferrous screening material will also reduce inductive coupling as well as capacitive coupling.

The reference of a converter should be decoupled to ground as near to the integrated circuit as possible. This does not prevent inductive coupling to the lead frame and the wire to the chip itself. In the future converters with on-chip references may be developed to overcome this problem.

In summary, spectral analysis of converters gives a useful insight into design weaknesses. If the noise floor is affected by the signal level, reference noise is a possibility. If the noise floor is affected by signal frequency, clock jitter is likely. Should the noise floor be unaffected by both, the noise may be inherent in the signal or in analog circuit stages.

12.14 Operating levels in digital audio

Analog tape recorders use operating levels which are some way below saturation. The range between the operating level and saturation is called the headroom. In this range, distortion becomes progressively worse and sustained recording in the headroom is avoided. However, transients may be recorded in the headroom as the ear cannot respond to distortion products unless they are sustained. The PPM level meter has an attack time constant which simulates the temporal distortion sensitivity of the ear. If a transient is too brief to deflect a PPM into the headroom, it will not be heard either.

Operating levels are used in two ways. On making a recording from a microphone, the gain is increased until distortion is just avoided, thereby obtaining a recording having the best SNR. In post production the gain will be set to whatever level is required to obtain the desired subjective effect in the context of the program material. This is particularly important to broadcasters who require the relative loudness of different material to be controlled so that the listener does not need to make continuous adjustments to the volume control.

In order to maintain level accuracy, analog recordings are traditionally preceded by line-up tones at standard operating level. These are used to adjust the gain in various stages of dubbing and transfer along landlines so that no level changes occur to the program material.

Unlike analog recorders, digital recorders do not have headroom, as there is no progressive onset of distortion until converter clipping, the equivalent of saturation, occurs at 0 dBFs. Accordingly many digital recorders have level meters which read in dBFs. The scales are marked with 0 at the clipping level and all operating levels are below that. This causes no difficulty provided the user is aware of the consequences.

However, in the situation where a digital copy of an analog tape is to be made, it is very easy to set the input gain of the digital recorder so that line-up tone from the analog tape reads 0 dB. This lines up digital clipping with the analog operating level. When the tape is dubbed, all signals in the headroom suffer converter clipping.

In order to prevent such problems, manufacturers and broadcasters have introduced artificial headroom on digital level meters, simply by calibrating the scale and changing the analog input sensitivity so that 0 dB analog is some way below clipping. Unfortunately there has been little agreement on how much artificial headroom should be provided, and machines which have it are seldom labelled with the amount. There is an argument which suggests that the amount of headroom should be a function of the sample wordlength, but this causes difficulties when transferring from one wordlength to another. The EBU[25] concluded that a single relationship between analog and digital level was desirable. In 16 bit working, 12 dB of headroom is a useful figure, but now that 18 and 20 bit converters are available, the new EBU draft recommendation specifies 18 dB.

12.15 Introduction to the AES/EBU interface

In all the above interconnects, there is enough similarity due to the common purpose to make interfacing possible with a little extra hardware, but enough difference to be irritating.

The AES/EBU digital audio interface, originally published in 1985,[26] was proposed to embrace all the functions of existing formats in one standard. The goal was to ensure interconnection of professional digital audio equipment irrespective of origin. The EBU ratified the AES proposal with the proviso that the optional transformer coupling was made mandatory and led to the term AES/EBU interface, also called EBU/AES by some Europeans. The contribution of the BBC to the development of the interface must be mentioned here. Alongside the professional format, Sony and Philips developed a similar format now known as SPDIF (Sony Philips Digital Interface) intended for consumer use. This offers different facilities to suit the application, yet retains sufficient compatibility with the professional interface so that, for many purposes, consumer and professional machines can be connected together.[27,28]

The AES concerns itself with professional audio and accordingly has had little to do with the consumer interface. Thus the recommendations to standards bodies such as the IEC (International Electrotechnical Commission) regarding the professional interface came primarily through the AES whereas the consumer interface input was primarily from industry, although based on AES professional proposals. The IEC and various national standards bodies naturally tended to combine the two into one standard such as IEC 958[29] which refers to the professional interface and the consumer interface. This process has been charted by Finger.[30]

Understandably with so many standards relating to the same subject differences in interpretation arise leading to confusion in what should or should not be implemented, and indeed what the interface should be called. This Chapter will refer generically to the professional interface as the AES/EBU interface and the consumer interface as SPDIF.

12.16 The electrical interface

Many of the older interconnects have separate lines for bit clocks and sampling-rate clocks, which is acceptable for the short distances required for simple dubbing, but causes problems in the broadcast environment where long lines might be needed in a studio complex. It was desired to use the existing analog audio cabling in such installations, which would be 600 ohm balanced line screened, with one cable per audio channel, or in some cases one twisted pair per channel with a common screen. At audio frequency the impedance of cable is high and the 600 ohm figure is that of the source and termination.

If a single serial channel is to be used, the interconnect has to be self-clocking and self-synchronizing, i.e. the single signal must carry enough information to allow the boundaries between individual bits, words and blocks to be detected

Figure 12.28 Recommended electrical circuit for use with the standard two-channel interface

reliably. To fulfil these requirements, the AES/EBU and SPDIF interfaces use FM channel code (see Chapter 5) which is DC-free, strongly self-clocking and capable of working with a changing sampling rate. Synchronization of deserialization is achieved by violating the usual encoding rules.

The use of FM means that the channel frequency is the same as the bit rate when sending data ones. Tests showed that in typical analog audio-cabling installations, sufficient bandwidth was available to convey two digital audio channels in one twisted pair. The standard driver and receiver chips for RS-422A[31] data communication (or the equivalent CCITT-V.11) are employed for professional use, but work by the BBC[32] suggested that equalization and transformer coupling are desirable for longer cable runs, particularly if several twisted pairs occupy a common shield. Successful transmission up to 350 m has been achieved with these techniques.[33] Fig. 12.28 shows the standard configuration. The output impedance of the drivers will be about 110 ohms, and the impedance of the cable used should be similar at the frequencies of interest. The driver was specified in AES-3–1985 to produce between 3 and 10 V peak-to-peak into such an impedance, but this was changed to between 2 and 7 V in AES-3–1992 to reflect better the characteristics of actual RS-422 driver chips.

The original receiver impedance was set at a high 250 ohms, with the intention that up to four receivers could be driven from one source. This has been found to be inadvisable because of reflections caused by impedance mismatches and

Figure 12.29 The minimum eye pattern acceptable for correct decoding of standard two-channel data

AES-3–1992 is now a point-to-point interface with source, cable and load impedance all set at 110 ohms.

In Fig. 12.29, the specification of the receiver is shown in terms of the minimum eye pattern (see Chapter 5) which can be detected without error. It will be noted that the voltage of 200 mV specifies the height of the eye opening at a width of half a channel bit period. The actual signal amplitude will need to be larger than this, and even larger if the signal contains noise. Fig. 12.30 shows the recommended equalization characteristic which can be applied to signals received over long lines.

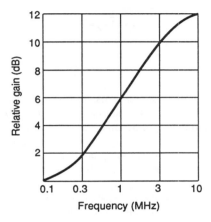

Figure 12.30 EQ characteristic recommended by the AES to improve reception in the case of long lines

The purpose of the standard is to allow the use of existing analog cabling, and as an adequate connector in the shape of the XLR is already in wide service, the connector made to IEC 268 Part 12 has been adopted for digital audio use. Effectively, existing analog audio cables having XLR connectors can be used without alteration for digital connections. The AES/EBU standard does, however, require that suitable labelling should be used so that it is clear that the connections on a particular unit are digital. Whilst the XLR connector was never designed to have constant impedance in the megahertz range, it is capable of towing an outside broadcast vehicle without unlatching.

The need to drive long cables does not generally arise in the domestic environment, and so a low-impedance balanced signal is not necessary. The electrical interface of the consumer format uses a 0.5 V peak single-ended signal, which can be conveyed down conventional audio-grade coaxial cable connected with RCA 'phono' plugs. Fig. 12.31 shows the resulting consumer interface as specified by IEC 958.

It is common knowledge from practice and from the original proposals and standards that professional audio devices use balanced signals on XLR connectors and consumer devices use unbalanced signals on RCA connectors. Unfortunately there is nothing in IEC 958 to require it. This is a grave omission because it is possible to build equipment having the professional signal structure

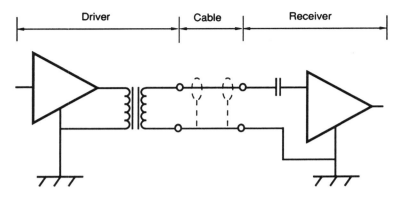

Figure 12.31 The consumer electrical interface

yet outputting an unbalanced signal. Although this conforms to IEC 958 the resultant device is as much use as the proverbial chocolate teapot because it is no use to either type of user. Consumers cannot use it because the professional channel-status information is meaningless to consumer equipment, and professionals cannot use it because it will not drive long cables and reject interference. It is to be hoped that this matter will be rectified in the next revision.

There is a separate proposal[34] for a professional interface using coaxial cable for distances of around 1000 m. This is simply the AES/EBU protocol but with a 75 ohm coaxial cable carrying a 1 volt signal so that it can be handled by analog video distribution amplifiers. Impedance-converting transformers are already on sale to allow balanced 110 ohm to unbalanced 75 ohm matching.

12.17 Frame structure

In Fig. 12.32 the basic structure of the professional and consumer formats can be seen. One subframe consists of 32 bit cells, of which four will be used by a synchronizing pattern. Subframes from the two audio channels, A and B,

Figure 12.32 The basic subframe structure of the AES/EBU format. Sample can be 20 bits with four auxiliary bits, or 24 bits. LSB is transmitted first

alternate on a time division basis. Up to 24 bit sample wordlength can be used, which should cater for all conceivable future developments, but normally 20 bit maximum length samples will be available with four auxiliary data bits, which can be used for a voice-grade channel in a professional application. In a consumer RDAT machine, subcode can be transmitted in bits 4–11, and the 16 bit audio in bits 12–27.

Preceding formats sent the most significant bit first. Since this was the order in which bits were available in successive approximation converters it has become a *de facto* standard for interchip transmission inside equipment. In contrast, this format sends the least significant bit first. One advantage of this approach is that simple serial arithmetic is then possible on the samples because the carries produced by the operation on a given bit can be delayed by one bit period and then included in the operation on the next higher-order bit. There is additional complication, however, if it is proposed to build adaptors from one of the manufacturers' formats to the new format because of the word reversal. This problem is a temporary issue, as new machines are designed from the outset to have the standard connections.

The format specifies that audio data must be in two's complement coding. Whilst pure binary could accept various alignments of different wordlengths with only a level change, this is not true of two's complement. If different wordlengths are used, the MSBs must always be in the same bit position otherwise the polarity will be misinterpreted. Thus the MSB has to be in bit 27 irrespective of wordlength. Shorter words are leading zero filled up to the 20 bit capacity. The channel-status data included, from AES-3–1992, signalling of the actual audio wordlength used so that receiving devices could adjust the digital dithering level needed to shorten a received word which is too long or pack samples onto a disk more efficiently.

Four status bits accompany each subframe. The validity flag will be reset if the associated sample is reliable. Whilst there have been many aspirations regarding what the V bit could be used for, in practice a single bit cannot specify much, and if combined with other V bits to make a word, the time resolution is lost. AES-3–1992 described the V bit as indicating that the information in the associated subframe is 'suitable for conversion to an analog signal'. Thus it might be reset if the interface was being used for non-audio data as is done, for example, in CD-I players.

The parity bit produces even parity over the subframe, such that the total number of ones in the subframe is even. This allows for simple detection of an odd number of bits in error, but its main purpose is that it makes successive sync patterns have the same polarity, which can be used to improve the probability of detection of sync. The user and channel-status bits are discussed later.

Two of the subframes described above make one frame, which repeats at the sampling rate in use. The first subframe will contain the sample from channel A, or from the left channel in stereo working. The second subframe will contain the sample from channel B, or the right channel in stereo. At 48 kHz, the bit rate will be 3.072 MHz, but as the sampling rate can vary, the clock rate will vary in proportion.

In order to separate the audio channels on receipt the synchronizing patterns for the two subframes are different as Fig. 12.33 shows. These sync patterns begin with a run length of 1.5 bits which violates the FM channel coding rules and so cannot occur due to any data combination. The type of sync pattern is

Figure 12.33 Three different preambles (X, Y and Z) are used to synchronize a receiver at the starts of subframes

denoted by the position of the second transition which can be 0.5, 1.0 or 1.5 bits away from the first. The third transition is designed to make the sync patterns DC free.

The channel-status and user bits in each subframe form serial data streams with 1 bit of each per audio channel per frame. The channel-status bits are given a block structure and synchronized every 192 frames, which at 48 kHz gives a block rate of 250 Hz, corresponding to a period of 4 milliseconds. In order to synchronize the channel-status blocks, the channel A sync pattern is replaced for one frame only by a third sync pattern which is also shown in Fig. 12.33. The AES standard refers to these as X, Y and Z whereas IEC 958 calls them M, W and B. As stated, there is a parity bit in each subframe, which means that the binary level at the end of a subframe will always be the same as at the beginning. Since the sync patterns have the same characteristic, the effect is that sync patterns always have the same polarity and the receiver can use that information to reject noise. The polarity of transmission is not specified, and indeed an accidental inversion in a twisted pair is of no consequence, since it is only the transition that is of importance, not the direction.

12.18 Talkback in auxiliary data

When 24 bit resolution is not required, which is most of the time, the four auxiliary bits can be used to provide talkback.

This was proposed by broadcasters[35] to allow voice coordination between studios as well as program exchange on the same cables. Here 12 bit samples of the talkback signal are taken at one-third the main sampling rate. Each 12 bit sample is then split into 3 nibbles (half a byte, for gastronomers) which can be sent in the auxiliary data slot of three successive samples in the same audio channel. As there are 192 nibbles per channel-status block period, there will be

Figure 12.34 The coordination signal is of a lower bit rate to the main audio and thus may be inserted in the auxiliary nibble of the interface subframe, taking three subframes per coordination sample

Byte

Byte	
0	Basic control data (see Figure 12.36)
1	Mode and user bit management (see Figure 12.37)
2	Audio wordlength (see Figure 12.38)
3	Vectored target from byte 1 (reserved for multichannel applications)
4	AES11 sync ref. identification (bits 0–1), otherwise reserved
5	Reserved
6	
7	Source identification (4 bytes of 7 bit ASCII, no parity)
8	
9	
10	
11	Destination identification (4 bytes of 7 bit ASCII, no parity)
12	
13	
14	
15	Local sample address code (32 bit binary)
16	
17	
18	
19	Time-of-day sample address code (32 bit binary)
20	
21	
22	Channel status reliability flags (see Figure 12.39)
23	CRCC

Figure 12.35 Overall format of the professional channel-status block

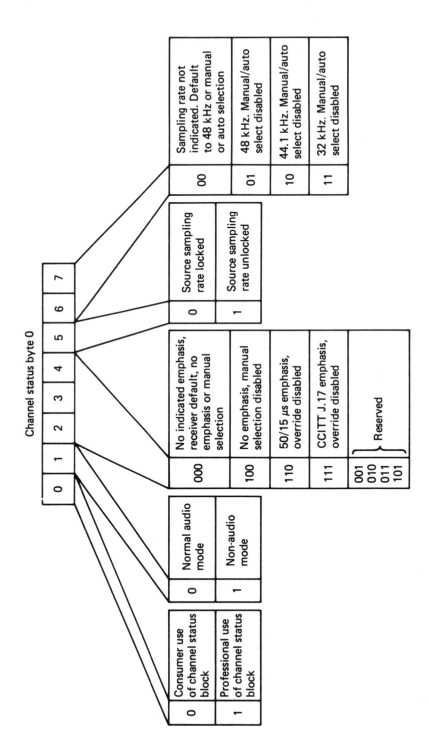

Figure 12.36 The first byte of the channel-status information in the AES/EBU standard deals primarily with emphasis and sampling-rate control

exactly 64 talkback samples in that period. The reassembly of the nibbles can be synchronized by the channel-status sync pattern as shown in Fig. 12.34. Channel-status byte 2 reflects the use of auxiliary data in this way.

12.19 Professional channel status

In both the professional and consumer formats, the sequence of channel-status bits over 192 subframes builds up a 24 byte channel-status block. However, the contents of the channel-status data are completely different between the two applications. The professional channel-status structure is shown in Fig. 12.35. Byte 0 determines the use of emphasis and the sampling rate, with details in Fig. 12.36. Byte 1 determines the channel usage mode, i.e. whether the data transmitted are a stereo pair, two unrelated mono signals or a single mono signal, and details the user bit handling. Fig. 12.37 gives details. Byte 2 determines wordlength as in Fig. 12.38. This was made more comprehensive in AES-3–1992. Byte 3 is applicable only to multichannel applications. Byte 4 indicates the suitability of the signal as a sampling-rate reference and will be discussed in more detail later in this chapter.

There are two slots of 4 bytes each which are used for alphanumeric source and destination codes. These can be used for routing. The bytes contain 7 bit ASCII characters (printable characters only) sent LSB first with the eighth bit set to zero according to AES-3–1992. The destination code can be used to operate an automatic router, and the source code will allow the origin of the audio and other remarks to be displayed at the destination.

Bytes 14–17 convey a 32 bit sample address which increments every channel-status frame. It effectively numbers the samples in a relative manner from an arbitrary starting point. Bytes 18–21 convey a similar number, but this is a time-of-day count, which starts from zero at midnight. As many digital audio devices

Figure 12.37 Format of byte 1 of professional channel status

Bits states 3 4 5	Audio wordlength (24 bit mode)	Audio wordlength (20 bit mode)
0 0 0	Not indicated	Not indicated
0 0 1	23 bits	19 bits
0 1 0	22 bits	18 bits
0 1 1	21 bits	17 bits
1 0 0	20 bits	16 bits
1 0 1	24 bits	20 bits

Figure 12.38 Format of byte 2 of professional channel status

do not have real-time clocks built in, this cannot be relied upon. AES-3–92 specified that the time-of-day bytes should convey the real time at which a recording was made, making it rather like timecode. There are enough combinations in 32 bits to allow a sample count over 24 hours at 48 kHz. The sample count has the advantage that it is universal and independent of local supply frequency. In theory if the sampling rate is known, conventional hours, minutes, seconds, frames timecode can be calculated from the sample count, but in practice it is a lengthy computation and users have proposed alternative formats in which the data from EBU or SMPTE timecode are transmitted directly in these bytes. Some of these proposals are in service as *de facto* standards.

The penultimate byte contains four flags which indicate that certain sections of the channel-status information are unreliable (see Fig. 12.39). This allows the transmission of an incomplete channel-status block where the entire structure is not needed or where the information is not available. For example, setting bit 5 to a logical one would mean that no origin or destination data would be interpreted by the receiver, and so they need not be sent.

The final byte in the message is a CRCC which converts the entire channel-status block into a codeword (see Chapter 6). The channel-status message takes 4 ms at 48 kHz and in this time a router could have switched to another signal source. This would damage the transmission, but will also result in a CRCC

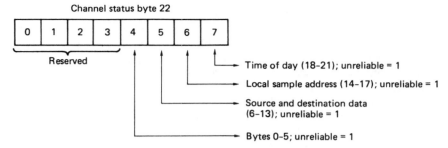

Figure 12.39 Byte 22 of channel status indicates if some of the information in the block is unreliable

failure, so the corrupt block is not used. Error correction is not necessary, as the channel-status data either are stationary, i.e. they stay the same, or change at a predictable rate, e.g. timecode. Stationary data will only change at the receiver if a good CRCC is obtained.

12.20 User bits

The user channel consists of 1 bit per audio channel per sample period. Unlike channel status, which only has a 192 bit frame structure, the user channel can have a flexible frame length. Fig. 12.37 showed how byte 1 of the channel-status frame describes the state of the user channel. Many professional devices do not use the user channel at all and would set the all-zeros code. If the user channel frame has the same length as the channel-status frame then code 0001 can be set. One user channel format which is standardized is the data packet scheme of AES18–1992.[36,37] This was developed from proposals to employ the user channel for labelling in an asynchronous format.[38] A computer industry standard protocol known as HDLC (High-level Data Link Control)[39] is employed in order to take advantage of readily available integrated circuits.

The frame length of the user channel can be conveniently made equal to the frame period of an associated device. For example, it may be locked to film, TV or RDAT frames. The frame length may vary in NTSC as there are not an integer number of samples in a frame.

12.21 Synchronizing

When digital audio signals are to be assembled from a variety of sources, either for mixing down or for transmission through a TDM (Time Division Multiplexing) system, the samples from each source must be synchronized to one another in both frequency and phase. The source of samples must be fed with a reference sampling rate from some central generator, and will return samples at that rate. The same will be true if digital audio is being used in conjunction with VTRs. As the scanner speed and hence the audio block rate is locked to video, it follows that the audio sampling rate must be locked to video. Such a technique has been used since the earliest days of television in order to allow vision mixing, but now that audio is conveyed in discrete samples, these too must be genlocked to a reference for most production purposes.

AES11–1991[40] documented standards for digital audio synchronization and requires professional equipment to be able to genlock either to a separate reference input or to the sampling rate of an AES/EBU input.

As the interface uses serial transmission, a shift register is required in order to return the samples to parallel format within equipment. The shift register is generally buffered with a parallel loading latch which allows some freedom in the exact time at which the latch is read with respect to the serial input timing. Accordingly the standard defines synchronism as an identical sampling rate, but with no requirement for a precise phase relationship. Fig. 12.40 shows the timing tolerances allowed. The beginning of a frame (the frame edge) is defined as the leading edge of the X preamble. A device which is genlocked must correctly decode an input whose frame edges are within ±25% of the sample period. This is quite a generous margin, and corresponds to the timing shift due to putting about a kilometre of cable in series with a signal. In order to prevent tolerance build-up when passing through several devices in series, the output timing must be held within ±5% of the sample period.

The reference signal may be an AES/EBU signal carrying program material, or it may carry muted audio samples, the so-called digital audio silence signal. Alternatively it may just contain the sync patterns. The accuracy of the reference is specified in bits 0 and 1 of byte 4 of channel status (see Fig. 12.35): 00 indicates the signal is not reference grade (but some equipment may still be able to lock to it); 01 indicates a Grade 1 reference signal which is ±1 ppm accurate; whereas 10 indicates a Grade 2 reference signal which is ±10 ppm accurate. Clearly devices which are intended to lock to one of these references must have an appropriate phase-locked-loop capture range.

Modern digital audio devices may also have a video input for synchronizing purposes. Video syncs (with or without picture) may be input, and a phase-locked loop will multiply the video frequency by an appropriate factor to produce a synchronous audio sampling clock.

12.22 Timing tolerance of serial interfaces

There are three parameters of interest when conveying audio down a serial interface, and these have quite different importance depending on the application. The parameters are:

(1) The jitter tolerance of the serial FM data separator.
(2) The jitter tolerance of the audio samples at the point of conversion back to analog.
(3) The timing accuracy of the serial signal with respect to other signals.

The serial interface is a digital interface, in that it is designed to convey discrete numerical values from one place to another. If those samples are correctly received with no numerical change, the interface is perfect. The serial interface carries clocking information, in the form of the transitions of the FM channel code and the sync patterns, and this information is designed to enable the data separator to determine the corect data values in the presence of jitter. It was shown in Chapter 5 that the jitter window of the FM code is half a data bit period in the absence of noise. This becomes a quarter of a data bit when the eye

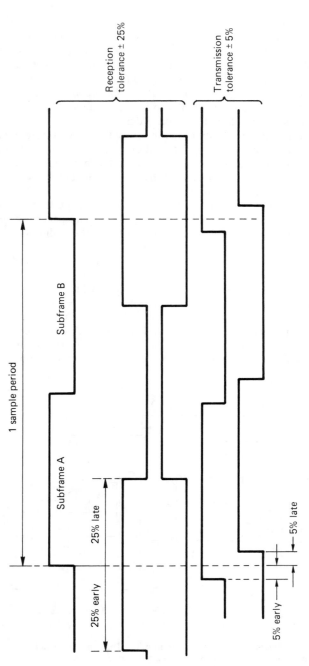

Figure 12.40 The timing accuracy required in AES/EBU signals with respect to a reference (a). Inputs over the range shown at (b) must be accepted, whereas outputs must be closer in timing to the reference as shown at (c)

opening has reached the minimum allowable in the professional specification as can be seen from Fig. 12.29. If jitter is within this limit, which corresponds to about 80 nanoseconds peak-to-peak the serial digital interface perfectly reproduces the sample data, irrespective of the intended use of the data. The data separator of an AES/EBU receiver requires a phase-locked loop in order to decode the serial message. This phase-locked loop will have jitter of its own, particularly if it is a digital phase-locked loop where the phase steps are of finite size. Digital phase-locked loops are easier to implement along with other logic in integrated circuits. There is no point in making the jitter of the phase-locked loop vanishingly small as the jitter tolerance of the channel code will absorb it. In fact the digital phase-locked loop is simpler to implement and locks up quicker if it has larger phase steps and therefore more jitter.

This has no effect on the ability of the interface to convey discrete values, and if the data transfer is simply an input to a digital recorder no other parameter is of consequence as the data values will be faithfully recorded. However, it is a further requirement in some applications that a sampling clock for a converter is derived from a serial interface signal.

The jitter tolerance of converter clocks is measured in hundreds of picoseconds. Thus a phase-locked loop in the FM data separator of a serial receiver chip is quite unable to drive a converter directly as the jitter it contains will be as much as a thousand times too great.

Fig. 12.41 shows how an outboard converter should be configured. The serial data separator has its own phase-locked loop which is less jittery than the serial waveform and so recovers the audio data. The serial data are presented to a shift register which is read in parallel to a latch when an entire sample is present by a clock edge from the data separator. The data separator has done its job of correctly returning a sample value to parallel format. A quite separate phase-locked loop with extremely high damping and low jitter is used to regenerate the sampling clock. This may use a crystal oscillator or it may be a number of loops

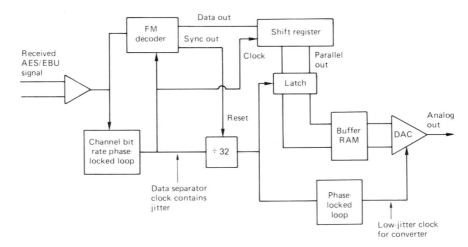

Figure 12.41 In an outboard converter, the clock from the data separator is not sufficiently free of jitter and additional clock regeneration is necessary to drive the DAC

in series to increase the order of the jitter filtering. In the professional channel status, bit 5 of byte 0 indicates whether the source is locked or unlocked. This bit can be used to change the damping factor of the phase-locked loop or to switch from a crystal to a varicap oscillator. When the source is unlocked, perhaps because a recorder is in varispeed, the capture range of the phase-locked loop can be widened and the increased jitter is accepted. When the source is locked, the capture range is reduced and the jitter is rejected.

The third timing criterion is only relevant when more than one signal is involved as it affects the ability of, for example, a mixer to combine two inputs.

In order to decide which criterion is most important, the following may be helpful. A single signal which is involved in a data transfer to a recording medium is concerned only with eye pattern jitter as this affects the data reliability.

A signal which is to be converted to analog is concerned primarily with the jitter at the converter clock. Signals which are to be mixed are concerned with the eye pattern jitter and the relative timing. If the mix is to be monitored, all three parameters become important.

12.23 Asynchronous operation

In practical situations, genlocking is not always possible. In a satellite transmission, it is not really practicable to genlock a studio complex half-way round the world to another. Outside broadcasts may be required to generate their own master timing for the same reason. When genlock is not achieved, there will be a slow slippage of sample phase between source and destination due to such factors as drift in timing generators. This phase slippage will be corrected by a synchronizer, which is intended to work with frequencies which are nominally the same. It should be contrasted with the sampling-rate converter which can work at arbitrary but generally greater frequency relationships. Although a sampling-rate converter can act as a synchronizer, it is a very expensive way of doing the job. A synchronizer can be thought of as a lower-cost version of a sampling-rate converter which is constrained in the rate difference it can accept.

In one implementation of a digital audio synchronizer,[41] memory is used as a timebase corrector as was illustrated in Chapter 2. Samples are written into the memory with the frequency and phase of the source and, when the memory is half-full, samples are read out with the frequency and phase of the destination. Clearly if there is a net rate difference, the memory will either fill up or empty over a period of time, and in order to recentre the address relationship, it will be necessary to jump the read address. This will cause samples to be omitted or repeated, depending on the relationship of source rate to destination rate, and would be audible on program material. The solution is to detect pauses or low-level passages and permit jumping only at such times. The process is illustrated in Fig. 12.42. Such synchronizers must have sufficient memory capacity to absorb timing differences between quiet passages where jumping is possible, and so the average delay introduced by them is quite large, typically 128 samples. They are, however, relatively inexpensive. An alternative to address jumping is to undertake sampling-rate conversion for a short period (Fig. 12.43) in order to

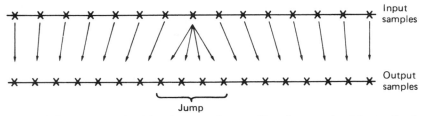

Figure 12.42 In jump synchronizing, input samples are subjected to a varying delay to align them with output timing. Eventually the sample relationship is forced to jump to prevent delay building up. As shown here, this results in several samples being repeated, and can only be undertaken during program pauses, or at very low audio levels. If the input rate exceeds the output rate, some samples will be lost

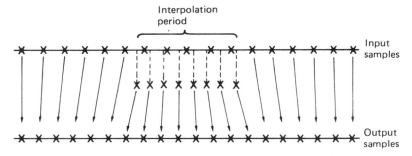

Figure 12.43 An alternative synchronizing process is to use a short period of interpolation in order to regulate the delay in the synchronizer

slip the input/output relationship by one sample.[42] If this is done when the signal level is low, short-wordlength logic can be used.

The difficulty of synchronizing unlocked sources is eased when the frequency difference is small. This is one reason behind the clock accuracy standards for AES/EBU timing generators.[43]

12.24 Introduction to NICAM 728

This system was developed by the BBC to allow the two additional high-quality digital sound channels to be carried on terrestrial television broadcasts. The performance was such that the system has been adopted as the UK standard, and is recommended by the EBU to be adopted by its members, many of whom have put it into service.[44]

The introduction of stereo sound with television cannot be at the expense of incompatibility with the existing monophonic sound channel. In NICAM 728 an additional low-power subcarrier is positioned just above the analog sound carrier, which is retained. The relationship is shown in Fig. 12.44. The power of the digital subcarrier is about one-hundredth that of the main vision carrier, and so existing monophonic receivers will reject it.

Vision carrier

Analog FM
sound carrier

Digital sound
signal

2   1   0   1   2   3   4   5   6   7   8 MHz

1.25 MHz   6.552 MHz

8 MHz

Channel

Figure 12.44 The additional carrier needed for digital stereo sound is squeezed in between television channels as shown here. The digital carrier is of much lower power than the analog signals, and is randomized prior to transmission so that it has a broad, low level-spectrum which is less visible on the picture

Since the digital carrier is effectively shoehorned into the gap between TV channels, it is necessary to ensure that the spectral width of the intruder is minimized to prevent interference. As a further measure, the power of the existing audio carrier is halved when the digital carrier is present.

Fig. 12.45 shows the stages through which the audio must pass. The audio sampling rate used is 32 kHz which offers similar bandwidth to that of an FM stereo radio broadcast. Samples are originally quantized to 14 bit resolution in two's complement code. From an analog source this causes no problem, but from a professional digital source having longer wordlength and higher sampling rate it would be necessary to pass through a rate converter, a digital equalizer to provide pre-emphasis, an optional digital compressor in the case of wide dynamic range signals and then through a rounding circuit incorporating digital dither as explained in Chapter 3.

The 14 bit samples are block companded to reduce data rate. During each 1 millisecond block, 32 samples are input from each audio channel. The magnitude of the largest sample in each channel is independently assessed and used to determine the gain range or scale factor to be used. Every sample in each channel in a given block will then be scaled by the same amount and truncated to 10 bits. An eleventh bit present on each sample combines the scale factor of the channel with parity bits for error detection. The encoding process is described as a near instantaneously companded audio multiplex, NICAM for short. The resultant data now consist of $2 \times 32 \times 11 = 704$ bits per block. Bit interleaving is employed to reduce the effect of burst errors.

At the beginning of each block a synchronizing byte, known as a frame alignment word, is followed by five control bits and 11 additional data bits, making a total of 728 bits per frame; hence the number in the system name.

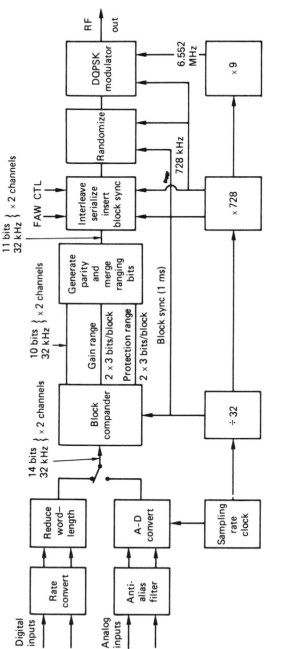

Figure 12.45 The stage necessary to generate the digital subcarrier in NICAM 728. Audio samples are block companded to reduce the bandwidth needed

As there are 1000 frames per second, the bit rate is 728 kbits/s. In the UK this is multiplied by nine to obtain the digital carrier frequency of 6.552 MHz; some other countries use a different subcarrier spacing.

The digital carrier is phase modulated. It has four states which are 90° apart, as was described in Chapter 5. Information is carried in the magnitude of a phase change which takes place every 18 cycles, or 2.74 μs. As there are four possible phase changes, 2 bits are conveyed in every change. The absolute phase has no meaning, only the changes are interpreted by the receiver. This type of modulation is known as differentially encoded quadrature phase shift keying (DQPSK), sometimes called 4-phase DPSK. In order to provide consistent timing and to spread the carrier energy throughout the band irrespective of audio content, randomizing is used, except during the frame alignment word. On reception, the FAW is detected and used to synchronize the pseudo-random generator to restore the original data.

12.25 NICAM 728 frame structure

Fig. 12.46 shows the general structure of a frame. Following the sync pattern or FAW is the application control field. The application control bits determine the significance of following data, which can be stereo audio, two independent mono signals, mono audio and data or data only.

Control bits C_1, C_2 and C_3 have eight combinations, of which only four are currently standardized. Current receivers are designed to mute audio if C_3 becomes 1.

The frame flag bit C_0 spends eight frames high then eight frames low in an endless 16 frame sequence which is used to synchronize changes in channel usage. In the last 16 frame sequence of the old application, the application control bits change to herald the new application, whereas the actual data change to the new application on the next 16 frame sequence.

The reserve sound switching flag, C_4, is set to 1 if the analog sound being broadcast is derived from the digital stereo. This fact can be stored by the receiver and used to initiate automatic switching to analog sound in the case of loss of the digital channels.

The additional data bits AD_0 through AD_{10} are as yet undefined, and reserved for future applications.

12.26 The NICAM sound/data block

The remaining 704 bits in each frame may be either audio samples or data. The two channels of stereo audio are multiplexed into each frame, but multiplexing does not occur in any other case. If two mono audio channels are sent, they occupy alternate frames. Fig. 12.46(a) shows a stereo frame, where the A channel is carried in odd-numbered samples, whereas Fig. 12.46(b) shows a mono frame, where the M1 channel is carried in odd-numbered frames. The format for data has yet to be defined.

The sound/data block of NICAM 728 is in fact identical in structure to the first-level protected companded sound signal block of the MAC/packet systems.[45]

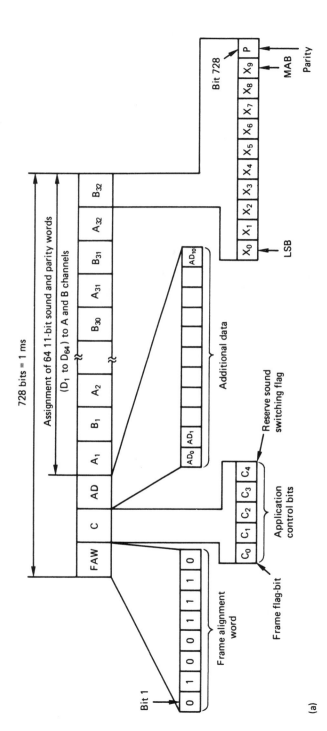

Figure 12.46 In (a), the block structure of a stereo signal multiplexes samples from both channels (A and B) into one block. In mono, shown in (b), samples from one channel only occupy a given block. The diagrams here show the data before interleaving. Adjacent bits shown here actually appear at least 16 bits apart in the data stream

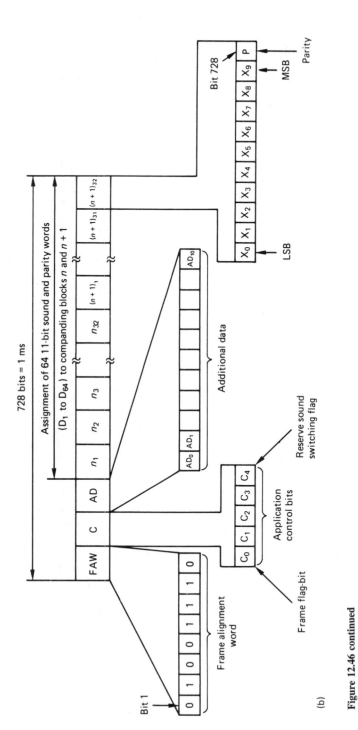

Figure 12.46 continued

12.27 Companding, scaling and parity

These three subjects are intimately related in NICAM 728. Fig. 12.47 shows how the companding works. The 14 bit samples are examined to extract the sample magnitude. Clearly the sign bit plays no part in determining magnitude, and so the diagram has a certain vertical symmetry. The most significant nine of the remaining 13 bits will be used, along with the sign bit, to produce a 10 bit mantissa. As there are only five shifted positions in which 9 bits can reside within 13 bits, clearly there are only five scaling factors; 3 bits are required to describe five scaling factors, and 3 bits actually allowss eight combinations.

The error-protection strategy of a companded channel is subtle. In NICAM 728 there is no error correction. The channel is sufficiently reliable that errors are rare. If an error occurs, it is not corrected, but it is detected so that concealment can be used. The subjective effect of a bit error is roughly proportional to its significance in the companded sample, and so it is only necessary to detect errors in the most significant bits, as errors in the low-order bits only will experience the same masking effects which allow the use of companding in the first case. In NICAM 728, the six most significant bits of each companded sample are protected by an additional parity bit. This works perfectly until the lowest-magnitude samples occur in the fifth coding range. When the sample is 6 dB below the fifth coding range, the MSB of the companded sample will no longer be active, and when the sample is 12 dB below the fifth coding range the two most significant bits will not be active. It makes more sense to slide the 6 bits which are protected by parity down by 1 or 2 bits respectively, giving an improvement in SNR on quiet signals in the presence of errors of up to 12 dB. This explains the fact that although there are only five different scale factors, there are seven different protection ranges.

In order to convey the scale factor to the receiver during a stereo broadcast, 3 bits must be transmitted for each channel of each block. These data cannot be sent unprotected, as their loss would effectively prevent the scaling of an entire block. The scale factor bits are actually merged with the parity bits. In the case of the most significant scale factor bit R_2, reference to Fig. 12.47(b) will show that when R_2 is 1, the parity bits of samples 1, 7, 13, 19, etc., are inverted, but when R_2 is 0 they are left unchanged. Similarly if R_1 is 1, the parity bits of samples 3, 9, 15, 21, etc., are inverted, and so on for bit R_0. As stated, errors in transmission are relatively few, and so on reception the presence of an apparent parity failure in bits 1, 7, 13, 19, etc., is interpreted as R_2 being set to 1. An actual error would cause the parity check to succeed, but this would still be interpreted as an error because if, for example, sample 7 had no parity error yet samples 1, 13, 19, 25, etc., did, it is more likely that R_2 is 1 and sample 7 has a parity error than that sample 7 is correct, R_2 is 0 and all the other samples are wrong. The receiver requires majority decoding logic correctly to interpret the received parity and ranging bits. An odd number of parity checks is employed to prevent the decoder needing to toss a coin. It is possible to convey two more bits in the same way using the parity modification of samples 55 through 59 and 60 through 64, although this is not needed in the NICAM 728 application.

Fig. 12.47(c) shows how the scale factor is merged with the parity on a mono transmission. In mono, each frame contains two blocks from one audio channel, and needs a separate scale factor for each. Note that some of the samples (28–32) from the first block are used to carry the scale factor of the second block. This

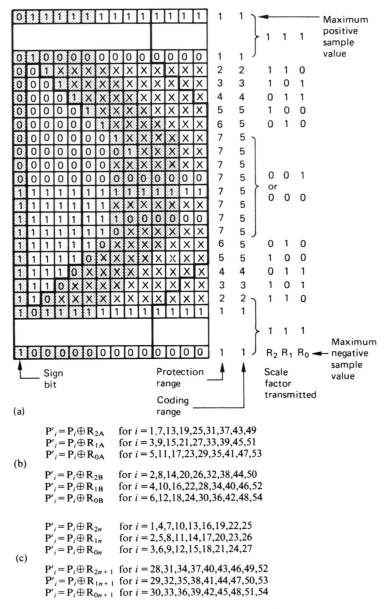

(a)

$P'_i = P_i \oplus R_{2A}$ for $i = 1,7,13,19,25,31,37,43,49$
$P'_i = P_i \oplus R_{1A}$ for $i = 3,9,15,21,27,33,39,45,51$
$P'_i = P_i \oplus R_{0A}$ for $i = 5,11,17,23,29,35,41,47,53$

(b)

$P'_i = P_i \oplus R_{2B}$ for $i = 2,8,14,20,26,32,38,44,50$
$P'_i = P_i \oplus R_{1B}$ for $i = 4,10,16,22,28,34,40,46,52$
$P'_i = P_i \oplus R_{0B}$ for $i = 6,12,18,24,30,36,42,48,54$

$P'_i = P_i \oplus R_{2n}$ for $i = 1,4,7,10,13,16,19,22,25$
$P'_i = P_i \oplus R_{1n}$ for $i = 2,5,8,11,14,17,20,23,26$
$P'_i = P_i \oplus R_{0n}$ for $i = 3,6,9,12,15,18,21,24,27$

(c)

$P'_i = P_i \oplus R_{2n+1}$ for $i = 28,31,34,37,40,43,46,49,52$
$P'_i = P_i \oplus R_{1n+1}$ for $i = 29,32,35,38,41,44,47,50,53$
$P'_i = P_i \oplus R_{0n+1}$ for $i = 30,33,36,39,42,45,48,51,54$

Figure 12.47 The companding of NICAM 728 is shown here. As the programme material becomes quieter, the high-order bits no longer play any part, since they become the same on the sign bit. In a companded sample, the sign bit and nine other bits are transmitted, as the heavy lines indicate. There are only five gain ranges (1–5) possible. However, parity is only generated on the six most significant bits of the sample, except at low levels where the bits checked are slid down one or two places. Thus there are five gain ranges but seven protection ranges which are conveyed for each block by the scale factor bits R_0–R_2. Scale factor is transmitted by reversing parity at predetermined bit positions. These are shown in (b) for stereo and in (c) for mono causes no concern, as a frame can never be transmitted without both blocks present, and it allows samples 55–64 to be used for other purposes as before. The interleaving is performed as follows: columns of an array are assembled, each of which contains four 11 bit samples; 16 columns are necessary to hold the 64 samples of each frame. The data bits are read out in rows, and transmitted. As a result, bits in the same sample are never closer together than 16 transmitted bits. See Chapter 6 for a further discussion of interleaving.

12.28 Audio in the scrambled serial video interconnect

In this interconnect, which was described in Chapter 7, there is provision for auxiliary data to be sent during vertical and horizontal sync pulses.[46,47] Fig. 12.48 shows that following the usual TRS-ID, there will be an auxiliary data flag whose value must be $3FC_{16}$. Following this is a code which identifies the kind of data which are being sent. In the case of digital audio, it will be all ones. Next, a symbol count parameter specifies how many symbols of user data are being sent in this packet. The audio data proper follows, and at the end of the packet a checksum is calculated.

Fig. 12.49 shows that the system wordlength is 9 bits, and that three 9 bit symbols are used to convey all of the essential bits of the 32 used in the AES/EBU subframe. Since DVTRs have four audio channels, there are two

Figure 12.48 Ancillary data format (see text)

Address \\ Bit	x3	x3 + 1	x3 + 2
B9	$\overline{B8}$	$\overline{B8}$	$\overline{B8}$
B8	A (2^5)	A (2^{14})	P
B7	A (2^4)	A (2^{13})	C
B6	A (2^3)	A (2^{12})	U
B5	A (2^2)	A (2^{11})	V
B4	A (2^1)	A (2^{10})	A MSB (2^{19})
B3	A LSB (2^0)	A (2^9)	A (2^{18})
B2	CH (MSB)	A (2^8)	A (2^{17})
B1	CH (LSB)	A (2^7)	A (2^{16})
B0	Z	A (2^6)	A (2^{15})

Figure 12.49 AES/EBU data for one audio sample is sent as three 9 bit symbols. A = audio sample. Bit Z = AES/EBU channel-status block start bit

Figure 12.50(a) Ancillary data locations for PAL

channel bits which specify the channel number to which the subframe belongs. A further bit, Z, specifies the beginning of the 192 sample channel-status message. V, U and C have the same significance as in the normal AES/EBU standard, but the P bit reflects parity on the three 9 bit symbols.

In component systems the audio is placed according to the ancillary data specified for the parallel standard. Fig. 12.50(a) shows the position of ancillary data for PAL and (b) shows the location for NTSC. The exact positions of the packets in the video structure are not specified, but it is only necessary to provide a little RAM buffering at both ends of the link, and this becomes unimportant, as the receiver can determine the sampling rate from the video timing and demultiplex the channels according to the symbol labelling.

12.29 Digital audio in VTRs

The audio performance of video recorders has traditionally lagged behind that of audio-only recorders. In video recorders, the use of rotary heads to obtain sufficient bandwidth results in a wide tape whose longitudinal audio tracks travel relatively slowly by professional audio standards. In all rotary-head recorders,

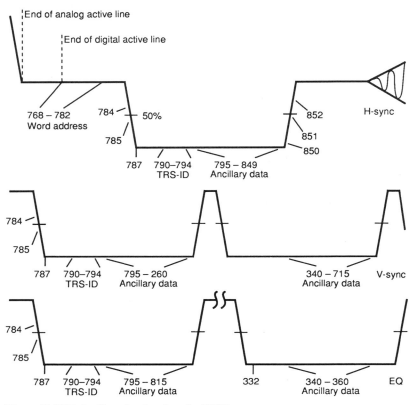

Figure 12.50(b) Ancillary data locations for NTSC

the intermittent head contact causes shock-wave patterns to propagate down the tape, making low-flutter figures difficult to achieve. This is compounded by the action of the capstan servo which has to change tape speed to maintain control track phase if the video heads are to track properly.

The requirements of lip-sync dictate that the same head must be used for both recording and playback, when the optimum head design for these two functions is different. When dubbing from one track to the next, one head gap will be recording the signal played back by the adjacent magnetic circuit in the head, and mutual inductance can cause an oscillatory loop if extensive antiphase crosstalk cancelling is not employed. Placing the tracks on opposite sides of the tape would help this problem, but phase errors between the channels can then be introduced by tape weave. This can mean the difference between a two-channel recorder and a stereo recorder. Crosstalk between the timecode and audio tracks can also restrict performance.

The adoption of digital techniques essentially removes these problems for the audio in a DVTR. Once the audio is in numerical form, wow, flutter and channel-phase errors can be eliminated by timebase correction; crosstalk ceases to occur and, provided a suitable error-correction strategy is employed, the only degradation of the signal will be due to quantizing. The most significant advantages of digital recording are that there is essentially no restriction on the number of generations of re-recording which can be used and that proper crossfades can be made in the audio at edit points, following a rehearsal if necessary.

Digital audio recording with video is rather more difficult than in an audio-only environment. The special requirements of professional video recording have determined many of the parameters of the format, and have resulted in techniques not found in audio-only recorders.

The audio samples are carried by the same channel as the video samples. The audio could have used separate stationary heads, but this would have increased tape consumption and machine complexity. In order to permit independent audio and video editing, the tape tracks are given a block structure. Editing will require the heads momentarily to go into record as the appropriate audio block is reached. Accurate synchronization is necessary if the other parts of the recording are to remain uncorrupted. The sync block structure of the video sector continues in the audio sectors because the same read/write circuitry is used for audio and video data. Clearly the ID code structure must also continue through the audio. In order to prevent audio samples from arriving in the frame store in shuttle, the audio addresses are different from the video addresses.

Despite the additional complexity of sharing the medium with video, the professional DVTR must support such functions as track bouncing, synchronous recording and split audio edits with variable crossfade times.

The audio samples in a DVTR are binary numbers just like the video samples, and although there is an obvious difference in sampling rate and wordlength, the use of time compression means that this only affects the relative areas of tape devoted to the audio and video samples. The most important difference between audio and video samples is the tolerance to errors. The acuity of the ear means that uncorrected audio samples must not occur more than once every few hours. There is little redundancy in sound when compared with video, and concealment of errors is not desirable on a routine basis. In video, the samples are highly redundant, and concealment can be effected using samples from previous or subsequent lines or, with care, from the previous frame.

Whilst subjective considerations require greater data reliability in the audio samples, audio data form a small fraction of the overall data and it is difficult to protect them with an extensive interleave whilst still permitting independent editing. For these reasons major differences can be expected between the ways that audio and video samples are handled in a digital video recorder. One such difference is that the error-correction strategy for audio samples uses a greater amount of redundancy. Whilst this would cause a serious playing time penalty in an audio recorder, even doubling the audio data rate in a video recorder only raises the overall data rate by a few per cent. The arrangement of the audio blocks is also designed to maximize data integrity in the presence of tape defects and head clogs. Chapters 8 and 9 showed that the audio blocks are at the ends of the head sweeps in D-2 and D-3, but are placed in the middle of the segment in D-1, D-5, Digital Betacam and DCT.

The audio sample interleave varies in complexity between the various formats. It will be seen from Fig. 12.51 that the physical location of a given audio channel rotates from segment to segment. In this way a tape scratch will cause slight damage to all channels instead of serious damage to one. Data are also distributed between the heads, and so if one (or sometimes two) of the four heads clogs the

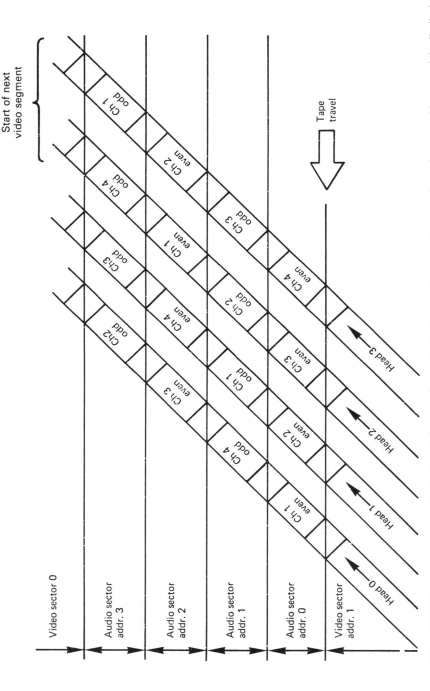

Figure 12.51 The structure of the audio blocks in D-1 format showing the double recording, the odd/even interleave, the sector addresses, and the distribution of audio channels over all heads. The audio samples recorded in this area represent a 6.666 ms time slot in the audio recording

audio is still fully recovered. The D-2 and D-3 formats differ considerably between PAL and NTSC versions owing to the difference between the subcarrier frequencies of the two standards. In PAL one field requires eight tracks, and so the track rate will be 400 Hz, and since there are four audio blocks in each track, the audio block rate will be 1600 Hz. In NTSC one field requires six tracks, so the track rate will be 360 Hz (minus 0.1%) and the audio block rate will be 1440 Hz (minus 0.1%). Since the audio sampling rate is unchanged by the video format, the number of samples in each audio block will be different in the two versions of D-2 and D-3.

12.30 Audio strategy of D-1

The actual mechanism of video editing is simply to start recording the new data at a field boundary, the result appearing as a cut in the picture. This is also the most basic way of editing the audio; at an interleave block boundary the new recording is substituted for the old. It is to be expected that this will result in step discontinuities of the audio waveform, audible as clicks, but this may well be acceptable in a portable machine whose tapes will be the raw material for post production. In order to allow click-free editing without read–modify–write D-1 simply records all audio data twice.[46] Thus the same audio data appear in two versions which are physically separate on tape. Double recording is much less error resistant than using the same space for error-correcting codes, but this arrangement allows a more satisfactory edit to be performed by initially updating only half of the blocks with new data. During this overlap period, the end of the previous recording and the beginning of the new will both be present, and the DVTR can perform a crossfade in the digital domain between the two sample streams on replay. At the end of an insert, the reverse crossfade would take place. The overlap period is flexible, because the best crossfade time varies subjectively with the material recorded. Clearly on performing the edit, the crossfade period is simply the time for which only half of the sample blocks are recorded. On replay, the crossfader needs to know how its coefficients should vary with time to match what has been recorded. This is neatly solved by incorporating a gain parameter in the audio blocks, which will change during the overlap period and control the replay crossfader. The format is such that machines which do not support this mode record zeros in the parameter position, and this code results in no action in any player. There is a flaw in this simple crossfading approach because the 100% redundancy is absent during the overlap period, and dropouts or mistracking during crossfades caused the machine to interpolate using the odd/even interleave. The problem can of course be overcome by using read–modify–write.

The error-correction system of D-1 uses product codes as described in Chapter 6. Codewords are formed prior to interleaving – the so-called outer code – and further codewords are formed after interleaving, known as the inner code. The inner code is optimized to correct random errors, so that these will not be seen by the outer code. Burst errors will overwhelm the inner code; it will simply declare all data in the codeword as bad, and attach error flags to it. Following de-interleave, the outer code can use the error flags to perform erasure correction, which will not be impaired by random errors. The product coding is done by writing data into an array in columns, and adding column redundancy to form the outer code. The array is then read in rows, which interleaves the data, and row redundancy is added to form the inner code. Fig. 12.52 shows the details of the audio product code generation. The inner code is the same as for video, because common circuitry can then be used, but the outer code is different from the video outer code which is not discussed here. The audio data are contained in 20 bit words, and 168 of these form one audio-write block. Most of these are audio samples, but there are also control words and housekeeping data which will be detailed later. The data are written into columns which are seven words high. The columns are written non-sequentially to produce the maximum distance between adjacent samples after interleave; 24 columns are necessary. Each column is then treated as five columns of 4 bits each, and 3 nibbles of redundancy are added to each column, so that there are now ten rows. Redundancy is now produced along

Figure 12.52(a) Data are written into an array as 20 bit columns, and read out as rows. The column redundancy is produced in 4 bit wide columns, and forms the outer codewords of 40 bits each

Figure 12.52(b) The row redundancy forms the inner code, as four check bytes are added to the data to produce ten codewords of 64 bytes each. The relationship to the tape track is such that two inner codewords occupy one sync block. Five sync blocks can hold the entire interleave block

each row, and 4 bytes are added, making the total length of a row 64 bytes. One sync block holds 128 bytes; thus the rows are written sequentially, and can be accommodated in five sync blocks, which is one audio-write block. Although it is common to use a further interleave between the inner code and the actual recording stage in digital audio-only recording, this is not practicable in the DVTR because it contradicts the requirement for blocks to be read randomly in shuttle.

12.31 Audio strategy of D-2

In D-2 the double audio recording of D-1 was retained, although the odd–even separation was no longer employed. In order to prevent the increase in concealments when editing, D-2 did not update one copy of the audio and then the other, but updated both copies at once. This made a crossfade impossible, and a Vee-edit (a brief fadeout followed by a fadein) is employed instead to avoid clicks. A Vee-edit is of no use for editing in music as it is audible. Read–modify–write was therefore essential for quality work. With no provision to update the audio copies individually, there is then no reason to use double recording.

Unfortunately the opportunity to use the doubled recording area for proper error-correction coding was not taken. This left D-2 with a flawed audio error-correction strategy, which combined with the lack of flying erase on early machines to cause difficulties.

A product code is used, and the interleave is generated by the usual memory array, as Fig. 12.53 illustrates. The 20 bit audio samples are written into the array in rows, where 2½ rows of bytes are needed for one row of samples.

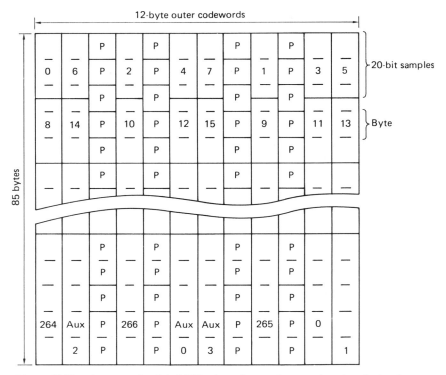

Figure 12.53 In the composite digital VCR, the audio samples are written into the interleave array in rows to produce outer codewords, and read out in 85 byte columns to form sync blocks as shown in Fig. 12.54

Sync	1D	Data	Inner check	Data	Inner check
2 bytes	2 bytes	85 bytes	8 bytes	85 bytes	8 bytes

Inner codeword (95 bytes)   Inner codeword (93 bytes)

Figure 12.54 One sync block of the composite digital format contains two inner codewords formed from columns of Fig. 12.53. Six sync blocks are necessary to hold the entire interleave block, and form one audio sector (NTSC)

Each row of the array is loaded with eight samples, and then 4 bytes of Reed–Solomon redundancy are added to form an outer code. Reading the array in rows and adding 8 bytes of R–S redundancy produces inner codewords. Two of these inner codewords can be accommodated in one sync block as shown in Fig. 12.54. Accordingly six sync blocks are necessary to record one audio block.[47,48]

12.32 Audio strategy of D-3

D-3 is probably the first DVTR format properly to address the problem of audio recording in the company of video data. D-3 uses 100% redundancy, but double recording is not used. Instead, for every data byte there is a byte of Reed–Solomon code redundancy.[49]

As in other formats, each audio channel is recorded independently. A product code is used, but in D-3 the interleave is generated over a period of one complete field by a memory array, as Fig. 12.55 illustrates for PAL. The 20 bit audio samples are written into the array in rows, where 2½ bytes are needed for one sample. A block of 30 samples requires 75 bytes to which 1 byte of auxiliary data is added to make the 76 byte data content of a sync block. It will be seen from the figure that four of these are formed across each row, and eight rows are necessary to contain the 960 samples required in a field period. The interleave process alters the sequence of samples in the block as shown. Reading the array in byte-sized columns and adding 8 bytes of R–S redundancy produces outer codewords. The inner coding is then performed by adding eight R–S redundancy bytes to each 76 byte data symbol to make a sync block. Accordingly 64 sync blocks are necessary to record one audio block (eight sectors per field × eight sync blocks per sector).

In NTSC, the audio sector rate is lower, so each sector contains more samples. The field interleave block remains the same except that the rows contain only three sync blocks of 85 bytes. Accordingly 48 sync blocks are necessary to record one audio block (six sectors per field × eight sync blocks per sector).

In both line standards, the sync blocks associated with one audio product code are distributed over all of the tracks in the field. As there is as much outer redundancy as data, full error-correction performance is maintained up to the point where half of the audio recording area in a field is lost. A clogged replay head only loses one-quarter of the audio and is not a problem. Two clogged heads are fully correctable except that tape dropouts will now be concealed. Insert edits with mistracking only damage the first or last track in a field, and this represents only one-sixth (NTSC) or one-eighth (PAL) of the product code even if the whole track is unreadable. D-1 and D-2 do not have this ability because the product blocks are restricted to individual segments.

D-3 supports simple editing whereby a new recording is commenced and a Vee-edit is used to conceal the click. The field-sized product block means that this type of edit is only field accurate. This is adequate for ENG cameras and cart. machines which can be built to perform assemble edits without using flying erase. This cuts complexity and scanner noise.

The simple crossfade mode of D-1 is not supported as there is no double recording. Thus all production editing is performed by read–modify–write. Edits can then have any crossfade period and can be sample accurate.

Figure 12.55(a) D-3 audio block (PAL). Audio samples of 20 bit length are written non-sequentially along rows of an array as shown here; 30 samples and one auxiliary data byte can be accommodated in one 76 byte block. Outer codes are formed vertically

Column blocks: 2½ bytes | block 0 (76 bytes) | block 1 (76 bytes) | block 2 (76 bytes) | block 3 (76 bytes). The "30 samples" span covers blocks 0–1.

Row				0					1					2					3		
PCM data 8 byte																								
0	0	32	64	********	928	AUX 0	4	36	68	********	932	AUX 4	8	40	72	********	936	AUX 8	12	44	76	********	940	AUX 12
1	16	48	80	********	944	AUX 16	20	52	84	********	948	AUX 20	24	56	88	********	952	AUX 24	28	60	92	********	956	AUX 28
2	29	61	93	********	957	AUX 29	1	33	65	********	929	AUX 1	5	37	69	********	933	AUX 5	9	41	73	********	937	AUX 9
3	13	45	77	********	941	AUX 13	17	49	81	********	945	AUX 17	21	53	85	********	949	AUX 21	25	57	89	********	953	AUX 25
4	26	58	90	********	954	AUX 26	30	62	94	....	958	AUX 30	2	34	66	....	930	AUX 2	6	38	70	********	934	AUX 6
5	10	42	74	********	938	AUX 10	14	46	78	********	942	AUX 14	18	50	82	********	946	AUX 18	22	54	86	********	950	AUX 22
6	23	55	87	********	951	AUX 23	27	59	91	********	955	AUX 27	31	63	95	********	959	AUX 31	3	35	67	********	931	AUX 3
7	7	39	71	********	935	AUX 7	11	43	75	********	939	AUX 11	15	47	79	********	943	AUX 15	19	51	83	********	947	AUX 19
Outer ECC 8 byte																								
8	PV0	PV0	PV0	********	PV0	PV0	PV0	PV0	PV0	********	PV0	PV0	PV0	PV0	PV0	....	PV0	PV0	PV0	PV0	PV0	********	PV0	PV0
9	PV1	PV1	PV1	********	PV1	PV1	PV1	PV1	PV1	********	PV1	PV1	PV1	PV1	PV1	....	PV1	PV1	PV1	PV1	PV1	********	PV1	PV1
10	PV2	PV2	PV2	********	PV2	PV2	PV2	PV2	PV2	********	PV2	PV2	PV2	PV2	PV2	********	PV2	PV2	PV2	PV2	PV2	********	PV2	**PV2**
11	PV3	PV3	PV3	********	PV3	PV3	PV3	PV3	PV3	********	PV3	PV3	PV3	PV3	PV3	********	PV3	PV3	PV3	PV3	PV3	********	PV3	PV3
12	PV4	PV4	PV4	********	PV4	PV4	PV4	PV4	PV4	********	PV4	PV4	PV4	PV4	PV4	********	PV4	**PV4**	PV4	PV4	PV4	********	PV4	PV4
13	PV5	PV5	PV5	********	PV5	PV5	PV5	PV5	PV5	********	PV5	PV5	PV5	PV5	PV5	********	PV5	PV5	PV5	PV5	PV5	********	PV5	PV5
14	PV6	PV6	PV6	********	PV6	PV6	PV6	PV6	PV6	********	PV6	PV6	PV6	PV6	PV6	********	PV6	PV6	PV6	PV6	PV6	********	PV6	PV6
15	PV7	PV7	PV7	********	PV7	PV7	PV7	PV7	PV7	********	PV7	PV7	PV7	PV7	PV7	********	PV7	PV7	PV7	PV7	PV7	********	PV7	PV7

(a)

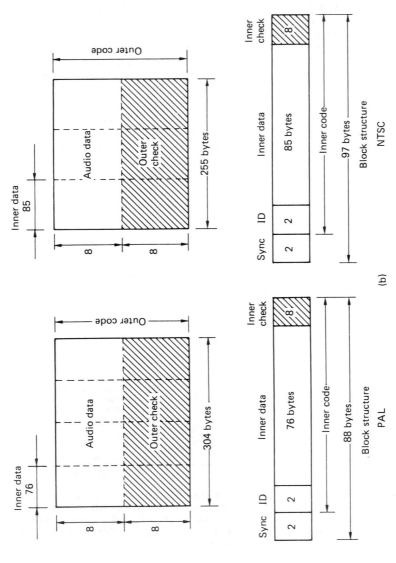

Figure 12.55(b) Audio block structure for D-3. As audio sampling rate is common, but scanner speed differs between PAL and NTSC, the audio blocks are different. Although outer coding is specific to audio, the size of the sync block is common to audio and video and the same inner code generator is timeshared between the two functions

12.33 Writing audio sectors

In each sector, the track commences with a preamble to synchronize the phase-locked loop in the data separator on replay. Each of the sync blocks begins, as the name suggests, with a synchronizing pattern which allows the read sequencer to deserialize the block correctly. At the end of a sector, it is not possible simply to turn off the write current after the last bit, as the turnoff transient would cause data corruption. It is necessary to provide a postamble such that current can be turned off away from the data. It should now be evident that any editing has to take place a sector at a time. Any attempt to rewrite one sync block would result in damage to the previous block due to the physical inaccuracy of replacement, damage to the next block due to the turnoff transient, and inability to synchronize to the replaced block because of the random phase jump at the point where it began. The sector in a DVTR is analogous to the cluster in a disk drive. Owing to the difficulty of writing in exactly the same place as a previous recording, it is necessary to leave tolerance gaps between sectors where the write current can turn on and off to edit individual write blocks. For convenience, the tolerance gaps are made the same length as a whole number of sync blocks. Fig. 12.56 shows that in D-1 the edit gap is two sync blocks long, as it is in D-3, whereas in D-2 it is only one sync block long. The first half of the tolerance gap is the postamble of the previous block, and the second half of the tolerance gap acts as the preamble for the next block. The tolerance gap following editing will contain, somewhere in the centre, an arbitrary jump in bit phase, and a certain amount of corruption due to turnoff transients. Provided that the postamble and preamble remain intact, this is of no consequence.

Figure 12.56 The position of preambles and postambles with respect to each sector is shown along with the gaps necessary to allow individual sectors to be written without corrupting others. When the whole track is recorded, 252 bytes of CC hex fill are recorded after the postamble before the next sync pattern. If a subsequent recording commences in this gap, it must do so at least 20 bytes before the end in order to write a new run-in pattern for the new recording

12.34 Synchronization between audio sampling rate and video field rate

Clearly the number of audio sync blocks in a given time is determined by the number of video fields in that time. It is only possible to have a fixed tape structure if the audio sampling rate is locked to video. With 625/50 machines, the sampling rate of 48 kHz results in exactly 960 audio samples in every field.

For use on 525/60, it must be recalled that the 60 Hz is actually 59.94 Hz. As this is slightly slow, it will be found that in 60 fields, exactly 48 048 audio samples will be necessary. Unfortunately 60 will not divide into 48 048 without a remainder. The largest number which will divide 60 and 48 048 is 12; thus in 60/12=5 fields there will be 48 048/12=4004 samples. Over a five-field sequence the fields contain 801, 801, 801, 801 and 800 samples respectively, adding up to 4004 samples.

12.35 AES/EBU compatibility

In order to comply with the AES/EBU digital audio interconnect, wordlengths between 16 and 20 bits can be supported, but it is necessary to record a code in the sync block to specify the wordlength in use. Pre-emphasis may have been used prior to conversion, and this status is also to be conveyed, along with the four channel-use bits. The AES/EBU digital interconnect uses a block-sync pattern which repeats after 192 sample periods corresponding to 4 ms at 48 kHz. Since the block size is different to that of the DVTR interleave block, there can be any phase relationship between interleave block boundaries and the AES/EBU block-sync pattern. In order to recreate the same phase relationship between block sync and sample data on replay, it is necessary to record the position of block sync within the interleave block. It is the function of the interface control word in the audio data to convey these parameters. There is no guarantee that the 192 sample block-sync sequence will remain intact after audio editing; most likely there will be an arbitrary jump in block-sync phase. Strictly speaking a DVTR playing back an edited tape would have to ignore the block-sync positions on the tape, and create new block sync at the standard 192 sample spacing. Unfortunately the DVTR formats are not totally transparent to the whole of the AES/EBU data stream, as certain information is not recorded.

As a DVTR can individually edit audio channels, it does not require a great leap of the imagination to see that a multitrack audio-only machine could be made by filling the tape tracks with audio sectors. The number of channels this would permit is staggering and it may be more useful to incorporate a reduced-resolution or monochrome video channel. It should be pointed out that such a machine is outside the intentions of the formats described here.

References

1. Nakajima, H. and Odaka, K., A rotary-head high-density digital audio tape recorder. *IEEE Trans. Consum. Electron.*, **CE-29**, 430–437 (1983)
2. Fielder, L.D., Human auditory capabilities and their consequences in digital audio convertor design. In *Audio in Digital Times*. New York: Audio Engineering Society (1989)
3. Moore, B.C.J., *An Introduction to the Psychology of Hearing*. London: Academic Press (1989)
4. Muraoka, T., Iwahara, M. and Yamada, Y., Examination of audio bandwidth requirements for

optimum sound signal transmission. *J. Audio Eng. Soc.*, **29**, 2–9 (1982)

5. Muraoka, T., Yamada, Y. and Yamazaki, M., Sampling frequency considerations in digital audio. *J. Audio Eng. Soc.*, **26**, 252–256 (1978)

6. Fincham, L.R., The subjective importance of uniform group delay at low frequencies. Presented at 74th Audio Engineering Society Convention (New York, 1983), preprint 2056(H-1)

7. Anon., AES recommended practice for professional digital audio applications employing pulse code modulation: preferred sampling frequencies. AES5–1984 (ANSI S4.28–1984), *J. Audio Eng. Soc.*, **32**, 781–785 (1984)

8. v.d. Plassche, R.J., Dynamic element matching puts trimless convertors on chip. *Electronics*, 16 June 1983

9. v.d. Plassche, R.J. and Goedhart, D., A monolithic 14 bit D/A convertor. *IEEE J. Solid-State Circuits*, **SC-14**, 552–556 (1979)

10. Adams, R.W., Companded predictive delta modulation: a low-cost technique for digital recording. *J. Audio Eng. Soc.*, **32**, 659–672 (1984)

11. Hauser, M.W., Principles of oversampling A/D conversion. *J. Audio Eng. Soc.*, **39**, 3–26 (1991)

12. Cutler, C.C., Transmission systems employing quantization. US Pat No. 2,927,962 (1960)

13. v.d. Plassche, R.J. and Dijkmans, E.C., A monolithic 16 bit D/A conversion system for digital audio. In *Digital Audio*, ed. B.A. Blesser, B. Locanthi and T.G. Stockham Jr, pp. 54–60. New York: Audio Engineering Society (1983)

14. Gerzon, M. and Craven, P.G., Optimal noise shaping and dither of digital signals. Presented at 87th Audio Engineering Society Convention (New York, 1989), preprint No. 2822 (J-1)

15. Wannamaker, R.A., Psychoacoustically optimal noise shaping. *J. Audio Eng. Soc.*, **40**, 611–620 (1992)

16. Lipshitz, S.P., Wannamaker, R.A. and Vanderkooy, J., Minimally audible noise shaping. *J. Audio Eng. Soc.*, **39**, 836–852 (1991)

17. Adams, R.W., Design and implementation of an audio 18-bit A/D convertor using oversampling techniques. Presented at the 77th Audio Engineering Society Convention (Hamburg, 1985), preprint 2182

18. Adams, R.W., An IC chip set for 20 bit A/D conversion. In *Audio in Digital Times*. New York: Audio Engineering Society (1989)

19. Richards, M., Improvements in oversampling analogue to digital convertors. Presented at 84th Audio Engineering Society Convention (Paris, 1988), preprint 2588 (D-8)

20. Inose, H. and Yasuda, Y., A unity bit coding method by negative feedback. *Proc. IEEE*, **51**, 1524–1535 (1963)

21. Naus, P.J., *et al.*, Low signal level distortion in sigma-delta modulators. Presented at 84th Audio Engineering Society Convention, (Paris, 1988), preprint 2584

22. Stikvoort, E., High order one bit coder for audio applications. Presented at 84th Audio Engineering Society Convention (Paris, 1988), preprint 2583(D-3)

23. Lipshitz, S.P. and Vanderkooy, J., Are D/A convertors getting worse? Presented at 84th Audio Engineering Society Convention (Paris, 1988), preprint 2586 (D-6)

24. Harris, S., The effects of sampling clock jitter on Nyquist sampling analog to digital convertors and on oversampling delta-sigma ADCs. *J. Audio Eng. Soc.*, **38**, 537–542 (1990)

25. Moller, L., Signal levels across the EBU/AES digital audio interface. In *Proc. 1st NAB Radio Montreux Symp.*, 16–28 (1992)

26. Audio Engineering Society, AES recommended practice for digital audio engineering – serial transmission format for linearly represented digital audio data. *J. Audio Eng. Soc.*, **33**, 975–984 (1985)

27. EIAJ CP-340, *A digital audio interface*. EIAJ, Tokyo (1987)

28. EIAJ CP-1201, *Digital audio interface (revised)*. EIAJ, Tokyo (1992)

29. IEC 958 *Digital audio interface, first edition*. IEC, Geneva (1989)

30. Finger, R., AES3–1992: the revised two channel digital audio interface. *J. Audio Eng. Soc.*, **40**, 107–116 (1992)

31. EIA RS-422A, Electronic Industries Association, 2001 Eye St NW, Washington, DC 20006, USA

32. Smart, D.L., Transmission performance of digital audio serial interface on audio tie lines. *BBC Des. Dep. Tech. Memo.*, 3.296/84

33. European Broadcasting Union, Specification of the digital audio interface. *EBU Doc. Tech.*, 3250 (1985)

34. Rorden, B. and Graham, M., A proposal for integrating digital audio distribution into TV production. *J. SMPTE*, 606–608 (Sept. 1992)

35. Gilchrist, N., Co-ordination signals in the professional digital audio interface. In *Proc. AES/EBU Interface Conf.* 13–15. Burnham: Audio Engineering Society (1989)
36. AES18–1992, Format for the user data channel of the AES digital audio interface. *J. Audio Eng. Soc.*, **40**, 167–183 (1992)
37. Nunn, J.P., Ancillary data in the AES/EBU digital audio interface. In *Proc. 1st NAB Radio Montreux Symp.* 29–41 (1992)
38. Komly, A and Viallevieille, A., Programme labelling in the user channel. In *Proc. AES/EBU Interface Conf.* 28–51. Burnham: Audio Engineering Society (1989)
39. ISO 3309, *Information processing systems – data communications – High level data link frame structure* (1984)
40. Dunn, J., Considerations for interfacing digital audio equipment to the standards AES3, AES5 and AES11. In *Proc. AES 10th International Conf.* 122. New York: Audio Engineering Society (1991)
41. Gilchrist, N.H.C., Digital sound: sampling-rate synchronization by variable delay. *BBC Res. Dep. Rep.*, 1979/17
42. Lagadec, R., A new approach to sampling rate synchronisation. Presented at 76th Audio Engineering Society Convention (New York, 1984), preprint 2168
43. Shelton, W.T., Progress towards a system of synchronization in a digital studio. Presented at the 82nd Audio Engineering Society Convention (London, 1986), preprint 2484(K7)
44. Anon., NICAM 728: specification for two additional digital sound channels with System I television. BBC Engineering Information Dept. (London, 1988)
45. Anon., Specification of the system of the MAC/packet family. *EBU Tech. Doc.*, 3258 (1986)
46. Gregory, S., *Introduction to the 4:2:2 Digital Video Tape Recorder*. London: Pentech Press (1988)
47. Ampex Corporation, Ampex digital format for video and audio tape recording of composite video signals using 19mm type D-2 cassette. Redwood City, CA (1988)
48. Watkinson, J.R., *The D-2 Digital Video Recorder*. Oxford: Focal Press (1990)
49. Watkinson, J.R., *The D-3 Digital Video Recorder*. Oxford: Focal Press (1992)

Index